HODGES UNIVERSITY
LIBRARY - FT. MYERS

D1257605

The Origins and Role
of Same-Sex Relations
in Human Societies

The Origins and Role of Same-Sex Relations in Human Societies

JAMES NEILL

McFarland & Company, Inc., Publishers

Jefferson, North Carolina, and London

LIBRARY OF CONGRESS CATALOGUING-IN-PUBLICATION DATA

Neill, James, 1940–
The origins and role of same-sex relations in human societies / James Neill.
p.   cm.
Includes bibliographical references and index.

ISBN 978-0-7864-3513-5
illustrated case binding : 50# alkaline paper ∞

1. Homosexuality — History.
2. Sexual orientation — History
I. Title.
HQ76.25.N45   2009   306.76'609 — dc22   2008027100

British Library cataloguing data are available

©2009 James Neill. All rights reserved

*No part of this book may be reproduced or transmitted in any form
or by any means, electronic or mechanical, including photocopying
or recording, or by any information storage and retrieval system,
without permission in writing from the publisher.*

On the cover: *The Tyrannicides,* Roman copy of a Greek original
by Kritios and Nesiotes, marble, 477 BC, Museo Archeologico Nazionale,
Naples, Italy (Bridgeman Art Library)

Manufactured in the United States of America

*McFarland & Company, Inc., Publishers
Box 611, Jefferson, North Carolina 28640
www.mcfarlandpub.com*

Acknowledgments

This book could not have been written without the work of a host of historians, sexologists, anthropologists, psychologists and other researchers whose industry and insight opened up vast areas of knowledge about human sexuality and the sexual customs and traditions of widely diverse societies — an area of study that had been all but off limits to scholars up until the 1970s. I would like to acknowledge my debt to all of the scholars who have contributed to the ever-expanding documentation of social attitudes to sex and same-sex love in societies around the world and throughout history, but a half dozen deserve special mention for the contribution of their work to my understanding. A pioneer in the area of research into the sexual customs of past historical periods, and a giant in his field, was the late Vern L. Bullough who, despite risk to his professional reputation, published his *Sexual Variance in History* in 1976, a work that opened up the field of cross-cultural sexual research to academic scholars, and that still remains a standard work in the field. John Boswell's groundbreaking *Christianity, Social Tolerance and Homosexuality*, published in 1980, examined enormous previously overlooked evidence showing that social attitudes to same-sex love were not uniformly negative during the first millennium of Christianity, as has been uniformly assumed, and that the rigid enforcement of sexual conformity associated with Western history emerged only as a by-product of the Church's efforts to enforce celibacy among its clergy in the Middle Ages. Thanks to the astute study of the sexual traditions of ancient Greece provided by Sir Kenneth Dover in his *Greek Homosexuality*, the subject of same-sex love among the Greeks, studiously ignored by most classicists before him, became a respectable field of study. Further illuminating the previously shrouded area of homosexual practices in the classical world is Eva Cantarella's *Bisexuality in the Ancient World*, a comprehensive and informative analysis of Greek and Roman sexual laws and mores that brought much needed clarity to our understanding of the laws and moral codes governing homosexual conduct in the classical period. David F. Greenberg's *Construction of Homosexuality*, which includes an encyclopedic survey of sexual customs around the world and throughout history, provided many perceptive insights into the forces that shaped sexual attitudes and customs in the West, not the least of which is the role of psychological conflict within the clergy over sex in the vehemence with which the church denounced homosexuality in the late Middle Ages. Stephen O. Murray's prodigious compilation and analysis of research into homosexual customs in societies around the world, consolidated in his *Homosexualities*, supplemented the cross-cultural contributions of Bullough and Greenberg while providing much new detail and incisive commentary.

A partial list of other scholars whose work I am indebted to include Wayne R. Dynes, editor of the *Encyclopedia of Homosexuality* with Warren Johansson and William A. Percy, and the latter for the insights he provides into Greek homosexuality in *Pederasty and Pedagogy in Archaic Greece*; Walter L. Williams for his *The Spirit and the Flesh*, an engrossing study of sexual diversity in the Native American culture; Bret Hinsch for his *Passions of the Cut Sleeve*, which introduced Western readers to the astonishing 3,000 year documented history of same-sex love in China; Tsuneo Watanabe and Jin'ichi Iwata, for *The Love of the Samurai*, which introduced Western readers to the hitherto unknown venerable homosexual traditions of Japan; Gary P. Leupp for his *Male Colors*, a detailed treatment of Japan's homosexual traditions that greatly expands on the material presented by Watanabe and Iwata; the great French Medievalist Georges Duby for the light he throws on Medieval sexuality, particularly in the world of the knighthood; German theologian Uta Ranke-Heineman for her informative examination of the treatment of sex in the development of canon law in the Middle Ages, *Eunuchs for the Kingdom of Heaven: Women, Sexuality and the Catholic Church*; James A. Brundage, for *Law, Sex and Christian Society in the Medieval Europe*, a comprehensive examination of the evolution of church doctrine and civil law on sexuality in the Middle Ages; Michael Goodich, for his *The Unmentionable Vice: Homosexuality in the Later Medieval Period*, a lucid dissection of church's successful drive to demonize non-procreative sexuality in late Medieval Europe. Allen J. Frantzen for his *Before the Closet*, which includes a much-needed examination of Anglo-Saxon attitudes to same-sex relations; Louis Crompton for his *Homosexuality and Civilization*, an elegant and magisterial survey of homosexuality throughout world history; Byrne Fone, for *Homophobia: A History,* the historical survey of the development of anti-homosexual religious doctrine and the development and spread of the harsh persecution of people for committing homosexual acts that characterizes much of Western history since the Middle Ages; Rictor Norton, for *The Myth of the Modern Homosexual*, an incisive critique of social constructionist theory, and also the insightful and informative material provided on his web site; Jonathan Ned Katz, for his *Gay American History*, a treasure trove of information about the surprising history of homosexuality in America; Weston La Barre, for *Muelos: A Stone Age Superstition about Sexuality*, which documents the persistence of primitive notions about the power and role of the phallus and semen in the beliefs of ancient societies; Thorkil Vanggaard, for *Phallos: A Symbol and Its History in the Male World*, an intriguing work predating La Barre's work by more than a decade that examines the beliefs about semen, the phallus and homosexuality in early warrior societies; Edward O. Wilson for the stimulating insights he provided in *On Human Nature* on the possible the patterns of exclusive homosexuality in humans; John J. McNeill, for his *The Church and the Homosexual*, an illuminating re-evaluation of Roman Catholic doctrine on homosexual love; Bishop John Shelby Spong, for his *Living in Sin? A Bishop Rethinks Human Sexuality*, an astute re-examination of the scriptural and theological bases of the traditional Christian teaching on sexuality; and Paul Halsall, for the large and enormously helpful collection of original historical source documents dealing with homosexuality and religious and social attitudes to sex on the web sites he maintains, People with a History and Medieval Sourcebook.

    I would like to thank the many friends who have supported me in the ten years I have worked on the book, especially the late Dr. Laura Bigman, who provided invaluable help in getting the book started, Bobbie Brewster who played a critical role in getting the ball rolling, and Dr. Barbara von Mettenheim, an early supporter, who patiently read the chapter manuscripts and provided helpful critiques and comments. Other friends whose support played an important role in moving the project forward way include Jerry Fujimoto, Phil Cullen, Rey Aguirre, Dr. Alice Worley, Jane Lamb, Suzanne Tobin and P.P.S.R. And last, but not least, I would like to acknowledge and thank the support of my family members, particularly Dr. Thomas Steven Neill, who read an early draft and provided helpful comments, as well as John Neill, Diane Tincher and Patrick Franey, whose encouragement helped propel the book along during the years it took to complete.

Table of Contents

Preface

The Origins and Role of Same-Sex Relations in Human Societies delves into the heart of one of the most controversial and emotionally charged issues in contemporary life — homosexuality and its role in society. We have seen recent political campaigns pander to the homophobic fears of voters to avoid dealing with more substantive issues, while at the same time mainline religious organizations continue to be polarized over the issue of gays in the clergy. In the meantime, violence against gay people continues, and the military continues to lose the service of thousands of highly skilled and capable personnel because of its anti-homosexual culture.

As I observed the ongoing controversies over homosexuality and the campaigns of gay rights advocates from my position (in a previous lifetime) in a news organization in Washington, D.C., I was struck by how the parties in the political debates over gay rights talked past each other. It was also clear to me that the debate over gay rights was being conducted before a public with a profound ignorance about the nature of homosexuality, its origins, and its role in nature. Conservatives denounced homosexual behavior as a sin and an abnormality and used that argument to justify restrictions on homosexuals. On their side I heard the questions: how can homosexuality be natural if homosexuals can't have children? How can it be moral if it's not natural? On the other side of the debate, gay rights advocacy groups based their assertion of rights on the fundamental principles of justice and equality for all guaranteed by the U.S. Constitution, but generally bypassed the moral argument made by the opponents of gay rights. It seemed to me that it would be difficult to adequately resolve the debate in the minds of the public without a better understanding of homosexuality, how it is that it appears in so many otherwise healthy, spiritually dedicated and hardworking people, and how it came about that a fierce condemnation of homosexuality became such a prominent feature of the Judeo-Christian tradition.

I was fortunate enough to be able to take a sabbatical in the mid–1990s and spent a good portion of that time at the Library of Congress to pursue answers to the questions that had been on my mind on the nature of homosexuality and how it came to be an aspect of human sexuality. As I studied the available literature on the psychology and physiology of sex, the history of sexuality in human cultures and on the sexual practices of societies around the world I was astonished to discover how widespread homosexual practices have been in other societies around the world throughout history. I was also not prepared to find that exclusive homosexuality accounted for a only small portion of the varieties of homosexual customs and traditions reported by anthropologists and historians, and that in a great number of societies homosexuality was practiced by nearly all the males and females most of whom would move on to heterosexual marriage or were already married. I was also struck by the amazing prevalence and variety of homosexual behavior among a broad range of animal species, especially those higher on the evolutionary tree. As I digested this material it became apparent to me that the understanding of sexuality taken for granted in modern life was only part of the story, and the portrayal of sex in Western tradition as a force that

1

draws only a man and a women together for the purpose of procreation amounted to a cultural myth.

As I worked my way through the many recent historical and anthropological studies and scientific research on sex and homosexuality it also became apparent to me that a major barrier to appreciating the degree to which homosexual customs were interwoven into the social traditions of non–Western societies is the powerful imprint of the assumptions about sexuality in which people in the West have long been indoctrinated. For example, in many of the studies that examined the homosexual traditions of the ancient world, the authors seemed to assume that homosexuality was either not present or was disapproved by the respective societies, unless clear cut evidence was demonstrated that showed that homosexual practices were present or approved. To take a specific example, because the fragmentary evidence we have on the daily life of the Mycenaean Greeks does not mention homosexual customs, it is assumed by many academic scholars not only that homosexuality was not practiced within that society, but that it must have been disapproved of as well. In a similar way many academic classicists maintain that homosexuality among the ancient Athenians was a limited phenomenon, restricted to one way relationships between an unmarried adult and an adolescent who derived no sexual pleasure from the relationship, that it occurred only among youths and young men for a very limited period of their lives, and that after that limited period all sexual expression was strictly heterosexual. Their understanding is based on evidence drawn from laws instituted to protect the educational character of homosexual practices, and philosophical treatises and moral commentaries on homosexuality rather than seeing those documents as a reaction to what was happening in the society. Their conclusions were drawn based solely on the documents and artifacts from the period without taking into consideration the influence of human nature in sexual behavior.

The approach followed in this book takes a different tack from conventional historical or anthropological studies relating to homosexuality which collect evidence on the historical period or society studied and then draw conclusions based solely on the evidence gathered. It seemed to me that it would be advantageous to first establish some general observations about human sexuality and the place of homosexuality within it — if it, in fact, can be shown that it does play a role in human sexuality — and then review the evidence we have on human societies to see the degree to which those initial observations are borne out. Therefore, to set the natural context, the book starts with a review of homosexual behavior in the animal world, the patterns in which it appears, and the beneficial role, if any, that homosexual behavior seems to play in the life of those species. In reviewing the material in Chapter 1, it should become apparent to the reader that an overwhelming case can be made, based upon the abundant evidence of homosexuality in the animal kingdom, not only that homosexuality is a product of nature, but that it is evident that homosexual behavior plays an important role in the reproductive success of many species.

The naturalness of homosexuality being concretely established, the suggestion was made that since humans evolved from a branch of the primate family, and because homosexual behavior is widespread among all primates, homosexuality should also be a trait found among humans. The review of the sexual customs of indigenous tribal peoples that follows demonstrates that, as expected, homosexuality is indeed widespread among peoples of all races on all continents. Analyzing and comparing patterns of homosexual expression among the different societies, and drawing on findings of research into the psychology and physiology of sex, some general conclusions are then drawn about the place of homosexual behavior in the life of the human species. Of course, the suggestion that the patterns of sexual behavior found among primitive tribal peoples can be used to draw conclusions about human sexuality might seem a bold assumption to some, and would probably encounter fierce arguments among others. The next step, then, was to review the sexual behavior patterns among all the world's civilizations starting with the first stirrings of civilization in Mesopotamia and Egypt to see if the conclusions about sexuality based on observations of tribal peoples and scientific research are validated.

As noted earlier, it is often assumed by historians and scholars that homosexuality is either scarce or disapproved among human societies unless specific positive evidence can be found to the contrary. Thus, where historical evidence is fragmentary or sketchy, most historians and researchers have been reluctant extrapolate beyond the bare facts the evidence supports. However, when even fragmentary evidence is examined from the perspective of observations about human sexuality based on the research of psychologists and sex researchers and the general patterns in which homosexuality has repeatedly manifested among human societies, the outlines of consistent patterns can often be discerned, patterns that appear again and again in different societies around the world with only local variations. In the case of the classical Greeks, most American and British classicists have focused on the Greek traditions in isolation from the Greeks' Indo-European heritage which can be seen in many areas of Greek life. Taking my lead from the French Indo-Europeanist Bernard Sergent, who traced Indo-European themes through the great number of Greek myths telling the stories of homosexual loves of Greek gods or heroes, I found it productive to consider the evidence of Greek homosexual customs in the context of similar traditions of the Greek's Indo-European cousins and arrived at conclusions that go beyond the current accepted view.

The sum of these reviews, observations and analyses leads to some truly provocative conclusions about human sexuality, and our ambisexual nature, which will most likely seem outrageous and absurd to people inured in the family-centered/procreation-oriented understanding of sex that is so deeply engrained in Western culture.

After laying out the compelling evidence that human sexuality is ambisexual in nature and that it seems probable that this fundamental trait of human nature was inherited from our animal ancestors, the next task was to examine how it came about that the sexual traditions in Western society diverged so radically from every other society around the world and down through history. In pursuing the answer to this question, I found that some astute scholars have already been down that road. With the help of the insights provided by the recent scholarly work of a number of theologians and historians who have cut through the religious haze that has obscured the true origins of Western moral dogma, it was possible to arrive at a coherent narrative of how it was that Western religion developed what is essentially an adversary relationship with a fundamental aspect of human nature, and the role of neurosis in shaping Christian moral attitudes to sex.

If the material gathered and arranged in this book can be of help in furthering the understanding of homosexuality and its place in human life, I will have achieved my purpose.

James W. Neill
Reston, Virginia

Introduction:
The Heterosexual Myth

myth. 3. An invented story, idea or concept. 4. An imaginary or fictitious thing or person. 5. An unproved or false collective belief that is used to justify a social institution.[1]

A shotgun blast to the chest killed Scott Amedure on the morning of March 9, 1995. A friend of Amedure's, 26-year-old Jonathan Schmitz, purchased a 12-gauge shotgun and drove to Amedure's home that morning. Finding Amedure in his kitchen, Schmitz fired two shots at close range into his friend's chest. The motivation for this cold-blooded murder? Schmitz had been embarrassed and enraged three days earlier when the 32-year-old Amedure told a television audience on the *Jenny Jones* TV show that he was sexually attracted to Schmitz. Looking at the case rationally, it is hard to imagine why Amedure's admission, which some males might find flattering, and which Schmitz himself admitted on the show, would drive a young man to murder his friend in cold blood. The notorious 1995 *Jenny Jones* talk show murder cast a sharp spotlight on the enormous tension that exists in modern society surrounding homosexuality.

Yet the case is hardly unique. A few years later the nation was shocked by the brutal beating of Matthew Shepard, an elfin 21-year-old gay college student, by two drinking acquaintances who left him tied to a fence, mortally injured, on a cold Wyoming night. Not content to let the community heal from the tragedy, the Westboro Baptist church in Topeka, Kansas, announced plans to erect a monument "Dedicated to Matthew Shepard's Entry to Hell," in the victim's home town, which it promoted on its web site, God Hates Fags.

What is it about homosexuality that would so disturb a young man that it would cause him to murder a friend when the friend's sexual interest in him was publicized? What explains the deep hatred that is seen among moralizing opponents of homosexuality? For that matter, why does homosexuality exist? How could it be natural if it doesn't lead to reproduction? How could it be moral if it's unnatural?

The knowledge of most people about sex comes from what they've learned in their families, what they've heard preached from pulpits, what they see on television or in movies and what they learn from their peers or in school. The overwhelming message that is heard and that frames everything people see and experience about sex in modern society is that sex is about a man and a woman and its purpose is propagation of the species. Against this backdrop of a heterosexual world, the homosexual comes in like an unwanted guest at dinner.

According to our cultural assumptions and Judeo-Christian moral tenets, homosexuality should not exist at all in the Western world, and, indeed, until very recently, homosexuality was rarely visible to the public eye. If homosexuality was portrayed in literature or films at all it was usually cast in a negative light. We are still told by moral leaders that it is unnatural, a moral depravity, "an objective disorder," according to the Catholic Church. The uncontested line is that heterosexuality is the way of the natural order, and that procreation is the sole and self-evident purpose of sex.

In the meantime political campaigns pander to the homophobic fears of voters to avoid dealing with more substantive issues, and mainline religious organizations are polarized over the issue of gays in the clergy. Violence against gay people continues, while the American military loses the service of thousands of highly skilled and patriotic men and women because of its homophobic culture. As the issue of homosexuality in society is exploited and debated, the general public remains profoundly ignorant of the nature of homosexuality, its origins, its role in nature, and the circumstances leading to the harsh condemnation of homosexual practices that has been one of the defining characteristics of Christian sexual morality. Yet at the same time a new and startling understanding of homosexuality and its place in human sexuality is beginning to emerge. The results of the efforts of a host of scholars and researchers, working in fields ranging from anthropology and history to sexual psychology and the physiology of sex, promise to profoundly change the way our society thinks about sex and homosexuality.

Until the mid–20th century, when the groundbreaking Kinsey Report was released amid great controversy, human sexuality itself was not deemed a proper subject for research or academic study. Even as late as the 1970s, the topic of homosexuality remained taboo among academic researchers outside the fields of psychology and criminology. A pervasive anti-homosexual bias reigned in the academic world, which regarded homosexual behavior as a pathological illness or aberration restricted to a tiny deviant minority and a sign of social and moral decay. Historians and social scientists risked damaging their careers if they devoted too much attention to the topic. As a result, the state of knowledge about homosexuality even among academic scholars was meager, and restricted primarily to theories of homosexuality as a mental disorder or social deviance. When confronted with evidence of homosexuality among the subjects of their research, anthropologists and historians either ignored the topic altogether, or sidestepped the issue with terse references to "moral perversions" or "unnatural relations."

Fortunately, the gradual liberalization of attitudes to sexuality and homosexuality in the academic and scientific establishments in the last decades of the 20th century has allowed scholars to pursue research into sexual practices among other societies and in past historical periods, work that would have posed a risk to their careers as recently as the 1970s. At the same time new research into the psychology and physiology of sex has begun to illuminate this vital area of human behavior and experience that was until recent times the exclusive province of religious dogma. The insights provided by these accumulating studies shine much needed light on the hitherto little understood subject of homosexuality, and taken together present a radically new picture of human sexuality, dramatically different from the family oriented heterosexual model to which Western social and moral tradition has long sought to restrict all sexual expression.

* * *

It is stating the obvious to say that an intense hostility to homosexuality has been ingrained in Western culture for many centuries. Former Chief Justice Warren Burger summed up the popular view, writing in an opinion upholding a state sodomy statute that "the condemnation of these practices is firmly rooted in Judeo-Christian moral and ethical standards."[2] Put more bluntly by Floyd Cochran, a former member of the white supremacist group Aryan

Nation, "It was taught from the beginning that homosexuality was evil, that homosexuals were evil perverts, and there was no alternative but death."[3] But no such extreme reaction occurs in response to many other evils of our day, be they the conning of the elderly out of their retirement savings, the neglect or abuse of children, wanton or sadistic murders or even genocide. The deep repugnance to overt homosexuality that has long been a feature of Western society is, indeed, a special case.

A clue to why this is so can be found in the nature of the reaction itself. As the oft-quoted line from Shakespeare's *Hamlet* would put it, our culture "doth protest too much."[4] The uneasiness many feel when confronted with homosexuality, extreme in some cases, occurs, researchers are beginning to recognize, because it strikes close to home. Recent research at the University of Georgia by a team led by Dr. Henry Adams has found that there is a direct correlation between the degree of dread or hostility that people experience regarding homosexuality and the level of a person's same-sex responsiveness.

The study selected a group of males who graded themselves in a prescreening assessment as exclusively heterosexual in both orientation and experience. The research team deliberately excluded heterosexual men who admitted any experience of homosexual feelings or activity in the past. The resulting group of men was further assessed to gauge the level of homophobia or discomfort that each experienced when confronted with homosexuality. The responsiveness of the subjects to various erotic stimuli, homosexual and heterosexual, was then measured. The researchers found that "individuals who score in the homophobic range and admit negative affect toward homosexuality demonstrate significant sexual arousal to male homosexual erotic stimuli."[5] That is, overt homophobia masks *significant* same-sex responsiveness.*

The hostility to homosexuality exhibited by the homophobic men in the study is a product of the sharp psychological conflict that occurs between the strict social and moral conditioning dictated by traditional Western sexual morality and innate homosexual responsiveness within the individuals. Psychologists have long recognized that when people's beliefs or value systems conflict with aspects of themselves, they develop psychological defenses to shield the conscious mind from the reality of the disliked characteristic. One such defense mechanism is denial, the refusal to consciously acknowledge an undesirable reality. But because denial absorbs a lot of psychological energy, it is usually accompanied by another defense mechanism, such as reaction formation, in which a person avoids the stress of confronting the unacceptable trait by taking on the opposite trait or emotion. A classic example of reaction formation would be a person in denial about homosexual desires or feelings within himself engaging in aggressive hostility to homosexuality.

The research findings linking overt hostility to homosexuality with repressed homosexual responsiveness would obviously suggest that the visceral hostility or disgust that has been the reaction of so many people throughout Western history to homosexuality is not simply due to the shock of being faced with a gross violation of their moral beliefs. In earlier times, when superstition, rather than science, governed society's understanding of the world, peo-

---

*The researchers inadvertently provided evidence that a complete lack of same-sex responsiveness may be relatively rare in males. The team had originally planned to divide the men into four groups, based on the level of their homophobic score, but they ended up dividing the men into only two groups because of an inability to find a sufficient number of exclusively heterosexual men with a very low homophobic score. Because of the strong correlation the research found between homophobic scores and the level of same-sex erotic responsiveness, the difficulty of finding an adequate number of heterosexual men with very low homophobic scores suggests that men with very low or no homosexual responsiveness at all may be relatively rare. The finding is all the more remarkable when it's considered that heterosexual men who admitted any level of sexual response to other males at any time in the past were deliberately excluded from the study.

ple certainly would have felt threatened by the affront to natural order they saw in homosexual behavior and fearful of divine retribution on a town for the acts of a few, especially during periods of plague or warfare. But heretics or those accused of witchcraft, or those engaging in "unnatural" heterosexual practices like oral or anal sex, all of whom could, presumably, have brought divine wrath on a community, were not attacked with anything like the same vehemence or deep-seated repugnance that were the norm in condemnations of sodomists by either civil or church authorities. And while it's not unusual for people to be uncomfortable with behavior unfamiliar or odd to them, the special intensity of negative reactions to homosexuality in Western history is in a class by itself.

It seems highly likely, therefore, that the ferocity of denunciations of homosexual behavior, a vehemence absent from responses to most other evils in European history, was driven in large part by the same psychological conflict revealed in the men in the Adams study. If aggressive or visceral hostility to homosexuality is a sign of same-sex responsiveness in a person, then it would follow that the widespread repugnance of homosexuality vociferously expressed in Western society over many centuries of its history would be an indicator of some significant level of latent homosexual responsiveness in the population. Put another way, the intensity of negative reactions to homosexuality in Western culture is by itself suggestive of some degree of underlying homosexual responsiveness in modern society.

Such a conclusion is supported by one of the most controversial findings of the Kinsey Report which found that homosexual inclinations or responsiveness are not limited to a tiny, deviant minority, but are found among a much broader portion of the population. The Kinsey researchers found that many of the 20,000 subjects interviewed in the study had had varying amounts of both heterosexual and homosexual experiences. As stated in the report, "males do not represent two discrete populations, heterosexual and homosexual. The world is not to be divided into sheep and goats. It is a fundamental of taxonomy that nature rarely deals with discrete categories.... The living world is a continuum in each and every one of its aspects."[6] To illustrate the varying proportions of heterosexual and homosexual experience found among each of the study's thousands of subjects, the team devised a seven-point scale, with zero representing someone with exclusively heterosexual experiences, and six representing exclusively homosexual experiences. The Kinsey team found that most people fall somewhere between the two extremes.

The Kinsey Report's findings about homosexuality have been fiercely attacked by religious and social conservatives. In fact, in the half century since the report was published it has spawned a cottage industry of conservative-funded research studies aimed at discrediting not only the work of Kinsey's Institute of Sex Research but Alfred Kinsey personally. Yet the understanding of human sexuality emerging from the historical, anthropological and clinical research performed in recent decades suggests that, if anything, the Kinsey Report's estimation of the incidence of same-sex responsiveness in human society as a whole is conservative.

For example, it would surprise many to learn that homosexual practices were a common aspect of human life throughout the world in the past, and were recognized by many cultures as making a positive contribution to the health of society. Many people have some notion about the ancient Greeks practicing homosexuality, but few are aware of the prevalence of homosexual practices and general ambisexuality in many ancient societies. In widely diverse cultures around the world throughout human history, and continuing in some parts of the world even today, homosexual practices have existed alongside heterosexual marriage and have been experienced by nearly everyone in the society at some point in their lives.

In a surprisingly large number of societies it was assumed that everyone was capable of homosexual attraction, and in many of those societies same-sex relationships were a primary form of sexual relations before or outside of heterosexual marriage. In other societies, specialized roles existed for exclusively homosexual individuals who were credited with special gifts in spirituality, healing, art and music. The accumulated evidence from numerous anthropological and historical studies makes clear that the overwhelming predominance of heterosexuality in Western society, rather than being the rule, is actually the exception among human societies over the vast range and history of human cultures around the world. Furthermore, it becomes evident that the attempt of Western moral traditions to suppress or deny the place of homosexuality in human sexuality is one of the chief causes of the widespread sexual neurosis that afflicts modern society.

More astonishing, still, the results of sexual research in the last several decades show that the exclusive heterosexuality held up as the norm in Western society is actually not the inevitable consequence of the human sexual drive, as is universally assumed today, but is a socially conditioned phenomenon unique in world culture. As explained by the veteran sexual researcher C.A. Tripp: "Most people see their heterosexual responses as innate and automatic, but trained observers understand that people are specifically heterosexual because they have been geared by their upbringing to expect and to want to be."[7] In other words, the exclusive heterosexuality prevalent in modern society is not a natural product of the human sexuality, but is entirely the result of the intensive heterosexual conditioning of Western culture and a corresponding harsh condemnation of any hint of homosexual inclinations.

The picture that emerges from the anthropological and historical research, combined with insights from studies in the psychology and physiology of sex, is that of a multifaceted human sexuality in which same-sex activity plays an important and complementary role in support of the vitality of heterosexual procreation. The inescapable conclusion, that the human race is an ambisexual species* and has been one for a very long time, is a radical departure from the exclusively heterosexual vision of sex presented in religion and popular culture. The belief that human sexuality is exclusively heterosexual, or should be, an assumption that still weighs heavily on academic studies of sexuality and that saturates popular culture in the modern world, *is simply a myth.*

Many people will no doubt find this assertion absurd, even outrageous. Yet the factual evidence presented in this book pointing to a multifaceted human sexuality is plentiful and persuasive. Through a survey of the patterns of sexual expression found among animals and among societies around the world throughout history, and an examination of the functional role homosexual behavior has played among animal species and human societies alike, we will see that the heterosexual assumptions that have governed the portrayal of sexuality in popular culture and that have defined the scientific and historical approach to sexuality are incorrect. By demonstrating not only the immutable nature of this trait among humans, but also the complementary role homosexual behavior has played in supporting the reproductive harmony of the human species, this material reveals homosexuality to be an important aspect of the sexual nature inherited by the human species from its animal ancestors.

---

*The term ambisexuality *is now regarded as a more accurate designation than* bisexuality *of the variability sexologists have found in sexual orientation among humans. It was first used by Erwin J. Haeberle in 1978 in his textbook* The Sex Atlas *as an alternative, more precise term for* bisexuality. *Several problems with the precision of and adequacy of the term* bisexual *were noted in the Kinsey Report (Kinsey et al., op. cit., page 615). Vern L. Bullough's* Human Sexuality, An Encyclopedia, *suggests that* "ambisexuality rather than bisexuality is the better term to use. Ambisexuality would recognize the continuum and be defined as 'a person's ability to eroticize both genders under some circumstances,' since equal attraction to males and females is virtually nonexistent" *(Erwin J. Haeberle, Ph.D., Ed.D.,* The Sex Atlas *[New York: The Continuum Publishing Company, 1983]; Vern Bullough,* Human Sexuality, An Encyclopedia *[New York: Garland Publishing Company, 1994]; quoted from online version edited by Erwin J. Haeberle, maintained at http://www2.hu-berlin.de/sexology/GESUND/ARCHIV/SEN/INDEX.HTM). This material reveals homosexuality to be an important aspect of the sexual nature inherited by the human species from its animal ancestors.*

How, then, could our society and its social institutions be so wrong about such a basic element of our nature? Given the degree to which this heterosexual myth has saturated our culture it would surprise many to find that its dominance in our society dates only from the Middle Ages in Europe, and that it required several centuries of violent repression of dissent and non-conformity to make it stick.

In probing the origins of this heterosexual myth, we will examine the historical circumstances and philosophical influences that shaped the development of sexual attitudes in the West, and the conditions under which homosexual love, honored and idealized in some societies, became for the West "the sin whose name we dare not speak." In following these developments, we will see the unfolding of the peculiar confluence of historical forces that, within the space of 150 years, transformed a somewhat sexually tolerant and easygoing early Medieval Europe into a late Medieval society so hounded by the demands of sexual abstinence and sexual conformity, and so fearful of divine retribution for the sins of a few, that in the words of the historian Rattray Taylor, it "came to resemble a vast insane asylum."[8] The impact of those forces and the sexual neuroses and phobias that were engendered in their wake are still with us today in myriad ways, from a homophobic military and the anti-gay hysteria of conservative religionists, to the distorted hyper-machismo of males paranoid about their sexual image and the corresponding demands that society places on young women to see themselves as little more than sex objects for the male.

While the reader may find the assertions presented in this introduction to be outrageous or absurd, the vast and varied material examined in the following chapters makes a compelling case. What emerges is a revolutionary view of the human race as an ambisexual species whose complex sexual harmony is being thwarted by the imposition of what is essentially an artificial and outmoded understanding of nature.

PART I. THE INHERITANCE OF NATURE

One of the principal arguments used by Western religion to condemn homosexual behavior is the contention that same-sex love is unnatural. The notion of the unnaturalness of homosexuality originated in the work of the ancient Greek philosophers at a time when the Greeks were trying to define natural principles and the order of the cosmos. Observing animals in nature, some Greek writers assumed that the "natural purpose" of sex was reproduction. This simplistic philosophical postulation, based on a limited view of animal behavior, found its way into the developing dogma of the early Christian Church where it became a central principle of Christian moral teaching. However, in Chapter 1 a survey of sexual behavior in the animal world will show that not only is homosexual behavior a prominent aspect of animal sexuality, but among many species the level of homosexual activity far exceeds heterosexual activity, and among some species homosexual behavior appears to play a beneficial role supporting the reproductive success of those species.

In Chapter 2 a review of sexual practices among the indigenous tribal cultures that were discovered in the undeveloped regions of the world during the expansion of Western colonialism will show that homosexuality in one form or another was virtually universal among pre–Westernized tribal peoples of all races, and that in t hose cultures homosexuality seemed to harmoniously complement the heterosexual relations of married couples. The widespread homosexual behavior in the animal world, of course, refutes the argument that same-sex love is unnatural, or for that matter, an aberration, an abnormality or a psychosexual disorder. If homosexuality among humans is natural, the question then arises as to what role it plays in the reproductive success of the human species, since features or characteristics of an animal that persist through multiple generations are presumed by evolutionary biologists to be there because they support the survival of the species.

To seek answers to that question, the material surveyed about homosexual behavior among animals and among tribal cultures will be examined in Chapter 3 and summed up and considered with the help of insights into human sexuality provided by recent research. The results are a radically new vision of the place of same-sex relations in human society.

1

Against Nature? Homosexual Behavior in the Animal World

> Billy-goats mount nannies. That is very right indeed, but no one has ever seen a billy mount a billy; nor rams mount rams instead of ewes, nor cocks tread cocks instead of hens.[1]

So the hero of the third century tale of Daphnis and Chloe lectures a would-be seducer after fending off a homosexual advance. Since early Christian times, disapproval of homosexual behavior by moral leaders has been based in large part on the contention that sex between individuals of the same sex was "against nature." Supporters of the argument maintained that the purpose of sex was propagation of the species, and pointed to animals in nature as illustration of the intended function of sexuality. Though this notion persists in the popular mind to the present day, accumulating research shows that, contrary to the traditional view, billy-goats do indeed mount billies, rams do mount rams instead of ewes and cocks do tread cocks. Homosexual behavior not only occurs in the animal world, it is a common and widespread phenomenon among a vast range of species: "The impression that infra-human mammals more or less confine themselves to heterosexual activities is a distortion of the fact which appears to have originated in a man-made philosophy, rather than in specific observations of mammalian behavior."[2]

Farmers have long been aware of same sex behavior among domestic animals. This behavior is so common in domestic stock it is mostly ignored by handlers, though they do take advantage of it for specific purposes. Cows in heat will mount other cows so frequently that farmers use this as a signal the cows are ready for breeding or insemination.[3] Young bulls or steers are often used as "teasers" to arouse mature bulls in order to collect semen for use in artificial insemination. In fact, if a bull won't respond sexually to a cow, a young male is put into the pen with the bull in order to get the bull sexually aroused.[4]

Homosexual behavior also occurs in flocks of chickens. Animal behaviorists found that among the social hierarchy of chickens, males high in the "pecking order" had breeding rights, while high-ranking hens seemed exempt from breeding activity. In breeding, the rooster climbs, or "treads," onto the back of a subordinate bird. A subordinate male will usually avoid being tread upon by facing an approaching dominant rooster and raising its hackles, but if a rooster comes upon an unsuspecting male facing the other way, perhaps taking a dust bath, it will not hesitate to mount it. Younger males will also respond to the courting waltz of a rooster and allow mounting. Males low in the pecking order can be trodden upon to such an extent they are injured or killed. Among hens, those higher in the social hierarchy will often mount other hens. Similar behavior has been observed among turkey hens, where the dominant hens were able to bring the passive females to "orgasm" and subsequent temporary reduction in sex drive.[5]

Same-Sex Activity Among the Lower Animals

Homosexuality is not limited to animals confined in domestic situations. Sexual contact between individuals of the same sex has been observed among animals across the range of evolutionary complexity, from fish and reptiles to primates. Among sticklebacks, a fish that mates in nests of water weeds constructed by the males within tightly defended territories, other males will sometimes enter the territory of an established male, respond to its courting dance, and enter its nest, sometimes even pushing out a female already there. At this point the courting male will attempt mating with the interloping male.[6]

In a species of Jamaican lizard, *Anolis garmani*, in which the males also defend established territories, a smaller male will sometimes live within the territory of a larger male, who will mount and copulate with the younger male. It is not certain whether the dominant male is mistaking the smaller male for a female, or whether he finds the other male to be just as sexually attractive. However, since sexual copulation among the species is very involved, taking approximately 25 minutes, there can be no doubt that the passive male knows what is going on. And inasmuch as the smaller male could easily avoid the encounter by running away, it seems clear he readily submits to the attention of the older male. It is likely the smaller lizard benefits from his association with the larger male, perhaps enjoying better food availability or the opportunity to sneak a mating with one of the resident females. Thus, writes the naturalist who made these observations, an "occasional buggery might be a small price to pay for the advantages of remaining within the large male's territory."[7]

For another lizard, the *Teiidae* sexual activity can start with an active male masturbating by rubbing his genital area on the ground, at which point he then seeks a mate of either sex. If he comes upon a male, he will mount and copulate with the passive male, who may in turn become aroused by the homosexual copulation and then engage in intercourse with the previously dominant male. Lizards of this type may pile up three deep in copulation. Among iguanas, ten of twenty-one observed copulations in one study were male homosexual, with weaker or smaller males falling automatically into the passive homosexual role. Female homosexual behavior, though much less common than male homosexuality in lizards, has been documented among American chameleons, where one female takes a male role in mounting another female.[8]

In many animals, especially among the lower orders, homosexual activity closely follows the patterns heterosexual behavior takes in that species. Homosexuality frequently arises in situations in which an individual is sexually aroused by exposure to or involvement in heterosexual mating, or where an absence of sexual outlets has caused a buildup of sexual tension. In such cases a male may attempt copulation with the first appropriate partner he encounters, male or female. In a similar way, cases of females mounting females are often a result of increased sexual excitement associated with the estrous cycle.[9]

However, even in animals of relatively primitive evolutionary development there is evidence that preference may be a factor in choosing a same-sex partner. Among many bird species, whose heterosexual mating involves bonding among pairs who may stay together for years, homosexual activity takes place within similarly bonded pairs. Such same-sex pair bonds have been observed among birds for over a century. Many of these reports were of free-living individuals who could easily have mated with an opposite-sex partner, which implies that an element of choice or preference is present. Konrad Lorenz, one of the pioneers of animal behavioral studies, frequently mentioned male pair bonds among the greylag geese he studied. Female-female pairs of swans have been reported in England, with the pairs nesting together for several years, one of them playing the male role in sexual activity. A male-male pair of nesting swans was also reported by English birdwatchers. Among ostriches in South Africa, elaborate homosexual courtship displays among males have also been observed.[10]

In one group of Western gulls studied, up to 14 percent of the population consisted of female-female pairs nesting together. These pairs displayed most of the courtship and territorial behaviors shown by heterosexual pairs, a few performed mounting and attempted copulation, and most of the pairs stayed together for more than one breeding season. Similar behavior has been reported in other gull species.[11] Naturalists studying gulls in the Patagonia region along the southern Pacific coast of South America have found that there is an increase in female homosexuality during El Niño weather cycles. With the rise in water temperature associated with the abnormal currents, local fish stocks from which the gulls feed are reduced. When this occurs, a number of females refuse to mate with males, bonding instead with other, impregnated females. They then assist the mothers in feeding the smaller population of young from the reduced fish supply.[12] Without this remarkable adaptation, the competition of the normal number of brooding chicks for a reduced food supply would result in serious malnourishment of the entire chick population, making it difficult for the chicks to survive into adulthood.

While there is no question that heterosexual mating is the predominant sexual activity among reptiles and birds, and that same-sex mounting can often be seen as an adjunct to normal heterosexual activity, it is nonetheless also clear that behavior of a distinctly homosexual character is well established among these relatively primitive species.

Same-Sex Activity Among Mammals

Homosexuality is even more widespread among mammals. In fact, frequent homosexual activity has been observed for all species of mammals which have been carefully studied.[13] Homosexual activity has been reported by scientists among rats, mice, guinea pigs, bats, porcupines, raccoons, dogs, cats, hyenas, lions, elephants, horses, donkeys, cattle, porpoises, and whales, not to mention all varieties of primates.[14] Exclusive homosexual behavior has been found among hedgehogs, lions, dolphins, monkeys, baboons and chimpanzees, among others.[15] One authority in mammalian sexuality has even argued that a biological tendency to homosexual behavior is an inherent characteristic of mammals.[16]

Homosexual behavior has been frequently observed among rats in captivity and will typically be present among males in overcrowded situations or where females are absent. As with many other species of lower mammals, the males will often try to avoid being mounted, either by attempting to escape or by retaliating aggressively. However, several researchers have reported that some male rats will invert their normal sexual role in response to the sexual advances of a male, displaying reactions typical of a female in heat. Contrary to what one might expect, these were not "effeminate" males, but proved to be vigorous copulators of high virility when placed with receptive females. When one of these males was castrated, leading to a gradual elimination of male hormones, its role inversion response disappeared quickly, while the heterosexual coital activity tapered off gradually. While injection of small amounts of male hormones reawakened the rat's ordinary masculine sexuality, restoring the hormones to their previous healthy levels produced a reoccurrence of the rat's willingness to invert its sexual role. Injection with female hormones in this neutered rat produced some female-like receptivity, but the responses were less intense than those under the influence of male hormones.[17] Other studies have confirmed that readiness of males to play the passive role in homosexual copulation is directly linked to levels of testosterone: the greater the level of virility, the more likely it is to display sexual versatility with other males.[18] In a similar way, female mammals are more likely to mount each other when feminine hormones are elevated, as occurs when they are in heat. The direct correlation that has been observed between levels of testosterone in males and estrogen in females and homosexual behavior has led animal behaviorists to conclude that homosexuality and inversion of sexual roles are not an aberration, but are a normal part of a sexually healthy animal's behavioral repertory.[19]

Among herding animals in the wild, homosexual activity seems to be a natural complement to heterosexual behavior. In many such species, ranging from gazelles to mountain sheep, heterosexual mating is performed by a dominant male who earns his position by demonstrating his superiority to the other males in sparring matches. Thus, only the genes of the strongest individuals will be passed to the next generation. Among mountain sheep, male-male battles end with the losing ram being mounted, with an erection, by the winning ram. The mounting male usually achieves full penetration, which is followed by pelvic thrusts probably leading to ejaculation in most cases.[20] In feral goats, among which similar behavior has been observed, penetration and ejaculation have been confirmed in male-male mounts after dominance fights.[21] Once the dominant ram has established his position, he will then court and mount subordinate rams as well as estrous ewes. If a female is not in heat, she will simply walk away from the ram, but a subordinate ram will allow himself to be mounted, assuming the swaybacked mating posture taken by receptive females. The dominant ram will often court a subordinate male with horn displays, just as he does with females; he will also frequently lick and sniff the genital area of his sex object. Among English sheep, a dominant ram, when courting a subordinate male, will take the subordinate's penis into his mouth. When the dominant ram is courting and copulating with females, the subordinate rams, evidently aroused by the activity, will mount each other indiscriminately.[22] Among bighorn and thinhorn sheep, the males live in what one zoologist has characterized as "homosexual societies," in which homosexual courtship and mounting routinely occur among all members.[23] Inasmuch as it is likely some of the males will never rise to become the dominant ram, it is inevitable that homosexuality will be the exclusive sexual outlet of a significant percentage of the males.

Homosexual activity is clearly an integral part of the sexual life of these species. In one herd of mountain sheep studied, for every 100 copulations observed, 69 were homosexual. Same-sex courtship is such a fundamental part of mating patterns among bighorn and thinhorn sheep that females will even mimic the behavior of males in order to mate with them. Females in heat will often adopt behavioral patterns typical of young males being courted by more senior males, which will then arouse the interest of the older males because, ironically, it makes them resemble young males.[24] Similar homosexual mounting by dominant males has been observed in many other hierarchical animal societies.[25]

Same-sex mounting is frequent among blackbuck, Thompson's and Grant's gazelles on the plains of Central Africa, among American and European bison, and among African buffalo. Male blackbuck gazelles, who live in same-sex herds, only leave their groups during mating season, when males over three years old attempt mating with females. At other times, most males remain in the all-male herds, where much homosexual activity takes place. Among blackbucks, mounting may occur during play-fighting, friendly sparring matches with erotic overtones, which may involve three males at a time. Adult Blackbuck males will also perform elaborate courtship displays toward younger males before mounting them.[26]

American bison males also live in small same-sex groupings of up to 12 individuals, where homosexual activity is frequent. Mounting may occur during play-fighting, but also following aggressive interaction between two bulls. American bison bulls, especially younger animals, sometimes form temporary bonds with other males, where one male may closely follow another male, defend him and mount him. Among some pairs, the mounting is reciprocal, while in others, only one of the two bulls does the mounting. Homosexual activity is very frequent among American bison bulls, especially during mating season, when it may occur several times a day. In fact, since females rarely allow mounting by males more than once a year, and males may mount other males several times a day, heterosexual copulation represents a small fraction of total sexual activity.[27]

Homosexual mounting by dominant males in these herding species seems to play an important role in dissipating tensions and reducing injuries in dominance-submission interactions, just as the homosexual mounting among subordinates provides sexual release for individuals who are precluded from heterosexual activity. However, among many species homosexuality has nothing to do with dominance interactions, and appears to be more an expression of affection or playfulness between individuals. For example, homosexual behavior is a primary characteristic of male giraffes and is much more frequent than heterosexual behavior. In one study in Africa, same-sex mountings among males accounted for 94 percent of all observed sexual activity. Male giraffes, especially younger animals, tend to congregate in all-male groups, where homosexual activity is the rule. Male giraffes are very affectionate with one another, and have a unique courtship or affectionate activity called "necking." Two males will typically initiate such affectionate contact by standing side by side, usually facing the opposite direction, and then gently rubbing their necks on each other's body, head, neck, loins, and thighs, sometimes for as long as an hour. One male may lick the other's back or sniff his genitals during necking. Necking usually leads to sexual arousal, with one or both males developing erections, followed by mounting which often leads to orgasm.[28]

Homosexual activity among females has also been observed among several species of African antelope. Among kob antelopes, virtually all females engage in homosexual activities ranging from simple mounting to elaborate courtship displays, which usually occur during the mating season. A female usually initiates courtship of another female by prancing, approaching the other female with short, stiff-legged steps with tail and head raised high. The courting female will then sniff the vulva of other female, who crouches and urinates while her partner sniffs the stream of urine. Her courtship dance continues with her raising her foreleg and gently touching her partner between her legs from behind, and the partner will respond with a ritual mating-circling in which she circles tightly around the courting female, sometimes nipping or butting her hindquarters. This activity leads to mounting in which the courting female climbs onto the back of her partner. Similar female homosexuality also occurs among other closely related species of antelope, the waterbuck, lechwe and puku. In contrast to kob antelopes, homosexual activity among waterbuck females frequently occurs among females who are not in heat.[29] Same-sex activity is also known among females among other species of herding animals. For example, female elephants in single-sexed groups have been observed spending much of their time masturbating each other with their trunks.[30]

Homosexuality, as a sexual outlet in the absence of heterosexual opportunities, has been observed in a variety of species. Sea manatees, sometimes called sea cows, are large aquatic mammals that inhabit the coastal waters of Florida. When a female manatee comes into heat, she may be pursued by three or four males until she accepts one of them for mating. The frustrated males will often turn to each other for sexual relief, rubbing against each other, penises erect, sometimes four at a time.[31] Similar group sex has been observed among blue whales. When the resident bull of a group of blue whales engages in sex with the females, young adult and adolescent males will also become sexually excited and will cavort with each other, rubbing their erect penises against each other, leaving clouds of sperm in the water.[32]

Homosexual interaction is frequent among gray whale males during their northward migration, and when they are summering in northern waters. Sexual activity occurs close to the surface of the water in sessions that can last from 30 minutes to more than an hour and a half. The sessions often include more than two whales, and sometimes four or five. The whales may start the activity by rolling around each other and onto their sides amid much splashing of water and blowing. Two whales will run their bellies together and position themselves so that their genital areas are in contact, often with erect penises. Often two whales will intertwine their penises above the water's surface, or one of the whales may nudge the other whale's penis with his head. Sexual interactions between females have also been observed. Gray whales will also form same-sex pairs or trios who remain together as companions, traveling and feeding together throughout the summer. These companions cruise together, side by side with their fins touching, and will often perform synchronized blowing and diving maneuvers, including breaching, dramatically leaping out of the water and landing on their sides or backs.[33]

Same Sex Activity Among the Higher Animals

While much of the homosexual behavior among lower species for the most part either mimics or seems a substitute for heterosexual behavior, among higher species same-sex behavior takes on a character of its own, distinct from heterosexual patterns. In fact as the tree of evolutionary development is ascended, not only is homosexual behavior more frequent, but the types of sexual interaction are more varied than in heterosexual situations. Much of the activity has nothing to do with dominance-submission interactions, an element of playfulness is often present, and the appearance of preference in choice of partner is more pronounced. And among those animals with highly developed and convoluted cerebral cortexes — dolphins, monkeys and apes — homosexual relations readily occur without the stimulus of heightened sexual drive or the unavailability of partners of the opposite sex that is often associated with same-sex activity among lower animals.[34]

Dolphins are very active sexually throughout the year and much of the activity is homosexual. Adult male dolphins seem particularly attracted to younger males and repeatedly attempt to engage in sexual relations with them. Adult males may swim up against the younger males, masturbating against their flanks or attempting copulation. Even in cases where male dolphins have been courted by a receptive female, they may avoid her and promptly attempt to copulate with other males.[35] Among bottlenose dolphins, the most well-known species, homosexual activity is frequent among both males and females. Two males or two females often rub their bodies together, mouthing or nuzzling each other, and may also caress and stroke each other with their fins or snouts. This activity is sometimes accompanied by playful rolling, chasing, pushing and leaping. During this play, which can last anywhere from minutes to several hours, males often display erect penises. More explicit homosexual activity may take a variety of forms. One dolphin may gently probe another's genital area with the soft tips of its flippers. Female spinner dolphins sometimes ride on each other's dorsal fin: one inserts her fin into the other's vulval or genital slit, and then the two swim together in this position. Female bottlenose dolphins often take turns rubbing each other's clitoris, using their snouts, flippers or flukes. Females will also clasp each other, belly to belly, in a manner similar to heterosexual mating, which may also involve thrusting against each other. Male dolphins will sometimes rub their erect penises against a partner's body or genital area. This activity often leads to copulation, in which one male swims upside down underneath the other, pressing his genitals against the other's, and often inserting his penis into the other male's genital slit or anus. Single-sexed groups of a dozen or more spinner dolphins have been observed gathering together in group sessions of caressing and sexual behavior.

Among bottlenose dolphins, males frequently form lifelong pair-bonds with each other. Adolescents and younger males usually live in all-male groups, in which homosexual activity is frequent. A male within one of these groups will usually begin to develop a strong bond with another male, usually the same age, with whom he will spend the rest of his life. The pair of dolphins becomes constant companions, traveling widely together. While sexual activity between the two of them gradually declines as they grow older, it usually continues to be a regular feature of their relationship. Bonded pairs will sometimes take turns guarding or remaining vigilant while the other partner rests, just as the partners will defend each other against sharks, and protect their mates while they are healing from wounds inflicted during predators' attacks.[36]

The strength of the attachment that male dolphins develop with each other has been demonstrated between a bonded pair of males which was studied in captivity. As part of the study, one of the males was removed from the tank for three weeks. When he was returned to the tank, the two dolphins greeted each other with enormous excitement. The pair swam side by side for hours, rushing frenziedly through the water, leaping completely out of the water together on several occasions. For several days the two males were inseparable, neither paying any attention to a female, who was in heat. At other times the two males seemed bent only on preventing the other's mating with the female.[37]

Homosexual activity is a major part of the social life of the orca, or killer whale, the largest member of the dolphin family. During the summer and fall, when large numbers of Orcas assemble to feast on the salmon runs, males of all ages frequently spend entire afternoons courting and engaging in sexual activity with each other. Sexual interaction is usually between pairs, though three or four may sometimes join together. The males will roll around with each other on the surface, splashing, and making frequent body contact as they rub, chase, and gently nudge one another. The males pay special attention to each other's belly and genital area. Often one male will swim underneath the other upside down, touching or nuzzling the other's genital area with his snout. The two males then swim together in this position, continuing the snout genital contact as the upper one surfaces to breathe, following which the two dive together, spiraling down in an elegant double helix. When the pair surfaces again, three to five minutes later, they repeat the sequence, reversing positions. During all these interactions, the orcas will often have erect penises. Though males of all ages participate in these homosexual interactions, the activity is most common among adolescent orcas, that is, sexually mature individuals 12 to 25 years old. Some of the males have favorite partners with whom they interact year after year, and some may even form long-lasting "friendship" pairs.[38]

Among monkeys and apes homosexual activity is frequent and in most cases unrelated to dominance. Not only does the homosexual behavior exhibited by primates bear little resemblance to heterosexual mating, but same-sex interactions occur in an astonishing variety — a tribute to the vitality and creativity of these animals. Immature and adolescent males show a wide range of sexual responses. They may sexually "present" like females, engage in mutual masturbation or mount one another. Homosexual behavior is so common in adolescent monkeys one prominent primatologist has argued that male monkeys go through a homosexual phase during development.[39]

Sexual versatility is also exhibited by adult monkeys. In one instance, a smaller male macaque was observed climbing up the hindquarters of a larger male, pulling the penis of the large male backwards and sucking it. In another situation, two male macaques bent over, back to back, and each reached between the other's legs to manipulate the other's penis.[40] Sometimes the male playing the passive role in anal intercourse reaches back and handles the penis of his male partner. In other situations, the receptive male masturbates while a dominant male is copulating with him — a technique also employed among human males engaged in intercourse.[41] In fact, homosexual copulation among monkeys can be quite human-like. A detailed description of one such encounter written by an early primate specialist reads like the clinical observations of humans by sex researchers:

> If the exposure of the visual, olfactory and tactile receptors generated more sexual affect it was manifested in the more vigorous play of the aggressor and more animated smacking of the lips. Its intensification was often further expressed by the voice sounds. This usually aroused like responses in the sexual object [the second male] and the play continued until the summation of affect ... had generated a very active sexual craving. Insertion of the penis into the anus was finally made, followed by rapid strokes and kissing of the lips until mild general convulsive movements resulted.... The transitory functional paralysis attending a complete orgasm seems to be the ultimate reaction sought for as the erotogenic play advances from one stage to another, and after a period of rest the play begins all over again.[42]

Homosexual behavior among female primates, while less frequent than among males, is nonetheless a widespread phenomenon. Typically one female mounts another in a way that stimulates her own and/or her partner's genitals, often to the point of orgasm. As might be expected, a female's estrous state often correlates with homosexual activity. While most or all females also engage in heterosexual activity, individual females seem to have preferences, and pursue them, among both males and females.[43]

In homosexual interaction among female chimpanzees, sexual activity might include oral/genital contact, and mounting, with one partner dominating the other. Pairs of females among a group of rhesus macaques being studied at the Boston Zoo engaged in homosexual relations in a position closely approximating ordinary heterosexual mating, where one mounts the other from the rear, but also in five other positions not usually seen in heterosexual copulation. One female-female pair seemed to enjoy "ventral hugging" in which the two hugged face to face while one of them rubbed her genitals on her partner. Similar behavior has been observed among female rhesus monkeys living in the wild.[44]

Much homosexual activity among primates takes place between favorite partners. Female Japanese macaques often form intense, exclusive pair-bonds with each other based on mutual sexual attractions. Female bonded partners will often sit together, huddling or in close physical contact, frequently spending long periods grooming one another. They often synchronize their movements, traveling in tandem or following one another closely, sometimes cooing to each other, and will also defend each other should one of them be threatened by another animal. Such pairs of females engage in a variety of sexual behaviors, ranging from mutual genital stimulation to mounting, which they also perform in a number of different postures. Courting behavior among pairs of female rhesus macaques involves five distinct pursuit games: "hide and seek," in which two females peek at each other from around a tree trunk; "kiss and run," in which one female rushes up to another and briefly kisses or nuzzles her and then quickly runs off with the other one in pursuit; "follow the leader," in which the females alternate positions following one another; "lipsmack and circle," where one female circles closer and closer to the other while making lipsmaking noises; and "present and run," in which one female invites the other to mount her and then teasingly runs off. Similarly intense pair-bonds are common among male stumptail macaques, who will also engage in a variety of sexual activities. These male pairs will huddle together, embracing, with one gently nibbling at the other's mouth. The partners may even sleep together, with one closely hugging the other from the back, while holding his partner's penis. Sexual activity between the pair includes oral sex, mutual masturbation and mounting, all of which can be performed in a variety of positions.[45]

While among some species, pairs of males or females may form intense pair-bonds, among other species pairs will form less intensive type of relationships, sometimes termed "friendships" by behaviorists.[46] These sorts of friendship relationships, less inclusive than pair-bonds, but much more than incidental interactions, might occur between young bachelor males, or between older females. Often relationships occur between an older male and a smaller adult or adolescent male. Aggressive adults tend to protect their homosexual favorites from assault by other monkeys and the favorites soon learn to seek this protection. One observer described a friendship between two such macaques which was accompanied by frequent intercourse, mutual embracing and protection of the younger male by his partner.[47] Similar relationships have been reported among other species of monkeys.[48]

Homosexual behavior is common among both male and female gorillas. These animals, the largest members of the primate family, live in small groups of eight to fifteen individuals, usually made up of a dominant older male, three to six adult females, one or two juvenile males, and five to seven immature offspring. All-male groups are also common, and are formed by the banding together of males who leave their home groups upon reaching maturity. Among the all-male groups, which can persist for years, homosexual behavior is frequent. In fact, sexual activity is greater among the all-male groups than among mixed-sex groups. Each male has preferred partners with whom they sexually interact. Some males have sex with only one other male of the group, while others may have as many as five different partners. Pairings, likewise, vary considerably, and may last for a few months or go on for years. There is often intense competition among the group for preferred partners, usually the younger males. Older, higher-ranking males frequently guard their younger partners, and will fight off other males who attempt to make sexual advances to their partners. Males will copulate with each other either face to face, or with one mounting the other from the rear. Touching and fondling each other's genitals is also frequent. Male gorillas are, thus, primarily homosexual unless they are able to achieve the dominant-male status within a family group, at which time their sexual activity becomes predominantly, though not exclusively, heterosexual.

Within the mixed-sex groups, the adult female gorillas sometimes form pair bonds with other females, and such a female will spend as much time with her female partner as with the breeding male of the group. The two females will remain in close physical contact while they spend time together, sitting with each other, or lying one against the other, and they will spend much of this time in mutual grooming. After sitting quietly together for a while, they may begin sexual activity by fondling each other's genitals, after which one of them may bring her face into contact with the other's vulva, smelling or touching it with her mouth. This is usually followed by face-to-face embracing, usually lying down, with rubbing of the genitals against each other. Sexual interaction between female gorillas is distinctly different from heterosexual interaction, usually lasting much longer, involving the face-to-face position, which is rare in heterosexual mating, and generally being more affectionate, with much more embracing and mutual grooming.[49]

Among baboons, which live in highly ordered societies, sex plays an important role in defining and regulating the relationships among members of varying ranks of the social hierarchy. A troop of baboons may number 50 to 100 individuals or more, and is governed by a small group of older, dominating males who stick together and support one another's authority. Subordinate males acknowledge the authority of the dominant males by sexually presenting to them, just as the dominant males will assert their authority by mounting subordinate males. The use of sex as a gesture of power also occurs when a troop finds their territory encroached by another troop of baboons; the males will respond by sitting on the outside of their troop, legs apart, displaying their penises, often erect, as a warning to the competing group.[50]

The troop is organized into families, each of which is presided over by a dominant male and includes a number of females and their young as well as several bachelor males. Homosexual activity is frequent and is engaged in by all members of the group, male and female. Mutual grooming, genital examination and mounting may take place between the overlord and a favorite bachelor, or between either of these and any male of the troop, regardless of age, with whom temporary friendly relations are established.[51] Bachelor males occasionally pair off in friendship bonds with each other, and for a time a pair will be seen constantly together. Relationships also exist between older and younger males. One such relationship was observed to last three years and was ended only by the death of the younger baboon. This young male rarely mixed with the other adolescents of the troop, and whenever it was harassed by other baboons and squealed, it was immediately rescued by its older partner, with whom it often engaged in sexual intercourse.[52]

It can be clearly seen that among primates sex has acquired functions completely unrelated to reproduction. As is the case with many other mammal species, sex mediates dominance interactions between males, diffusing aggression and preventing injuries. Homosexuality also provides a sexual outlet for adolescents and non-breeding adults of both sexes and contributes to harmony among the groups by cementing friendship alliances. But it must be said also that at times primates seem to engage in sex for no other reason than the fun of it, that sex is but one expression of the exuberant vitality of these creatures.

Among bonobos, a close relative of chimpanzees, the development of non-reproductive functions for sex is even more explicit. Bonobos, until recently very little known, were at first thought to be a variety of chimpanzee, and were only recognized as a separate species in 1929. These animals, which share more than 98 percent of their genetic material with humans,[53] have sparked considerable interest in the scientific community in recent decades because of some remarkable similarities to humans. Like humans, and unlike all other mammals, bonobo female sexual receptivity is not restricted to the estrous cycle, and so females are sexually receptive nearly all the time. Bonobos are also the only animals besides humans in which heterosexual mating occurs in the face to face "missionary position"; the bonobo vulva and clitoris are oriented more frontally than in other primates which suggests that bonobos have adapted to this position. Bonobo adult males are also subject to that bane of middle aged human males, pattern baldness, and the females have breasts with no hair on them. One of the more notable features of bonobo behavior is its ability to walk upright with ease, which it will do so that it can carry food in its hands. In fact, bonobos standing upright strongly resemble artists' conceptions of the first hominid, *Australopithicus*— the pre-human better known by the nickname "Lucy," which is considered to be the transitional animal between primates and humans. Comparisons of bonobo skeletons with those of Lucy show close resemblance in size and body proportions. These factors have prompted some scientists to propose bonobos as the prototype ancestor from whom both chimpanzees and humans evolved.[54]

In bonobo societies, a primary role of sex is in establishing and maintaining peaceful relations between members of groups.[55] Unlike many other species, in which sex is a fairly distinct category of behavior, among bonobos, sex is an integral part of social relations, serving an important function as a substitute for aggression. When a food source is encountered, a situation which normally results in squabbles and aggression among other primate species, bonobos will first engage in sexual relations and then peacefully share the food. Sex is also used in establishing friendships, to help new members of a group become acquainted with the other group members, and for reconciliation after altercations — a practice not unknown in human relationships.[56]

As might be expected when sex is involved in so many interactions, bonobos engage in sexual relations in virtually every partner combination, heterosexual and homosexual. In one group of bonobos studied less than a third of sexual matings involved sexually mature individuals of the opposite sex.[57] The variety of sexual contacts in bonobos include oral sex, massage of another individual's genitals and intense tongue-kissing. Among males sexual patterns range from cursory mounting to intensive face-to-face embracing with thrusting and mutual penis rubbing. A favorite sexual position female bonobos will take with each other is unique to their species; one female will cling with arms and legs to another, face to face, and then the two will rub their genitals sideways together, accompanied by grins and squeals of delight. The face to face position is preferred by juveniles of both sexes and by adult females; adult males seem to prefer mounting from the rear, though they will adopt the frontal position frequently as well.[58]

Recognizing the close relationship between bonobos and early humans, some scientists have raised the possibility that sex may have played a similar tension-reducing role in early hominid groups, contributing to the development of the monogamous family unit, and, by reducing competition among males, allowing the cooperative hunting and gathering and food sharing that is thought to have been essential to the survival of early human societies.[59]

An Evolutionary Development in Animal Sexuality

As this brief survey has shown, sexual behavior between members of the same sex is a widespread phenomenon throughout the animal world. This incontestable fact eliminates one of the principal arguments used to prove that homosexual behavior is unnatural and that the purpose of sex is procreation. In fact, the very dynamics of heterosexual interaction seems to have been a contributing factor to the development of homosexual behavior. A characteristic element of the sexuality of vertebrate species is the opposing role the male plays with the female in reproduction. In many species the female is very selective in choosing a sexual partner, only permitting mating with individuals that meet certain standards of strength and vitality. In other species mating rights are won by a male who succeeds in demonstrating superiority in physical strength through dominance fights. This selectivity, by the female, and through dominance competition among males, insures that the genes of the strongest and fittest individuals are passed on to the next generation. As a consequence of this nearly universal reproductive strategy, males evolved with a highly competitive and promiscuous nature. While it is the female's nature to resist mating except under certain conditions and with the right mate, it is the male's nature to aggressively seek opportunities for sexual release.

This inherent characteristic of the male would account for a male of even such primitive species as reptiles taking sexual advantage of another male. The male would recognize the other animal as a member of its own species, hence, within the range of possible sex objects. It may not matter to such a male seeking release whether the sexual object is of the opposite sex or not; he may find males as sexually attractive as females. During dominance competitions, it would have been inevitable that stronger males would recognize the opportunity for sexual release in defeated males. The emergence of a passive sexual response in the defeated male as a defense would reduce the chance of injury. By eliminating excessive violence and reducing the incidence of injuries, the diversion of aggression into sex would have contributed to the health of the species, and thus would have become favored as an adaptation in natural selection. This in turn would have set the stage for the emergence of a non-procreative function of sex in mitigating aggression and reducing tensions. Because of its beneficial effects, this non-reproductive sex paradoxically had the effect of enhancing the reproductive success of the species. It is therefore possible to see a progression in the evolutionary development of homosexual behavior purely as by-product of the dynamics of heterosexual reproduction.

Janet Mann, a psychologist and researcher in animal behavior, has argued that homosexual behavior among dolphins developed as an evolutionary adaptation because of its positive role in minimizing aggression, particularly among males of the species.[60] Other researchers have proposed that homosexual behavior evolved within various animal species because of its role in social tension regulation, reconciliation, social bonding and alliance formation between members of animal groups.[61]

Whatever its genesis, the fact remains that homosexual behavior is deeply ingrained in the genetic heritage of the animal world, playing a part in the lives of mammals, especially those higher on the evolutionary tree, to a degree not generally appreciated. While providing a tension-reducing function, and a sexual outlet in the absence of heterosexual opportunities and for non-breeding adults, homosexual behavior has also been shown to facilitate social relationships and contribute to harmony within groups, and seems to be the primary form of sexual expression for adolescents and young adults of many species. As evolutionary biologists have observed, characteristics of a species do not evolve in response to a need of the species; rather evolutionary selection often favors the adaptation of existing features to uses or purposes that may have no relation to their original function in the species, but which provide a reproductive advantage of some sort. Such appears to be the case with the widespread occurrence of homosexual behavior among mammals.

Implications for Human Sexuality

Homosexual behavior, then, is not only "natural," and not a corruption of nature as has long been argued, but a product of evolutionary development that plays an important role in the lives of many species of animals. Considering the prevalence of homosexual behavior among the primates, one would naturally expect homosexuality to be a significant characteristic of the most prominent of primates, humans. In fact, homosexual behavior is so well established among mammals, especially those of the higher orders, that it would be odd if homosexual behavior did not play a significant role in human sexuality. As will be seen from the anthropological and historical material surveyed in the following chapters, a tendency to homosexual behavior is indeed a primary characteristic of the sexuality of the human species, though that fact has been obscured by centuries of Western religious dogma about sex and its attendant misconceptions about the natural world.

The implications of homosexual behavior among animals on the study of human sexuality has been largely overlooked by sexual researchers. One might suppose, for example, that the patterns of adolescent homosexuality and same-sex pair bonds between non-breeding adults, which are quite common among primates, would be a prominent aspect of human sexuality, inasmuch as humans evolved from a branch of the primate family and share all but a tiny fraction of genetic material with primates. And, indeed, a review of patterns of sexual behavior that have been observed among aboriginal tribes and non–Western cultures shows that homosexuality is also a widespread phenomenon of non–Christianized societies throughout the world, and in patterns quite similar to those documented among primates.

However, until the advent of Gay Liberation in the late 1960s and 1970s, homosexual behavior has been rarely visible in the modern West. In fact, until very recently the scientific establishment has regarded homosexuality among humans as deviant behavior and a sign of pathology — a view that is still maintained by conservative religious bodies. Among Western societies research into homosexuality in the past was for the most part devoted to documenting and investigating the causes of homosexual behavior on the assumption that it arose from deficiencies in psychological development or some sort of personality disorder. The problem with this approach is obvious when one applies the same assumptions to animals: it is absurd to think that the widespread and frequent same-sex behavior among such diverse species as mountain sheep, dolphins, and primates has anything to do with a developmental disorder or any form of psychopathology. The widespread homosexual behavior among animals makes it abundantly clear that homosexuality among humans is not a phenomenon invented by humans, nor a psychosexual disorder, but an aspect of sexuality that the human species inherited from millions of years of evolutionary development in animals.

2

The Nature People: Same-Sex Behavior Among Indigenous Peoples

When the Spanish began exploring the New World in the years that followed Columbus's epochal voyages, they encountered a people living in a culture quite different from their own. Throughout Central America and along the Pacific Coast of South America the explorers found a civilization of cities with large populations living around towering temples dedicated to exotic gods. Since the time of the Crusades, Europeans traveling in far off lands had brought back reports of strange lands and peoples, but what the Spanish saw in the Americas was unlike anything Westerners had known elsewhere. In fact, what the Spanish found was like a much earlier stage of their own cultural development. Though they couldn't know it, they were encountering a civilization comparable to that of the earliest developments in Mesopotamia.

Among the strange habits that the Spanish found among these peoples was one for which they were not prepared. To their horror, they found homosexuality to be a widely practiced custom among the inhabitants of this New World. Not only were natives of every social stratum involved in what to Spanish eyes was a heinous crime against nature; homosexual acts even figured in the art objects displayed in temples and worn as jewelry.

Bernal Díaz del Castillo, who accompanied the conquistador Hernán Cortés on his conquest of Mexico in 1519, commented frequently on the widespread homosexual behavior they encountered. Cortés, in his first report to Emperor Charles V, wrote that the Indians of Mexico "are all sodomites and have recourse to that abominable sin." Another writer, López de Gomara, called the Indians "sodomitic like no other generation of men."[1] Father Pierre de Gand found sodomy to be virtually universal among the Aztecs. Bernal Díaz described numerous male prostitutes among the Aztecs, as well as unmarried temple priests engaging in sodomy.[2] Montezuma, the Aztec god-king, was reported to have had sexual relations with the young warriors who were about to be ritually sacrificed.[3] There was even an Aztec god, Xochipili, who was the patron of homosexuality and male prostitution. Bartolome de las Casas reported that Mayan parents supplied their adolescent sons with young males to use as sexual partners before marriage.[4] Other missionaries also reported widespread homosexuality among the Mayans.[5] Pedro Cieza de León, in his "Chronicles of Peru," described sodomy as among the worst sins of the people there.[6]

In the high cultures of Mexico and Peru the Spanish found a rich tradition of erotic art, much of it depicting homosexual activity. Bernal Díaz, while exploring the coast of Yucatan in 1517, wrote of discovering numerous clay figurines in which "the Indians seemed to be engaged in sodomy, one with the other." Fernandez de Oviedo, a royal chronicler, wrote of an expedition to an island off the Yucatan coast by Diego Velazquez, who reported entering a Mayan temple and being shocked to see a large wooden statue of two males engaged in intercourse. Ovieda himself saw some of the erotic art work in Panama in 1515, which he described: "In some parts of these Indies, they carry as a jewel a man mounted upon another in that diabolic and nefarious act of Sodom, made in gold relief. I saw one of these jewels of the devil, twenty pesos gold in weight.... I broke it down with a hammer and smashed it under my own hand." Most appalling to the Spanish was that homosexuality was frequently associated with cross-dressing, and that these practices often had religious connotations. Cieza de León wrote in disgust of the customs he witnessed in temples in Peru:

> The devil has introduced this vice [sodomy] under a kind of cloak of sanctity, and in each important temple or house of worship they have a man or two, or more, depending on the idol, who go dressed in women's attire from the time they are children.... With these, almost like a rite, and ceremony, on feast [days] and holidays they have carnal, foul intercourse, especially the chiefs and headmen.... The devil held such sway in this land that, not satisfied with making them fall into so great sin, he made them believe that this vice was a kind of holiness and religion.[7]

The widespread homosexual practices encountered by the Spanish were an affront to everything they believed about sexuality. Citing biblical authority, the Spanish held that any sexual act other than that designed for reproduction was "against nature." In line with centuries of European religious thought, they believed anything outside their conception of what was natural to be associated with sin and the Devil, and so used the "sinfulness" of the natives as a justification of their conquest and subjugation of the population. Setting up a branch of the Inquisition in the New World, the Spanish set about prosecuting and executing those found guilty of sodomy wherever they found them. Vasco Núñez de Balboa was praised when during his expedition across Panama, he had forty "sodomites" eaten alive by his dogs.

Almost as soon as the Spanish had established their control, their missionaries began converting the natives and imposing on them their notions of proper, Christian moral behavior. When the diseases the Europeans carried with them to America began decimating native populations, the Spanish saw that as God's punishment for their homosexuality. Fernandez de Oviedo wrote, "It is not without cause that God permits them to be destroyed. And I have no doubt that for their sins God is going to do away with them very soon." In 1552 the historian López De Gomora reported that sodomy in the New World was being successfully wiped out by the Spanish. But the Spanish found that homosexual practices were not limited to the inhabitants of the old Meso-American civilizations of Central America and Peru. In Florida, Spanish missionaries found widespread homosexual practices among the Timucua Indians and tried to get them to confess their sodomy and repent. When Spanish missionaries arrived in California, they found homosexuality common among the tribes there as well, and waged a campaign over several centuries to try to wipe it out.[8]

As European explorers spread throughout the Americas, Africa and the Pacific in the next three centuries, their explorations of new lands were accompanied by similar unexpected discoveries about the sexual customs of these primitive, undeveloped peoples, who the Germans called the naturvölker, the nature people. In contrast to the rigid sexual morality focused on procreation held by the Europeans, native peoples in many areas displayed no discomfort with sexual interaction among members of the same sex, and seemed to take such behavior for granted. Early explorers were taken aback by the casual acceptance of homosexual behavior among tribal peoples and confounded by the seemingly universal presence of androgynous homosexual individuals, whom they often found playing important leadership roles in many tribes. Though in most cases the reaction of the other Europeans wasn't as drastic as that of the Spanish conquistadors with their Inquisition, the missionaries who later accompanied the colonists nonetheless labored industriously to enforce their European sexual morality among the natives.

What is one to make of the sexual practices these early explorers encountered? Certainly to many modern Westerners the sexuality described by the Spanish would be as foreign and as perplexing as it was for the Spanish. But as recent anthropological and historical research makes clear, it is the Western cultural attitude toward sex, as being solely for the purpose of procreation, which is unique. In a vast range of societies around the world throughout human history and in some parts of the world even today, homosexual behavior has existed alongside, and complemented, heterosexual activity, making an important contribution to the health and vitality of those societies. What the Spanish conquistadors saw among the native peoples of the Americas, then, was merely glimpses of the diversity of sexual expression that has characterized many societies throughout the non–European world.

The Survival of Homosexual Traditions in Central America

There is evidence that the homosexual customs of the pre–Columbian cultures were quite old. The Toltec civilization which preceded the Aztecs had a reputation for homosexuality among the Mayans and Aztecs, and it may be from the Toltecs that the Aztecs got their god Xochipili, who was associated with homosexuality and male prostitution.[9] In Peru, a large amount of pottery survives from the Chimu culture, which preceded the Incans, and the Moche culture, which preceded the Chimu, and the surviving pieces include numerous depictions of homosexual intercourse between males.[10] The homosexual traditions of these peoples, therefore, seem to be as old as the cultures themselves, which date back to the beginning of the first millennium, nearly 1,500 years before the arrival of the Spanish.

From what can be gleaned from the accounts given by the Spanish, homosexual behavior occurred in a variety of forms and seemed to play a part in the lives of many men. Spanish accounts complain about what seemed to them effeminate men who would take the passive role in intercourse, and who seemed quite numerous throughout the region, often playing key roles in religious rituals. But homosexuality was found not just among cross-dressing religious functionaries involved in exotic worship rites. Among those prosecuted by the Inquisition during a visit to Bahia, California, in 1592 were pairs of young men, such as one young pair who the records said had "sinned" together more than two hundred times — evidently homosexual lovers.[11] A 17th century Franciscan friar, Juan de Torquemada, wrote of a practice among the Mayans of providing teenaged sons with pubescent males as sexual partners. Torquemada wrote that the Mayans told him they learned the practice from a god who came down to earth and taught males to have sex with each other. The custom thereafter arose for a boy at puberty to become the "boy-wife" to an older teenager, and then to graduate in his teenage years to being the husband of a younger boy, and then in his twenties to becoming the husband of a woman.[12] According to Mayan customs, then, all Mayan males would have had sexual relationships with both males and females at some point during their lives.

In the aftermath of the Spanish conquest, the Meso-American civilizations were completely destroyed. Remarkably, though, despite centuries of church and government hostility to homosexuality, vestiges of the sexual customs of the Mayans and Aztecs seem to have survived among the peoples of southern Mexico and Central America. In modern times Mayans continue to live in the rain forests of Yucatan and Guatemala that have overgrown the ancient Mayan cities and temples. The sexual tradition of a culture radically different from that of modern Western Europe is evident in some of the ruins, where the Mayan fascination with the penis is displayed in huge stone phallic symbols that occupy prominent positions in the ceremonial grounds. Likewise, the same casual acceptance of homosexuality that so appalled the Spanish authorities persists among the Mayan villagers. Homosexuality is very open and common, particularly among males between the early teens and the mid-twenties. After that point, the young men are expected to marry and settle down, but homosexual behavior often continues nonetheless. In fact, marriage to a woman does not seem to have much effect on the occurrence and amount of homosexual behavior.[13]

While Mayan society allows males seemingly unrestricted freedom to pursue sexual relations with other males, general norms do exist which regulate the roles they may play within those relationships. A Mayan male will be seen either as *hombre*, one who plays the active masculine role in sex, or as *mayate*, one taking the passive role with another male. Surprisingly, an individual might take either role in sex, depending on the particular relationship established with the other partner. Some males, called *internationales*, take both roles sexually, but most males identify with one role or the other. Generally the one who is perceived as more masculine will take the active role with his partner. The passive males usually effect an androgynous appearance, not particularly feminine, but not macho either, and are completely accepted by macho men, who show no reluctance to be seen flirting with them. The masculine hombres do not see themselves as homosexual, and as long as they display a macho demeanor and express at least the desire to get married to a woman at some time in the future, they are free to pursue their sexual interest in other males.[14] While the homosexuality that is such a part of the adolescence and young adulthood of modern day Mayans is not institutionalized as it was when the Spanish arrived, it nonetheless demonstrates a remarkable continuity of the social attitudes and customs of a people concerning sexuality.

The relaxed attitude toward homosexuality shown by the Mayans is shared by many other native peoples in Central America. According to anthropologists the friendships among bachelors in Southern Mexico and among Guatemalan Indians usually contain a strong homosexual component.[15] Among the Zapotec Indians of southern Mexico homosexual behavior is common among males of all ages. Boys typically begin having sex with other males during puberty and will continue having sex with other young men through their twenties. By the time they are thirty most males marry and have children, but as with the Mayans, homosexual relations can continue even after marriage. In fact, it is not uncommon for a Zapotec man to leave a marriage after his children are grown and move in with a male lover.[16]

Same-Sex Customs in South America

Male homosexuality in adolescence and extending into adulthood is a common occurrence in many tribes in South America as well. In the Central Amazon region, homosexual relations are a routine aspect of male camaraderie among both bachelors and young married men. Among the Barasana of Colombia a young man's relations with his in-laws include considerable sexual intimacy. Young men can be found together in each other's hammocks, nuzzling each other and fondling each other's genitals. Sexual relations are also reported to be the norm among young males of the Yanamano, a large tribe of the rain forest of southern Venezuela and Brazil, among Cubeo men in the Northwest Amazon, and also among young men of the Araucanian tribes of Chile and Argentina. After they complete initiation, youths of the Bororo tribe in Central Brazil were reported to move into the men's house, where they formed sexual relationships with one another. An ethnologist visiting the region in 1894 reported that "couples in love could be seen amusing themselves under a communal red blanket."[17]

Men on hunting, fishing and trapping expeditions in the region often engage in homosexual relations with each other. When going on hunting trips, men of the Tapirape Indians of Central Brazil bring along as receptive sexual partners other adult males, some of whom might even be married. Homosexuality is clearly a part of the behavioral vocabulary of these indigenous peoples. When youths of tribes in the Central-Northwest Amazon visit other villages, the young men of the host villages will try to seduce the visitors to try to keep them away from their women.[18]

In some tribes homosexual relations among adolescents are institutionalized. Among many tribes, marriage arrangements between a boy of one family or clan and a girl of another are often undertaken to establish ties or renew bonds between the two groups. Among the Nambikwara of Brazil, the brother of the bride-to-be is brought together in a sexual relationship with the groom-to-be, his future brother-in-law. The ceremony that unites the two youths is more festive and given greater notice than the heterosexual union that will later follow. Unabashed about their passion for each other, the young men do not seek secluded spots in the forest for love making as will heterosexual lovers, but will make love to each other out in the open by a campfire with their neighbors looking on in amusement. These "crossed cousins" or "cousins who make love," as the Indians call them, continue their relationships after marriage. Men in such relationships, though married and fathers of children, can be seen in the evening walking lovingly together, arm in arm.[19]

While homosexuality seems to be an accepted facet of adolescence and young adulthood among the indigenous groups of the region, it is generally expected that the young men will eventually marry and have children, and most of them do. However, many tribes throughout the Americas acknowledge some males as having a separate, exclusively homosexual status. Among the Zapotec of southern Mexico these men are called *ira'muxe*. They are seen as neither men nor women, but as *muxe*, which means male-female, and are sometimes viewed as more of a third sex. Somewhat androgynous, they do both women's and men's work, but unlike most males they develop especially close friendships with women.[20] While their apparel can be somewhat flamboyant, they are more masculine than feminine in dress. An ira'muxe's status is recognized in childhood, and as Zapotec parents consider the ira'muxe to be the brightest, most gifted children, they will keep them in school longer than other children.[21] Like the Mayan mayate the ira'muxe takes the passive role in sex with masculine males who will sometimes take an ira'muxe as a spouse.[22]

Males who played similar passive homosexual roles were observed by the early Spanish explorers in many tribes. One Spaniard reporting on the Lache Indians of Colombia wrote that if a woman bore five consecutive male sons without bearing a female she could raise one as a *cusmos*. The youth would be trained in feminine skills and when he reached the proper age he would be given in marriage to another man. The Lache men, the explorer wrote, preferred them to true women. Spanish priests in California in the 1820s described a similar practice among the Luiseno and Gabrielino Indians, and wrote that the chiefs greatly valued these feminized men as auxiliary wives.[23]

Since homosexual relations among males seem to be an accepted part of life among many of these indigenous peoples, it would not be necessary for a male to acquire feminine characteristics or adopt the feminine role in sex simply to be able to have sex with other males. For many of these tribes, the mixing of the sexes that these roles involve has less to do with sexuality, and is generally believed to be an indication of a special spiritual status or the presence of supernatural power in the person. As such, these individuals were often thought to have healing abilities and were frequently consulted by tribal elders on important tribal issues.

In many tribes throughout South America the religious leader, or shaman, is often a similar, sexually ambiguous male who plays the passive role in sex with other males. In fact, shamans were so often found to be cross-dressing, passive homosexuals that early ethnographers thought potential shamans were identified by their sexual proclivities and feminine characteristics.[24] In the sixteenth century transvestite shamans were reported by the Spanish among the Araucanians in Chile and Argentina. A Spanish missionary in the late 1700s described transvestite "wizards" among the Moluche and Puelche tribes in the Rio Negro Valley of Argentina. Transvestite shamans seem to have been virtually universal among tribes throughout South America at the time the Spanish arrived, but because of the vigorous efforts of Spanish authorities and missionaries to eradicate their "diabolical" rituals and sexual practices, they have survived in modern times for the most part in tribes living in more remote areas. Anthropologists working in recent times have reported male-transvestite shamans among the cattle-herding Guajire people of northwestern Venezuela and northern Colombia, among the Tehuelche, a tribe of hunter-gatherers in Argentina, among the Caduveo of the southern Brazilian rain forest and among the peoples surrounding Lake Titicaca on the Peruvian-Bolivian border.[25]

Native Reactions to European Homophobia

While homosexual practices similar what the conquistadors described continue to be present among many of the descendants of peoples conquered by the Spanish, that is not to say that the hostility of the Spanish to homosexual behavior did not have a profound effect on the ways of the subjugated populations. Many tribes responded to the anti-homosexual attitudes of the colonial authorities by adapting their rituals to remove highly visible homosexual elements or by concealing their homosexual activities from missionaries and other outsiders. The Araucanian and Mapuche tribes, whose religious leaders were all homosexual shamans at the time of the Spanish conquest, had by the early 20th century switched to female shamans in order to protect their transgenderal males from targeting by the authorities. Other tribes used secrecy to shield their homosexual traditions. Beverly Chinas, an anthropologist who studied the sexuality of the Zapotec Indians, lived among them for several years before they would talk to her about their homosexual ways and the role of the ira'muxe.[26]

In fact, secretiveness about homosexuality has been the response of many native peoples throughout the world once they learned of the negative responses of Europeans to homosexual customs. Gilbert Herdt, who produced a major study on homosexuality in initiation rituals in New Guinea, says that when he first lived among the tribe he studied they unanimously denied same sex practices, and it was only after he lived among them for six months that they developed enough trust in him to discuss their homosexual traditions.[27] Anthropologist Nancy Lurie has reported that among the Winnebago, a Plains Indian tribe, knowledge of their transgenderal two-spirit was supposed to be kept secret from whites.[28] A Cheyenne elder, reflecting a desire among traditionalist Indians to shield aspects of their culture which have been disparaged by whites, told anthropologist Walter Williams, "I am not much interested in talking about our traditions to non–Cheyenne researchers. We want to keep our history within the Cheyenne people."[29]

In other cases, native peoples, when talking to Westerners, will feign disgust for homosexual practices that other reports showed were commonplace among them. A researcher working among rubber plantation workers in the Solomon Islands reported that his subjects described homosexual behavior as bizarre, while at the same time volunteering that it is more enjoyable than heterosexual intercourse — knowledge of which all of them claimed was from secondhand information.[30]

Because of Western aversion to homosexual behavior and the assumption that it is relatively rare, many anthropologists have accepted their subjects' denials at face value.[31] As a consequence colonial authorities, missionaries and anthropologists have for years reported the absence of homosexual practices in areas where later studies have shown that homosexuality was pervasive. The understandable reluctance of indigenous peoples to acknowledge or discuss their sexual customs has thus made it difficult for many anthropologists to appreciate the degree of diversity of sexual expression that exists among native peoples.

Obstacles to the Study of Homosexuality Among Native Peoples

Another problem in the study of the sexual customs of non–Western cultures has been the reluctance of many anthropologists to report practices they find abhorrent, or indifference of the profession to behavior that wasn't considered the proper purview of formal studies. As recently as 1975, the Executive Board of the American Anthropological Association voted "not to endorse anthropological research on homosexuality across national borders."[32] Though later rescinded, the statement reflected deeply held Western cultural biases which have inhibited research into sexual customs in other cultures. In his field studies on the Australian Tiwi, the anthropologist Arnold Pilling amassed considerable information on homosexual behavior among tribal members. Yet the topic was not even mentioned in a book Piling later co-authored on the Tiwi. Another anthropologist, Kenneth Read, says it never occurred to him to ask about homosexual practices in one New Guinea village he studied even though numerous reports had been published on ritual homosexuality in New Guinea going back to the late 19th century. Read commented later that even though he had observed a lot of same-sex physical contact, he just assumed that "homosexuality could not be a part of the culture.[33] Anthropologists who did write openly about homosexual customs sometimes found their work censored. In the 1930s E. Evans-Pritchard, who worked among the Azande tribe of Central Africa, wrote detailed reports about the homosexuality he found practiced by both men and women. His reports, however, were withheld from the public by the American Anthropological Society until the early 1970s when they were finally published.[34]

The pioneering anthropologist Margaret Mead, in commenting on the unreliability of statements that claim the absence of homosexuality in primitive societies, emphasized the difficulties that arise when anthropologists attempt to assess the sexuality of a given culture. Homosexual behavior, she said, may go unnoticed by some investigators because of such factors as language barriers, unbreakable cultural taboos, needs for personal privacy, distrust of Caucasian investigators, and conventions of courtesy that require telling a questioner what he presumably wants to hear.[35] In some instances, the cultural prejudices of the anthropologists themselves serve as a barrier to communication; the anthropologist F.E. Williams, working among the Keraki in New Guinea in the 1930s, at first inquired about homosexual intercourse among his subjects by asking if "they had ever been subjected to unnatural practice." Evidently not understanding what Williams meant by the phrase, the natives answered in the negative. Williams was only awakened to the prevalence of homosexuality among the Keraki when he was propositioned by a young Keraki male in the forest.[36] In other cases, what can only be called willful denial by anthropologists prevented them from acknowledging homosexual customs among the people they studied. In a 1971 study of sexual practices among the Bala, an African people, the anthropologist Alan Merriam stated in one sentence that homosexual behavior was not present in Bala society, and in the very next sentence reported that the Bala described the *kitesha,* a third-gender social role similar to the Zapotec ira'muxe, as homosexual.[37]

Some researchers don't report sexual relations between same-sexed partners because those relations may only appear incidental or situational, and therefore not really "homosexual." Other anthropologists have ignored homosexuality when it didn't involve deviations from normal gender roles, that is, transvestite shamans. In some cases researchers are concerned only with homosexual behavior that is promoted or institutionalized by the group. Hence, informal homosexual relationships may go unnoticed or unreported.[38] Adding to the problem is that some developing third world nations, in order to improve their image in the West, have not only made homosexual practices illegal, but have prohibited research into the subject.[39] All of these factors suggest that reports that claim the absence or disapproval of homosexuality in various third world societies should be treated with great skepticism.

In a well-known study on sexual behavior published in 1951, Clellan Ford and Frank Beach reported that of 76 societies for which information on sexuality was available, homosexuality was present and considered an accepted form of behavior in 63 percent.[40] While this high percentage may be surprising to many in the West, it is very probable that this number is a serious understatement of the true incidence of homosexual practices in societies around the world. Given the reluctance of native peoples to be open about homosexuality and the prejudice many anthropologists have displayed in dealing with same-sex relations, it is unlikely that many of the studies that claim the absence of or intolerance of homosexual practices among various societies accurately reflect the sexual attitudes and behavior of those peoples. The sociologist David Greenberg examined a study on the relation of homosexuality to population control which cited 39 societies for which information on sexual behavior was known, 19 of which (nearly half), were categorized as "not accepting" homosexual behavior. Greenberg found other evidence showing that in 15 of the 19 "not accepting" societies homosexual practices were indeed accepted and present, bringing the number of "accepting" societies in that particular study to 90 percent of the total.[41] Thus, homosexuality seems to characterize the sex lives of the indigenous peoples of the developing world to a degree that would evidently astonish even many anthropologists.

It is apparent that before the introduction of Western sexual morality, homosexuality in one form or another seems to have been virtually universal among the tribal cultures of the aboriginal lands colonized by European explorers. Not only is homosexual behavior nearly always present among primitive cultures, but the striking similarity of the patterns in which it appears over a broad variety of peoples suggests that the forms in which it is expressed reflect deeply intrinsic characteristics of human sexuality.

Homosexuality Among Native American Peoples

As the early explorers and pioneers made their way across the North American continent they were often mystified by the sexuality they saw expressed among the native population. Henri de Tonti, who accompanied La Salle's expedition in the upper Mississippi Valley in the 1690s, described the Indian men as being sexual toward women "with excess, and boys, above women, so that [those boys] become by that horrid vice, very effeminate." The French explorer Pierre Liette wrote of the Illinois Indians in 1702 that "The sin of sodomy prevails more among them than in any other nation." The young men, Liette continued, didn't seem satisfied by women alone, so "there are men who are bred for this purpose from their childhood." Father Francois Charlevoix, a Jesuit missionary, also writing in the Mississippi Valley in the early 1700s, decried the passive male homosexuals he encountered: "Effeminacy and lewdness were carried to the greatest excess in those parts; men were seen to wear the dress of women without a blush, and to debase themselves so [in sex with other men] from whence followed a corruption of morals past all expression; it was pretended that this custom came from ... religion." The official account of the expedition of Lewis and Clark across the continent included descriptions by members of the expedition of the encounters they had with these "men dressed in squaws' clothes." Among the Hidatsas, William Clark reported that, "If a boy shows any symptoms of effeminacy or girlish inclinations, he is put among the girls, dressed in their way, brought up with them, and sometimes married to men. They submit as women to all the duties of a wife. I have seen them — the French call them Berdaches."[42]

Sexual Relations Between Masculine Braves

But as in Central and South American cultures, homosexual behavior was not limited to sex with what Europeans considered effeminate men. Joseph Francois Lafitau, a French Jesuit missionary in early 18th-century Canada, wrote of intense and socially recognized "special friendships" among young men, which he compared to the homosexual loves of the ancient Greeks, and which he said

> are instituted in almost the same manner from one end of America to the other.... They are highly ancient in their origin, highly marked in the constancy of their practice, consecrated, if I dare say as much, in the union which they create, whose bonds are as close as those of blood and nature.... They become Companions in hunting, in war and in fortune; they have a right to food and lodging in each other's cabin. The most affectionate compliment that the friend can make to his friend is to give him the name of Friend.

Lafitau suspected "much real vice" in these relationships, which the missionaries, he said, suppressed because of the sodomy they associated with them.[43] Francis Parkman, a pioneer on the Oregon Trail in 1846, described a similar relationship among two Lakota males, writing that they were "inseparable; they ate, slept, and hunted together, and shared with one another almost all that they possessed. If there be anything that deserves to be called romantic in the Indian character, it is to be sought for in friendships such as this which are common among many of the Prairie tribes." A nineteenth century army officer reporting on these "brothers by adoption" among Arapaho warriors said that, "They really seem to 'fall in love' with men; and I have known this affectionate interest to live for years." The devotion these pairs felt for each other, the officer wrote, sometimes inspired extraordinary heroism deserving of "mention alongside the heroic exploits in the legends of Greece and Rome and the Norseland."[44] The union of such pairs was often formalized in a Friendship Dance they would perform together.[45]

So uninhibited were the American Indians about homosexuality that a masculine warrior could take the passive role in sex with another warrior without it having any effect on his gender identity or reputation as long as he retained a masculine personality. White men living on the frontier were sometimes sexually approached by Indian warriors, who did so in public and without any effect on their masculine image among other warriors.[46] Victor Tixier, a writer who lived among the Osage Indians in 1839–1840, wrote of being sexually approached by warriors while he was bathing in a river. Tixier wrote, "The warriors bothered us with indiscreet questions.... If we swam along beside them, they asked us to let them examine our bodies; we had to tell them very sternly to be of more decent behavior." Tixier was annoyed by their "habits of sodomy, which their curiosity seemed to announce and which they exercise, according to what they say, on their prisoners. These sons of nature are extremely lascivious."[47]

The indigenous North American Indian culture was characterized by a freedom of sexual expression and affection totally foreign to the modern Western cultural tradition. Homosexual relationships from adolescence through adulthood were common in tribes throughout North America. George Devereux, an ethnographer who lived among the Mohave in the 1930s, wrote that "Mohave sex life is entirely untrammeled by social restraint." The Mohave, he said, view sexual activity as an enjoyable gift from nature to be freely indulged. Without social restraint, Mohave children grew up with an adventurous attitude toward sex, and so casual same-sex relations from early childhood were frequent. "There is little or no objection to homosexuality among the Mohave," Devereux wrote.[48]

Same-sex experiences beginning in childhood were reported to be common for most males in many other tribes as well.[49] An anthropologist writing in the 1920s reported that casual same-sex relations among both men and women were well known among the Yuma Indians though more common among men. Richard Grant, a researcher who worked among the Hopi Indians in the 1970s has reported that similar attitudes continue among that tribe. "Everyone considers homosexual behavior normal during adolescence, and nearly all boys form special bonds which include sexual behavior. It is expected that all will 'grow out of it' however, so that by adulthood marriage and the production of children will occur," but until their 20s, males are free to participate in homosexual relationships without social disapproval. After years of direct study of traditionalist Indians of various tribes, anthropologist Omer Stewart has concluded: "My impression is that the American Indians were fairly unconcerned one way or the other regarding homosexual behavior."[50]

The Institution of the Two-Spirit

Certainly the most perplexing aspect of Native American sexuality to the Europeans was the role of the berdaches, who seemed to be present in tribes throughout continental North America. As William Clark noted, the name *berdache* was applied to these individuals by French explorers, and comes from the French word for a young male who would take the passive role in sex with another male, who might keep him as a sexual companion the way other men might keep mistresses — a practice not uncommon in 17th-century France. Like their counterparts in Central and South America, the berdaches, or two-spirits, as they were called by Native Americans, normally took on an androgynous appearance, a mixing of the sexes, which often appeared effeminate to the Europeans. While two-spirits often wore some feminine attire, their dress was usually more androgynous, or a mixture of masculine and feminine, though in some tribes, such as the Navajo, they dressed like other males.

Most puzzling to the Europeans, though, was the respect that these individuals received within the tribes. Joseph Lafitau, the French Jesuit, condemned the two-spirits for acting like women, yet he admitted this was not the way they were viewed by their tribes: "They believe they are honored ... they participate in all religious ceremonies and this profession of an extraordinary life causes them to be regarded as people of a higher order and above the common man." The French explorer Jacques Marquette reported that among the Illinois tribe and its neighbors the two-spirits were always included in solemn ceremonies: "They are summoned to the Councils, and nothing can be decided without their advice.... They pass for Manitous — that is to say, for Spirits — or persons of consequence."[51] G.L. Davydov, a Russian explorer who visited the southern Alaskan coast in 1812, wrote in amazement about the androgynous Kodiak males who were frequently kept as sexual companions by Kodiak men: "They are not looked down upon, but instead they are obeyed in a settlement and are not seldom wizards."[52] Coming from the Western Christian tradition in which sensuality is seen as antithetical to spirituality, the European explorers and missionaries could not comprehend the linking of sexuality and religion that came together in the role of the two-spirit. Yet it is their spiritual role, more than their homosexuality, which distinguishes the two-spirits among their tribes.

Insight into the spiritual significance Native Americans attached to the sexuality of the two-spirit can be gleaned from the religious beliefs of the Indians. Among many tribes the Supreme Being is conceived of as neither male nor female, but as a combination of both male and female.[53] Hence a male who takes on characteristics of a female, and who is thus viewed as being of both sexes, was seen as an indication of the favor of the Great Spirit on that tribe. The creation myths of many tribes tell stories of how the intercession of a man-woman spirit was crucial for the tribe's survival and prosperity. Sometimes the tribal name for the two-spirit is a reflection of the tribe's recognition of the two-spirit as embodying the presence of that patron spirit. For example, the Zuni word for two-spirit, *lhamana*, is derived from *ko'l-hamana*, a male-female spirit who played a key role in the Zuni creation story. A constant theme from tribe to tribe is the notion that the two-spirit's presence is a gift of the Great Spirit, that two-spirits were created to provide the tribe with a better quality of life.[54] Among many tribes these two-spirit individuals were thought to have been present from the time of the tribe's creation. As a Mohave elder explained to George Devereux: "From the very beginning of the world it was meant that there should be [two-spirits] just as it was instituted that there should be shamans. They were intended for that purpose."[55]

The two-spirit role is not considered to be one of choice, but of a reflection of the inborn nature of the individual. Males who would become two-spirits were usually identified in childhood by an interest in feminine things or a tendency to play more with girls than boys. The child would be allowed to learn feminine skills, such as cooking and sewing.[56] Because of the spiritual gifts believed to reside in them, special care would be shown in raising such children that was not shown other children, and as they grew older they were shown great respect, almost to the point of reverence. When a family had a two-spirit among its members, its success and wealth were believed to be assured.[57]

Females filling a cross-gender role comparable to the male two-spirit were also known in a number of groups in both North and South America. In fact, it was the Spanish encounter with female warriors in rain forest tribes in South America that led to their naming the Amazon River after the mythical women warriors of Ancient Greece. In North America female two-spirits were known among tribes of the northern Plains, the Southwest, California and the Pacific Northwest. Among the Cocopa tribe in California such girls played with boys, made bows and arrows and hunted birds and rabbits. Wearing their hair like men, they also had their noses pierced, as men did, and went to war and fought with the men. Confining their sexual relations to women, they usually had wives.[58] Called *kwe'rhame* by the Yuma Indians, these females were described as having muscular builds and dressing like men. A Yuma *kwe'rhame* who married a woman and set up a household with herself as husband also went to war, where she was known for bravery in battle.[59] In other tribes these women might take up traditional male occupations, but still dress as women. A Crow female two-spirit in the mid-nineteenth century achieved renown for her exploits in combat against the Blackfoot, was a highly successful hunter, became a chief, married four wives, but during her whole life dressed like the rest of the women, except for hunting arms and accoutrements.[60]

More common, though, were male two-spirits, who were valued for their contributions to the quality of life of tribes throughout continental North America. Male two-spirits were regarded as very hard workers, and especially talented in crafts. The Zunis considered them the finest potters and basket weavers in the pueblo. Among the Winnebago, Hopi, Lakota, Mohave, Assiniboine and Crow tribes they had a reputation for doing women's tasks better than any woman could do them. They were universally praised for their beadwork, pottery, weaving, saddle-making and tanning, and being good providers for their families. Handicrafts made by Ogalala two-spirits were valued as masterpieces, and brought high prices.[61] In 1903 an ethnologist reported that the Crow two-spirits, called *bade*, were known for being the best cooks, and were highly regarded for their charitable acts. They were also, he added, known for having the "best-decorated" tipis.[62]

Considered to be especially gifted with children, two-spirits were recognized as having special talents in teaching children. Steven Powers, after visiting the Yuki and Pomo reservations in California in 1871 and 1872, wrote of meeting Yuki and Pomo two-spirits. "They are set apart as a kind of order of priests or teachers.... [They] devote themselves to the instruction of the young by the narration of legends and moral tales." Even in recent times two-spirits maintain their reputation as the best teachers. Ruth Landes, an ethnographer working with the Potawatomi Indians in Kansas, wrote of one such young man teaching in the primary school on the reservation. He was admired by the other Indians because "he loved to care for the children, to advise their parents and to scrub the school house till it [shone]." The anthropologist Walter Williams has written of another such two-spirit teacher among the Lakota tribe, who is recognized as the best teacher in the elementary school on his reservation. Williams describes the young man as very spiritual in nature, active in traditional Lakota religion, but especially devoted to teaching and his students. Considering their talents, it is not surprising that two-spirits sometimes assume parental roles, adopting orphaned children or children from over-crowded families.[63]

While male two-spirits often did "women's work," they also had other roles that went beyond what women did. Not puny effeminates, two-spirits were often described as strong and tall, athletic in build and able to carry heavy burdens. A French explorer wrote in 1805 that they were taken on hunting expeditions, "to watch over the horses, to skin or carry the pelts of game that are killed, to carry the meat, cut the wood, light the fire and, in the absence of women, to satisfy a brutal passion abhorrent to nature." On a French expedition in Florida in 1564 Jacques Le Moyne de Morgues sketched berdaches among the Timucua Indians and noted that they were quite common. Because of their strength, he said, they carried the provisions when a chief went to war, carried the dead for burial, and transported the sick on their shoulders so they could care for them. Two-spirits were often taken on war parties: among the Lakotas, the two-spirits, called *winkte*, did the cooking, took care of the camp and tended to the wounds of the warriors. The Cheyenne *he man eh* were an integral part of war parties, where their presence was valued because of their spiritual powers and the good luck they were thought to bring to raids. According to George Grinnell, a 19th century ethnographer, large Cheyenne war parties "rarely started without one or two of them. They were good company and fine talkers. When they went with the war parties they were well treated. They watched all that was being done and in the fighting cared for the wounded."[64] Two-spirits were especially revered for their healing abilities, which were credited to their spiritual powers, but they were also noted for their skill in setting broken bones and in the use of medicinal herbs for healing — hence, their reputation as "medicine men" among whites.[65] Considering the manifest talents of the two-spirits and the unquestionable contribution they have made to the quality of life of their tribes it is no wonder their presence was viewed as a gift of the Great Spirit.

The most controversial aspect of the two-spirit — at least among Europeans — is the sexual role they take with Indian men. Two-spirits were often married to masculine Indian men, but among many tribes there was encouragement for a two-spirit to remain single so that his favors could be shared with the rest of the men in the group. Their availability for sex was one of the reasons two-spirits were taken along on hunting expeditions and war parties, but sex with two-spirits was not limited to time away from the village, and even married men would regularly visit the two-spirit for sexual encounters. Because of their spiritual powers, sex with a two-spirit was often considered to bring good luck. Lakota men would visit a winkte for sexual purposes before a raid, believing it would increase their ferocity. If a Lakota wanted the two-spirit to give his son a sacred name — a kind of blessing — he would engage in sex with the winkte. There was even ceremonial recognition of the sex life of the two-spirit. George Catlin, who traveled among the Sauk and Fox Indians in the 1830s, recorded a sacred feast which was given each year in honor of the two-spirit, during which the young men of the tribe who had had sex with the two-spirit would perform a ceremonial dance and publicly announce their sexual involvement with him.[66]

Even today two-spirits are highly regarded for their sexual attractions and have followings among masculine Indian men. Among the Hopi, a 20-year-old two-spirit was observed by an anthropologist at a religious ceremony. "A real queen" the observer wrote, "he was accompanied by four other young men, all of whom were very good looking while simultaneously looking rather tough." It was not uncommon for young Indian men to boast among themselves about their exploits with a two-spirit the way young American men might boast about their sexual accomplishments with women. In the decades after World War II young men of some of the eastern tribes frequently went to New York City and Boston to work in the high rise steel construction industry. Walter Williams has reported that one such group of four young men from the Micmac tribe was accompanied by a young two-spirit. They got an apartment together, with the two-spirit keeping house, doing the cooking and caring for anyone who got sick. The two-spirit would choose which of the other young men he wanted to sleep with, and they would retire to the privacy of his room, where they would sleep together and make love often. The other young men, though they considered themselves heterosexual, were eager to have sex with him. This two-spirit did have one favorite over the years, about whom he said "I really feel in love with him. He married a woman, but we have sex periodically. We're still the best of friends."[67]

It is remarkable that the sexual role of the two-spirit has continued to be valued among some Native American groups, despite several centuries of religious and government campaigns against this native social institution. In the American Indian cultures, where personal freedom of choice in all matters is highly valued, men are not forced to restrict their sexual life to heterosexual marriage, and usually are emotionally closer to other men than to their wives. While sexual relations between masculine men can occur, the role of the two-spirit provides a socially recognized way to serve the sexual needs of many men without competing against the institution of heterosexual marriage. And if a masculine male desires a mate of the same sex, a number of tribes provide the option of becoming the husband of a two-spirit.[68]

Because of their spiritual connection, there is a strong association between two-spirits and shamanism. While the word *shaman* refers to an office or religious role that a number of individuals could fill, the two-spirit is distinguished by inborn male-female characteristics unique to the two-spirit. Thus, the shaman, or spiritual leader of a tribe, was not necessarily a two-spirit, but because of their perceived spiritual powers, two-spirits were considered to be especially powerful shamans. However, in those instances where the shaman was not a two-spirit, the two-spirit was still often deferred to at crucial points in ceremonies.[69] But in many tribes the role of shaman was filled by a two-spirit whose man-woman spirit was considered crucial for the power of the magic that was invoked in sacred ceremonies.

In fact, sexual acts involving a two-spirit-shaman were an integral part of some of the most important sacred rituals. The climax of a traditional Hopi ceremony performed to insure a bountiful maize harvest came when young men in turn mounted and anally inseminated the *katcina*, the Hopi two-spirit, who represented in the ceremony the "Virgin of the Maize," a spirit whose fertility was required for the success of the harvest.[70] George Catlin described a similar ritual he witnessed among the Mandan Sioux in the 1830s. Many of the Plains Indian tribes were highly dependent on the buffalo, whose meat was a prime source of nutrition and whose hides they used for clothing and shelter. In preparing for the hunt, and in order to draw the herds to them, the Mandan would perform a Bison's dance in the course of which a two-spirit, portraying a spirit, would be repeatedly mounted and anally inseminated by warriors wearing bison's heads and skins, playing the role of bulls. The Mandan believed that this homosexual rite was essential if the Great Spirit was to send the bison the tribe needed.[71]

The Paleolithic Origins of the Two-Spirit Tradition

Native American rituals and beliefs such as these are thought to stem from very ancient origins. Joseph Campbell, who has called the ritual complex of the North American Plains Indians "the twilight of the Paleolithic Great Hunt," has pointed to amazing continuities between practices attributed to Paleolithic hunting peoples on the plains of Europe during the period of the last Ice Age, 10,000–30,000 B.C., and those observed among Plains Indians in the last century. George Grinnell, writing in the 1870s, reported a Blackfoot ritual where the shaman, wearing the head and hide of a buffalo, would lure a herd of buffalo over a cliff, where waiting tribe members would butcher them when they fell on the rocks below. Not only is there evidence that a similar technique was used by Paleolithic peoples in Europe to capture buffalo, but among the great cave paintings, dating from 18,000 B.C., is a painting of a shaman, similarly garbed in the head and skin of a buffalo, apparently engaged in a shamanic dance, surrounded by 30 bison. The evocation in this Paleolithic cave painting of a ritual world comparable to that of the North American Plains Indians is unmistakable.[72] Scholars who have examined this and other illustrations of shamans in cave paintings have identified a number of characteristic features of Paleolithic shamans also found among tribal shamans throughout the world in historic times. These include the shaman's ritual dance, the wearing of animal costumes such as the head and hide of a bison or stag, and his role as "master of game animals," through which the shaman assured a plentiful supply of game for his tribe.[73] In several cave paintings of the period, the shaman is shown displaying an erect phallus, indicating that a sexual element of some kind also existed in the rituals.

A similar antiquity of the homosexual two-spirit-shaman tradition and the related linkage between sexuality and spirituality is suggested by the enormous geographic range of the cultures in which this tradition has been found. Two-spirit type individuals have been reported among a vast number of tribes throughout South and Central America, and before European colonization were apparently universal among tribes in North America and Alaska.* But the tradition extends further, across the Bering Strait into Siberia, where homosexual shamans were historically prominent among the Asiatic Eskimos, the Chukchi, Koryak and Yukaghir peoples, and inland into Western Siberia, where they have been reported among the Yakut.[74] Homosexual shamans have also been reported among tribal peoples in Korea, in Southeast Asia, where transvestite shamans were known in the Vietnamese countryside, among tribal

---

*Homosexual shamans have been reported in tribes ranging from the Araucanians and Puelshe in southern South America, to tribes of the Amazon basin and coastal Peru. In North America the two-spirit tradition has been noted among tribes ranging from the Seminoles of Florida, the Choctaw and Muskogee tribes of the southeastern United States, through the Illinois, Chippewa, Saux-Fox, Dakota, Mandan, Crow, Ponca, Omaha, Kansas, Oto and Osage tribes of central North America and the Great Plains to the Zuni, Acoma, Laguna, Navajo, Yuma and Mohave tribes of the western United States. In Alaska two-spirits are universally present among tribal peoples in the southern and Pacific coastal regions, while two-spirit-like shamans are universal among Eskimo tribes.

peoples in Burma, Malaya and Borneo, and among the Pardhi and Lloosais peoples of India.[75] A rural homosexual shaman figured in commentary from 13th-century China,[76] and as far back as the time of the ancient Greeks, the historian Herodotus described transvestite shamans among the Scythian tribes who inhabited the steppes of Central Asia north of the Black Sea.

Aside from the association of homosexuality with spirituality, there are other commonalities in the traditions which seem to indicate a common ancient origin. For example, among the various Siberian peoples, a prominent element of the shaman's ritual is the use of a sacred drum, an implement that is also an important part of the shaman's craft among tribal peoples across the Americas, from Alaskan Eskimos, to the Blackfoot of Montana, all the way down to the Puelche of the Rio Negro Valley in Argentina. Because of the similarity in the traditions among peoples so widely scattered, across an arc from Central Asia down through North America to the Patagonian Coast of South America, it seems probable that the homosexual shaman-two-spirit belief complex originated among Paleolithic clans on the Eurasian landmass, and was brought to the Americas with the peoples who migrated there, who are thought to have come across the Bering land bridge to America sometime between 12,000 and 20,000 B.C.—which would take this homosexual tradition back to the same era as the paintings in the great temple caves.

Homosexual Customs Among the Peoples of the Pacific

The peoples of the island cultures of Polynesia are also believed to have migrated from the Asian mainland in prehistoric times, and it is probably not coincidental that among them is found a similar two-spirit-type tradition, in addition to the same relaxed attitude toward same-sex relations found among native peoples of the Americas. Western explorers in the South Pacific were often as startled as their counterparts in the Americas when they came across what a number of the island cultures called *mahus*. An English ship's captain in Tahiti in 1789 wrote that one of his men was very much smitten by what he thought was a dancing girl, "but what was his surprise when the performance was ended, and after he had been endeavoring to persuade her to go with him on board our ship, which she assented to, to find this supposed dancer, when stripped of her theatrical paraphernalia [was] a smart dapper lad."[77] Captain Bligh of the *Bounty* wrote that nowhere in the world were these feminized men so common, observing that they were as highly respected and esteemed as women.[78] James Wilson, a missionary in Tahiti during the 1790s, reported that mahus wore women's clothing and sought "the courtship of men the same as women do." A sailor from the HMS *Bounty*, in describing mahus, said they "pick their beards out and dress as women, dance and sing with them. They are generally excellent hands at making and painting of cloth, making mats and every other woman's employment. They are esteemed valuable friends in that way."[79]

Mahus were found among Polynesian cultures from New Zealand to Hawaii. Linguistic evidence from Polynesian languages suggests that mahus may at one time have been shamans. In the language of the Maori of New Zealand, mahu means "to heal"; in Samoan the related word, mafu, means both "to heal a wound" and a "a male homosexual." Like the two-spirits in North America, mahus played an important role in traditional religion. In Hawaii, mahus were the principal dancers in the *tahiku* dance, an ancient religious ceremony performed with chanting. Despite the decline in traditional Hawaiian religion under the influence of Western European culture, mahu dancers are still highly prized among native Hawaiians because of their skills and devotion to the tradition.[80] Also like the two-spirits, mahus are devoted to their families, and are usually the ones who care for aging parents. According to early explorers all the principal chiefs took them as spouses,[81] and even today mahus are popular with young native Tahitian men, who say sex with a mahu is more pleasurable than sex with a woman.[82] Female counterparts to the mahu have also been reported among some Polynesian peoples. Sometimes referred to by the male term for cross-dressers, *bayot*, and sometimes by their own, *lakin-on*, these females wore male clothes and engaged in male occupations.[83]

As in the Americas, though, homosexuality was not restricted to transgenderal or effeminate individuals. Reports going back to the 18th century indicate that homosexual relations were quite common among masculine men as well throughout the region. Captain Bligh of the *Bounty*, who visited Tahiti in the late 18th century, reported seeing a chief perform oral sex on a male attendant. Other travelers reported that Tahitian chiefs used their wealth to attract young men to their court, and made them available to guests for sexual purposes.[84] Extensive male and female homosexuality has been reported by anthropologists among the New Zealand Maori and among the peoples of the Society Islands, which includes Tahiti. In the 1930s Margaret Mead described frequent casual homosexual relations among adolescent males and females on Samoa. On the Marquesan Islands homosexual relationships in adolescence were reported to be the norm, and would continue into adulthood for young men of marriage age who had not found a wife. Reports of early explorers indicate homosexuality was also common in Hawaii before Western colonization.[85] In fact, among the Hawaiians, Western explorers encountered a second institutionalized homosexual tradition in addition to that of the mahu.

In his diary, John Ledyard, who visited Hawaii in 1779, wrote of the

> sodomy, which is very prevalent if not universal among the chiefs.... The cohabitation is between the chiefs and the most beautiful males they can procure about 17 years old. These they call Kikuana, which in their language signifies a relation. These youths follow them where ever they go and ... [the chiefs] are extremely fond of them, and by a shocking inversion of the laws of nature, they bestow all those affections upon them that were intended for the other sex.[86]

These *aikane*, as they were known in the Hawaiian language, were not effeminate males or cross-dressers. Sometimes having wives of their own in addition to their sexual relationships with older men, they were also not restricted in their relations to playing the passive role.

"All the chiefs had them," wrote James King, one of Captain Cook's officers. According to Cook's second in command, Charles Clerke, the young men were kept "for the amusement" of the chiefs. "They talk of this infernal practice with all the indifference in the world, nor do I suppose they imagine any degree of infamy in it.... They are profligate to a most shameful degree in the indulgence of their lusts and passions."[87] David Samwell, the expedition's surgeon, also wrote of these aikane, and noted that their "business is to commit the sin of Onan upon the old King.... It is an office that is esteemed honorable among them." The Hawaiians they encountered evidently assumed that attractive young sailors on Cook's crew played similar roles with the senior officers. "They have frequently asked us on seeing a handsome young fellow if he was not an *aikane* to some of us." In fact, Samwell, wrote that as their expedition was about to depart the islands, a chief sought to pay six hogs as a bride price for temporarily leaving behind, "a handsome young fellow whose appearance he liked much."[88] Cook's young officer, James King, was similarly propositioned, writing that a chief proposed to Captain Cook "very seriously to leave me behind; I had had proposals by our friends to elope, and they promised to hide me in the hills till the ships were gone, and to make me a great man."[89] This last point is a reference to the special roles aikane often played in Hawaiian society. In addition to serving as sexual companions of the chiefs, the aikane were often honored emissaries from the chiefs to visitors. And as political protégés, they could rise to great stature among their people, as did King Kamehameha the Great, a former aikane.[90] Similar sexual relationships were also reported between young men and chiefs in Tahiti.[91]

Though the highly visible relationships aikane had with chiefs earned for them a prominent place in the accounts of Western explorers, aikane could become sexually involved with males of lesser rank, males of their own age, and even other aikane. According to one scholar, "There are stories where the ages and ranks are the same, others where they are radically different, and still others where they are not even stated."[92]

Several American writers in the 1840s described their own special friendships with young Polynesian men. In his classic, *Two Years before the Mast,* Richard Henry Dana wrote of his young Hawaiian "friend and *aikane*" who, he said, "adopted" him, and who considered "himself bound to do everything" for his older companion. Several years later the great novelist Herman Melville, known for his homosexual interests, wrote of Tahiti's "extravagant friendships, unsurpassed by the story of Damon and Pythias: in truth, much more wonderful.... Mine was Poky, a handsome youth, who never could do enough for me." Other writers indicated that in such cases the young man himself chose or "adopted" the older visitor; the relationship would begin with the young man's invitation for the man to sleep at his family's house, where the youth "wore no clothes after dark."[93]

Another such relationship between an American and a young Tahitian was described in a surprisingly frank account which appeared in the American magazine, *Overland Monthly,* in 1869. In "A South-Sea Idyll," Charles Warren Stoddard wrote of his romance with a Tahitian youth, Kana-ana. The relationship began, according to Stoddard, when "he placed his two hands on my two knees, and declared, 'I was his best friend, as he was mine; I must come at once to his house, and there live always with him.' What could I do but go?" Sleeping in a bed "big enough for a Mormon," the naked youth

> never let loose his hold on me.... His sleek figure, supple and graceful in repose, was the embodiment of free, untrammeled youth.... If it is a question of how long a man may withstand the seductions of nature and the consolations and conveniences of the state of nature, I have solved it in [this] one case; for I was as natural as possible in about three days.... Again and again he would come with a delicious banana to the bed where I was lying and insist upon my gorging myself.... He would mesmerize me into a most refreshing sleep with a prolonged manipulation.[94]

Such an account leaves no doubt about the unaffected attitudes toward sex of these native cultures, which stand in such a contrast to the restrictions and inhibitions that surround sexual matters in Western society. With the coming of Western colonial powers and the missionaries who accompanied them, the aikane tradition vanished, leaving the mahu as the sole remaining vestige of Polynesian aboriginal homosexual customs.

The Stone Age Homosexual Traditions of the Western Pacific

The native peoples of the Pacific are a racial composite of considerable diversity, with varying degrees of Negroid, Caucasoid and Mongoloid elements. The diversity reflects the effects of the ebb and flow over thousands of years of successive waves of migrations. Movement into the Pacific region from Asia is thought to have started as far back as 40,000 B.C., when some of the Negroid peoples who inhabited large parts of South Asia during the last Ice Age began migrating into the continent that then combined New Guinea and Australia and into nearby islands. By the end of the Pleistocene, Mongoloid peoples had moved into southern Asia, pushing the remaining mainland Negroid population into isolated pockets. Around 4,000 B.C., movements of tribes of Mongoloid Asians from Southeast Asia into the Indonesian Archipelago and the coastal areas of New Guinea inhabited by aboriginal Negroid peoples was producing racial mixing in those areas, while rugged terrain and impenetrable tropical forests in the interior of larger islands allowed their inhabitants to evolve in isolation from foreign elements. By 2,000 B.C. the migrations had reached the Caroline and Marshall Island chains of Micronesia, and by early in the first millennium A.D. Polynesia was being populated — making the islands of the eastern Pacific the last habitable parts of the earth to be settled by humans.

By historic times, then, the racially mixed Pacific population ranged from dark-skinned, kinky-haired Australoids in Australia, New Guinea and nearby island groups to wavy- or straight-haired and lighter-skinned Mongoloid-looking peoples in the Philippines, Micronesia and Polynesia. As might be expected, language and cultural differences correspond loosely to the racial variation. The lighter-skinned, more Mongoloid Oceanic populations speak a variety of languages of the Austronesian family in common with some of the peoples of Southeast Asia, while the languages of most of the darker-skinned Austroloid peoples of New Guiunea and Australia are classified as Non-Austronesian and subdivided into Papuan and Australian groups. Similarly, the two-spirit/mahu tradition has not been found among the darker-skinned non–Austronesian speakers, who were the original inhabitants of the region, though homosexual shamans and two-spirit-like individuals were reported among Mongoloid Austronesian speakers on the Southeast Asian mainland and throughout the wide range of their migrations, from Madagascar to the eastern Pacific.

Because of the darker pigmentation of its inhabitants, the island region of the Western Pacific running southeast of the Philippines has been termed Melanesia, from the Greek *melanos*, "black pigment," and *nesos*, island. The largest of the Melanesian islands, New Guinea, is, after Greenland, the second largest island in the world, running 1,400 miles from tip to tip and 400 miles wide in its central portion. Bisected by a rugged mountain range reaching 16,000 feet, the lowland areas of the island are covered with dense tropical forests and swampland. This varied and difficult terrain discouraged travel, which not only led to the development of hundreds of separate languages among its isolated tribes, but prevented any significant intrusion of outsiders until well into this century. However, when Europeans finally did penetrate the dense forests of the island they discovered an enormous, hitherto unknown, population of head-hunting warrior tribes living lifestyles that seem to have been little changed since the Old Stone Age. As a result of the tremendous interest this discovery engendered among Western scholars, New Guinea and the adjacent Melanesian islands have since been more intensively studied by anthropologists than any other place on earth — a fact that has led to some resentment among the natives.

As among the islands of the eastern Pacific, homosexual behavior seems to be a common characteristic of the indigenous population of Melanesia, especially among adolescents and young adults. Casual homosexual relationships have been reported to be routine among youths between puberty and marriage among the Kanaka Popinee of New Caledonia and among males and females of the Manus of the Admiralty Islands.[95] In the Santa Cruz Islands, east of the Solomons, male homosexuality seems to have been quite extensive. According to anthropologist William Davenport, who studied the peoples of the Santa Cruz Islands in the 1960s, nearly every male engages in extensive homosexual activities at some time during his life. Sexual activity, he wrote, would usually begin with foreplay, which may consist of mutual or unilateral masturbation, and end with anal copulation culminating in orgasm. Adolescents or young men who are friends or even relations are expected to take turns accommodating each other sexually. Even married men are involved; though married men of the islands consider heterosexual intercourse pleasurable and average two copulations a day, most also pursue sexual relations with adolescent males. In relations with youths, the adult male always plays the active role, though it is considered obligatory for him to give the youth presents in return for the youth accommodating him. According to Davenport, a man would not engage his own sons in such a relationship, but fathers do not object when friends pursue sexual relations with their sons, provided the adult is kind and generous.[96]

Among the Big Namba tribe on Malekula Island in the New Hebrides, homosexual customs were reported to be not only quite pervasive, but highly developed. A.B. Deacon, who studied the customs of the Big Namba in the 1930s, wrote that "every chief had a number of boy-lovers, and it is said that some men are so completely homosexual in their affections, that they seldom have intercourse with their wives, preferring to go with boys." Until a boy's coming of age initiation he is proscribed from taking a boy-lover himself, but must serve as a lover for an older man, in relationships that are governed by kinship rules, i.e., for a man to have as a lover a youth of his own genealogical line would be considered incest. The relationships are very close, and, at least in regard to the boy-lover, monogamous — his older lover has complete sexual rights over him. The youth accompanies his older lover everywhere, works in his garden, and if one of the two were to die, the other would "mourn him deeply."[97]

Sexual relationships among women are also reported to be very extensive among the Big Namba. According to Deacon, "Between women, homosexuality is common, many women being generally known as lesbians, or in the native term, *nimomogh iap nimomog* ('woman has intercourse with woman'). It is regarded as a form of play, but at the same time, it is clearly recognized as a definite type of sexual desire, and that women do it because it gives them pleasure."[98]

In New Guinea itself, homosexuality has also been reported by anthropologists among its numerous tribes. Brian DuToit, an anthropologist who worked among the Akuna of the Eastern Highlands in the early 1970s, wrote of frequent reciprocal sexual relations among adolescent boys in which they take turns playing the passive and active role in anal intercourse with each other. He described similar relations among adolescent girls, in which two girls become intimately associated, caressing and petting the breasts and genitals of the other, and then one lies on top of the other as in heterosexual intercourse.[99] Homosexual relations among adolescent pairs have also been reported among the Kwoma, a tribe of the Sepik River district,[100] and among youths[101] and even adult men[102] of Wogeo Island, off the mouth of the Sepik River. Another anthropologist noted extensive casual homosexuality among adolescents of the Highland Gebusi, and also apparently exclusive and sexually reciprocal relationships among male peers in their mid–20s, an age at which most men have married women. Among the Gebusi, he found that homosexuality is a common topic for joking among men, all of whom in their youth would have engaged in homosexual relationships. Homosexual relationships are such a routine part of Gebusi adolescence that they are governed by tribal incest rules.[103] In fact homosexuality seems to be the standard sexual outlet for unmarried males of a large number of tribes. T.N. Barker, who studied the Ai'i of Oro Province in the east, wrote that among that tribe "a homosexual relationship with a brother or a cousin is deemed suitable for the uninitiated and unmarried boys and men and for spinsters," and seems to play an important role in bonding among the males.[104]

A lifelong sexual relationship with a male age-mate is a major aspect of life for men of the Asmat, a people occupying a large area along the southwest New Guinea coast. Among the Asmat it is considered normal for children to play with each other sexually, but as they grow into adolescence, boys usually acquire a partner, called an *mbai*, or bond-friend, with whom an exclusive sexual relationship is established. According to Tobias Schneebaum, who lived among the Asmat for an extended period, "Asmat culture in some regions not only allowed for sexual relationships between men, but demanded that no male be without his companion, no matter how many wives he had, or how many women he might be sleeping with." These relationships are often established by the families when the boys are very young in order to strengthen clan ties or as part of marriage arrangements, though in some villages the two boys choose each other.[105] As an Asmat friend described the relationships to Schneebaum,

> Mbai are always friends and always help one another when there is trouble. They remain mbai all their lives, until one of them dies. Sometimes one is jealous because his mbai has been with another man. He is not jealous when he goes with a woman ... only when he is with another man. It is all right to play with another man. He may suck his penis or even enter his ass; that is all right. But he may not have an orgasm. Then, his mbai is very angry.

Conversely, the wives of the men are not jealous of the sexual relationship their husbands have with their mbai, only sexual activity with other women.[106]

The Asmat emphasize reciprocal balance in the relationships among these bond-friends. As Schneebaum's Asmat friend describes it,

> There must always be balance between mbai.... When one mbai sucks the penis of his friend, the two may not part until the friend turns around and sucks his penis. If one enters the ass of another, the other must turn around and enter [the first one's] ass. Mbai must always give back what they take. When I bring fish to the house of my mbai, he will bring me sago [a staple food of the region] the next time he goes into the jungle.... When I am angry at someone ... [my mbai] must come with me to fight him. When [my mbai] has a fight, I must help him. We must share what we have. Everything must remain in balance.

The sharing among Asmat mbai in the past even extended to wives. Wife exchange, an integral part of Asmat ritual, was regarded by the Asmat as an important means of restoring cosmic balance in times of stress or disturbance. Balance would be restored through the reciprocal exchange of semen, the all-important life substance of many aboriginal cultures throughout the region. Traditionally two mbai would exchange wives at feasts or at times of warfare with neighboring tribes, though at the time of Schneebaum's visit missionaries in some Asmat villages had put an end to the practice. According to Schneebaum's Asmat friend, "[the local] pastor has stopped us from ... exchanging wives, but we still have our mbai. He does not know this. He knows we have our exchange friends, but he does not know our relationship."[107]

Homosexuality among the aboriginal tribes of Australia has been described in numerous reports since the 19th century. Among the Tiwi of the Torres Strait, boys begin sexual relations among themselves at a fairly young age, eventually choosing as a regular partner someone who might become a future brother-in-law. Similar peer homosexuality has been reported among other Australian tribes.[108] Homosexuality among both men and women was reported among the Australian Aranda. In describing lesbian practices among the Aranda, the early anthropologist Geza Roheim wrote that sexual activity would begin with the women tickling each other's clitoris, and then "after having excited each other for some time like this, one of them will lie on top of the other like a man, and then rub the two chelia together."[109] Frequent homosexuality among women has also been reported among the tribes in the highlands of New Guinea.[110]

Homosexuality and Initiation

In many tribes in Melanesia, hierarchical sexual relationships between older, dominant males and younger males are an integral part of the rites of initiation that frame a boy's transition to manhood. In fact, it is universally believed among tribes that practice this initiatory homosexuality that a boy's physical growth and the development of sexual virility, hunting skills and warrior prowess cannot be achieved without the implantation of semen of an older male into the boy. This ritualized homosexuality is part of an elaborate set of secret rites whose aim is to transform the boy into a strong, skilled and courageous member of the warrior/hunter society of adult men, whose cohesiveness in times of conflict with neighboring tribes is crucial to the tribe's well-being. The rites of many of the tribes occur within the confines of a secret warrior society or club whose membership is restricted to initiated adult males and whose rituals are to be kept secret from women and children. The rites introduce the boy to residence in the men's house, and stem from the perception that it is necessary to masculinize the boy, to break the association with the mother, to cleanse him of feminine influences, and to grow the boy into a man through insemination by a masculine male, thereby preparing him for incorporation into the tightly knit brotherhood of masculine warriors.

One of the first tribes in which ritual homosexuality was studied was the Keraki of the Fly River basin in New Guinea. F.E. Williams, a government anthropologist working among the Keraki in the 1920s, wrote,

> The bachelors had recourse to sodomy, a practice which was not reprobated, but was actually a custom of the country ... fully sanctioned by male society and universally practiced. For a long time the existence of sodomy was successfully concealed from me, but latterly, once I had won the confidence of a few informants in the matter, it was admitted on every hand. It is actually regarded as essential to the growing boy to be sodomized. More than one informant being asked if he had ever been [sodomized] answered, "Why yes. Otherwise how should I have grown?"

According to Williams, a boy is introduced to the homosexuality at the bull-roarer ceremony, a key initiation ritual, and "when he becomes adolescent his part is reversed, and he may then sodomize his juniors, the new initiates to the bull-roarer." Williams, noting the role of erotic attraction in the practices, says, "some boys are more attractive and consequently receive more attention of this kind than others, but all must pass through it, since it is regarded as essential to their bodily growth."[111]

While the rites vary considerably from tribe to tribe, the boy's sexual initiation into the world of the adult men is typically started when he is approaching puberty. At this time the boy is separated from his mother, household and playmates, and is taken to live with other initiates under the guidance of the men, which may be in the men's house, or in a camp or lodge in the forest removed from the home village. This transition is marked in many of the tribes by ceremonies that include ritual implantation of semen into the boy, which is thought to foster the onset of puberty. In most of the tribes the transfer of semen into the boy is through anal copulation, though in a number of tribes fellation of the older male by the younger is preferred. In all cases it is the younger male who receives the semen from the older, either orally or anally.[112] Once initiated, the youths seem to take to the homosexual activities with enthusiasm. Daniel Gajdusek, who performed medical research among New Guinea tribes, said that wherever his research took him, adolescent males tried to seduce him. In the Upper Ruffaer Valley, Gajdusek wrote, friends greeted one another with such phrases as, "I will eat your genital organs," or "I will take your penis to my mouth."[113] From puberty until he reaches his mid-twenties the youth lives almost exclusively in the company of other males, and takes part frequently in homosexual relations, usually in a relationship with an older male who serves as his mentor and guide. During these developing years, the youth learns hunting and warrior skills, and has to endure ordeals meant to instill in him the strength, endurance and courage of a warrior.

Among the Etoro, a tribe of the New Guinea Highlands, a boy becomes involved in homosexual relations at around the age of ten, when he is given a partner, usually his sister's husband or fiancé. The boy engages in oral sex with the older male, consuming the semen when his partner ejaculates. The relationship between the two will continue until the youth reaches his early twenties. The youth's rapid body growth during this period, his sprouting of facial and body hair, and development of masculine skills and characteristics such as hunting ability and courageousness in battle are uniformly regarded by the Etoro as the direct results of insemination. Ceremonies marking the initiation of Etoro youths into manhood occur in their late teens or early twenties, when they go into seclusion from women at a lodge on the edge of the forest. The activities involve the participation of most adult Etoro men and include general insemination of the initiates by the men. Much of the time is spend hunting and trapping, and according to Raymond Kelly, who studied the Etoro rites, "everyone residing at the lodge goes about nude and, it is said, with their penises erect. This is part of a general celebration of masculinity, and especially that recently attained by the initiates." After his initiation is completed, the now-mature young man becomes the older partner of another pubescent boy, normally his wife or fiancé's younger brother, and continues in that relationship, playing the role of inseminator, until about the age of forty. His homosexual involvement ends at that point, except for initiation ceremonies, which include collective homosexual intercourse between all the initiates and all the older men. Because of numerous Etoro taboos and restrictions on heterosexual intercourse, which forbid heterosexual relations for more than half the year, homosexuality is the primary sexual outlet for Etoro males between the ages of ten and forty.[114]

Among the Sambia, a tribe in the Eastern Highlands studied by Gilbert Herdt, a boy's initiation begins when he is approaching puberty with his participation in a ceremony where he is taught how to practice oral sex on an older male. The boy then goes to live in the men's clubhouse and continues the initiation process, engaging in oral sex with an adolescent male somewhat older than him. Like the Etoro, the Sambia believe ingestion of semen is necessary to bring about puberty. In addition, according to the Sambia, the process of counteracting maternal influences and developing masculine qualities requires many years of semen ingestion. After some years the roles are reversed and the youth becomes the donor of semen for a younger boy who fellates him. For a number of years the youths continue living in the clubhouse where they engage exclusively in homosexual relations, lying down side by side, one youth practicing oral sex on the other. When a youth reaches his early 20s he usually marries a young girl not yet sexually mature who will practice oral sex on him until she begins to menstruate. During that period, which may be a year or two, the young man is essentially bisexual, being fellated by both younger males and his new wife. After the girl begins to menstruate, the young man is expected to replace his homosexual activities with heterosexual intercourse, though homosexual activity continues for some men.[115] One Sambian man told Herdt, "A married man who didn't play around (swallow semen) enough will die quickly like an airplane without gasoline." Another man, a father of ten, said, "I still never stop thinking about semen or eating it."[116] It is clear that the Sambia males derive much pleasure from their homosexual experiences.[117] According to Herdt, the Sambia refer to sex with youths as pleasurable "play," whereas sex with women is "work."[118] The youths, too, seem to enjoy the fellation of the older males: "They are fascinated with the forms, textures and tastes of semen, which they discuss frequently, like wine-tasters."[119]

Responding to anthropologists who have claimed that the homosexual acts involved in initiation rites are merely the mechanistic performance of ritual, Herdt has emphasized the role that the erotic aspect of these traditions plays in the lives of the participants. "Let us underline the obvious," he writes, "without erotic desire, arousal and consummation, any sexual intercourse is impossible."[120] Genuine erotic interest is necessary for there to be an erection and ejaculation, especially when the acts go on for a lifetime. The young males of many

Melanesian cultures grow up in a world in which the idealized object of physical beauty is the male, not the female, and so the male is easily seen as a kind of sex object, an object of desire.[121] Pubescent males readily accept the erotic interest of older males, who in turn eagerly avail themselves of the sexual attractions of the young initiates. The sexual bonding that is established by sexual contact during initiation can produce the same jealousies that arise in conventional heterosexual relationships. For the bachelors of many tribes, the homosexuality of initiation is the primary channel through which their sexual needs are met. In some tribes, such as the Marind-Anim, a male will continue to have erotic interest in and involvement with other males his whole life.[122] Thus, while the sexual acts and relationships between the participants are regulated and structured, the performance of required ritual goes hand in hand with the satisfaction of the sexual and emotional needs of the young males.[123]

Among the Marind-Anim, like most of the tribes practicing initiatory homosexuality, anal copulation is the preferred mode of sexual relations between males. The Marind, a people comprising approximately 50 related tribes occupying a large portion of South-Central New Guinea, had, at the time of their discovery by Europeans, a reputation as the fiercest head-hunters in the region. The Dutch anthropologist Jan Van Baal, an authority on the Marind, characterized their men as "homosexuals who practice institutionalized sodomy on an uncommonly large scale."[124] Like many New Guinea tribes, the Marind regard semen as magical, and have many uses for it. The Marind believe that rubbing it into the body made it strong, and put it in special concoctions to be added to food and drink to give health to children, relatives and friends. When spread on spears, bows, arrows and fishhooks, semen was believed to direct them straight to their target. A primary use for semen, though, was its role in the growth of boys into men. Like many other Melanesian tribes, the Marind believe that masculinity is stimulated in boys by the absorption of semen through anal copulation with older men, and, thus, a boy becomes increasingly masculine and grows more quickly as he takes in more and more semen.[125]

A Marind boy begins the initiation process when he leaves his mother's hut at age 12 to 13 and goes to live in the men's house. Initially he may engage in casual homosexual relations or more extended liaisons, though tribal incest rules restrict his involvement to those not sharing his ancestral lineage. Later he comes under the care of a man, usually his mother's brother, whom he is to obey completely, with whom he sleeps at night and to whom he submits sexually. The youth's older lover, called his *binahor* father, serves as his mentor and teacher, and inseminates him through anal intercourse. The relationships are exclusive, and the binahor fathers are often jealous of their sexual protégés except during cult ceremonies, during which unrestricted homosexual activity prevails among the males. The relationship between the two of them continues throughout the development of the younger male, until he reaches his early twenties. The progression of the youth through the years of initiation is punctuated by numerous ceremonies commemorating successive stages of the youth's growth, which include much homosexuality involving all the males of the tribe. The final act of initiation, which marked the formal incorporation of the young man into the warrior corps of the tribe, occurred when he participated in his first war raid, which usually took the form of a head-hunting expedition.[126]

Initiatory Homosexuality and Head Hunting

Since the first contact of Westerners with the aboriginal tribes of New Guinea and Melanesia, their head-hunting has been seized upon in the popular imagination as emblematic of the savage barbarity of these cultures. Yet head-hunting for these peoples is not a senseless expression of primitive brutality, but a sacred act central to their spiritual beliefs and cultural mythology, a practice closely related to the institution of initiatory homosexuality. The cult of head-hunting and the importance in a youth's development that these tribes attach to insemination by an older male stem from the same core belief— that semen, which carries the life force, originates in the brain, is stored in the brain marrow, and is transmitted along the spinal column to the phallus. As a consequence of this belief, these tribes see the skull as the locus of the mystical life force, and regard the phallus both as the avenue for expression of that power and as symbolizing that power, and so treat it with reverence.

Just as a youth could acquire virility through having the semen, the life substance, of a mature male implanted in him, tribes could enhance their fertility and add to their collective life force through the ritual consumption of the brains of fallen enemies. Similarly, the Marind and other New Guinea tribes associate the acquisition of an enemy's head by a young man with the acquisition of the dead man's virility and fertility, and thus that act served as the culmination of a young man's initiation into the warrior society of the tribe. The skulls of slain enemies, thought to contain the mystic life force, are also an integral part of many rites. During the initiation ritual of the Asmat of the Papuan Gulf, the skull of an adult male is placed in the groin of the youth being initiated, so that he can thereby absorb the life force and fertility they believe resides within it.[127]

The anthropologist Weston La Barre has argued that initiatory homosexuality and the related practice of head-hunting for the purpose of acquiring virility and fertility are extraordinarily old customs. The notion that the life force originates in the head and is transmitted via semen is one of the oldest mystical beliefs of the human race, and is believed to have developed several hundred thousand years ago following the discovery of the male role in the conception of children. For early peoples, who had little understanding of physiology, it would have been quite natural to associate the life force with the head, the seat of consciousness, and to regard the emission of semen through the phallus as the transmission of that force. A logical consequence of the belief would have been 1) the collecting of heads in order to obtain fertility and other prized qualities thought to be present in the brain matter, 2) initiatory homosexuality, through which the courage, virility and prowess in hunting and warfare of adult males could be transmitted through their semen to the next generation of males, as well as 3) the preoccupation with the phallus that appeared in cave paintings 20,000 years ago and continued throughout world religious cultures into historic times.[128]

Evidence of a Paleolithic skull cult is widespread. Numerous sites have been discovered throughout the Eurasian landmass going back 60,000 years to the time of the Neanderthals showing evidence of ritual treatment of skulls. In a number of sites that have been dated to Paleolithic times, skulls have been found with openings broken into the rear identical to those made in skulls by contemporary Melanesian tribesmen for the purpose of extracting the brains. Acquiring skulls in order to capture the power or life force of another person has been observed among primitive cultures around the world throughout historic times. When the colonists came to North America the Indians there collected not scalps, but skulls, and switched to scalping only when they began to use the horse and found the weight of heads awkward to carry. Head-hunting was widespread until recent times among tribes in the Amazon Basin, some of whom are also reported to have practiced initiatory homosexuality. Head-hunting for the purpose of acquiring fertility was widespread until recently among mountain tribes of eastern India and Burma* and persisted in some parts of the Philippines and Indochina into

In fact, during World War II British army officers in the Burmese theater, in an effort to harass Japanese units in the area, offered to pay the tribesmen bounties for the heads of Japanese soldiers they could collect. By the war's end, they had paid bounties for over 10,000 heads.

early in the 20th century. Head-hunting cults similar to those found in Melanesia have also been reported for tribes in Central Africa. Capturing the heads of enemies in order to possess their power continued among the peoples of Europe into historic times. According to Roman and Greek historians, the collection and ritual use of the skulls of enemies was routine among the Scythians north of the Black Sea, and among Celtic and Germanic tribes, peoples who made prominent use of phallic symbols and who, not coincidentally, are believed to also have had a tradition of homosexual initiation.[129] Thus, the initiatory homosexuality and related head-hunting of Melanesian tribes are a vestige of a primordial belief complex that appears to have had its origins deep in the Paleolithic period and that was once very widespread among early peoples.

In recent decades initiatory homosexuality has been declining among Melanesian peoples due to the combined effects of concerted efforts of the governments and missionaries to suppress it and the enormous social change that has swept the region since World War II.[130] Though these factors and the secretiveness of the tribes about the rites make estimates of the continued practice of ritual homosexuality in Melanesia difficult, Gilbert Herdt has assembled anthropological data which demonstrate the survival into recent times of a tradition of institutionalized ritual homosexuality among peoples along an arc from Fiji in the east through the Santa Cruz Islands, the New Hebrides, the Banks Islands, the Duke-of-York Islands, New Britain and onto New Guinea. In New Guinea itself Herdt determined the presence of a tradition of ritual homosexuality for tribes from the Ai'i people in the east, through the lowland and highland Anga peoples, tribes on the Great Papuan Plateau, groups along the northwestern coast and found it virtually universal in the south central and southwestern lowland regions.[131]

Ritual homosexuality may have been more extensive in the past, for some tribes for which initiatory homosexuality is not reported still retain imagery and mythic forms suggestive of the spiritual power of insemination. Initiation on Small Island, in the New Hebrides, for example, does not entail overt homosexual relations, though it does include mock anal penetration by ancestral spirits.[132] The initiation rites of the Orokaiva of the New Guinea Highlands include considerable homoerotic symbolism, yet homosexual acts, according to anthropologist Eric Schwimmer, are regarded as "the meaningless activity of bachelors."[133] Government agents and missionaries had been at work among many tribes long before the arrival of anthropologists, and so the absence of reports of initiatory homosexuality may be due to successful efforts to suppress these native sexual traditions. Using available anthropological reports, Herdt has established the survival of a tradition of ritual homosexuality in up to 20 percent of the tribes in the region. Citing cultural and linguistic evidence, Herdt and others have suggested that initiatory homosexuality was part of an ancient "root" ritual complex introduced to the Melanesian region by the earliest Non-Austronesian speakers as early as 10,000 years ago, which would place the origins of these Melanesian sexual traditions in the Paleolithic era.[134]

Since Australia and New Guinea were joined at the time of the immigration of their first inhabitants during the Ice Age, and were only separated by rising waters around 900 B.C., it is not surprising that similar homosexual customs have been reported among Australian tribes. Several anthropologists have noted striking similarities between the initiatory homosexual traditions of the Papuan coastal region and tribes in northern Australia. In fact, Jan Van Baal has maintained that the practices of the Marind-Anim are more similar to Australian traditions than they are to customs of other New Guinea groups.[135] As in New Guinea, many Australian tribes believed semen had magical effects, and in addition to its importance in initiation, it was fed to old men and those who were sick.

Homosexual Bonds and Marriage Arrangements

In many Australian tribes, as among many Melanesian tribes, a youth is usually paired in a sexual relationship with the young man to whom his sister is betrothed. In these groups, marriages are arranged through the exchange of women — a daughter of one clan is given in marriage to the son of another clan in exchange for a suitable girl to become the wife of a son of the first clan. Since very early times humans have been aware of the problems that result from inbreeding, and so consequently early peoples around the world adopted elaborate incest taboos and devised marriage rules and customs such as marriage exchange to insure that marriage partners were acquired from outside the kin or clan. The small size of many groups and the shortage of women often make marriage exchanges difficult, and so frequently a son is engaged to a girl in another clan still in her infancy. In such situations, providing the older brother of the girl as a sexual companion for the girl's fiancé until she matures provides sexual gratification and ties of affection to maintain the exchange obligation.[136] While the older male benefits from the wife he is to receive from the clan and the erotic gratification he gains from his relationship with her brother, the younger male receives in exchange the semen of his older brother-in-law, believed necessary to insure his masculine development, as well as his affection and support as he grows into manhood.

Among many of the indigenous peoples of Melanesia and Australia homosexuality has been thus intricately woven into the fabric of life, serving as a vehicle for the development of young males, and playing an important and complementary role to heterosexuality in marriage customs. The complementary role homosexuality plays to heterosexuality and the importance of balance between the two can be seen in the mystical beliefs of the Bedamini, a tribe of the New Guinea Highlands. Because of their association of homosexuality and insemination with the development of boys into men, the Bedamini believe homosexual activities promote growth, not just in humans, but throughout nature, particularly in gardens. On the other hand, the Bedamini believe excessive heterosexual activities lead to decay in nature, as well as in society, and so balance between these forces is necessary for human survival. The Bedamini are, of course, aware that the birth of children is a result of heterosexual relations, but they stress that it is heterosexual activity in excess of what they consider necessary for producing a child that will have these negative consequences, that is, excessive heterosexuality leads to decay.[137]

But the balance between heterosexuality and homosexuality that seems to have existed for thousands of years in so many of these tribes may soon be a thing of the past. The region has undergone enormous change since World War II, prompted by the work of Western missionaries, the efforts of regional governments to assert their authority over the tribal populations, and the opening of the region to commercial development. From the time they first appeared on the scene in Melanesia, Western Christian missionaries have been attempting to convert the native peoples and replace their ancient customs with Western religious traditions. Western colonial and modern post-colonial governments have understandably sought to eradicate head-hunting practices, but they have in addition waged vigorous and lengthy campaigns to suppress native sexual practices that don't conform to Western standards.[138] Contributing to the disruption of traditional lifestyles has been the emergence of large scale commercial operations, from rubber plantations in the Solomon Islands to timber operations in the New Guinea rain forests, which have recruited workers from tribes throughout the region, separating thousands of natives from their home cultures. William Davenport, who studied the sexual practices of the Santa Cruz Islanders in the 1960s, returned there two decades later and found that the pervasive same-sex relations he studied were being replaced with extensive extra-marital heterosexual permissiveness. According to Davenport, "Despite a great deal of public indignation about this, the traditional sanctions against such permissiveness cannot be applied. Both government and church, oddly, have worked hard and successfully against the application of severe sanctions against heterosexual offenses. It is my impression that with this permissiveness toward extramarital heterosexual relations, there has been a distinct decline in peer same-sex relations."[139]

Frequency of Hierarchical Homosexuality Among Native Peoples

While the socially sanctioned pederastic traditions of Melanesia would be shocking to many in the West, such hierarchical male homosexuality is hardly unique. Homosexual relations between older and younger males are surprisingly common among tribal cultures in other parts of the world. Among the Batak, a tribe of former head-hunters in northern Sumatra, homosexuality between bachelor adults and adolescent males is universal. Whether it has significance in initiation is not known, since these Batak customs have not been studied.[140] A tradition of initiatory homosexuality similar to Melanesian customs has been also reported for tribal cultures in the Amazon basin, though there, too, little is known about it because of the lack of research into the customs.[141] The notion that special skills or qualities can be transmitted through sexual intercourse is also found among disparate peoples. Among the Coerunas and Bororo Indians of Brazil an apprentice healer was taught by going into the forest for an extended period with an older healer who would teach him healing skills and herbal lore while communicating his healing power through sexual intercourse. The early 20th century sociologist and philosopher Edward Westermarck wrote of the common belief among the mountain peoples of Northern Morocco that "a boy cannot learn the Koran well unless a scribe commits pederasty with him. So also an apprentice is supposed to learn his trade by having intercourse with his master."[142]

Homosexual Apprenticeships in Africa

A sexual relationship with a warrior was a central element of the military apprenticeship of youths of the Azande, a tribal people whose kings ruled in pre-colonial times parts of what is now the Central African Republic, southern Sudan and northern Zaire. Before the imposition of European colonial rule there was frequent fighting between rival tribal kingdoms, and so a portion of the Azande adult male population was organized into military companies, divided between married warriors and bachelor warriors. In addition to their military duties, the companies served at the royal courts in various capacities and were called upon for labor in the royal gardens, and so therefore a large portion of the bachelor warriors lived a great deal of the time in barracks at court. According to E.E. Evans-Pritchard, who studied the customs of the Azande in the 1920s, each of the bachelor warriors was accompanied by a young lover, who would get his meals, assist him in his work in the royal gardens, and carry his shield for him when his company went to battle. At night, the youth slept with his older lover who, according to Evans-Pritchard, "had intercourse with him between his thighs. The boys got what pleasure they could by friction of their organs on the husband's belly or groin. However, even though there was this side to the relationship, it was clear from Zande accounts that there was also the comfort of a nightly sharing of the bed with a companion." When a boy was 12 he would be given in such a relationship to a bachelor warrior who would present the boy's father with a spear in exchange. The youth would live with his warrior "husband" until he reached his early twenties, at which time he would graduate to warrior status, become a member of the company to which his older lover belonged, and take on a young lover of his own.[143]

Homosexuality among the Azande extended beyond these apprentice relationships. Same-sex relationships were not uncommon among members of the noble ruling class, though according to Evans-Pritchard these were mainly "young sons of princes who hung about the court until their fathers saw fit to give them wives and districts to administer." The princes, too, would sleep with youths on occasions when heterosexual intercourse was forbidden, as before consulting an oracle. Evans-Pritchard also mentions a senior prince who habitually slept with boys, though he had several wives, commenting that "for this and other reasons he was regarded by the Azande as slightly crazy." Kings and princes were always accompanied by youthful pages, who were treated with great affection in contrast to the aloofness with which the older courtiers were treated.[144] Extensive homosexuality also was customary among women, especially in households where the husband had several wives. According to Evans-Pritchard, such wives would "cut a sweet potato or manioc root in the shape of the male organ, or use a banana for the purpose. Two of them would shut themselves in a hut and one would lie on the bed and play the female role while the other, with the artificial organ tied round her stomach, played the male role. Then they reversed roles."[145]

Widespread Homosexual Customs Among Native African Societies

Because of the widespread assumption that homosexuality was a deviance limited to advanced, urbanized societies, the conventional wisdom among academic anthropologists until very recently has been that homosexuality was a phenomenon largely unknown in Sub-Saharan Africa, despite voluminous evidence to the contrary. To rebut this notion, the historian Wayne R. Dynes compiled and published a list of articles and monographs found in professional journals on various aspects of homosexuality among Sub-Saharan African peoples. That the list he published contained over 500 citations underscores the stubborn refusal of mainstream academic scholars to come to grips with the reality of homosexuality as a phenomenon of human behavior around the world.[146] Homosexual behavior, then, appears to have been just as common among the indigenous peoples of Africa as it has been among tribal peoples in other parts of the world. Not only is homosexuality usually present, but the patterns in which it appears show great similarity to patterns of homosexual behavior among other indigenous peoples.

The range and scope of homosexual behavior among African native cultures can be illustrated by some examples from the reporting of researchers across the continent. An early researcher in Africa, John Weeks, reported in 1909 that sodomy between men was very common among the Bangala of the Congo and was "regarded without shame." Homosexuality was reported to be commonplace among unmarried Tutsi and Hutu men of Rwanda and also among unmarried Nkundo men and women of the Congo. According to other researchers, it was common for Hottentot men to enter into mutual assistance pacts, which frequently developed into sexual relationships. In Dahomey male and female homosexuality were reported to be frequent and considered normal in adolescence. Lesbian relationships were also reported to be common among the Nandi of Kenya, and virtually universal among unmarried Akan women of Ghana, sometimes continuing after marriage. In fact, whenever possible, the Akan women would purchase extra large beds to accommodate group sex sessions involving as many as a half dozen women.[147]

As in other parts of the world, homosexuality among adolescents appears to be a universal practice among African peoples. In Tanzania, boys of the Nayakyusa tribe were reported to leave their parents home at about ten and live with other boys and young men in a camp on the outskirts of the main village, where they would have sexual relationships with other age mates until they married.[148] According to other researchers, shepherd boys of the Qemant and Amhara of Ethiopia commonly develop homosexual relationships with each other, which include frequent anal intercourse, up until the time they are married.[149]

In addition to the Azande tradition of homosexual apprenticeships for youth training to be warriors, researchers have also reported hierarchical homosexual relationships between dominant adult males and youths among numerous tribal peoples, an example being the Fang, a large tribal group living in what is now Cameroon, Equatorial Guinea and Gabon.[150] During periods when religion forbids heterosexual intercourse, Mossi chiefs in Burkina Faso will indulge in sexual relations with adolescent males.[151] Anthropologists have reported that among the Ubangi tribes of the Congo the men regarded women as existing essentially for procreation, and adolescent males for pleasure.[152] Among Berber speaking tribes of the Siwan Oasis area in the Libyan desert, all the men pursue sexual relations with adolescent boys, with whom they engage in anal intercourse. This activity is so common that males are regarded as peculiar if they do not take part in these homosexual relationships. Siwan men will even lend their sons to each other, and they talk about their masculine love affairs as openly as they discuss their love of women.[153]

In Lesotho, age-differentiated sexual relationships between young women were reported to be a normal part of growing up. Called "mummy-baby" relationships, these romantic and sexual friendships were entered into in early adolescence and could continue even after the older partner had gotten married to a man. These sexual bonds involved increasing levels of intimacy, including open expressions of kissing, and often led to lifelong bonds. The older partner took on the responsible role in the relationship, and provided her younger partner with gifts and advice. The relationships might continue for some time after the marriage of the older women, though at some point the sexual relationship would cease. When that occurred the younger partner would reverse roles and take on a younger woman of her own. These relationships were believed to play an important role in the growth and social development of the women.[154]

Transgenderal two-spirit-like individuals are also common among a number of African tribal peoples, where they often play roles as shamans or healers. The *mugawe*, a powerful religious leader of the Meru of Kenya, cross-dresses and is usually a passive homosexual, sometimes marrying a masculine man. Among the Kwayama of Angola, two-spirit-like men serve as diviners and healers. Like the two-spirit of Native American peoples, they appear feminine in dress, do women's work and become auxiliary wives to men who may have other female wives. The diviners of the South African Zulu are usually women, but the 10 percent who are men are all cross-dressing passive homosexuals. Members of a spirit possession cult among the Hausa in northern Nigeria practice cross-dressing and take the passive role in homosexual intercourse. Brazilian and Haitian cults derived from West African religions also involve cross-dressing and homosexuality. Non-religious two-spirit type homosexuals have also been reported among a large number of Africa tribes.*

Among the many tribes for which transgenderal or two-spirit-like homosexual roles have been reported are the Nandi of Kenya, the Dinka and Nuer of the Sudan, the Konso and Amhara of Ethiopia, the Ottoro of Nubia, the Fanti of Ghana, the Ovimbundu of Angola, the Thonga of Zimbabwe, the Tanala and Bara of Madagascar, the Wolof of Senega and the Lango, Iteso, Gisu and Sebei of Uganda, among others.

Societies Where Homosexual Behavior
Has Been Reported to Be Uncommon

While homosexual behavior in one form or another seems to have been a commonly accepted part of life among the vast majority of the aboriginal cultures of the Americas, the Pacific and Africa, there are some native societies where homosexuality is reported to be absent or uncommon. In most cases the infrequency of homosexual behavior seems to be due to either an overriding emphasis on heterosexual expression, or prohibitions against same-sex involvement. In some tribes, the potential for homosexuality is precluded by strong heterosexual conditioning, such as marriage between children, sometimes as young as five years of age, and other types of encouragement of overt heterosexuality among children. Often, though, a lack of homosexuality appears to stem from especially intense expectations of heterosexual conformity among tribal members.[155] Among the Mbuti, a tribe of pygmies in central Africa, the rarity of homosexual behavior has been explained as a consequence of the extreme importance the Mbuti place on the conception of children. Since children cannot be conceived through homosexual intercourse, it does not make sense to them. Despite this attitude, homosexual behavior is still known to occur on occasion among the Mbuti.[156] Most of the societies in which homosexuality is reported to be rare have severe sanctions against such behavior. Among the Nuer and Lango tribes of Uganda, tribal laws required that anyone engaging in a homosexual act be killed. However, if one of the partners assumed the gender identity of the opposite sex, they would be allowed to live together undisturbed.[157] Among a Bantu tribe in northern Kenya, homosexual acts are considered to be a source of ritual impurity requiring purification. Similarly, among the Santal, a tribal people in India, a person committing a homosexual act is fined, but after an act of ritual penance and purification is accepted back into normal tribal life.[158]

In some tribes the reported absence or disapproval of homosexuality can be linked to the influence of Western colonial authorities and missionaries. Recent anthropological studies report that among the Aymara, a large Indian group living on the Andean plateau of Peru and Bolivia, "sex perversions" are now uncommon, though male and female homosexuality, as well as male transvestism, was reported to be widespread among them in the early 19th century. This change has been attributed to vigorous repression on the part of the Roman Catholic church.[159] However, it is indicative of the strong predisposition toward homosexuality among humans that even among societies with strict sanctions against it, homosexual behavior is still often reported to go on in secret.

Conclusion

In the sexual customs of aboriginal cultures we can see an accommodation of the intrinsic ambisexual characteristics of the human species in ways that promoted the survival and prosperity of those societies. The patterns of sexual behavior seen among these cultures demonstrate how these inherent sexual inclinations, probably present in humans from the origins of the species, often coalesced into social traditions where homosexual behavior complemented heterosexuality in a natural harmony that contributed to the reproductive success and quality of life of those societies.

This survey of the sexual customs of aboriginal cultures, then, reveals a dramatically different picture of sexuality from the view maintained in modern Western culture. Taken together with the widespread homosexual behavior among animal species, the near universal appearance of same sex relationships among tribal peoples strongly argues that an intrinsic ambisexuality was present during the evolution of humans as a species. As human evolved from clans of primitive hunger-gatherers into progressively more complex cultures, the complementary role homosexual behavior plays in the species evolved with them, often becoming incorporated into social institutions. The two-spirit of the hunter-gatherers and early agriculturalists became temple priests in socially more complex societies, such as those of the pre–Columbian civilizations. Adolescent homosexuality became enshrined in traditions such as the Mayan custom where teen-aged males were given pubescent boys to serve as partners until marriage, at which time the younger partner was given a pubescent boy of his own. What the Spanish encountered when they arrived in the Americas, then, was not a depraved society of sodomitical heathens, wallowing in sin and vice, but the manifestation of a complex sexual harmony, the results of tens of thousands of years of social and cultural evolution of a species for which homosexuality was as natural and played as important a place in the lives of its members as heterosexuality.

3

The Inheritance of Nature: The Ambisexual Harmony of Human Sexuality

In Chapter 1 we briefly surveyed the range of same-sex behavior that occurs throughout the animal kingdom, looking at the recurring patterns in which it appears among various species, and taking note of the apparent functional role homosexual behavior plays in supporting the evolutionary success of a wide range of species. Heterosexual reproduction is obviously the primary form of sexual behavior among animals, but the sheer abundance of same-sex behavior in the animal world, not to mention the benefits it appears to bring to many species, should establish with finality, for all who are willing to look at the evidence, that homosexual behavior is an integral part of the natural order of life.

Similarly, the virtually universal presence of same-sex behavior among indigenous peoples in all geographic regions and among all races, where it has appeared regardless of the availability of partners of the opposite sex or the encouragement of social traditions, should likewise remove all doubt that homosexuality is a deeply rooted feature of human sexuality. As the sex researcher C.A. Tripp has observed, where homosexuality "is merely approved, it tends to be prevalent."[1]

The Functional Role of Homosexuality Among Humans

According to evolutionary biologists, "if a structure, function or behavior occurs in a number of individuals or species, and if it persists through several generations, then that feature can be presumed to serve some evolutionarily advantageous function. That is, it must contribute to the persistence of the species."[2] The question therefore naturally arises as to the function such a non-procreative sexual trait as homosexuality would serve in promoting the reproductive success of the human species.

Because the lifestyles of tribal peoples before the intrusion of Western missionaries and colonial governments were uniformly free of the kind of religious or philosophically-based restrictions on sexuality found in the West, it can be argued that the sexual behavior and traditions of those societies more purely reflect the sexual inclinations or predispositions intrinsic to human sexuality. While it is true that many tribal societies have a collection of taboos, restrictions or customs relating to sexual behavior, the restrictions or traditions that appear, aside from mandatory initiatory homosexuality among some tribes, are primarily concerned with maintaining healthy reproduction. Examples of such customs include menstrual taboos, tribal incest rules, and marriage exchanges between different tribes which are aimed at preventing conception between close relatives as well as securing wives for the males of the tribe.

Except for rare exceptions, homosexual behavior is not disapproved, and, in fact, among most tribal peoples, social attitudes toward homosexuality are essentially neutral. This stands in stark contrast to social attitudes in the West, which have been shaped by a sexual morality based on scriptural interpretation and a philosophically based definition of "natural law" that would seem absurd to indigenous peoples, whose understanding of sexuality is based on their observations of nature itself. If homosexuality among humans has an "evolutionarily advantageous function," as evolutionary biologists would suggest, the patterns of homosexual behavior found among these "nature peoples," being unaffected by philosophical or scripture-based restrictions, should give us insight into whatever functional role is played by homosexuality in support of reproductive success of the human race.

Adolescent and Young-Adult Homosexuality

In looking at the way homosexuality has manifested in various indigenous societies around the world, the pattern which stands out as most common, as nearly universal, in fact, is homosexual behavior among adolescents and young adults. More striking, still, is the large number of societies with institutionalized sexual traditions in which every single male without exception spends a portion of his life in a homosexual relationship. While initiatory customs for young women like those for males have not been documented, there have been reports of analogous customs, such as the "mummy-baby" relationships of Lesotho, in which all girls participate. If every male and female experience homosexual relations for a segment of their lives among the indigenous societies with such traditions, there is no reason to believe that young people among all other societies in the world would not be capable of similar homosexual responsiveness.

The tendency to homosexuality in adolescence and young adulthood is also a key characteristic of primate sexuality and would seem to be one of the most obvious of the behavioral traits inherited by humans from their immediate animal ancestors. While homosexuality among adolescents and non-breeding adults is common among many other animal species with strongly developed social behavior, such as bison, giraffes, dolphins, whales and primates, it is found most frequently among the males of the species because of the limitations that the females' estrous cycle places on their sexual activity. Among primates, however, such homosexuality is nearly as common among females as among males. Among these social animals, homosexuality among younger or non-breeding animals promotes sociability and provides a tension-reducing outlet for sexually mature individuals where sexually ready females are not available either because none are in estrous or because breeding rights are controlled by dominant males.

In a great number of tribal societies observed around the world in recent times, homosexual relationships among adolescents and young adults have produced a similar social benefit by providing companionship and sexual gratification for those sexually mature males and females of the society who are either too young for marriage, or for whom a suitable marriage partner is not yet available. Among most tribal societies marriage for the males occurs after they have come of age, usually in their early to mid–20s, and before that age sexual expression flows naturally toward companions of the same sex. In some tribes, heterosexual opportunities for young men are restricted because of the unavailability of marriageable women due to polygamous practices of the chiefs or other senior males. However, in a large majority of tribal cultures the availability of partners of the opposite sex is not an issue, and homosexuality among adolescents and young adults is nonetheless common. Among traditional North

American Indian cultures, for example, homosexuality among youths has been considered normal and has been commonly accepted by the tribes as long as the individuals grow out of it and get married by the time they are in their mid-twenties.

A similar understanding about adolescent homosexuality has long been held by medical authorities, who regarded it as a transitory phase of normal sexual development. Sigmund Freud wrote in 1905 that a homosexual tendency at puberty is normal among both boys and girls, and commented that "I have never carried through any psychoanalysis of a man or a woman without discovering a very significant homosexual tendency."[3] Freud's judgment on adolescent homosexuality has been seconded by most authorities since.[4] For example, Frank Richardson, a former surgeon general of the British army, and author of a handbook on sexuality widely used by army medical officers, described adolescent homosexuality as a normal phase of development. Though he was writing in the 1960s, when adult homosexuality was still regarded by the medical establishment as a psychosexual disorder, Richardson took homosexuality in adolescence as a given, and held that it was only abnormal, what he called a "form of immaturity," when it extended into the individual's adulthood.[5] So while the unavailability of sexual partners of the opposite sex would certainly encourage homosexual behavior, it cannot be denied that there is a natural predisposition among adolescents and young adults to homosexual behavior regardless of circumstances. Put another way, every human being is capable of some degree of homosexual responsiveness and expression, especially in youth.

This observation, by itself, dramatically rebuts the common assumption in modern Western culture that homosexual proclivities are restricted to a small minority. If every human has some capacity for homosexual responsiveness to some degree or other, then the imposition of a moral order harshly condemning homosexual expression, such as has long prevailed in Western society, would inevitably lead to the large-scale propagation of same kind of the psychological conflict and resulting homophobic neuroses exhibited by the subjects of the Adams study discussed in the Introduction.[6]

Conditions Contributing to Homosexuality Among Young People

Several factors work to delay heterosexual involvement until later in the development of an individual and encourage homosexual behavior, even where members of the opposite sex are available. The first of these is the intrinsic homosexual responsiveness that Freud and others have noted is experienced by boys and girls alike during the onset of puberty. Sex researchers have found that "young boys frequently associate what is male with what is sexual in such a way as to arrive at a powerful homosexual thrust before realizing that heterosexual possibilities even exist." Researchers have noted that pubescent boys are fascinated with the male genitals, and often associate their first orgasms with maleness, male genitalia "and all that is sexually valuable and exciting," an association that easily leads to sexual interest in other males.[7] A similar homosexual responsiveness has been noted among girls as they become sexually aware of themselves and their peers during puberty.

Contributing to this inherent homosexual responsiveness is the high level of testosterone in adolescent males and estrogen in teenaged girls which are produced in large quantities with the onset of puberty and reach their peak levels in the late teens. High levels of sex hormones have been shown to trigger homosexual behavior in a variety of mammals, and are likely a contributing factor in the widespread homosexuality among adolescent and young adult animals of many species. Sex researchers have also identified high levels of sex hormones as a condition that can bring about homosexual responsiveness in humans. The natural same-sex responsiveness that comes with puberty and the compounding effect of high hormonal levels would certainly explain the readiness of adolescents and young adults to engage in homosexual relations that has been observed in societies around the world, even among individuals who later demonstrate a strong heterosexual drive.

A second factor contributing to a natural delay in heterosexual activity is the strong tendency of both males and females to associate exclusively with members of their own sex, beginning in childhood, and continuing through adolescence and young adulthood. In most aboriginal societies, social companionship and emotional intimacy are primarily experienced with others of the same sex. Segregation of the sexes is also a widespread phenomenon among many species, such as mountain sheep, giraffes, elephants, dolphins, baboons and gorillas. The widespread appearance of sexual segregation among a vast range of social animal species suggests that segregation of the sexes is an elemental trait of the behavior of social mammals. Among traditional Native American cultures, both males and females remain emotionally closer to others of their sex their whole lives, even after marriage.[8] In many aboriginal societies in the Amazon, Melanesia and parts of Africa, men and women spend most of their time apart, and rarely, if ever, even sleep together. Men frequently occupy entirely different quarters from the women and children, with sexual intercourse between husband and wife being relegated to brief periods and unrelated to any sense of companionship.[9] This tendency to segregate along sexual lines reduces the likelihood that an individual will develop strong sexual interest in members of the opposite sex until the customary age for marriage, which in most indigenous societies comes when the individuals are in their 20s.

Due to the strong cultural emphasis on heterosexual romance in modern Western societies, and the pressure this exerts on adolescents to show they are "normal," involvement with members of the opposite sex usually begins when individuals begin to date in the teen years. However, except for dating, adolescent socializing is almost exclusively among members of the same sex. Among adults in Western society, social companionship between members of the opposite sex outside of sexual relationships is very rare. Except for heterosexual involvement, then, humans, like many other species of mammals, seem prone to segregate themselves along sexual lines.

The natural homosexual responsiveness that emerges with the onset of puberty, the high levels of sex hormones characteristic of the adolescent and young-adult years, and the strong tendency of individuals to associate solely with members of their own sex in the absence of contrary societal pressures are the probable explanations for the near universal appearance of adolescent and young adult homosexuality observed in aboriginal societies around the world.

A Functional Benefit of Adolescent Homosexuality

As among primates, some adolescent homosexuality can be viewed as play or experimentation. Sexual bonds can also provide adolescents with a stabilizing companionship during what can be a difficult period of their lives. These youthful relationships give adolescents a way to learn about the emotional aspects of sex and bonding without the risk of pregnancies with which they are not equipped to deal. Indeed, the very fact that adolescent same-sex relationships *are not procreative* represents a significant benefit to the species. While humans generally reach sexual maturity in their early teens, and are at the peak of their sexual drive in their late teens, psychological, emotional and physical maturity are not generally achieved until the early twenties.

It is no small irony that the tendency to sexual activity is the greatest at an age when the individuals are ill prepared to deal with the natural consequence of heterosexual coitus, that is, the conception of a child. By diverting the sex drive away from inappropriate heterosexual involvement, the strong predisposition toward homosexual behavior among adolescents and young adults works to prevent pregnancies among these immature individuals, and helps to insure that the conception of children occurs within stable relationships between psychologically and emotionally mature adults. Therefore, adolescent and young adult homosexuality, as a trait of human sexuality, can be said to play a useful role in regulating reproduction, mitigating against the possibility of conception among those who are less capable of providing children with the care they need, thereby helping to insure stronger and healthier offspring for the species as a whole.

In Western cultures where homosexual activity is still widely stigmatized, and is often viewed as sinful or deviant, most adolescents learn to successfully suppress this latent homosexual responsiveness. In fact, they frequently go to great pains to avoid being perceived as homosexual by their peers, often to the point of engaging in gay-baiting and other homophobic activities. In addition, modern Western culture places high expectations on teens to demonstrate heterosexual interest, bombarding them with heterosexual images and role models, whether in song lyrics or teen movies, which pound in the theme that to be normal is to be heterosexual — a powerful message for impressionable and socially insecure teenagers still developing an identity. As a result adolescents in Western societies and in westernized cultures of the Third World direct their sexual energies for the most part toward the opposite sex. It is telling that in recently westernized areas of the Third World, where the introduction of Western moral values and influences has resulted in a sharp curtailment of previously widespread homosexual traditions, there has been a corresponding explosion of extramarital heterosexual permissiveness and its attendant problems.[10]

Among pre-westernized indigenous tribal peoples, where sexuality is seen as a part of the bounty of life, and not something to be tightly restricted, homosexual behavior readily manifests as a part of adolescent life. With no need to seek sexual outlets with members of the opposite sex, as is expected in Western societies, the young people of most tribal cultures find sexual and emotional companionship with members of their own sex, and do not become heterosexually involved until they are in their twenties and ready for marriage and raising a family. As a result, the problems of teen pregnancies and single mothers are virtually unknown among those aboriginal societies still unaffected by Western cultural and moral values. Looking from the perspective of the ambisexual patterns of our primate ancestors and the functional benefits demonstrated by the adolescent homosexuality among indigenous peoples, the involvement with the opposite sex that is the norm among teenagers in Western culture represents a *premature heterosexuality* at variance with the ambisexual harmony observed among a wide variety of animal species and among many human societies.

The Phenomenon of Pederastic Homosexuality Among Males

A distinctive form in which homosexual behavior has appeared among the indigenous peoples in many parts of the world is hierarchical relationships in which an older male plays a dominating role with a younger, sexually passive male partner. In addition to Melanesia, where hierarchical homosexuality plays a central role in male initiation rites, initiatory homosexuality has been reported among tribal societies in the Amazon Basin and in Africa. Informal pederastic homosexual relationships have also been frequent in native societies throughout the world, ranging from the Siwan Berbers of North Africa and the Fang and Ubangi peoples of Central Africa to the Batak of Sumatra and the natives of the Santa Cruz Islands in the Pacific. Scattered reports from ethnographers working in Melanesia, Polynesia and Africa indicate that such hierarchical relationships can occur among women, as well, though they do not appear to be nearly as common as those among males. In fact, the potential for pederastic or asymmetrical relationships among males is so deeply engrained in male sexuality that it seems to be an aspect of human sexuality that is rooted in the primordial past of the species.

The tendency of males to couple in these asymmetrical relationships appears to be a byproduct of the intrinsic dominant/aggressive characteristic of male sexuality. Males of many species, ranging from iguanas to dolphins, will not hesitate to take sexual advantage of younger or smaller males. For a male to express his dominance over another male sexually is a trait that has been observed in such disparate species as mountain sheep and baboons. Likewise, subordinate males of many species will respond in a sexually submissive way when challenged by a dominant male. The willingness of subordinate males to yield to the sexual advances of larger males is even seen in such relatively primitive species as lizards, chickens and rats.

Animal studies have shown that the tendency of males to invert their sexual roles with other males correlates to high levels of testosterone. The association of passive homosexual receptivity in a male with high testosterone levels is significant because it is testosterone that stimulates the development of male characteristics in a fetus, that leads to the development of male genitals and secondary sexual characteristics in puberty, and that drives male sexual behavior. That testosterone is responsible for males inverting their sexual roles with other males has led animal biologists to conclude that the capacity for a passive homosexual response is an inherent characteristic of the sexuality of male animals.

Sexual researchers have determined that high testosterone levels can lead to passive homosexual behavior among human males, as well. In fact, researchers have found that it is the super-masculine, swashbuckling, he-man type of male that is more likely to engage in such passive behavior rather than the timid or effeminate, un-athletic type that popular culture stereotypes as a passive male.[11] Traditional psychoanalytic theory has maintained that the desire of a male to be sexually penetrated by another male is due to femininity in the individual.[12] Considering the role that male sexual inversion plays among many animal species, discussed in Chapter 1, it seems much more likely that such a desire, and the development of a passive sexual response, originated as a defensive response of male animals in dominance confrontations realizing the superiority of their opponents. The correlation of testosterone levels to passive sexual receptivity would support such a conclusion, because male animals with higher testosterone levels would be more aggressive, and thus more likely to end up in violent dominance confrontations.

Sexual researchers have long recognized that masculine men can experience great pleasure in playing a passive role in sexual intercourse, and that males possess a "passive genital zone" associated with the prostate.[13] Indeed, the sexual and emotional satisfaction that human males can derive from being dominated sexually is illustrated by the abundant pornographic material widely available in Western societies featuring bondage and submission themes which is marketed to heterosexual as well as homosexual audiences. And while it is an aspect of male sexuality little known or appreciated outside the gay community, human males can become so aroused and experience so much pleasure when subjected to deep anal penetration that they can be brought to orgasm with very little other stimulation.[14]

The fact that this sexual responsiveness of males to smaller or younger males and a corresponding submission on the part of the subordinate male to the dominant male has been observed among animal species across the range of evolutionary complexity, from lizards to humans, suggests that this trait is more basic to animal sexuality than other instinctual traits we take for granted, such as bonding between heterosexual mates or the paternal instinct —

traits which are not found among many animal species, and which are not even found among primates.

The potential for such asymmetrical relationships among human males is strong. Older males show a natural capacity for sexual attraction to younger males. In many indigenous societies around the world, the sexual appeal of adolescent males to adult males is taken for granted. Sexual responsiveness to adolescent males has even been demonstrated in normally adjusted heterosexual males in the West, most of whom would be loath to admit such an attraction. In studies measuring the sexual responsiveness of males by monitoring blood flow through the penis, which increases with even slight sexual arousal, a variety of normal, heterosexually conditioned males were shown pictures of males and females of various ages and in various stages of undress. The studies found that these heterosexually "straight" males, who responded sexually to images of women of all ages, also displayed arousal when viewing pictures of nude adolescent males.[15]

Conversely, adolescent males show a strong potential for sexual attraction to older males. In describing a boy's admiration for masculine prowess and his desire to emulate older males, the Kinsey Report states, "the anatomy and functional capacities of male genitalia interest the younger boy to a degree that is not appreciated by older males who have become heterosexually conditioned, and who are continuously on the defensive against reactions which might be interpreted as homosexual."[16] Researchers have noted that "although a stealthy interest in the genitals of the father is the rule with small boys, it is suppressed as they grow older, and in boys in pre-puberty and later, conscious interest is directed towards the genitals of other men and youths."[17]

Concurrent with a boy's or young adolescent's fascination with the sexual characteristics of other males is his psychological need to select role models to admire and imitate among older youths and men. The prototype of the fixation boys and young adolescents have for older males is the boy's relationship with his father. As described in a standard psychoanalytic text by Otto Fenichel, "Every boy loves his father as a model whom he would like to resemble; he feels himself the 'pupil' who, by temporary passivity, can achieve the ability to be active later on. This type of love could be called the apprentice love."[18]

This tendency to identify with the traits of admired role models assists boys in their acquisition of desirable qualities and plays a crucial role in their development. In such a situation, it is not unusual for a young adolescent to be awestruck by the seemingly miraculous achievement of an even slightly older youth.[19] These relationships are often accompanied by strong feelings of attachment and love, which contribute to the development of the boy.[20] Therefore, a boy or adolescent who develops an intense admiration for another male may easily find his adoration becoming eroticized, particularly when it is centered on a particular individual.[21] Such a youth would be especially receptive if the admired male were to initiate sexual contact. Though this fact is little understood by the public, police authorities, psychologists and others who work with juvenile populations are well aware of the receptivity of teenaged males to sex with older teens or adult males. In fact, it is not unusual for the younger males to initiate the relationships.[22]

The Psychological Impact of a Dominant Male Lover on a Developing Adolescent

While Melanesian tribesmen attribute the development of virility and courage in a youthful initiate to the mystical power of semen injected into him during initiation, there is in fact a psychological basis to the transformation from child to virile adult that the tribesmen believe occurs as a result of these homosexual relationships. Whatever tendency there is in an adolescent to imitate characteristics of an admired model would be reinforced by the physiological and psychological consequences of sexual involvement. This is because the establishment of a sexual relationship between two individuals triggers a number of physiological and psychological changes within the individuals that are associated with the phenomenon of "falling in love." The individuals find the presence of their lovers euphoric and tend to idealize the characteristics of their partners. This is due to chemical changes in the brain that result in a flood of endorphins and a lowering of the ego boundaries, part of the mechanics of a developing physical/sexual bond. Consequently, a youth sexually and emotionally involved with an admired older male would be even more likely to emulate his lover's admirable traits, and would be particularly influenced by his personality and attitudes.

Gilbert Herdt, in his analysis of ritual homosexuality in New Guinea, has underscored the power of sexual submission to bring about psychosocial changes in a youth's identity, in internalizing tribal beliefs and norms, and in the assimilation of such warrior traits as courageousness and aggression.[23] A tribal youth in a sexual relationship with an adult warrior would therefore be all the more receptive to his teaching and training, would be eager to please his teacher-lover, would seek to emulate his virile nature, and would more easily internalize the ideals and beliefs the lover is seeking to pass on to the youth. In addition, the affection and support of his lover/mentor during this crucial stage of his development would provide needed affirmation and positive reinforcement as he faced the challenges involved in the training of a hunter/warrior, and underwent ordeals meant to instill in him the strength and courage expected of a warrior. By submitting to the sexual as well as psychological dominance of the older male, the youth would be more likely to acquire the desirable traits of his older lover. Therefore, a sexual relationship between a warrior and a youth could indeed be instrumental in the development of the youth into virile manhood, not as a result of the injection of semen into him as is believed by many primitive warrior cultures, but because of the psychological consequences of the sexual relationship.

Since the basis for these hierarchical relationships lies in the inherent characteristics of male sexuality, the potential for this type of sexual involvement is not limited to those individuals more or less inclined to exclusive homosexuality. The Danish psychiatrist Thorkill Vangaard, drawing on his own clinical experience as well as observations of New Guinea tribes and accounts of ancient Greek customs, has argued that all normal, heterosexually adjusted males have the capacity for such homosexual relationships at some time in their lives, either as a receptive, junior partner, or, later, as a mentoring older lover.[24]

There is no question that hierarchical relationships between males have been widespread across a vast range of human cultures. In fact, the historian John Boswell has pointed to the irony in the horror with which pederastic relationships are viewed in the modern West, inasmuch as relationships between men and youths have been the single most common type of homosexuality throughout human history. In fact, in a great number of societies throughout history such relationships were as common as heterosexual marriage.

The Variability of Homosexual Expression Among Humans

As widespread as hierarchical homosexuality seems to have been, it is also true there are great numbers of tribes where the pattern does not exist, at least as a recognizable custom involving most members. While homosexual behavior among adolescents and young adults of both sexes seems to be virtually universal to some degree or other among aboriginal societies, the manner in which it manifests among tribal societies varies considerably. It occurs most frequently in the sort of informal peer relationships that are common among both male and female adolescents in tribes in every geographic region, but also in more formalized peer relationships, such as among the bond-friends of the New Guinea Asmat. In many instances adolescent homosexual relationships are included in marriage exchange arrangements, not just in Melanesia and Australia, but also in the Amazon, among such tribes as the Nambikwara of Brazil. Among societies which have a tradition of homosexual initiation the sexual energies of adolescents and young adult are channeled through those rigidly structured relationships. So while there appears to be a strong intrinsic predisposition among humans to homosexual behavior beginning at puberty and continuing into young adulthood, there is also some fluidity in the patterns in which it manifests. The specific causes of the variance in sexual customs that have been observed among different societies have been the subject of considerable debate among academic scholars in recent years.

A number of sexual historians in the last several decades have argued that the sexual behavior of people in a society is determined by how sexuality is "constructed" by that society, i.e., the social attitudes, sexual morality and laws that shape the way people look at and understand sex. This is obviously true to a certain extent, and would certainly apply to those cultures with institutionalized sexual traditions. Yet there are numerous examples throughout history where actual sexual behavior differs markedly from the forms specified by a society's social and moral strictures. For example, it is conventional wisdom among mainstream academic historians, particularly among those influenced by the social constructionist school, that homosexuality in classical Athens was limited to temporary, one-sided educational relationships between older men and beardless youths who, it is argued, don't share the sexual pleasure their older lovers find in the relationships. These historians base this definition of Greek homosexuality primarily on Greek laws and the commentaries of a handful of Greek writers who were discussing what they believed constituted honorable, socially approved relationships. However, as will be seen in a later chapter, a traversal of Greek literature and art objects turns up scores of exceptions to this limited definition of Greek homosexuality, from relationships that extend throughout the lifetime of the lovers, to examples of younger males who obviously enjoy the sexual relationships, and even of youths attempting the seduction of older males. After a review of this material it becomes obvious that the Greek writers cited by the social constructionist historians were describing the moral ideals that proper Athenian society expected in sexual relationships, not cataloging what actually occurred in their society.

A most obvious example of the inadequacy of social constructionism in explaining the sexual behavior of a society is the persistence of homosexuality in Western culture. Same-sex behavior was harshly condemned and punished for centuries, and was hardly visible at all until recent decades, while a strictly heterosexual, family-oriented sexual morality has for centuries dominated religion, civil law and social customs. If, as social constructionism argues, a society's sexuality is constructed by the society's attitudes and set of sexual mores, then homosexuality should not have existed in Western society at all, which is obviously not the case either in modern times, or as will be seen, throughout Western history since Roman times. So while a society's laws, traditions, moral teachings and social expectations are certainly influential in shaping the sexual behavior of a society, we must look to other factors for an explanation of the diversity of sexual behavior among human societies.

Sexual researchers have found that an individual's lifelong sexual tastes and preferences are strongly influenced by initial sexual experiences in adolescence. The patterns established in an adolescent's first sexual experiences, then, act as a template through which sexual possibilities are viewed and imagined, and which steers sexual fantasies and subsequent sexual activity. These initial sexual patterns can even determine what a person may prefer to do in bed many years later. Even in societies with tightly "constructed" sexual customs, the imprint of initial sexual experiences can continue to have a strong influence on later sexual behavior.

For example, among the New Guinea Sambia studied by Gilbert Herdt, whose elaborate tradition of initiatory homosexuality would be considered a classic of socially constructed sexual behavior, adult men still enjoyed playing the initiate role in sex with other men, practicing oral sex on them and swallowing their semen, long past the period in which they as initiates practiced oral sex on adult warriors, and at an age when their sexual role according to social tradition was as a husband to a wife and a "donor" of semen to young male initiates. One man, a father of ten, told Herdt, "I still never stop thinking about semen or eating it." Another told him, "A married man who didn't play around (swallow semen) enough will die quickly." It is obvious that the imprint of their first sexual experiences, where they as initiates practiced oral sex on older males, continued to exert a strong influence on their sexual imaginations throughout their lives.

In societies without tightly structured sexual traditions, the imprint of early sexual experiences on an individual's sexual outlook would help to explain the relative uniformity of sexual patterns within those groups. It would, for example, explain why hierarchical male homosexuality would be the rule among such peoples as the Siwan Berbers, yet uncommon among traditional Native American cultures where peer relationships have dominated. It would also explain how adolescents could come of age and progress through life in an intensely heterosexually oriented environment such as the modern West, where initial sexual experiences are most often heterosexual, without being consciously aware of homosexual possibilities, desires or fantasies despite the intrinsic homosexual responsiveness that substantial empirical evidence has shown to be latent within most people.

However, this initial template of sexual preferences is not immutable for most individuals. A person can in later years discover or be abruptly introduced to different modes of sexual activity or lovemaking that the individual could not even have imagined in earlier life and that prove to be enormously satisfying. There are also numerous examples of mature adults coming to a realization of homosexual desires and preferences in mid-life, despite an earlier sexual life in which sexual desires, fantasies, and relationships were exclusively heterosexual. The patterns of sexual preferences imprinted in adolescence, then, constitute a set of behavioral habits that, left alone, might never change, but that can be modified, added to or replaced entirely under varying circumstances.

Because of the intense heterosexual expectations and exclusively heterosexual role models presented in popular culture in Western societies, not to mention the fairly uniform disapproval or negative view of homosexuality even in contemporary Western culture, the great majority of adolescents acquire heterosexual attitudes and behavioral habits at an early age and thus regard the idea of homosexual activity as alien or perverse. On the other hand, this template of heterosexual identity and behavior can mask significant homosexual responsiveness within many individuals that can manifest in neurosis or homophobic attitudes. The research correlating homophobic attitudes and anti-homosexual hostility with levels of repressed homosexual responsiveness discussed in the Introductory Chapter is a compelling demonstration of the potential for neurosis caused by the conflict between socially conditioned behavior and contrary sexual feelings or desires within individuals.

Therefore, despite the influences of social attitudes, sexual morality and the heterosexual expectations and role models presented to developing adolescents in Western society, and the equally influential imprint of early sexual experiences, significant same-sex responsiveness can persist in many heterosexually conditioned individuals, and homosexuality can even emerge later in life as a viable sexual option for others. The persistence of the intrinsic homosexual responsiveness of human sexuality, then, transcends both social influences and the imprint of personal sexual experience even in individuals who develop satisfying heterosexual sex lives — a clear demonstration of the immutable character of this aspect of human sexuality.

Variability in Sexual Orientation

In most native societies it is normal for young people participate in homosexual activity and relationships. Most move on to heterosexual marriage, usually by the mid-or late twenties, though some do not. The exclusively homosexual orientation of some individuals has been recognized by a great number of tribal societies around the world in the acceptance and respect shown for the role of berdache-like individuals in tribal life. But predominantly homosexual inclinations do not necessarily imply feminine characteristics in a male. Sex researchers have found that effeminate mannerisms in men are unrelated to their sexual preference, and so whether an individual appears "masculine" or "feminine" has little to do with his sexual orientation. Indeed, feminine traits deemed necessary to demonstrate the male-female aspects of a berdache spirit were often deliberately cultivated in boys who might otherwise not appear particularly different from other boys.[25]

There are also numerous examples of masculine men among tribal cultures who pursue homosexual relationships with peers in adulthood, such as the socially recognized "special friendships" between warriors that were reported by early explorers and frontiersmen to be universally present among tribes across the North American continent. We have also seen examples of men who maintain homosexual relationships alongside their marriage to a woman, such as among the Asmat "bond-friends" of Southwest New Guinea or the "cross-cousins" among the Nambikwara of Brazil. Among the Zapotec of Southern Mexico some men will leave their wives after the children are grown, to move in with a male lover.

The broad appearance in indigenous societies throughout the world of primarily or exclusively homosexual individuals, in addition to the differing degrees of the bisexuality of adolescents and young adults who later move on to heterosexual marriage as well as adults, male and female, who pursue same-sex relationships while married shows that not only is there variability in the way homosexual inclinations are expressed, but also in the degree of sexual orientation of individuals. Even in societies where the progression through sexual patterns for all males is structured and regulated, this variability is evident. Gilbert Herdt reported that among the New Guinea Samba some males showed a strong heterosexual interest early with a corresponding diminished interest in the homosexual activities of initiation, while other males were primarily homosexual in preference, and continued frequent homosexual relations after their marriages. Herdt estimated that the total number of these males — strongly heterosexual, and predominantly homosexual — represented about five percent of the total population of males.[26]

As we saw in the Introductory Chapter, this variability in sexual orientation was one of the most controversial findings of the Kinsey Report when it was published. The percentage of otherwise heterosexual males who participated in homosexual relations at some point in their lives came as a great surprise to Alfred Kinsey and his team as they began to sift the study data.

"We ourselves were totally unprepared to find such incidence data when this research was originally undertaken. Over a period of several years we were repeatedly assailed with doubts as to whether we were getting a fair cross section of the total population.... It has been our experience, however, that each new group into which we have gone has provided substantially the same data. Whether the histories were taken in one large city or another, whether they were taken in large cities, in small towns, or in rural areas ... the incidence data on the homosexual have been more or less the same."[27]

Because the percentage of men who reported some homosexual experience was much larger than any previous estimate, the Kinsey team subjected the data to a dozen different validation tests, stricter scrutiny than was applied to any of the other data in the study. After completing the analysis, the team concluded that the actual incidence of the homosexual experience is at least 37 percent of the total interview population and 50 percent of males single through age 35, and added, "The tests show that the actual figures may be as much as five percent higher, or still higher."[28] The figures are especially remarkable when one considers the strict social and sexual conservatism of the 1930s and '40s period in which the study interviews were conducted, and the fact that the interview subjects verbally reported their homosexual experiences to the researchers in face to face sessions. It cannot be doubted that such face to face interview sessions, especially in that conservative early 20th-century social climate, would have had an inhibiting effect on the candor of some of the subjects in discussing experiences they might consider acutely embarrassing. After reviewing the Kinsey Report's findings on the incidence of homosexuality among males, Wainwright Churchill, a physician and sex researcher, wrote, "Surely we cannot continue to imagine that homosexual interests are rare among American males, or even that the tendency to act upon these interests is rare. Indeed, it is not too much to say that homosexual responsiveness constitutes a part of the sexual experience of a very great number of males even within most cultures that attempt to minimize or to suppress completely such responsiveness." Noting the stridently anti-homosexual social environment of the men interviewed in the study, Churchill remarked that "Because they are drawn from a highly homoerotiphobic environment, the Kinsey data perhaps more than any other tend to bring into focus *the likelihood that homosexual behavior is rooted in tendencies that are characteristic of mammalian sexuality.*"[29]

To illustrate the variability in sexual orientation evident in the sexual experience of many of the 20,000 men interviewed in the study, the Kinsey team devised the sliding scale of sexual orientation discussed in the Introductory Chapter and found that most people placed somewhere between the two extremes.[30] Though the findings and methodology of the Kinsey Report were harshly attacked in the years since the report's publication,* the psychiatric community has in recent years come to accept the report's finding that homosexual activity commonly occurs among many individuals well outside the confines of the gay community at some point in their lives.[31] The variability of sexual orientation that the Kinsey team addressed with their scale has also found acceptance among researchers, and, in fact, Kinsey's

*Addressing some of the criticisms of the Kinsey Report's statistical methods, Paul Gebhard and A.B. Johnson of the Kinsey Institute published a retabulation of the original report's data in 1979, which included additional interviews that had been collected after the report's first publication, and excluded groups, such as prisoner populations, that were thought to bias the sample. After this "cleansing" of the data, Gebhard and Johnson concluded that "the major findings of the earlier works ... remain intact. Adding to and cleansing our samples has markedly increased their value, but has not as yet caused us to recant any important assertion." Despite the continued attacks on the Kinsey Report's methodology and credibility by conservative organizations, and in spite of the original study's flaws, which the Kinsey Institute readily admits, the study is regarded by sex researchers and social scientists today as a monumental contribution to society's understanding of human sexuality, easily eclipsing in depth and scale anything done in the realm of sex research before or since.

original scale has been modified and is now used to capture a broader measure of an individual's sexual orientation.

In the 1970s, the psychiatrist and sex researcher Fritz Klein concluded that Kinsey's linear scale did not completely reflect the actuality of a person's true orientation because it was focused purely on a person's sexual experiences, and did not take into account the individual's sexual feelings, fantasies or emotional and social preferences. Klein built upon Kinsey's linear scale by scoring not just a person's same sex or opposite sex experiences, but by using Kinsey's 0–6 scale to score the relative sexual orientation of the individual's sexual attraction, sexual fantasies, and emotional and social preferences. Klein then expanded the scale into two dimensions by plotting those scores against a horizontal line of the individual's past and present experiences and what they would consider their ideal.[32] The result, the Klein Sexual Orientation Grid, has found broad acceptance among researchers, psychologists and clinical practitioners. The insights provided by Klein's research, demonstrating the multiple factors that can shape a person's sexual desires and object choice, would help explain the great variability in sexual orientation seen among aboriginal groups, especially those without institutionalized sexual practices.

The Genetic Basis of Exclusive Homosexuality

While exclusive homosexuality has been reported among lions, dolphins, monkeys, baboons and chimpanzees, among humans the trait is more pronounced. Until recently, many scientists were skeptical about whether exclusive homosexuality was an inherited, genetic trait. In line with the stubborn persistence in popular culture of Freudian assumptions about psychosexual development, it was usually contended that homosexual development in an adulthood had a psychological basis. The removal in 1976 of homosexuality from the list of psychological disorders maintained by the American Psychiatric Association did not dissuade all academic scientists from their arguments about the psychological basis for homosexuality in an individual. However, a growing body of research conducted over the past several decades strongly supports the conclusion that a tendency toward exclusive homosexuality is heavily influenced by genetic factors.

Studies of twins have established that there is a high probability that a predisposition toward exclusive homosexuality is inherited. In one study of over a hundred pairs of male twins, it was found that where one twin had a homosexual orientation, the other twin was also homosexual in 50 percent of the cases where the twins were identical — that is, they grew from a single sperm and egg. In the case of biological twins — twins growing from separate fertilized eggs — if one sibling was homosexual, it was found that the other was also homosexual in 24 percent of the cases, less than half the incidence observed for genetically identical twins. It is interesting to note that even in the case of the biological twins the proportion of twins who are both exclusively homosexual is much greater than that found in the general population. Several other large-scale studies of twins were carried out since the original studies, confirming the results. As a result of these studies on twins there is increasing consensus among researchers that sexual orientation is substantially influenced by hereditary factors.[33]

There has also been genetic research at the National Institutes of Health by a team lead by Dr. Dean Hammer which examined DNA markers on the X chromosomes of members of the same family and found certain markers present on the X chromosomes of homosexual members of the family, but not on the X chromosomes of non-homosexual family members.[34] Though the findings are not conclusive, they provide additional support for the view that genetic factors play a role in sexual orientation. In addition, recent research into the physiology of the brain has shown that there are several notable anatomical differences between the brains of homosexual and heterosexual men, which could only be explained by genetic differences between exclusively homosexual and non-homosexual individuals.

In 1991, Dr. Simon LeVay made headlines when he reported that a part of the hypothalamus in the brain was smaller in homosexual men than in heterosexual men. Other studies since then have shown not only additional structural differences, but also functional differences in the brains of homosexual and non-homosexual individuals. Since scientists began studying the anatomic functioning of the brain, it has been recognized that certain psychological abilities are controlled in one of the cerebral hemispheres and other activities in the other. For example, visual-spatial ability, the ability to visualize and analyze three-dimensional space, and to control the position and orientation of the body and the limbs in space, is controlled, or lateralized, in the right hemisphere. On the other hand, verbal abilities, language skills and the ability to organize ideas are controlled in the left hemisphere. Studies have shown that men and women differ in various mental abilities, especially in those traits that are highly lateralized — those that tend to be controlled by one side of the brain more than the other. Men generally perform better in tasks that require visual-spatial ability, such as throwing or catching objects, or visualizing directions from maps. Men also tend to be better at mathematical reasoning and problem solving. Women, in contrast, are generally more proficient in verbal and language skills, and in fine and complex motor movements requiring precision and pinpoint accuracy, such as in fine needlework.

Several studies have demonstrated differences between homosexual and non-homosexual individuals in certain of the lateralized psychological functions. In a study that measured the accuracy with which individuals of both sexes and differing sexual orientations could hit a target with a projectile — a right brain function — it was found that non-homosexual men did better on average than homosexual men, and lesbians performed better than non-lesbian women. Additional studies have shown that homosexual men have greater verbal abilities — a left brain trait — than non-homosexual men. Other research has identified differences in the brain structure itself between exclusively homosexual men and other men that would indicate that in homosexual men brain functions are more evenly divided between the two cerebral hemispheres. The studies have found that in gay men the bundles of fiber that connect the two halves of the brain, the *corpus callosum* and the *anterior commissure*, are larger than in non-gay men, a difference that according to scientists would correlate to greater functional symmetry in the brains of gay men.[35]

Within these general trends, though, there is also great variability. There are numerous instances of predominantly homosexual men who are also great athletes, just as there are heterosexually oriented men gifted in verbal abilities. Adding to the mix are the powerful behavioral influences of testosterone in men and estrogen in women on behavior. The greater balance between masculine and feminine mental capacities of a homosexual male when combined with the masculine physical development and aggressive behavioral tendencies brought on by testosterone could account for the exceptional athletic performance of some homosexual men. These various factors and the varying mixture of inherited masculine and feminine mental traits in all individuals would certainly help explain the enormous variety in talents and personalities found among humans.

The North American Indian attribution of the traits and skills of a berdache to a male-female spirit shows a striking correspondence to the greater functional balance scientists have discovered between the "masculine" and "feminine" halves of the brain in exclusively homosexual individuals. This greater functional symmetry in the brain could explain qualitative differences that have been observed in mental capacities between exclusively homosexual individuals and the rest of the population. Native American peoples considered berdaches to be the most intelligent of their members and often relied on their advice in tribal matters. Studies in Western industrial societies have shown that homosexual men score higher than heterosexuals on intelligence tests, are upwardly mobile to an exceptional degree and generally excel in their careers.[36] Among Native American peoples berdaches were renowned for the quality of their artistry and handicrafts, for their storytelling, and for their abilities in roles that relied on intuitive faculties, such as healers, shamans and seers. Likewise, the greater functional balance in the brains of homosexually oriented men and women in Western culture may also explain the disproportionate numbers of homosexuals prominent in the creative arts and design, and in such helping professions as teaching, nursing and the clergy — all roles which, as the Indians said about the berdache, have added immeasurably to the quality of life of society.

The Evolutionary Development of Exclusive Homosexuality in the Human Species

Though studies into the anatomical differences in the brain associated with sexual orientation are in their infancy, they have added considerable support to the contention that the tendency to exclusive homosexuality is a product of genetic development. The growing evidence for a genetic basis of exclusive homosexuality has nonetheless puzzled geneticists, who wonder how a non-reproductive trait would enter the gene pool if its carriers did not reproduce.

However, the human species is not like other mammal species, where individuals go about the tasks of survival, from seeking food to raising their young, more or less independently. Even among herding species, individual animals get their needs met independently of others, and group together mainly because of the safety afforded by membership in the herd. In contrast, humans provide for most of their needs in cooperation with others. Paleoanthropologists studying the development of early humans believe that one of the primary factors in the success of the human species was its evolution of group behavior and interdependence. It is thought that division of labor was crucial to the survival of the early hunter-gatherers, whether in bringing down game much bigger and more powerful than they were, or managing the daily tasks of gathering nuts, berries and vegetables, caring for children, and providing for the safety and security of the clan. As the species developed, each little society or clan functioned as one organism, with individual members contributing in varying ways and in different roles to the common welfare.

Natural variations in the personalities and talents of individuals would have complemented the division of labor and diversity of roles of early societies. Individuals with less inclination for heterosexual mating or for whom a marriage partner was unavailable, who would, then, have continued the homosexual patterns of adolescence rather than progressing to heterosexual relationships as others did, would have nonetheless contributed to the welfare of the clan. Exclusively homosexual males could have helped on hunting or scouting parties, or contributed to the defense and protection of the clan, a role similar to that played by the young men in "special friendship" sexual bonds that frontiersmen reported among warriors of Native-American tribes. Homosexual men and women could also have assisted in gathering nuts, berries, tubers and firewood, or helped in the camp sites, serving as midwives, assisting with childcare, caring for the sick, or tending to other domestic needs. Berdache or two-spirit like men and women may also have taken on the roles of seers, shamans, artisans, healers and keepers of tribal knowledge, roles whose contributions, though less tangible, would have been nonetheless important to the psychological and spiritual health of the clan.

With no children of their own to absorb their energies, these homosexual members would have been better able to assist their close relatives. The presence of these non-reproducing adults would have had the effect of increasing the proportion of productive workers in the total population of adults and children, thereby raising the per capita productivity of the group in their efforts to bring in such necessities as food and firewood, and in tending to domestic chores. Because of the extra help these individuals would have provided, their close relatives would have been able to successfully raise more children, and the ability of the group as a whole to survive would have been enhanced.

Considering the marginal existence of many early hunter-gatherer societies, this greater per capita productivity could have provided a decisive advantage in the struggle for survival. Hence, the presence of non-reproducing homosexual individuals would have, paradoxically, contributed to the reproductive success of the clan. Put another way, *the presence of exclusively homosexual individuals may have been critical to the survival of the human race* during a very difficult period. Because of the higher survival and reproduction rates of the close relatives of homosexual individuals, the genes they shared with their homosexual relatives would have been passed on in greater numbers. While the homosexual individuals would not have reproduced, their genes would have been passed down in collateral lines of descent. Evolutionary biologists have thus argued that a genetic predisposition to exclusive homosexuality would have found its way into the human gene pool because of the reproductive advantage gained by early clans with exclusively homosexual members.[37]

This "kin-selection hypothesis," as the theory is called, is supported by the existence of a specialized non-reproductive role for exclusively homosexual individuals that has been observed among tribal groups throughout a broad geographic range. The specialized non-reproductive role played by these exclusively homosexual individuals, such as the berdache of Native American cultures or the transvestite shamans of Siberian tribes, constitutes a venerable social tradition among these peoples which is thought to have its origins deep in the Paleolithic period. The widespread occurrence of exclusive homosexuals and berdache-like social roles among aboriginal peoples of all racial lines suggests that exclusive homosexuality and the emergence of this specialized role for exclusively homosexual individuals would have occurred before the development of racial differences among humans, which would place the origins of those traditions more than 40,000 years ago, and the emergence of a genetic trait for exclusive homosexuality even farther back than that.

The berdaches and homosexual shamans of the Paleolithic and Neolithic periods, then, with their skills in handicrafts, artwork, storytelling and tribal lore, and the intuitive abilities in healing and spiritual matters that won them such a high regard among later aboriginal cultures, can be seen as the *genetic prototypes* for the exclusive homosexuals of modern times. The varying mixture of male and female mental abilities, which Native Americans attributed to a male-female spirit, but which is most likely a result of the greater balance in lateralized brain function that has been discovered in exclusive homosexuals, is very probably responsible for the prominence of gay people in art and design, the performing arts, and in such helping professions as counseling, teaching, nursing and the clergy, where intuitive abilities are essential.

The homosexual interior decorator, hair dresser or theater designer has become a cliché, but our modern world would be immeasurably poorer without the very real contribution of these modern berdaches to the quality of life of society. Human civilization is studded with the luminous contributions and pivotal influences of many individuals who are now believed to have had a marked homosexual preference.*

Homosexuality Among Paleolithic Peoples

It is inevitable that homosexual practices would have been widespread among Paleolithic peoples. In addition to the exclusive homosexuality of individuals who would have carried out shaman or other non-reproductive roles among early clans, homosexuality would have occurred in sexual relationships between pairs of adolescent males or females, between male youths and older males and between adult pairs of men or women, similar to what has been observed among many of the world's indigenous tribes. Aside from the natural tendency of adolescents and young adults of both sexes to become involved in such relationships, and the high probability that this kind of homosexuality was one of the behavioral traits inherited from our primate ancestors, there are several other factors that would make such a conclusion inevitable.

As we saw in Chapter Two, the social hierarchy of some highly socialized primate species, such as gorillas and baboons, is organized entirely around the dominant males and the sexually mature females they control and their offspring. Among gorillas, which along with chimpanzees and bonobos are the closest animal relatives to humans, the alpha male serves as *pater familias* of a small clan consisting of him, the breeding-age females and their young. The sexually mature adolescent and young adult males separate themselves from the alpha's clan and form their own troop, spending a significant amount of their time courting each other and in homosexual activity. The females in the alpha's troop also develop homosexual bonds with each other, sitting or lying with each other, grooming each other, and engaging in sexual activity.

It is interesting to note that among some indigenous tribal peoples a very similar system has occurred, under which a polygamous chief and perhaps a few other senior males have a monopoly over the women of the tribe, with the result that the other males, adolescents and adults, divide up into homosexual pairs. Homosexual relationships also develop among the wives of the chief, and provide them with emotional support not possible from the chief because of the division of his affections among multiple wives. The occurrence of remarkably similar sexual behavioral patterns of tribal communities with such a polygamous chief or leader and gorilla troops is not, of course, because tribal peoples are genetically closer to primates — a notorious slander of racists in the past — but is entirely a consequence of the play-

---

Lists of prominent individuals with homosexual preferences have frequently been cited by writers defending the naturalness of same-sex love. Since the widespread appearance of homosexual behavior among animal species and human societies alike is powerful testimony to the naturalness of same-sex expression, a list is provided here only to illustrate the variety of personalities, talents and contributions of primarily homosexual individuals: Socrates, Plato, Aristotle, Sappho, Sophocles, Alexander the Great, Augustus Caesar, Virgil, Hadrian, Alcuin, Abu Nuwas, Richard the Lion Heart, Saladin, Erasmus, Rumi, Suleiman the Magnificent, Donatello, Leonardo Da Vinci, Michelangelo, Raphael, Benvenuto Cellini, Caravaggio, Michel de Montaigne, Christopher Marlowe, William Shakespeare, Francis Bacon, Molière, Queen Christina of Sweden, Peter the Great, Jean-Baptiste Lully, Frederick the Great, George Frederick Handel, Goethe, William Blake, Alexander von Humboldt, Napoleon Bonaparte, Ludwig von Beethoven, Lord Byron, Franz Schubert, John Henry Newman, Hans Christian Andersen, Gustave Flaubert, Ralph Waldo Emerson, Herman Melville, Florence Nightingale, Susan B. Anthony, Henry David Thoreau, Emily Dickenson, Peter Tchaikovsky, Walt Whitman, Auguste Rodin, Paul Gaugin, Thomas Mann, Willa Cather, Manuel de Falla, Marcel Proust, George Santayana, Maurice Ravel, Karol Szymanowski, John Maynard Keynes, T.S. Eliot, Sergei Diaghilev, Vaslav Nijinsky, Ludwig Wittgenstein, Federico Garcia Lorca, Aaron Copeland, Margaret Mead, Vladimir Horowitz, W.H. Auden, Francis Poulenc, Benjamin Britten, Samuel Barber, Tennessee Williams, Leonard Bernstein and Rudolf Nureyev.

ing out of the dynamics of sexual and social dominance against the backdrop of the strong latent homosexual responsiveness within members of each species.

It is easy to imagine that such a sexual organization would have been likely among early hominids as they evolved from a primate species into the early human antecedents — *Australopithecus*, and *Homo Erectus* — and then into modern humans, because the same dynamics of sexual dominance would have been at play. The basic family unit that we take for granted, the male and female parent together rearing their offspring, is not found among any of the primate species, nor for that matter among most other species in the animal kingdom except for birds, which are only distantly related to humans. Inasmuch as human social and sexual behavior evolved from that of our primate ancestors, it would be incorrect to assume that such a family unit would have been characteristic of early hominid groups or even clans of early *Homo Sapiens*. In the absence of a nuclear family unit, it is probable that heterosexual opportunities would often, if not universally, be controlled by the dominant males, leaving the younger males with homosexuality as their only sexual option. At whatever point along the way of human social evolution it was that nuclear families developed — though the fact that a system of polygamous chiefs controlling the women survived among some aboriginal tribes into the 20th century shows that the nuclear family system would hardly have been universal — the predisposition of adolescents and unmarried adults to homosexuality inherited from the primates would have remained.

Another factor faced by early societies which would have encouraged homosexual relationships among young males, even in the absence of polygamous senior males, may have been a limited availability of heterosexual partners. The Paleolithic population lived in small bands widely scattered across vast territories, and so suitable marriage partners for sexually maturing males were not always available. The scarcity of marriage partners was apparently exacerbated by a skewed ratio of males to females in the population. Paleoanthropologists have found that skeletal remains from the period show that among Paleolithic societies the ratio of adult men to adult women was approximately 5 to 4. A similar 5 to 4 ratio of men to women has been observed in the New Guinea societies which practice initiatory homosexuality,[38] and, in fact, in his discussion of ritual homosexuality in New Guinea, Herdt has cited the probability of a skewed sex ratio as a factor in the development of homosexual traditions among those tribes.[39] The relative scarcity of suitable marriage partners among Paleolithic peoples may have led to the development of the type of marriage exchange customs such as are seen among aboriginal tribes in Australia, New Guinea and the Amazon, which often include homosexual ties between brothers-in-law.

It seems beyond doubt, then, that homosexual behavior in forms similar to what has been observed among indigenous societies around the world in recent times would have been widespread among Paleolithic clans throughout the many millennia of their development, not only among exclusively homosexual members playing shaman or other helper roles, but among other members of the groups. By providing a means of sexual gratification and companionship for young males at or near the peak of their sexual drive, homosexual relationships would have contributed to harmony within those early societies by protecting against the conflicts that could arise from adventurous, but sexually frustrated, young males seeking outlets among inappropriate or unavailable females. Because heterosexual partners, if available, would not generally have been acquired until the individuals were physically and psychologically mature, the children produced would have been more likely to receive the care and nurturing they required. In clans with polygamous chieftains, sexual relationships among the leader's wives would have contributed to solidarity and harmony among the women, while providing emotional support for them that was not available from the chief because the division of his attentions among several wives, just as homosexual relationships among the other males would have provided them sexual satisfaction and emotional companionship.

During periods of severe hardship, the increased ratio of adults to children resulting from the presence of exclusively homosexual individuals would have increased the prospects for survival of the clan because of the greater efficiency of the clan as a whole in procuring the necessities of life. During less difficult times, the exclusively homosexual members, because of their creative abilities and intuitive skills, would have enhanced the quality of life of the clans with their healing abilities, skill with crafts, and spiritual contributions. The substantial benefits these homosexual individuals provided to early societies is suggested by the recognition and respect that tribal societies throughout the Americas traditionally accorded to their berdaches, a homosexual social institution which is thought to extend back as far as 20,000 years ago, to the distant period before the ancestors of the first Americans migrated over the Bering land bridge from Asia.

Additionally, where hierarchical mentor-student homosexuality was present, this form of homosexuality would have strengthened the ability of those societies to inculcate the crucial skills upon which the clans depended into each new generation of males, thereby contributing to the health and prosperity of the group. Early societies must certainly have observed the beneficial effects of hierarchical homosexual relationships in guiding the development and training of adolescent males, particularly hunter or warrior societies, where great valor and a high degree of proficiency in learned skills was required among adult males. With no understanding of the psychological aspects of sexual relationships, it would have been natural for those early clans to attribute the transformation of a pubescent boy into a skilled and courageous hunter or warrior to the magical effects of semen implanted into the youth by a virile male. As a result, these hierarchical homosexual relationships would have become incorporated into social customs, playing a central part of a boy's initiation into manhood.

Initiation rites such as these are thought to be among the oldest customs known among human societies. As noted in Chapter 3, anthropologists believe that the initiatory homosexuality among the aboriginal peoples of Melanesia and Australia may extend back 10,000 years or more, well into the Paleolithic era, and a growing number of scholars believe that a similar tradition of initiatory homosexuality existed among the prehistoric ancestors of modern Europeans.[40] There is even evidence of puberty rites in the caves at Montespan, France, dating from more than 15,000 years ago.[41]

Homosexuality and Reproductive Strategies in Nature

Contrary to what conservative religious bodies preach, and what many traditional scientists have assumed, the high level of same-sex activity that appears to be a natural and inevitable product of human sexuality is not only *not* a threat to the successful reproduction of the human race, but can, in fact, be shown to be supportive of the reproductive vitality of the species. The examples of numerous indigenous peoples with long-established homosexual traditions demonstrate that even though same-sex activity is not procreative, and that exclusive homosexuals do not reproduce, homosexual behavior can still make substantial contributions to the reproductive health of those societies in the various ways outlined in this chapter. It is clear, then, that homosexual behavior plays a significant role in the reproductive strategy of the human species as it evolved from its animal ancestors, a reproductive strategy that is similar to and entirely consistent with modes of reproduction found among many other species.

There are many examples of reproductive strategies among animal species which do not depend on the successful reproduction of each individual, and in which non-reproductive sexual activity is extensive. Among bonobos, one of the primate species most closely related to humans, both non-reproductive heterosexual and homosexual behavior outnumber actual reproductive heterosexual behavior by a vast margin. Non-reproductive hetero- and homosexual activity is also common among another close human relative, chimpanzees. Among gorillas, sexual activity in the all-male groups is significantly greater than in the mixed sex groups presided over by the alpha males. Among bottlenose dolphins, where homosexual activity is also far more frequent than heterosexual activity, most of the males become involved in pair-bonds with other males during adolescence in relationships which involve much homosexual activity, and which persist their entire lives. Similarly, females of the species live in small, all-female pods, where they raise their young while engaging in homosexual activity with other members of the group.

Among herding species such as bighorn sheep, where breeding rights are also controlled by a dominant male, and among which homosexual copulations outnumber heterosexual mountings by two-to-one or more, it is inevitable that a significant number of the males will never achieve dominant status and so will never mate with a female, with the result that their entire sex lives will be homosexual. Even though they don't pass on their genes, the subordinate males support the reproductive success of the species by contributing to the safety of the herd by their numbers, and by acting as a genetic reserve ready for mating in the event of the demise of the current dominant male. In human conception, itself, the millions of sperm that do not fertilize the egg still contribute to the reproductive success through the protective effect of their sheer numbers, which make it more likely that at least one sperm will be able to travel all the way through the chemically hostile environment of the woman's uterus to the egg. Indeed, a significant number of the sperm end up bonding with each other, but are still valuable for the reproductive effort because of the contribution of their mere presence to the total protective mass of sperm. The successful fertilization of the egg is due to the results of the entire mass of sperm working in aggregate, just as the reproductive success of such species as bighorn sheep and gorillas is achieved in the aggregate, not through the successful reproduction of each animal.

In view of the many species with reproductive strategies involving extensive non-reproductive sexual behavior, and the significant role homosexual behavior plays among primates, it seems perfectly natural that the human species would evolve with a reproductive strategy where the successful reproduction of the species is likewise achieved in aggregate, not in the propagation of each individual member, and where non-reproductive homosexual activity plays a supportive role. The multifaceted sexuality inherited from the primate ancestors of the human race, then, constitutes a complex sexual harmony, consistent with sexual patterns found among many other species.

The Ambisexual Inheritance of the Human Race

A survey of the extensive homosexual behavior in the animal world, a review of the virtually universal homosexual practices among pre-westernized indigenous peoples, and a consideration of the general patterns and characteristics of that sexual behavior in light of what is known of the psychology and physiology of sex and the results of recent research in sexuality make inevitable some provocative conclusions about human sexuality.

- Homosexuality among humans is an integral aspect of the multifaceted sexuality inherited by the human race from its primate ancestors, not a perversion of nature, an invention of degenerate urban inhabitants, a psychosexual disorder or a biological anomaly. The evidence that humans are an ambisexual species and inherited that trait from the primate ancestors of the human race is overwhelming.
- As is the case among the primate relatives of the human race, and many other mammal species, homosexuality plays a complementary role to heterosexuality in the reproductive strategy of the human species
- All human beings are capable of some degree of responsiveness to homosexual stimulus, whether acknowledged or not, especially in the adolescent and young adult years.
- A strong tendency to homosexual behavior is a normal aspect of adolescence and young adulthood for all individuals, and provides a positive benefit to the species by diverting the sex drive away from heterosexual partners for people too young or otherwise unable to shoulder the responsibilities of parenthood, the natural consequence of heterosexual activity. Same-sex relationships among young people supports the reproductive success of the species by helping to insure that human conception occurs under more ideal conditions between psychologically and emotionally mature individuals. Conversely, the socially and culturally promoted heterosexual involvement of adolescents in Western societies represents a premature heterosexual development of the individuals.
- Because the multifaceted sexuality the human race inherited from its animal ancestors includes a homosexual component that would be latent to a greater or lesser degree within all individuals, it could be expected that any social and moral codes that strictly prohibit, harshly condemn or otherwise demonize homosexual expression would engender considerable psychological conflict and resulting defenses and neurosis within a significant number of those subject in response to such a social or moral code.
- Exclusive homosexuality, which has also been observed to a limited degree among other mammals, very probably became widely established in the genetic line of the human race because the extra help provided by non-reproducing homosexual members of early hunter-gatherer clans gave them a reproductive advantage that enabled them to survive during periods when human existence was marginal.
- The special abilities and spiritual powers of berdaches and transvestite shamans that indigenous peoples attributed to a male-female spirit is very likely in large part the result of a greater functional balance between the right and left hemispheres of the brain that scientists say would be supported by anatomical differences that have been discovered in the brains of exclusively homosexual individuals.
- While the presence of non-reproducing exclusive homosexuals among early hunter-gatherer clans may have been critical to the survival of the human species, exclusively homosexual individuals have continued to support the quality of life of human societies through the aesthetic and spiritual contributions made possible by the special mental abilities resulting from the greater functional balance in their brain structures. The homosexual shamans and berdaches (both male and female) of the Paleolithic hunter-gatherers are, therefore, the genetic prototypes of the exclusive homosexuals of modern times.

Conclusion

The picture of human sexuality that emerges from an examination of the material considered in this chapter is obviously radically different from the understanding of sex prevailing in Western societies. However, some might argue that surveying the sexual customs of primitive tribes is hardly the way to assess the sexual nature of a morally based, civilized society like the modern West. Is the near universal presence and acceptance of homosexual behavior among tribal peoples around the world simply a reflection of their "uncivilized," "barbarous," or "primitive" nature, as conservative moralists might argue? Or is it because they are un-baptized heathens, wallowing in sin and vice, who haven't yet been "saved," as the Spanish conquistadors saw them, a view that would undoubtedly be shared by many conservative Christians?

In the next section of the book we will look at the sexual practices and moral attitudes towards sex throughout the world's civilizations, using the product of recent historical scholarship that has pierced the barriers of taboos and prejudice that have until the last several decades prevented a candid examination of sexual customs and attitudes of past historic periods. This survey of sexual customs and traditions of the world's civilized cultures will show that the sexual practices of aboriginal tribes are not, in fact, any different from those found around the world through most of human history, and that it is the sexual attitudes of European society, specifically the West since the Middle Ages, that are at variance from the norm, not the traditions of the "nature peoples."

Part II. Ambisexual Traditions in World Civilizations

The liberalization of attitudes to the study of sex and homosexuality in the last decades of the 20th century has fostered historical scholarship that has uncovered an enormous amount of previously unknown or overlooked evidence of same-sex practices among societies throughout the world going back to the earliest developments of civilization in Mesopotamia and Egypt. Despite the abundance of such evidence, it is still widely assumed that homosexual practices were either unknown or were rare and were always emphatically condemned among societies around the world in past periods. Though clearcut evidence of homosexual customs can be found in the literature and artifacts of the vast majority of historical societies, many scholars have been seemingly unwilling to admit the implications of evidence of well-entrenched homosexual traditions among those societies. Even scholars who have no personal bias against homosexuality are powerfully affected by the indoctrination into a strictly heterosexual understanding of sex that results from the exclusively heterosexual depiction of sex that permeates every aspect of Western life from moral teaching to popular culture.

Consequently academic historians frequently deny a sexual component in the relationship depicted between the hero of the ancient Sumerian Epic of Gilgamesh and his beloved male companion despite explicit references in the text to the sexual character of the relationship. In a similar way, it has often been assumed 1) that an apparently negative reference to homosexual relationships in the Egyptian Book of the Dead shows that the ancient Egyptians disapproved of homosexual relationships, despite considerable evidence to the contrary found among burial artifacts in their tombs; 2) that the story of the destruction of Sodom and an injunction against homosexual acts in Leviticus proves that the ancient Israelites always and uniformly condemned homosexuality; 3) that even though the classical Greeks took for granted that a sexual bond existed between the Homeric heroes Achilles and Patroclus, the failure of Homer to explicitly refer to the relationship between Achilles and Patroclus in the *Illiad* as sexual means that the famous love depicted between those two heroes was chaste; 4) that a few scattered critical remarks about same-sex love in classical Greek literature show that the ancient Greeks did not tolerate homosexuality and ridiculed males who practiced it; 5) that the claims of a couple of Roman historians living under the early Empire that the rustic farmers of the early Roman Republic prohibited homosexual relationships demon-

79

strate a disapproval of homosexuality under the Roman Republic; 6) that the anti-homosexual screed of early Christian writers proves a uniform condemnation of homosexual acts among the early Christians; 7) that because of the influence of the family-oriented philosophy of Confuscius Chinese society traditionally disapproved of homosexuality; and 8) that negative judgments on homosexual acts in Islamic scripture, and the anti-homosexual campaigns of contemporary Islamic fundamentalists illustrate a long-running intolerance of homosexuality under Islam. While there is surprisingly abundant evidence of a variety of homosexual practices and customs among the great civilizations of world history — including the Sumerians, Babylonians, Egyptians, Greeks, Romans, Chinese, Japanese, Muslims and even the ancient Hebrews and Christian Europe — it is also clear that the powerful influence of Western moral and social sexual conditioning has prevented many scholars, even today, from fully appreciating the degree to which same-sex love has been intertwined with the sexual traditions of societies around the world.

Indeed, so powerfully do the assumptions about sex ingrained in Western culture shape perceptions about sex that a truly objective evaluation of historical and documentary evidence of sexual practices in past periods would be very difficult if restricted to evidence reported and evaluated under the constraints of the same Western intellectual tradition that has shaped modern society's exclusively heterosexual understanding of sex. Though the heterosexually-oriented cultural and moral tradition of the modern West has imposed a restrictive lens through which historians have had to view the evidence of sexual customs among other societies, objective measures from clinical observations and empirical research into the psychology and physiology of sex, discussed in the previous chapter, have provided an unambiguous baseline of facts about human sexuality against which historical evidence can be considered that can serve as an objective reference in considering historical evidence of sexual customs. Moreover, the findings of science about the latent homosexual responsiveness within humans as well as the widespread same-sex practices documented among indigenous peoples would argue that, rather than the prevailing assumption that homosexuality has been rare in human societies, a strong potential for same-sex expression should be taken into account in any examination of evidence of sexual customs among historical societies. When the growing body of historical evidence attesting to the persistent appearance of same-sex relationships among the ancient Mesopotamians and Babylonians, Egyptians and Israelites, the Indo-European tribes, the Greeks, Romans, Chinese, Japanese, Muslims and post–Roman European population is considered in light of what researchers and clinicians have discovered about human sexuality, we shall see that the varieties of patterns of same-sex expression found among pre–Westernized tribal cultures around the world reviewed in Part I, and their complementary role to heterosexual marriage customs are remarkably consistent with the patterns of sexual relations found in the world's great civilizations.

4

Same-Sex Behavior at the Dawn of Civilization

In the years following the end of the last Ice Age some of the early hunter-gatherer societies began to supplement their diet of game and nuts and berries with grains they learned to cultivate in small patches adjacent to their dwelling sites. At about the same time they began to keep and raise young animals taken from wild herds of cattle, sheep and goats, which greatly simplified their acquisition of meat. The development of agriculture and animal husbandry had a profound effect on these early tribes. Scholars, in fact, have used the appearance of agriculture to signal a major demarcation in the development of human culture, assigning the term Paleolithic, or Old Stone Age, to the primordial hunter-gatherer phase, and Neolithic, or New Stone Age, to stone age cultures who acquired knowledge of agriculture.

The cultivation of crops tied the early agriculturalists to land in specific locations, and led to a more settled way of life, in contrast to the nomadic wanderings of the Paleolithic hunter-gatherers. Similarly the myths and rituals of the hunter-gatherers, which involved a mystical contract with the spirits of the game animals they depended on, gave way to rituals seeking to promote the fertility of their animals and an abundant harvest. A similar transition from Paleolithic to Neolithic can be seen in the lifestyles of the North American Indians before the encroachment of European settlers. The Indians of the Great Plains continued a way of life similar to that of the Paleolithic clans who hunted the great herds of grazing animals on the plains of Eurasia that lay south of the Pleistocene ice fields. The Plains Indians hunted the herds of bison which roamed the North American plains and depended on their meat for sustenance and on their hides for clothing and shelter. Tied more to the bison herds than to the land, Plains Indian tribes would move their encampments to be closer to the herds if necessary. In contrast, the Pueblo Indians in the American Southwest cultivated crops of maize, and so developed settled communities of mud brick dwellings close to their crops. While the Plains Indians used animal hides for clothing, and made straw baskets for storage, the Pueblo Indians wove cloth for clothing and produced ceramic pottery for use in grain storage and for water vessels.

Starting around 9,000 B.C., similar settled communities began to develop in the fertile river valleys of the Middle East. Cultivating crops of wheat and barley, grains that at the time grew wild in a belt from Asia Minor to northern Iran, the early farming communities thrived in the mild climate and regular rainfall of the upland areas of the region. In the eighth millennium, towns of mud brick houses, not unlike those of the Pueblo Indians, began to appear, first around 8,000 B.C., at Jericho, the site of a large oasis in Palestine, and shortly thereafter at Jarmo, in northern Mesopotamia.[1] Around 6500 B.C., at Catal Huyuk, in southern Anatolia (modern Turkey), ceramic pottery first appeared,[2] and by the beginning of the next millennium tools of copper were being used in eastern Anatolia.[3]

It is, of course, impossible to know with certainty to what degree homosexual behavior figured in the lives of these early clans and tribes. However, given the ramifications of the widespread homosexual behavior among primates on human sexual evolution, and considering what the virtually universal appearance of homosexuality among aboriginal tribal societies around the world reveals about human sexuality, there seems to be little doubt that homosexual behavior would have been widespread among these Neolithic tribes, as well as among their Paleolithic forebears, most likely in patterns similar to those found among tribal peoples around the world in recent times.

Over the next several thousand years, as knowledge of crop cultivation and stock-raising slowly spread throughout the region, an increasingly refined lifestyle developed among these Neolithic peoples. The division of labor and role specialization became increasingly complex, with a multitude of occupations emerging, ranging from farmers and shepherds to craftsmen and traders. By 4500 BC fine ceramic pottery, painted in sophisticated geometric designs, was being made throughout northern Mesopotamia, and spread via trade as far away as the Mediterranean coast.[4] The rituals of the Paleolithic shamans evolved into complex rites of worship presided over by a priesthood who began to exercise increasing influence and authority in the communities. Serving as mediators with the goddess, who was believed to control the fertility of the crops and livestock the communities depended on, the priests gradually took on the role of managing and coordinating the labor required in agricultural production.

In the early fourth millennium B.C., the people who settled on the fertile delta that was formed where the Tigris and Euphrates Rivers meet the Persian Gulf discovered the techniques of crop irrigation. As a result of this advance they were able to grow crops of such abundance that for the first time a people was producing more food than it needed for survival. The subsequent surpluses, which were traded with distant peoples for goods ranging from timber to precious stones, served as a basis of accumulating wealth and propelled the growth of the delta farming villages into cities. With the achievement of economic surpluses, a portion of the society was freed from the day-to-day struggle for survival that had characterized humans since earliest times, and was able to spend time on political administration and on intellectual and artistic pursuits. Writing was invented, the sciences of astronomy and mathematics were developed, monumental architecture was erected, and representational art replaced the largely decorative art of earlier periods. The resulting political, economic and cultural attainments form the basis for that blossoming we have come to know as the Sumerian civilization. The economic and political infrastructure developed in these city-states served as the prototype of the Babylonian and Assyrian civilizations that were to succeed them and of the high civilizations that were to later develop in Egypt and around the Mediterranean and eastward in the Indus Valley of India and in China.

During a thousand years of flourishing development, the Mesopotamian city-states remained an island of civilization in a sea of Neolithic tribal cultures. Over time, the prosperous Sumerians became targets for increasing predation and invasions by bordering mountain tribes and nomadic peoples from the arid steppes north and south of the Sumerian civilization. From the south, nomadic tribes of Semites moved north in search of greener pastures and attracted by the wealth of the Sumerian city-states. Around 2300 B.C. Sargon the Great, a warrior-king who was descended from Semitic nomad tribes who had settled in the north and west of the river valley, conquered the Mesopotamian city-states and brought them together under the rule of what became known as the Akkadian Empire. Toward the end of the Third Millennium, after a brief resurgence of Sumerian rule, Amorite Semites from the south conquered the region, setting up the Babylonian Empire, which was to endure, in one form or another, for nearly two thousand years. In succeeding centuries, Sumerian culture retained a strong influence on Babylonian life, with much of the literature and documents continuing to be written in the Sumerian language. Likewise, the Assyrians, who succeeded the Amorite Semites in Babylon, adopted with little change the political structure and legal tradition of the Babylonians, and continued rites of worship similar to those practiced since earliest Sumerian times. Because of the continuities in the artistic, political, legal and religious traditions from Sumerian to Assyrian times, it is possible to view the successive Mesopotamian cultures as one continuous civilization.

Homosexual Practices of the Mesopotamians

Archeological remains from these Mesopotamian cultures reveal a complex, stratified society, with a ruling class living in luxury, supported by an organized and prosperous working class. Graceful pottery, luxurious domestic goods, beautifully crafted jewelry and art objects testify to an elegant and comfortable lifestyle. Glimpses into the social and sexual lifestyles of the people are provided by art objects, legal and religious texts, and literature that survive from the period. This material abundantly demonstrates that at the dawn of the historic period homosexual customs, most likely the continuation of practices of their Neolithic forebears, were already well established among the inhabitants of this most ancient of civilizations.

Among the art objects found among archeological remains are numerous terra cotta figurines showing couples in sexual intercourse, many of which depict two males engaging in anal intercourse. These statuettes, dating from as early as the beginning of the third millennium B.C., have been found at Uruk, Assur, Susa and Babylon and provide solid evidence of the familiarity of the people of this early civilization with homosexuality.[5] Another source of knowledge of the attitudes of the Mesopotamian peoples is found in the law codes, which have been found from Sumerian, Babylonian and Assyrian periods. The Code of Hammurabi, which dates from around 1700 B.C., has provisions dealing with aspects of sexuality such as adultery and prostitution, but makes no mention of homosexual behavior. The absence of prohibitions against homosexual behavior in the face of evidence that homosexuality was present demonstrates the acceptance of homosexuality among these cultures. An Assyrian law code, which dates from the middle of the second millennium B.C., contains two provisions which mention homosexuality. Paragraph 19 provides a penalty for a man who slanders a neighbor by starting "a rumor against his neighbor in private, saying, 'people have lain repeatedly with him,' and who is unable to prove his charge." This is similar to another provision which penalizes a man for making unproven slanderous accusations against a neighbor's wife, to the effect that she behaved like a prostitute by taking many lovers.[6] Another section specifies that a man who forcibly rapes another man is to be himself subjected to forcible penetration.[7] These laws would make no sense if homosexual behavior were not a familiar aspect of daily life of early Mesopotamia.

Other evidence survives that shows that homosexual behavior played a role in the lives of the Mesopotamians. King Hammurabi, himself, is known to have had male lovers, as did Zimri-lin, king of Mari, in western Mesopotamia, whose wife refers to them in a letter.[8] An Assyrian astrological text, which deals with the effect of the stars on potency and lovemaking, includes verses indicating that the region of Libra is auspicious for the love of a man for a woman, Pisces, for the love of a woman for a man, and Scorpio, for the love of a man for a man.[9] An Almanac of Incantations from the Babylonian period contains prayers to be said by a man seeking the love of a woman, a woman for a man, and also prayers for a man to seek another man. Other religious tablets have been found which contain text referring to homosexual relations, such as "if a man has intercourse with his male companion."[10] Lesbian relations between women are also mentioned in similar texts in contexts that suggest they were also commonplace.[11] The references in these texts to homosexual love, alongside and in the same context as references to heterosexual love, show that same-sex relationships must have been a commonly accepted aspect of daily life, and that to the Mesopotamians the sexual love of a man for a man was seen as a legitimate alternative to love between men and women.

A Babylonian religious text used for divining the future contains predictions based on sexual acts, some of which include homosexual acts. For example, "If a man has intercourse with the hindquarters of his equal (male), that man will be foremost among his brothers and colleagues." Another reads, "If a man has intercourse with a (male) cult prostitute, trouble will leave him." And another, "If a man has intercourse with a male courtier, for one whole year the worry which plagued him will vanish." Some foretell negative consequences: "If a man yearns to express his manhood while in prison and thus, like a male cult prostitute, mating with men becomes his desire, he will experience evil," perhaps an admonishment against passive homosexuality among ordinary citizens. Or, "If a man has intercourse with a male slave, care will seize him."[12] While the homosexual behavior itself is not viewed negatively, it does appear that the context in which it was carried out and the social status of the partners were matters of concern for the Babylonians.

Homosexuality and Religious Practices

The sexual intercourse with male cult prostitutes and courtiers mentioned in this text is a reference to specialized roles for exclusively homosexual men that bear a fascinating similarity to the transvestite priests encountered by the Spanish conquistadors in Meso-America more than three thousand years later. From earliest Sumerian times, a significant percentage of the personnel of both temples and palaces were individuals who, like the two-spirit of the American Indians, were viewed as being neither male nor female, but more like a third sex. Sumerian temple records from the middle of the third millennium refer to *gala* priests, who were created, according to a Babylonian text, by the god Enki to sing "heart-soothing laments" for the goddess Inanna. Their homosexual inclinations are made clear by a Sumerian proverb that reads, "when the *gala* wiped off his ass, he said, 'I must not arouse that which belongs to my mistress [i.e., Inanna].'" The word *gala*, in fact, was written using the signs "penis-anus," an explicit reference to the sexual role taken by these male priests with other men.

A similar role which appears in Sumerian mythology and liturgical texts from 2000 B.C. onward is that of the *kur-gar-ra*, a role which also appears in Akkadian texts as *kurgarru*. In Babylonian and Assyrian texts the kurgarru usually appear in association with another closely related role, the *assinnu*.[13] The sexual nature of the assinnu is also made obvious by the fact that the noun, *assinnu*, has the same root as *assinutu*, to practice anal intercourse.[14] The gala are also referred to in texts describing Babylonian and Assyrian ritual, where their role appears to be even greater than in Sumerian ritual. These various homosexual priests played a central role in Mesopotamian goddess worship throughout the development of those civilizations, down to Roman times.

The Mesopotamian worship of the goddess derived from earlier Neolithic cults, which themselves descended from Paleolithic cults. The oldest representations of a deity known among human cultures are female goddess figurines and carvings which have been found across the Eurasian landmass from Western Europe to Siberia in sites from as far back as

25,000 B.C.[15] Evidence of the veneration of the goddess has been found from the earliest periods of the Neolithic agricultural settlements in Anatolia and the Middle East.[16] Excavations under the direction of the famed archeologist James Mellaart at Catal Huyuk in Turkey, the site of a settlement that dates to 7500 B.C., established the continuity of mother goddess worship from the Sumerian period back as far as the Upper Paleolithic.[17] With the pursuit of agriculture and animal husbandry, an abundant harvest and the fertility of their animals became of prime importance to Neolithic peoples and were thus a focus of worship rites. Among the Neolithic farming villages, the goddess, who symbolized the generative power of nature, was usually found in association with the image of a bull, who represented the moon-god, and whose fertilizing role with the goddess was thereby believed to result in the multiplication of the herds and abundance of harvests. The imagery of the cow-mother fertilized by the moon-bull was a reflection of the importance of their herds to the livelihood of the people. Numerous figurines of the goddess accompanied by images of the bull have been found from village remains dating to 6500 B.C.[18]

With the invasions of the Middle East by fierce Bronze Age warrior peoples, the Semites of Akkad under Sargon the Great in Sumer, the Indo-Europeans in Anatolia and Persia, the Amorite Semites of Hammurabi in Babylon, and the Hebrews in Canaan, goddess worship was supplanted in importance by the patriarchal male deities the invaders brought with them.[19] Nonetheless, the various forms of the mother-goddess and her associated fertility cults and male homosexual attendants remained an important part of worship throughout the ancient world, from the Mediterranean to India, up until early Christian times. Known as Inanna, or the Queen of Heaven, by the Sumerians, she was called Ishtar by the Akkadians and Babylonians. In Egypt, where the goddess was worshiped as Isis, the ceremonial dress of the pharaoh included a representation of the tail of a bull, signifying his role as consort of the goddess. The worship of the Phoenician goddess Astarte included male homosexual temple personnel called *kelev*, as did the worship of the Anatolian goddess Cybele, whose homosexual priests were called *galli*. Few are aware that goddess worship was also a feature of the religion of the early Israelites, and, in fact, the temple compound in Jerusalem contained a building to house the *kadesh*, her male homosexual attendants, as late as the seventh century B.C. In parts of India the goddess, known as Sakti, is still venerated by transvestite devotees called *hirjas*, and her temples included male and female cult prostitutes until well into the 20th century.[20]

A key part of the Mesopotamian worship of the goddess was a ceremony held on special feast days called the sacred marriage, in which the sexual union of the goddess and the moon-bull were enacted through the persons of the king, serving in the role of the bull-consort, and a temple attendant, playing the role of the goddess. The sexual consummation that occurred during this rite was believed necessary to insure the success of the city's crops and the fertility of its livestock. The sort of sympathetic magic invoked by this sexual ritual is characteristic of the worship rites of primitive tribal cultures and as such is indicative of the primordial origins of Mesopotamian religion. In the Sumerian city of Uruk the sacred marriage rite is believed to have been performed annually between an attendant who represented Inanna and the king, who represented Dumuzi, the Sumerian moon-god. Numerous sensuous songs celebrating the love between Inanna and Dumuzi have been found from the period, as well as illustrations of the rite on cylinder seals. A cylinder seal from the Sumerian city of Elam from early in the second millennium depicts Inanna and Dumuzi as a nude couple on a bed. The sexual focus of Mesopotamian goddess worship is made explicit by an early Babylonian hymn which describes Ishtar as a sacred prostitute whom 120 men cannot exhaust. Similarly, the Syrian goddess Qudshu, who was associated with love and fertility, was called "the Prostitute" on a monument erected in her honor in Egypt, where her worship was popular in the second millennium.[21]

Similar sexual rituals were also performed throughout the year with laymen seeking divine protection or benefit. An important function of the homosexual temple attendants was to stand in for the goddess in copulation with ordinary male worshipers, whose semen would be deposited in the bodies of the temple attendants as an offering to the goddess, while the fee that was paid for the services would go to the upkeep of the temple. This custom has been called "temple prostitution," a somewhat misleading term, since the practices were an integral part of worship and not merely the retailing of sexual pleasure. Some scholars have expressed skepticism about whether the male temple attendants actually played such a sexual role with worshipers. However, the sexual nature of the titles for some of them — *gala*, written in a hieroglyphic that combines the signs for penis and anus, and *assinnu*, derived from the verb for anal intercourse — and the numerous references in texts to intercourse with them in ritual contexts, as well as to divine favors or good fortune coming to males who have intercourse with them, make such a conclusion inevitable.

Third-gender or transgenderal individuals also played major roles in the palaces. Court officials were called either *sa'ziqni*, bearded, or *sa res*, a term that has sometimes been translated as "eunuch." These men were almost certainly not physical eunuchs, but passive homosexuals. An important class of sa res were the *girsequ*, who in late third millennium B.C. Sumerian texts appear as domestics of palaces or temples, are frequently described as attached to kings, and appear in dream omen texts in the same context as assinnu, as sexual objects for men. Similar beardless figures appear in Assyrian reliefs as musicians or royal attendants.[22]

As we saw in Chapter 2, sexual rites involving third-gender or transvestite priests that were remarkably similar to the Mesopotamian customs were also commonplace among the Meso-American cultures conquered by the Spanish conquistadors. Cieza de Leon wrote with disgust about the temple priests he witnessed in Peru: "In each important temple or house of worship they have a man or two, or more, depending on the idol, who go dressed in women's attire from the time they are children.... With these, almost like a rite, and ceremony, on feast [days] and holidays they have carnal, foul intercourse, especially the chiefs and headmen."[23] The homosexual rituals of Mesopotamian goddess worship also bear a striking resemblance to a ritual of the Hopi Indians in the American Southwest, in which the Hopi berdache, or two-spirit, playing the role of the "Virgin of the Maize," is anally inseminated by Hopi braves in order to guarantee a successful maize harvest.[24] A similar ritual occurred among the Mandan Sioux, in which the two-spirit was ritually inseminated via anal intercourse by the young braves of the tribe in order to bring about a plentiful supply of bison.[25]

This ritualized homosexual intercourse is only one of a number of remarkable similarities between the mythic beliefs and third-gender priests of Mesopotamia and their counterparts among the indigenous peoples of the Americas. The Mesopotamians believed the gala, assinnu and kurgarra were called into service and sexually transformed into women by the goddess. Similarly, among some American tribes, the berdaches were believed to take up their calling at the command of a female spirit or goddess.[26] Just as American Indians believed the berdaches were created by the Great Spirit for the betterment of their tribes, cult prostitution was listed by the Sumerians along with kingship, justice and truth as one of the divinely ordained institutions.[27] Many of the Plains Indians believed sex with a berdache before a battle brought good luck. Likewise, sex with an assinnu or kurgarra was believed to bring good fortune. Like the berdache, the assinnu were considered to have magical powers: according to one text, "if a man touches the head of an *assinnu*, he will conquer his enemy," and to ward off the threat posed by an eclipse of the moon, the king would ritually touch the head of an assinnu.[28] Also like the berdache, the assinnu was believed to have the power to heal illnesses and foretell the future. One of the functions of the berdache was to serve as keepers of the knowledge of tribal ritual dances and chanting, a role also filled by the gala, assinnu and kurgarra, who sang hymns to the goddess, performed ritual dances, and served as musicians in the temples. In sum, both the Native American two-spirit and the third gender priests of ancient Mesopotamia were believed by their people to be divinely ordained institutions, were thought to have been called to their professions by a goddess who transformed their sexuality, were sexual objects for masculine men, who would experience good fortune through intercourse with them, were believed to have magic powers, and so served as healers and seers, and were the principal performers of ritual dance and song.

Linguistic and cultural evidence suggests that these specialized third-gender roles originated in prehistoric times. In fact, some scholars believe that the kurgarru may date back as far as 5600 B.C., well before the development of the temple culture, which would indicate that the role most likely originated in berdache-like transvestite shamans among Neolithic tribes.[29] Considering the remarkably close similarities to the berdache-two-spirit, and in view of the apparent antiquity of these specialized third-gender roles in Mesopotamia, it's hard to avoid the conclusion that they evolved from the same Paleolithic origins as the two-spirit tradition, which is believed to have come to America from the Eurasian continent with the Paleolithic ancestors of the indigenous American peoples.

Homosexual Love Between Masculine Men

The specialized third-gender roles comprise only one aspect of the diversity of sexual expression among the people of ancient Mesopotamia. The numerous references in religious and astrological texts to love between members of the same sex make it clear that homosexual experiences were a part of the lives of ordinary men and women as well as the transgendered attendants of the temples and palaces. Indeed, the sexual love between two super-masculine heroes is a central focus of the Epic of Gilgamesh, an extraordinary early work of literature that had its origins in early Sumerian legends and was popular for thousands of years throughout the ancient Near East.

The historical period of human existence began with the invention of writing, which occurred around 3200 BC among the Sumerian city-states. The Epic of Gilgamesh, the earliest known work of literature, first written around the middle of the third millennium B.C., and drawn from a Sumerian legend which existed in oral tradition long before that time,[30] deals in large part with the love of the hero, Gilgamesh, for a male companion, Enkidu.

Gilgamesh, the legendary king of the Sumerian city of Uruk, was born of the union of a mortal man with a goddess. Through his goddess mother he was endowed with not only tremendous physical strength, but great beauty, with a great chest, and adorned, the texts say approvingly, with a large phallus.[31] As the story opens, Gilgamesh is in full manhood, "superior to all other men in beauty and strength, and the unsatisfied cravings of his half-divine nature, for which he can find no worthy match in love or in war."[32] Possessed of tremendous sexual vigor, Gilgamesh's unrelenting sexual pursuit of both the sons and daughters of the city has been causing problems for the people of Uruk.

Seeking relief, the people prayed to the goddess for protection of their sons and daughters from Gilgamesh's rapacious sexual appetites. In their prayers to the Goddess Aruru, the people called, "Thou, Aruru, did create Gilgamesh; now create his equal; to the impetuosity of his heart let him be equal; let them strive with each other, and let Uruk thus have rest." In response the goddess "washed her hands, pinched off clay, and threw it on the steppe ...

Valiant Enkidu she created." Gilgamesh was fascinated when he heard tales of a great hairy wild-man seen on the steppe and sent a temple courtesan to lure the wild-man to him. The courtesan describes Gilgamesh to Enkidu, as one "who seeks a friend, one who understands the heart.... I will show you Gilgamesh, a joyful man.... Comely is his manhood, endowed with vigor is he. The whole of his body is adorned with pleasure." She goes on to say, "Shamash (the great god) has conferred a favor upon Gilgamesh.... Before you will arrive from the open country, Gilgamesh will behold you in his dreams."[33]

As predicted, Gilgamesh dreamed of Enkidu before meeting him, which he then related to his mother. "There were stars in the heaven ... one of them, a meteorite, fell down to me. I tried to lift it, but it was too heavy for me; I tried to move it away, but I could not remove it.... I bent over it as over a woman, and put it at your feet, and you yourself did put it on a par with me."

His mother, a goddess, interpreted the dreams for him, telling Gilgamesh that the star he could not lift and which was too heavy for his strength was the man she had made into his companion, who would watch over him as would a wife. This companion, she said, would never abandon him, would always come to his aid, and the weight of his strength would bear down on the entire country. His mother stated, "I myself put him on a par with you, over whom you did bend as over a woman. He is a strong companion, one who helps a friend in need.... That you did bend over him as over a woman means that he will never forsake you. This is the meaning of the dream."

Gilgamesh then dreamed about a great axe, and, telling his mother about it, said: "I looked at it (the axe) and I rejoiced, loving it, and bending over it as over a woman. I took it and put it at my side." In another translation of this passage, by the great Babylonian scholar, Thorkild Jacobsen, the sexual character of the relationship is even more explicit: "I loved it and cohabited with it, as if it were a woman."[34] His mother explained that it was not an axe. "The axe you did see is a man. That you did bend over him as over a woman means that he is a strong companion, one who helps a friend in need."

Lest there be any doubt about the sexual implications of the dreams, there are several puns which underscore the sexual nature of the relationship that is foretold for Gilgamesh. In the first dream, *kisru*, the word for the meteorite which fell from the sky and which Gilgamesh "bent over as over a woman," is a play on the word *kezru*, a male prostitute. Similarly, *hassinu*, the word for the axe of the second dream, plays on the word *assinnu*, one of the homosexual temple attendants.[35] The sexual connotations in the puns made on the very objects Gilgamesh made love to in the dreams and which represent the companion foretold for him would not have been lost on the epic's ancient audience.

When Enkidu arrived in Uruk, the men of the town were enthralled at his sight: "The men rejoiced; 'A mighty one has arisen as a match for the hero whose appearance is so handsome; for Gilgamesh, an equal like a god has arisen.'" Enkidu found Gilgamesh about to enter a wedding party where he was intending to deflower the bride, but Enkidu barred his way. The two of them wrestled, and "grappled, holding each other like bulls.... They shattered the door posts and the walls shook." But finally, Gilgamesh prevailed. Enkidu responded, "there is not another like you in the world.... Enlil (one of the gods) has given you the kingship, for your strength surpasses the strength of men."[36] "They kissed one another and formed a friendship." Delighted with his new companion, Gilgamesh began acting more like a hero-king, pursuing adventures with the intent of benefiting his city and his people.

Since it is inconceivable that the central figure in a legend or epic would not reflect the values and sentiments of its intended audience, it follows that homosexual relationships between masculine men were known and even admired among the Sumerian city-states where the Gilgamesh legend originated, and among the later Akkadian and Babylonian civilizations which wrote down the legend. As mythology generally reflects in a metaphorical way the values of a people, the story of Gilgamesh and Enkidu can be seen as representing for the people of that culture nature's way of providing unbridled sexual energy (Gilgamesh) with focus and satisfaction (companionship with Enkidu) in a way that promotes the well being of society.

From the way the relationship is presented it appears that the role such a relationship plays in society and the benefits it would bring to that society are clearly anticipated. In their prayer to the Goddess Aruru, the people were very specific about what they had in mind: "Thou, Aruru, did create Gilgamesh; now create his equal; to the impetuosity of his heart let him be equal; let them strive with each other, and let Uruk thus have rest." It should be noted that in the languages of the ancient Near East — and continuing today in the Arab world — a common phrase used to denote sexual arousal is "a rising of the heart." So in praying for someone who could match "the impetuosity of (Gilgamesh's) heart," the people of Uruk clearly wanted Gilgamesh to have a sexual companion suited for him, so they could "thus have rest." As summarized by Thorkild Jacobsen, "Aruru hears their prayers and creates Enkidu, a being whose sexual vigor is a strong as Gilgamesh's so that when falling in love with each other they may neutralize each other and the inhabitants of Uruk may return to tranquility."[37]

It is also significant that the people were not praying for a wife for Gilgamesh, for in that culture, and considering Gilgamesh's royal status, he probably already had one. Thus, the epic also makes clear that people of the period did not regard propagation as the sole purpose of the sexual drive. In a stable, prosperous society with a steadily growing population, there was no need to restrict sexual activity to propagation, and the very desirability of diverting the more than ample sexual drive that nature has endowed in humans away from heterosexual situations may have been apparent to the Sumerians and Babylonians.

Indeed, the great emphasis the epic devotes to the loving friendship between the two men underscores the recognition that one of the primary ends of sexual desire in humans is not sexual gratification itself, nor procreation necessarily, but companionship. In fact, it is through the loss of that which Gilgamesh cherished the most — his beloved companion, Enkidu — that the hero is impelled to set out on a search for immortality and the meaning of life, the central theme of the epic. This theme, of the transitory character of life and the nature of existence itself, is one of the most profound questions humans have faced, and recurs repeatedly in some of the greatest art and literature that human culture has produced. That the loss of a beloved male companion by this hyper-masculine hero is used as the predicate for the unfolding of the major theme of this epic is eloquent testimony to the appreciation of the Mesopotamians for this type of love relationship between masculine men.

At the center of the oldest great work of literature in the world, then, we see what amounts to the delineation of an archetype: a same-sex relationship, born out of the stated need for an outlet for sexual capacity that was obviously over and above that needed for propagation — a relationship that diverted that excess sexual drive in a way that benefited society, not only by providing a wholesome outlet for it, but through bringing happiness and satisfaction to the partners, thereby supporting creative and productive endeavors by these partners which worked to the betterment of the society.

Denial of the Sexual Character of the Relationship

Despite the ample evidence of the sexual bond depicted in the epic between Gilgamesh and Enkidu, mainstream academic scholars have frequently denied that the relationship was sexual. That these writers can refuse to acknowledge a sexual relationship between the two heroes can only be attributed to bias resulting from modern Western presumptions about sexuality, because the evidence for it is very strong.

First, the epic was produced by a society where homosexuality was a common feature of life, as illustrated by the numerous terra cotta figurines found in archeological sites depicting anal intercourse between men, by the role of homosexual attendants and homosexual acts in temple worship, and in the multiple references to homosexual love in astrological and religious texts in contexts that place same-sex relationships as parallel alternatives to heterosexual relationships. In such a culture, a sexual relationship between two males would be seen as quite ordinary, in contrast to the disgust with which such a relationship between masculine heroes would have been seen until only very recently in the West.

Secondly, the sexual character of the relationship between the two is very explicitly portrayed in the epic. Enkidu is created, in the first place, by the goddess Aruru in response to the pleas of the people of Uruk for someone to match Gilgamesh's sexual vigor, to divert his sexual energies away from not just their daughters, but their sons as well, which in itself is an indication of the hero's homosexual interests. That Enkidu is created as a solution to the problem posed to the people of Uruk by Gilgamesh's excessive sexual appetite strongly implies that Enkidu is to absorb Gilgamesh's sexual attention, that he is to play a sexual role with Gilgamesh.

The sexual nature of the relationship that is foretold for Gilgamesh with Enkidu in his dreams could not be clearer. When Gilgamesh dreams about making love to the "star that fell down from the sky" and, then, the axe, there is no question that these objects are symbols for Enkidu. After all, the courtesan in the interlude on the steppes had just predicted to Enkidu that he would appear in Gilgamesh's dreams. And then when Gilgamesh's mother interprets the dreams for him, she confirms that the objects in the dream that Gilgamesh made love to symbolize a companion created for him. As his mother states: "I myself put him on a par with you, over whom you did bend as over a woman. He is a strong companion.... That you did bend over him as over a woman means that he will never forsake you." When in the latter phrase she links the sexual act between the two with the formation of an undying loyalty in the partner, she is certainly alluding to the consequences of a sexual bond. Thus, she is describing Enkidu as a life companion, which most people would understand as meaning a mate or lover. And, as we saw earlier, the sexual nature of the relationship foretold for Gilgamesh is underscored in the sexual puns that are employed in the words for the objects to which Gilgamesh made love. So, therefore, for Gilgamesh to make love in his dreams to objects symbolizing a man ordained by his goddess mother as a mate for him doesn't leave much room for doubt that what is being foretold is a sexual relationship.

Finally, the presence of a physical bond uniting the two heroes is unmistakably demonstrated in the intense grief displayed by Gilgamesh at Enkidu's death. Gilgamesh, who loves Enkidu "like a wife," veils his dead friend's body "like a bride," and mourns over him, "like a widow," for six days and seven nights, not allowing him to be buried "until a worm fell out of his nose."[38] The death of Enkidu, whose friendship was more important to Gilgamesh than anything else, had an enormous impact on him, causing him to question the values that had directed his life, and impelling him to leave everything and embark on his search for the meaning of life. While the death of a beloved colleague or comrade can provoke much grief, the loss of a spouse or lover often has a devastating effect on the surviving partner, an impact due to the physical nature of the bond that develops as a result of sexual love, and the enormous pain that occurs when such a physical bond is ruptured. Judging by the level of Gilgamesh's grieving, Enkidu was certainly no ordinary colleague or comrade to Gilgamesh, but occupied a place in the king's emotional life of the sort most readers would associate only with a lover or spouse.

It would obviously be difficult for even those writers who deny a sexual component in the relationship to ignore the sexual implications in the description of the relationship in the text. But instead of accepting the obvious, that a sexual relationship is being described, some academic scholars insist on interpreting the sexual language used in the description of the relationship merely as a literary device employed to emphasize the intensity of a non-sexual friendship between the two. The historian George Held argues that the use of sexual language in the epic in describing the relationship is no different from the use of sexual imagery to describe non-sexual relationships in such works as the *Song of Solomon* or the religious poetry of the ascetic monk, Saint John of the Cross.[39]

Held's use of the *Song of Solomon* as an example of the non-sexual intent of sexual language ironically illustrates the problem with his interpretation: the projection of modern religious sensibilities and attitudes toward sexuality onto the literature of an ancient people with a radically different view of sex. The *Song of Solomon* is a set of love songs, believed to date to 1,000 B.C., which feature frankly erotic language spoken alternately by a man and a woman. While conventional biblical interpretation in modern times holds that the sexual imagery contained in the work is meant as an allegorical treatment of the relationship between, say, God and Israel, or between God and an individual soul, that interpretation is of relatively recent origins. In the Middle Ages, and at least until the time of Martin Luther, the work was regarded literally as the wedding song of King Solomon, and even today that is how the text is titled in German biblical translations.[40] Some modern scholars, however, believe the work actually originated as a collection of songs associated with the rite of sacred marriage, which was ritually consummated as part of goddess worship throughout the ancient world by a king and a temple prostitute representing the goddess. The existence of goddess worship among the ancient Israelites for much of their history before the Babylonian exile establishes without doubt the cultural context that would make such an interpretation plausible. Thus, the Song of Solomon, rather than being an example of the non-sexual use of sexual language, is, in the use made of it by Held, yet another example of the same projection of modern cultural and religious attitudes onto an ancient text that Held brings to his interpretation of the relationship between Gilgamesh and Enkidu.

Held's comparison of the sexual language in Gilgamesh to the mystical poetry of Saint John of the Cross is particularly odd, and displays the same lack of differentiation between the approach that two enormously different societies bring to sexuality. It's hard to see a greater contrast than between the literary expression of an ancient culture where homosexual behavior was evidently widely practiced, and where homosexual acts even had a place in worship, and the ascetic, mystical writings of a 17th-century Spanish monk, a member of a religion that viewed sexuality as antithetical to spirituality, that condemned any sexual activity outside of marriage, and in a time when men were still being burned at the stake for homosexual acts. But the fact that Held would make the comparison underscores the degree to which modern Western attitudes towards sexuality shade the perceptions of otherwise astute academic scholars.

Another example of how contemporary scholars are prone to project Western Christian religious conceptions about sexuality onto ancient cultures is found in a well-received study of homoeroticism in the biblical period by the Finnish scholar Martti Nissinen. In his discussion of the thematic structure of the epic, Nissinen argues that Gilgamesh, after an earlier life of sexual dissipation, was spiritually transformed by his friendship with Enkidu, with whom he found a love "purified of any indecency," so that in their relationship the two heroes achieved "an accentuated masculine asceticism."[41] The absurdity of this interpretation is obvious when one considers the fact that the ideal of sexual asceticism, not to mention the association of homosexual love with "indecency," did not emerge as moral concepts until at least *two thousand years* after the epic was first written down.* Such an anachronistic interpretation could not have been intended by the writers of the epic, nor would it have been understood by epic's ancient audience.

Why these writers seem impelled to find an alternative meaning to the sexual language used in the epic to describe the relationship may be due to their inability, reflecting the deeply ingrained attitudes of modern Western culture, to accept the possibility that masculine heroes could find true sexual fulfillment in any way other than through heterosexual marriage. But, as has been observed about overzealous psychoanalytic analysis, sometimes a cigar is just a cigar. And so in the epic, when Gilgamesh meets Enkidu, he is transformed from a sexual predator to hero-king, not because of any ascetic or spiritual development triggered by the friendship, but because of the harmony and satisfaction that arises from the sexual fulfillment he found in companionship with a partner suited to him. Likewise, the eventual spiritual development of Gilgamesh was triggered, not by his relationship with Enkidu, but by the devastating loss of that relationship. It was only after the death of his partner Enkidu, whose company meant so much to him, that he was impelled to embark on his search for meaning in life, during which he underwent his spiritual transformation.

In succeeding centuries the Epic of Gilgamesh became widely disseminated throughout the Middle East. Copies were produced over a period of nearly 2,000 years and have been found in several languages in locations as diverse as the remains of the Hittite capital in what is now Turkey, and in Palestine. The influence of the epic can even be seen in the *Illiad* and *Odessey* of Homer. The popularity of the legend over a wide area for such a long time indicates a familiarity and acceptance of homosexual relationships like that between Gilgamesh and Enkidu throughout the Middle East for much of ancient history.

**As noted earlier, the oldest extant text of the epic dates to the middle of the third millennium* B.C. *The sexual nature of the relationship between Gilgamesh and Enkidu is apparent in the Akkadian version which dates from 2400–2200* B.C. *(see Kilmer, op. cit). The prohibition against homosexual behavior in Hebrew scripture, which is discussed in detail later in the chapter and was the first such prohibition in the ancient world, occurs in the Book of Leviticus, which was written after the return of the Israelites from Babylonian captivity in the late sixth or fifth century* B.C., *nearly two millennia after the dating of the Akkadian version of the epic. Some historians have pointed to a prohibition against homosexual acts in the teachings of the Iranian prophet Zoroaster, who is thought to have lived around 1200* B.C. *However, the Zoroastrian prohibitions against homosexuality did not appear until the third century* B.C., *during the Parthian rule of Persia. The* Vendidad, *a Zoroastrian text written around 250* B.C. *in Persia, contains provisions that prohibit homosexual acts as part of a sexual code promoting procreative sexuality. However, a strong homosexual tradition in Persia is attested to by Greek historians from the fifth century onward, and so the prohibition apparently had little effect on Persian attitudes or sexual behavior outside the ranks of devout Zoroastrians in rural eastern Persia (see Greenberg, pages 186–189). The concept of sexual asceticism had its roots in Greek Stoicism, which developed in the third century* B.C., *roughly two thousand years after the Akkadian Gilgamesh. However, the Stoics did not disapprove of sexual pleasure or homosexuality — indeed, the school's founder, Zeno, had a male lover, Parmenides — but advocated moderation and self-control. The word asceticism, in fact, is derived from the Greek word,* askesis, *which refers to disciplined practice, or exercise, as in athletic training. Stoic concepts, however, as interpolated with precepts of Mosaic Law by the late Hellenistic Jewish writer Philo Judaeus, and combined with the antimaterial attitudes of dualistic cults and the anti-sexual teachings of late classical Neo-Platonism, were the basis of the strident anti-sexual asceticism that developed in the early Christian church in the third and fourth centuries* A.D. *The origins and embrace of sexual asceticism as an ideal of Christian sexual morality — an attitude totally foreign to the teachings in the Gospels — is examined in Chapter 9.*

Evidence of Homosexuality Among the Ancient Egyptians

Around the time of the flowering of the high civilization of the Sumerian city-states, what would become an even grander civilization was beginning to take shape in Egypt, again growing amid the verdant fertility of a river valley. But, protected from nomadic invasions by vast deserts which surrounded it, the indigenous Egyptian culture developed into a unique and elaborate civilization, largely unsullied by outside influence. And here, too, scholars have found evidence that homosexuality was common and accepted, in practices not any different from those common in ancient Southwest Asia.

Since an enormous amount of Egyptian wealth and attention revolved around funerary rites for the pharaohs and other dignitaries, owing to the Egyptian obsession with the after-life, most of what is known of Egyptian culture and customs is derived from surviving tombs and the wide variety of material deposited with the mummified bodies of the dead. Conse-quently there is not a lot of evidence relating to the erotic life of the ancient Egyptians. Another reason for the sparseness of any kind of material on Egyptian sex life may be due to the ancient Egyptian sense of privacy, which restricted discussion of erotic themes. As a result, Egyptologists and historians have usually maintained that homosexuality did not occur among the Egyptians and that they, in fact, disapproved of homosexual acts.

However, enough evidence from the tombs survives to show not only that homosexual-ity was a phenomenon familiar to Egyptians, but that it seems to have been a generally accepted aspect of daily life. A hieroglyphic inscription in one tomb, which dates from the third mil-lennium B.C., tells of King Pepys II Neferkare paying nightly visits to the house of one of his generals, Sisine, a top royal administrator, who was unmarried, for the purpose of sexual encounters.[42] Many ecstatic erotic drawings have survived showing tender embraces between pharaohs and young men. A drawing carved into a pillar in the temple of Amon at Karnak and dating from the 12th Dynasty depicts the Pharaoh Senusret I in an intimate embrace with his male friend Phtah.[43] A homosexual relationship has been imputed between Egyptian Pharaoh Akhnaten and his son-in-law, Smenkhare, whom the Pharaoh is shown caressing in a carving on a stele. The two men are shown together nude, a convention very rare in Egypt-ian depictions of royalty. Smenkhare was also given titles of endearment like those previously used for Akhnaten's concubines. An Egyptian tomb from the third millennium B.C. was found to have been prepared for two male courtiers, one of whom was apparently a court hairdresser. The two men are depicted in bas-reliefs on the tomb walls in intimate and affectionate poses.[44]

There was also a belief in Egyptian culture that homosexual intercourse with a god was auspicious. The text on one coffin reads: "I will swallow the phallus of Re." Another, refer-ring to the earth god Geb, says "his phallus is between the buttocks of his son and heir." Instructions from the Vizier Ptahotep, from around 2600 B.C., warn against forcing a youth to submit to sodomy after he protests, suggesting 1) anal sex between males was common enough that a need arose to guard against abuses, and 2) there was nothing wrong with sodomy with the youth if he was willing.

An episode in Egyptian mythology involving anal intercourse between two deities, Horas and Seth, is further evidence of the familiarity of Egyptians with homosexual behavior.[45] As related in a Middle Kingdom papyrus, dating from the third millennium B.C. and cited by Vern Bullough,

> The Majesty of Seth said to the Majesty of Horus, "How beautiful are thy buttocks! How robust...." The Majesty of Horus said, "Wait that I may tell it (in) the palace." The majesty of Horus said to his mother Isis ... "Seth desires to have intercourse with me." And she said to him, "Take care, do not approach him for that; when he mentions it to thee a second time, say thou to

him, It is altogether too difficult for me because of (my) nature, since thou art too heavy for me; my strength will not be equal to thine, thou shalt say to him. Then, when he shall have given thee strength, do thou place thy fingers between thy buttocks.... Lo, he will enjoy it exceedingly.... This seed which has come forth from his generative organ without letting the sun see it.[46]

Horus, following the directions of his mother, Isis, caught the semen ejaculated by Seth in his hand, and when Seth was not looking, threw it into a nearby stream. When Horus told Isis about what happened, she told him to produce some semen of his own, and give it to her. She took Horus's semen, spread it on some lettuce, and gave it to Seth, who ate it. When Seth later bragged to the other gods about how he had dominated Horus in a sexual act, Horus denied it. To settle the argument, the gods summoned the seeds of both Horus and Seth. The seed of Seth replied to the gods from the depths of the stream where Horus had thrown it, while the seed of Horus came forth from the forehead of Seth in the form of a golden disc. The gods, therefore, believed Horus's version of the incident. Then one of the gods, Thoth, took the golden disc from the head of Seth, placing it on his own head as an ornament, an action that was seen in Egyptian mythology as the birth of Thoth as the moon-god. The birth of Thoth as the moon-god from the result of the homosexual union between Seth and Horus is referred in other sources where Thoth is described as the "son of the two lords."[47] This legendary episode, which recounts the homosexual desire of Seth for Horus, Seth's description of Horus' buttocks as beautiful, and the subsequent intercourse between them, is an unambiguous demonstration of the everyday familiarity of the Egyptians with homosexual desire and anal intercourse.

While there is not enough information from ancient Egypt to understand the role homosexuality played in Egyptian culture, it is certain that homosexual practices were accepted, and familiar enough so that where reference is made to homosexual behavior it is done in a casual way, with the behavior being treated as unremarkable.

The Ancient Israelites

Homosexuality throughout the ancient Near East is also attested to in Hebrew scripture, which contains numerous references to homosexuality both among the people and in the ritual in the lands surrounding the Israelites. Many will probably be surprised to find that there is strong evidence that homosexual practices were a facet of life of the early Israelites as well. In fact, the evidence from the Bible shows that the sexual attitudes and life styles of the early Israelites were little different from that of other nations of the ancient Near East. There are a number of biblical passages that speak of the recurring participation of the early Israelites in the kinds of homosexual worship practices documented among the neighboring peoples of the region.[48]

Moreover, we know that the early Israelites had no prohibitions against homosexuality of any kind. According to the Hebrew scriptural scholar Louis M. Epstein, "sodomy is not prohibited in the pre-exilic section of Scripture." Not only that, Epstein says, "there is a distinct lack of preaching on sexual matters among the Hebrews of the pre-exilic period."[49] Therefore it is unlikely that the sexual practices of the early Israelites were any different or less accepting of homosexuality than those of the people of Egypt, or their neighbors in Mesopotamia, from where Abraham was said to have emigrated and where homosexual practices were commonplace.[50] The hostility to homosexuality that is associated with Hebrew scripture came relatively late in the history of the Israelites, appearing for the first time in the period after the return from Babylonian exile, in the late sixth century B.C.

Goddess Worship and Homosexual Rituals Among the Early Israelites

The early Israelites were of a Semitic warrior culture similar to the Semitic warrior tribes who conquered the Sumerians and founded the Akkadian and Babylonian Empires. Originating in the arid desert lands in the south, the Hebrew tribes, led by a caste of warrior-priests, invaded Canaan in the second millennium B.C., and mounted a series of wars of conquest in order to overcome the resistance of the Canaanite natives.[51] The violence with which the invading Israelites subdued the indigenous peoples of Canaan is amply attested to by numerous passages in the Bible which describe the wholesale slaughter of populations who resisted the Israelites.[52] Like other Bronze Age warrior invaders, the Hebrews brought with them a fierce and jealous god of war, and sought for several centuries to impose their religion and patriarchal ideology on the conquered goddess-worshiping Canaanites.[53] However, as was the case of the Indo-European invaders in the Middle East and the Aegean, who imposed their male tribal deities on the conquered peoples while at the same time assimilating many of the conquered peoples' worship rites, the Hebrew tribes absorbed native Canaanite cults and rituals into their worship along with continued devotion to Yahweh. As a result, Hebrew worship practices in the period after the conquest and settlement of Canaan were notably polytheistic, with a blending of the worship of the Israelites' tribal deity, Yahweh, with the sexual rituals associated with the worship of Asherah, the Canaanite name for the goddess, and Baal, her son and consort.[54]

Like the Sumerian goddess Inanna and her consort Dumuzi, the two Canaanite gods were believed to control the fertility of the livestock and the coming of the rains that were critical to the success of the crops. The animal representation for Baal was the bull, a symbol representing his fertilizing role with the goddess. As we saw earlier in the chapter, the association of the bull with the goddess as a symbol of the consort's fertilizing role with the goddess was widespread in the region and has been dated back as far as 6500 B.C. The bull was also a symbol of the ancient God of the Hebrews, and perhaps not coincidentally the earliest Hebrew name for God is Baal. Some biblical scholars, in fact, believe that the original God of the Israelites was Baal, and that the development of the cult of Yahweh was largely an outgrowth of the Baal cult, instigated as a nationalistic response to the goddess worship that prevailed in the region. The earliest depiction of Yahweh as the mighty warrior god, in fact, uses language lifted almost unchanged from a Canaanite text describing Baal as the storm god.[55] At a minimum, the early Israelites in the period before their arrival in Canaan would have been well aware of worship rites for the goddess and her consort to ensure the abundance of crops and livestock because of the universal presence of goddess worship throughout the ancient Middle East.

In the period before the arrival of the Israelites in Canaan, Yahwah was known to the Israelites primarily as a mighty warrior god. Yahweh had defeated the Pharaoh, parted the waters of the Red Sea and guided them safely through the Sinai desert. Yahweh brought down the walls of Jericho enabling the Israelites entry into Canaan, and destroyed the armies of the Philistines and the Canaanites. Yahweh was, therefore, seen as the powerful and fearsome protector of the Israelites, who would smite their enemies and mete a terrible punishment on those who offended him. Yahweh was not seen, however, as involved with the everyday aspects of life like farming and animal husbandry.[56] As the conquering Hebrew tribes established themselves in Canaan and began a life of farmers and herders, it would have been natural that they would also take up local rites and rituals for the goddess and her consort to promote an abundance of crops and fertility among their herds. Because Yahweh was not identified with the success of their crops and livestock herding, it would have seemed logical to the newly settled Israelites to rely on Yahweh for protection in times of national crisis, but to turn to the goddess and the fertilizing power of her divine consort for help with their crops and herds.

That the early Israelites embraced the fertility rites associated with goddess worship after their arrival in Canaan cannot be denied. Numerous references in Hebrew scripture show that participation of the Israelites in the worship of Baal and Asherah, with its homosexual rituals and temple prostitutes, was extensive and continual. In fact, the worship of Baal and Asherah persisted among the Israelites for over seven centuries, from the period after the conquest and settlement of Canaan, which most biblical scholars place at around 1400 B.C., to the time of the destruction of Jerusalem by Nebuchadnezzar and the exile of the Israelites in Babylon in the 6th century B.C.

The involvement of the Israelites in rites for Baal and the goddess appear in Hebrew scripture as early as the time of the Judges, the period immediately after the invasion of Canaan.[57] Scriptural passages also contains a number of references to the presence in the religious places of *Asherim*, images or symbols of Asherah, along with "sacred pillars" or "Asherah poles," thought by scholars to be phallic symbols, related to the fertility rites that were an element of goddess worship in the region.[58] References in the scripture frequently describe Baal worship in conjunction with rites for Asherah, which would be expected given the interrelated roles of the two deities in bringing about an abundance of crops and livestock.[59]

The degree to which the worship of Baal and the goddess was entrenched in the life of the early Israelites after their settlement in Canaan is shown in the inclusion of Baal in a number of place names.[60] Widespread participation of the Israelites in rites for Baal and Asherah is suggested by the large number of priests associated with their worship. According to 1 Kings 18, during the time of King Ahab, in the 9th century, B.C., there were 450 priests of Baal and 450 priests of Asherah among the Israelites, a number that would have required the support of a significant segment of the population.[61] According to recent scholarship, it now appears that the Ark of the Covenant, the most important symbol of Hebrew religion, did not originally hold within it the Ten Commandments, but instead housed a bronze statue of a serpent, a symbol associated with the goddess throughout the ancient Middle East.[62] Such a bronze serpent, according to 2 Kings 18, was worshipped in the Temple in Jerusalem alongside an image of Asherah, and remained within the Temple until the time of King Hezekiah, in the early seventh century B.C.[63]

There is also substantial archeological evidence of goddess worship among the ancient Israelites. At an excavation at Tell Beit Mirsim, near modern Hebron, the most abundant religious artifacts found from the levels preceding the invasion of Canaan were ceramic figurines of Asherah. Yet even in later layers, corresponding to the centuries after the invasions when the town was rebuilt under the Israelites, the figurines were plentiful. According to the biblical archeologist Rabbi Raphael Patai, "The archeological evidence leaves no doubt that these figurines were very popular among the Hebrews." Considering both the archeological and scriptural evidence, Rabbi Patai concluded that up until "the very end of the Hebrew monarchy [i.e. the time of the Babylonian invasion] the worship of the old Canaanite gods was an integral part of the religion of the Hebrews."[64]

As in the case of goddess worship in neighboring Mesopotamia, where rites for the goddess involved the practice of sympathetic magic believed necessary to promote the fertility of the crops and livestock, the worship of the goddess and her consort included a significant amount of sexual activity. Copulation with both male and female temple prostitutes, proxies for the goddess, would be performed to fertilize the goddess and thus ensure the health and expansion of their herds, or to bring about other favorable events. References to the *kadesh*, the male temple prostitutes, and *kadeshem*, the female temple prostitutes, appear eight times in Hebrew Scripture,[65] and, as noted earlier in the chapter, the temple compound in Jerusalem included a building to house the kadesh which was not removed until the late seventh century B.C., under the reign of King Josiah (640–609 BC).[66] Another ritual involving masturbation before the idol of Baal was performed to arouse the god, who would thereby bring rains to make Mother Earth fertile. The rites also included the initiation of young men into the "sexual-religious exaltation of orgasm" in the temple and ceremonies including oral-genital contacts between priests and worshippers. The latter have survived even into modern times in some orthodox circumcision ceremonies which include a ritualistic fellation of the newly cut penis.[67]

The majority of followers of the Baal and Asherah cults seem to have been women. In addition to having a role in the fertility of the fields and livestock, the goddess was also the patron of childbirth. As such, she was a source of comfort for women undergoing pregnancy and facing the ordeals of childbirth, a process fraught with risk in a time long before the advances of medicine. In Jeremiah 44, when the prophet is preaching before a crowd of men and their wives predicting the destruction that will fall on the people for their worship of "the Queen of Heaven," a reference to the goddess, the scripture states that his message was addressed "particularly to all the women."[68] The women followers of Baal and Asherah would no doubt have included the rural farm wives, whom one might expect would be more likely to participate in local rituals, but they also included some high-ranking women. Maacah, the mother of King Asa of Judah, was denounced in 1 Kings 15:13 for erecting an *Asherim* for Asherah.

Contrary to the widespread assumption that the Israelites repeatedly abandoned Yahweh for the worship of Asherah and Baal, an impression fostered by statements in the scripture itself, it is apparent that the worship of the goddess and her consort continued side by side with the worship of Yahweh for many centuries. The parallel worship of the goddess and her consort alongside rites for Yahweh is well illustrated by the worship of the bronze serpent in the Temple, mentioned above, and the building housing the male temple prostitutes in the temple compound that was not removed until the time of King Josiah.

While devotion to the goddess and her consort was practiced alongside rites for Yahweh for much of the Israelites early history, that is not to say that there was harmony between the two competing cults. The fierce opposition of the priests of Yahweh to the worship of Asherah and Baal is plainly evident in the scripture.[69] The principal source of the hostility to goddess worship was the priesthood, the Aaronite priesthood of the Southern Kingdom of Judah, who controlled the Temple worship in Jerusalem, and the Shiloh, or Mushite priests of the Northern Kingdom of Israel, who were arch-rivals of the Aaronite priests. Though they were bitter competitors for preeminence in matters of Hebrew worship, they shared with each other a longstanding contempt for the rituals of the goddess and her consort, and would have regarded the widespread participation of the Israelites in her rituals as a continuing threat to their prestige and authority.

The historic animosity of the priesthood to the goddess worship of the Canaanites was a product of the long running attempt of the Hebrew priestly leadership to impose their tribal god, Yahweh, and their patriarchal ideology on a resistant, goddess-worshipping Canaanite people.[70] The priesthood's ire would certainly have been inflamed by the evident embrace of rites for Baal and Asherah by a large portion of the Israelite population, into which the native Canaanite population was being assimilated. The historian Christopher Witcombe has remarked that, in the light of the struggle to establish Yahweh as the one and only god of the Israelites, "much of the Old Testament can be read as an extended Yahwist propaganda tract" against the native cults of Baal and Asherah. As Witcombe observes, "the tactic adopted by the Yahwists in their efforts to defeat Baal was to demonize the cult and to represent Baal as an evil god, a demon hostile to humankind."[71] Hence, the animal symbols for Baal and Asherah, the bull and snake, became incorporated into images of Satan — the horns and hoofed feet of the bull became distinguishing marks of Satan, while the Devil takes the form of a snake to trick Adam and Eve into eating the forbidden fruit.

It is noteworthy that the passages condemning or denigrating the rites of Baal and Asherah in Hebrew scripture are found almost exclusively in books among those that were written, compiled, edited and amended by the Aaronite priesthood in the period after the return from Babylonian exile in the late sixth or early fifth century B.C. Those books are Exodus, Numbers, Deuteronomy, Joshua, Judges, 1 and 2 Samuel, and 1 and 2 Kings, all of which are composed of texts that were written or compiled from earlier texts by members of the Aaronite or Shiloh priesthoods. According to the widely accepted Documentary Hypothesis explanation of biblical authorship,* they were compiled and edited into their final form by an Aaronite priest or group of priests in the period after the return from exile. Some biblical scholars suspect the editor was Ezra,[72] an Aaronite priest and religious leader of the Israelites after their return from Babylon. Such a conclusion would also be consistent with rabbinical tradition, which holds that Ezra edited the texts that became the Torah in 440 B.C. Shortly after the

---

*Based on extensive and detailed textual analysis, biblical scholars starting in the late 19th century came to the conclusion that the books comprising most of what we know today as the Old Testament of the Bible were compiled from a number of different texts written by different priestly authors over a period of several hundred years beginning somewhere around the early eighth century B.C. The first of the texts, called the J text, was written by a member or members of the Aaronite priesthood of Jerusalem, and contained an account of events from the Creation to the arrival of the Israelites in Canaan. The narrative was told from the Aaronite perspective, i.e., stressing the significance of Aaron and his priestly descendants, and de-emphasizing the role of Moses, from whom the rival Shiloh priesthood claimed descent. The text, which approximates much of what became the first four books of the Torah, also included the first Hebrew law code, a lengthy list of rules ranging from dress to diet, which provided the Aaronite priesthood a means of codifying their authority over Hebrew worship. The second text, the E text, was written in response to the Aaronite text by the Shiloh priests in the Northern Kingdom of Israel, and provided a similar historical narrative, but slanted to the perspective of the Shiloh priests, as well as a competing law code. It therefore accentuated the role of Moses and diminished the role of Aaron.

In the period after the destruction of the Northern Kingdom of Israel by the Assyrians in 720 B.C., when Jerusalem was flooded with refugees from the north, the two texts were joined, most likely in an effort to ease the assimilation of the refugees from Israel with the people of Judah. In the late seventh century, King Josiah initiated religious reforms which centralized Hebrew worship around the rites in the Temple in Jerusalem, controlled by the Aaronite priesthood. The Aaronites accordingly produced an edited version of JE, called the P text, which reasserted the Aaronite viewpoint in the text and removed texts favorable to the Shiloh priests remaining in JE from the Shiloh's E text. In response, a member of the Shiloh priesthood, a writer many scholars believe to be Jeremiah, produced a long historical narrative starting with the arrival of the Israelites in Canaan down through the invasion of Nebuchadnezzar, the destruction of Jerusalem and the Temple, and the exile of the Israelites in Babylon. The text, called by scholars the Deuteronomic History, includes the text in what is now the book of Deuteronomy plus the books of Joshua, Judges, 1 and 2 Samuel and 1 and 2 Kings.

After the defeat of Babylon by the Persians and the liberation of the Israelites from captivity, the Persian monarch, Artaxerxes, appointed Ezra, a member of the Aaronite priesthood, as religious leader of the Israelites, an act which sealed the Aaronite control of Hebrew worship practices. In the following years, a writer whom scholars call R, or the Redactor, possibly Ezra himself, and certainly a member of the Aaronite priesthood, performed a final recompilation, amending and editing of the texts and formed them into the first four books of the Torah. In the process, he added eleven chapters to Genesis, doubled the size of Exodus, wrote most of Numbers, and created the entire book of Leviticus from scratch. He then integrated the books of the Deuteronomic History with the rest of the texts, and organized the whole into the books of the Bible as they are known today. Around the same time, an Aaronite scribe added I and II Chronicles, presenting an Aaronite response to the Deuteronomic texts, which put a final Aaronite stamp on the historical narrative of the Bible. The Books of Ezra and Nehemiah pick up the historical narrative with the return of the Israelites from exile, the rebuilding of the Temple, and the reconstitution of the nation of Israel, again from the Aaronite perspective. The remaining books of the Bible, the books of the Prophets and the Wisdom books, were compiled from numerous other sources, including the writings of the prophets themselves, and other texts handed down through the generations.

Torah and Historical books were assembled, 1 and 2 Chronicles, which also contain negative references to Baal and Asherah, were added by an Aaronite scribe. Jeremiah, which includes condemnation of Baal and Asherah, is understood by most scholars to have been written by Jeremiah himself, a Shiloh priest.

Only a handful of references to Baal and Asherah appear in books not written by the priesthood. Five negative references to Baal appear in the Book of Hosea, which contains the writing of the minor prophet Hosea, a contemporary of Isaiah and Amos. The great prophet Isaiah, not a member of the priesthood, rails against Israel for her sins, but contains only three passing references to Asherah poles[73] and none to Baal. It is interesting to note that Amos, who like his contemporary Isaiah was not a member of the priesthood, but was a farmer and herder from humble origins, makes no references at all to the worship of Baal or Asherah. Instead, Amos emphasizes compassion and social justice, concepts that receive minimal treatment in the books written by the priesthood. The writings of the latter have, on the other hand, an overriding emphasis on obedience to Yahweh and the Law, as interpreted by the priesthood, and the negative consequences of straying from the Law.

Considering the long-running participation of a large segment of the Israelite population over many centuries in rites for Baal and Asherah, participation that often occurred under the authority of and with the participation of the kings of Israel and Judah, it is hard to accept the contention that the ancient Israelites as a nation identified themselves solely with the worship of Yahweh, and because of moral weakness repeatedly abandoned Yahweh for idolatry, like a faithless wife committing adultery, a recurring theme in the books written by the priesthood. Rather, it is clear that the religious practices of the Israelites were overtly polytheistic for a long period of their early history, with concurrent rituals for Yahweh that sought divine protection from the Israelites' enemies alongside the fertility rites and homosexual rituals of Baal and Asherah thought necessary to ensure good harvests and healthy herds.

The well-documented rivalry between the Aaronite and Shiloh priesthood also demonstrates that religious piety and devotion to Yahweh were not the only concern of the priesthood, but that eliminating rivals for the religious leadership of the Israelites was a conscious aspiration, whether the competitors were priests of Yahweh or of another god. Given this competition, it seems likely that the priesthood would have regarded the worship of Baal and Asherah as a convenient foil against which to portray the righteousness of their role in calling the Israelites from heathen worship to avoid Yahweh's punishment.

Also noteworthy is the fact that in many of the passages condemning the cult of Baal and Asherah, it is women who get the blame for leading Hebrew men astray.[74] As related in 1 Kings 11:4–5, "when Solomon was old, his wives turned his heart away after other gods," including Asherah. King Ahab "sold himself to do evil in the eyes of the Lord, urged on by Jezebel his wife."[75] The king "went to serve Baal and worshiped him. So he erected an altar for Baal in the house of Baal," and "also erected an *Asherim*" for Asherah.[76] Because of Jezebel's highly visible support for the worship of Baal and Asherah and opposition to the priests of Yahweh, she received especially harsh treatment from the priestly authors. In fact, her name has come down as a term for "a wicked or shameless woman"[77] or a woman who is "evil and scheming."[78] As a result of the prominent role of women in goddess worship among the Israelites, women came to be viewed in the eyes of the priests of Yahweh as weak, prone to sin and responsible for leading men astray. In the sectarian conflict between the Yahweh priests and the followers of the goddess, therefore, can be found the beginning of a decline in the status of women among the Hebrews, particularly in the eyes of the Aaronite priesthood.

The continuing campaign of the priesthood to purge Hebrew worship of rituals of Baal and Asherah may have also been spurred on by nationalism. Several historians have argued that the hostility of the Hebrew leadership toward these cults was less a moral crusade than a nationalist rejection of the indigenous Canaanite religion in favor of a strictly Hebrew national god.[79] The historian David F. Greenberg has observed that vigorous efforts under the Judean monarchs to quash the goddess worship in many cases closely corresponded to periods when the kings were asserting Jewish nationalism.[80]

It is important to note that in the many passages containing negative references to Baal and Asherah the priests' disapproval of the rites did not single out the homosexual rites involving the *kadesh*, the male sacred prostitutes, as sexual offenses. Where the kadesh are mentioned, the texts state the disapproval with the Hebrew term for idolatry, *to-ebah*.[81] Similarly, when the kadesh, misleadingly translated as "sodomites" in some modern biblical translations, were finally removed from the temple, the emphasis, as Epstein writes, "was not on sexual morality, as on the idolatry involved."[82] Given the total absence of condemnation of homosexual practices in pre-exile scripture, and the extensive participation of the Israelites in the rituals of Asherah and Baal, which included a significant amount of homosexual activity, the nearly universal assumption among scriptural scholars that the early Israelites always and uniformly condemned homosexuality is therefore completely without basis.

The Sin of Sodom

One of the oldest stories in the Bible, and one of the most notorious, is the account of the fiery destruction of Sodom and Gomorrah. Christians have believed for many centuries that the punishment meted by God on the people of Sodom and her sister city, Gomorrah, was done because they practiced homosexuality, one of the most serious of sins according to Aquinas, and an act commonly referred to by the name of that city since Medieval times. However, the association of homosexual practices with the sin of Sodom is another of the many myths that have grown up around sex and homosexuality since early Christian times. If as biblical scholars have noted there is a total absence of preaching about sexual morality and no prohibition against homosexuality in the pre-exile portion of the Old Testament, homosexuality could not be the sin for which the two cities were destroyed. The story in Genesis of Lot's sojourn in Sodom and the subsequent destruction of that city would have occurred during Abraham's lifetime, which according to most reckonings of the biblical timeline would be around 1,500 years before the Babylonian conquest and the subsequent exile of the Hebrews. The popular understanding that the sin that caused the destruction of Sodom and Gomorrah was homosexuality is, therefore, a misconception at odds with both the evidence in the Bible and the traditional interpretation of the story in both Christian and Jewish teachings.

The Book of Ezekiel defines the sin of Sodom very differently: "This was the sin of your sister Sodom: she and her daughters lived in pride, plenty, and thoughtless ease; they neglected the poor and those in need; they grew haughty, and committed idolatries before me, and therefore I cast them out of my house" (Ezekiel 16:49–50). A similar interpretation occurs in Wisdom: "They suffered for their crimes, since they evinced such bitter hatred towards strangers. Others had refused to welcome unknown men on their arrival, but these had made slaves of guests and benefactors" (19:13–14). Likewise Ecclesiasticus: "He did not spare the people with whom Lot lived, whom he abhorred for their pride" (16:8).[83] Jesus makes clear his own understanding of the sin of Sodom in several of the Gospels: "But whenever you enter a town and they do not make you welcome ... I tell you, on that day it will not go as hard with Sodom as with that town."[84] Most scholars — Jewish as well as Christian — have traditionally held that the sin for which Sodom was destroyed was arrogance and uncharitableness, callousness, inhospitality or cruelty to strangers or those in need.

In the passages in question in Genesis 18 and 19, the story is told of angels sent by God to Sodom to investigate the wickedness of the inhabitants, whether they "have done all that is alleged in the outcry against them" that has come to God's attention. The angels, appearing as men, arrived at the city and Lot took them into his house for the night. A crowd gathered around Lot's house, demanding that Lot bring out the men so that they might "know" them. The verb, to know, is used in a number of places in the Old Testament to refer to having sexual intimacy with another.* Lot refused, saying, "Do no such wicked thing. I have two daughters who are virgins. I am ready to send them out to you, to treat as it pleases you. But as for the men, do nothing to them, for they have come under the shadow of my roof." The crowd rejected Lot's pleas and when they attempt to bash in the door of Lot's house the angels struck them blind, and then warned Lot and his family to flee, after which the town was destroyed.

That the meaning of the destruction of Sodom had less to do with sexual practices than with mistreatment of travelers who had been given shelter is clear in the passage. Lot *offers the unruly mob his virgin daughters to do with as they please*, but demands the crowd leave the men alone, "for they have come under the shadow of my roof." The sort of brutish mistreatment of the visitors attempted by the men of Sodom, which many biblical scholars see as an attempt at homosexual rape, was a gross violation of the age-old tradition in the Near East, continuing today in much of the Arab world, of offering food, shelter and protection to travelers whose survival in that arid land literally depended on the kindness of strangers. The association of homosexuality by itself with the destruction of Sodom did not come until much later in Jewish history. In fact several scholars have asserted that the sexual elements in the story were inserted at a much later date.[85]

On the other hand, the reaction of the men of Sodom to the entrance of the two angels, who we can assume would have manifested as young men of exceptional good looks, shows that the writers of Genesis were well aware of homosexual proclivities among the men of Canaan, Sodom and Gomorrah being Canaanite cities. A similar episode recounted in the Book of Judges that occurred in the Judean town of Gibeah shows that the scriptural authors were also aware that Hebrew men could have an interest in homosexuality.

In the story, a traveler and his female concubine arrived in Gibeah late in the day and were putting their bedding down in the town square to sleep for the night. An old man approached them and urged them to spend the night in his house, an invitation the traveler accepted. After the traveler and his concubine had arrived at the old man's house, a crowd of men surrounded the house, demanding, "Bring out the man who came to your house that we may know him." The host refused. "No, my brethren," he said, "do not act so wickedly; seeing that this man has come into my house, do not do this vile thing. Behold here are my virgin daughter and his concubine; let me bring them out now. Ravish them and do with them what seems good to you; but against this man do not do so vile a thing." The men

---

*Many biblical interpreters have assumed that the desire of the men to "know" the visitors meant that they desired sexual intercourse with them, and that their intent was homosexual rape. While the word for "know," yadha, is used in ten places in biblical scripture to indicate sexual intercourse, the expression is used far more often, in 924 passages, in fact, to mean "to get acquainted with." The historian Rictor Norton has observed therefore that "the odds against the homosexual usage of this term are nearly 1000-to-1," and notes that many modern biblical scholars have now rejected the sexual interpretation of "know" in the story. According to these scholars, what occurred in the incident is that Lot, who was not a citizen of the city, but the equivalent of a resident alien who had no rights in the city, had brought two strangers into the city without permission. The men, according to this interpretation, were seeking to check the strangers out, to see their credentials, so to speak. However, Lot's offer of his two virgin daughters to the men in place of the angels implies that Lot understood the intent of the men of Sodom to be sexual (Rictor Norton, A History of Homophobia, "1 The Ancient Hebrews," 15 April 2002 <http://www.infopt.demon.co.uk/homophol.htm>

refused the offer of the man's virgin daughter and the concubine, and still insisted on having the traveler come out, which seems a strong indication of the homosexual interests of the men. If the men were normal heterosexuals, as scholars uniformly assume of men in biblical times, one would think they would have been pleased with the offer of the man's virgin daughter and the concubine. After the men rejected the offer of the two young women, the traveler threw his concubine out anyway to the men, who "knew her, and abused her all night until the morning." When dawn came, the traveler went out and found his concubine dead. Outraged by the savage treatment of his concubine, the traveler sent news of the crime to the Twelve Tribes of Israel, who came and destroyed the town.[86]

As in the case of the attempted rape of the angels by the men of Sodom, the intent of the men of Gibeah to rape the traveler was regarded by the Hebrews as an egregious violation of the obligation of kindness and hospitality to strangers. The old man in the story said so himself when he told the men, "seeing that this man has come into my house, do not do this vile thing," a response nearly identical to what Lot told the men of Sodom. While it seems clear that the men of Gibeah intended to commit homosexual rape of the traveler, there is no question that the most serious of the offenses of the men of Gibeah in the eyes of the Hebrews, aside from the rape and murder of the concubine, was their violent disregard for the tradition of kindness and hospitality to strangers or those in need. At no time were the men of Gibeah denounced for the homosexual nature of the acts they intended with the traveler. The main issue was not the homosexual acts that were intended, but the violent and coercive manner with which the men of Gibeah intended to carry them out. Rather than showing that the Hebrews disapproval of homosexuality, the episode of the traveler in Gibeah, then, provides evidence that Hebrew men of the period were aware of homosexual attraction and would be inclined under some circumstances to take advantage of opportunities for homosexual gratification.

Love Between Heroes: David and Jonathan

Given what is now known about the homosexual potential in human sexuality, and the lack of any prohibition against homosexual acts in Hebrew scripture before the time of the exile, it should not be surprising to find evidence of homosexuality among major Hebrew figures mentioned in the Bible. The most prominent example of a same-sex relationship among the early Israelites is the relationship described in I and II Samuel between the great Israelite hero, David and Jonathan, the son of Saul, the first king of Israel. The contention that there was a sexual relationship between David and Jonathan has been fiercely rejected by traditional Biblical scholars, both Jewish and Christian. However, a close reading of the description of their relationship in the text, which contains a number of references to the sexual nature of the friendship, leaves little room for interpreting the relationship any other way.

Saul came to the throne in the 11th century B.C., not long after the Israelites had settled in Canaan. During this period they were under frequent attack by neighboring powers, most particularly, the Philistines, an Indo-European warrior people who had settled on the Palestinian coast and who had occupied some of the Judean hill country. Saul was a strong and arrogant warrior-leader, whose prideful temperament brought him trouble with Yahweh. After defeating a neighboring tribe, he felt that he could disregard a command of Yahweh to slaughter all the people and livestock of the vanquished enemy, and instead took the king captive alive as well as the fattest of the sheep and goats. Because of this act of defiance he was "rejected by Yahweh" and consequently was beset with fits of anxiety and melancholy. To relieve his distress, Saul's servants sought a skilled harp player, whose sweet music they thought would restore the king's spirit. Therefore, David, "a skilled player, a brave man and a fighter," was brought to the king. David, who is described in the scripture as exceptionally good looking, entered the king's service. "Saul loved him greatly, and David became his armor-bearer.... And whenever the spirit from God troubled Saul, David took the harp and played."[87]

Not long afterwards, the Israelites found themselves again facing the Philistines in battle. The great hero of the Philistines, Goliath, whose size and ferocity struck terror among the ranks of Saul's army, came out every day and taunted the Israelites, challenging one of them to come down and try to defeat him. David answered Goliath's challenge, and meeting him in battle, slung a stone which penetrated the giant's forehead, bringing him to the ground, whereupon David, using Goliath's own sword, cut off his head. Seeing their champion defeated, the Philistines fled, with the Israelite army in pursuit, and in the ensuing rout the enemy was driven out of the land.[88]

David was brought before an amazed King Saul, with Goliath's head still in his hand. With Saul was his son, Jonathan, a warrior-hero in his own right, who had previously led the Israelite army in a significant victory over the Philistines. After David and Saul finished talking, the scripture says that Jonathan was smitten with the good looking young hero, and "the soul of Jonathan was knit with the soul of David, and Jonathan loved him as his own soul.... Then Jonathan and David made a covenant, because he loved him as his own soul. And Jonathan stripped himself of the robe that was upon him, and gave it to David, and his garments, even his sword, and his bow."[89] Saul then brought David to live in the royal house with him and his son. Later, when Saul gave his daughter, Michal, in marriage to David, he remarked that when David married Michal, he would be the king's son-in-law "through two."[90] By this Saul meant that David would be his son-in-law through two of his children, that is, through David's relationship with his son, Jonathan, and through David's marriage to his daughter, Michal. This implicit acknowledgement by Saul of his son's sexual relationship with David has been overlooked by most biblical scholars.

David quickly proved himself a superior soldier, for "whenever David went out, on whatever mission Saul sent him, he was successful, and Saul put him in command of the fighting men. He stood well in the people's eyes, and in the eyes of Saul's officers, too."[91] David's growing popularity with the people caused Saul to become jealous of David, whom he saw as a threat to his kingship. Saul turned against David and told Jonathan and his servants he wanted to have the young hero killed. Jonathan, because of his love for David, warned him of Saul's plot, and sent David into hiding. Jonathan told David he would sound out his father, to find out if he really meant to kill David, and arranged to meet David in a secret place, to let him know what he found out.

At the dinner meal one night, Saul, seeing David's place empty, asked of his whereabouts. Jonathan covered for his friend, telling his father that David had to go to his home in Bethlehem for a family religious ritual. Not believing his son, Saul raged in anger against Jonathan:

> You son of a perverse, rebellious woman. Do not I know that you are in league with the son of Jesse (David) to your own disgrace and the disgrace of your mother's nakedness? As long as the son of Jesse lies on the earth neither your person nor your royal rights are secure. Now, send and bring him to me. He is condemned to death. Hot with anger, Jonathan rose from the table and took no food that second day of the new Moon, being grieved on David's account.[92]

Jonathan then went to meet David in their hiding place to tell him that he would have to flee. At their meeting "they kissed and both shed many tears."[93]

David subsequently fled from Saul, became for a while an outlaw, and then took refuge in the territory of the Philistines. While there, he heard news of the death of Saul and Jonathan in a battle. Weeping over his friend's death, David lamented, "O Jonathan, in your death I am stricken. I am desolate for you Jonathan, my brother. Very dear to me you were, your love to me more wonderful than the love of a woman."[94] The language David used in his lament, comparing his feelings for Jonathan to heterosexual love, is strikingly similar to the description of the love of Gilgamesh for Enkidu. In his dreams before meeting Enkidu, Gilgamesh makes love to Enkidu's symbols "as over a woman." After Enkidu's death, Gilgamesh, "like a widow, mourns Enkidu," and "veils his dead friend like a bride."[95]

It has, of course, been argued that two men can have a close friendship without homosexual involvement. However, the character of the relationship as described in the story, set against the context of what we know about attitudes toward homosexuality among Middle Eastern cultures during that period, make it clear that the relationship between David and Jonathan went beyond the bonds of ordinary friendship. First, the evidence from Mesopotamia and Egypt shows that it was not unusual for masculine men to have sexual relationships during this period; therefore, a sexual bond between Jonathan and David would have been consistent with contemporary practices elsewhere in that region. Second, since there was no prohibition on homosexual acts in the pre–Exile portion of Hebrew scripture, there would have been no moral impediment to a sexual relationship between the two.

Third, the dramatic intensity of the language used in the text to describe their developing bond, "the soul of Jonathan was knit with the soul of David, and Jonathan loved him as his own soul," is an unmistakable reference to the most total love of which humans are capable, sexual and emotional union. Fourth, the singular nature of the love between the two is unambiguously displayed by Jonathan when he ostentatiously bestows on David his clothes and armor, and then the two of them declare a lifetime covenant with each other. Indeed, the Hebrew word in the text for the "covenant" is the same word that is used to denote a marriage covenant elsewhere in Hebrew scripture.[96] Likewise, the word "brother," with which David addresses the dead Jonathan in his famous lament, was commonly used in Jewish scriptures as a term of endearment for a spouse or lover.[97] Also suggestive of a spousal or "family"-type relationship is David's taking Jonathon's son to live with him in his household after Jonathan's death, which he said he did "for Jonathan's sake."[98] Finally, Saul's quip that through David's marriage to Michal he would become Saul's son-in-law "through two" is an overt acknowledgment of a sexual bond — tantamount to a marriage, in Saul's eyes — between David and Jonathan.

The sexual relationship between Jonathan and David was also alluded to by Saul, in his angry outburst at Jonathan in 1 Samuel 20:30, though that fact is not apparent in modern biblical translations. In the King James Version, Saul says: "Do not I know that thou hast chosen the son of Jesse to thine own confusion, and unto the confusion of thy mother's nakedness?"[99] The Hebrew word translated as "chosen," which the Jerusalem Bible quoted earlier translates as "in league with," has also been translated as "have sided with," "have made friends with," and "are a comrade of." However, the Septaugint text, the oldest extant version, renders the word as *metecho*, which means "partner" or "companion." The great 19th century Oxford Biblical scholar Samuel Rolles Driver concluded that the wording used in the Septaugint manuscript is the only logical rendering of the passage, which would then yield the translation: "For do I not know that you are an intimate companion to the son of Jesse?" In a similar way, the Latin Vulgate, translated by Saint Jerome, uses the verb *diligo* which means "to love" or "to cherish" and was used by Ronald Knox as a basis for his translation of the passage, which reads, "Dost thou think I have not marked how thou lovest this son of Jesse, to thy own undoing and hers, the shameful mother that bore thee."[99]

The sexual import of Saul's accusation is reinforced by last part of the clause, "to the shame of thy mother's nakedness." The words "shame," and "nakedness" in the passage are derogatory allusions to sex which appear frequently in the Old Testament. Their use by Saul in his accusation indicates that the intimate companionship he is referring to between David and Jonathan is of a sexual nature. The indirect use of "shame" and "nakedness" to refer to sex is a result of a convention in Semitic languages of avoiding a direct reference to a person or group being criticized.[100] Similarly, in the same passage David, the object of Saul's hatred, is not named, but is referred to indirectly as the "son of Jesse." A close look at the text of the passage therefore leaves no doubt that Saul is referring to a sexual relationship between Jonathan and David.

If the relationship between the two was no more than a Platonic friendship, it would have made no sense for Saul to point that out when confronting his son since that fact would have been obvious from the beginning. But it would have been natural for Saul, in his anger, to call attention to the sort of bond between the two that would cause his son to favor his friend over his father. And so the cause of Saul's anger with Jonathan is made clear: Saul is accusing his son of assisting in David's escape because of his sexual involvement with David. Jonathan's reaction to Saul's outburst, angrily leaving the table and not eating, "being grieved on David's account," underscores his intense emotional involvement with the young hero.

The historian John Boswell has noted that writers of the Jewish Mishnah, compiled during the early centuries of Christianity, cited Jonathan and David as a paramount example of lasting love (Aboth 5:16), in contrast to the heterosexual passion between Amnon and Tamar, also detailed in 2 Samuel, that is described as transitory. Boswell maintains that the direct comparison between the two couples seems a striking acknowledgment of a physical bond between David and Jonathan. Indeed, the word used to describe the love between the members of each couple is the same throughout the Mishnaic text.[101]

A psychological analysis of the relationship between David and Jonathan cited by the scriptural scholar Tom Horner concluded that the Jonathan, the royal prince, was the aggressor, and the ambitious young David a willing seductee. The study found David as "unreservedly responsive" to Jonathan's advances, and though his homosexuality was only a passing phase, it was one that David turned to good advantage by cementing a close alliance between him and the royal family.[102] Whatever the circumstances of their involvement or the motives of the partners, the love between David and Jonathan is another example of the kind of masculine love between heroic comrades that was very probably frequent among the military aristocracy of the ancient Middle East. As Rabbi Raphael Patai, the biblical archeologist, has written, "The love story between Jonathan, the son of King Saul, and David, the beautiful hero, must have been duplicated many times in royal courts in all parts of the Middle East in all periods."[103]

Ruth and Naomi

Several historians have also read a physical relationship in the story of Ruth and Naomi, described in the Book of Ruth.[104] Naomi, a Hebrew woman, went with her husband and two sons and settled in Moab, a kingdom east of the Dead Sea in what is now Jordan. Eventually her husband died, and her two sons married Moabite women, Orpah and Ruth. Some time later both of her sons died, leaving the three women alone. Noami urged her daughters-in-law to go back to live with their families, which would have been the normal custom in such circumstances. Orpah kissed Naomi good-bye and left for her family, but Ruth "clung to her" and refused to leave the older woman, making a solemn vow never to desert Naomi as long as she lived. Her passionate statement to Naomi has been described as one of the most eloquent pledges of love that has ever been made by one human to another:

> Entreat me not to leave thee,
> > or to return from following after thee;
> For whither thou goest I will go,
> > And where thou lodgest I will lodge.
> Thy people shall be my people,
> > And thy God my God:
> Where thou diest, will I die,
> > And there will I be buried.
> The Lord do so to me, and more also,
> > If aught but death part thee and me.[105]

In this extraordinary statement, Ruth shows her willingness to abandon her family and even her faith to remain with Naomi. Few would doubt that this statement reveals an attachment that goes beyond mere friendship. Though there is little indication in the scripture of a romantic interest between them, it should be noted that the Hebrew word in the passage where Ruth refused to leave Naomi, and "clung to her" is the same word used in Genesis (2:24) in describing the attachment of husband and wife.[106]

In the ancient world, as in many other societies, the segregation of the sexes caused women to spent most of their time with other women, who thus were often forced to turn to each other for emotional companionship. Sexual relations between women are not prohibited in Hebrew scripture, as later occurred with homosexuality among men. As has been observed among women in similar circumstances in other societies, a sexual attachment between Ruth and Naomi would not have been unusual. Indeed, lesbianism in the harems of the ancient Near East and India was well known.[107] So while a sexual relationship between Ruth and Naomi cannot be proven from what it said in the scripture, such a relationship would have been certainly possible under those circumstances and in that period, and, as the Biblical scholar Tom Horner put it, "the right words were said."[108]

Sexual Implications in the Book of Daniel and the Babylonian Captivity

Elsewhere in the Bible, some scholars have suggested a sexual component in the "favor and compassion" bestowed upon the Prophet Daniel by the "chief eunuch" in the court of Nebuchadnezzar.[109] In earlier times the men whose titles have often been translated as court "eunuchs" were usually not castrated, but were most often passive homosexuals, who frequently made themselves sexually available to masculine men. This tradition of homosexual court attendants and officials extended back to the earliest periods of Mesopotamian civilization. The castration of court officials was first reported among the Assyrians in the fifth century B.C. by the Greek historian Herodotus.[110] Herodotus wrote of this custom a little over a century after the time of Nebuchadnezzar, so it is possible that it was practiced in the Babylonian court at that time. Castration usually involved the removal of the testes only, and was often performed after puberty, so that the individuals retained sexual function, if not procreative capacity. In fact, in harems in the Islamic world, where they were often employed as guards, eunuchs were said to have been popular with the women because they could sustain erections for great lengths of time because they never experienced an exhausting emission like normal men.[111] Notwithstanding their later popularity in harems, eunuchs in the ancient Middle East are usually associated with homosexuality wherever they are mentioned. Whether or not the chief eunuch was actually castrated, his only sexual role, according to tradition, would have been to serve the sexual needs of masculine men. So when such a man confers "favor and compassion" on a young man such as Daniel, the customs of the time strongly suggest a sexual meaning in the episode.

The phenomenon of castrating boys or men for service in royal courts, though little understood by modern Westerners, was a widespread custom in late antiquity. Because castrated officials were not capable of siring offspring, monarchs had no reason to fear dynastic ambitions among powerful officials who were eunuchs. According to the Greek writer Xenophon, the Persian king Cyrus the Great, who reigned in the sixth century B.C., preferred eunuchs as his officers, because men without wives would be loyal only to him. Xenophon writes that under Cyrus's successor, Darius, eunuchs "acquired a vast political authority and appeared then to have filled all the chief offices of state. They were the king's advisors in the palace, and his generals in the field."[112]

As might be expected given the sexual customs of the period, young eunuchs were often sexually used by the aristocracy. One of the effects of castration is to prolong the youthful looks of a young man, because the development of a beard and pattern baldness is brought about by testosterone, which is eliminated when the testes are removed. The tribute paid by Babylon to Darius consisted of a thousand talents of silver as well as 500 castrated boys.[113] The harems of the Persian kings Darius III and Artaxerxes included both concubines and eunuchs. One of Alexander the Great's lovers was Bagoas, a beautiful young Persian eunuch who had previously been a lover of Darius.[114]

It is also interesting to note the circumstances under which Daniel appeared in the court of Nebuchadnezzar. After the Babylonian conquest of Jerusalem, the king ordered his chief eunuch "to select from the Israelites a certain number of boys of either royal or noble descent; they had to be without any physical defect, good looking … suitable for service in the palace of the king." Thus, Daniel and three other good looking Israeli captives were brought into the royal service.[115] For thousands of years, conquerors throughout the region had the practice of taking good looking boys and young men, indenturing them into service in their courts, or selling them into slavery. It was understood that a principal function of handsome boys captured and sold in this way was to meet the sexual needs of their masters. The *Odyssey* of Homer mentions the practice of Phoenician shipmasters purchasing or kidnapping boys to be sold for such purposes to wealthy purchasers.[116] There is also a reference in Hebrew scripture, in the book of Joel, to the sale of young males into sexual slavery.[117] The trade in sexually attractive boys and young men was widespread in the ancient Middle East, and in the Greek and Roman world, and continued in the Islamic world into modern times. The fact that the good looks and physical perfection of the young men was one of the prime qualifications specified by the king in their selection from among the Hebrew captives strongly suggests that what we see in the opening of the Book of Daniel is a glimpse of this widespread and ancient sexual custom.

There is also the possibility that Daniel and his handsome compatriots would have been turned into eunuchs for service in the Babylonian court. Flavius Josephus, a first-century A.D. Jewish scholar and historian, maintained that Daniel had been castrated and sodomized by Nebuchadnezzar. Such a scenario would certainly have been possible, given the practices of the times. David Greenberg has observed that though Josephus is not always considered a reliable source, his account does provide evidence that the castration of court personnel was so common in the empires of the East that it could be assumed in such cases.[118] Similarly, it has also been argued that the remarkable success of Joseph, the son of Jacob, in the court of the pharaoh was due to his being a eunuch who provided sexual services, first to Potiphar, and then to the pharaoh.[119]

Hebrew Hostility to Homosexuality After the Babylonian Exile

The exile of the Hebrews in Babylon began in 587 B.C. when the Babylonians under Nebuchadnezzar conquered and destroyed the city of Jerusalem, razed the Temple to the ground, enslaved the Jewish people, and brought a vast number of them back to Babylon. When the Persian monarch, Cyrus the Great, overthrew the Babylonians in 539 B.C. he dealt with the captured Hebrews sympathetically, allowed a large contingent of Israelites to return to their homeland and helped them in rebuilding the Temple in Jerusalem. During the nearly five decades they spent in Babylon, which spanned several generations, the ability of the Israelites to continue the observance of Hebrew rites and practices was naturally diminished. The Babylonian rulers had allowed the Israelites a measure of rights and participation in Babylonian society, and a number of Israelites even rose to prominent positions in the government. Many Israelites participated in non–Hebrew worship rituals and marriages between Hebrews and Babylonian natives were common. When Cyrus defeated the Babylonians and extended an invitation to the Hebrews to return to their homeland, the process of assimilation that started in Babylon did not cease upon their return to Canaan.

When the Israelites returned to their homeland after the Babylonian exile, they found themselves in a land without secure borders and without the religious and tribal institutions that had bound them together as a people since their conquest of Canaan centuries earlier. In fact, the only thing that still identified them as a distinct nationality was their worship of the Israelites' tribal God, Yahweh, and with the effects of assimilation over the years in Babylon, even that tie was being seriously weakened. Many of the Israelites returned with Babylonian wives, and the continuing participation of the returning Israelites in Babylonian religious cults and goddess worship was extensive. Because of the dilution of Hebrew religious practices among the Israelites, the priestly leadership would certainly have recognized the imperative of re-establishing a Hebrew religious order for all the Israelites as a critical step in reasserting the Israelites' national identity. A fundamental step in achieving that end would have been the gathering of the competing strands of Hebrew religious writing together into one unified scripture for a united Jewish people.

In a fateful decision that heavily influenced the direction of the Jewish religion, the Persian King Artaxerxes, in the early 5th century, appointed one of the Aaronite priests still remaining in Babylon, Ezra, as the religious leader of the Israelites in Judah and Jerusalem. Artaxerxes directed Ezra to "make an inspection of Judah and Jerusalem according to the Law of your God, which is in your possession." The king empowered Ezra to draw on the funds in the provincial treasury to spend as he deemed appropriate, to direct Hebrew worship and to instruct the people in the Law, which the king said was "the law of the king," Artaxerxes further decreed that anyone who did not obey the Law, as interpreted by Ezra, would have judgment "strictly executed on him: death, banishment, confiscation or imprisonment."[120] This set the stage for the assembly and revision of the numerous Hebrew religious texts, as interpreted by the Aaronite priesthood with the backing of the Persian monarch, into the body of scripture we know as the Old Testament.*

The Aaronites' compilation and editing of the religious texts came at a pivotal juncture

---

*When Artaxerxes appointed Ezra to be religious leader of the Jews and sent him back to Jerusalem with substantial funds to support his leadership, he was not just being magnanimous towards the Jews, but had specific political objectives in mind. In 460 B.C. a Greek confederation under the leadership of Athens had defeated the Persians at Memphis in Egypt, and had taken a large strip of the coastline of Palestine and Phoenicia, which created a serious military threat to the Persian empire. Establishing a strong pro-Persian religious and civilian establishment in Judah would serve as a bulwark against further encroachment of the Greeks from the Palestinian coast.

in the history of the Jewish people. The trauma of their captivity in Babylon, during which the identity of the Hebrews as a people had narrowly escaped extinction, had a profound effect on the concerns and religious attitudes of the Israelites as they went about rebuilding their society back in Israel. The religious precepts compiled during and after the Babylonian Captivity under the leadership of the Aaronite priesthood, and the social organization that resulted afterwards brought together both the principal elements of the Judaic religion as it has been known since, and the integration of the Twelve Tribes of Israel into one Jewish people.

Although they were back in their homeland, the Israelites were a changed people. Long a people of farmers and herders living an insular, agrarian lifestyle, many of them had been uprooted by the disastrous upheavals of the Assyrian invasion of the Northern Kingdom. The subsequent cataclysm of the Babylonian invasion and exile effectively ended the traditional farming and herding lifestyle for the vast majority of the Israelites. Instead, out of necessity they became a nation of city-dwelling craftsmen and merchants dependent on trade with foreign nations. No longer the confident heirs of Abraham claiming their inheritance in the Promised Land, the Jews saw themselves as a small part of a much broader world of more powerful nations, subject to wars of invasion and living under the ever present threat of subjugation by neighboring powers.

The stresses and uncertainties of their new condition led to a pessimistic outlook toward the world and worldly things in Hebrew thinking, in which "man was conceived as a weak, helpless creature, heir to inborn, evil tendencies from his original father, Adam, constantly tempted and irresistibly lured by evil, personified in Satan."[121] Among man's weaknesses, the greatest, in the opinion of the priesthood, was the lure of sex, an attitude that began to be expressed frequently in Jewish writings in the post-exile period. Such a negative view of sex is seen, for example, in the Testament of the Patriarch Reuben, which states that sex "leads the youth as a blind man to a pit and as a beast to a precipice."[122] Women, already suspect in the eyes of the male priesthood for their association with goddess worship in the pre-exile period, were depicted by the post-exile priesthood as moral weaklings, and the cause of the moral failings of men which they brought about by tempting them into evil with the lure of sex. This attitude resulted in both the distinctly negative treatment of women found in post-exile scripture, and the stringent code on sexual behavior that was included in the law codes that were developed in the period after the disasters of the Assyrian and Babylonian invasions.

The devastation of the Northern Kingdom of Israel by the Assyrians, and then the catastrophe of the Babylonian captivity, were interpreted by the priesthood as Yahweh's punishment of the Israelites for their failure to keep his Law. This was not surprising, since the priestly prophets had repeatedly predicted that lack of devotion to Yahweh and participation in the worship of Baal and Asherah would lead to disasters and the destruction of their nation.* The pessimistic view of man's moral frailty, vulnerable to the ever present temptations of Satan and the moral dangers posed by the tantalizing attractions of sex, likewise persuaded the priesthood that only adherence to a strict and ascetic moral code could secure God's protection.[123] The most obvious affront to the Law in the eyes of the priesthood was, of course, the continued participation of many Jews in the worship of Baal and Asherah, in which sexual rites including male homosexual acts were prominently featured.

The vulnerability of the Israelites as a people, the urgency of controlling man's sinful nature to secure the protection of Yahweh, the dilution of Hebrew religious practices resulting from assimilation in Babylon, and the persistence of goddess worship among the people

---

It hardly needs to be pointed out that religious authorities down through history have routinely blamed the sins of the people for catastrophes from floods, plagues and earthquakes to defeat of a country's army in battle.

were all factors that would have weighed heavily on the priesthood as they began the process of compiling and editing the different source documents into one religious text. In performing these tasks, the Aaronite priestly editors would have held up as a primary objective purifying Hebrew religious practices by first, defining the ritual and behavioral norms that set the Hebrews apart as the chosen people of Yahweh, and then, once and for all, outlawing the rituals of goddess worship and the religious practices of neighboring peoples that were still being embraced by many of the Israelites.

The resulting code of religious and behavioral standards is found primarily in the Book of Leviticus, named after the priestly tribe of the Aaronites, the Levites, and the only book of the Torah composed entirely after the exile. A number of historians have concluded that the strict regulations on dress, diet and behavior contained within the Book of Leviticus represented an attempt of the priesthood to re-establish a national Hebrew religion and identity after the years of assimilation in Babylon by distinguishing Hebrew religion and practices from those of their neighbors.[124] Among the strictures included are two provisions prohibiting male homosexual acts, the first such prohibition in the Bible. Leviticus 18:22, as translated in modern versions of the Bible, reads, "For a man to lie with another man as with a woman is an abomination." The injunction is repeated in Leviticus 20:13, but adds the punishment, "They shall be put to death."

The condemnation of male homosexual acts in Leviticus is taken by many to be a straight forward prohibition, like the commandments of Moses. However, the origins and context of the provisions as well as the choice of words used make it clear that their original intent had more to do with religious and ethnic purity than with sexual behavior, and that the primary focus was cleansing Jewish worship and practices of foreign elements, chiefly the rituals of Baal and Asherah. Leviticus 18, in fact, begins and ends with exhortations against following the practices of the Egyptians and the Canaanites, which implies that the prohibited practices listed in the chapter, which include the injunction against male homosexual acts, represent the forbidden customs of those neighboring peoples.

Among the disapproved religious practices of the Israelites' neighbors, and a longstanding concern to the priests of Yahweh, was, of course, goddess worship which in that period included the sacrifice of pigs in her honor along with its homosexual rites. Accordingly, the writers of Leviticus included prohibitions on the consumption of pork, associated with goddess worship, and on homosexual acts, a common practice among the Israelites' neighbors, and a highly visible element of goddess worship.*

Though modern Christians and Jews would read the passage in Leviticus 18:22, "For a man to lie with another man as with a woman is an abomination," as an injunction as clear-cut as "Thou shall not kill," the Hebrew text has a very different slant. The word in the text translated as "abomination" in modern Christian and Jewish translations is to-ebah, which means "unclean," "ritually impure" or "idolatrous." The expression had its origins in the Egyptian word for "holy" or "sacred," which the priests appropriated and then used in a negative sense when condemning rites or practices that were holy or sacred to non–Hebrews, practices which the priests of Yahweh regarded as idolatry.[125] The sense of the meaning is clear in its use in the phrase to-ebah ha goyem, "the uncleanness of the Gentiles." The term is used 116

---

*Some scholars think that it is possible that the Hebrew elders were also influenced by the strict religious precepts of the Zoroastrian religion that they observed practiced by their Persian benefactors, which placed great emphasis on the production of children and therefore condemned all non-procreative sexuality, including homosexual practices. Given the weakened condition of the Israelites as a nation, such a prohibition could have been seen as desirable. However, as noted earlier, the Zoroastrian prohibition of homosexuality was contained within the Vendidad, which was not written until the third century B.C., two centuries after the prohibition in Leviticus is thought to have been written.

times throughout the Old Testament, nearly always in reference to idolatry. For example, when the people of Judah are denounced in I Kings, Chapter 14 for idolatrous worship, *to-ebah* is used in verse 24 in reference to the homosexual rites of the kadesh, the male temple prostitutes associated with the goddess worship alluded to in the preceding verse 23. On the other hand, in condemning common prostitution, a strictly sexual offense, Leviticus 19:29 uses a different term, *zimah*.[126]

A second flaw in modern translations is the failure to accurately render the meaning of the Hebrew words used for the sexual act being disapproved. The modern translation of the sexual act in the verse "to lie with another man as with a woman" is an imprecise and misleading reading of the Hebrew text and because of that loses a critical element of its meaning. The prohibited act is indicated by the words *miskebe issa*, which is a very unusual construction, unique in Hebrew scripture. However, a similar term appears in a number of passages to refer to the male act in intercourse (literally, "to lie the lying-down of a man") (Genesis 20:15, 16; Exodus 22:15; Numbers 31:17, 18, 35; Judges 21:12). Because the word *issa* means "woman" a number of scholars have concluded that the phrase *miskebe issa* would translate as, "to lie the lying of a woman," or to take the female or receptive role in intercourse. The rendering of the act in most modern translations "to lie with another man as with a woman," does not specify a particular act, and, if anything, seems to point to the male role. If the intent of the scriptural authors was to prohibit a male sexually penetrating another male, the writers could have used the frequently used term, "lie the lyings of a man" rather than a very unusual term used nowhere else in Hebrew scripture. Why the Aaronite authors of Leviticus would single out the act of a male taking the passive role in sex with another man can be explained by their centuries-long animosity towards the male temple prostitutes, the *kadesh*, who performed that sexual act as part the rituals of goddess worship. The sense that the provision is directed against the male cult prostitutes is strengthened by the use of the Hebrew word *zakar* to refer to the male with whom the act is performed, rather than the word *ish*, the most commonly used term for a male. While the term *zakar* can refer to a male, it is primarily used to refer to males with sacred associations, such as priests or men with special religious duties, or males dedicated to Yahweh in some sense. It is used in Deuteronomy 20:13 to refer to Canaanite males who lead Israelites into idolatry (priests or religious functionaries), and is even used twice (Deuteronomy 4:16 and Ezekiel 16:17) for male pagan idols. The Hebrew word *ish* is used to refer to males in ordinary, non-religious contexts, and in fact appears more than 2,100 times in the scripture, whereas *zakar* is used only 86 times. When one considers 1) the cultic or sacral connotations of *zakar*, the male with whom the act is performed, 2) the fact that the prohibited act is a male taking the female role in intercourse, 3) the priesthood's historic animosity towards goddess worship and her homosexual attendants, and 4) the religious associations of *to-ebah*, and its use to condemn idolatry elsewhere in the scripture, it is hard to avoid the conclusion that the writers of the text had male sacred prostitutes specifically in mind in composing the verse.[128]

The exhortations against following the idolatrous practices of the Canaanites and Egyptians in the preamble and conclusion to Leviticus 18, and the use of the religious vocabulary in stating the prohibition on a male taking the passive role in sexual copulation, make it clear that conformance to religious and ethnic norms, not regulation of sexual behavior, is the principal emphasis of the provision.[129] The Hebrew scriptural scholar Louis Epstein made the same point in discussing the expulsion from the Temple of the *kadesh*, whose activities are also described as *to-ebah*, that the emphasis "was not on sexual morality, as on the idolatry involved."[130] Jewish moral writings in the period after the exile also repeatedly link homosexual practices with idolatry.[131]

The derivation of the word *to-ebah*, from the Egyptian term for sacred or holy, which underscores the religious connotation of the expression, calls into question, in fact, the choice of the English word "abomination" for *to-ebah*, which appears in Christian as well as Jewish Biblical translations. The 2006 edition of the Random House Unabridged Dictionary defines abomination as "1. anything abominable; anything greatly disliked or abhorred; 2. intense aversion or loathing; detestation: He regarded lying with abomination; 3. a vile, shameful, or detestable action, condition, habit, etc.: Spitting in public is an abomination." According to the Random House Unabridged Dictionary, then, the word has nothing to do with idolatry or foreign worship practices. Rather, it refers to an object or practice that causes an intense *reaction* of a person, a reaction of abhorrence, aversion or loathing. This, of course, calls to mind the loathing and abhorrence for homosexuals exhibited by homophobic men in the University of Georgia study discussed in the Introductory Chapter.

It is clear, then, that in using an English word, *abomination*, that refers to a visceral reaction of disgust or loathing, to translate a Hebrew religious term, *to-ebah*, used in numerous places in Hebrew scripture to refer to the worship of foreign gods or idolatry, the translators were reading their own meaning of the provision into the translation. The translation is therefore more a reflection of the religious and cultural prejudice of the translators than literal accuracy. The findings of the University of Georgia study suggest, in fact, that the translators were describing *their own reactions* to the homosexual acts denounced in the verse rather than providing an accurate literal translation of *to-ebah*.

Given the derivation of the term from an Egyptian term for *sacred*, its use elsewhere to condemn the religious practices of the Canaanites, the literal rendering of the words for the sex act in the text, and the cultic associations of the term used for the male with whom the act is performed, there can be little doubt that the provision was a product of the priesthood's long campaign to rid Hebrew worship of goddess worship and its sexual rituals.

The proscription against homosexual behavior in Leviticus, then, is just one element of a code which prohibited such other acts as men cutting their hair and beards, wearing garments made of two kinds of cloth and eating shellfish. These and many other strictures in the code were unique to the Hebrew culture of the period, and were clearly aimed at distinguishing Jewish ritual and ethnic practices from that of the other peoples of the region. How strictly the provisions prohibiting homosexual acts were enforced is questionable. Though the death penalty was prescribed in the code as a punishment for those violating the ban on homosexual practices, it is telling that there is absolutely no evidence that the punishment was ever carried out.[132]

After the conquests of Alexander the Great in the fourth century B.C., and the diffusion of Greek culture throughout the Near East, the Israelites again found themselves under the influence of foreign religious and social customs, which in the case of the Greeks included a long homosexual tradition. Just as many of the Israelites took up Babylonian customs during the exile, many Jews in the period of Greek rule began to ignore the sexual and ritual prohibitions in the Torah and were offering sacrifices to Greek gods. According to the Book of Maccabees, a Greek-style gymnasium, featuring nude athletics, an anathema to devout Jews, was even built in Jerusalem. As related in 1 Maccabees, the Jews "disguised their circumcision, abandoned the Holy Covenant, submitting to the heathen rule as slaves to impiety," and "prostituting themselves to all kinds of impurity and abominations,"[133] which implies a widespread disregard for the sexual injunctions in Leviticus. This, of course, would have provoked a stern reaction of the priestly leadership, and, indeed, Jewish writers in the period were especially vehement in their denunciations of the sexual "idolatry" of the Greek conquerors. With the Greeks' homosexual customs replacing the passive homosexual acts of the cult prostitutes as the target of priestly condemnation, the Levitical injunction originally prohibiting males taking the passive role in copulation with another male began to be applied to all homosexual acts.

There can be no doubt that the negative judgment of passive homosexual acts in Leviticus had its origins in their association in the minds of the priests of Yahweh with the homosexual rituals of goddess worship. The linkage with goddess worship cannot be avoided because of the choice of the religious term, *to-ebah,* in the text to relate the disapproval, and the language in the Hebrew text which specifies the prohibited act as a male taking the passive role in sex with a man, The broadening of the condemnation to include all same-sex acts that occurred after the Jews were inundated with the detested homosexual traditions of the Greeks set the stage for the histrionic and visceral language that was commonly used in later periods against homosexuality. This is because once the notion that a natural aspect of a person such as homosexual feelings is evil is established in the consciousness, the inevitable psychological conflict between the person's natural impulses and their beliefs will result in an emotional or visceral discomfort with the subject whenever it is encountered. The stronger the homosexual feelings, the more acute will be the discomfort and consequent expression.

Indeed, Jewish moral writings over the next several centuries began to display exactly the kind of visceral disgust for homosexual practices that has characterized much of Judeo-Christian sexual teaching ever since, a reaction to homosexuality totally absent from Hebrew teachings prior to the appearance of the anti-homosexual provisions of Leviticus. The anti-homosexual injunctions in Leviticus, therefore, which the historian Rictor Norton attributed to "the historical accident of a local sectarian feud," sowed the seeds of what would become a peculiar preoccupation with homosexuality in Western moral teaching, a response driven, as Norton says, by "a sometimes-not-very-subtle form of neurosis, often reaching the proportion of mass hysteria."[134]

While a condemnation of homosexuality became codified in Judaic Law as part of the response of the Aaronite priesthood to the dramatic post-exilic changes in Hebrew life, the extent to which it was strictly observed among the post-exilic Jewish community is open to question. In this regard, Rabbi Raphael Patai, the biblical scholar and archeologist, has remarked, "as opposed to the Law, in actual practice male homosexuality was rampant in Biblical times and has so remained in the Middle East down to the present day."[135] Nonetheless, the proscription against homosexuality in Leviticus, which represented the final triumph of the patriarchal Yahweh cult over competing native religious cults at a very late date in the development of the Jewish religion, was to have far reaching effects throughout the Western world, well beyond the concerns of the tiny Jewish community of ancient Palestine.

Conclusion

From the earliest point at which anything at all is known about the sexual life of the peoples of the ancient Middle East, there is evidence that homosexual behavior was already a well established part of the lives of the population. As nothing happens in a vacuum, it can be presumed that homosexual behavior characterized the lives of these people long before the written documents or art objects that provide evidence of homosexual behavior in Mesopotamia, ancient Egypt or among the Hebrews were produced. Just as the ancient Near Eastern civilization did not happen spontaneously, but was a product of thousands of years of incremental development, so, too, homosexual behavior would certainly have played a part in the lives of the indigenous peoples of the region over the course of time of the development of their culture. The homosexuality and mythical beliefs associated with the third-gender priests and cult prostitutes very probably descended from berdache-like shamans among their Stone Age ancestors. Similarly, the homosexual relations that occurred between ordinary men and women would most likely have been present among their tribal ancestors, just as homosexual relationships among men and women have been observed among aboriginal tribal cultures around the world in more recent times. The similarity of the patterns of sexual behavior found in the ancient Near East to those of aboriginal culture in modern times reinforces the perception that these patterns of behavior stem from deeply intrinsic characteristics of the inherited sexuality of the human species.

5

Love Between Warriors: Homosexual Customs of the Early Indo-Europeans

In the early third millennium BC, Indo-European tribes began a series of migrations out of their ancestral homeland in the steppes of Central Asia, moving, over the next thousand years, into a vast area, from India on the east, through Persia, the Mesopotamian river valley, northern Syria, Anatolia and into Greece and Europe proper. These Indo-European invaders had a profound impact on the conquered lands, overlaying indigenous cultures with their deities and mythology, and setting up ruling structures based on a warrior aristocracy, a system which was to dominate not only the Hittite, Kassite, Mitanni and Persian kingdoms of the ancient Near East, but upon which would be built the social and political structures of Greece, Rome and even Feudal Europe. Peoples descended from these invaders include the Greeks, Celts, Hindus, Persians, Romans, Scythians, French, Spanish, Slavs, Germans and the Scandinavians.

The notion that these disparate peoples could have a common origin first emerged when it was discovered that the varying languages they spoke shared numerous elements of basic structure and vocabulary that could not be explained by parallel development. Sir William Jones, who first made the discovery while serving as a British colonial judge in India in the late 18th century, concluded that Sanskrit, the ancient Indian classical language, is more closely related to European languages than had previously been thought possible. Jones observed that Sanskrit bore to both Latin and Greek "a stronger affinity, both in the roots of verbs, and in the forms of grammar, than could possibly have been produced by accident; so strong, indeed, that no philologer could examine all three of them without believing them to have sprung from some common source."[1]

Further scholarly investigation established eleven clearly interrelated language families spoken from northern Europe to the Indian subcontinent. Through analysis of common elements, the linguists were able to reconstruct the basic structure of the mother Indo-European language itself. Having a language naturally gave rise to the conviction that there must have been some ancient people who spoke it, who would be the common ancestors of all the varied Indo-European-speaking peoples. Investigation then turned to identifying the probable motherland of all these different groups. Coinciding as it did with the rise of nationalist movements in Europe in the late 19th century, the search for the Indo-European homeland produced proposals for various parts of Europe, usually geographically close to the residence of the proponent of each proposed homeland. The idea of a common Indo-European ancestry fell into disrepute among some scholars when Nazi propagandists tagged onto the Indo-European theory their own debased version trumpeting the glories of the "Nordic super-race."[2]

Fortunately, continuing scholarship along both linguistic and archeological avenues has

115

yielded credible results. By analyzing word forms common to all the languages of the Indo-European family, philologists deduced that sheep and horses were important to the common ancestors, that they were pastoral nomads. As for timing, scholars observed that the Indo-European languages share a root for "copper," but have varying words for "bronze." This implies that these peoples were still in the region of their homeland during the late copper age, but had begun to disperse by the time copper was being combined with tin to produce bronze, which would place their first movements out of that region in the late fourth or early third millennium B.C.[3] Looking for a region suitable for pastoral nomads that would have given them easy access to the range of their wanderings, which stretched from India and Persia on the east to Anatolia, Greece and Northern Europe on the west, brought their focus to the steppes of southern Russia. It was further noted that the early Indo-European language has affinities with other linguistic groupings — with Uralic, associated with peoples of the Urals Mountains, and with Trans-Caucasian-Mediterranean, spoken in ancient Anatolia. Interestingly enough, the Volga basin in southern Russia is situated exactly between the Urals and the Caucasus.[4] The linguistic findings pointing to the lower Volga basin of the fourth millennium B.C. as the homeland were significantly reinforced by archeological evidence assembled by Marijas Gimbutas in the early 1960s.

Gimbutas, summarizing archeological discoveries from sites that dated from the beginning of the third millennium B.C., described a simple farming people, of squat stature, who lived in the area just north of the Black Sea, along the banks of the Dneiper and Don Rivers, raising cattle and pigs. They apparently had no horses, and buried their dead in mass graves flanked by flat-bottomed jugs. Gimbutas dubbed these people the North Pontic, after the Latin name for the Black Sea. To the southeast, on the slopes of the Caucasus Mountains, lived a different culture, also squatly built farmers, but unlike the North Pontians, they already had carts. Battle-axes and polished mace-heads found in the remains of their mountain villages point to a more warlike character of this people, whom Gimbutas calls the Trans-Caucasian Copper Age culture. Not far to the east, in precisely the same steppe land between the lower Volga and the Caspian Sea identified as the possible Indo-European homeland, lived a distinctively different people. Taller and more gracefully built, with narrower and longer skulls than the Pontians or Trans-Caucasians, they were probably originally hunters, but by the third millennium B.C. they had taken to raising sheep and cattle and had domesticated the horse, which greatly increased their mobility. These equestrian steppe dwellers buried their dead singly, in burial mounds called *kurgans*, and so Gimbutas named them the Eurasian Kurgan culture.[5]

By the middle of the third millennium B.C. the Kurgans had conquered, first, the North Pontians, and then the Trans-Caucasians, sharpening their warrior skills in the process and assimilating some of the cultural advances the Trans-Caucasians had apparently acquired from the Mesopotamians to their south. Thus began a process that would characterize the descendents of the Kurgans, or the Indo-Europeans as they are now recognized, as they spread out across Eurasia in later periods: constantly developing, through the combination of inherited strengths and acquired elements, a new and superior way of living. The success of their advances can be seen in graves of Kurgan princes that have been found, filled with jewelry and ornaments of gold and silver, hammerhead axes of semi-precious stones, turquoise, pearls, copper daggers and lance points. Similar treasure-stocked tombs were later assembled for the warrior aristocracy of the Hittites, Mycenean Greeks and Scythians, direct descendants of these Kurgan warriors. By the end of the third millennium B.C. Indo-Europeans were consolidating power in Anatolia, at the same time other Kurgan descendents, now called the Battle-Axe people, were establishing themselves in Northern Europe.[6]

The earliest sources describing the Indo-European invaders invariably depict them as tall, blond or fair-haired, blue or gray-eyed warriors of great skill and ferocity. Not only did these Indo-Europeans introduce the use of the horse to warfare, but it is they who perfected the battle chariot, which they used to great effect in their movements into the Near East. Demonstrating their common Neolithic tribal ancestry, remarkable commonalities survived among these peoples in mythology, ritual and culture, even thousands of years after their emigrations from Central Asia. The Indo-European scholar Edgar C. Polome has remarked, "It is undeniable that a set of striking correspondences emerge in which myths preserved in the Rigveda (India) will find parallels in the legendary history of the kings of Rome as reported by Livy, and in Scandinavian mythology ... as well as in some passages of Irish epics."[7] Along with common mythological roots, the various Indo-European peoples retained similar deities. When Alexander the Great went into India, he recognized among the Indian gods counterparts to those of the Greek pantheon; similarly when Julius Caesar drove the Celts from Gaul he wrote in his Gallic Wars of Celtic counterparts to each of the Roman gods.

Another set of customs common to Indo-European peoples were sexual practices, particularly patterns of homosexual behavior. According to Bernard Sergent, an authority in Greek and Indo-European myth, "initiation, typically and essentially in the form of the promotion from adolescent to adult status, was universal in the Indo-European family of peoples, which stretched from the Atlantic to the Ganges, just as it has been found to be widespread more recently in a majority of tribal peoples in many different parts of the world."[8] A growing number of scholars now believe that among the early Indo-European tribes the training of a youth in hunting and warrior skills that was part of the initiation process took place in the context of a homosexual relationship between the youth and an adult warrior, and that this tradition dated back to the early Neolithic tribal origins of these groups.[9] Many of the rituals, spiritual practices and sexual beliefs found among early the Indo-European tribes have, in fact, an astonishing similarity to rituals and sexual beliefs observed among aboriginal peoples in recent times. There is abundant evidence that the early Indo-European tribes shared the same Stone Age beliefs, about the life force being resident in the head, contained in semen and expressed through the phallus, that undergird the head-hunting and initiatory homosexuality among the warrior tribes of Melanesia, and that have been observed among tribes in other parts of the world. Another prominent feature that the Indo-European warriors shared with aboriginal tribes are the closely knit warrior societies, among which meals were eaten, camaraderie was shared, and into which young men gained membership through ritual initiation.

While the information we have about the Celtic and Germanic warriors, who were known for their pederastic homosexuality, is not adequate to confirm that they, like the Melanesians, also believed that a warrior's virility and courage were passed into a youth through sexual intercourse, it is evident that their beliefs in every other respect were remarkably similar to those of the Stone Age head hunters of the Southwestern Pacific. In fact, the strong correspondences between the beliefs and practices of these two widely separated societies strongly hint at a widespread primordial belief system combining both skull rituals and initiatory homosexuality. Because of the light that these beliefs could shed on their sexual traditions, it is worth examining the customs of the Indo-European in this regard in more detail.

Stone Age Cults of the Early Indo-Europeans

The Indo-European tribes were widely known in the ancient world for their head-hunting.* The Celts, the first Indo-European group to establish themselves as a power in western Europe, emerged as a recognizable people near the end of the second millennium B.C., and were at the peak of their dominance toward the end of the first millennium, when their territory stretched from Galatia in Asia Minor, across northern Italy, into Switzerland, Gaul (France), Spain and the British Isles. Diodorus Siculus, a Sicilian-born Greek historian of the first century, B.C. described Celtic warriors as formidable:

> Their aspect is terrifying.... They are very tall in stature, with rippling muscles under clear white skin. Their hair is blond, but not naturally so: they bleach it, to this day, artificially, washing it in lime and combing it back from their foreheads. They look like wood-demons, their hair thick and shaggy like a horse's mane. Some of these are clean-shaven, but others, especially those of high rank, shave their cheeks but leave a moustache that covers the whole mouth."

The warriors adorned themselves with jewelry, gold necklaces, and most particularly the famous torcs, large rings of gold or brass fitting closely around their necks. And, Diodorus added, "They go naked into battle."[10]

The Celts were fierce warriors who struck terror among the inhabitants of the regions they invaded, not least because of their reputation for head-hunting. According to Diodorus,

> they cut off the heads of enemies slain in battle and attach them to the necks of their horses. The blood-stained spoils they hand over to their attendants and carry off as booty, while striking up a paean and singing a song of victory. And they nail up these first fruits upon their houses. They embalm in cedar oil the heads of the most distinguished enemies, and preserve them carefully in a chest and display them with pride to strangers, saying that for this head one of their ancestors, or his father, or the man himself refused the offer of a large sum of money.[11]

The collection of the heads of enemies by Celtic warriors was not the mere accumulation of trophies of war, for the symbolism associated with the head was central to Celtic religious mythology, and represented divinity, otherworldly powers and fertility. To the Celts the head symbolized the very essence of being, and consequently something that could exist in its own right. In possessing someone's head, one could take ownership over that person's power and spirit.[12] The similarity of these Celtic beliefs to those of New Guinea tribesmen is striking. Like Melanesian warriors and tribesmen in the Amazon Basin, the Celts often posted the heads of defeated enemies on their houses or on stakes around their camps.

To take advantage of the power residing in the heads of their most distinguished foes, the Celts would clean out the skulls, gild them, and use them as sacred drinking cups in religious rituals. This was the fate of Lucius Postumius, a Roman consul whose army met catastrophic defeat at the hands of the Celts in the third century B.C. As described by the Roman historian Livy, "the (Romans) got no report of the disaster until some Gallic horsemen came in sight, with heads hanging at their horses' breasts, or fixed on their lances, and singing their

---

*Few are aware that head-hunting was widely practiced in Eurasia in prehistoric times, and extended back at least to the time of the Neanderthals. There was apparently a widespread belief that the life-power of a man, resident in the skull, could be obtained by eating the brains of other men. A Neanderthal skull has been found which shows a deliberate breaking away of the bone at the base of the skull almost identical to those made by contemporary Melanesian tribesmen for the purpose of extracting and consuming the brain. Similarly treated skulls have been found from Stone Age sites in Southeast Asia as well as in recent times among primitive tribes ranging from Africa to Borneo. Several skulls from Saxony in northern Germany, dating from around 2000 B.C., which have similar openings broken into the base, provide evidence that head-hunting for the purpose of eating the brain survived in Europe into late prehistory. Weston La Barre, Muelos: A Stone Age Superstition about Sexuality (New York: Columbia University Press, 1984), pages 14–15.

customary songs of triumphs." As for the unfortunate Lucius Postumius, "(the Celts) stripped his body, cut off his head, and carried their spoils in triumph to the most hallowed of their temples. There they cleaned out the head, as their custom, and gilded the skull, which thereafter served them as a holy vessel to pour libations from and as a drinking cup for their priests and other temple attendants."[13]

Other early Indo-European peoples had similar practices. The Greek historian Herodotus, in the fifth century B.C., wrote of the Scythians: "As for their enemies they overcome, each man cuts off his enemy's head, and carries it away to his house where he impales it on a tall pole and sets it standing high above the dwelling, above the smoke-vent for the most part. These heads, they say, are set aloft to guard the whole house."[14] Like the Celts, the Scythians would make sacred cups out of the skulls of enemies, so as to drink of their strength and power. Another classical writer, Plutarch, reported that warriors of the Germanic tribes likewise cut off the heads of their opponents and drank from cups made from their skulls, in order to "imbibe their courage."[15]

It is important to note that the motive underlying these practices was not to debase the victim, or give vent to hatred of an enemy, but to bring substantial supernatural benefit to the drinker.[16] A skull found at Pompeii, mounted in precious metals, had on it the inscription in Greek, "drink and you shall live for many years," implying that longevity could be enhanced by drinking of the life-stuff of the skull. This superstition has even survived in modern times, in the familiar toasts, "to your health," or, in northern Europe, "skål," which derives from "skull." In fact, in many of the Indo-European languages the words for cup and skull are closely related. The Anglo-Saxon *hafala* and the Sanskrit *kapala* mean both cup and skull; the Scandinavian *skoal* means both skull and drinking bowl; the Scottish *skull* means goblet for liquor; the French *tete*, which means head, also means a pottery bowl. According to the anthropologist Weston La Barre, the association of "cup" and "skull" is so universal in Indo-European languages that it must go back to the original undivided Indo-European stock, which would date it back to the fourth millennium B.C.[17]

The mystical importance of drinking from skulls eventually became transferred to cups, which is seen in the ritual significance attached to drinking wine or mead in the warrior's societies of the various Indo-European tribes, in which only initiated members were allowed to drink. Whereas among Melanesian head-hunting tribes, the acquisition of the skull of an enemy by an initiate conferred on him membership in the brotherhood of warriors, among the Indo-European group, the consumption of an alcoholic beverage from a ritual cup, the mystical successor to the skull, signaled a young man's accession to membership in adult male society.[18]

Artifacts dating from Neolithic times have been found which underscore the life-enhancing symbolism of the cup/skull by combining it with another symbol of the life force, the phallus. In archeological sites in southern Europe from the Adriatic to the Danube, hundreds of drinking cups have been found with representations of phalluses for stems.[19] The phallus, whose symbolism in fertility is obvious, is one of the most common mythic images found from Stone Age cultures. Phallic representations have been found from all periods throughout prehistoric Europe and Asia. Among the Celts, the phallus, as an avenue of the life force, had a strong association with the head, thought to be the repository of semen, which was in turn believed to be present in the brain matter. A statue of a Celtic deity from France, with a phallus coming out of the top of the head, illustrates this belief. Likewise, antlers or horns growing directly from the life force-containing head are viewed as signs of phallic power and fertility. The annual growth and shedding of stag antlers was, accordingly, associated by the Celts with fertility and reproductive potency, and with the seasonal rebirth and immortality they saw in nature. The connection between antlers or horns and fertility is also widespread, found among peoples as diverse as the American Indians, and also the ancient Chinese, who used ground animal horns as a fertility potion. One of the principal Celtic gods, Cernunnus, the lord of fertility and "master of animals," is depicted with deer's antlers. The similarity of Cernunnus to the antler-crowned shaman in the famous cave painting, the *Dancing Sorcerer of Trois Frères*, which dates from 18,000 B.C., is suggestive of the deep Paleolithic origins of these associated beliefs.[20]

The phallic power evoked by horns growing out of the head is also seen in the horned helmets which Celtic warriors often wore into battle, which no doubt added to their ferocious appearance.[21] Similar horned helmets were worn by Scandinavian and Germanic warriors, who shared the Celts' beliefs about the connection between the life force, the skull and the phallus. Bronze statuettes of gods wearing horned helmets have been found dating from 1000 B.C. in Sweden and Denmark. The prominence of phallic imagery among the Scandinavians is evident in rock carvings from southern Sweden dating from the same period, which show horned warriors with swords, axes and blowing battle trumpets, all with erect phalluses.[22] Like the Celts, the Scandinavians viewed the phallus as a symbol not only of fertility, but of power, and so associated the phallus with swords, lances, axes and plows — all implements of manly power and accomplishment. The association of the phallus with divine power is seen in a statute of the Nordic god Frey, from the 11th century, which has a phallic-shaped head. Even after Scandinavia was Christianized in the 12th century, large phallic shaped pillars continued to be erected outside churches in the region.[23]

Homosexual Initiation

Considering the remarkable consistency between the beliefs of the Stone Age tribes of Melanesia and those of the early Indo-European tribes about the mystical power residing in the skull and transmitted through the phallus, it should not be surprising to also find evidence of a tradition of homosexual initiation among Indo-European warriors comparable to the ritual homosexuality of New Guinea tribesmen. Like their head-hunting counterparts in Melanesia, the early Indo-European warriors are believed to have initiated young males into their warrior societies through the framework of homosexual relationships between the young initiates and adult warriors. Whether these sexual customs were related to the same mystical beliefs which underlay their skull cults and phallic worship is impossible to confirm. Because these warriors did not have writing, and actually viewed as unmanly the need to commit anything to writing rather than relying on memory, they left no written records to shed light on their traditions. However, Greek and Roman writers have left references to these sexual customs, and while they are no more than brief glimpses, they do provide enough details to establish without doubt the basic initiatory context of the homosexual relationships they describe.

The fourth-century A.D. Roman writer Ammianus Marcellinus described homosexual relationships between youth and adult warriors among the Taifali, a Germanic tribe related to the Goths. The Taifali, who at the time of Marcellinus' observations lived along the northeastern frontiers of the Roman Empire, had been causing considerable problems for the Romans because of their repeated incursions into Roman territory. Marcellinus became familiar with the Taifali when he was posted as a soldier in the region. Their youth, Marcellinus wrote, remained in these homosexual relationships until they became adults and had killed a boar or a bear, a typical initiatory ordeal. Similar homosexual customs were described by the late Roman historian Procopius in the sixth century A.D. among another Germanic tribe, the

Heruli.[24] Among the Heruli, the youth, who were called *douloi,* literally "slaves," had to serve their elders and fight without a shield until they proved their courage in battle. The use of terms such as "slave," and "servant," when used for young men and warriors, was typical of Germanic men's societies. Such a distinction in status between novices, who were being tested for demonstrations of courage, and adult warriors is also characteristic of initiation.[25]

Among many Germanic tribes, who were ruled by a land-owning warrior elite, land was not divided upon the death of the father, but went to the oldest son, and only the son who inherited his father's land could marry. The other sons left home as adolescents, and began initiation into the *mannerbunde,* the men's society of their tribe. As part of their initiation, they were trained as warriors, and had to undergo hazardous ordeals and tests. If they passed, they dedicated themselves to the god Wotan and became a member of the mannerbunde. These young warriors wore animal skins, engaged in sword dancing and spent their time "hunting, fighting, robbing, drinking and in other idleness." In fighting they were known to intimidate their opponents with ecstatic frenzies, which may have been drug-induced. If through the death of a brother they were able to inherit the family homestead, they left the mannerbunde, and only then could they get married. If not, the warriors remained bachelors for life. Because in Germanic tribal society the women were expected to adhere to strict rules of chastity, and were punished severely for violating them, heterosexual outlets for the warriors were virtually nonexistent. As a result, homosexuality in the form of institutionalized pederasty of the sort described by Ammianus Marcellinus and Procopius is understood to have been the rule within the Germanic warrior societies.[26]

Remarkably similar societies of unmarried warriors existed in Norse and Celtic society. The members of the Norse warrior societies also dedicated themselves to their god, Odin, dressed likewise in the skins of wolves or bears, and were said to fight with the furor of one possessed of the spirits of those animals. The English word *berserk,* in fact, comes from the Old Norse *berserkir,* which means "having a bear garment," a reference to the frenzy of these animal-skinned fighters. Like the Germanic peoples, Celtic society was ruled by a warrior aristocracy supported by a farming peasantry who gave them allegiance in return for protection. A youth of the Celtic warrior elite entered initiation to the men's society, called the *fianna,* at the age of 14, and upon completion of his initiation was given an animal name.[27] The newly initiated warrior would join his comrades at common meals, where the choicest cuts of meat went to the most illustrious of the fighters. Frenzied fighting is also described among Celtic warriors, which, according to Diodorus Siculus, was the feature of the Celts that most terrified their opponents.[28] While the references by classical writers to homosexual relationship between Celtic warriors and youth are not detailed enough to be able to establish an initiatory context, the pederastic relations that they described would almost certainly have occurred within the fianna, the principal social venue of Celtic warriors. Indeed, given the close similarity of Celtic and Germanic tribal customs, and the well documented esteem of the Celts for male homosexuality, it would have been odd if the Celts did not practice a similar type of initiatory homosexuality.

The ancient writers leave no doubt as to the Celtic warriors' enthusiasm for homosexuality in general. According to Aristotle, the Celts held homosexuality in high esteem[29] and publicly honored homosexual relations.[30] Diodorus writes that despite the charm of Celtic women, "The men will have nothing to do with them. They long instead for the embrace of one of their own sex, lying on animal skins and tumbling around with a lover on either side. It is particularly surprising that they attach no value to either dignity or decency, offering their bodies to each other without further ado. This was not regarded as at all harmful; on the contrary, if they were rejected in their approaches, they felt insulted."[31] Celtic youth evidently shared the attitudes of their elders. The Greek writer Strabo described the young Celts of Gaul as "shamelessly generous with their boyish charms."[32]

In the Celtic warrior societies one can see the same cult of male beauty that holds up males as sexual objects among Melanesian tribes. The Celtic warriors took great care in their physical appearance, and, according to Strabo, "tried to avoid becoming fat or potbellied, and they punished any boy whose waist was larger than the standards they set."[33] They adorned their muscular bodies with gold arm bands and their famous torcs, and even went to the extent of dying their hair. Once an adolescent left home to begin initiation to the men's society, he was in the constant company of other males. These young men learned riding, swordsmanship, hunting, and drinking, all in the company of others of their own sex. It is natural that these sons of the warrior elite of the tribe would see each other as the only suitable companions. In a society where great emphasis is placed on male virtues and achievement, it is easy for what is masculine to become associated with what is erotic, for admiration of masculine attainment in others to become mixed with desire, and for comradely affection to acquire erotic dimensions.

Love Among Comrades

The lack of sexual inhibitions that the Celtic warriors displayed toward each other amid such an atmosphere of masculine eroticism suggests that homosexuality was not limited to pederastic relations, and that love between comrades was also a part of Celtic warrior life. In fact, it is the warriors, not the youth, whom Diodorus describes as "offering their bodies to each other without further ado." Such a relationship between warrior peers even appears in an Irish Celtic saga of the late first millennium. The hero, in explaining why he does not want to fight his foster-brother and former comrade-in-arms, says, "Fast friends, forest companions, we made one bed, and slept one sleep."[34]

Sexual bonds between adult warriors were common among some of the other Indo-European groups as well. The Roman writer Lucian, in the second half of the first century A.D., described lifelong bonds between Scythian warriors whose union was recognized in a formal ceremony. Called "blood-brothers," these relationships were known for the extraordinary devotion the partners showed for each other. Lucian relates the description a Scythian gave of these relationships:

> We consider appropriate to [these relationships] what you do in regard to marriage — wooing for a long time and doing everything similar so that we might not fail to obtain the friend, or be rejected. And when a friend has been preferred to all others, there are contracts for this and the most solemn oath, both to live together and to die, if necessary, for each other, which we do. From the point at which we have both cut our fingers and let the blood run into a chalice, dipped the tips of our swords in it, and both drunk from it together, there is nothing that could dissolve what is between us. It is allowed to enter into such contracts at most three times, since a man who had many such relations would seem to us like a promiscuous and adulterous woman, and we would not consider that his devotion was as strong if it was divided among many affections.

Herodotus, writing five hundred years earlier, had also described these ceremonies among the Scythians, evidence that blood-brother relationships were a deeply engrained tradition among these fierce warriors.[35]

Blood-brother relationships also existed among Scandinavian warriors. A blood-brother ceremony, comparable to that described for Scythian warriors, is described in the Nordic *Saga of Gisli Sursson*. In this ceremony, a long strip of turf is cut in such a way that both ends remain attached to the ground. In the center of the cut, a spear is placed to lift the turf above the ground. The two men then crouch underneath the turf, and each cuts a vein and lets the blood run into the soil under the turf, mixing blood and soil. The blood-brothers then kneel and swear to avenge each other, calling on the gods as witness. The Danish psychiatrist Thorkil Vanggaard, in describing this union, has noted the symbolism in the ceremony: "By going under the turf, which is fast to the ground, they pass, as it were, through an opening in the earth, thereby being reborn as brothers. Mixing their blood in the soil makes them one in flesh and blood."[36]

There is evidence that these blood-brother relationships among Scandinavians may have very ancient origins. The region of Denmark was invaded about 2000 B.C. by the Battle-Axe people, the Indo-European ancestors of the Scandinavians, who subdued the indigenous Neolithic population then living in the area. The Battle-Axe people brought the horse to Denmark, and also a new burial custom in which the dead were buried singly or in pairs. In the double graves, remains have been found of men and women, but also of two men buried together. According to the Danish archeologist P.V. Glob, the burial of two men together in the same grave and in the same position as man and woman is an indication that there was a sexual union between the two men, that they were blood-brothers.[37] Also noteworthy is a rock carving from Bohuslan, in southern Sweden, dating from around 1000 B.C., which shows two adult males engaged in anal intercourse.[38] Since rock carvings were not graffiti, but usually carried ritual significance, the drawing may have been an indication that blood-brother ceremonies uniting two warriors were carried out at that site. At a minimum, the drawing of the pair, amid illustrations of other warriors carrying battle implements, demonstrates that homosexual relationships between warriors was a significant enough aspect of warrior life in Scandinavia three thousand years ago that they would be commemorated in rock carvings.

Among the Norse, the blood-brother relationships were lifelong unions between men who may have been predominantly homosexual. In *The Blood-Brother's Saga*, the story is told of Thorgeir and Thormod, two warriors who never married. In fact, in the saga it states unambiguously of Thorgeir that "he cared little for women." Thormod, on the other hand sought their company, evidenced by a poem he sings in praise of a girl named Kolbrune, but the saga never states that he ever had carnal knowledge of a woman. Instead, the opposite seems to be the case, that he was never able to involve himself with a woman, a fact he states himself.[39]

Though Nordic and Germanic warriors seemed prone to homosexuality, there was at the same time a tremendous stigma attached to being *argr*, that is, allowing oneself to be used "as a woman." The insult was so powerful that the use of the term was outlawed under later Norse, Icelandic and Swedish law. Accordingly, men could be humiliated by forcibly subjecting them to anal penetration.[40] Thorkil Vanggaard, in his analysis of the blood-brother relationships, says that sexual bonds between warriors were possible only when they were established on the basis of equality, the equality serving to maintain undisturbed the dignity and self-esteem of both parties. Such a balance is also critical in the peer-bond relationships between Asmat warriors of New Guinea, in which neither partner can assert sexual dominance over the other, and sexual relations are always reciprocal.[41] When the balance is upset, the relationships cannot survive, and that is what occurred with the blood-brothers Thorgeir and Thormod. In the saga, when Thorgeir in a fit of prideful boasting asked his partner, "Which of us would overcome the other if we two fought together?" Thormod answered, "That I know not; but I know that this question of yours will put an end to our comradeship and fellowship, and that we can no longer go along together." Thorgeir said, "I had not thought at all of trying to see who was the better man of us two." Thormod replied, "You were surely thinking of it while you spoke, and this will part our fellowship," which indeed was the outcome. Vanggaard states that given the attitudes of the time, Thorgeir's question was the equivalent of asking, "Which of us, do you think, would be able to make the other one argr?" which was enough to destroy the relationship. It is a testament to the respect for their blood-brother's oath, that when, later, Thorgeir was killed, Thormod, in spite of their long separation from each other, went to battle to avenge his death.[42]

The Stigma of Argr and the Claim That the Germanic Tribes Condemned Homosexuality

It goes without saying that Indo-European warriors prided themselves on their virility and their ability to prevail over another, whether in war or in sex. But the warriors' contempt for one who willingly accepted the passive role in homosexual copulation was not merely the machismo of warriors, but an attitude that had much deeper roots in the closely related Germanic and Nordic cultures. The enormous stigma attached to being argr is thought to stem from a division in Germanic and Nordic societies between the warrior class and the farmers, the two principal divisions of Indo-European society. The split between the warrior class and the farmers was reflected in a division in the gods between the Aesir, the gods who were associated with the arms-bearing activities of hunting, warfare and government rule, and the Vanir, the gods of fertility, prosperity and sensual pleasure.

There is evidence that in early Germanic society, fertility rites, which are religious rituals of primary importance to early farming populations, were officiated by shaman-like transvestite priests, and that their rituals involved cult homosexuality.[43] Herodotus, in the fifth century B.C., described similar transvestite shamans among the Scythians, Indo-European cousins of the Germans. It appears that the Vanir would have been associated with just such a farming society. Among the rituals of the Vanir cult were magical techniques known as *seidr*, which evidently involved passive homosexual acts. In a Nordic saga relating a war between the Aesir and the Vanir, Freya, one of the Vanir, came to live with the Aesir as a hostage following a negotiated settlement. While there, she taught Odin, one of the chief Aesir gods, the seidr techniques, about which the saga states, "it was by this means that he could fathom the fate of men and of events still to come, and also to speak to men of their deaths or misfortunes or illnesses, and also to take away from men their intelligence or strength in order to give it to others. But the use of this magic is accompanied by so great a degree of effeminacy that men were of the opinion that they could not give themselves up to it without shame."[44]

The description of the rituals required to invoke the magic, involving "effeminacy" of such a character that the warriors could not practice it without "shame" strongly implies that the magic involved passive homosexual acts similar to those employed in the rituals of Native American two-spirits and the transvestite priest of Mesopotamian rituals. Such passive homosexuality would, of course, have been anathema to Germanic warriors whose world-view would have been shaped by their patriarchal ideology and powerful masculine deities. The association of effeminacy and passive homosexuality with magic and soothsaying, which has also been found among North American Indians with respect to their two-spirits, and the ancient Mesopotamians with respect to their third-gender priests, suggests that the seidr beliefs derived from a common Paleolithic ancestry. The degree of repugnance felt by Nordic warriors toward these rites may be seen in an episode in another saga, the *Heimsrkingla*. When Haraldr learns that one of his sons, Rognvaldr, has become a seidr master, he sends another son, who "burned his brother Rognvaldr together with eighty *seidmenn*, and this action was much praised."[45] In addition to the role of the warriors' patriarchal sexual attitudes in shaping the disgust they felt for males taking the passive sexual role, the warriors' response was very likely reinforced by a division in social and cultural attitudes between the warrior class and the farming class that had its roots in the early history of the Indo-Europeans in Europe.

As we saw in the previous chapter, the rituals and mythology of early Neolithic farming societies from Europe to Central Asia primarily revolved around the worship of the mother-goddess and her associated fertility cults.[46] It is probable that in most places the rituals would have been overseen by two-spirit-like shaman/priests, and that such rituals would have most likely prevailed in the ancestral motherland from which the early Indo-European tribes originated. With the rise of the warrior culture that accompanied the movement of Indo-Europeans out of their Neolithic homeland, increasing emphasis would have been placed on the masculine deities who were the patrons who supported their military efforts. This would have inevitably produced tension with the adherents of the mother-goddess and her fertility cults, who would have been mostly the members of the agricultural class of the society, which though reduced in status, were still nonetheless crucial to the survival of the tribes. A parallel development can be seen in the ancient Mesopotamian cultures, in which the goddess worship that dominated ritual of the earlier periods was supplanted in importance with the ascension of the male deities brought in by conquering Bronze Age warrior peoples. A more extreme example of this divergence can be seen in the ancient Israelites, who with the pre-eminence of the patriarchal Yahweh cult, suppressed the mother-goddess worship of earlier times, eventually condemning her passive homosexual attendants as idolatrous.

The legend of the war between the Aesir and the Vanir is thought by a number of scholars to be a mythical portrayal of the armed conquest of Northern Europe by Indo-European tribes, with the Aesir representing the conquering Indo-European warriors, and the Vanir, the goddess-worshiping native agricultural peoples. By the time the Indo-European invaders reached Northern Europe, the goddess worship and fertility rites associated with their Neolithic past would most likely have been long forgotten, while the worship of the agricultural communities they conquered would have still focused on the goddess and her fertility rites. Linguistic analysis of early Indo-Germanic religious terms associated with each group of gods, in fact, supports the view of a cultural and ethnic division between Indo-European speaking warrior conquerors, associated with the Aesir, and goddess-worshipping farmer natives, associated with the Vanir. As the society developed and evolved under the rule of the warrior class, a common culture and language would have developed, without necessarily replacing ancestral beliefs and attitudes specific to each social class. Thus, beliefs and rituals originating in the distant Neolithic past of the farming class could have survived under the rule of the warrior aristocracy who most likely would have had little interest in the rituals of their social inferiors and, like the warriors in the *Heimsrkingla*, would have felt contempt for sexual rites they could not comprehend.

The tensions between the warrior elite and the agricultural class may also have been exacerbated by the contempt warriors felt for farmers, who were often reluctant to go to war because they were needed at home to tend their crops and livestock. The Roman historian Tacitus wrote that during annual fertility rites of the Suiones, a Scandinavian agricultural people who had a peace-loving reputation, all weapons were to be put away and warfare was prohibited for the duration of the rites. Such a scenario would have been, of course, anathema to the full-time warriors of the Germanic ruling class, whose very *raison d'être* was fighting, and who would have regarded the pacifist attitudes of the farmers as cowardly.[47] So the contempt for one who willingly takes the passive role in homosexual copulation reflected an age-old antipathy of the warriors for the despised rituals of the agriculturalists, epitomized by their transvestite priests, whose values they saw as unmanly and as the polar opposite of their own.

Whatever disapproval there was for a warrior being known for offering to take the passive role in sex, there was evidently no stigma attached to taking the active role in homosexuality. In one of the *Edda*, the great cycle of Nordic mythic poems, a warrior, Sinfjotli, in an angry dispute before a battle, heaps accusations on his opponent, Gudmundr, for being argr. Sinfjotli calls Gudmundr a disgusting hag who offered himself to other warriors "for love's pleasure." In a later stanza, Sinfjotli says all of the *einherjar*, Odin's warriors in Valhalla, fought with each other over the right to make love to Gudmundr. Finally he states that Gudmundr was pregnant with nine wolf cubs, and that he, Sinfjotli, was the father. While the accusations that Gudmundr offered himself for sex to other warriors was a grievous insult, Sinfjotli's claim that he himself had fathered Gudmundr's wolf cubs shows that there was clearly no disgrace attached to playing the active role in sex with another male. To the contrary, it was something to boast about. And Sinfjotli certainly implied no disrespect for the masculinity of Odin's warriors in Valhalla over their purported competition for Gudmundr's favors.[48] In another saga, in which revenge was sought on a disloyal priest, Bjorn, and his mistress, Thorunnr, "it was decided to put Thorunnr into bed with every buffoon, and to do that to Bjorn the priest, which was considered no less dishonorable."[49] Again, there was no dishonor to the warriors who engaged in homosexual intercourse with Bjorn to carry out his punishment.

It is also clear that there was no stigma attached to one of lesser rank than a warrior, such as a youth, who hadn't yet risen to warrior status, who took the passive role in homosexual intercourse. The accounts by Ammianus and Procopius of the pederastic relations between the warriors and youth of the Taifali and Heruli confirm this. After living for a period of time in sexual submission to warriors, the youth were honored by elevation to warrior status once they had successfully completed their initiation. Another illustration of the lack of concern over passive homosexuality in youth appears in an anecdote that Procopius related about the capture of Rome by the Vandals. Procopius wrote that that these Germanic warriors selected from their tribe three hundred boys of good birth, "whose beards had not yet grown, but who had just come of age," and offered them as house slaves for Roman patricians. These Roman men were more than willing to accept the services of these good looking young males, no doubt because in accordance to longstanding Roman customs, these services would also have included the youths' sexual submission to their masters. On a predetermined date, the youthful servants rose early in the morning and killed their masters, facilitating the Vandals' capture of the city. It is evident that the Vandals' disapproval of passivity in males, reported by the Roman writer Salvian a century earlier, did not extend to sexual passivity among their youth.[50]

An observation of the Roman writer Tacitus has sometimes been used to claim the Germanic tribes condemned homosexuality. Tacitus stated that the Germans drowned in swamps those who were *ignavos et imbelles et corpore infames*, usually translated as "slothful and unwarlike and infamous in body." The latter expression has been taken by some to mean passive homosexuals, perhaps those above a certain age. However, this seems to be a superficial reading which comports nicely with the anti-homosexual prejudice of its adherents, including the Nazis, who used the passage to justify their persecution of homosexuals. To apply the phrase, "those of infamous bodies" to homosexuals would not have made any sense to readers of the period in which Tacitus wrote, the Roman Empire of the first century A.D., where homosexuality was taken for granted, participated in by a vast majority of the population at some point in their lives, and where male homosexual prostitutes were so well established that their earnings were taxed and they had their own national holiday.[51] A description of homosexuals as *corpore infames,* in fact, resembles more the anti-homosexual preaching of ascetic Christian clerics of later periods. The phrase more likely was meant by Tacitus to refer to the deformed, or those who avoided military service by maiming themselves,[52] which would be consistent with the first two categories of individuals named by Tacitus, the slothful and unwarlike, and who would be people who would have no place in the rigidly ordered scheme of things contemplated by the Germanic military ethic.

The Shared Homosexual Customs of the Indo-Europeans in Europe

Evidence about the customs and practices of these Indo-European groups, inhabiting a vast area from the Black Sea to northern Europe, reveals a remarkable uniformity across a broad expanse of time. These tribes without exception shared a social organization led by a warrior elite infused with a restless, warlike temperament, worshiped common deities, and held to ritual beliefs and practices from skull cults to phallic worship that can be traced to a distant Stone Age ancestry. Sexual relations between youth and warriors were described by ancient observers over a span of a thousand years among Scythian, Celtic and Germanic tribes from the Black Sea to northern Europe. Likewise, sexual relationships between Indo-European warrior comrades are demonstrated by archeological evidence as early as 2000 B.C. in Northern Europe, were described by Herodotus among the Scythians north of the Black Sea in the fifth century B.C., again by Lucian in the first century A.D., were attributed to the Celts by Greek writers from the fifth century B.C. to the first century A.D., and were enshrined in the sagas of the Norse that were passed down through innumerable generations in oral tradition and finally recorded in the early Middle Ages. There is little doubt that these Indo-European peoples inherited their shared traits from common ancestors, and brought them with them in their emigration out of their Neolithic homelands.

Indo-Europeans in the Ancient Middle East

Though the tribes who moved into the forests of northern and western Europe retained much of the character of their Neolithic tribal forebears, the Indo-European groups who invaded the old civilizations of the ancient world assimilated many of the customs of their conquered subjects, with the resulting blend producing among their descendents the distinctively cosmopolitan cultures that were seen among the Hittites, Persians, Greeks, Romans and Aryan Indians.

While tribal groups related to the Neolithic ancestors of the Indo-Europeans were probably responsible for many of the raids during the third millennium B.C. that the ancient Mesopotamians blamed on "barbarians from the north,"[53] the first Indo-European people to establish a significant presence in the ancient Middle East were the Hittites. The most prominent of the Indo-Europeans in the ancient Middle East, the Hittites first appeared as a force in Anatolia in the late third millennium B.C., about the time of the establishment of the Amorite rule in Babylon. The Hittites quickly established themselves as a power in the area, and by 1800 B.C. they had captured the city of Hatussa, which became their capital, and had extended their rule over most of Anatolia, expanding in the following centuries down into northern Syria.

The Hittites, like other Indo-European groups, were skilled warriors, who perfected a method of producing carbonized iron, a major military advance, which led to the development of the Iron Age. In the early 16th century B.C. they captured the Babylonian capital, and it was the Hittites who stopped the expansion of the Egyptian empire under Ramses III into the Middle East. After this peak the Hittites' empire gradually declined, with western Anatolia coming under the dominance of the Indo-European kingdoms of Phrygia and Lydia, and the lands along the Aegean coast being colonized and settled by Mycenaean Greeks. By 1200 B.C. the Hittite capital at Hattusa was overthrown by the Phrygians leaving only northern Syria under Hittite control. After the turmoil of the 12th and 11th centuries, which saw the overthrow of traditional power structures throughout the Middle East, the Hittite kingdom dwindled until the 8th century B.C., when it was absorbed into the expanding Assryian Empire.

What is known of Hittite life is derived from archeological ruins, artifacts, and written tablets. It was only in the early 20th century, when Hittite ruins in Turkey began to be excavated, that the prominence of Hittite power and culture in the ancient Middle East began to be appreciated. Numerous clay tablets have been recovered inscribed with the cuneiform script of the Mesopotamians which the Hittites borrowed and adapted to their own language to record their laws. Some of these laws provide insight into the sexual life and attitudes of the Hittites. Like the Code of Hammurabi, whose influence can be seen in Hittite laws, there is no prohibition against homosexual behavior.[54] There is a law prohibiting father-son incest, a stricture that seems to imply that homosexual relations between men and youths were common. Since incest laws, by their nature, are intended to prohibit among kin behavior that is acceptable with others, there would be no need for an incest law prohibiting homosexual relationship between fathers and sons if adult-youth relationships were not known among other non-related pairs. Fragments of a Hittite play have been found which seem to deal with these sorts of pederastic relationships.[55]

Another law has been interpreted as regulating homosexual relationships between adults and youths, though that reading is controversial among scholars. The standard translation of the text in question reads, "If a slave gives the bride-price to a free youth and takes him to dwell in his household as husband (of his daughter), no one shall surrender him." The phrase in parentheses, "of his daughter," was inserted into the text by the translator, E. Neufeld, who seemingly could not accept the homosexual implications of the text as it originally appeared. Without the added phrase, the law appears to protect the rights of a slave who purchases a sexual relationship with a free youth. Neufeld, himself, wrote, "It would seem that such a relationship among free men did not require any special legal provisions." The custom of purchasing a male sex partner by a free male was apparently so common that no law was needed, but that granting the privilege to a male slave required a law.[56] Neufeld's insertion of the phrase into the text, which completely alters its meaning, has been sharply criticized by other scholars.[57] Nonetheless, many academic Hittologists have accepted Neufeld's version.[58] Despite this controversy, it is generally agreed by scholars of the period not only that the Hittites "did not object to homosexuality,"[59] but that "homosexuality was a practice well known to the Hittite world and culture."[60]

According to Herodotus, homosexual relationships between men and youths were also common among the ancient Persians, the descendants of Indo-Europeans who conquered the region of modern day Iran in the early second millennium B.C. Herodotus attributed the customs to influence from the Greeks, an assertion Plutarch later disputed, and which seems very unlikely considering the prevalence of homosexuality from the earliest periods throughout the region. Recent scholarship has shown that the early Indo-Europeans of Iran had men's associations comparable to warriors' clubs of the other Indo-European groups, within which hierarchical homosexuality may have played a role in the initiation of youths into the ranks of adult warriors.[61] Some scholars, in fact, maintain that early Persian warriors practiced homosexual initiation rites, like other Indo-European groups.[62] In any event, pederastic homosexuality among the Persian ruling class seems to have been well established many centuries before Herodotus wrote of the practices.

Other Indo-Europeans in the Ancient World

By the middle of the second millennium B.C. Indo-European groups had made their presence felt throughout the civilizations of the ancient world. Around 1760 B.C. Indo-Europeans known as Kassites, introducing the use of chariot warfare, invaded the Babylonian Empire ending the rule of the Amorite line of Hammurabi.[63] By 1600 B.C., as Aryan tribes were moving into India, overthrowing the old Indus Valley civilization, another Indo-European people, the Hyksos, took control of Egypt, disrupting fifteen centuries of Pharaonic rule.[64] At about the same time the Indo-European ancestors of the Greeks first appeared in the Aegean, where they quickly established their rule over the indigenous Minoan civilization that had been flourishing in that region for over a thousand years.

While little is known of the sexual practices of the Kassites, Hyksos or Aryans, that is not the case with the Greeks. The extent of the prevalence and social importance of homosexual behavior among the ancient Greeks is so thoroughly documented that it is possible to get a clear picture not only of the character of homosexual relationships in Greek society, but of the important role homosexuality played in that society. Through the perspective provided by Greek homosexuality, which is examined in the next chapter, the fragmentary glimpses we have of homosexual behavior among the other Indo-European peoples can be recognized as revealing a unified pattern of sexual customs and beliefs that seems to have prevailed among all the Indo-European ancestors of modern Europeans.

Conclusion

The sexual practices of the Indo-European tribes represent a further elaboration in the patterns of homosexual behavior displayed among the peoples of the ancient world. These patterns, which are shared by many of the aboriginal cultures surveyed in Chapter 2, are aspects of sexual behavior seemingly universal among the human species, and as such must reflect deeply intrinsic characteristics of human sexuality. The pederastic relationships between warriors and youth seen among the Celts and Germanic tribes, and which were also evidently common among the Hittites and Persians, illustrate the strong predisposition for this type of homosexuality among males. This hierarchical homosexuality has also been observed among numerous aboriginal tribes in recent times, particularly those with a prominent warrior culture. Sexual bonds between peers, seen in the blood-brothers of the Norse and Scythians, which were relationships marked by intense devotion and loyalty to their partners, were also widespread among braves of the North American Indian tribes before their lands were taken over by Europeans, and have been observed in recent times among tribes in the Amazon, Africa and Melanesia. The striking similarities in these patterns of behavior seen among peoples separated by enormous geographic distances and by thousands of years in time could not be coincidental, and strongly imply that they reflect basic characteristics of the inherited sexuality of the human race.

6

Greek Homosexuality:
The Age of Heroes—
Love-Inspired Valor

The pervasive homosexuality in the world of the ancient Greeks is well known, better understood than that of any other ancient people. Abundant evidence shows not only that virtually all male citizens during classical Greece engaged in homosexual relations at some point in their lives, but that homosexuality itself played a major role in society: a sexual relationship between a youth or young man with an older man was, for over a millennium, the primary vehicle for the education of young men of the ruling class in military skills, social values, and literature and the arts. Homosexuality pervaded Greek culture, figured in the decoration on vases, was expressed in love poetry and praised in philosophy. Plato and other Greek philosophers rhapsodized on the virtues of love between men, seeing it as superior to heterosexual love because it was love, not for the propagation of the species, but for its own sake, an avenue to the experience of the highest of ideals. Similarly, love and devotion between warrior-comrades was idealized, and was celebrated in poetry and literature.

The existence of homosexuality among the Greeks was not even acknowledged by classical scholars until Eric Bethe, in 1907, wrote a celebrated article directly addressing the institution of educational homosexuality between adults and youths, an area most other scholars had previously avoided or euphemistically explained away as "Platonic love." Building on the work of the 19th-century German scholar C.O. Mueller, the first modern scholar to frankly discuss the homosexual customs of the Greek, Bethe in his paper compared Greek homosexual customs and beliefs to the initiatory homosexuality of tribal cultures in Melanesia, and wrote that the Greeks, like Melanesian tribesmen, believed the noble qualities of the tutor-lover were passed into the youth in his semen via anal intercourse. Noting the prominence of these ritualized homosexual customs among the Dorian Greeks of Sparta and Crete, and citing classical Greek authors, Bethe argued that this tradition was introduced by tribes of Dorian Greeks who moved into Greece during the 11th century B.C., and spread from the Dorian areas to other Greek regions.[1]

When Bethe's article was published it was greeted with derision by many academic scholars. Typical was Anatol Semenov's reaction, which displayed the religious and cultural bias that until very recently so often infected academic consideration of homosexual issues: "In fact, how then was it possible for such a simple, ... primitive folk like the Dorians already in quite ancient times to have reached such a refinement of moral corruption as to extend the protection of the state to an unnatural vice? This is patent nonsense!"[2] Like Semenov, most other early classicists, if they admitted homosexuality among the Greeks at all, blamed it on influence from what they regarded as the decadent cultures of the ancient Middle East.[3]

So reluctant were scholars in the 18th and 19th centuries to admit among the Greeks, whom they so highly admired, sexual behavior they abhorred that translators of Greek classics routinely censored or rewrote passages dealing with love between members of the same sex — a practice that continued well into the twentieth century.[4] Indeed, most standard histories of the ancient Greeks written before 1950 contain absolutely no references to homosexuality. Considering what is now known about the central role same-sex relationships played in classical Greek society, this omission can be seen as yet another example of the obtuse denial of homosexuality that has been frequently found among scholars, even in the face of overwhelming evidence.[5]

Even as the homosexuality of the Greeks came under more widespread study in the late 20th century, many academic scholars still held on to a restricted view of Greek homosexuality, insisting that it was a limited and peculiar phenomenon of classical Greece, existing only for a specific educational purpose, and that it occurred only among youths and young men for a very limited period of their lives, after which all sexual expression was strictly heterosexual. Perhaps because of the modern Western mindset that can only comprehend sexuality in terms of the heterosexual norms prevailing in Western culture, it seems that these scholars could admit homosexual practices among the Greeks only to the extent they are specifically referred to in laws and social commentaries that are so unambiguous that not even the most Victorian of readers could deny their implication. In effect these scholars were using laws instituted to protect the educational character of homosexual practices, and philosophical treatises and moral commentaries on homosexuality to define the sexual practices that occurred, rather than seeing those documents as a reaction to what was happening in the society. The understanding of sexuality that emerges from such an approach is no more accurate a picture of sexual life in ancient Greece than what could be gleaned of sexual practices in the United States from a reading of state sodomy laws, many of which have forbidden any non-procreative sexual relations, whether between men or between men and women, or religious handbooks on sex, none of which are accurate reflections of what actually occurs in modern Western society.

However, the considerable scholarship that has continued in the area of Greek life and sexuality in the last several decades makes it clear that homosexual behavior was present in Greek culture from the earliest periods of Greek society, and that it was not necessarily restricted to the pedagogical relationships that were so important to the society of classical Greece. Just as the miraculous explosion of art, drama, science, mathematics and philosophy of classical Greece did not appear in isolation, but emerged from a civilization that had been developing in Greece for over a millennium, it is now clear that the homosexual practices on view in Periclean Athens were part of a continuum extending back to the first presence of Indo-Europeans in Greece, and probably much further into the Indo-European tribal origins of the Greeks.

The Early Greeks

In the early second millennium B.C., as Indo-European warrior-peoples began to emerge as a powerful force in the lands across the ancient Middle East, the first Indo-European ancestors of the Greeks arrived on the Greek mainland. Though at that time Greece and the surrounding Aegean Islands had been long populated by a mixture of various Indo-European and Mediterranean peoples,[6] the Indo-European warriors who suddenly appeared in approximately 1600 B.C.[7] quickly established a distinctive presence, first on the mainland, and then, within the next two centuries over the islands of the Aegean and on Crete. Prototypically

Indo-European, these conquerors were of a larger build than the earlier residents, and brought with them a characteristically Indo-European warrior culture, which, combined with their religious and mythical heritage, became the foundation on which later Greek culture would grow. Like the Indo-European Kassites in Babylon and the Hyksos in Egypt, these Indo-Greeks employed chariot warfare in their conquest of the native population, establishing a ruling warrior-aristocracy. Also like their Indo-European cousins in the Middle East, they assimilated many of the religious and cultural elements of the conquered people into their own tradition, thus producing the uniquely Greek culture that grew from their Indo-European roots. These early Greeks were particularly influenced by the venerable culture of Minoan Crete, which had dominated the Aegean for over a thousand years, and adopted many of the artistic, cultural and religious forms of the Minoans. Likewise, the proto-Indo-European language spoken by these conquerors quickly developed, under the influence of the indigenous Aegean languages, into the unique form we know as the Greek language.[8]

As their Hittite neighbors were reaching the peak of their power and prestige, the small principalities that had emerged from the conquering tribes of mainland Greece experienced rapid increases in wealth, a flowering of culture, and the development of elaborate government organization, with palace bureaucracies supplanting the traditional rule of the Indo-European warrior-aristocracy. The most prominent of these principalities, Mycenae, soon achieved dominance over the rest, thereby giving its name to the people and culture of that period. In the same period, the early Greeks spread throughout the Eastern Mediterranean, developing a presence as traders, and carrying back with them to Greece cultural influences from the ancient kingdoms of Mesopotamia, Asia Minor, and Egypt. In approximately 1450 B.C., not long after the Minoan civilization was weakened by the catastrophic volcanic explosion that destroyed much of the Island of Thera (modern day Santorini), the Mycenaean Greeks took over the island of Crete, setting up a ruler in the palace at Knossos. In the following century the Mycenaeans continued the expansion of their trade, spurring colonization, first in the eastern Mediterranean at Rhodes and Cyprus, and later in the western Mediterranean.[9]

A characteristic of Indo-European rulers of this period was the close relations they cultivated and maintained with other Indo-European rulers, in contrast to the traditional monarchies, like those in Egypt and Babylon, who ruled in imperial isolation with little personal contact with other rulers. The Hittites in Anatolia, the Kassites and Mittani in Mesopotamia and the Hyksos in Egypt all maintained ties with each other and with the Mycenaeans. Indo-European rulers not only exchanged lavish gifts, but also sisters and daughters in marriage. Thus, the historian James Breasted has called this Late Bronze Age period "the first international civilization."[10]

The Mycenaean Greeks maintained especially close relations with their Indo-European neighbors across the Aegean Sea in Anatolia, particularly the Hittites. The Greeks carried on extensive trade with the Hittites, exchanged ambassadors, and young Greek princes were sent to the royal Hittite court at Hattusas to study chariot warfare. In addition to the close commercial and political interaction between the Mycenaeans and the Indo-Europeans of Anatolia, there were close cultural ties. A number of early Greek myths show strong association with Anatolian traditions. A Greek myth relating the divine succession of kingships, set to writing by the poet Hesiod in the eighth century B.C., has close parallels with an earlier Hittite myth in which exact counterparts to Greek gods are found among the Hittite divinities. Several Greek myths depicting homosexual love involve heroes of apparent Anatolian origins.[11]

Most of what is known of the Mycenaean Greeks comes from archeological ruins and their treasure stocked shaft graves, which attest not only to their warrior culture, but their success as traders and conquerors. While evidence of their military success is abundant, little is known of their day to day lives. Numerous tablets have been discovered inscribed in the Proto-Greek language of the Mycenaeans, but, except for an enumeration of gods and heroes, they contain mostly military and palace inventories — lists of horses, chariots and the like — and provide little or no evidence of their cultural life or sexual practices. However, given their close relationship to the Hittites, their ethnic cousins across the Aegean in Anatolia, with whom they shared a common cultural and mythical tradition, it is reasonable to assume that the Mycenaeans would have shared the Hittites' homosexual customs, as well. It is quite likely, therefore, that homosexuality, most probably in the form of age-differentiated sexual relationships between older and younger males, which seem to have been common among the Hittites and which were later documented among other Indo-European groups, was also a familiar part of Mycenaean life.

The Downfall of the Mycenaeans and the Arrival of the Dorian Greeks

The late thirteenth century B.C. brought a period of enormous tumult to the civilizations of the eastern Mediterranean and the Near East. After a rule of nearly four centuries, the Mycenaean world was destroyed by a series of invasions which left their cities in ruins and their populace scattered. Similar convulsions resulted in the overthrow of ruling dynasties throughout the Middle East, and even reached into Egypt, where hieroglyphic records blamed the disorders on invasions of "the Sea Peoples." While the exact origin of these mysterious invaders has never been determined, their arrival and the destruction that ensued brought to an end the era of the great Bronze Age warrior conquerors.

Amid the turmoil of the 12th and 11th centuries B.C., tribes of Dorian Greeks moved down into areas of Greece that appear to have become depopulated as a consequence of the destruction of the Mycenaean world. Until recently, most scholars have characterized the arrival of the Dorians as an invasion, and some even attributed the fall of the Mycenaeans to the Dorians. However, recent scholarship demonstrates that the Dorians' appearance occurred well after the destruction of Mycenaean rule had begun. It seems most likely that the Dorians simply took advantage of the weakness or departure of the Mycenaean ruling class to conquer the richest and most productive of the Mycenaean lands, and with them the peasant population who had formerly served the Mycenaean aristocracy.[12]

The Dorians were Indo-Europeans whose ancestors came to Greece in the early second millennium B.C. as part of the Indo-European invasion that brought the ancestors of the Mycenaeans. Living for centuries on the northern fringes of the Mycenaean world, the Dorians had considerable interaction with the Mycenaeans and shared many of their religious customs and mythical traditions.[13] Because of their remoteness from the Aegean world that so influenced the development of the Mycenaean culture, these early Greeks retained the pastoral culture under a warrior aristocracy that was characteristic of the early Indo-European peoples, but had been abandoned by the cosmopolitan Mycenaeans. The Dorians took over most of the western mainland, much of the Peloponnesian Peninsula, Crete and a few of the Aegean Islands, while the descendants of the Mycenaeans remained in cities in eastern Greece, on the islands of the Aegean and in cities on the Aegean coast of Anatolia. Thus, when Greece emerged from these tumultuous times, sometimes called the "Greek Dark Ages," and prosperity returned, Greece had become divided into two principal cultural spheres associated with these two contrasting societies: the more militaristic, tribal Dorians speaking the Doric dialect, whose most prominent center was Sparta; and the more sophisticated and urbane Ionians, whose world was dominated by Athens.

Love Between Heroes in the Homeric World

The turmoil that saw the destruction of the Mycenaean world and the subsequent arrival of the Dorians was a watershed from which the political and cultural landscape of what we know as classical Greece began to take form. But while the Mycenaean world was gone, the age lived on in myth and legend. By the beginning of the eighth century B.C., as prosperity and cultural development resumed and the art of writing was rediscovered, the first substantive literature of the Greeks appeared. Stories and legends that had been handed down for countless generations through oral tradition were given poetic treatment. Through the literature that resulted, the themes and values that reverberated through the myths of the Mycenaean Greeks coalesced into a written summation of the philosophy and values of a unified Greek people. In the *Iliad* and *Odyssey* of Homer, events which may have been historical, like the destruction of the ancient Anatolian city of Troy, became enmeshed with myth, with heroes and gods alike playing roles in the epochal events that preceded the emergence of classical Greece. These epic poems, among the greatest ever written, were seen by the Greeks as symbols of Hellenic unity and heroism, and were held up as sources of moral and practical guidance.

While the Homeric epics were set in the Mycenaean age, scholars are generally agreed that the epics actually depict life in the period following the decline of Mycenaean power and culture, an era that has been called the Greek Feudal Age. In this period of warfare and invasion, the warrior culture that characterized the early Indo-European conquerors of Greece regained dominance, replacing the settled, urban world of commerce and trade ruled by palace bureaucracies that had been flourishing under the Mycenaeans. With the re-emergence of the warrior ethos, it was inevitable that the virtues and ideals that are prized among warriors would become embodied in the legends of heroes that were gathered by Homer into the *Iliad*. And central to the story of the *Iliad*, amid the tales of battles and heroic exploits of the legendary war against Troy, are the love and devotion between two great warrior heroes.

The passionate love between Achilles, the mortal son of a goddess, and Patroclus, his lifelong companion, provides another example of the masculine love between heroic comrades that was celebrated in the ancient world in the stories of Gilgamesh and Enkidu, and David and Jonathan. Like the blood-brother relationships of the Indo-European warriors, the love between Achilles and Patroclus was marked by intense devotion, a devotion that was to play a pivotal role in the eventual triumph of the Greeks over the Trojans. Since the *Iliad* is a compilation of stories and legends passed down from generation to generation through oral tradition, the customs and attitudes depicted in the epic are considered to be a reliable reflection of actual practices and beliefs of the Greeks in the centuries preceding the composition of the epic by Homer. Thus, the relationship between Achilles and Patroclus suggests not only that a tradition of sexual love among warrior-peers was a part of Greek ancestral culture, but that in Homeric times such a love still had sufficient appeal to the people that a passionate relationship between two archetypal heroes would play a central role in the epic.

Achilles and the War Against Troy

Achilles was the son of Peleus, the mythic king of the Myrmidons, a tribe of Thessaly, in northeastern Greece. His mother was the sea nymph Thetis, an immortal. According to Homer, Achilles was raised at Phthia with his cousin and inseparable companion, Patroclus. Another legend about Achilles' childhood relates that his mother dipped him in the water of the River Styx which made him invulnerable, except for the portion of his heel by which his mother held him—the proverbial "Achilles' heel." Like other mythical heroes with immortal parentage he was exceptionally handsome and famed for his super-human warrior prowess.

Achilles was the greatest hero of the Greek armies under the Mycenaean king, Agamemnon, who led the Greeks in their legendary assault on Troy. The war was ostensibly fought to recover Helen, the wife of Agamemnon's brother, Menelaus, who had been abducted by Paris, the son of the king of Troy. Though the Achaeans' war with the Trojans is the central event around which the narrative of the *Iliad* revolved, the role of Achilles is so central to the story, and the space devoted to the unfolding of his character is so great, that the epic could almost be called the "Achilliad."

During the first nine years of the war, Achilles led the Greeks to decisive victories, capturing all the lands around Troy and taking 12 cities. But in the tenth year a dispute broke out between Achilles and Agamemnon. Agamemnon had taken as part of his portion of the spoils of war Chryseis, the daughter of a priest of Apollo, Chryses. Chryses went to Agamemnon and, invoking his sacred office, begged the release of his daughter, which Agamemnon refused. So Chryses prayed to Apollo to send a pestilence into the Greek camp until they returned his daughter. Apollo granted the request, and an epidemic broke out in the Greeks' encampment, killing many men.

The Insult of Agamemnon

When a council was called by the Greeks to deliberate how to appease the wrath of Apollo, Achilles charged Agamemnon with causing their misfortune by refusing to release Chryseis and insisted that Agamemnon return the young woman to her father, the priest. An irate Agamemnon consented to release the priest's daughter on the condition that in order to replace his loss of Chryseis, Achilles had to turn over to him Briseis, a slave-concubine who had fallen to Achilles as part of his share of the spoils of war. Infuriated by this slight to his honor, Achilles refused to take further part in the campaign against Troy and pulled his army, the Myrmidons, out of the war. Without Achilles, the Greeks were greatly demoralized—an oracle had earlier prophesied that Troy could not be taken without Achilles. The Greeks made little progress, began to lose ground, and were at last repulsed to the area around their ships with many of the warriors killed or injured.

Realizing the importance of bringing Achilles back into the fight, Agamemnon decided to send a mission to placate Achilles. Agamemnon would agree to return Briseis to Achilles, offer his daughter in marriage, and send him a trove of other gifts, if Achilles would return and serve under him: "And let him yield place to me, inasmuch as I am the kinglier and inasmuch as I can call myself born the elder."[14] Agamemnon, therefore, sent a party composed of Achilles' closest friends, including Odysseus and the aging hero, Phoenix, Achilles' boyhood tutor and guardian, to relay his message and to persuade Achilles to return.

Achilles was not swayed by the offer, recognizing the refusal of Agamemnon to acknowledge the injury to his honor: "Go back and proclaim to him all that I tell you openly, so other Achaeans may turn against him in anger if he hopes yet one more time to swindle some other

Danaan.... I will join with him in no counsel, and in no action. He cheated me and he did me hurt. Let him not beguile me with words again."[15] Odysseus reminded Achilles that his father had pleaded with him that he not give vent to his anger. Achilles even resisted a lengthy entreaty of Phoenix, his old teacher. Finally, with the Trojans closing in and beginning to set fire to the Greeks' ships, Achilles' companion, Patroclus, distraught over the suffering of the Greek armies, came in tears to Achilles. Patroclus implored the angry hero to at least let him put on Achilles' armor and lead the Myrmidons out into battle so the Trojans would think Achilles had returned, and the Greeks would be heartened and be rallied to victory. Though Achilles was unmoved by Agamemnon's offer of the return of the concubine Briseis and the great treasure, and even the pleadings of his closest friends and comrades, he could not bear the anguish of his beloved companion. Though he himself would still remain on the side-lines, Achilles agreed to Patroclus' request, lent him his armor, and prayed that the gods would protect his beloved in battle.

The Death of Patroclus

Patroclus therefore, clad in the famous armor of Achilles, led the Myrmidons out against the Trojans and pushed them back to the gates of the city. The Greeks would then and there have taken the city were it not for the intercession of the god Apollo, who personally repulsed the charges of Patroclus. The great hero of the Trojans, Hector, whose battlefield perform-ance thus far had been distinctly lackluster, was standing by, pondering what to do, when Apollo berated him for not fighting and urged him to seek glory by slaying Achilles/Patro-clus. Hector went out to engage Patroclus, made little headway against his fury, but finally, and only with the help of Apollo, succeeded in killing him.

Hearing the news of Patroclus' death, Achilles was devastated: "And the black cloud of sorrow closed on Achilles. In both hands he caught up the grimy dust, and poured it over his head and face, and fouled his handsome countenance.... And he himself, mightily in his might, in the dust lay at length, and took and tore at his hair with his hands, and defiled it." His friend Antilochos "held the hands of Achilles as he grieved ... fearing Achilles might cut his throat."[16] When his friends came to comfort him, Achilles mourned, "There is nothing worse than this I could suffer, not even if I were to hear of the death of my father ... or the death of my dear son."[17]

The death of Patroclus, the one life Achilles valued as his own, eclipsed the question of honor that had caused Achilles to sit out the war. Swearing that with Patroclus gone his only aim in life was to avenge the death of his companion, Achilles returned to the war, killed Hector along with many Trojans, and in so doing ensured the defeat of Troy. Thus, the fate of the epochal campaign begun to restore a heterosexual union, that of Menelaus with Helen, turned on the passionate love between two men.

The Denial of the Sexual Bond Between the Two Heroes by Modern Scholars

Though Greeks in the classical era took for granted that a sexual relationship existed between Achilles and Patroclus, many modern writers, particularly in the academic world, have dismissed the idea that the two heroes were lovers, apparently taking their lead from Xenophon, a fourth-century B.C. Athenian writer.[18] Xenophon, who seems to represent an anti-homosexual strain in Greek thought,[19] was unique among the ancient Greeks in this view of Achilles and Patroclus. Another indicator that Xenophon's writings were not a particularly reliable reflection of Greek thought on sexual matters was his view on the famous myth of the abduction of Ganymede by Zeus, who carried off the beautiful youth to live with him among the gods. Xenophon claimed that Zeus was attracted to Ganymede, not because of his beauty, but because of his mind, an absurd assertion, plainly in contradiction to centuries of Greek tradition.[20]

Proponents of the opinion that the two heroes were not lovers point to the heterosexual interest shown by both Achilles and Patroclus for their slave-concubines, and argue that Homer's text never directly states that there was a physical relationship between the two.[21] In regard to the first point, demonstration of heterosexual interest certainly does not preclude homosexual desire, as is shown in the lives of many prominent Greeks, like the lawgiver Solon, the playwright Sophocles, the great orator Demosthenes, and the philosopher Socrates, all of whom had heterosexual unions, but nonetheless pursued homosexual loves. In fact, some scholars have seen as confirmation of Achilles' homosexual inclinations the several noble youths, referred to twice in the poem, who are included among gifts made to Achilles by Agamemnon when they were finally reconciled.[22] In addition, in the *Odyssey,* after Patroclus' death, Homer depicts another warrior, Antilochus, taking his place in Achilles' affections, implying that Homer cannot conceive of the great hero of the *Iliad* without a favorite male companion.[23] As to the lack of a specific reference to a sexual relationship between the two warriors, the respected classicist Gilbert Murray suggested that the poem is not more explicit about Achilles and Patroclus because the text was censored.[24]

Other scholars have maintained that the relationship between Achilles and Patroclus is never directly mentioned because the conventions of the epic form require discretion in regard to such intimate matters as sexual relations.[25] In a similar way, while there are numerous references to homosexual love in fifth- and fourth-century B.C. comedy and in the works of Greek philosophers, homosexual relationships are rarely alluded to in Greek tragedies written in the same period. That discretion in regard to sexual relations was the rule in Greek upper class society is also illustrated in the writings of several classical authors. When in Plato's *Symposium* Alcibiades describes for the guests his failed attempt to seduce Socrates, he makes it clear that he was breaking the rules of polite conversation with his direct references to the nature of his intentions with Socrates. Similarly, in Xenophon's work of the same name, Socrates apologizes for his "coarseness" in mentioning homosexual body contact, even though he was only referring to kissing and caressing.[26]

The Unique Intensity of the Love Between Achilles and Patroclus

Regardless of the reasons for the reticence of Homer in regard to the nature of the relationship between Achilles and Patroclus, the intensity of the feelings between the two heroes is so evident from the description of their behavior in the text that a statement that they were lovers is not necessary to prove the nature of their love.[27] As the fourth-century B.C. Athenian orator Aeschines put it, though Homer never speaks directly of the nature of the relationship between the two, their love "is obvious to the educated among his readers."[28]

The relationship depicted between Achilles and Patroclus goes far beyond the normal comradeship of warriors. Achilles' attachment to Patroclus, and the space in the narrative devoted to it, are unique among all the figures in the epic.[29] Achilles described Patroclus as one "whom I loved beyond all other companions, as well as my own life."[30] The first words Patroclus says in the poem are addressed to Achilles asking if Achilles has any needs, and the last word he utters is Achilles' name.[31] When Hector mortally strikes Patroclus, the dying hero understands intuitively that Achilles will avenge him, regardless of the dispute with Agamemnon, and so warns Hector. In Book Twenty-Three, when Patroclus comes back from the dead to speak to Achilles, he recalled the intimacy and affection the two had shared, and asked Achilles to hold his hand to comfort him in his sorrow, regretting that the two would no longer "sit apart from our other beloved companions, making our plans." Patroclus then asked that they be buried together, so that they could remain together just as they were together since childhood.[32]

Throughout the text of the *Iliad* the two heroes are constantly shown in each other's company. In fact they are separated from each other only twice in the epic, in Book Eleven, when Achilles sends Patroclus out to check on the wounded, and then in Book Sixteen, when Patroclus goes into battle wearing Achilles' armor. Patroclus was a part of Achilles' household and performs a role for Achilles that underscores their domestic arrangement. When the elderly Phoenix is to sleep in Achilles' tent it is Patroclus who gives the orders to the household servants in making arrangements for Phoenix.[33] Patroclus is also described as setting dinners before Achilles. The sort of domestic involvement depicted between the two men is unique in the *Iliad* and is the sort usually only seen in love relationships. Even when the two are sleeping with their female concubines, they are in beds across from each other.

The intensely exclusive nature of their relationship is made clear in Book Sixteen in Achilles' passionate prayer to the gods for Patroclus' safety — an expression of concern again unparalleled in the poem. In the prayer Achilles expresses the wish that only he and Patroclus would survive the war, with all the Trojans and even all the Greeks perishing, so that the two comrades, alone together, would share the glory of taking Troy.[34] This declaration of Achilles is astounding: it would be fine with him if everyone else in the entire epic were to perish as long as he could remain together with Patroclus. And when Patroclus is killed, Achilles declares he has only one aim in life, to avenge his beloved's death, and after that, to lie with him in the same grave, forever united, as they were in life.

Allusions to the Physical Nature of Their Relationship in the Poem

There are, in fact, several allusions in the text to the physical relationship between Achilles and Patroclus. During the visit of the emissaries from Agamemnon to Achilles, Phoenix, in attempting to persuade Achilles to accept the gifts from Agamemnon, relates the story of another legendary hero in similar circumstances. Meleager, a great hero of the Aetolians, had withdrawn in a rage from a war his people were fighting against the neighboring Couretes because his mother had cursed him. With the war going badly for the Aetolians, his mother and father beseeched him to return to the battle to save their city, but Meleager would not relent. His dearest friends implored him to return, but to no avail. Finally, when the Couretes were setting fire to the city, Meleager's wife came to him in tears, describing the suffering that was overtaking the city. Only then did he yield, unable to bear the pain of his beloved partner.

The story told by Phoenix exactly parallels the events that were to take place in the *Iliad*. After withdrawing from the war against Troy because of the insult of Agamemnon, Achilles resisted the return of the slave-concubine whose loss had started the dispute, the vast treasure offered by Agamemnon, and even the pleadings of his closest friends. Achilles yielded only when his beloved companion came to him, in tears, relating the suffering that was befalling the Greek armies. In each case it was only the power that arises from a love relationship that could overcome the intransigence of the hero. The parallel between Phoenix's story and the unfolding events of the epic would certainly have been recognized by Homer's audience, who would have seen the comparison between Patroclus and Meleager's wife as underscoring the enormity of the loss Achilles was to suffer in the death of Patroclus.

A more direct allusion to the physical relationship between Achilles and Patroclus comes from the hero's mother, Thetis. Visiting Achilles after the funeral of Patroclus to urge him to end his grieving, Thetis makes an explicit reference to the nature of the relationship between the two, saying that with Patroclus gone, he might now find comfort with a woman: "My child, how long will you go on eating your heart out in sorrow and lamentation, and remember neither your food nor going to bed? It is a good thing *even to lie with a woman in love.*[35]

If the sexual nature of the attachment between the two heroes is not apparent from these examples, the enormity of Achilles' grief over his fallen friend, and his expression of it, lying with Patroclus' corpse, repeatedly embracing it and declaring his "longing" for his companion, unmistakably demonstrates the presence of a bond that could only be physical. Indeed, what but a sexual bond could account for Achilles' exclamation on hearing of Patroclus's death that, "There is nothing worse than this I could suffer, not even if I were to hear of the death of my father ... or the death of my dear son"?[36] Who but a lover could be emotionally more important to the hero than either his father or young son?

In Book Nineteen, his goddess mother finds her son lying in the arms of the dead Patroclus, embracing the corpse, "crying shrill."[37] Remembering Patroclus, and the meals he had brought him, Achilles mourns to the corpse, "But now you lie here torn before me, and my heart goes starved for meat and drink, though they are here beside me, by reason of longing for you."[38] When at last Achilles gave the body of Patroclus up to the funeral pyre, he again embraced the body, saying good-bye and vowing to avenge his death.[39] After the funeral rites and games were over, and the rest of Patroclus' friends were returning to their routines, Achilles still remained in grieving, unable to sleep. "Only Achilles wept still as he remembered his beloved companion, nor did sleep who subdues all come over him, but he tossed from one side to the other in longing for Patroclus, for his manhood and his great strength and all the actions he had seen to the end with him."[40] Achilles' grief at the death of Patroclus was so extreme that even Zeus and Athena took pity.[41]

The classicist W.M. Clarke has cited the remarkable behavior of Achilles toward the body of Patroclus, repeatedly embracing it and lying with it, as unmistakable evidence of a sexual bond between the two heroes. Noting that the implications of Achilles' behavior toward the body of Patroclus have been all but ignored by scholars, Clarke remarked that none of the writers who emphasize the fact that Homer makes no reference to a physical relationship between the two heroes have attempted to explain the nature of the feelings that would compel Achilles to embrace and lie with the dead body of Patroclus. Adds Clarke, "It is senseless to assume that Achilles would lie in the arms of a dead man whom, living, he had kept at the discreet distance appropriate to one who is no more than a 'companion.'"[42]

Parallels with Other Hero-Lovers

The prolonged mourning of Achilles for Patroclus recalls the intensity of the grief the Sumero-Babylonian hero Gilgamesh felt over the death of his lover, Enkidu, who, like Patroclus, was killed through the machinations of the gods.[43] When Enkidu died, Gilgamesh was devastated. "He began to rage like a lion.... This way and that he paced round the bed, he tore out his hair and strewed it around."[44] For seven days and seven nights Gilgamesh wept over his companion's body, until it began to rot. Enkidu, like Patroclus, also came back from the dead to speak to Gilgamesh. And for both Achilles and Gilgamesh the death of their male companion was a pivotal point in their lives.

Indeed, scholars have found a number of parallels, not only between the two pairs of hero-lovers, but between the Gilgamesh epic and the Homeric epics in general, evidence of the broad influence of the Epic of Gilgamesh in the Bronze Age, and general Greek familiarity with the heritage of the Near East. The parallels in the relationships between the two sets of heroes, in fact, suggest that the relationship between Achilles and Patroclus may have been patterned after that between the two Sumerian super-heroes. The Homeric poems were products of Ionian Greeks, living on islands in the Aegean and along the coast of Asia Minor, who had long been exposed to the cultures of the ancient Middle East. It must be remembered that the story related in the *Iliad* was not an invention of Homer — or the group of bardic poets we know as "Homer" — but is a synthesis of stories and legends handed down through centuries of oral tradition, rooted in ancestral legends, but also influenced by the encounters of the early Greeks with the ancient cultures surrounding them. Thus, the similarity of the relationships between Achilles and Patroclus and Gilgamesh and Enkidu may be no accident, reflecting a widespread ancient tradition which recognized and admired love and devotion between valiant heroes.

Homosexual relationships are known to have existed among warrior peers among other Indo-European groups, such as the Celts and Scandinavians in Europe and the Scythians, who lived in a neighboring region to the northeast of the Greek mainland. That sexual bonds among Indo-European warriors in northern Europe extended back to at least 2000 B.C. is attested to by double burials found from that period in which two males are laid beside each other in the same position as husband and wife.[45] The desire of Achilles and Patroclus to be buried together, which is stated several times in the poem, is no doubt a reflection of this warrior tradition, as was the example in classical times of the great warrior Epaminondas who was buried together with his lover Caphisodorus.[46]

A Warrior Ideal: Love-Inspired Valor

In the face of the vivid description of Achilles' passionate love for Patroclus, it seems pedantic to insist that because Homer never states "Achilles and Patroclus are lovers" there could have been no sexual bond between the two men. As a popular axiom would put it, if it walks like a duck, and quacks like a duck, one does not need an affirmative statement that it is a duck to conclude that it is one. So, like the sagas of the Norse, which sang of the heroic acts of warriors inspired by devotion to a beloved comrade, the climax of this great epic turned on the valiant deeds unleashed by the passionate love of a hero for a fallen companion. Indeed, no less an acute observer of human nature than Dante pinpointed the central role that Achilles' love for Patroclus played in the epic when, in describing Achilles, he wrote: "Achilles/who through love was brought at last to fight." About this line of Dante's, the great 19th-century classicist John Addington Symonds commented, "In this pregnant sentence Dante sounded the whole depth of the *Iliad*. The wrath of Achilles for Agamemnon, which prevented him at first from fighting; the love of Achilles, passing the love of women, for Patroclus, which induced him to forego his anger and to fight at last; these are the two poles on which the *Iliad* turns."[47]

Another classical scholar, E.F.M. Benecke, added, "how thoroughly suitable a motive of this kind would be in a national Greek epic. For this is the motive running through the whole of Greek life."[48] As Benecke observes, love-inspired valor, epitomized by the warrior-lovers Achilles and Patroclus, was a frequent theme in later Greek culture. It was exemplified by the acts of numerous heroes throughout the history of the Greeks, among them, Diocles of Athens, who fell in a battle near Megara, fighting for his beloved; the great Thessalian hero, Cleomachus, who, inflamed with passion for the youth he loved, led his Chalcidian compatriots to victory over the enemy Eretrians, losing his life in the process; and the lovers Harmodius and Aristogeiton, whose love was credited by the Athenians with the overthrow of the Pisistra-did tyranny in the late sixth century B.C. In his *Symposium* Plato praised the courage and valor that were inspired by such love relationships as a great ideal and one of the great benefits to society of homosexual love. Plato wrote that an army composed of pairs of noble lovers, inspired by their love for each other, would surely demonstrate the greatest of virtue and courage. Indeed, such an army as Plato described was formed by the Theban general, Gorgidas, in the 4th century B.C. Called the Sacred Band of Thebes, the force of 300, composed of pairs of lovers, was renowned during the period for the valor of its warriors and its extraordinary military successes.

It is not surprising, then, that Greeks in the classical era would find it natural and inevitable that such an intense relationship as that described between Achilles and Patroclus would include a sexual bond. Not only were sexual love between masculine heroes, and the valor that such love inspired, probably a familiar part of ancient oral tradition, but the sentiments expressed by the two lover-heroes would certainly have been shared by many men in the Greek audience who may have had similar experiences in their own lives, not only in the almost obligatory teacher-student relationships that most of them would have experienced, but in less formalized love relationships as well.

The devotion between Achilles and Patroclus became something of a standard for the classical Greeks. The orator Aeschines, in his famous prosecution of Timarchus, cited their relationship as an example of noble love as did Plato in the *Symposium*.[49] The poet Theocritus wrote to his lover that their union should be lifelong, that age didn't matter, and that as they grew older they would become like Achilles and Patroclus.[50] The playwrights Aeschylus and Sophocles both wrote plays about the two lovers. The only difficulty the classical Greeks had with the relationship between Achilles and Patroclus was in the attempts by some of them to fit the two hero-lovers into the asymmetrical teacher-student model that characterized the educational homosexuality that came to dominate Greece in the centuries following the Homeric age. According to the writer Athenaeaus, the orator Aeschines and the playwright Aeschylus, Achilles was the *erastes*, or lover-tutor. On the other hand, Plato felt that Patroclus was the erastes, largely because of a tradition that Patroclus was older than Achilles,[51] which was also reflected in a vase painting which shows Achilles binding a wound of Patroclus who was wearing a beard, an indication of age.[52] That the two warriors were both old enough to be famous heroes, and therefore, adult peers, doesn't seem to have been considered in these debates.

Their Relationship—A Pattern Found Elsewhere

The relationship between the two actually resembles the kind of peer relationships found among other Indo-European groups, some of which were even formalized, such as the blood-brother relationships found among warriors of the Scythian and early Scandinavian tribes discussed in the previous chapter. The peer bond pattern is also found among aboriginal societies throughout the world. As seen in Chapter 3, these male pairs, like the "special friendships" of warriors among the North American Plains Indians, the bond-friends of the Asmat in New Guinea or the crossed-cousins of the Amazonian Nambikwara, often develop a physical relationship in adolescence which lasts for the rest of their lives. Among the Asmat and Nambikwara, the two men continue to have sexual relations on a regular basis even after they have taken wives. In the lives of the bond-friends of New Guinea, or the crossed-cousins in South American tribes, the primary relationship which commanded the greatest loyalty was to the male-lover, regardless of other relationships that might develop.

Similarly, Achilles and Patroclus became companions in their adolescence and were insep-arable ever since, even while engaging in sexual relationships with the slave-concubines men-tioned in the *Iliad*. That Achilles' relationship with Patroclus was at all times more important to him than his heterosexual relationship with his concubine, Briseis, is clear in the story. Agamemnon's taking of Briseis from Achilles was the affront which set off their dispute and Achilles' subsequent withdrawal from the war. But when, to appease Achilles, Agamemnon offered to return Briseis in addition to giving Achilles considerable treasure if he would return to the war, Achilles still refused, demonstrating that his interest in Briseis was not as impor-tant to him as his pride. It was only his love for Patroclus which was greater than his pride and impelled the hero to rejoin the fighting. The intensity of the relationships that develop between male peers in tribal societies would explain the passionate devotion between Achilles and Patroclus that could exist side by side with relationships with concubines or even wives, but still remain supreme in the hearts of the heroes.

While these peer-bond homosexual relationships between masculine men have been insti-tutionalized in tribal societies in New Guinea, North and South America and Africa, as well as among the Greeks' Scythian neighbors and the ancient Scandinavians, there is no evidence of formal, ceremonial recognition of peer-bonds between warriors in Greece in Homeric or later times. However, as the lover-heroes of the *Iliad* demonstrate, and as the presence of these warrior-bonds in other Indo-European groups suggest, love between warrior-peers must have been a traditional presence among the early Indo-Europeans in Greece. Otherwise, such a compelling image of passionate devotion between two heroes could not have become enshrined in the centuries of oral tradition from which was distilled this great epic, regarded by the Greeks as a summation of the Greek heroic tradition.

Other Sexual Friendships in Homer

The love between Achilles and Patroclus is not the only example of homosexual love in the world of Homer. There is a hint, in the *Iliad*, of a similar relationship between the great warriors Sthenelus and Deipylos, "his close friend, whom beyond all others of his own age he prized, for their hearts were intimate."[53] However, after that passage, no further mention is made of Deipylos. Some writers have also seen a sexual relationship in the close, intimate friendship bonds that are described in the *Iliad* between the warriors Orestes and Pylades, and between Theseus and Pirithous. And several scholars[54] have called attention to what appears to be a sexual relationship depicted in the *Odyssey* between Telemachus, the son of Odysseus, and Pisistratus, the youngest son of Nestor, king of the Pylians and a senior com-mander and counselor in the Trojan war.

When Telemachus visits the palace of Nestor, the king entertains his old comrade's son at dinner. After dinner, when Nestor is retiring to bed with his wife, he sends Telemachus to bed with his only unmarried son, Pisistratus.[55] The two become close companions, and when Telemachus later travels to Sparta, Pisistratus accompanies him, riding in the chariot beside Telemachus. After being entertained in Sparta by Menelaus at dinner, Telemachus addresses Pisistratus as "you, who delight my heart,"[56] and, later, the two young men are again found in bed together. While Menelaus sleeps with his wife, Helen, Telemachus again sleeps with Pisistratus.[57] The repeated parallels in the sleeping arrangements between the young men and their hosts and the sexual implications therein could be no accident in such a finely crafted poem. When the goddess Athena appears to Telemachus to urge him to return to Italy, she finds the two young men in bed together. After Athena leaves, Telemachus wakes up Pisis-tratus, "touching him with his foot."[58]

While Pisistratus is young, he is old enough to be called "captain of Spearmen" and a "leader of warriors." W.M. Clarke has observed that if Pisistratus is old enough to deserve the epithets of a man, but is still unmarried, the poet evidently meant to picture him "in that bloom of young manhood which later authors regard as ideally attractive from a homosexual standpoint."[59] To put a young hero like Telemachus in bed with such an attractive young man would not have been much different from putting him in bed with a young woman.[60] So the two young men who sleep together were young adult males of similar ages, with no appearance of the traditional hierarchical mentoring relationship that has often been assumed to be the sole type of homosexual relationship that existed in ancient Greece.

As we saw in Chapter 2, sexual relations between unmarried males is virtually universal in tribal societies, being less common mostly in those rare societies which had prohibitions against homosexual behavior, strictures that were entirely absent in ancient Greece. The casualness with which the relationship of Telemachus and Pisistratus is treated clearly implies an attitude in Homer's time that would find such an informal, non-pedagogical sexual relationship between two young men completely unremarkable and perhaps even inevitable. The epics of Homer, therefore, provide us with a view of a world in which homosexuality, though discretely kept in the background as befitting the seriousness of the form, is nonetheless taken for granted, whether in passionate bonds between warrior-comrades or in informal sexual relationships between young men.

7

Greek Homosexuality: Educational Homosexuality in Classical Greece

In the years following the Homeric age, the prosperous and relatively stable Greek world was marked by a profusion of art and literature, the beginnings of an age of extraordinary artistic expression unparalleled in the ancient world, and which was to continue unabated until early Christian times. Among the first products of this creative output was the poetry of the Lyric poets, much of it celebrating homosexual love. One of the earliest was Alkaois, of the Ionian island of Lesbos, who composed poetry "singing of the loves of youths," in the late seventh or early sixth century.[1] Another poet, Anacreon, born in the early sixth century B.C. on the Ionian isle of Teos off the coast of Asia Minor, wrote poetry with frequent references to the objects of his desire: "I long to enjoy the fun of youth with you for you have graceful ways," he writes to one youth.[2] To another, "Come, pledge me, dear boy, your slender thighs." But the poet's love is sometimes spurned: "See, I fly up on light wings to Olympus in search of Love; for [the boy] does not wish to enjoy the fun of youth with me." One of the most famous of the Lyric poets was Pindar, born in 519 B.C. in Boetia. Pindar's verses, too, show the power that the beauty a young male could hold over an adult male: "Who from the pupils of Theoxenus looks at the sparkling rays and does not tumble into desire, ... I am undone in the grip of the rays like the wax of the sacred bees, when I see in the fresh limbs of young boys the grace of love."

Two books of verses survive from the mid–6th-century B.C. poet Theognis, born in the Dorian city of Megara. The second book, which is devoted to the love of youths, details the poet's infatuation with and pursuit of a youth named Cyrnus and the pain of his eventual rejection. "Listen to me, boy, you who have bent my heart," but Cyrnus resists: "Boy, how long will you flee me? I search for you, I follow you: I wish I could reach the goal." But Cyrnus has other loves: "I saw you in silhouette, and your deception has not escaped me, boy. You have grown intimate with them; and this love of mine you have left, despised.... Very well, have yourself another man." Finally, the inevitable: "I love him no more, the boy: I've kicked out all that pain, I have happily survived the harshest sorrows, I am free of the passion of lovely Aphrodite. For you, boy, nothing more from me." Though the love of youths inevitably brings sorrow, it is a passion whose pleasures the poet cannot live without. In verses that seem to sum up the sentiments of the age in this regard, Theognis writes: "Loving a boy, having him, losing him, all are fine. Easier to discover than enjoy him. Endless woes come from this, endless good: There is something fine even thus."

As is demonstrated by work of the Lyric poets, who came from all the varied regions of the Greek world, the sexual pursuit of young men by adult males was a passion that was seemingly universal among Greek men in the centuries following the Homeric period. Even Solon, the great Athenian statesman and legislator, whose virtue and propriety were legendary among Athenians, was not immune to the attractions of young males. "Till he loves a lad in the flower of youth, bewitched by thighs and by sweet lips," reads a surviving fragment of Solon from the early sixth century B.C.

The pursuit of these hierarchical homosexual relationships was not merely the decadent pastime of an idle aristocracy. As in many tribal cultures, sexual relationships between men and youths were felt by the Greeks to play a crucial role in the training of young men in warrior arts and social responsibilities, and in the induction of young men into adult society. As the historian Werner Jaeger has written, "It must be recognized that the love of a man for a youth or a boy was an essential part of the aristocratic society of early Greece, and was inextricably bound up with its moral and social ideals."[3] The Greeks shared the belief of many tribal societies that a youth could acquire a noble warrior's manly virtues and valor, what the Greeks called his *arete,* through sexual submission to him. A sexual relationship with an adult male was, therefore, central to the passage of a young man from childhood into adulthood, a transformation that in early Greek society was expressed in rites of initiation that symbolized the rebirth of the youth as an adult and that served as a framework for his education.

Homosexuality and Initiation in Greek Myth

The transformational role of these relationships in initiating a youth into noble adulthood is illustrated in a number of Greek myths in which a noble youth's progression to manhood is made possible through the agency of a sexual relationship with a god or mythical hero. These myths, which were part of the ancestral heritage of all the regions of Greece, show how deeply these hierarchical relationships were ingrained in Greek culture, and are suggestive of the deep antiquity of this homosexual institution among the Greeks. Bernard Sergent, an authority in Greek and Indo-European mythology, has argued that this tradition of educational homosexuality even predates the Greeks' arrival in the Aegean region. According to Sergent, the customs derived from homosexual initiation rites practiced by the early Indo-Europeans warriors, and were brought to Greece by the Indo-Europeans when they settled there in the early second millennium.[4] The presence of traditions of homosexual initiation among other early Indo-European groups, discussed in the previous chapter, lends credence to Sergent's argument.[5]

Sergent has identified more than sixty of these myths, and has demonstrated an initiatory character and a distinctly Indo-European structure in many of the stories. A number of the myths, according to Sergent, can be traced to Mycenaean times or earlier. The myths of Apollo and Hyacinthus, Ameinias and Narcissus, and Heracles and Iolaus may have predated the arrival of the Indo-Europeans in Greece. The names Hyacinthus and Narcissus come from the same pre–Hellenic linguistic stratum, and are probably of Anatolian origin,[6] and if so would provide another example of the close cultural association between the early Greeks and their Indo-European cousins in Anatolia. The transformation from youth to noble adult that the Greeks believed resulted from these love relationships can be seen in a brief review of four of the most famous of the myths.

Apollo and Hyacinthus

The Spartans saw in the mythical love of Apollo for Hyacinthus the archetype of the initiatory relationship.[7] An important festival, the Hyacinthia, which was in part a celebration of initiation[8] and was celebrated annually in southern Spart at Amyclae, was named for this young beloved of Apollo. Bulfinch describes Apollo as the god of light, healing, music, poetry, and archery, the incarnation of the Greek ideal of youthful manhood.[9] Famous for his pursuit of Daphne, who was turned into a tree as she fled from him, Apollo is the god to whom the largest number of male loves is attributed, according to Sergent.[10] With his youthful beauty, and his association with the hunt and warrior prowess, Apollo represented the ideal tutor-lover, which the Greeks called the *erastes*, and a number of myths portray his love and mentoring of a beautiful young man, the *eremenos*. The sexual nature of these relationships is made explicitly clear by the use of these words to describe each partner. The Greek word *erastes* refers to the active partner in a sexual relationship, and was used to refer to a married man's role with his wife as well as to the active partner of a homosexual relationship. The word *eremenos*, used to describe the young beloved, literally means "one who is sexually desired"; the word is the past participle of the verb *eramai*, which means "to desire sexually."[11]

Hyacinthus was the youngest and most handsome of the sons of Amyclas, an early king of Sparta. The youth's great beauty caught the attention of Apollo, who fell in love with him. In other myths Hyacinthus is also pursued by Zephyr, the god of wind, and depictions of this winged god lying with Hyacinthus making love was a popular theme of Athenian potters during classical times. Apollo became Hyacinthus's instructor, and taught the young prince archery, music, the art of the lyre, and the exercises of the gymnasium, and it was through Hyacinthus, the Spartans believed, that knowledge of these subjects came down to humans. As part of his tutoring of Hyacinthus, Apollo took the young man out into the wilderness of the countryside, "along the rough mountain peaks of the rugged ridges," where he taught him hunting.[12] As among many tribal cultures, removal of the youth from home and family into the wilderness or an alien environment was an important element of initiation, as was hunting. For in learning to kill a wild predator, whether it be a boar, bear or lion, the youth showed he was equal or superior to the power of the animal, and had grown from the stage of helpless child to powerful adult.

One day, while Apollo was teaching Hyacinthus discus throwing, the youth was accidentally killed when a discus thrown by Apollo hit Hyacinthus in the head. In some versions of the myth, the god Zephyr, jealous of Apollo's relationship with Hyacinthus, caused a wind to blow the discus into Hyacinthus. The young man, mortally stricken, fell to the ground, blood running out of his head. Apollo was so distraught at the death of his beloved that he caused a plant to grow out of the blood that flowed from his wounds, the hyacinth. This flower, whose petals had markings similar to the Greek letters spelling the mournful exclamation, "AI, AI," — "alas" in Greek — was considered by the Greeks to be the most beautiful of all flowers. Hyacinthus's death was commemorated by the Spartans in the Hyacinthia, their second most important festival, celebrated in the Spartan month of Hyacinthia, in early summer. Beginning with mourning songs and dances for Hyacinthus, the festival gradually evolved into a joyous celebration of the glory of Apollo. But according to the Spartans, Hyacinthus's story did not end with his death.

As related by the poet Pindar, there was an enormous statue of Apollo with helmet, shield and bow at Amyclae, where the Hyacinthia festival was celebrated. The base was covered with paintings, one of which shows Hyacinthus with a beard, an indication of Spartan adulthood. In the painting, the goddesses Aphrodite, Athena and Artemis are shown carrying the adult Hyacinthus to Heaven. The painting, then, depicts the completion of the initiation of Hyacinthus, his transformation from youth to adult peer of his lover-tutor.[13]

Through his initiatory relationship with Apollo, the youthful Hyacinthus dies, and then, as is symbolically enacted in initiation rites in tribal societies around the world, he is reborn as an adult.[14] But since his erastes was an immortal god, and since through submission to his lover the youth, in an initiation, acquires the qualities of his lover, it would be only natural for this eremenos to have acquired the immortal, god-like qualities of his erastes. Indeed, that is what happened to Hyacinthus, according to the Spartans, and that is what is represented in the painting, where Hyacinthus is shown being carried up by the goddesses to take his place among the immortals. The deification of Hyacinthus was commemorated by the Spartans in rites that were performed for centuries. On the Aegean island of Thera, a Spartan colony since the early first millennium, there was even a temple honoring Hyacinthus.

Poseidon and Pelops

In the story of Poseidon and Pelops we see another example of how the beloved grew in strength and power — and acquired a marriage appropriate to noble adulthood — through his relationship with his lover. Poseidon, brother of Zeus and Hades, was one of the oldest and most powerful of the Greek gods, and, according to most scholars, his legend was brought to Greece by the early Indo-European invaders. In earliest times, he was the god of horses, war and the chariot, a deity of principal importance to the Indo-European warrior culture. After Poseidon and his two brothers succeeded in dethroning their father, Cronos, as master of the gods, they drew lots to divide up the world, and Poseidon ended up with the kingdom of the sea, while Hades got the underworld, and Zeus the world. In later times Poseidon was associated mainly with the sea — he was the Roman Neptune — but it is in Poseidon's earlier manifestation, as god of horses, war and the chariot, that he is linked with Pelops. Pelops and his father, Tantalus, were mythical heroes thought to be brought by the early Indo-European colonizers of the Anatolian coast. Associated with Mount Siplus on the border between Lydia and Phrygia in western Anatolia, these two heroes are of Asian Indo-European origin, Tantalus being the Greek version of Atlas. Sergent has, thus, traced the origins of the legend of Pelops and Poseidon to earliest Mycenaean times.[15]

According to this early myth, Tantalus, who was a favorite of the gods, invited the gods to a feast at his home. Tantalus, deciding to test the gods' omniscience, chopped up his son, made a stew of his body, and offered it to the gods to eat to see if they could perceive what they were eating. Only one of the immortals, Demeter, apparently distracted by the recent loss of her daughter, Persephone, actually ate a portion. Zeus was not duped and was enraged by the arrogance of Tantalus, who dared test the gods' powers, and so Tantalus was punished by the gods and was later raped by Poseidon. Zeus restored Pelops to life, and when it was found that Pelops was missing a shoulder — apparently eaten by the distracted Demeter — a new one was made for him out of ivory.[16]

After Pelops was brought back to life, Poseidon, taken with the beauty of the youth, fell in love with him and took him from his home to Olympus to live with him among the gods. Pelops was educated by Poseidon and served as Poseidon's page, fulfilling the initiatory requirement that the apprentice must serve his master.[17] Then, according to the poet Pindar, "When at the time of life's blossoming, the first beard came to darken his cheek," the point at which he came of age as an adult, "he thought of winning a bride ready at hand, Hippodamia, the glorious daughter of a king in Pisa," a city in southwestern Greece, ruled at that time by the king Oenomaus. To win the prize of Hippodamia's hand, Pelops would have to triumph in a challenge Oenomaus had set for suitors of his daughter, to beat the king in a chariot race, and lose his life if he failed. Pelops called out to his erastes, "Look you, Poseidon, if you have had any joy of my love, block the brazen spear of Oenomaus, and give me the fleeter chariot by Elis's river, and clothe me about in strength. Thirteen suitors he has killed now, and ever puts aside the marriage of his daughter." In response, the god gave Pelops a golden chariot drawn by magical winged horses that never tired. Pelops went to demand the hand of Oenomaus's daughter, and was the victor in the subsequent chariot race, which also saw the death of Oenomaus. Pelops thereupon assumed the throne of Pisa, married Hippodamia, and fathered six sons by her, "lords of the people, blazing in valor." Thus was formed the myth of Pelops as the founder of the royal dynasties of Greece, and it is for him that the Peloponnesian peninsula was named. The story of Pelops' duel with Oenomaus was also thought by some Greeks to be the founding myth of the Olympics, the premier event of the games in ancient times being the chariot race.[18]

Zeus and Ganymede

Probably the best-known mythical example of homosexual love among the gods was the love of Zeus for the youthful Ganymede, which was widely depicted in Greek art. Ganymede is another one of the mythical figures going back to the time of the earliest Indo-European settlement in Greece and the Aegean. Later, the Mycenaean Greeks brought the story of Zeus and Ganymede with them when they conquered Crete, where a later tradition substituted the Cretan god-king Minos as the lover of Ganymede. According to Greek tradition, Ganymede was the beautiful son of Tros, a legendary king of Troy. As the *Homeric Hymn of Aphrodite* tells the story, "It was for his beauty that Zeus carried off the blond Ganymede, who lived among the immortals and served as cup bearer to the gods in Zeus' abode."

After his abduction by Zeus, Ganymede became an immortal, frozen in immortality as the eternal eremenos. As such, he served his lover as cup bearer, again in line with the tradition that the student-beloved serve his master. In Greek society, through classical times, the drinking of wine was reserved for noble male adults; a cup bearer was not a mere servant, but an honored position for noble youth on the threshold of entrance to adult society. The myth of Zeus and Ganymede thus served as a divine archetype for the Greek pederastic tradition, and was regarded as the founding myth of educational homosexuality in much of early Greece.[19]

Heracles and Iolaus

Not all Greek legends dealing with sexual/educational relationships involved tutoring by immortals. The most famous and popular of Greek mythical figures was the hero Heracles (the Roman Hercules). This legendary superman was a war hero and military leader whose appearance in Greek myth also dates from the earliest period of Indo-European presence in the lands around the Aegean. Heracles is among those gods and heroes named in the famous Mycenaean "Linear B" tablets, which date to around 1500 B.C., but is probably of even earlier origin. Similar to other Indo-European warrior heroes, Heracles also incorporates elements of Minoan and Asian mythology, and may also be a direct heir of the Sumerian super-hero, Gilgamesh.[20]

According to Plutarch, Heracles had so many lovers it would be impossible to name them all.[21] Among them were Jason, of the famous Argonauts, Hylas, Adonis and Iolaus. The latter, among the Greeks the most well-known of Heracles' lovers, also had origins in very ancient myth. According to Sergent, in early Greece going back to Mycenaean times, the second syllable of Iolaus' name, *laus*, referred to people in arms. This syllable is a very archaic compound, and, like many other words in the Greek military vocabulary, is of Indo-European origin. The primitive Greek form of that syllable, "isw-o" is very close to the Sanskrit "isu," which has the same meaning, and illustrates the close relation of Iolaus' name to the Indo-European ancestral language.[22]

The son of Heracles' brother, Iolaus is depicted as the youthful assistant of Heracles in his exploits. Euripides describes Iolaus as Heracles' squire, a role similar to that which Pelops played for Poseidon. Iolaus accompanied Heracles in the expedition against Troy, the voyage of the Argonauts, and in many of the famous "labors of Heracles." According to the Greek writer, Diodorus Siculus, Heracles even shared his wife, Megara, with his lover Iolaus.

Iolaus learned well from his lover-tutor. He was a master chariot driver, and when Heracles organized the Olympic games (according to this legend), it was Iolaus who won the main event, the chariot race. Iolaus became the leader of a troop of youths, in an army commanded by Heracles, and when Heracles died, Iolaus became commander of the army.[23] Thus, Iolaus, through submission and subservience to his lover-master rose to the stature of his lover, the classic transformation from youth to heroic manhood. The love between Heracles and Iolaus remained a powerful image for the Greeks for many centuries. As late as the second century A.D., according to Plutarch, lovers went to Iolaus's tomb in Thebes to swear an oath of loyalty to each other.[24]

Not only do these early myths demonstrate the presence of homosexuality as a cultural institution among the Greeks as far back as the time of their first appearance in the lands around the Aegean, but in them we see the outlines of the sexual educational relationships that played such an important social role in the society of the ancient Greeks: 1) An adult male with heroic or noble qualities would pursue the love of a young male based on his manly beauty and virtue. 2) The youth submits to the love of the adult and becomes the adult's companion, apprentice or squire. 3) The youth is tutored by the adult in warrior skills, the arts, and other desirable attributes. 4) The youth acquires the power and qualities of adult. 5) The youth, now an adult, takes his place in adult society — is transformed. Hyacinthus, Pelops, Ganymede and Iolaus were chosen by their masters because of their virile beauty, and each served his master as an assistant or apprentice. Pelops achieved the status of a king and his royal wife through his relationship with his lover. Hyacinthus and Ganymede became immortal peers of their lovers. Iolaus became Heracles' equal, succeeding him as commander of an army. Throughout these myths runs the common theme: transformation of a youth, through the love of a superior, into the equivalent status of the superior.

Some modern writers, who maintain that homosexuality in ancient Greece was a phenomenon limited to the late archaic and classical periods, have insisted that these myths were "homosexualized" in the classical period, that the homosexual themes were not originally present in the myths, but were introduced by classical poets and writers. There are certainly some stories involving sexual relations between mythical figures which were contrived in classical or later times. However, it doesn't seem likely that the classical writers and poets who wrote of the love relationships between mythical heroes would have been able to inject precisely the same archetypal initiatory elements, which sometimes are quite subtly built into the stories, into each and every one of the great number of myths in which they appear. In these myths the sexual relationships that are depicted invariably serve as the framework of a story that includes such initiatory features as the separation of the youth from family and society, the subservient role of the youth as squire or apprentice to his lover, instruction of the youth in hunting or other manly skills, the youth's symbolic — and sometimes explicit — death, and the resurrection or emergence of a new adult individual to take the place of the adolescent in adult society. Rather than simply recounting the romantic pursuit of some beautiful youth by a legendary figure, these early myths describe love relationships that in all cases coincide with an ennobling transformation of the youth into adulthood.

Aside from the initiatory character common to the myths, there are references to the myths in Homeric and archaic literature, which significantly predate the classical authors who supposedly invented their homosexual elements. A reference in the *Iliad* to the myth of Zeus and Ganymede, which emphasizes the beauty of the young prince in a way that suggests, as Sergent says, an "erotic preoccupation on the part of the poet,"[25] shows that in Homeric times, the ninth century B.C., that famous myth was understood to be a story of homosexual love. Another reference to the relationship of Zeus and Ganymede that appears in the *Homeric Hymn of Aphrodite*, a poem of the early archaic period, is even more explicit about the erotic nature of that relationship. In the poem, the Trojan Prince Anchises is trying to escape being seduced by Aphrodite, because since the love of gods is fatal to mortals, that would mean his death. Aphrodite, in trying to reassure him, compares their relationship to that of two other mortals loved by immortals, Tithonus, who was loved by the goddess Aurora, and Ganymede, who was carried off by Zeus "because of his beauty."[26] It's clear, then, that the sexual nature of Zeus' attraction to Ganymede was appearing in literature well before the period of the classical writers, who some scholars claim are responsible for the homosexualization of Greek myths.

Additionally, Sergent has demonstrated that in many of the myths the initiatory themes as well as the love relationships that are depicted between legendary figures can be dated to the time of the earliest Greek presence in the lands around the Aegean. For example, the figures of Hyacinthus, Ganymede and Iolaus, whose names are derived from pre–Greek Indo-European elements, and most probably date from before the arrival of the Greeks in the Aegean, exist in the myths for no other reason than as archetypes of the ideal eremenos, and as protégés of their lover-masters.[27] Moreover, cultural details depicted in the myths, as well as the importance given to hunting prowess, which was a much more critical masculine skill in earlier periods than in classical times, point to origins in the Dark Ages or earlier.[28]

The Question of the Origins of the Greeks' Homosexual Customs

The Greeks themselves were divided on the origins of the homosexual customs in their societies. Many of the city-states attributed the introduction of the practices to legendary heroes associated with their past. For example, the Thebans regarded Laius, the father of Oedipus, as the founder of the homosexual tradition in their city, just as the Spartans traced their homosexual customs to Apollo and Hyacinthus. On the other hand, two passages in Plato's *Laws* and a reference in Aristotle's *Politics* show that some classical Greeks believed that their homosexual customs were introduced to Greece by the Dorians, and that the other Greeks learned the practices from them. However, the classicist K.J. Dover has noted that Plato was not a historian "either by trade or temperament" and so has cautioned against regarding these remarks of his as authoritative.[29] It should be added that the same could be said for Aristotle.

Nonetheless, based on these passages, as well as the prominence of institutionalized homosexuality as a social custom among the Dorian Greeks, the prevailing consensus among many traditional classicists, starting with the early 19th-century German scholar C.O. Mueller, has been that Greek homosexuality originated in the military structure of the Dorian states, principally Sparta and Crete, and spread from there to other regions of the Greek world.[30] As described by Ulrich von Wilamowitz-Moellendorff, the dean of German philologists in the early twentieth century, the Dorians brought boy-love with them, which in their wandering hordes had the same cause as among the Celts and among many Germanic tribes of the great migrations. It was the urgency of the situation, the close intimacy on the campaigns of plunder that allowed no female camp-followers.... The boy who is received into the community and has so much to learn needs the older comrade who initiates and protects him, since in such a society a cruel form of hazing usually prevails. The knight has need of a page, and in a circle of members of the same social stratum this cannot be a slave.[31]

On the other hand, the French historian H.I. Marrou argued that "It [institutionalized homosexuality] was bound up with the genuine Hellenic tradition as a whole," and not a peculiarity of the Dorians. According to Marrou,

It is one of the most obvious and lasting survivals from the feudal 'Middle Ages' (i.e., the Homeric Age). In essence, it was a comradeship of warriors. Greek homosexuality was of a military type.... Love between men is a recurring feature of military societies, in which men tend to be shut in upon themselves. The exclusion — the utter absence — of women inevitably means an increase in masculine love.... The phenomenon is more accentuated in a military milieu, for here, with the glorification of an ideal made up of masculine virtues like strength and valor and loyalty, with the cultivation of a distinctly masculine pride, there goes a tendency to depreciate the normal love of a man for a woman.[32]

However, the homosexual practices of the Greeks were not confined to those times when Greek armies were away from home and the men were "shut in upon themselves," but pervaded Greek society regardless of circumstances. In classical times, the homosexual pursuit of male youths existed side by side with heterosexual marriage.

Other writers have attributed the widespread homosexuality of ancient Greece to the inferior position of women in classical times. According to this view, women of Athens, who were confined mostly to the households, and who were denied the opportunity to familiarize themselves with philosophy, politics or civic affairs, would have been regarded by their highly educated husbands as uninteresting companions, with whom they had little in common. Hence, the males would have pursued sexual companionship among other males. However, the extreme segregation of women and their diminished status only occurred in classical times, whereas male homosexuality was certainly well established in much earlier times.[33] In addition, it is not intellectual achievement or public accomplishments that cause men generally to pursue women, but other qualities, quite independent of their cultural or political education.

It is also clear that upper-class Athenian women were not ignorant homebodies, fit only for household management. They frequently accompanied their husbands to cultural events, such as performances of the great tragic dramas of Aeschylus, Sophocles and Euripides, which cannot be appreciated by the ignorant or narrow-minded. In Sparta and the other Dorian states, in contrast to Athenian practices, women had greater freedom and relative equality with the men. Spartan girls were trained, like the boys, in exercises, including discus throwing, and in music and dancing. They often attended games and festivals with boys, and so had opportunities to develop common interests. Thus, the argument that homosexuality developed because of the segregation of women or because of their ignorance and inferior status would not explain the situation in Sparta, where male homosexuality was universally practiced.[34]

The historian William Percy has advanced a theory that the homosexual customs of classical Greece had their origins in legislation enacted in Crete to combat overpopulation. During the eighth century B.C., there appears to have been a population explosion in Greece, which particularly affected Crete. Since the estates of the Dorian nobility of Crete were customarily divided equally among all surviving legitimate sons, the rapidly growing upper class of Dorian knights would have found it increasingly difficult to provide estates for their sons adequate to maintain their aristocratic lifestyle. In response, Percy says, the Cretan governing body instituted measures to curb the exploding population. According to Aristotle, "The Cretan lawgiver regarded abstemiousness as beneficial and devoted much ingenuity to securing it, as also to keeping down the birth-rate by keeping men and women apart, and by instituting sexual relations between males."[35] In addition to the segregation of women, Percy notes that the Cretan population reforms included raising the marriage age to 30, from 18 or 19, which, aside from encouraging homosexuality, would have reduced the number of upper-class births because of two factors. First, because of natural mortality rates among the young warriors, fewer males would be marrying, which would in turn produce fewer offspring; secondly, raising the marriage age to 30 would reduce the number of years a male could father children, which would also contribute to a decline in the birthrate. As population pressures mounted, Dorian knights all over Crete gradually accepted these laws. The customs then spread, according to Percy, via the Spartans, the Dorian cousins of the Cretans, to other areas of Greece.[36]

One problem with this theory is that at least in some regions of Greece the prescribed marriage age for males was already 30 some time before 650 B.C., when Percy says the legislation was enacted in Crete, and, presumably, well before the customs would have spread to other areas. The late eighth-century B.C. poet Hesiod, from the region of Boetia in central Greece, wrote in his *Works and Days* (considered a moral tract), that men should not marry until the age of 30.[37] Boetia was regarded by the Greeks as the most backward region in Greece, and if so, its marriage customs would most likely be a reflection of the practices of earlier times. Hence, Hesiod's view on the appropriate age for marriage may based on a long-standing Boetian tradition that significantly predates the legislation of the Dorians of Crete.

It is also hard to believe that men would have begun to pursue other males simply because of legislation. Homosexuality in one form or another was almost certainly always present among the Greeks, just as it was prevalent in other ancient cultures contemporary with the beginnings of Greek presence in the Aegean. As noted earlier, there is evidence that homosexuality, particularly pederastic practices, was common among the Hittites, the Mycenaean Greeks' ethnic cousins across the Aegean in Anatolia, with whom they had extensive interaction and with whom they shared divinities and mythology. It seems unlikely that the Mycenaeans, who had many cultural traits in common with the Hittites, would not have also shared their sexual customs. The early initiation myths, some of which show strong association with the Indo-Europeans of Anatolia, seem to confirm the presence of a tradition of hierarchical homosexuality among both the Indo-Europeans of Anatolia and their Mycenaean Greek cousins. Homosexuality, whether in bonds between warriors, or casual relationships among youth, must also have been known in the Greek feudal period depicted by Homer.

There are also examples in the Homeric epics of references to the physical or sensual beauty of youths or young men that demonstrate without a doubt that in that period men regarded them as sexual objects. The example of Zeus' attraction to the Trojan prince Ganymede has already been mentioned. In Book X of *the Odyssey*,[38] the hero, Odysseus, while exploring the island of Circe, encounters, but does not recognize, the god Hermes, "in the form of a youth with the first down of his beard upon his chin, in whom the charm of youth is fairest," the sort of description that in later times signified a young man at the peak of sexual attractiveness to other males. In the *Iliad*, Homer speaks of the beauty of Nireus, second only to that of "perfect Achilles."[39] A striking example of the appreciation that the men of Homer's world had for the beauty of younger men appears in the poignant scene where the aging King Priam comes in great distress to Achilles to beg for the return of the body of his son, Hector. Despite the heart-rending emotion of his task, the king still cannot help glancing with admiration upon the beauty of the same young man who had slain his son. On this passage, the German classicist Rainer Gerlach observed, "We must accordingly form a higher idea of the beauty of Achilles than of the charms of Helen; for Priam, on whom the most unspeakable sorrow has been inflicted by the former, admires it and is able to be surprised at it, at the very moment when he is begging for the dead body of his son."[40]

While the legislation Percy cites, which is documented only in Crete, could have contributed to the prominence that homosexuality had in Greece beginning in the late seventh century and onward, it seems improbable that the legislation—if there was such legislation on the Greek mainland, which is not documented—would have caused men to suddenly begin pursuing youths. It seems more likely that such legislation may have reflected a growing appreciation of the utility homosexual customs played in serving social needs, in this case, curbing overpopulation. Since sex researchers have found that among human societies where homosexuality is "merely approved, it tends to be prevalent," the social sanction provided by the legislation Percy cites could have contributed to the high visibility homosexuality had in art, literature and society beginning in the late seventh century B.C. However, it is clear that the homosexual customs of the Greeks derived from much older traditions.

The Initiatory Homosexuality of the Dorian Greeks

Whether or not the prominence of homosexuality among the classical Greeks was due to any of the above reasons, none of the circumstances raised by these various scholars in their arguments can explain the distinctly initiatory character of the homosexual customs among the Greeks most known for holding on to ancient traditions, that is, the Dorian Greeks of Crete and Sparta. Many scholars now recognize that before the rise of the Greek city-states the progression of a male youth into adult society was accompanied by rites of passage, or initiation.[41] These initiation rites, which are thought to be part of the Indo-European inheritance of the Greeks, and which gave rise to the great number of myths of initiation documented by Bernard Sergent, are regarded today by an increasing number of scholars as the source of the educational homosexuality of classical Greece.[42] One such initiation rite, still being practiced by the Dorian aristocrats of Crete as late as classical times, centers around an explicitly sexual relationship between an adult warrior and a youth, and bears an uncanny resemblance to homosexual initiation rites observed among aboriginal tribes in recent times. The ritual is described in the work of the Greek historian Strabo, who had taken it from an account of the fourth-century B.C. writer Ephorus, whose works have not survived. Since the time of the Dorian invasion, much of Crete was dominated by powerful, culturally conservative noble families who maintained ancient traditions long past the time they were abandoned by other Greeks.[43] Thus, the homosexual initiation ritual described by Ephorus is considered to be a relic of ancient practices that were widespread in earlier times.[44]

In this Cretan ritual an armed noble warrior took a youth away from his home into the wilds of the countryside for two months, where he taught him hunting and warrior arts, while engaging in sexual relations with him. In the manner of Zeus, who took on his lover, Ganymede, by kidnapping him, the Cretan rite began with a mock abduction. As Strabo writes,

> [The Cretans] have a peculiar custom in regard to love affairs, for they win the objects of their love, not by persuasion, but by capture. The lover tells the friends of the boy three or four days beforehand that he is going to make the capture. But for the friends to conceal the boy, or not to let him go forth by the appointed road, is indeed a most disgraceful thing, a confession, as it were,

that the boy is unworthy to obtain such a lover. And when they meet, if the abductor is the boy's equal or superior in rank or other respects, the friends pursue him and lay hold of him, though only in a very gentle way, thus satisfying the custom. And after that they cheerfully turn the boy over to him to lead away. If, however, the abductor is unworthy, they take the boy away from him. And the pursuit does not end until the boy is taken to the *andreion* (men's house) of his abductor.

Like Apollo, who took Hyacinthus out "along the rough mountain peaks of the rugged ridges," the Cretan warrior then took the youth into the wilderness of the countryside, where the warrior taught his young lover hunting, and engaged in sexual relations with him. Then, "after feasting and hunting with them for two months — for it is not permitted to detain the boy for a longer time — they return to the city."[45]

According to Ephorus, at the end of the period in the countryside, the lover presented his beloved with a set of military armor, a drinking cup and an ox for sacrifice to Zeus. The presentation of a drinking cup to the youth signified his being accepted into adult male society, since in Greek culture women and children were not allowed to drink wine.[46] Then, continues Ephorus, "the youth sacrifices the ox to Zeus and gives a feast for those who came down with him from the mountains. He then declares, concerning his relationship with the lover, whether it took place with his consent or not; the convention encourages this in order that, if any violence is used against him in the abduction, he may restore his honor and break off the relationship." This last point indicates that in the absence of coercion, the relationship between the lovers would normally continue, that the initiation ceremony marked the beginning of the sexual relationship. After the conclusion of the ritual, the young man, like the lover apprentices of Azande warriors, became the shield bearer for his lover, and took up residence with his lover in the andreion, the men's house, where he joined in the common meals, and continued his training.

In this ritual of the Dorian Greeks of Crete can be found all the principal elements of sexual initiation found in aboriginal tribal cultures. Participation in the ritual was compulsory. It was a requirement for youths of noble families to undergo this initiation in order to gain acceptance in adult society; for a handsome youth of a good family not to be chosen by a lover would be a disgrace to the boy and his family. The removal of the youth from home and family into a foreign or alien environment was meant to break his association with his childhood, to cleanse him of maternal influences, and symbolized the death of his child self.

The instruction in hunting is a vestige of a much earlier time when hunting was an important food source, and a principal role of the adult male was as a hunter, not only to provide food, but to protect domestic animals from wild predators.[47] Hunting in many tribal cultures is closely associated with initiation, and was an opportunity for the initiate to prove his mettle. As among the Germanic tribes, a youth was required to kill a boar or bear as an initiatory ordeal, because in killing such a powerful animal, the young man would prove he was the equal of the powerful animal. The killing of a boar also persisted as an initiatory requirement in the time of Alexander the Great in neighboring Macedonia, where a man could only recline at dinner with other adults after he had killed a boar without a hunting net. Cassander, the son of one of Alexander's generals, had to sit upright at the table at the age of thirty-five, because he had not yet accomplished this feat.[48]

At the end of the two month period, the young man re-emerged from the wilderness, reborn as an adult. His transformation to adult status was commemorated by his being given the three gifts prescribed in the ritual — the suit of armor, which marked his ascension to the status of an adult warrior, the ox, which he sacrificed to Zeus and thus assumed the ritual responsibilities of an adult, and the cup, symbolizing his entry to the confraternity of adult warriors. Like the youth of the Germanic or Celtic tribes, who upon initiation left their homes and joined the *mannerbunde* or *fianna*, the recently initiated Cretan youth took up residence in the andreion of his lover, where he served in an apprentice capacity to his lover, and lived until he married at the age of 30.

Finally, the sexual submission of the youth to his teacher played an integral role in the attainment of adult status by the young man. Like Melanesian tribesmen, the Greeks believed that a noble warrior's desirable manly qualities — his virtue, courage and skill with weaponry, what the Greeks called his *arete*—were transmitted to the youth in his semen via anal intercourse.

The Sexual Transmission of Noble Manhood

The importance of these homosexual relationships in the acquisition of manly virtues by a youth was first described in the modern West by the 19th-century German scholar C.O. Mueller, who had no knowledge of the similar beliefs of Melanesian warriors.[49] Mueller's views were developed by Eric Bethe in his 1907 paper in which he was the first scholar to note the similarity between these Greek and Melanesian customs, which at that time were only beginning to be reported in the West. While Bethe's claim that the Greeks believed a warrior's arete was transmitted via sexual intercourse into his student lover was ridiculed by his academic contemporaries — and is still vigorously rejected by many academic classicists — the work of some modern scholars has revived interest in this understanding of Greek homosexuality.[50]

Bethe found support for Mueller's views in inscriptions discovered in the late 19th century on the Aegean island of Thera, which seem to commemorate the sexual climax of an initiatory ritual. Like Crete, Thera had been under the rule of Dorian aristocrats since the time of the Dorian arrival in the Aegean. The inscriptions, dating from the seventh century B.C., were found carved into a rock wall adjoining a temple of Apollo, which itself is significant. From very ancient times Apollo had been closely associated with male initiation; the poet Hesiod, in the late eighth century B.C., wrote in his *Theogony* that "the Lord Apollo brings young boys to manhood."[51]

The inscriptions announce the completion of anal intercourse with a youth. "Invoking the Delphic Apollo, I, Crimon, here copulated with a boy, son of Bathycles," states one inscription. These inscriptions have been dismissed by some academic scholars as obscene graffiti.[52] However, the sacred site and the invocation of the name of Apollo, whom the Dorians believed to be the patron of male initiation, strongly argue that the sexual act just performed was in conjunction with the performance of a ritual. The Greek word used in the inscription for the sexual act, *ophein*, means to copulate "in accordance with the law," and in legal texts was used to indicate the marriage act.[53] Thus, the inscriptions are an announcement of the formal consummation of the relationship between erastes and eremenos — the climax of a sexual initiation rite.

The certainty of the Greeks that such intangible qualities as courage and manly skills could be transmitted via semen has its roots in the same primordial superstitions about the life force residing in the skull and being transmitted through the phallus that underlie the head-hunting and initiatory homosexuality in New Guinea and that have been documented among the Celtic, Scythian and Germanic tribes. Aspects of this primitive belief complex can be seen in many areas of Greek life, ranging from ritual to philosophy.

Weston La Barre has shown how among the early Indo-European tribes the life-giving

powers thought to reside in the skull became associated with the cup.[54] The symbolic importance of the acquisition of a cup in the initiation of a young Cretan Greek very likely had its
origins in the skull rituals of the Indo-European ancestors of the Greeks. Like the other Indo-
European peoples, the Greeks had a reverence for the power and fertility represented by the
life-force transmitting phallus. The phallus itself was a religious symbol believed to possess
magical properties which enabled it to break the spell of evil spirits — the belief being that
evil spirits were so enchanted by the sight of the phallus that they ignored everything else.[55]
Every temple and house in Athens had standing in front of it a herma, a four-sided column
with a man's head and a protruding, erect phallus. The hermas, which were placed there for
protection of the building and its occupants, were also found at crossroads. Similar hermas
are still found at the doorways of houses in the Southwest Pacific, a region where homosexual initiation, head-hunting and attendant skull cults and phallic worship were widespread
until very recently.[56]

Dionysus, the god of fertility, was associated with the phallus, and processions in his
honor included large phalluses carried by participants, who also had large artificial phalluses
strapped onto them. Dionysus is called both *phales,* which means the phallus personified, and
paiderastes, which means a lover of boys, and, in fact, sexual initiation was closely associated
with phallic worship. According to the German philologist Ulrich von Wilamowitz-Moellen-
dorf, "for the Hellenes, the phallus symbolized the full force of manliness, not just procreative power," and, thus, because of its powerful symbolism, the act of being sexually penetrated
by a virile warrior had an enormous psychological impact on the life of the initiated youth.[57]
Like the Celtic Cernunnus and the Nordic Frey, who are depicted with phallic horns growing out of the life-force-containing head, Apollo Carneius, a Dorian variant of Apollo, was
originally depicted with horns. The name Carneius, in fact, means "the horned." An archaic
stele dedicated to Apollo has been found with the horns of a ram coming out of the head. In
a combination of phallic symbolism, the image of Apollo Carneius has also been found on a
herma. Not coincidentally, the temple where the Thera inscriptions announcing the completion of sexual initiations were found was dedicated to Apollo Carneius.[58]

The information we have on the beliefs of the Celtic, Germanic and Scythian tribes
about the life force being resident in the skull and expressed through the phallus, which in
every other respect are closely similar to those of Melanesian tribes, is not sufficient to confirm
that they, too, believed that a warrior's virility was passed with his semen into his young lover.
But if these interrelated beliefs, which they shared with the Greeks, were part of a common
Indo-European inheritance, which seems likely, it would follow that that they also believed
that the sexual initiation that was reported among them was responsible for the transformation of youth into courageous warriors, because such a belief system is reflected in the work
of a variety Greek writers.

The Greeks believed that qualities of a man's character, such as courage, virtue and wisdom, resided in his psyche, his consciousness or soul. According to Plato, "the psyche is itself
seed (*sperma*), or perhaps more precisely it is in the seed, and the seed is in the skull and in
the spinal 'generative marrow' and *breathes* through the genital."[59] As astonishing as it may
seem, in this passage Plato succinctly and precisely stated the very same concept that is the
basis for the head-hunting and initiatory homosexuality of the Stone Age tribes of Melanesia. In the *Symposium,* Plato cites as a benefit of homosexual love the transmission of the special qualities of artists, poets and statesmen *in their seed* to their young lovers. "And he who
in youth *has the seed of these implanted in him* and is himself *inspired*" — as a result of having
their seed implanted in him — goes on as an adult to likewise seek to propagate wisdom and
beauty in suitable youth via homosexual love.[60]

The Pythagorean philosopher Diogenes of Apollonia taught that "the seed is a drop of the brain containing in itself warm vapor" and that this vapor becomes the psyche of the new creature. The Stoic philosophers taught that the seed is breath, or *pneuma*. The impregnation of the goddess Io by the breath of Zeus is referred to several times in the plays of Aeschylus. Aristotle refers to procreation as "blowing," an association also found in English — the slang term used to describe oral sex performed on a male. The fact that there is a similar expression in Hindi suggests that the association goes back to early Indo-European times.[61]

C.O. Mueller, in his examination of Spartan rituals, wrote that the older lover's sexual love for the youth "was termed a *breathing-in* or *inspiring*."[62] The word "inspire," in fact, is derived from *spirare*, Latin for "breathe." Xenophon wrote that the development of virtue in youths was brought about "by the very fact that we *breathe our love* into beautiful boys."[63] Or, as Plato described it, "He who in youth *has the seed of these implanted in him* and is himself *inspired*." Thus, a word used for the older lover in Sparta, *eispnelas,* according to Eric Bethe, should be translated as "in-blower" of seed.[64] The Greek historian Aelian wrote that Spartan youth asked their lovers to "breath into them."[65] And what was passed into them through this "breathing-in," as Xenophon notes, were qualities of the man's psyche, itself, his virtue, courage, wisdom and manly skills, which, as Plato wrote, were contained in his seed (*sperma*) and "breathe through the genital."

This Greek belief is another amazing illustration of the seeming universality of this primordial belief complex among early peoples. While the initiatory rituals of the Dorian Greeks of Crete very probably originated in Indo-European prehistory, the beliefs underlying their sexual customs are evidently much older, and complete the picture we have of a generalized Indo-European tradition that, in its remarkable similarity to the customs and beliefs of the Stone Age tribes of Melanesia, evokes an ancestral lineage that surely descended from deep in the Paleolithic past.

Military Initiation in Sparta

Among the Dorians of Sparta, the training of a youth in warrior skills and social responsibilities was also incorporated into homosexual customs. The Spartans were extraordinarily secretive about their rites, and the only accounts that survive of these institutions are those written by outsiders who would not have been privy to the details. Nonetheless, the consensus of modern scholars is that the available evidence leaves little doubt that sexual relations between a youth and a young adult warrior who served as his mentor and teacher were an integral part of Spartan military education.[66]

Sparta, like Crete, preserved ancient traditions that had long disappeared in other city-states. Indeed, many aspects of Spartan customs concerning homosexuality and marriage strongly resemble those reported in recent times among tribal cultures which practice sexual initiation.[67] As in many primitive tribal societies, the men were segregated from the women and children, sleeping in a men's house, or barracks. Also in common with tribal initiation rituals, participation in the rites was compulsory for youths, involved separation from home and family, was carried out under rigorous conditions, required the successful completion of difficult ordeals, and was accomplished under the guidance of an adult warrior whose sexual love for the youth was regarded as crucial to his acquisition of the qualities of a noble warrior. Under the auspices of the pre–Olympian Mother Goddess cult of Rhea and Zeus, the boys were cleansed of maternal influence and reborn as men. Also like the rituals of primitive tribes was the use of bull-roarers, devices which simulated the sounds of thunder or bulls, which were used to terrify the initiates.[68]

Spartan society, famous for its military regimentation, divided the boys into age classes reminiscent of those which the youths of the Marind-Anim of New Guinea progress through during initiation. A boy's training started at the age of seven when he joined a troop of boys under the leadership of an older boy or youth who was in turn supervised by adults. He lived with the other members of his age class in barracks and ate his meals in a common mess hall like those of the adults. The boys were encouraged to visit the men's mess hall, where the adults reclined, and each had a boy as wine-pourer next to him who would fill his cup when he emptied it. The boys were expected to listen to the political discussions and the reports of the men's heroic exploits, and were even permitted to ask questions, which had to be answered. According to the legendary Spartan leader Lycurgus, the experience gained by the boys from observing the men's meals was an important supplement to their education.[69]

When a boy reached 12, according to Plutarch, he was entrusted to the care and control of a lover chosen among the noblest warriors of adult age.[70] Thereafter the boy lived in the men's house with his lover, who supervised his military training and was held accountable for the youth's performance and behavior. The older lover had an authority over his young lover similar to that of parent over a child. Indeed in many ways the authority of a lover over his beloved was considered superior to parental authority, for it came at the age when the youth was beginning to ripen into manhood and cast off the bonds of family authority and tradition.[71] While his family brought the boy into the world, it was his adult lover who parented his entry into world of the adult citizen. The lover was thus fully responsible for the growth and educational development of his beloved, and shared the youth's honor or shame.[72] According to Plutarch, the lover of one youth was punished after the young man screamed in pain from an injury suffered in a mock battle.[73]

While the sexual bond between the youth and his warrior lover was the principal relationship he had during these years, it may not have been exclusive. In listing the types of relationships a Spartan male could have, K.J. Dover notes, "first, loyalty to the males of his age-group, with whom he competed for recognition of his male virtues, and with whom he may have had frequent and casual homosexual relations."[74] The bond that grew between a Spartan and others of his age class was apparently so strong that Spartan warriors were known to share their young lovers and even their wives with age-mates.[75] That the young Spartan could remain an eremenos well into his 20s is implied by a passage from Plutarch in which during a discussion of the Spartans' everyday activities he states that those under the age of thirty "absolutely never went to the market, but had the transactions necessary for the management of their households carried out for them by their kinsmen and *erastai*." In other words, according to Plutarch, a young Spartan might remain the beloved of a warrior even after he was elevated, at the age of 20, to the status of an adult warrior and had joined the membership in a common mess with other adult warriors.[76]

Like the Dorians of Crete, who only allowed the "abduction" of a youth by a warrior of sufficiently noble character, the Spartans placed paramount importance on the qualities and virtue, the arete, of the older lover. This is because the acquisition of arete was the primary goal of educational development throughout ancient Greece for males of the ruling class, and it was from a youth's lover that the Greeks believed he acquired it. A man of insufficient nobility would be incapable of passing on true arete to a youth.

Arete, a word that sums up the Greek ideal of noble adulthood, is a term which has no precise equivalent in present day language. It was arete from which a man derived power of mind, body and spirit, skill in weaponry and argument, and the character underlying his courage and steadfastness in battle. Arete was the source of a man's hardiness, his faithfulness to duties, his obedience, his sense of solidarity with his fellows and his country, his honesty, integrity and power of judgment, as well as his fairness, temperance and generosity.[77] To the ancient Greeks, arete was interwoven with honor, and its cultivation in its citizens was regarded as crucial to the survival of their society.

Arete manifested itself in the nobility of ancestry, and so fathers and forefathers were often enumerated when a man was described. This is why, in the Thera inscription cited earlier, the name of the youth is not mentioned, only that he is the "son of Bathycles," and thus, as the son of man of known nobility, worthy of the cultivation of arete.[78] In line with this admiration of the Dorians for the arete of a male, it was not a youth's beauty that made him attractive, but his incipient nobility and virility. In his description of the Cretan ritual, Ephorus notes that, "it is not the boy who is unusually handsome whom they regard as a worth object of love, it is the boy who is eminent in respect to manliness and decency." This emphasis on the qualities of a youth is reflected in the adjective the Dorians used to describe an attractive or desirable youth, *agathos*, which means good in a noble or virtuous sense.

As a consequence of these beliefs, the sexual relationships which the Spartans saw as responsible for the development of arete in their youth were not private affairs, but were regarded as of great importance by the state, and were supervised by its legal authorities. According to Xenophon, the Spartan leader Lycurgus considered it important for men of quality and nobility to seek the love of youths so that their qualities, their arete, could be passed on. In fact, a noble warrior could face punishment for not taking a youth as a lover. The Greek historian Aelian wrote of an incident where the Spartan authorities punished a man, who in his virtue and arete was suitable as a tutor, but who did not want the trouble and responsibilities involved in a pederastic relationship. Similarly, a youth could be punished for refusing to take on a lover, or for preferring a rich, but base man to a poor though noble man.[79] Thus, to the Dorians, the attainment of their highest social aims was intertwined with sex, which is one reason many traditional scholars have found the homosexuality of the Greeks so perplexing: the expression and achievement of the greatest of ideals was found though the pursuit of sexual relations these scholars found repugnant and antithetical to their concepts of virtue.

The rigor and consistency with which the Dorians educated their young men was admired throughout Greece, as was the remarkable military proficiency that resulted. From 669 to 371 B.C., a span of nearly three centuries, the Spartans were defeated in battle only once.[80] There is no doubt that the homosexuality that was central to Spartan military education played a role in the heroic achievements of the Spartan army. Not only would the beloved have striven for excellence in his training to please his lover, but the older lover, in order to maintain the admiration of his beloved, was inspired to live by the highest standards, and to demonstrate the greatest courage in battle, lest his beloved see him falter. Accordingly, before a battle, the Spartans offered sacrifices not to Ares, the god of war, but to Eros, the god of love.[81]

Plutarch recounts an instance of a Spartan falling before an enemy in battle, crying out to his adversary to let him turn and take the fatal thrust in his chest, so that his beloved would not find him wounded in the back, as if struck down while fleeing. A similar story is told of a Dorian warrior in Crete by Aelian.[82] The desire of an erastes to display valor before his beloved is illustrated in the story of the legendary hero, Cleomachus, who was called in by the citizens of the city of Chalcis to help defend them from the cavalry of an enemy. Cleomachus first called his eremenos to watch the battle. The young man kissed Cleomachus and put his helmet on his head for him. Cleomachus, with his beloved watching, then joined the battle and successfully broke through the ranks of the enemy, ensuring their defeat, but losing his life in the process. The citizens of Chalcis thereafter honored his grave, and attributed the founding of educational homosexuality in their city to Cleomachus.[83]

The belief about the sexual transmission of arete from lover to beloved was not simply the survival of a primeval superstition about sex. It is clear that the Greeks saw tangible results from the educational homosexuality of these relationships, and as a result there was great concern throughout the history of classical Greece for protecting the ennobling aspects of these relationships and guarding against their deterioration into base sexual pursuits. The Greeks didn't have the understanding of psychology to be able to appreciate that the effectiveness of educational homosexuality in inculcating values and skills in their youth was in large part due to the powerful psychological influence that a dominant lover and admired role model would have on a developing youth. However, the Greeks intuitively understood the role that emotions stirred by love played in inspiring virtue and excellence in both the lover and the beloved. The nobility and valor that was inspired by love between erastes and eremenos was highly regarded throughout Greece, and was even praised by Plato in one of his dialogues:

> Without these feelings it is impossible for city or person to perform any high and noble deeds. Let me then say that a man in love, should he be detected in some shameful act or in a cowardly submission to shameful treatment at another's hands, would not feel half so much distress at anyone observing it, whether father or comrade or anyone in the world, as when his beloved did. And in the selfsame way we see how the beloved is especially ashamed before his lover when he is observed to be about some shameful business. So that if we could somehow contrive to have a city or an army composed of lovers and their favorites, they could not be better citizens of their country than by thus refraining from all that is base in a mutual rivalry for honor. And such men as these, when fighting side by side, one might almost consider able to make even a little band victorious over all the world. For a man in love would surely choose to have all the rest of the host rather than his favorite see him forsaking his station or flinging away his arms. Sooner than this, he would prefer to die many deaths. While as for leaving his favorite in the lurch, or not succoring him in his peril, no man is such a craven that Love's own influence cannot inspire him with a valor that makes him equal to the bravest born.[84]

Such a military corps composed of pairs of lovers fighting side by side was indeed formed, just as Plato described it, by the city of Thebes in the fourth century. Called the "Sacred Band of Thebes," this unit of 300 warriors was credited with remarkable military feats. The Sacred Band was the heart of the Theban army that gave the Spartans their first defeat in nearly two centuries, at Leuctra in 371 B.C. This army of homosexual lovers remained undefeated until it was vastly outnumbered by the forces of Philip of Macedon at Cheironeia in 338 B.C. The practice of lovers fighting in pairs may have been customary in Crete, as well, because there the younger lover was called *parastathens*, which means he who stands by another's side.[85]

Love Among Women in Early Greece

Plutarch wrote that "this type of love" was so well thought of by the Spartans that even "the young girls had love relations with beautiful and good women," and that "the most respectable women became infatuated with girls."[86] This rare reference to life among Greek women sheds light on a sexual tradition that seems to have been as firmly implanted in early Greek culture as love relations between men.[87]

Though among the early Greeks women had enjoyed relatively high status in society, as seen in the importance of goddesses in Greek mythology and the relative prominence of women in the Homeric epics, by the Classical age and the development of the male-oriented polis their status became secondary. Further, since the purpose of educational pederasty in post–Homeric Greece was the creation of a virtuous and capable body of citizens, which was by definition restricted to free males, love among women was of little interest or importance to the dominant male society, and thus little was written about it.[88]

However, according to Plutarch and other writers, initiation ceremonies for young women in Sparta were nearly equal in importance to those for young men. Women played an important part in the Hyacinthia, the great Spartan festival that was in part a celebration of the tradition of sexual initiation. According to Bernard Sergent, pedagogical relations among women similar to those symbolized by Hyacinthus and Apollo among men, date from very early periods.[89] Initiation rituals among women share some of the features of those for males, for example, segregation from the town or community and the love of a woman. But in contrast to educational homosexuality among males, which occurred in relationships between younger and older men, love in the female rites could either be between girls, or between a girl and the headmistress, the education occurring within the experiences of life in the community of women. These female rites were not restricted to Sparta. There were special sanctuaries for these rites outside Sparta at Limnai, between Laconia and Messenia, but also at Brauron, in the Attic countryside near Athens.[90]

In fact most of what is known about love between women in ancient Greece comes not from Sparta, but from the great poetess, Sappho, of the Aeolian island of Lesbos. Born of an aristocratic family in 612 B.C., Sappho was a poetess of such stature that Plato called her the "Tenth Muse," Socrates called her "Sappho the Beautiful," and Strabo called her "miraculous."[91] Unfortunately, most of her work was destroyed under instructions of early Christian leaders, and so we have today only a small fragment, six hundred out of twelve thousand verses Sappho composed.[92] For most of her life she was the head of a *thiasoi*, an association of young women, found not only on Lesbos, but in other areas of Greece. These were not merely finishing schools, as has sometimes been written. It is true that they were communities in which adolescent girls learned dance, music and singing, and the graces which would make them desirable women. But the thiasoi were more than that: they were groups with their own divinities and rituals where girls went through a transforming experience of life that was somewhat analogous to that experienced by males in initiation rituals.[93]

In the thiasoi, the young women learned the joys and vicissitudes of love through relations with other women, which we can see, quite clearly, in the poems which Sappho wrote over the years to various girls. "Once again limb-loosening Love makes me tremble, the bitter-sweet, irresistible creature," she writes of one such young woman. Of another: "For as soon as I look at you, my voice at once fails me, my tongue is silent, and an intangible fire circulates beneath my skin. My eyes can no longer see. My ears buzz. I am bathed in sweat. A quivering overcomes me."[94] To another friend she makes this request: "I bid you, Abanthis, take your lyre and sing of Gonglya, while desire once again flies around you, the lovely one. For her dress excited you when you saw it; and I rejoice."[95] One cannot deny the sexual passion that wells from Sappho's words.

In the seventh and sixth centuries love relations between women were not only an accepted feature of life in the thiasoi, but they were formalized in an initiation-type ritual that brought two girls together in a sexual union similar to a marriage.[96] One such union between two young women has been immortalized in a *parthenion*, a song for a chorus of virgins, written by the Spartan poet Alcman on commission for the ceremony. Two girls in the thiasoi, Agido and Hagesichora, are in love, and in the song, the chorus, which represents the others girls in the thiosos, regret that through no temptation or gift will any of the other girls be able to detach Agido from Hagesichora and persuade her to love another: "For abundance of purple is not sufficient for protection, nor intricate snake of solid gold, no, nor Lydian headband, pride of dark-eyed girls, nor the hair of Nanno, nor again god-like Areta nor Thylacis and Cleisithera."[97] Apparently it was not uncommon for the girls in the thiasoi to ask for the intervention of the headmistress in winning the favor of another girl. And so when the chorus turns to address Agido, they make reference to Aenesimbrota, the headmistress of the Spartan thiasoi where the ceremony was being held: "Nor will you go to Aenesimbrota's and say, if only Astaphis were mine, if only Philylla were to look my way and Damareta and lovely Ianthemis; no, Hagesichora guards me."[98]

In the post–Homeric world, then, it is clear that sexual love among women was accepted and even institutionalized to some extent. That it was not confined to the thiasoi is illustrated by numerous vase paintings and plates from throughout Greece illustrating love between women, such as a plate from Thera shows two women courting, and a red-figured vase from Athens shows a kneeling woman fingering the genital region of another.[99] In addition, there is abundant evidence that women frequently used *olisboi*, dildo-like objects made of leather, to satisfy themselves, either by themselves, or not infrequently together with another woman.[100] However, by Classical times the thiasoi had disappeared and with them any literate references to the world of women. With the subordination of women and their confinement to household roles that came with the ascendancy of the male-oriented polis, a silence fell on the world of women. That is not to say, however, that homosexuality ceased to be practiced among women. There is evidence that neglected Greek women found the comfort and solace denied to them by husbands with other women,[101] and that these relationships may have taken on something of the character of a counter-culture reaction to their cloistered segregation.[102]

Educational Homosexuality in Classical Athens

The sexual practices of the Dorian Greeks bear all the hallmarks of traditions that descended from earlier tribal rituals.[103] The homosexual customs of Ionian Athens and other regions of Greece, while shorn of most of the vestiges of a tribal past, nonetheless retained the same educational character and ennobling ideals that underlay the traditions of the Dorian Greeks. In contrast to the military emphasis of education in Sparta, however, the goal of education in Athens was in developing good citizens, educated not only in the use of arms, but in the other areas thought necessary for the cultivation of well-rounded citizens, which included philosophy, music and the arts. The differences in approach that the Athenians took to male homosexuality can also be seen in the word they used to describe a desirable young male. While the Dorians praised a young man with the word, *agathos*, which means good in a noble or virtuous sense, the Athenians used the word, *kalos*, which means beautiful in a sensual or aesthetic sense. Beauty was not, however, merely seen as a physical attribute, but was a quality that went hand in hand with the Greeks' conception of virtue.[104] To the Greeks beauty had spiritual resonance, as a reflection of the perfection of forms, which, as Plato wrote, was the essence of the divine. Thus, the Athenians regarded the pursuit of beauty in youths as consonant with the pursuit of virtue.

The work of the Lyric poets demonstrates that young males were sexually pursued with great passion and enthusiasm by men throughout Greece in the post–Homeric period, and that the pursuit of beautiful young men was a major preoccupation of many upper class men. The Greeks of the late seventh and sixth centuries B.C. left abundant evidence of their appreciation of the beauty of young males: by one count the Greeks in this period erected more than 60,000 statues of nude male youths. As the classicist Jan Bremmer has observed, "This staggering amount can only be understood in terms of an overriding preoccupation with the beauty of the youthful male nude."[105] This preoccupation can also be seen in the paintings on vases. During the sixth century, a great number of vases were produced in Athens painted with illustrations of young males, usually in the nude, many of which were inscribed with the word, *kalos,* or "beautiful." The young males are shown in a variety of activities, from hunting to athletics, and in many cases are depicted being courted by or in a sex act with older men. The overwhelming preference for young males as subjects on vases in this period is demonstrated by the fact that vases with nude males vastly outnumber those painted with scenes of women.

However much the pursuit of younger males by older men was an exercise in sexual passion, it was also an institution of principal social importance to the Athenians, just as it was for the Dorians and other Greeks. While for the Dorians, the purpose of the love relationship was the development of a warrior, for the Athenians it was the vehicle through which males were educated in the values, beliefs and manners important to the Athenians, and through which the young man was introduced to adult male society. The relationship served a socializing function, whereby the youth, as companion to the older man, learned how to comport himself in society, how to enjoy the pleasures of life, and how to bring self-control and moderation to enjoyment of those pleasures.[106] With the guidance of his mentor/lover, the boy began the cultivation of what were to the Greeks the all-important virtues of courage, temperance, justice and wisdom. Though a boy received a basic education in such areas as reading and writing from a tutor, or in later times in a primary school which he would attend until his early teens, it was through his relationship with his lover that he acquired knowledge of and experience in the world of the Athenian citizen, became conversant in politics, civic virtues and philosophy, and acquired an appreciation of the arts. This educational emphasis reflected the Athenian view that civic strength rested not just on military might, but on a citizenry composed of educated and virtuous men.

The broadening of the focus of education in Athens beyond the development of military skills that had been the central aim of training in earlier times, and that continued to dominate education among the Dorians, coincided with a change in military tactics that eclipsed the role of the Athenian aristocracy in battle, and transformed them from warrior-aristocrats to denizens of a leisure class. In earlier times, the effectiveness of an army was based largely on the ability of individual warrior-champions, as illustrated in the tales of individual heroism in the battle scenes in the Homeric epics. In post–Homeric times, Greek armies began to use heavily armored foot soldiers, called hoplites, arrayed in tightly spaced phalanxes in battle. From that point on, it was the compactness and weight of the massed hoplite phalanxes breaking through enemy ranks that proved to be decisive in battles, not the individual brilliance of warrior-aristocrats.

The appearance of the hoplite tactics heralded the decline of the feudal aristocracy in many areas of Greece and contributed to the rise of a middle class. Deprived of their dominant positions in battle, the warrior elites turned their competitive energies to sports. Instead of the fierce display of warrior skills and manly courage in battle, the cultivation of sporting prowess through which one could assert oneself and outclass others became a source of prestige. Thus, distinction in battle, which was for so many centuries the glorious ideal of the Indo-European warrior aristocracy, was supplanted by accomplishment in sport. The growing popularity of sports among the upper class in the early sixth century is illustrated by the fact that in the course of a single decade three major athletic festivals were founded, the Pythian in 582 B.C., the Isthmian in 581 B.C. and the Nemean in 573 B.C.[107]

The shift in the focus of the Athenian aristocracy from military to cultural and athletic activities may have been accelerated by the establishment of a tyranny in 561 B.C. under Pisistratus and his family which reigned for nearly 50 years. With the monopoly of political power by the tyrant, the members of the upper class found themselves further removed from their traditional leadership roles. Like the French aristocracy, who under Louis XIV found their power diminished by the centralizing of authority under the king, and so diverted their competitive spirit into artistic patronage and the cultivation of such divertissements as courtly dancing, the Athenian nobility channeled their energies into athletics, cultural activities and an increasingly refined social life-style. The transformation of the Greek upper class from a warrior caste to a leisure class, and its subsequent preoccupation with cultural pursuits set the stage for an explosion of artistic and intellectual achievement, particularly in Athens, of a brilliance unparalleled in the ancient world, which laid the foundations for the intellectual development of Western civilization. The central role of athletics and its cult of male beauty found expression in the art of the period in the numerous statues of athletically developed male nudes, sculpted by the fifth century B.C. with a grace and naturalness not surpassed until the Italian Renaissance, which served as icons for the age, and with which classical Greece has since been closely identified.

The sort of sexual educational relationship through which a youth was made ready for and introduced to this cultivated upper class society is epitomized by the relationship described by the Lyric poet Theognis between himself and his young lover, Cyrnus. Through his poetry, the reader follows Theognis through a lengthy courtship in pursuit of Cyrnus and witnesses the poet's erotic infatuation with the youth, expressed by declarations of romantic ardor and lamentations over the poet's powerless in the face of such youthful beauty. That part of Theognis' verse which is not concerned with the erotic is given over to lengthy lectures and admonitions about the character and behavior of a true gentleman.[108] Many of the vases produced in the sixth century B.C. in Athens are illustrated with such courting scenes, in which a bearded adult is shown caressing a youth's chin with one hand, and with the other hand fondling his genitals. On some of the vases, the suitor is shown offering gifts which indicate the qualities expected of an eremenos, such as a cockerel, which symbolizes fighting spirit; a hare, hunting skills; and a lyre, musical abilities. Vases from earlier periods show youths being given helmets, which recalls the suit of armor given to the eremenos on Dorian Crete, a gift also given to young men by their lovers in Thebes.[109] On other vases, the adult is shown embracing or kissing his beloved, or performing the sex act with him by placing his erect penis between the youth's thighs.[110]

Some of the vases illustrate this sexual interaction between men and youths against the background of a symposium, a principal setting for socializing among upper class Athenian male society. The symposium was a banquet which featured political discussions, poetry reading and entertainment from musicians and dancers, all accompanied by much drinking. Filling a social role roughly analogous to that of the *andreion* of Dorian Crete and the men's messes of Sparta, scholars have recently shown that the symposia were descended from the warrior's clubs of earlier times, the early Greek counterparts to the *mannerbunde* of the Germanic warriors and the *fianna* of the Celtic tribes.[111] Also like the andreion of Crete and the men's messes of Sparta, the symposium was a venue for the education of youth who were brought there by their lovers.[112] Much of the early poetry, a great deal of which, like the verses of Theognis, was addressed to youths and was frequently didactic in nature, was composed for delivery at such banquets.[113] At the symposia, the youths had to learn and sing songs glorifying the deeds of mythical and historical heroes so that they could learn by their example, a practice that was also widespread in the men's common meals in other regions of Greece.[114] In addition, the youth had to serve, like the mythical eremenos Ganymede, as cup-bearers or wine-pourers for the men, a custom that is mentioned in literature as early as the Homeric epics.[115]

At the point when the young men came of age, they at last were allowed to have their own cups and to join in the drinking with the men. Thus, under the polished veneer of classical Athenian society can still be seen the skeletal vestiges of a primordial initiatory tradition. The youth, under the sponsorship and guidance of a noble adult lover, is introduced into membership in adult male society, symbolized by the symposium, the social descendant of the Indo-European warriors' associations, where he is educated in the values of his elders, and passes from the apprentice status of wine-pourer to full fledged membership, signified by his gaining the privilege of drinking wine with the other men from a cup, the ritual descendant of the skull. The symposium, transformed from a warrior's association into a stage for political and philosophical discussion and cultural activities, was the setting for one of Plato's most famous dialogues, not coincidentally dealing with homosexual love.

Sexual Norms, Mores and Etiquette

While the Athenians had no memory of the ritual origins of their homosexual customs, sexual relationships between adult males and youth performed precisely the same function in Athenian society that sexual rites performed in tribal societies. Instead of the ritual traditions seen in tribal societies, however, the sexual relationships of the Athenians were surrounded by laws, social mores and rules of etiquette whose purpose was nonetheless the same as that of tribal traditions — the preservation of a sexual institution believed to be crucial to the survival of the society.

An Athenian boy could be introduced to such relationships as early as his early teens, though he would never be courted before the age of 12. Many modern Westerners would be outraged at the idea of adults pursuing sexual relations with individuals in their early teens, but it should be noted that in ancient Greece girls were normally married at the age of 12 or 13.[116] The introduction of a male to sexual relations at this stage in his development, when he was, after all, sexually mature, was considered to the Greeks to be part of the normal course of life. Though the age at which a youth was considered most attractive was to some extent a matter of taste, it appears that many Greek men were most drawn to youths in their later teens. As the writer Strato put it,

> The youthful bloom of the twelve-year-old boy gives me joy, but much more desirable is the boy of thirteen. He whose years are fourteen is a still sweeter flower of the Loves, and even more charming is he who is beginning his fifteenth year. The sixteenth year is that of the gods, and to desire the seventeenth does not fall to my lot, but only to Zeus. But if one longs for one still older, he no longer plays, but already demands the Homeric "but to him replied."[117]

However, it was believed by many Greek men that a youth lost his sexual appeal when his beard and body hair began to grow thickly.[118] The poets often threatened reluctant youths who did not give in to their approaches with the specter of what their beard and body hair would do to them: "Thy beard will come, the last of evils but the greatest, and then thou shalt know what scarcity of friends is," wrote Strato to one youth.[119] The poet Julius Diocles wrote of another youth, "And so Damon, who excels in beauty, does not even say good-day now! A time will come that will take vengeance for this. Then, grown all rough and hairy, you will give good-day first to those who do not give it you back."[120]

But it also clear that not all Greek men felt that way. In Plato's *Protagoras*, Socrates is taunted by a friend who pointed out that he was continuing to pursue Alcibiades, his youthful lover, even though his beard had grown. Socrates replies, "But you are not a follower of Homer, then. Homer says that a youth is most seductive at the moment when his beard begins to grow."[121] Some men found young males most attractive at the stage when they were *ephebes*, that is, between the ages of 18 and 22, and in fact there were terms to describe men with a taste for young men of this age, *philephebos* or *philoboupais*— one who is fond of bull-boys (husky young men).[122] In another of Plato's dialogues, *Charmides*, a young man lauded by Socrates as exceptionally appealing, was described as a *neaniskos*,[123] a term signifying a male who had come of age, and who could be anywhere between the ages of 18 and the mid-twenties.[124] One modern writer has concluded that the youths Greek men considered most attractive from a sexual standpoint were those who were the equivalent of college-aged males in today's society. When a young man had reached his mid-twenties, however, he was expected to reverse roles, to stop taking the passive role in sex, and to begin to pursue the active role with a younger lover of his own. By the time a young man reached the age of thirty, marriage to a woman and the fathering of children were the norm, though it is clear that the pursuit of younger males rarely stopped there.

So widespread was the sexual pursuit of younger males by the men of Athens that virtually every prominent Athenian was known for his homosexual loves. The legendary Athenian statesman Solon loved his nephew Pisistratus. The philosopher Socrates was loved by his teacher, Archelaos, and in turn was famous for his pursuit of beautiful young men, most significantly Alcibiades, who later became an Athenian general. In fact, the accusation against Socrates which led to the philosopher's trial and eventual death was made by Anytus, Socrates' rival for the love of Alcibiades. Plato was the lover of Alexis of Dion, and for three generations the position of head of the academy he founded passed from lover to beloved. Aristotle loved a young man named Hermias, whom he immortalized in a hymn. The love relationship between the philosopher Zeno and his lover, Parmenides, continued for most of their lives. The most famous of Greek sculptors, Phidias, loved his pupils Agoracritos of Paros and Pantarces of Airgos. The tragic poet Agathon became the beloved of Pausanias when he was 18, and their relationship was still going strong a dozen years later when Agathon was firmly established as a dramatist. The playwright Sophocles, who married twice and produced two sons, was still pursuing young males when he was in his 60s. The renowned orator Demosthenes, after he married his wife, fell in love with a handsome youth named Knossian, and even moved the young man into his household to live with him.[125] It is perhaps a testament to the preoccupation of Athenian men with the sexual pursuit of younger males that a law attributed to Solon required that men who were married have sex with their wives at least three times a month.[126] As in other societies, though, there is also evidence of a variability in sexual preference among men: the great statesman Pericles, though in a minority among Athenian upper-class males, expressed no interest in the love of young men, but preferred women.

A favorite site for men seeking sexual relationships with youth was the gymnasium, another major social center for Athenian men, particularly those of the leisure class, who would pass the time there exercising, gossiping and ogling the naked adolescents performing their exercises. At the gymnasium a man might seek an opportunity to attract the attention of a youth in a way that could lead to their introduction, or to even touch a boy in a seductive way, as if by accident, while wrestling with him.[127] A man might also offer to rub a particular youth with oil after exercise, another frequently used tactic for initiating a sexual relationship.[128] There are numerous references in Athenian literature of the classical period to the sexual encounters sought by men in gymnasia. The playwright Aristophanes refers to men "hanging around the *palaestra* (wrestling school) trying to seduce boys," and in his comedy *The Birds,* he has a character look upon an encounter with a handsome young man who has "left the gymnasium, after a bath" as an occasion for sexual seduction.[129]

Some of the flavor of the sexually charged atmosphere that was present in the gymnasia is conveyed in the opening of Plato's dialogue, *Charmides*, which recounts the commotion created by the arrival of an exceptionally good-looking youth. In the dialogue, Socrates has just arrived at a wrestling school after a long absence from Athens. He asks a companion, Kritias, to bring him up to date on who among the youth is now

> outstanding in accomplishment or beauty, or both. Kritias glanced towards the door, where he had seen some young men coming in, quarreling with one another, and a crowd following behind them. "So far as the good-looking (kalos) ones are concerned," he says, "I think you'll soon know. The people coming in are the advance party, the erastai (suitors) of the one who is regarded as the best-looking of all at the present time.'"

When the youth, Charmides, after whom the dialogue was named, arrives, Socrates relates, "I marveled at his stature and beauty, and I felt everyone else in the room was in love with him; they were thrown into such amazement and confusion when he came in, and there were many other erastai following after him, too."[130] It appears that the competition among the men for the better looking youths was often heated, and sometimes resulted in quarrels and even fights. The orator Aeschines, in his prosecution of Timarchos, admits that in his own sexual pursuit of such youths he made himself "a nuisance at the gymnasia," and was consequently involved in "hard words and blows arising out of this activity."[131]

Apparently many of the youths' fathers regarded the attention given to their sons by suitors as a nuisance, too, for many men hired tutors whose job in part was to protect their impressionable sons from unwanted pursuit. This was not an expression of disapproval for the homosexuality involved in these relationships, but was an effort to weed out among their sons' pursuers those who were unworthy or motivated solely by base sexual desires.[132] In his dialogue *The Symposium*, Plato distinguishes this undesirable kind of sexual love from that which was considered elevated and praiseworthy. The first, inspired by Aphrodite Pandemos, is common or base love, and this, according to Plato, is the type of love which inspires men of little worth, who pursue women and youths without distinction, who are more in love with bodies than with souls. The second type of love is inspired by Aphrodite Urania. A person inspired by this "heavenly" love does not pursue boys who are too young, who have not yet developed any discernment, nor does he pursue a boy and then abandons him when he finds a new love object more desirable than the last. This sort of lover loves a youth in a stable manner, courts him with perseverance, trying constantly to demonstrate the seriousness of his intentions.[133] It is only this sort of lover, who has demonstrated patience, moderation, self-restraint, piety and other qualities admired by Athenians, who was felt to be capable of guiding a youth's development into virtuous manhood. For his part the youth was expected to resist courtship, to test the seriousness of the lover. According to Aeschines, courtship provided the free youth with an opportunity to demonstrate his propriety and good manners. To give in too easily would show his lack of virtue. Somewhat like a Victorian maiden, he was to affect disinterest, only yielding when the nobility and steadfastness of his suitor had been established.[134]

Some modern writers have maintained that the eremenos derived no pleasure from sex with an older lover. This view is based, in part, on a passage by Xenophon, whose peculiar notions on Greek homosexual traditions were noted earlier. In it he wrote, "A youth does not share in the pleasure of the intercourse as a woman does, but looks on, sober, at another in love's intoxication. Consequently it need not excite any surprise if contempt for the lover is engendered in him."[135] These remarks of Xenophon's have elicited skepticism from other scholars, however. A great amount of courtship literature survives which shows that the boys enjoyed the attention of their suitors and often manipulated them, playing off rivals against each other.[136]

In addition, a passage in Plato's *Symposium,* which describes in detail the attempts of the youthful Alcibiades to maneuver Socrates into seducing him, shows that it was perfectly conceivable to classical Greeks that a youth could desire sex with an older male. First, says Alcibiades,

> I allowed myself to be alone with him ... and I naturally supposed that he would embark on conversation of the type that a lover usually addresses to his darling .... Nothing of the kind; he spent the day with me in the sort of talk which is habitual with him, and then left me and went away. Next I invited him to train with me in the gymnasium, and I accompanied him there, believing that I should succeed with him now. He took exercise and wrestled with me frequently, with no one else present, but I need hardly say that I was no nearer my goal.... So I invited him to dine with me, behaving just like the lover who has designs upon his favorite.... When the light was out and the servants had withdrawn ... I nudged him and said: "Are you asleep, Socrates?" "Far from it," he answered. "Do you know what I think?" continued Alcibiades. "No, what?" "I think that you are the only lover that I have ever had who is worthy of me, but that you are afraid to mention your passion to me. Now, what I feel about the matter is this, that it would be very foolish of me not to comply with your desires in this respect."

But Socrates still ignored the advances of Alcibiades. So, Alcibiades continued,

> Without allowing him to say anything further, I got up and covered him with my own clothes ... and then laid myself down under his worn cloak, and threw my arms round this truly superhuman and wonderful man, and remained thus the whole night long.... But in spite of all my efforts.... I swear by all the gods in heaven that for anything that happened between us when I got up after sleeping with Socrates, I might have been sleeping with my father or elder brother.[137]

Thus in this humorous way, Plato demonstrates the supreme self-restraint of his mentor, Socrates, in the face of the determined advances of a beautiful youth.

The contention that adolescent males would not enjoy sex with an older male is also contrary to the sexual nature of young males. Sex researchers have recognized that males from boyhood onward are fascinated with the sexual characteristics of older, admired males and have displayed a high degree of receptivity to sexual advances from such males.[138] It seems highly unlikely that in a society such as ancient Greece, where male beauty was idealized and homosexuality was institutionalized, adolescents at the peak of their sexual drive would not enjoy the sexual attention of virile and athletically developed older males. Indeed, in some of the vase paintings in which intercrural copulation is depicted between lover and beloved, the younger partner is shown with an erection, an obvious sign of sexual arousal.[139] It's also clear from vase paintings that the youths were willing partners in courting scenes. A standard depiction found in courting scenes is an older male stroking the chin of a youth with one hand while he fondles the genitals of the youth with the other. But on some vases a youth is shown stroking the chin of an adult suitor, or grabbing his arm, seemingly to guide it to his genitals.[140]

Suggestions of the pleasure the eromenos received from anal intercourse also comes from poetry. In the fifth Idyll of Theocritos, the shepherd Komatas reminds his former eromenos, Lakon, of his enthusiasm for the sexual acts they shared: "Don't you remember the time I was up you, and you with a grimace, wiggled your bottom deliciously, holding on tight to that oak tree."[141] A vase painting from the classical period showing two youths preparing to engage in anal copulation[142] demonstrates that they were well aware of the pleasure males could derive from anal sex. It is also likely that adolescent males of classical Athens, as in many other societies, were inclined to casual homosexual relations with peers whenever the opportunity presented itself—in situations such as was illustrated by the same vase.

There was, on the other hand, some concern about the youth appearing to yield too easily to the pleasures of the sexual act, as the Greeks believed a woman would. Plato, in the

Laws, asks, "Who will not blame the effeminacy of him who yields to pleasures and is unable to hold out against them?"[143] So the statement of Xenophon that the eremenos would not share the pleasure of sexual relations with his older lover, which has been accepted by some academic scholars as factual, was merely the opinion of a conservative and somewhat prudish aristocrat, though consistent with the decorum expected of the youth of a mannered and refined upper class society. In a similar way, it was commonly believed in the Victorian period that women did not experience pleasure in sex, a suggestion that would not be taken seriously today.

The Athenians, like the Dorians, closely associated these noble love relationships with courage and civic virtue, and, in fact, attributed the overthrow of the tyranny of the Pisistradid family in the late sixth century B.C. to the noble love of two young men, Aristogeiton and his eromenos, Harmodius. This legendary episode began when Hipparkhos, the younger brother of the tyrant Hippias, son of Pisistratus, attempted to seduce Harmodius. Resentful of the advances made by Hippias towards his lover, Aristogeiton concocted a plot to slay both Hipparkhos and Hippias. The plot was not successful, however, and they succeeded in killing only Hippias. Harmodius was killed on the spot, and Aristogeiton was arrested and died under torture. Though the plot may have been inspired more by Aristogeiton's jealousy than patriotism, and the tyranny endured for five more years until it was finally overthrown, the two lovers were nonetheless celebrated in popular tradition as heroes who freed Athens from tyranny. Nude statues of the two lovers commemorating their sacrifice were erected all over Athens, and both Plato and Aeschines cited them as exemplars of the noblest kind of love. Because of the valor inspired by these elevated relationships, Plato wrote, homosexual love shared the evil reputation of philosophy and gymnastics in "countries which are subject to the barbarians," because "they are inimical to tyranny." And, continued Plato, "Our own tyrants learned this lesson through bitter experience, when the love between Aristogeiton and Harmodius grew so strong that it shattered their power. Whenever, therefore, it has been established that it is shameful to be involved in sexual relationships with men, this is due to evil on the part of the legislators, to despotism on the part of the rulers, and to cowardice on the part of the governed."[144]

Because of the importance they attached to the role of these sexual relationships in molding noble and virtuous citizens, the Athenians and other Greeks went to great pains to protect the ennobling character of these relationships, and prevent their deterioration into base sexual affairs. A law attributed to Solon forbade a slave from seducing or courting a free youth in any way. Plutarch explained that, through this law, Solon placed the homosexual love of youths "in the category of what was honorable and worthy, thus in a way prompting the worthy to that which he forbade the unworthy."[145] Several Greek laws prohibited classes of people considered unfit to love boys from entering the gymnasia — those hotbeds of sexual pursuit. These included those engaged in commercial activities (regarded as of a lower social class), male prostitutes, slaves, slaves who had been freed as well as their sons, drunks, lunatics and the infirm. Also excluded were those "older than the boys," a reference to the young males who had reached the *neaniskos* age class. These were young men who had come of age, but were still in the transitional years between youth and adulthood, and in sexual matters, as capable of taking the passive role as they were desirous of pursuing the active.[146] Xenophon wrote of one such young man, Critobulos, who "while still an eromenos nevertheless desires the other youngsters."[147] While in their majority, these young men were felt to be not yet mature enough, still too unruly and irresponsible to be allowed the important responsibilities that came with loving a youth of the ruling class.

The refined mores that the Athenians attached to homosexual love were apparently not shared by all the Greek city-states. A character in Plato's *Symposium* alludes to the variations in attitudes to homosexual love among the other Greek states when he contrasts the situation in Athens, which he characterizes as "complicated" due to the restraints imposed upon the partners, with the customs in Elis and Boetia, where he says homosexual love is unfettered by the sort of moral considerations present in Athens.[148] Xenophon, in fact, wrote that in Boetia and other Greek states homosexuality was so unrestrained that men and boys "were living together like married couples."[149] The Athenians, then, were the "high Victorians" of ancient Greece, having developed an elaborate etiquette and set of laws and social mores whose criteria reflected the sort of sensibilities that evolved over a long tradition — recognizing the virtues and benefits of the institution of educational homosexuality, while also showing long experience with its abuse.

While a set or rules or etiquette grew up around educational homosexuality in Athens governing the manner of courting, the ages of the lover and beloved, the transition from eremenos to erastes, and eventual marriage, there is much evidence that there was considerable variation beyond these norms. Academic scholars have usually maintained that in classical Athens homosexual activity was restricted to one-sided educational relationships between an adult and a youth, and that a male would remain an eremenos only until his late teens or early twenties at the latest, at which point he was expected to switch roles, taking the dominant role in a relationship with a youth, and that all homosexual activity ceased once a man was married at the age of 30.[150]

However, there is abundant evidence that these norms represented only an ideal, and one that may have been more honored in its breach. For example same-sex relationships between youths of a similar age seem to have been relatively common in Athens. A number of vase paintings survive which depict the sexual pursuit of a young male by another young man, who is depicted without a beard, a sign of youth.[151] Xenophon, too, makes several references to sexual relationships between youths of similar ages, the first, in his history, *Anabasis*, to the relationship that Menon of Thessaly had, as a youth, with a barbarian youth, and, second, in his *Symposium*, to two youths among the guests at the banquet who are depicted as in love, and who actually kiss during the course of the discussion. In reference to the passion of one of the youths, the character of Socrates says: "This hot flame of his was kindled in the days when they used to go to school together," leaving no doubt that the sexual relationship described was between youths of similar ages.[152]

There is also evidence that sexual relationships between erastes and eremenos could continue well into the adulthood of the younger man, as illustrated by the famous examples of Socrates and Alcibiades, and Pausanias and Agathon, but also by the case of the philosopher Zeno, who was still eremenos of Parmenides when he was 40. Zeno even argued that a young man should be kept as an eremenos until he was 28.[153] Harmodius and Aristogeiton, the two lovers who assassinated the tyrant Hippias, were both old enough to be married when that legendary episode occurred, clearly over the threshold beyond which some writers assumed homosexual behavior would cease. Aristotle, in his *Politics*, described as admirable, not odd or unusual, the relationship between two male lovers who remained together their whole lives. These men, Philolaus, a great statesman of Thebes, and Diocles, a famous Olympic athlete, maintained a single household where they lived together, and even arranged to be buried beside each other.[154]

It is also clear that it was common in classical Athens for married men to continue to pursue homosexual relationships. Socrates carried on his pursuit of Alcibiades despite his marriage to Xanthippe. The playwrights Sophocles and Euripides, both of whom were married, continued their love relationships with younger men into old age. In fact, Euripides was still in love with Agathon when he was 72 and the latter was 40.[155] The case of Demosthenes, who moved his young lover into the house he shared with his wife, has already been mentioned. The orator Lysius was 50 when he wrote in his oration, *Against Simon,* of his love for the youth Theodotus, and his rivalry with his protagonist Simon over the youth.[156] Aeschines, who was 42 and long married at the time of his famous prosecution of Timarchos, told the jury that he was still pursuing sexual relations with younger men. The fact that Aeschines would mention in a matter of fact way his continuing affairs with young men, despite his marriage, at the same time that he was trying to prove the sexual immorality of Timarchos is strong proof that such a practice was not considered by the Athenians to be out of the ordinary or in any way unacceptable.

Not only was it accepted behavior for a married man to pursue youthful male lovers, but it is also clear that these homosexual loves were not considered a violation of the husband's faithfulness to his wife. The Greek myth of Orpheus and Eurydice relates that after the legendary singer was unable to rescue his wife from Hades, this hero, who was famous as an example of conjugal fidelity, consoled himself by turning to the love of youths, "since he was unwilling to be unfaithful to his wife."[157] Further proof that homosexual love was not considered a threat or affront to family life was the practice of men erecting statues of favorite male lovers in the temple of Hera, the goddess protector of the family.[158]

There is also strong evidence that the ancient Greeks were aware of exclusively homosexual inclinations in some men. Plato, in the *Symposium*, related a myth explaining the origins of human sexuality that specifically describes the creation of men and women who desire only their own sex. Originally, according to this myth, humans were all double creatures, like two people joined together, with two heads, two backs, two sets of arms, two sets of legs, and so on. One kind was male and male, a second was female and female, and the third was a mixture of male and female, "hermaphrodites." These beings had a good life, but they were proud and arrogant, and so Zeus decided to punish them by slicing them in half. And therefore, Plato writes, mankind became such that

> each of us then is the mere broken half of a man, the result of a bisection which has reduced us to a condition like that of a flat fish, and each of us is perpetually in search of his corresponding half. Those men who are halves of a being of the common sex, which was called ... hermaphrodite, are lovers of women, and most adulterers come from this class, as also do women who are mad about men and sexually promiscuous. Women who are halves of a female whole direct their affections towards women and pay little attention to men; Lesbians belong to this category. But the men who are a section of the male follow the male and while they are young, being a piece of the man, they love men and delight in lying down beside and being entwined with men. And they are themselves the best of boys and youths, because they have the most manly nature.... And these when they grow up are our statesmen, and these only, which is a great proof of the truth of what I am saying. When they grow to be men, they become lovers of youths, and it requires the compulsion of convention to overcome their natural disinclination to marriage and procreation; they are quite content to live with one another unwed; and such a one is born a lover of youths and fond of having lovers. And when one of them finds his other half, whether he be a lover of youth or a lover of another sort, the pair are lost in an amazement of love and friendship and intimacy, and one will not be out of the other's sight ... even for a moment. These are they who pass their lives with one another.[159]

Plato's description of those who are halves of the male-male creatures who yearn for their other half would certainly be recognized by modern readers as describing what contemporary society understands to be "gay" people. And it also describes very accurately the intense attachment exhibited by Achilles and Patroclus as described in the *Iliad*.

Because of the "compulsion of convention," as Plato describes it, which required Greek upper class men to marry, it is difficult to identify many figures of ancient Athens who would fall into the category of exclusive homosexuals. It is known that Plato, whose high regard for homosexuality is obvious, never married — a rarity in classical Athens. And at least one scholar has argued that Plato was exclusively homosexual.[160] The relationship Aristotle described between the Theban statesman, Philolaus, and the Olympic athlete Diocles, who lived together their whole lives, was mentioned earlier. Scholars have also recognized in the relationship between Agathon and Pausanias as depicted by Plato in the *Symposium* a "relationship that sounds rather like a homosexual marriage," in the words of K.J. Dover.[161] Indeed, in the *Symposium*, shortly after the recounting of the myth of the origins of human sexuality, the speaker refers to Agathon and Pausanias as being "of the manly sort just as I have been describing," those beings who were halves of a male whole who seek only their own kind.[162] John Boswell has observed that the relationship between the two "was wistfully admired by the speakers in the dialogue as the state to which any male would aspire but only a lucky few would attain."[163] Aristotle, in his *Nicomachean Ethics* recognized that some men love only other men "by nature," and in his *Quaestiones* even attempted to explain why some men enjoy carrying out the active role in sex and others only derive pleasure from the passive role with another man.[164]

In a later passage in the *Symposium*, Plato contrasts heterosexual men with primarily homosexual men. The former, he writes, are creative, or "pregnant," only in body, and "betake themselves to women and beget children — this is the character of their love; their offspring, as they hope, will preserve their memory and give them the blessedness and immortality which they desire in the future." But those men who are more creative in their souls than their bodies, that is, those who yearn for their own kind, give birth to "that which is proper for the soul to conceive," that is

> wisdom and virtue in general. And such creators are all poets and other artists who may be said to have invention. But the greatest and fairest sort of wisdom by far is that which is concerned with the ordering of states and families.... And he who in youth has the seed of these implanted in him and is himself inspired, when he comes to maturity desires to beget and generate. And he wanders about seeking beauty that he may beget offspring.... And when he finds a fair and noble and well-nurtured soul, and there is union of the two in one person, he gladly embraces him, and to such a one he is full of fair speech about virtue and the nature and pursuits of a good man; and he tries to educate him; and at the touch and presence of the beautiful he brings forth the beautiful which he conceived long before ... and the man and his male lover tend that which he brings forth, and they are bound together by a far greater tie and have a closer friendship than those who beget mortal children, for the children who are their common offspring are fairer and more immortal.[165]

Plato's description of the role of primarily homosexual individuals in giving birth to progeny of a spiritual nature which benefit all of society is a fascinating parallel to the theory posited by evolutionary biologists of the evolution in the Paleolithic of a specialized non-reproducing role for exclusively homosexual individuals. It is also remarkably similar to the explanation North American Indian cultures give for the berdache, whose sexuality, they believe, was a manifestation of their spiritual nature, created to bring a better quality of life to their tribes.

A notable difference between the sexual traditions of ancient Greece and those of the other societies of the ancient world is the absence of a role for exclusively homosexual men comparable to the berdache of the American Indians, or the homosexual priests and temple prostitutes of the ancient Middle East. However, fragments of the writings of Archilochus, a seventh century B.C. poet, suggest that there may have been such a specialized role for exclusively homosexual priests in the worship of the distant past of the Greeks similar to the transvestite priests reported by Herodotus among the Scythian tribes, and the *seidr* priest believed to be associated with the fertility rites of the early Germanic tribes. In the fragments, Archilochus satirizes what he regards as the effeminate lewdness of a certain musician, probably a cult prostitute, associated with the worship of Cotytto, a pre–Olympian mother goddess, and Sabazios, a god of the Phrygians, an Indo-European people in neighboring Anatolia, who was later identified with the Greek Dionysius.

The link with Dionysius, one of the most ancient of Greek deities, is significant because of his association with fertility rites, which among the early Germanic tribes, as with the peoples of the Middle East, were attended by homosexual priests. Worship rites in honor of Sabazios/Dionysius were held in Athens during classical times by private associations, and were still being performed in the first century B.C. when Diodorus Siculus described their "shameless ceremonies," a clear reference to the sexual nature of their rituals.[166] By classical times institutionalized cult prostitution had long been foreign to the mainstream religious culture of Greece. However, if, as suggested by the fragments of Archilochus, the rituals of the early Greeks included the services of transgenderal homosexual priests, the existence of similar homosexual priests among two other Indo-European groups, the Scythians and the Germanic tribes, supports the conclusion that a berdache-like tradition was present in the worship of the common Neolithic ancestors of the Indo-Europeans comparable to that found in early Mesopotamian cultures. In contrast to the berdache-like transgenderal homosexuality of the priests associated with mother-goddess worship, though, the homosexual tradition of the Greeks was associated with a strong and assertive masculinity, whether among the hyper-masculine heroes of Homeric tradition, or in the educational homosexuality of later times whose principal aim was the cultivation of distinctly masculine virtues and identity in the beloved. Indeed, Plato wrote that those men who yearn for their own kind, that is, exclusive homosexuals, "have the most manly nature."[167]

The Denial of Greek Homosexuality by Modern Writers

Despite the overwhelming evidence of homosexuality in ancient Greece — the thousands of verses of love poetry, the inscriptions on Thera which describe in frank language copulation between males, the numerous depictions of homosexual courting and love-making in vase paintings — some modern writers, especially those of the 19th and the greater part of the 20th century, have maintained that the Greeks condemned homosexuality, a notion that still endures in some quarters. The British historian Rattray Taylor, the author of an influential work on sex in history, wrote as recently as the 1960s that among the Greeks homosexual acts were strictly forbidden and made a felony punishable by death.[168] The French classicist Robert Flaceliere concluded in 1962 that homosexuality was never prevalent in ancient Greece "except in one class of society and over a limited period, and that there is no evidence that homosexuality met with any social approval."[169] Arno Karlen, a psychiatrist who produced a widely read study of homosexuality in 1971, argued that homosexuality was never widely accepted by Greeks, only by a "tiny leisured upper class." Karlen wrote in 1980 that only "a minority, even of the Greek upper classes, encouraged, approved or easily tolerated homosexuality," and that "clearly heterosexuality was the encouraged norm, as it has been in every society past and present."[170] Like many traditional scholars, Karlen here repeats the common assumption which places homosexuality in opposition to heterosexuality, assuming that encouragement of heterosexuality proves a disapproval of homosexuality, and evidently unaware of the great number of societies where homosexual traditions play a complementary role to heterosexual marriage.

In supporting his claim that the Greeks punished a homosexual act with death, Rattray Taylor cites a law supposedly promulgated by the legendary Spartan leader Lycurgus. Not surprisingly, Taylor's source on this law is Xenophon, whose credibility on matters ranging from homosexuality to Athenian politics has been questioned by a number of scholars. The Spartan law Xenophon cites is mentioned nowhere else in classical literature, and was most probably invented by Xenophon to buttress an idealized portrayal of the customs of a city-state the conservative, anti-democratic aristocrat unabashedly admired. The classicist Eric Bethe has characterized Xenophon's description of Sparta's educational customs as chaste as a "whitewashing operation," carried out, despite his knowledge to the contrary, in order to make the Spartans appear to conform to the lofty ideals of Socrates' vision of spiritual love. What's more, the assertion is contradicted by Xenophon himself in other works in which Xenophon writes in a matter-of-fact way about the sexual customs of the Spartans that leave no doubt about the homoerotic preoccupation of Spartan males.[171]

Other writers have based their conclusions about the Greeks' attitudes toward homosexuality on a misinterpretation of laws and mores that were developed not to prohibit homosexual relations, as they assume, but to protect the educational and ennobling character of homosexual love. In analyzing laws which prohibited certain undesirable people from entering gymnasia, Eva Cantarella, an authority on ancient Greek and Roman law, has shown that they were put in place not to prevent homosexuality, as has been argued, but precisely because gymnasia were centers for the sexual courting of upper-class youth, and so access needed to be restricted to those felt worthy of taking such an influential role in the development of these future upper class leaders. While Aeschines stated that violation of the law was punishable by death, Cantarella could find no other evidence that that was the case, or that the death penalty was ever carried out, and so concluded that Aeschines was merely exaggerating the severity of the offense for rhetorical effect.[172] In her review of Greek laws and social mores concerning homosexuality, Cantarella concluded, "Faced with such evidence how can one avoid thinking that adult Greek males enjoyed almost untrammeled freedom, being allowed to devote time to pederastic relationships which were far more than an occasional variation, amounting to a normal, acceptable, natural alternative? How can we fail to conclude that these men were almost completely free to express their emotions and sexuality?"[173]

Also cited to prove the Greeks disapproved of homosexuality are negative comments about homosexuality such as those made by Xenophon, and the scathing parodies in the plays of Aristophanes of prominent Athenians known for their homosexual proclivities. Arno Karlen claims that the attitude of most Athenians toward homosexuality was revealed by Aristophanes, who, Karlen says, "in reality mocked homosexuality as harshly in his plays as any twentieth century burlesque comedian. It was he, not Plato, who spoke for the majority of the Greeks."[174] While it is true that in his comedies Aristophanes mercilessly pilloried well-known Athenians for homosexual acts, these barbs are in every case reserved for those men who continued the passive sexual role into adulthood. Sir Kenneth Dover, a prominent authority on Greek homosexual customs, has written that "There is no passage of comedy which demonstrably ridicules or criticizes any man or any category of men for aiming at homosexual copulation with beautiful young males or for preferring them to women."[175] The acceptance with which the ordinary Athenians regarded an adult male's sexual interest in a younger male is illustrated in a passage in Aristophanes' *Knights*. In the passage, a character called Demos, who is the personification of the Athenian people, appears in all his majesty after the defeat of a tyrant and is encountered by another character, Sausage-Seller:

> SAUSAGE-SELLER: Now that that's settled, here's a folding-stool for you, and a boy — he's no eunuch — who'll carry it for you. And if you feel like it sometimes, make a folding-stool of him!
> DEMOS: Oh, Joy! Back to the good old days!

Dover writes that passages such as this contradict the assumption that Aristophanes was critical of homosexuality among his fellow Greeks.[176] It was only men like the tragic poet Agathon, who maintained the passive role of an eremenos well into adulthood, who were targeted by Aristophanes' razor wit. In the opening scene of *Thesmophoriazusae*, when a character says he doesn't recognize Agathon, Aristophanes has the character Euripides say, "Well, you've fucked him, but perhaps you don't know him," implying that Agathon had worked as a male prostitute in the dark.[177] The viewpoint of much of Aristophanes' comedy is that of middle-aged or even elderly citizens, resentful of the bright, energetic, disrespectful young men who seem to them to dominate the assembly and be elected to military and political offices. These characters express this generational resentment by speaking of the young as "fucked" or "wide-arsed." As Dover describes it, "The man in the street consoles himself with the thought that those who run his life politically and order him about are in fact his inferiors, no better than prostitutes, homosexually subordinate."[178] Aristophanes' ridicule, then, is not for homosexuality per se, but for those who have deviated from the norms expected of an upright Athenian citizen by continuing the sexually passive role of an eremenos as an adult.[179]

Karlen, Flacelière and others have also argued that Plato's dialogues celebrating homosexual love do not reflect the sentiment of ordinary Greek citizens, but were written for an intellectual elite, and that their sophisticated arguments were designed to justify, for the purposes of an elite minority which practiced it, a custom generally unacceptable to the population at large. However, the same cannot be said about the famous oration given by Aeschines, a fourth-century B.C. Athenian and contemporary of Aristophanes who, in a denunciation of the immoral homosexual conduct of another Athenian before an audience composed of ordinary citizens, praises homosexual love that is conducted within honorable bounds. The prosecution that Aeschines carried out against Timarchos was initiated by Aeschines in retaliation for accusations that Timarchos and other Athenians had made against Aeschines. Aeschines had been accused of compromising the security of Athens while part of a delegation negotiating a treaty with King Philip of Macedon. In response, Aeschines leveled accusations against Timarchos, his leading accuser, that he had essentially prostituted himself as a youth by engaging in sexual relationships with older men in return for financial gain and other favors from his lovers. While the Athenians had no law against prostitution — and, indeed, homosexual brothels were common — their laws barred citizens who had prostituted themselves from engaging in public life, the feeling being that those who had sold themselves could just as easily sell out the interests of their city. Timarchos, according to Aeschines, had violated the law against those who had prostituted themselves from engaging in the public life of the city when he took his public stand against Aeschines. By raising his own charge against Timarchos, Aeschines hoped to deflect criticism against himself for his role in the treaty with Macedon.

Aeschines' speech is significant because he is trying to persuade a jury composed of ordinary citizens, who would be expected to disapprove of socially unacceptable behavior, to condemn Timarchos not for the fact that he had homosexual lovers as a young man, but for the character of those relationships. Aeschines did not accuse Timarchos of being a common prostitute, that is, selling himself on the street or in a brothel, but for carrying on lengthy relationships with older men in return for financial support and other benefits, essentially serving as a concubine, or a "kept" man. So it was Aeschines' task to describe for the citizen jury what it is that distinguishes dishonorable from honorable relationships between males, and where it was that Timarchos went over that line. Aeschines cites as examples of noble love famous relationships, such as those between Achilles and Patroclus, and Harmodius and Aristogeiton, and even discusses his own pursuit of youthful male lovers. In his lengthy oration, Aeschines substantially confirms the view of ennobling homosexual love put forth by Plato. Because of the thoroughness with which Aeschines discusses the sometimes fine line that separates acceptable and unacceptable homosexual behavior, his speech is regarded by scholars as one of the most complete and authoritative documents that survive on the homosexual mores of classical Athens. That his discourse was addressed not to aristocrats, but to common citizens, whose agreement he was attempting to gain, is convincing proof that the homosexual relationships praised by Plato in the *Symposium*, and described in Aeschines' speech, were not limited to "a tiny leisured upper class" but were the accepted norm for ordinary citizens as well.[180]

It is also misleading for modern authors to cite negative comments about homosexual behavior without taking into account the historical context in which they are given. The plays of Aristophanes and the writings of Xenophon came at a time of great crisis and tumult for Athens. The population of the city had been decimated by plague and the disasters of the Peloponnesian War, and the air was filled with recriminations and scape-goating for the ills that had befallen the city. It was a time, according to the historian Thucydides, when the morality of the city had undergone a complete upheaval, when ancient disciplines had been forgotten, and the institution of educational homosexuality had degenerated into vice. In this period the corrupt love of young men was exacerbated by the increasing habit of extending homosexual relations beyond the proper age limit — to the extent that, according to Aristophanes, all Athenian men had become *katapygones*, a slang term for passive homosexuals with connotations comparable to the modern "slut."[181] These men, by abdicating their virile role, symbolized to Aristophanes the degree to which Athens was no longer capable of ruling Greece.[182] And here Aristophanes was not condemning homosexuality; rather he was bitterly decrying the degeneration of a sexual institution that had for centuries played an important role in inculcating moral values and virtue in Athenian citizens.

Likewise, in this time of crisis, when the population of young males was nearly wiped out by war, the city sorely needed increased focus on the production of children, and it is in this context that Xenophon wrote several works that praised the institution of marriage and sought to deemphasize homosexual love. Thus can be seen the reason that Xenophon frequently expounded views that went against the grain of Greek thought on homosexual love: he had an agenda, not based so much on hostility to homosexuality, as on a deeply felt concern for the welfare of his city in a time of crisis. It was in this period, too, that Plato made comments in two of his late works, the *Laws* and the *Republic*, which have been interpreted by some writers as showing that the Greeks condemned homosexuality.

In the *Laws*, Plato distinguishes relations between men and women, which are defined as *kata physin* (which has been translated as "according to nature") from sexual relations between two members of the same sex, which he calls *para physin* (which has often been interpreted as meaning "against nature"). The latter phrase was more likely meant by Plato to signify "unrelated to birth," or "non-reproductive." The word *physis* was derived from the word *phyo*, "to grow," or "to be born." Similarly, in the *Republic* Plato distinguishes between "man-made" and the "natural," as contrasting "what is constructed" from "what is born."[183] Therefore, it is clear that Plato was not characterizing homosexual behavior as an aberration of nature, but was simply categorizing it as non-reproductive sexual expression.

In another passage in the *Laws*, Plato's spokesman proposes the idea of inventing a social order that would conform to "nature" as the Greeks believed it to be before the "invention" of the homosexual love of youth. Such a proposition would have required massive changes in Greek beliefs and practices relating to homosexuality, and was an idea so preposterous to the other participants in the dialogue that they regarded its implementation as inconceivable.[184] Plato goes on in the *Republic* to lay out the laws for an ideal city in which all sexuality would be repressed, except that specifically directed toward procreation. He does this not because he feels homosexuality is morally wrong, but in order to place all sexual expression at the service of social utility, that is, the production of children.[185]

It is clear that in laying out this theoretical model for a utopian republic Plato had no intention of branding love relations between men as "unnatural" in the sense with which that term is now understood, though that is an interpretation that has frequently been put forward for his words. The Greeks of Plato's day took it for granted that a man would be erotically moved by the beauty of a male youth. Indeed, even Xenophon wrote that sexual love between men was a part of "human nature."[186] Plato's comments contrasting procreative heterosexual love and non-procreative homosexual love are best understood in the context of utopian theorizing undertaken in a time of grave crisis in his city. Rather than being a reflection of Greek feelings on homosexual love, the views Plato expounds in these two late works, in the words of the historian John Winkler, "went utterly against the grain of the values, practices and debates of Plato's society."[187]

It is natural in a culture such as the modern West, where homosexuality has been strongly disapproved, and where because of intense social sanctions it has until recently rarely been visible, for people to project their own ingrained prejudices and assumptions about homosexuality onto other societies, and to view negative statements about homosexuality as confirming that their own views were shared by that society. This seems to have been the case with authors such as Taylor, Karlen and Flacelière. However, a close examination of the evidence, which is found in the literature, laws and vase paintings of ancient Athens, shows that ancient Greece was quite different from the modern West, in that it took the sexual response of someone for another of the same sex as natural and normal, and sought to restrict its expression only to the extent that social needs were served.

Alexander and the Hellenistic Age

By the 5th century B.C., Athens had come to dominate Greece not only culturally, but politically, having established a maritime empire and a powerful navy to go with it. But as its Golden Age was reaching its peak, Athens, in a bid to expand its political influence over the rest of Greece, instigated the Peloponnesian War with Sparta, which lasted on and off for 30 years. Rather than enlarging its dominance over Greece, the war was disastrous for Athens, and resulted in the dissolution of its maritime empire. Continuing armed struggles in the early fourth century B.C. among the increasingly fractious Greek city-states, particularly Athens, Thebes and Sparta, destroyed the sense of national unity that had earlier enabled the Greeks to repulse the invasion of the Persians under Xerxes. Seeing the Greeks weakened by the constant infighting, Philip of Macedon took advantage of the opportunity and gradually expanded his authority over all of Greece. Thus, during the lifetimes of some of the most famous of Greek historical figures — Socrates, Plato, Xenophon, Aristotle, Thucydides, Aristophanes and Demosthenes — Athens lost its preeminence among the Greek city-states, eventually becoming, as with other Greek cities, a mere vassal of the Macedonian kingdom of Philip and his son and heir, Alexander the Great. The emergence of a politically unified Greece under the Macedonian monarchs set the stage for Alexander's extraordinary military conquests, which brought under Greek rule all the lands of the ancient civilizations of the Middle East, from Egypt to the borders of India.

The sexuality displayed in the Macedonian court demonstrates the degree to which homosexuality pervaded relations between males in the period, and was not just a phenomenon limited to the military initiation of the Dorian Greeks, or the cultivated society of the Athenians. In contrast to the refined, almost effete society of the Athenian upper class, the Macedonian ruling class was a bawdy world filled with hard-drinking, fierce warriors. Philip, who had several marriages, and according to one writer "seems to have consorted with anything ambulatory,"[188] was also given to sexual affairs with members of his elite bodyguard. In fact, his death came at the hands of a jealous favorite, aggrieved by the failure of the king to adequately address an injury the young officer had suffered in a drunken episode brought on by another member of the court.

According to an account of the incident by Diodorus Siculus, the young bodyguard, a Macedonian named Pausanias, "was beloved by the king because of his beauty. When he saw that the king was becoming enamoured of another Pausanias (a man of the same name as himself), he addressed him with abusive language, accusing him of being a hermaphrodite and quick to accept the amorous advances of anyone who wished." The second Pausanias, unable to endure such insults, kept silent for a time, but after confiding in Attalus, one of his friends and an in-law to the king, "he brought about his own death voluntarily and in a spectacular fashion." During a battle a few days later, the second Pausanias stepped forward in front of the king, and received on his body all the blows directed at the king, meeting his death in the process.

The incident was widely discussed in court circles, and Attalus, who knew of the circumstances that had prompted the dead man's actions, invited the first Pausanias to dinner and plied him with wine. After getting him drunk, Attalus handed over the body of the unconscious young officer to the stable grooms "to abuse in drunken licentiousness." Waking from his stupor, Pausanias was outraged by the sexual assault he had suffered as a result of Attalus' prank, and so went to the king demanding punishment for Attalus. Philip, still fond of Pausanias, shared his anger at the barbarity of the act perpetrated on him, but did not wish to punish Attalus at the time because of his in-law relationship with him, and because Attalus was a brilliant warrior and he needed his services in a campaign he was planning against the Persians. So the king "tried to mollify the righteous anger of Pausanias at his treatment, giving him substantial presents and advancing him in honor among the bodyguards."

But Pausanias still seethed at the insult to his honor because of the incident, a situation only made worse when shortly afterward Attalus won praise for his role in early successes of the Macedonian advance party against the Persians. Finally, during a religious ceremony before the departure of the Macedonian army on its Persian campaign, Pausanias leapt in front of the king and stabbed him in the chest with a dagger, killing him instantly.[189] This was not the first time a Macedonian monarch had been assassinated by a male lover. In 399 B.C. the Macedonian king Archelaus was slain while hunting by two men who had been his lovers, Cratias and Hallanocrates of Larissa.[190]

Philip's son, Alexander, was even more prone to homosexuality than his father. Since there is evidence for institutionalized pederasty in court circles,[191] and considering that the Macedonian aristocracy consciously imitated the customs of classical Greece it is not improbable that the young Alexander would have had an older lover-mentor, probably one approved by his father. As he grew older, Alexander only reluctantly became involved sexually with women, which was a matter of concern to his parents, since it was extremely important for him to produce a male heir. At one point his parents, Philip and Olympias, became so concerned with Alexander's indifference toward women that they arranged a sexual encounter between Alexander and a seductive Thessalian courtesan named Callixeina, but to no avail — Alexander would not sleep with her.

Alexander's indifference to women was not borne out of dislike or hostility to them: he was for the most part uncommonly considerate and appreciative of women. But unlike many conquerors, Alexander apparently never took advantage of the tens of thousands of women captured during his campaigns. To the contrary, he was said to have walked past the most alluring of Persian women as if they were "lifeless images cut out of stone." While in his early 20s on a campaign in Persia, Alexander apparently had his first encounter with a woman, the daughter of a Persian official, who bore him an illegitimate son whom they named Heracles. At age 27 Alexander was married to Roxanne, the daughter of a Bactrian prince, who was said to be the most beautiful woman in Asia. Six years later Roxanne finally produced a male heir for Alexander, though the king did not live to see the birth. Alexander had two more marriages, to relatives of Persian royalty, but both were blatantly political, and did not seem to have engaged him emotionally in the slightest way.[192] It is clear that the principal love relationships in Alexander's life were all with other males.

While still in his youth, Alexander fell in love with a Macedonian aristocrat close to his own age named Hephaestion, who remained his closest friend and lifelong companion. Alexander liked to compare his relationship with Hephaestion to that between Achilles and Patroclus, and, in fact, while in Troy in 334 B.C. the king reportedly laid a wreath at the tomb of Achilles, while Hephaestion placed a wreath on the tomb of Patroclus. Alexander's fondness for the analogy between his relationship with Hephaestion and that of the Homeric heroes, who were commonly believed in that era to be homosexual lovers, is taken by scholars to confirm the presence of a sexual bond between Alexander and Hephaestion.[193] The two were close companions through all of Alexander's campaigns, and when Hephaestion died while on an expedition in Babylon in 324 B.C., Alexander was devastated. Such was his grief according to the Greek historian Arrian, "that for two days after Hephaestion's death Alexander tasted no food and took no care of his body, but lay either moaning or in a sorrowful silence." Like Achilles mourning over Patroclus, Alexander, "lay weeping on his comrade for a day and a night before being pried away." Also like Achilles before him, Alexander had funeral games staged on a grand scale for Hephaestion, and cut his hair in honor of his dead friend, as Achilles had done for Patroclus.[194]

Despite the enormity of his attachment to Hephaestion, Alexander was known to have sexual relationships with other males, most notably Bagoas, an exceptionally beautiful young eunuch who had previously been a lover of Darius III, the Persian monarch defeated by Alexander. Bagoas was presented to Alexander by the Persian Grand Vizier after the defeat of the Persians, and the king quickly developed an attachment for the beautiful youth. The extent of Alexander's affection for Bagoas is seen in the influence the young eunuch enjoyed in court. He was instrumental in the discrediting and death of Orsines, a member of the Persian royal family, who had slighted the eunuch. Once, while watching a dancing and singing competition, Alexander provoked delighted applause from the audience of Macedonians when he wrapped his arms around Bagoas and kissed him in full view of the crowd.[195] Alexander enjoyed relations with several other eunuchs who were part of the harem he had acquired through his defeat of Darius, and was also known to have purchased handsome male slaves to use for sexual purposes.[196]

An incident involving a plot to assassinate Alexander demonstrates that homosexuality was not a practice limited to royal circles, but was apparently commonplace among the Macedonian military aristocracy. For some unknown reason a small group of young Macedonians aristocrats in the army became disenchanted with Alexander's leadership and so formed a plot to assassinate the king. The plot came to light when one of the conspirators, a Macedonian youth named Dimnus, told his lover, Nicomachus, about the plot. He in turn told another officer, Cebalinus, who then went to a high-ranking court official named Philotas with the information and asked for an audience with the king. Philotas told him that the king was too busy, but gave Cebalinus assurances that he would inform the king of the situation. When Cebalinus discovered the next day that the king had still not heard about it, he himself told the king the news. When an angry Alexander demanded to know why Philotas had delayed in telling him about the plot, Philotas explained that he had lent no credence to the information because of its source, and claimed he was reluctant to say anything out of "fear that he would be ridiculed for taking a lover's quarrel too seriously."[197] The casual way in which the homosexual relationship of the young plotter was mentioned illustrates how ordinary such relationships must have seemed at the time.

Though his empire was quickly divided upon his death, Alexander's conquests ushered in the Hellenistic Age, an era when Greek language and culture spread throughout the ancient lands he conquered. Following Alexander's armies into the far-flung remnants of the Persian Empire were thousands of merchants, farmers and craftsmen fleeing the economic decline of the war-battered Greek mainland, who founded Greek-speaking cities, and brought with them the architecture, customs and cultural heritage of their homeland. In fact, many of the Greek classics from this period, such as those written by Strabo, Meleager and Callimachus, were written by Greeks living not in Greece, but in the Hellenized lands conquered by Alexander. The most prominent of the new cities was Alexandria in Egypt, which became a principal center of science and learning. Also in Egypt, a royal dynasty was established by the Ptolemies, cousins of Alexander, who were to rule as pharaohs until Roman times. Greek dynasties were also founded by associates of Alexander in Anatolia and Persia. Throughout the region Greek culture was consciously promoted by these Greek rulers, and the Greek language became commonly used, especially by the ruling class.

It goes without saying that the Greeks brought their homosexual customs with them into these conquered lands. It is certainly true that the Greeks did not introduce homosexuality to the region, since there is evidence of widespread homosexual practices throughout the region going back to the earliest periods of civilization. However, the particular pattern of homosexuality traditional to the Greeks, that is, the sexual pursuit of younger males by older men, seems to have become ubiquitous, though the educational or ennobling aspect of the relationships that was emphasized in classical Greece was largely forgotten. During this Hellenistic Age, then, it was common practice for ethnic Greeks and other upper-class males from Egypt to Babylon to participate in homosexual relationships before and even during marriage, just as was done in classical Greece. A great amount of Hellenistic literature survives, much of it written in Hellenized Egypt or the Middle East, which recounts the tormented love of a man for a *pais*, literally "boy" in Greek, but for centuries the common term for the younger partner in a homosexual relationship between males.

Callimachus, a prominent Greek poet and writer, who was born in 305 B.C. in Cyrene in North Africa, was appointed to run the royal library in Alexandria, the biggest and most famous in the ancient world. In one of his better-known verses, he describes how the love of youth has ruled him: "It is but the half of my soul that still breathes, and for the other half I know not if it be Love or Death that hath seized on it, only it is gone. Is it off again to one of the lads?"[198] Meleager, born near the end of the second century B.C., in what is now modern Jordan, lived for most of his life in Tyre, in what is now modern Lebanon. A composer of epigrams and poetry, Meleager began the literary compilation known as the *Greek Anthology*, and included in it many of his own verses, a great number of which celebrated the sexual pursuit of beautiful youths. So common was it for males of the period to pursue homosexual loves, that the writers of a marriage contract prepared in the first century B.C. in Egypt found it necessary to stipulate, among other requirements, that the husband was not to have a "concubine or male lover."[199]

That the homosexual pursuit of male youths continued to be a common aspect of the sexual life of the men throughout the region well into Christian times is illustrated in a third-century A.D. work, the *Amores,* by a writer known as pseudo-Lucian of Samosata, in what is now modern Turkey. In this dialogue, Lucian's characters debate the superiority of the love of youths versus the love of women. The comparison of the merits of loving a *pais* versus loving a woman seems to have been a popular literary topic in the period. Such a comparison previously appeared in the *Greek Anthology,* and was also treated by Plutarch in his *Amatorius,* a work of the early second century A.D. As might be expected, given the variability of sexual preferences among humans, which form of love emerges from these debates as superior varies from writer to writer, though in most of such works the homosexual love of youths is the victor. In Lucian's dialogue, the character Caricles, who favors the love of women, bases his argument on the contention that what has been created is intended to survive the death of the individuals, and so humans were divided for that purpose into two sexes, mutually attracted, so that by their attraction, the human race will be continued. Caricles concludes this familiar argument with the observation — mistaken, of course — that animals "in nature" only couple with those of the opposite sex. When he is finished, his opponent, Callicratidas, makes his argument. The love of men for youths, he says, is the only love that allows pleasure and virtue to be brought together. Echoing some of the arguments seen in Plato's *Symposium,* Callicratidas says that while heterosexual marriage is a remedy invented to insure the continuity of the species, and therefore something done out of pure necessity, loving a youth is superior because it is done because of aesthetic values. Loving women is "primitive necessity," he argues, whereas loving men was a "conquest of divine philosophy."[200]

However homosexual love was rationalized by late classical writers, these works illustrate the persistence of these sexual practices and attitudes several centuries after the Greek world had become incorporated into the Roman Empire, and nearly two thousand years after the Indo-European ancestors of the Greeks first brought their homosexual customs to the lands around the Aegean.

Conclusion

For many classicists and historians, whose understanding of sexuality has been shaped primarily by the heterosexual norms prevailing in modern Western culture, the homosexual practices of the ancient Greeks are an aberration, and a perplexing one at that. Considering the enormous contribution of the Greeks in laying the intellectual foundations for Western civilization, not to mention their seminal role in the development of Western moral philosophy and ethics, the exalted place occupied by homosexual love in Greek society has long posed a special problem to these scholars. Indeed, in an acknowledgment of this discomfort, one of the first scholarly works to deal directly with the prevalent homosexuality of the classical Greeks was titled *A Problem in Greek Ethics.** As a result, a number of writers have offered theories to account for the widespread homosexuality of the Greeks, as if it were an excep-

---

*John Addington Symonds, one of the foremost men of letters of the late Victorian period, produced his A Problem in Greek Ethics *in 1883. Because of the controversy of its subject, and to protect the author's scholarly reputation, its first publication was in a private printing of only ten copies. It was later incorporated, after his death, in Havelock Ellis' pioneering* Studies in the Psychology of Sex, *though at the insistence of Symonds' family, his name did not appear in the English edition.*

tional and abnormal phenomenon among these otherwise admirable moral paragons that needed to be explained or excused. Some have seen it as a consequence of the military structure of Greek society, while others have blamed it on the subordination and segregation of women. A recently posed theory is that the homosexual customs came about as a consequence of measures to curb overpopulation. One prominent Oxford scholar has even tried to explain Greek homosexuality in psychoanalytic terms.[201]

However, an increasing number of scholars are now persuaded that the homosexual traditions of the classical Greeks evolved from homosexual initiation rites among the Indo-European ancestors of the Greeks similar to those found among aboriginal cultures in historic times. Indeed, the customs among the Greeks which come closest to the ritual homosexuality of Melanesian tribes, the initiatory practices of Dorians of Crete and Sparta, show unmistakable signs of descent from initiatory ritual of earlier tribal periods. The fact that similar initiatory homosexuality was observed among warriors of other Indo-European groups strongly suggests that these homosexual traditions are among the many shared cultural traits that the Greeks and the other Indo-Europeans inherited from their common Neolithic ancestors.

The survey of the sexuality found among aboriginal peoples in Chapter 3 has demonstrated certain general characteristics of human sexuality that are quite widespread among human societies. While homosexual behavior among adolescents and non-married adults seems to be nearly universal among tribal cultures, there is also some variation in the character of the relationships, as well as evidence of a variability in degree of sexual orientation among individuals. In some societies bonding between peers is common, and sometimes institutionalized. Among other groups age-differentiated hierarchical relationships between males are the norm, and in some regions serve as the framework for initiation rites through which all males must pass. Thus, in the context of the sexuality displayed among the great breadth of aboriginal societies, as well as among other early Indo-European peoples, the homosexual practices of the Greeks, far from being exceptional phenomena, seem quite ordinary.

While adolescent and young adult homosexuality, so common among tribal cultures around the world, was, among the Greeks, channeled into a particular hierarchical form governed by social traditions, these homosexual customs are not nearly as elaborate or structured as those of some tribal cultures, such as the Marind-Anim of New Guinea. But it also appears that in a number of Greek city-states of classical times, if Plato and Xenophon are to be believed, the homosexual pursuit of younger males was as informal and unrestricted as that found among such peoples as the Siwan Berbers or the natives of the Santa Cruz Islands. And even in classical Athens, where homosexual practices were governed by social mores and rules of etiquette as demanding as those found in proper Victorian society, there is considerable evidence not only of frequent deviation from those norms, but of the same variability in sexual preference found in many other societies.

Though in Athens it was typical for a male to progress from the role of courted sex object in his youth to the role of pursuer of younger males, and then to marriage by the age of thirty, there is evidence that some males took more readily to the heterosexual alternative than others, while many others of their peers seemed to retain a primary preoccupation with homosexual love for their whole lives. It is also clear that the ancient Greeks were quite familiar with individuals with exclusive homosexual inclination. And, the example of Achilles and Patroclus in Homer strongly implies that a tradition of passionate love between warrior peers, of an intensity reminiscent of the blood-brother relationships of other Indo-European warriors, was a part of the ancestral tradition of the early Greeks. It is evident, therefore, that none of the aspects of the homosexual traditions found among the Spartans, Cretans, Athenians or any other Greeks are unique to the ancient Greeks. Every pattern of homosexual behavior found in the Greek world — from the intense love bonds between warrior comrades depicted in Homer, to casual homosexual relations among adolescents and young adults, to the educational or initiatory homosexuality between older and younger males of archaic and classical times — can be found among aboriginal tribal cultures or among other Indo-European peoples.

What is really unique about Greek homosexuality is not the prominence of same-sex love in their society, but the enormous amount of material that has come down to us dealing with their sexual customs. This can be attributed to the Greeks' dynamic literary tradition and the great number of prolific writers. While there is evidence of homosexuality in some Egyptian texts and tomb paintings, and in the writings and art objects of Mesopotamia, the literature that survives from those two cultures is much more limited. In Egypt most of the writings that have been found were associated with rituals for the dead and provide little insight into the sexual lifestyles of the people. Though we have from Mesopotamians the Gilgamesh epic, as well as laws and religious writings that provide evidence of their homosexual practices, the total output is sparse compared to what has come down from ancient Greece. The numerous volumes of poetry, philosophy and social commentary produced by the Greeks have given modern scholars a detailed knowledge of the sexual attitudes and practices of the Greeks, in contrast to the fragmentary evidence provided by the artifacts of other ancient cultures. If the Celtic and Germanic warriors had not had such a disdain for writing, it seems likely that modern scholars would also be analyzing and attempting to explain the homosexual traditions of those Indo-Europeans groups, given the evidence that we have of the homosexual practices that seemed to have been just as common among them.

Some modern writers have also argued that same-sex love as practiced in classical Greece was not real homosexuality, and insist that these Greek sexual customs should not be compared to the sexuality of gay people in modern society. These writers contrast the homosexual practices of ancient Greece, which they see as a temporary, hierarchical bisexuality restricted to adolescent and unmarried males, with the sexuality of modern gays, which they assume to be reciprocal relations between adult peers of permanent homosexual orientation. However, the distinction between the homosexuality practiced in the two societies is not as sharp as these writers would have it appear.

First, we have seen that the type of homosexual relationship assumed to be the norm in classical Greece, a temporary, one-sided relationship between an unmarried young adult and an adolescent, was in reality an ideal. There is no question that an educational relationship between a noble adult and a youth was the admired norm in classical Athens, and, indeed, was institutionalized as part of military education in Sparta and Crete. But there is also evidence of wide variation beyond this norm in many of the Greek city-states, from informal and apparently reciprocal relations between adolescent peers, to love relationships that extend well into the adulthood of the younger partner, to men continuing to pursue male lovers their whole lives, despite marriage to a woman. And not only do the works of both Plato and Aristotle display a familiarity with men of exclusive homosexual inclination, they also provide several examples of adult male couples in what appear to be permanent, committed relationships. That references to permanent homosexual relationships between adults should casually appear in the works of two different writers suggests that they are not isolated examples. Further, if the implications of the sexual bond that is evident between Achilles and Patroclus in the *Iliad* are accepted, there must have been a tradition of sexual relationships between warrior peers, comparable to that between Indo-European blood brothers, among the Greeks of Homeric and earlier times. While we have no evidence from classical Greece of adult peer relationships of the sort that was depicted between Achilles and Patroclus, it appears that such a peer bond did exist between Alexander the Great and his companion Hephastion, who themselves recognized the similarity between their love relationship and that of the Homeric heroes. And, of course, what evidence we have of homosexual behavior among Greek women shows no difference in sexual practices among women in modern times except for the fact that most Greek women of the upper class were placed in arranged marriages.

So while the social conventions of classical Greece mandated the channeling of homosexual expression through a structured, educational and, hopefully, ennobling love relationship, the literature and artifacts of ancient Greece provide evidence of the same variability in sexual preference and variety of expression that is seen in many other human societies. To insist that homosexual expression in ancient Greece was limited to temporary, educational relationships between unequal male partners just because such relationships were prescribed in moral commentaries is like saying that sexual expression in the modern West only occurs in marriage between men and women who were virgins before they were married.

Secondly, it is a mistake to assume that male homosexual behavior in the modern world is restricted to adult gay males in reciprocal relationships between peers. Though it is true that many gay men seek relationships with peers of a similar age, a significant percentage of gay males in contemporary society become involved in distinctly hierarchical relationships, where an older partner plays a sexually dominant role with a younger, passive lover who could be anywhere from eight to twenty or more years younger. Indeed, a number of slang terms are found in gay personal ads to describe the roles of the male partner, such as "daddy" for the older, dominant partner; and "son," or "little brother" for the younger partner; and in S&M contexts, "master" is used for the dominant partner, "slave" for the submissive partner. Similarly the term "Greek active" or "top" is used to distinguish a male who seeks the dominant role in sex, whereas "Greek passive" and "bottom" are used for males who prefer the passive role. So the tendency of males to seek these hierarchical, non-reciprocal relationships is just as pronounced in modern society as in the ancient world, though in the contemporary world such relationships would be mostly restricted to self-identified adult homosexuals, rather than a more general phenomenon. And of course, because of laws punishing sexual relations with minors, not to mention the horror with which contemporary society views pederastic homosexuality, examples of those relationships are rare in the modern world.

It is also incorrect to assume that homosexual behavior or responsiveness in the modern society only occur among gay people. One of the most provocative findings of Alfred Kinsey's studies on male sexuality was the significant percentage of males who engage in sexual activity "to the point of orgasm" with other males at some point in their lives, a figure Kinsey put at nearly 40 percent of the general population. When we add the percentage of men who admit to having same-sex fantasies or dreams to this figure, the number rises to more than half the population. Kinsey also found a range of intensity of sexual orientation that varied in people, from predominantly homosexual to predominantly heterosexual, and devised his well-known scale to measure it. Kinsey's findings, as well as the work of other sex researchers, has shown that the demarcation between "gay" and "straight" is not as clear-cut as many assume, but one with many shades of gray. The reason this is not more apparent in contemporary society is because of the intense opprobrium attached to the expression of homosexual desire, which discourages those who could otherwise act out the homosexual side of their bisexuality from any public display that could be perceived as queer. Thus, in modern society the only visible proponents of homosexual expression have been those on the far end of Kinsey's scale, predominantly or exclusively homosexual individuals, who, unlike many in the bisexual middle portion of Kinsey's scale, have no other viable sexual alternative but to go against the grain of social attitudes on acceptable sexual behavior.

When one considers these factors, the contrast that has been drawn between the homosexuality of the Greeks and what is seen in contemporary society begins to blur. Therefore, it becomes clear that the principal distinction between Greek homosexuality and homosexuality in the modern world is not in any essential or intrinsic difference in the nature of human sexuality between the two eras, but in the nature of social indoctrination about sexuality that occurs in each respective society.

Greek homosexuality, then, provides us with a uniquely detailed demonstration of how the intrinsic ambisexuality of the human species manifested in a complex, cultured society. The sexuality displayed by the Greeks demonstrates how readily homosexual behavior manifests among humans, requiring little or no encouragement, and provides further proof of the sexologist C.A. Tripp's observation that "where homosexuality is merely approved, it tends to be prevalent."[202] In the practice of educational homosexuality maintained by the classical Greeks we see another example of how the natural inclination of adolescents and young adult males to hierarchical homosexuality is harnessed in a way that promoted the well-being of society. But despite social conventions in the classical period which mandated such a mentoring or educational relationship between a young adult and a youth, there is, nonetheless, considerable evidence of the same variability in sexual expression and degree of sexual orientation that is seen in many other societies. That the homosexual practices displayed by the Greeks are consistent in basic ways with the sexual behavior seen among many other societies shows that it is not Greek culture that is exceptional with regard to sexuality, but that of the modern West, which, with its rigid heterosexual model, denies the existence of an aspect of human sexuality that many other societies have taken for granted.

8

Ambisexuality in Ancient Rome: Homosexual Customs in the Republic and Early Empire

[After a gathering of friends] the servants bring in sometimes courtesans, sometimes handsome boys, sometimes their own wives. When they have taken their pleasure of the women or the men, they make strapping young fellows lie with the latter.... They certainly have commerce with women, but they always enjoy themselves much better with boys and young men. The latter are in this country quite beautiful to behold, for they live lives of ease and their bodies are hairless.[1]

So wrote the fourth-century B.C. Greek historian Theopompus, not about the Greeks, but about the Etruscans. An Indo-European people who dominated northern and central Italy in the first half of the first millennium B.C., the Etruscans were flourishing as a wealthy and sophisticated regional power when Rome was still a muddy village. Theopompus wasn't the only ancient writer who took note of the Etruscans' enthusiasm for homosexuality. The Greek historian Athenaeus also wrote of the Etruscans' lack of sexual inhibitions, and the great pleasure Etruscan men found in the sexual pursuit of younger males.[2]

Under Etruscan rule, the crude peasant village on the banks of the Tiber that Rome was at that time began its evolution to eventual grandeur. From the sixth century B.C., and continuing throughout the fifth century, early Rome was powerfully shaped by Etruscan culture. Etruscan influences on the cultural and social development of Rome ranged from urban planning, art, and architecture to religion, technology and even dress, and it was from the Etruscans that the Romans learned the alphabet. The Etruscans built the first wall around the city, laid out an extensive drainage system, and erected many imposing stone monuments, including the Capitoline Temple of Jupiter, which later served as a symbol of the Roman Republic. There was considerable intermarriage between Etruscans and Romans, and as a result a strong Etruscan element became assimilated into the native Latin population of Rome. Under the Etruscans, Rome reached a level of economic and cultural splendor equal to that of nearby Etruscan cities. Though Rome remained a fundamentally Latin city in language and spirit, the transformation was so profound that writers of the period referred to it as an Etruscan city. The close association of Etruscan culture with early Roman history is illustrated by the fact that the family of Julius Caesar, one of the oldest of the Roman aristocratic families, claimed Etruscan origin. However, by the early fifth century B.C. the residents of Rome had overthrown the last of the Etruscan kings, and founded their Republic. Roman power gradually eclipsed that of the Etruscans in the region, and, in fact, the Etruscans and their territory were eventually incorporated into the growing Roman Republic.

While later Roman culture owed a great debt to the Etruscans, Roman writers of the late Republic and Empire painted a picture of early Roman life which overlooked the central contributions of the Etruscans to their culture. In addition, they saw their ancestors as exemplars of a simple agrarian piety and a virtuous sexual morality revolving around the family, a view which differed sharply from the description Theopompus offered of the pleasure-loving Etruscans, especially in regard to homosexuality. The evidence shows, however, that this Roman view of their early history was more myth than fact.

These writers were living in a time when Rome's territory had grown to what must have seemed enormous dimensions, when great new wealth was flowing into the Rome, when the city's population was greatly expanded with an influx of foreigners, and when old institutions and values were changing or being abandoned. It is common for people in such times to recall their humble origins with nostalgia, to pine for "the good old days" when they imagined life was simpler and moral values were always respected. Roman writers of the late Republic and early Empire often expressed such sentiments regarding a simpler time under the early Republic, glorifying their humble origins as farmers, and depicting their ancestors as devout, sober and monogamous.[3] This Roman ideal was epitomized by the legend of Lucius Quinctius Cincinnatus, who was elected consul in 460 B.C. Two years later, with Roman forces besieged by Celtic tribes, Cincinnatus was asked to assume dictatorial powers in order to lead the defense. When emissaries came to tell Cincinnatus that he had been selected to take control, they found him plowing his fields. According to the legend, he laid his plow aside, assumed command of Roman forces, and defeated the enemy in one day. Sixteen days later, after Rome had passed through the emergency, Cincinnatus resigned his powers and returned to his plow, an act of selfless patriotism that must have seemed unimaginable to later Romans who had witnessed the power struggles of the late Republic and early Empire.

Roman writers of the early Empire also liked to assert that, in contrast to the hedonism and sexual promiscuity of their times, the early Republic was a period of strict sexual mores and rigid concepts of decency, a world in which homosexual love was unknown. This idealized morality revolved around the family, with the father, *pater familias*, as supreme authority. It was a time, they believed, when the moral purity of every Roman wife was unquestioned, and when children accepted their father's decisions without argument.[4] The standards of behavior were summarized in the three concepts of *gravitas*, a sense of dignity and responsibility; *pietas*, a loyal respect for the established order; and *mos maiorum*, the authority of the father over the household. This picture of an idealized moral past portrayed by Roman writers came to be fervently believed by a great number of Romans living under the Empire. However, it's doubtful that early Roman life and morality were as simple and idyllic as later depicted. Nonetheless, traditional historians, from Edward Gibbon onward, have often accepted this picture of the early Republic, and have insisted that homosexual behavior was not present or approved among the Romans until much later times, and that when it finally did emerge, it was as a result of Greek influence. But this too, it now appears, is more myth than reality.

Roman Origins

The early Romans were descended from Italic tribes who had established themselves in central and southern Italy by the beginning of the first millennium B.C. The Italics are thought to have been closely related to the Celts, as their languages are more closely related to each other than to any other Indo-European language family. It is likely that both the Celts and Italics developed from an amalgam of Indo-European invaders who occupied Central Europe and the Balkans in the second millennium B.C., and whose movements westward brought them through the Alpine passes into northern Italy. While many of the Celtic tribes continued on into western Europe, the Italics remained in Italy, where separate bands spread out throughout the peninsula, eventually developing separate dialects. By 800 B.C. the Latins, one of a number of Italic groups who had settled in southern Italy, had become concentrated around the hills on the banks of the Tiber River, where their settlements eventually developed, under Etruscan influence, into the city of Rome.[5]

The Romans later credited the origins of their nation to two mythical events: first, the colonization of Latium, the territory surrounding Rome, in the 12th century B.C. by the Trojan hero Aeneas and a band of followers who had escaped the destruction of their city in the Trojan War; and, second, the founding of the city of Rome five hundred years later by the Latin leader Romulus, after whom the city is named. Until recent years the account of the arrival of Aeneas and his troops of Trojans on the Latin Plains was regarded by scholars as nothing more than myth. However, archeological research conducted in the last several decades has shown that there may be some truth to the story. Archeological evidence has been uncovered that demonstrates that in the early first millennium B.C. the area was visited by Late Bronze Age seafarers whose trading activities extended as far as southern Tuscany. It is in that period that the Etruscans are believed to have arrived from Asia Minor, the location of ancient Troy, and, indeed, some scholars believe the Etruscans could have been Trojans fleeing the destruction of their country.[6] The mythical figure of Aeneas was familiar to the Etruscans from at least as early as the sixth century B.C., and so the legend could have established itself among the early Romans during the period of Etruscan dominance.

While there is evidence for a tradition of initiatory-type homosexuality among other early Indo-Europeans, not to mention the well-documented interest of the Italics' Celtic cousins in homosexual activity, there are only fragmentary hints of similar homosexual customs among the early Romans. Mars, a principal god of the early Romans, was closely associated with Indo-European expansion, and played a role in early Roman mythology similar to that held by Apollo among the Greeks. A drawing on a box discovered in the ancient Latin city of Palestrina-Praeneste depicts a naked Mars with several youths. The Indo-European scholar Georges Dumezil has suggested that the drawing could be depicting an initiation scene.[7]

The Roman historian Livy wrote that Romulus and Remus, the founders of Rome, led bands of youth in hunting, warfare and the abduction of women, activities that were associated with male initiation rites among other Indo-Europeans.[8] According to Roman legend, Romulus and Remus were fathered by Mars, and raised in the forest and suckled by a she-wolf. The historian David Greenberg has suggested that the she-wolf of the legend could actually have been a male initiator wearing a wolf-skin. After initiation, Celtic and Germanic warriors took animal names and wore wolf and bear-skins to absorb the ferocity of those animals. Wolves were sacred to Mars, and so for the figure in the legend to have been not a she-wolf, but a warrior clothed in the skin of the very animal associated with the prime exemplar of hunting and warrior prowess among the gods, would be a type of mythical symbolism typical of initiation rituals. Greenberg also notes that semen was thought to have magical powers among many tribal peoples, particularly warrior cultures that employ homosexual initiation, and that among such cultures semen is often associated with milk, which is, like semen, a lifegiving substance. And, as we have seen in Chapter 7, the ancient Greeks believed that a warrior's courage and manly virtue passed into his youthful lover in his semen, and that this and other associated beliefs about the presence of the life force in the skull and its transmission through the phallus, which seemed to have been shared by other early Indo-European groups, very likely descended from a common Indo-European Stone Age past. Therefore, it is possible that the story of Romulus and Remus being suckled by a she-wolf could have originated in the ancient memory of a wolf-skin-clad warrior inseminating a youthful initiate, thereby "parenting" his development as a virile warrior.[9] Given the likelihood that initiatory homosexuality was a tradition shared by all the early Indo-Europeans, as some scholars believe, the interpretation of this famous myth as a myth of homosexual initiation is far from implausible.

There is evidence that the Romans shared other aspects of these primitive beliefs and superstitions surrounding the life force, the skull and the phallus. A gilded skull found at Pompeii with the inscription, "drink and you shall live for many years," testifies to the survival of the same primordial beliefs in the mystical life enhancing powers in the skull that are the basis for the head-hunting of both the Indo-European tribes and the peoples of Melanesia. Like the Greeks — and aboriginal cultures in the Southwest Pacific — the Romans also associated the phallus with mystical powers and believed that the image of a phallus brought protection from evil spirits, the idea being that the evil spirits would be so fascinated with the phallus that they would ignore everything else. The word *fascinate*, in fact, is derived from the Latin word for phallus, *fascinum*. Images of a phallus were placed on doorways, in shops, at city gates, on war chariots and were even worn as amulets around the necks of little children to protect them.[10]

We also know from an account of the Roman historian Livy of an incident that occurred in 186 B.C., involving the Bacchanalian initiation rites, that a belief in the mystical transmission of special knowledge or power through homosexual intercourse persisted among some Romans until relatively late periods. Bacchus, the Roman counterpart to the Greek god Dionysius, is one of the oldest representations of a divinity known among ancient cultures, and was known in various forms as far back as Neolithic times, when he was associated with fertility rites, which among many cultures included sexual acts.[11] Indeed, one of the names the Greeks gave Dionysius means "the phallos personified."[12] Secret cults devoted to observance of the Dionysian mysteries persisted in Greece throughout classical and Hellenistic times and, in the cities of Megara and Argos, were known to have included homosexual initiation.[13] Livy wrote that during the Bacchic rites celebrated in Rome young men being initiated into the mysteries were subjected to anal intercourse. Because of a prevailing cultural prejudice against sexual passivity in Roman males, the practices provoked outrage among tradition-minded Romans when the secret rites were made public. Livy's reference to this sexual ritual, which is undoubtedly of very ancient origin, shows that a tradition of ritual homosexuality was being practiced at least by some Romans as late as the second century B.C.[14]

The absence of any kind of literature from the early Republic that would shed light on the sexual customs or attitudes of the early Romans precludes us from knowing with certainty to what extent homosexuality played a role in their day to day lives. However, given their lengthy and intimate association with the Etruscans, whose enthusiasm for homosexuality was documented by ancient writers, and their close ethnic relationship to other Indo-Europeans whose homosexual customs were well known, it is doubtful that homosexual behavior would have been either foreign to the early Romans, or disapproved of by them. In any event, from the point in time when Roman literature first appeared, in the 3rd century B.C., it is clear that uniquely Roman homosexual customs were already well established.

Early Roman Sexual Traditions

The plays of Plautus, who wrote in the second half of the 3rd century B.C., contain numerous references to homosexual activity, mostly in a humorous vein. In his comedy *Casina*, homosexual horseplay between two characters, Lysidamus and Olympio, is used as a humorous allusion to the manners and habits supposedly typical of the two characters' rural, agrarian origins — so much for the myth of the sober and monogamous Roman farmer.[15] Male slaves are also repeatedly teased by reminding them what is expected of them, that is, to get down on hands and knees so that they can be sexually used by their master. The frequent joking references to sexual relations between males in Plautus's plays display a comfortable familiarity of the playwright and his audience with male homosexuality. Rather than ridiculing homosexual practices as foreign or bizarre, Plautus' easygoing jests poke fun at situations or encounters that must have brought knowing chuckles from many of the men in the audience.[16] In another play, *Truculentus*, Plautus makes a joking reference to sexual relations between a courtesan and her female slave, suggesting that same-sex relations between women and their slaves were also a familiar feature of life in the period.[17] While the comedies of Plautus are very probably patterned after the work of the Greek playwright Menander,[18] the humorous references to the sexual use of slaves points to a homosexual tradition that developed a unique and distinctive character among the Romans that bears little similarity to the homosexual customs of the Greeks.

We know from numerous sources that during the Republic, going back at least as early as the 4th century B.C., it was the custom for many unmarried Roman men to keep a handsome young male slave, called a *concubinus*, as a sexual companion. Also called *puer delicati*, one historian has described them as "a special type of handsome young voluptuaries ... on intimate terms with their masters."[19] Such good-looking young male slaves in the larger households were also expected to be available to take care of the sexual needs of other males in the house, as well as male guests. That young male slaves were routinely pursued for sexual purposes is shown in an anecdote related by the Roman historian, Valerius Maximus, who wrote of a young man named Calidius Bomboniensis who was caught one evening in the bed chamber of a married woman. According to Valerius, "The place was suspicious, the hour was suspicious, the woman herself was suspect, and his own youthfulness was incriminating." In cases of adultery, Roman law allowed the betrayed husband a variety of ways to punish the adulterer, from giving him over to the household slaves to be sodomized, to death. However, Bomboniensis was able to convince the husband of his innocence by claiming that he was in the room "on account of his passion for a slave-boy."[20] That such a defense would be credible illustrates how ordinary such relationships must have seemed. In fact, so closely were young male slaves identified as sexual objects that slave merchants often lifted the garments of boys and young men on display in their slave markets to show off their musculature and genital development for prospective purchasers.[21]

Roman men also frequently found sexual companionship in young male prostitutes, called *scorti*, who were drawn from the ranks of the legions of non–Romans who settled in Rome in increasing numbers as Roman territory expanded under the Republic. *Prostitute* is not actually the right word to describe these young males, many of whom were really more like high-class courtesans, pampered and indulged, and whose services often commanded high prices. The Roman writer Cato complained about the extravagances of his fellow citizens, who, he said, were willing to pay 300 drachmas for a jar of Black Sea caviar, and to pay a handsome youth "more than the value of a farm" for his services. These "kept boys" lived lives of luxury, accompanying their wealthy Roman patrons in their socializing and travels. Female prostitutes, in contrast, occupied the lowest social stratum, and lived for the most part in poverty, plying their trade in the doorways and alleyways of the city.[22]

The keeping of male slaves and prostitutes as sexual companions, aside from confirming the existence of homosexual customs among the Romans of the early Republic, illustrates how different the Roman mentality in regard to sexuality was from that of the Greeks, and shows persuasively that the Romans could not have gotten their homosexual customs from the Greeks as is often claimed. While the sexual use of slaves was taken for granted throughout much of the ancient world, among the Romans, sexual activity with slaves was often more than simply taking advantage of an easy opportunity for sexual release. In many cases, Roman men developed deep and loving sexual relationships with a particular slave-companion, and would even ply him with gifts and special favors — not the type of treatment normally given a typical domestic servant. The extent to which Roman men would go to please their slave-concubines is illustrated in another incident recorded by Valerius Maximus. He wrote of a Roman who took the slave-boy with whom he was having a sexual relationship on an outing in the countryside. The youth expressed a desire to eat tripe, but since there were no meat markets in the vicinity, the Roman, in order to please his slave-lover, had a domestic ox killed. Because of laws protecting domestic work animals, this led to his arrest and trial.[23] It is easy to see that the sexual attachments Roman men developed with their slave-concubines and with male prostitutes played a role in the emotional lives of many Roman men not much different from the place that pederastic loves occupied in the lives of Greek men.

Why the Romans of the Republic would keep handsome slaves or prostitutes as companions rather than court attractive free youths, as the Greeks did, is explained by the Romans' concept of sexual virility and the identity they had of themselves as a race of conquerors. Every Roman boy of the period was raised to believe he was part of a race that was destined to conquer the world. This cultural attitude is summed up by Virgil in the phrase, *Parcere subiectis et debellare superbos*, "spare those who surrender, overcome those who dare oppose us."[24] The Romans believed they were born to dominate — fellow citizens through the use of language for political gain, and non–Romans through the force of arms. So in order to become a true Roman citizen, a boy had to learn from the earliest age never to submit, but to impose his will on others — even including his sexual will — on men as well as women. A virile Roman male regarded himself, accordingly, first and foremost, as a sexual conqueror, which has led one scholar to characterize the Roman sense of sexual virility as "based on rape."[25] Indeed, what other people would glorify a legendary episode in their past like the Rape of the Sabine Women, as the Romans did? Feminist writers have justifiably criticized the classical Greeks as being the archetypal male chauvinists, but in this regard the Romans surely get the prize.

Being from a race of dominators, it was inconceivable to the Roman sense of virility that a free Roman male, even a youth, could submit to another male. For a free Roman male to willingly give himself to another male would have been seen as a threat to the identity of Roman males as conquerors, and hence tantamount to a threat to the foundations of the state. The seriousness with which the Romans of the early Republic viewed an attempt to sexually dominate another Roman male is illustrated by a scandal recounted by the Roman historian Livy which occurred sometime in the late fourth century B.C. According to Livy's account, a handsome youth, Gaius Publilius, had given himself up into slavery for a debt owed by his father to a usurer named Lucius Papirius. Regarding the youth's beauty as additional compensation for the loan, Lucius sought first to seduce him with "lewd conversation." But when the young man ignored his advances, Lucius began to threaten him, and reminded him of the implications of his condition, including the obligations of a slave for sexual service. Then, according to Livy, after Lucius saw that the youth "had more regard for his honorable birth than his present plight, he had him stripped and scourged." The young man broke away and ran into the streets, where his mistreatment was discovered by the people. Outraged by the abuse he had suffered, they marched to the authorities demanding retribution for Lucius, not for attempting a homosexual relationship with a male slave, which would have been acceptable, but because the particular young man in question was a Roman citizen, a status that was not altered by his enslavement to another Roman. According to Livy, it was because of this case that the consuls shortly thereafter abolished slavery for debt.[26] A similar story is reported by Valerius Maximus, who in commenting on the case, emphasized the importance of protecting the *pudicitia,* the sexual honor, of Roman citizens.[27]

The discomfort with which the Romans of the early Republic viewed sexual passivity in a Roman male, even a youth, is a striking illustration of the differences between the Roman and Greek approach to sexuality. While male homosexuality in the form of hierarchical sexual relationships between a dominant older male and a younger passive partner was widespread among both the Romans and the Greeks, the differences in the beliefs of the two societies about sexuality dictated distinctive differences in the character of those relationships. Whereas the Greeks believed a youth could be ennobled as a result of a sexual relationship with a noble adult, proper Roman society believed that for a youth to enter into such a relationship would only result in his degradation. Hence, the objects of affection of Roman men, if male, had to be non–Romans or slaves. Further, since Roman men believed their virility was based on domination through the exercise of power, the patient courting and persuasion of a youth in order to win him over, as practiced by the Greeks, would have made no sense to a Roman male. Conversely, because of the Greeks belief about the ennobling role of homosexual relationships, that is, the molding of a noble and virtuous adult citizen, to love young slaves or prostitutes, who by definition were excluded from the ranks of citizens, would have seemed pointless to them. Given the sharp differences between the two societies in the beliefs governing sexual relations between males, it is hard to see how it could be argued, as some historians have, that the Romans derived their homosexual customs from the Greeks.[28]

Aside from the differences in the attitudes each society brought to homosexual relationships, there is evidence that the Roman tradition of homosexual relationships with slave-concubines was well established several centuries before the Romans acquired their infatuation with Greek culture and subsequently began their large-scale imitation Greek arts and practices.[29] The casualness with which sexual relationships with slaves are mentioned in the comedies of Plautus implies that by his lifetime, the late third century B.C., the tradition of loving slaves was a long-standing tradition. The incident cited by Valerius Maximus that prompted the abolition of slavery for debt occurred during the Samnite Wars, around 330 B.C., which would take the tradition back to at least the fourth century B.C.[30]

That such homosexual relationships were widespread in Republican Rome is attested to by the Greek historian Polybius, who visited Rome in the early second century B.C. In his account, written during the height of the Republic, Polybius commented that "moderation" in sexual matters was nearly impossible for young men in Rome, since most of them were having affairs with male lovers or concubines.[31] Even the statesman Cicero, regarded as a paragon of Republican virtue, had his slave-concubine, a young man named Tiro. Cicero was reportedly so fond of Tiro that he wrote a love poem to him, and later freed him.[32] It was apparently not unusual for Romans to grant freedom to slave-concubines they greatly loved, as Cicero did. John Boswell cites a case, described by Seneca the Elder, where a former slave was criticized for continuing to serve as his patron's concubine, even after he was freed. The man's lawyer responded that "sexual service is an offense for the free born, a necessity for the slave, and a duty for the freedman." As Boswell observes, this inevitably gave rise to a line of jokes on the order of "You aren't doing your 'duty' by me," and "he has become very 'dutiful' towards so-and-so."[33]

It is also significant to note that the widespread homosexuality that existed in Republican Rome occurred without the strong social encouragement that was a feature of the educational homosexuality of classical Greece. Indeed, among the Spartans, it was essentially a legal obligation for a noble adult to take a youth under his wing in the sort of ennobling sexual relationship the Spartans considered a necessary element in the development of their warrior/citizens. Not only was there the complete absence of any such notions about the social benefits of homosexual love among the Romans, but young Roman men had ample opportunity to pursue sexual relationship with slave girls and female concubines, who were widely available, and many men did just that. But the fact that so many Roman men would freely choose young males as sexual companions, despite the easy availability of attractive young women, and in the absence of any sense of social obligation of the kind associated with Greek homosexual customs, is strong evidence of the inherent homosexual component of human sexuality.

Legal Protections for Minor Sons

Given the self-conception of Roman males as sexual conquerors and the pride they took in asserting their sexual dominance over others, it was probably inevitable that some Roman men would disregard social scruples about subjecting another Roman male to sexual penetration, and pursue sexual relationships with attractive young Roman males. Roman youth, along with married women and their unmarried daughters, had been traditionally excluded from the ranks of possible sex objects for Roman men, who were free to pursue males or females among slaves, prostitutes or among the increasing number of non–Romans settling in the city as Roman territory expanded. But by the late third century B.C., the sexual pursuit of young free-born Roman males had become so common that legal measures had to be taken to protect them.

The first of these, the Lex Scantinia, probably enacted around 226 B.C.,[34] does not survive in written form, and so not much is known about its provisions. In fact, so little is known about the Scantinian law that there is not even agreement as to the spelling of its name — some scholars prefer Scatinia, without the first "n." Because the few references to the law that survive in Roman literature seem to suggest that it had something to do with homosexual relationships, traditional historians have assumed that the law must have forbidden homosexual acts, and have cited it as further proof that homosexuality was unknown or disapproved under the Republic. However, such an interpretation seems to reflect a superficial reading of the sources, and, in fact, the Romans have left no other evidence that homosexuality was disapproved under the Republic.[35] To the contrary, the accounts of Greek and Roman historians, not to mention the comedies of Plautus, leave little doubt that homosexuality among males was widespread during the Republic. Cicero, whose knowledge of Roman law was exhaustive, would certainly have been familiar with the provisions of the Lex Scantinia. Yet not only did this notoriously upright statesman and jurist have his own male lover-concubine, which would have been inconceivable if homosexuality were illegal, but it is clear from his writings that homosexual behavior was not only legal, but was a common feature of life in his day. On one occasion Cicero, in defending a man accused of taking his male lover to the countryside to have sex with him, stated categorically that "this is no crime." On another occasion Cicero persuaded Curio the Elder to honor the debts incurred by his son on behalf of his boyfriend, to whom, Cicero stated, the younger Curio was "united in a stable and permanent marriage, just as if he had given him a matron's *stola*." Given the nature of the relationship between the two young men, Cicero believed that paying off the debts was the only proper course of action.[36]

It is clear, then, that the Lex Scantinia could not have prohibited all homosexual behavior. The work of recent scholars has shown that, rather than being a general prohibition of homosexuality, the law was intended to penalize only one category of homosexual behavior, the sexual seduction of a free-born Roman youth. In so doing, the law essentially codified existing social attitudes that held inviolate the sexual honor of Roman youth, male and female. But it is significant to note that even for this act, which apparently provoked deeply held sentiments among traditional Roman moralists, the proscribed punishment was merely a monetary fine.[37]

The enactment of the Lex Scantinia seems to have had little effect in deterring Roman men from their pursuit of free-born youth. Indeed, not only were Roman youths continuing to be seen as objects of desire, but their admirers were openly courting them on the streets. As a consequence, barely 30 years later another legal provision had to be enacted toward the same end. It was the custom under the Republic for a newly elected *praetor,* an official akin to a chief magistrate or judge, to issue an edict informing the citizens of the criteria he would use in his administration of the law. One such praetor, who came to office around the beginning of the second century B.C. and whose name is not known, declared that he would penalize anyone who accosted or harassed respectable women or male youth on a public highway. The title of the edict, *De adtemptata pudicitia,* and the inclusion of women along with male youth in its protection, demonstrate that it was not homosexual relationships, per se, that were to be penalized. The term *pudicitia* refers to virginity, or sexual honor, which applied not only to unmarried virgins and the honor of married women, but also to that of a male adolescent, who could lose his sexual honor as a result of taking the passive role in homosexual intercourse. In restating this traditional Roman concern for protecting the sexual honor of both respectable women and male youth, the edit punished those who followed them "silently and insistently" on the street, in a lewd manner, with clear sexual intent. The Roman jurist Ulpian, in a commentary on the law, emphasized that it was not everybody who behaved in this way who was punished by the law, for example, someone who might make a flirtatious remark while passing on the street, but only those who did it *contra bonos mores*— against the dictates of propriety. The edict, then, was another attempt to protect young free-born males from attempted seduction by cruising lechers, which must have been a common occurrence. However, it appears that the edit had little, if any, effect on the behavior of Roman men, because despite the edict, and the Lex Scantinia that preceded it, young Roman males continued to be the objects of sexual seduction throughout the remaining years of the Republic.[38]

Homosexual Love in Roman Poetry

While indigenous Roman homosexual customs certainly preceded the period of Greek influence, the sexual pursuit of free-born males that was increasingly common in the late Republic coincided with a gradual Hellenization of Roman culture that accelerated after the Greek states were annexed by Rome in the second century B.C. The Greek model of romantic homosexual love between a lover and beloved of the same social status further undermined attempts to prevent the sexual pursuit of free-born Roman youth. But the influence of this Greek institution, which became familiar to Roman men because of the widespread popularity of Greek literature, also brought about a transformation in the character of sexual relations between males in Rome. In earlier times, a Roman man's sexual relations with a slave-concubine amounted to the exercise of his masculine right for the body of his slave lover. Under the influence of Greek culture, homosexual relationships acquired a romantic character, involving the pursuit and seduction of the beloved, and the recognition of the power the beloved had over the feelings of the lover.

This change in the character of these relationships can be seen in the love poetry produced by Roman writers in the years of the late Republic and early Empire. "My soul has left me; it has fled, me thinks, to Theotimus; he its refuge is…. What shall I do? Queen Venus, lend me aid." It's hard to imagine such lines being uttered in earlier years by a slave-owner about a slave-boy. And the author of these lines was not a decadent member of an urban artistic elite of the sort who might be expected to flaunt social conventions, but is no less than the Roman general, Quintus Lutatius Catalus, elected consul in 102 B.C. and commander of the army that defeated the invading Cimbri tribes in 101 B.C. The romantic ardor that began to be expressed in such love relationships was compared by another writer, Valerius Aedituus, to a flame that no storm could extinguish: "Oh, Phileros, why a torch that we need not? Just as we are we'll go, our hearts aflame. That flame no wild wind's blast can ever quench, or rain that falls torrential from the skies; Venus herself alone can quell her fire, no other force there is that has such power."[39]

Some of the most intense expression of this new romantic sensibility is seen in the poetry of Gaius Valerius Catallus, born in 84 B.C. Considered the finest of the Roman lyric poets, Catallus is famous for his many poems expressing the passion and ultimate futility of his love for a woman named Lesbia. But overlooked by many readers are the love poems Catallus wrote for a youth named Juventius. This was not a mere slave-boy, but the free-born son of an old and aristocratic family from Verona, who was sent by his family to Rome. There he met Catullus, who started an affair with him to comfort himself after his rejection by Lesbia.[40] Some scholars have claimed that the homosexual love expressed by Catallus in these poems could not have been based on fact or his own experience, but was merely a literary exercise in imitation of the homosexual love poetry of the Greek lyric poets, which had become well known in late Republican Rome. This argument is primarily based on the assumption that homosexuality was outlawed during the Republic by the Lex Scatinia, which, as we have seen, is not true. Not only is there abundant evidence that homosexual love was a common occurrence during the period when the Roman lyric poets wrote, but the description of the passions and torment stirred by their love affairs that is found in their poetry rings true as an expression of human feeling that could only have come from their own experience. Whether or not the subjects of these love poems were real-life figures or literary concoctions, the language displays an experience with real-life passion that could not be mere poetic artifice. Indeed, jealous and violent outbursts toward rivals, which also appear in the poetry of Catullus, have no precedent in Greek poetry.

In his poetry Catullus provides a vivid picture of the varied experiences encountered by a lover in his pursuit of his beloved: the ardor of love, despair at rejection, angry outbursts at rivals, and resignation when he knows he's lost the boy. In one poem, Catullus writes of his passion for the youth: "Your honeyed eyes, Juventius, if someone let me go on kissing, I'd kiss three hundred thousand times, nor never think I'd had enough." These lines are similar to some he wrote for Lesbia, and, in fact, the feelings he had for Juventius and Lesbia and the role those loves played in his life were very similar. Lesbia was not his wife, but a romantic infatuation. Romans of Catullus' status rarely married for love, but rather in order to advance family interests, and so very often the relationship between husband and wife was secondary to financial and dynastic issues. Romans like Catallus, then, sought to meet their sexual and emotional needs through extramarital affairs with women, or, quite often, with handsome young males.

When two friends of the poet, Furius and Aurelius, joke about his feelings for the youth, and make derogatory suggestions about his masculinity, Catallus responds angrily: "I'll bugger you and stuff your mouths, Aurelius Kink, and Poofter Furius, for thinking me, because my verses are rather sissy, not quite decent.... Because you've read of my hundred thousand kisses you doubt my virility? I'll bugger you and stuff your mouths!"[41] While Catullus was pursing a Greek-style romantic relationship with a free-born youth, his response to the taunts of Furius and Aurelius was typically Roman — threatening them with forcible sodomy, and, even more degrading for a Roman, forcing them to perform fellatio on him, the better to demonstrate the virility they questioned. When Catallus discovers that Aurelius, in addition to mocking his feelings for Juventius, was even trying to steal the youth away from him, he again explodes in anger, threatening sexual revenge: "Aurelius ... you long to bugger my love, and not in secret. You're with him, sharing jokes, close at his side, trying everything. It's no good. If you plot against me, I'll get in first and stuff your mouth!" Though the Roman lyric poets were undeniably influenced by Greek poetry, the sentiments expressed by Catullus here are purely Roman and have no parallel in similar works of the Greeks.

In another poem Catullus provides us with a glimpse of the role that the traditional homosexual relationships with slave-concubines played in the life of a proper Roman gentleman. The setting for the poem is the marriage ceremony of a friend of the poet, Manlius Torquatus. As the bride arrives, a boy is distributing nuts to the wedding guests, a ritual supposed to bring fertility to the marriage. But the boy distributing the nuts is doing so sullenly and carelessly, for it turns out that he is the *concubinus* of the bridegroom, that is, the young slave-lover, the *puer delicati*, with whom his master has been having a long-standing sexual relationship. The slave-boy knows that by handing out the nuts he is marking not only the marriage of his master, but the inevitable end of the relationship the two of them enjoyed, and so Catullus addresses this young *concubinus*, urging him to carry out his duties more graciously: "[Let not] the boy concubine refuse nuts to the children when he hears of master's love abandoned.... For long enough you have played with nuts, but now it's time to serve Talassius (the god of marriage)." But it's not just the *concubinus* who has to undergo a change. Addressing Manlius, the bridegroom, the poem goes on: "You are said to find it hard, perfumed bridegroom, to give up smooth-skinned boys, but give them up.... Husbands have no right to [those] pleasures." The poet implies here that Manlius' only sexual interests up to this point have been with males, and that with his marriage these are pleasures he has to give up. Another poet, Martial, depicts a husband-to-be in a similar position, and even goes on to state that for him heterosexual intercourse is *ignortum opus*, "unfamiliar work."[42]

Catullus, then, through his poetry, has given us a description of the sexual options available to a male Roman citizen of the late Republic. The traditional sexual outlet before marriage for a respectable male was with a *concubinus*, as we see in the case of Manlius Torquatus. According to traditional Roman sexual mores, Roman women were to be had only in marriage, and free-born males, not at all. But by the late Republic these strictures has loosened to the point where Catallus could pursue, without social disapproval, not only an unmarried Roman woman (Lesbia), but a free-born youth of a noble family.

The poet Tibullus, born in 54 B.C., a generation later than Catullus, provides in his fourth elegy a vivid picture of the appeal handsome young males had for Roman men: "Avoid them; don't let yourself near a gang of blooming boys; in every one of them there'll be some ground for passion. One boy is delightful for his tight rein on a horse, another parts still water with a chest as white as snow; one captivates you with his bold effrontery; another boy's soft cheeks have virgin modesty standing guard." Tibullus' reference to the objects of his desire as "boys" should not be taken to mean, as modern readers might assume, that he was pursuing young teenagers. Roman writers used the term "boys" to describe attractive males even when they were serving in the Roman army. Like the Greeks' use of the word *pais,* literally "boy," for the younger passive partner of a homosexual pair, the Romans used the Latin for "boy," *puer,* and "girl," *puella,* generically to refer to sexually appealing love objects. This is no different than the use of the same words in contemporary culture — boyfriend, girlfriend. Thus, no one today would take the phrase, "I'm dating a beautiful girl," to mean the speaker was describing a pubescent female. There is evidence, in fact, that, like the Greeks, Roman men preferred male youth in their later teens or early majority.[43] Indeed, Queen Boadicea of Britain criticized Roman men as "profligate" because they bathed in warm water, ate artificial dainties, drank unmixed wine, and slept on soft couches with "boys past their prime."[44]

After his warning about avoiding the beauty of these "boys," Tibullus, acknowledging the futility of resisting their attractions, then offers advice on how to win a favorite:

> Even if at first he does refuse, don't you give in through lack of perseverance; he'll soon accept the yoke.... You now, give in to your young man's every whim; love wins a million victories by pandering. Agree to go with him, however long a road he contemplates.... If fencing's what he wants, then limber up your arm and take him on; occasionally presenting him your open flank, so he can win. Then he'll be kind, then you can grasp the precious kiss; he will resist, but snatch and you'll have it. At first you'll have to snatch; later you'll only have to ask; and finally he'll embrace you at his own desire.

This last point, bringing the youth to the point where "he'll embrace [the pursuer] at his own desire," is an aspect of these homosexual relationships, that is, the presence of reciprocal desire, that is not usually depicted in Greek art and literature, and its portrayal in Roman culture is another example of the divergence of sexual attitudes between the two societies. Whereas the sexual mores of classical Athenian society required that the youth display no eagerness for the relationship, and in paintings on vases the youth is often depicted as a passive onlooker to the sexual passions of his pursuer, representations of male-to-male intercourse in Roman art show the partners as mutually attracted to each other in scenes of lovemaking infused with a tender intimacy. The artists depict both lovers as attractive and dignified, even in scenes of anal intercourse, where the two partners are frequently depicted gazing into each other's eyes.[45]

Tibullus goes on in his elegy to lay out the rules of courtship, rules which very closely parallel the norms of homosexual courtship observed in classical Athens. As in Athens, the Roman youth was to play hard to get, requiring that he be flattered and courted. Likewise, the Roman lover had to persevere, proving his dedication, and swearing eternal love. With the appropriation of this Greek model by Roman lovers, the traditional relationship between lover and beloved had become exactly reversed. Whereas in earlier times, the *concubinus* was, literally, enslaved to the lover, in the late Republic it was now the lover who was enslaved, figuratively, to the beloved. But the Roman borrowing from the Greek was not complete: there was no sense that the relationship played a role in the youth's betterment, and instead of the modesty and decorum demanded of the *pais* in Athens, the young Roman was, more often than not, a "capricious, spoiled, pretentious brat."[46] Though Roman lovers were inspired in their romances by the idealistic loves of classical Greece, it was a hollow imitation at best, and in some cases verged on parody in its excesses.

By the mid-first century B.C., homosexual romances were such a common feature of the lifestyles of Roman men that references to them appear in the works of virtually all writers of the period. As in other societies, though, it is apparent that the degree of homosexual interest varied from individual to individual. Though Tibullus seems to have been drawn primarily to males, Catallus, as we have seen, was attracted to both women and young men. Sextus Propertius, a contemporary of Tibullus, seems to have had a definite preference: he prayed that his enemies would fall in love with women, and his friends with boys.[47] The poet Horace, like Catallus, seemed to have been attracted equally to both sexes. Horace wrote lively poetic commentary on the joys and tribulations of loving young males, but seemed to regard the sex of his love object as of secondary importance. When, in a letter to his patron, he tried to describe the emotional disturbance he was suffering as a result of a passionate affair with a woman, he compared his state to the pain he suffered in an earlier love affair with a beautiful young man.[48] One of the greatest of Roman practitioners of love poetry was Ovid, born in 43 B.C. Though he acknowledged the attractions of loving boys, Ovid seems to have been primarily interested in the love of women, which he celebrated in love poetry of such passion and beauty that he is remembered today as the "arch-poet" of love.

The greatest of all the Roman poets was Virgil, who is known principally for his national epic, the *Aeneid*, but who was also the author of several volumes of pastoral elegies and other poetry. Born in 70 B.C. of Celtic stock, in a rural area near Mantua in northern Italy, Virgil witnessed, along with Horace and others of the lyric poets, the disintegration of the Republican government, the rise to power of Julius Caesar, his assassination, and the subsequent decades of political turmoil and civil war that ended only with the ascension of Caesar's nephew, Octavian, to power as Augustus Caesar, the first emperor of Rome. After so many years of upheaval and destruction, Augustus sought to restore Roman strength, through repopulation of rural farming areas devastated by the years of war and neglect, and by attempting to reawaken in the Romans a sense of national pride, and renew in them an enthusiasm for the traditional Roman values of bravery, frugality, duty, and devotion to family. Virgil's work is a reflection of these times, both in his pastoral idylls, in which can be found a yearning for the simple peace of bucolic life in the midst of the upheaval of war, and in his monumental epic poem, the *Aeneid*, which glorified the heroic virtues of early Rome, and linked those legendary roots of Rome to the grandeur of Roman achievement in the Augustan age.

As in other literature of the period, the vision of human experience expressed in Virgil's poetry includes the passion and rapture of homosexual love. Virgil, who never married, and who seems to have been primarily homosexual himself, includes several pairs of devoted warrior-lovers in the *Aeneid,* among them, the Latin warrior Cydon and his beloved, Clytius, his "latest joy, whose cheeks were goldening with down,"[49] and the Trojan Nisus and his beautiful lover, Euryalus, "handsomer than any other soldier of Aeneas, ... a boy whose cheek bore though unshaven manhood's early down."[50] That Euryalus was only slightly younger than Nisus[51] shows that to the Roman mind a male couple need not be separated by a dozen or more years of age, as was often the case in classical Greece, but could, like the Homeric warrior couples of Achilles and Patroclus, Sthenelus and Deipylos, Orestes and Pylades, and Telemachus and Pisistratus, be essentially peers. Indeed, the pair of Nisus and Euryalus was clearly patterned after the example of warrior-lovers celebrated in Homer, and exemplified by the Sacred Band of Thebes. As described by Virgil, "One love united them, and side by side they entered combat,"[52] and in Book IX, the poet dwells at some length on the valiant courage their love inspired and their heroic deaths.[53]

One of Virgil's better-known poems, and, in the treatment of its homosexual theme, more typically Roman, is his second *Eclogue*, which describes the suffering of a shepherd, Corydon, over his love for a beautiful youth, Alexis. When it appears that Alexis will not reciprocate his love, Corydon consoles himself with the knowledge that he will find another male to love in the countryside. Thus, the famous lines the poet writes: "Love has no bounds in pleasure, or in pain.... Quench, Corydon, thy long unanswered fire.... And find an easier love, though not so fair."[54] The poem provides an interesting contradiction of the assumption made by traditional scholars that the homosexual love found in Roman lyric poetry was not a reflection of the poet's real feelings or actual practices of the period, but merely an imitation of Greek forms. Virgil patterned his story of the love between Corydon and Alexis not after a similar homosexual love in Greek literature, but after a *heterosexual* idyll of the Greek poet Theocritus. The rural setting of this poem, which was immensely popular in Virgil's lifetime, also effectively rebuts the notion advanced by some scholars that homosexuality was purely an urban phenomenon in Roman times, and shows that to the Romans a passionate homosexual romance set among farmers and shepherds was as plausible as one set in the city.[55]

The poetry of Catullus, Tibullus, Horace, Ovid and Virgil presents a lyrical vision of the varied experiences of love among Romans of the late Republic and early Empire. The work of the satiric poet Martial, who lived in the first century A.D., traverses the same material, but with an earthy humor that, to some scholars, approaches the pornographic. While Martial has been accused by some writers of having "a tabloid mentality, and of purveying scurrilous gossip for mere titillation,"[56] the attitudes and sexual practices he describes are consistent with the practices described in the work of the lyric poets and other writers of the period. Thus, in the view of Martial and other contemporary writers, it could be taken for granted that nearly all Roman men found younger males at least as attractive, if not more so, than women; that some men had a marked preference for their own sex in love; and that some Roman men of the period not only enjoyed, but preferred the passive role in sex with another man.[57] Martial, himself, professes to be mostly indifferent to the sex of his partners: "And when your lust is hot, surely if a maid or pageboy's handy, ... you won't choose to grin and bear it? I won't. I like a cheap and easy love."[58] But judging from his poetic output, however, he seemed to have been more preoccupied with loving boys,[59] as he makes clear in one of his verses: "May I have a boy with a cheek smooth with youth, not with pumice, for whose sake no maid would please me."[60]

Martial's predilection for young males may have been due to the increasing assertiveness of Roman women during the early Empire, many of whom had wealth of their own, which freed them from material dependence on their husbands. And so Martial writes: "Why am I unwilling to marry a rich wife, do you ask? I am unwilling to take my wife as husband. Let the matron be subject to her husband." Other women, even if they had no wealth, had grown arrogant, sexually demanding and insatiable: "You bid my penis, Lesbia, to be always standing for you; believe me, one's prick is not the same as one's finger. You may urge me with toyings and wheedling words, but your face is imperious to defeat you."[61] But beautiful boys, who could be counted on to be compliant and submissive, presented no such problems. In this respect Martial reflects the attitude of a traditional Roman male, insisting on being the dominating partner, whether with a male or a female. And so he informs a youth who wants to be courted: "You wish to be courted, Sextus; I wished to love you. I must obey you; as you demand, you shall be courted. But if I court you, Sextus, I shall not love you."

Loving young men, then, as Martial sees it, was, in part, the Roman male's response to the "battle of the sexes." And so it is not surprising that when it came time for a man to marry, he found it difficult to give up his male lovers. Like Catullus in his counsel to the bridegroom, Manlius Torquatus, Martial advises another bridegroom about the new sexual role he is to play: "Enjoy feminine embraces, Victor; enjoy them, and let your poker learn an activity unknown to it. The red bridal veil is woven ... and by now the newly wedded wife will crop close your boys." The reference here is to the custom of cutting the hair of slave-boys at a certain age to indicate the end of their time as sexual objects. Referring to the pleasure of anal intercourse with young males that the husband will have to give up, Martial continues: "Now, she will grant sodomy just once to her wishful husband, while she still dreads the first hurt of that strange new lance; nurse and mother will forbid it to be done more than once, and they will say, 'She's a wife to you, not a boy.' Oh dear! What terrible worries, what awful troubles you'll have to put up with!" With marriage, as Martial says, a man was supposed to give up the pleasure of loving young males, but this was only in theory. Wives had reason to fear competition from young males, who were still widely available, and, in fact, a woman could not sue her husband for adultery until the late Empire.

And so Martial pokes fun at a wife who thinks she can win her husband's affection by offering the same attraction for which men pursued male youths: anal intercourse: "Having caught me, wife, in a boy, in a harsh cross voice you rebuke me and tell me that you too have a backside." Martial's fictional husband then reminds his wife of all the gods and mythical heroes who preferred anal intercourse with a youth to the same with a woman.

> Juno said the same a lot of times to wanton Jupiter the Thunderer! He nonetheless lies with grown-up Ganymede. Hercules put down his bow and bent Hylas over instead. Do you believe Megara [his wife] had no buttocks? Phoebus Apollo was tortured by Daphne as she ran away; but a Spartan lad ordained that those passionate flames should depart. Although Briseis lay a lot with her back turned, a clean-shaven boy-friend was closer to Achilles. So refrain from giving masculine titles to your things wife, and believe you have two quims [vaginas].

Thus, Martial displays in this poem the prevailing belief of Roman men that that women can't satisfy all of a man's requirements, and that they might as well accept the fact.

Homosexuality of the Ruling Class

As illustrated by the literature produced in late Republic and early Empire, homoerotic interests and relationships were a dimension of the sex lives of most of the Roman men of the period. Virtually all the major political and military leaders of the late Republic and early Empire were known for their homosexual loves and affairs. Julius Caesar, the brilliant military commander and statesman, whose defiance of the old nobility in the Senate set in motion the events leading to the demise of Republican government and the emergence of the power of the emperor, was famous for the passive role he played in a homosexual affair as a young man. While in military service in the East, the youthful officer allowed himself to be seduced by Nicomedes, king of the Anatolian kingdom of Bithynia. Their affair was witnessed by Roman businessmen, who also reported that Caesar had played the role of cup bearer for the king at a banquet. Though only 19 years of age at the time, the reputation Caesar earned for the passive role he played in this relationship, a role particularly inappropriate for a Roman military officer, was to follow him his entire life.

After Caesar's triumphant conquest of the Celts in Gaul, his soldiers sang, "*Gallias Caesar subegit, Nicomedes Caesarem*," "Caesar conquered the Gauls, Nicomedes conquered Caesar." When in a debate in the Senate, Caesar was pleading a matter on behalf of Nysa, daughter of Nicomedes, and recalled some benefits Rome had received from the king, Cicero interrupted him, saying, "Enough of that, if you please! We all know what he gave you, and what you gave him in return." During a public assembly, Octavian turned to Pompey, addressing him as "king," then turned to Caesar, and addressed him as "queen." Bibulus, Caesar's co-consul, called him "the Queen of Bithynia."[62] Caesar seems to have been completely unaffected by this mockery, a mark of his self confidence, nor did his youthful affair with the king detract from his political stature. When after his triumph in Gaul his soldiers sang the song about Nicomedes conquering Caesar and Caesar conquering Gaul, they followed that verse with two more, "Behold Caesar now triumphs, who subjugated Gaul; Nicomedes, who subjugated Caesar, has no victories now." His soldiers recognized that whatever Caesar did in his private life as a young man, the real measure of his manhood as a Roman was his military conquests, and so, compared to Nicomedes, Caesar was the real man.[63] A bisexual, like many Romans, Caesar also had a considerable reputation as a womanizer. He seduced the wives of several of his Senate colleagues, in addition to carrying on an extended affair with Cleopatra of Egypt. Thus, we have Curio the Elder's famous reference to him as "every man's wife and every woman's husband."[64]

After Caesar's assassination, Mark Antony, Caesar's co-consul and ally, and the prime mover in the defeat and death of Caesar's assassins, took up an affair with Cleopatra, and eventually died with her after their later defeat by Octavian. While Antony was immortalized by Shakespeare for his romance with Cleopatra, and, like Caesar, was well known for his seductions of the wives of his Senate colleagues, he was also notorious for his homosexuality. Like Caesar, Antony had a reputation for homosexual passivity in his youth that was fully exploited by his detractors. According to Cicero, Antony, who was of a noble family, prostituted himself as a youth, and then became the lover of Curio the Younger, with whom, wrote Cicero, he was "established in a steady and fixed marriage.... No boy bought for the sake of lust was ever as much in his master's power" as Antony was in Curio's.[65] When he was older, Antony had a reputation as a seducer of younger males. The first-century A.D. Jewish historian Josephus wrote that Antony, who ruled the eastern provinces after Caesar's death, asked the Judean king, Herod, to send his young brother-in-law Aristobulos to the Roman court. But Herod refused, because "he did not think it safe for him to send one so handsome as was Aristobulus, in the prime of life, for he was sixteen years of age, and of so noble a family; and particularly not to Antony, the principal man of the Romans, and that would abuse him in his amours, and besides, one that freely indulged himself in such pleasures as his power allowed him without control."[66]

With Antony's defeat and death in 30 B.C., Octavian, Caesar's nephew and heir, gained total control over the Roman world, which he ruled, as Augustus Caesar, for the next 44 years. Octavian, like his uncle, Julius Caesar, also had a reputation for homosexual passivity in his youth,* and, in fact, Mark Antony claimed Octavian gave himself sexually to his uncle in return for being made his heir.[67] While Antony eventually became a rival and enemy of Octavian, he had been for many years a close associate and ally of both Julius Caesar and Octavian, had married into Caesar's family, and so may have been in a position to know about the character of their relationship. The young Octavian was also reported to have sold himself to Aulus Hirtius, governor of Spain, for a small fortune, and to have used red-hot walnut shells on his legs to soften the hair for his male admirers.[68] That the future emperor's reputation for homosexual passivity was widespread and well established is illustrated by inscriptions found on lead shot used in slings by Roman soldiers in the siege of Perugia, in 41 B.C., a battle between Octavian's forces and those of Antony. It was customary for soldiers to inscribe insults about the opposing commander on the lead shot they aimed at their enemy, and among the shot that have been found from that battle are numerous pieces referring to Octavian as "Octavia," the feminine form of the name, as well as inscriptions associating Octavian with

---

*It is interesting to note the similarity of the sexual histories of Julius Caesar, Mark Antony and Octavian, and the parallels in their patterns of youthful homosexual passivity followed by aggressive heterosexuality to the similar pattern found in male rats. As described in Chapter 1, researchers have found that some male rats will willingly submit themselves sexually to other males, but when presented with heterosexual opportunities, these same males were found to be "vigorous copulators." The researchers discovered that the willingness of these animals to submit themselves homosexually correlated with high levels of testosterone, a trait that could also be surmised from the markedly aggressive nature displayed by Caesar, Antony and Octavian in the conduct of their careers—aggression being an aspect of male behavior brought on by testosterone.

fellatio and sexual passivity.[69] Another indicator of the reputation Octavian had for sexual passivity comes from a story related by Suetonius. One day at the theater the audience heard a verse alluding to a priest of the goddess Cybele playing a drum with his fingers. Priests of the mother goddess were well known throughout the ancient world for homosexual passivity. The Latin word for drum, *orbs*, used in the verse, can also refer to the world. So when the audience heard the verse, "Look how this invert plays the drum with his finger," they interpreted it as, "Look how this passive (Octavian) rules the world with his finger," and so broke into thunderous applause.[70] Octavian, like his uncle Julius and Mark Antony, also had a reputation as a womanizer when he became an adult, though this was in part due to a public relations campaign he waged to consolidate his reputation as a defender of traditional Roman values.

Octavian wasn't the only powerful Roman said to have submitted himself sexually to other men in order to advance his career. The historian Tacitus wrote that several popular military commanders of the early empire began their rise to power by sleeping with powerful patrons, including Sejanus and Otho, who was briefly emperor. Suetonius wrote that Otho, who advanced his career through a sexual relationship with Nero, even wore a wig and massaged his face with a poultice of bread to keep his beard from growing in order to remain more attractive to his admirers. Otho's successor as emperor, Vitellius, aided his rise through the ranks through a sexual relationship with the Emperor Tiberius. Suetonius reports that Vitellius, who acquired the nickname of *Spintria*—a vulgar term for a prostitute—was a member of the harem of handsome young men kept by Tiberius for his amusement.[71]

The homosexual interests of Roman emperors is familiar to many modern readers. In fact, Edward Gibbon wrote in his *History of the Decline and Fall of the Roman Empire* that "of the first fifteen emperors, Claudius was the only one whose taste in love was entirely correct," that is, in Gibbon's view, heterosexual, though other historians have also noted that Claudius was "a moron."[72] Tiberius, who succeeded Augustus, had a large pleasure palace built for himself on the isle of Capri, where he had a number of young men and women trained in sexual practices who would perform sexual acts before the emperor, sometimes out in the open in the gardens, while dressed as nymphs and Pans. He also had boys trained as "minnows" to chase around him when he swam, to get between his legs and nibble him.[73] The Emperor Domitian was reported to have offered his body for hire *in writing* while a youth, and was also known to have had a sexual relationship with Nerva, his eventual successor.[74] The Emperor Elagabalus, who was unabashed about his preference for being anally penetrated, was said to have sent out emissaries all over the Empire to seek out men "hung like mules."[75]

According to the Roman writer Dio Cassius, Nero was supposed to have been introduced to homosexuality by the Stoic philosopher Seneca,[76] though this seems unlikely and entirely unnecessary given the sexual attitudes and practices prevailing in the period. In addition to his habit of seducing free born males and married women alike, Suetonius writes that Nero also "debauched the vestal virgin Rubria."[77] Suetonius goes on to describe a sexual game that Nero would force on members of his court, in which, "covered with the skin of some wild animal, he was let loose from a cage and attacked the private parts of men and women, who were bound to stakes, and when he had sated his mad lust, was dispatched by his freed man Doryphorus."[78] Nero had earlier fallen in love with and formally married a young man named Sporus, in a public ceremony complete with dowry that was recognized and celebrated separately in both Rome and Greece. Suetonius recounted a popular joke of the day, "that it would have been well for the world if Nero's father, Domitian, had had that kind of wife." Sporus, "decked out with the finery of the empresses," accompanied Nero on his litter to public functions where he was often embraced affectionately by the emperor.[79] Nero later married his freed man Doryphorus, but in this relationship the emperor took the role of the passive part-ner, and reportedly even imitated the cries and wailings of a virgin being deflowered on his "wedding night."[80] But with this second "marriage" Nero didn't get rid of Sporus, who remained with him throughout his reign and stood by him when he died. Accounts of the arrangement seem to assume that a *ménage a trois* was involved.[81]

Caligula, renowned for his depravity and excess, frequently participated in homosexual affairs. He had sexual relations with several male members of his court, and one of them, Valerius Catullus, even boasted that Caligula had submitted to him, and that he had worn out his groin in the process of satisfying the emperor. But Caligula's reputation for sexual depravity was not due to his homosexuality, though modern writers have often equated the two in treatments of the sex life of Caligula, as well as other emperors. A cruel and capricious despot, Caligula indulged in a wide range of degenerate pastimes, including incest with his sisters, whom he sometimes had sex with in front of his wife.[82] Thus, Caligula's homosexu-ality, taken in the context of the times, was one of the tamer aspects of his personality. Homo-sexuality, per se, then, was not the concomitant of imperial decadence, as it is frequently portrayed, but was a dimension of the sex lives of many men of the period, and consequently something that could be practiced to excess like any other pleasure.

Hadrian, one of the greatest of the emperors, and in many ways the opposite of Caligula, was for all appearances exclusively homosexual. A cousin of the Emperor Trajan, Hadrian became the ward of the emperor after his father died when he was only ten. Entering mili-tary service at the age of 15, Hadrian advanced rapidly through the ranks. According to Aelius Spartianus, the young Hadrian became a "favorite of Trajan's," and accompanied the emperor on his military campaigns, "on terms of considerable intimacy," and "falling in with his habits"— the emperor being known for his homosexuality.[83] Trajan was so fond of Hadrian that he later adopted him, and on Trajan's death in A.D. 117 Hadrian became emperor. A highly educated man who was devoted to his troops, Hadrian united and consolidated Rome's vast empire, began a reform of Roman law, and embarked on a massive building program that produced many of the architectural monuments we today associate with imperial Rome, including the Pantheon in Rome and Hadrian's Wall in Britain.

Hadrian had a wife, but his marriage didn't interest him, and he rarely saw her. Of the romantic attachments associated with the emperor during his life, none were with women. The great love of Hadrian's life was Antinous, a Greek youth who served as the emperor's traveling companion, and on whom Hadrian showered such affection that it was a cause for wonder for Romans of the period. When Antinous was drowned in the Nile in A.D. 130 the heart-broken emperor "wept like a woman." To commemorate their love, Hadrian ordered the erection of thousands of statues of his beloved of such beauty that for centuries they were regarded as the standard for representations of male beauty. In fact, according to one scholar, "Roman art attained its highest achievements in the portrayal of this youth."[84] Hadrian also put the image of Antinous on coins, established a city on the Nile to honor him, and had him deified.[85]

Reaction to Sexual Excesses

The sexual decadence and hedonistic lifestyles of the emperors were mirrored in some elements of the population, particularly among the upper classes. Roman military conquests had resulted in the influx of enormous wealth into the city of Rome, enriching many fami-lies, who flaunted their new status with ostentatious displays and the pursuit of sybaritic pleasures. The vulgar excesses of the *nouveau riche* were resented by many of the old line aristocratic families, whose fortunes had declined with the demise of the power of the Senate, which in former years, as the locus of power and influence for the old nobility, had ensured their social and financial position. Particularly offensive to conservative aristocrats was the shameless pursuit of sexual pleasure, especially the increasingly common practice of adult males assuming the passive role in homosexual affairs, which they viewed as a refutation of traditional Roman values, and symptomatic of what they saw as a decline in moral standards, though they may have actually been more aggrieved by the loss of their former prestige and prominence.

Reaction to the sexual excesses of the period can be found in the satires of Martial and Juvenal, as well as the works of such writers as Livy and Tacitus. Martial addressed some of his most withering satire against adult men who were *pathicus*, that is, homosexually passive. He mercilessly skewered the overtly passive men who shamelessly paraded their tastes in public, but he reserved his harshest criticisms for those who put on an outward show of moral probity, noisily decrying the decline in morals, but who in private played the passive role in their sexual affairs. Juvenal was similarly outraged by the sexual permissiveness he saw around him, writing caustically about the dissoluteness of women as well as men. Juvenal was especially critical toward women, taking them to task for arrogance and presumptuousness, for switching husbands frequently, and for abandoning themselves to homosexual lovemaking, "even going so far as to do it in front of the altar of chastity."[86]

Writing in relative poverty, Juvenal bitterly resented the excesses of the wealthy, which he saw as a betrayal of the values that made Rome great. Like Martial, Juvenal paid special attention to sexual hypocrites, who publicly railed against vice, but who betrayed their real nature with perfume, jewelry and other displays he regarded as effeminate.[87] Both Juvenal and Martial seemed fascinated by the idea that a particularly virile looking man might be eager for anal penetration, and saw in such a figure a symbol of the degenerate state to which, in their view, Roman virility had descended. In his ninth satire, Juvenal takes aim at such a target, a wealthy man named Virro — a play on the word for "manly" — who has employed a male prostitute named Naevolus to satisfy his needs. But Naevolus is not a homosexually passive prostitute, but a "stud" who services women as well as men. Encountering Naevolus wandering around the city in a black temper, the poet inquires as to the reason for his mood. Naevolus tells him that his client Virro is a miserable skinflint, who, though he certainly has the means to reward him well for his services, has denied him his just due. And Naevolous has served him well, for he has not only pleasured the man by playing husband to him, but he has done for his client something he couldn't do for himself — impregnate his wife. So, if it weren't for him, Naevolus complains, the man would have no children, which the man points to as proof of his virility. Naevolus asks, what is there to do about his sad state. "Don't be afraid," the poet responds. "A passive client will never be lacking to you as long as these hills are standing."[88]

Naevolus was but one of a number of types of male prostitutes who catered to the sexual needs of the citizens of imperial Rome. While there had always been a large population of male as well as female prostitutes in Rome, by the early Empire the profession had become so well established that their earnings were taxed and they had their own national holiday. In addition, a degree of specialization had developed to meet the varying tastes of Romans. Male prostitutes like Naevolus, who sexually penetrated their customers, were referred to with such terms as *exoleti, drauci, paedicatores*, and *glabri*. *Exoletus* is the past participle of the verb *exolesco*, "to grow up," "to come to maturity," and was also a general term for post-adolescent males. According to Suetonius, the Emperor Galba preferred *praeduros* (hardbodied) *exoleti*, meaning young adult male studs. *Drauci* were a kind of bodybuilder, often found within circuses, who also made themselves available for rent. The term *paedicator* referred to the active role of the male, and could also be applied to lovers of free born boys, as well as penetrative customers of passive male prostitutes. *Glabri,* which is the Latin for "without hair" and was used to refer to young pages and depilated, that is, effeminate, men, was a term for prostitutes playing the passive role. Male prostitutes who played the passive role were also called *pathicus*, again a term defining the sexual role played, and also *cinaedus*, the Greek word for passive, effeminate males. A youthful, boyish male who served as a passive lover for his customer was called *catamitus*—from which was derived the English word *catamite*. The latter term originated in the Latin name for Ganymede, the Trojan youth loved by Zeus.[89]

Regarding the decline in morals of the upper class as a threat to the strength of Roman society, Livy, a historian who wrote during the rule of Augustus, extolled the great Roman achievements of the past with the hope that future generations might learn from the example set by their noble and virtuous forebears. Livy fervently believed that "if any nation can have the right to hallow its own origin and to attribute its foundation to gods," it was the Romans,[90] but he was worried that the Romans of his own time were squandering their noble heritage: "I hope everyone will pay keen attention to the moral life of earlier times, to the personalities and principles of the men responsible at home and in the field for the foundation and growth of the empire, and will appreciate the subsequent decline in discipline and in moral standards ... down to the present day. For we have now reached a point where our degeneracy is intolerable."[91]

The emphasis placed by Livy and other writers on the supposedly virtuous past of the Romans was in part a defensive reaction to a profound sense of cultural inferiority they felt in the face of the sophistication and elegance of Greek art and culture that had inundated Rome in the late Republic and early Empire.[92] Some Romans responded to this cultural inferiority complex with an anti-intellectualism that boasted of Roman skill in military and government affairs, leaving achievements in art and literature to the Greeks. This attitude is expressed by Virgil, in Book VI of the *Aeneid*, when he has Anchises, the father of Aeneas, commend the Romans to specialize in governing, acknowledging that the Greeks, with their far older civilization, will always be superior to their own in the arts and sciences.[93]

Another response to the perceived inferiority of Roman culture was to assert moral superiority to the Greeks by claiming a primordial simplicity and purity of Roman society before it became corrupted by alien luxury. Accordingly, in his patriotic fables, Livy stressed the guileless virtue of early Romans, toiling in their fields and devoted to their wives and families. In a similar vein, Cornelius Tacitus, born a hundred years after Livy, in the mid-first century A.D., extolled in his writing the image of the noble farmer of early Rome, close to the soil and the family hearth, and criticized Romans of his day for slipping away from their virtuous past.[94] By contrasting the hedonism, rampant materialism and sexual excess of their day with an unspoiled, virginal Roman past, these writers found it convenient to blame decadent homosexual habits on Greek influence, when they more likely derived from the native Roman sexual mentality which took pride in sexual exploitation. Thus, we have in the works of these two writers the defensive portrayal of an idealized vision of early Rome, exemplifying all that Romans believed to be moral and virtuous. Though certainly based more on myth than reality, it was a picture of their past regarded as fact by many Romans, who, like Livy and Tacitus, were uneasy with the hedonistic excess and sexual laxness displayed by many of the rich and powerful of their time.

Love and Devotion in Homosexual Relationships

While it is undoubtedly true that there was more than a little sexual excess displayed during the early Empire, especially among the upper classes, the widespread impression held by many modern readers that Roman society in general was caught up in a loveless sexual degeneracy is incorrect. This false picture is based on extrapolation from some of the popular literature of the period, such as the satires of Martial, that sensationalized aspects of sexual behavior for the entertainment of its audience, just as soap operas and primetime law and order television programs in our day provide a distorted picture of modern life. Much evidence exists that shows that most Romans were as preoccupied with loving relationships, fidelity and family as people today. In fact, the emphasis in most popular Roman literature of the Empire was on love and companionship of the partners, whether it be heterosexual or homosexual, not on aimless sexual gratification.

The *Satyricon* of Petronius Arbiter, a brilliant satire often called the first European novel, portrays precisely the sort of hedonistic and sexually promiscuous culture that many today associate with ancient Rome. Yet the principal sexual preoccupation of Encolpius, the comic anti-hero around whom the work revolves, is his relationship with his young boyfriend, Giton. Attributed to a wealthy Roman nobleman and intimate of the Emperor Nero, who came to rely on him as an arbiter of taste — hence his appellation "Arbiter"— the *Satyricon* is a sophisticated satire that parodies the sort of vulgar ostentation and sexual promiscuity of the wealthy class that was so deplored by Juvenal, Livy and Tacitus. The novel follows Encolpius, a young Roman commoner, through a series of misadventures and disasters which parallel in a satiric way the travails of the Homeric hero Odysseus.[95] Along the way Encolpius finds himself in situations which provide Petronius the opportunity to brilliantly parody various aspects of the life of first-century, A.D. Roman society, from literary genres to the sexual pursuits and pretentious displays of the *nouveau riche*. Though Encolpius is repeatedly thrust into sexual encounters with women or men who lust after him, his primary sexual interest is in his boyfriend Giton, living with him, sharing affection with him, or, after losing him, winning him back.

Indeed, throughout the story the relationship between the two is depicted as tantamount to a common law marriage, and, in fact is referred to by Petronius as a *contubernium*, a form of marriage involving non-citizens that, though it provided the partners with only minimal legal rights under Roman law, was nonetheless legally recognized.[96] Their relationship was not simply a case of an older man keeping a younger male, which was a common pattern throughout the Greco–Roman world, but was more of a relationship of mutual interest between peers. While Giton was 16 years old, Encolpius, though he was a former gladiator, could not have been much older. In the scene where he is seduced by the voluptuous Circe, but is embarrassed to find he is unable to sexually perform, his excuse to her is that he is still *iuvenis*, a youth.[97] When Giton is coerced into participating in a heterosexual marriage ceremony, it is clear that all the parties viewed it as a farce. In contrast, Encolpius regarded his relationship with Giton as "so long established that it had become a bond of blood."[98] When, in a voyage at sea, their ship sinks in a storm, Giton and Encolpius bind themselves together with a belt to insure they will be buried together. The touching devotion of the two partners to each other acts as a foil against which the sexual promiscuity of the other characters plays out in stark relief.

Devoted love between sexual partners, whether heterosexual or homosexual, is a theme found in much of the literature of the period. In the romance novel *The Ephesiaca* by Xenophon of Ephesus, the principal characters are Habrocomes and Anthia, a heterosexual couple who are brought together through an arranged marriage. The development of a loving relationship between them, and their subsequent misadventures, in which they each are tempted but nonetheless resist sexual involvement with other partners, is the principal plot of the novel. But running as a counterpoint to the relationship of the main characters are the homosexual romances of Hippothoos, an ex-pirate and devoted friend of the hero. The great love of his life was Hyperanthes, a young man of the same age as himself. After Hyperanthes' parents arrange, for economic reasons, a sexual relationship for him with an older man, Hippothoos undertakes an adventure to take back his lover. Selling all his possessions, he sails to the older man's home, and rescues his partner from the clutches of the older man by abducting him at sword point from the latter's house. Later in the story, after Hyperanthes is tragically killed, Hippothoos settles down with another young man, Cleisthenes, who is both beautiful and of a good family. Hippothoos and Cleisthenes then live as a permanent couple on terms of equality and friendship with their friends, the heterosexual couple of Habrocomes and Anthia.[99]

In *Clitophon and Leucippe*, a novel of Achilles Tatius, a Greek writer of the eastern Empire, the stories of homosexual and heterosexual romance are nearly indistinguishable, except for the gender of the partners. In one scene, a heterosexual male turns to his older homosexual cousin for advice on love; the cousin then assists him in escaping with the woman he loves. Three men who meet on a ship are all lovers who have tragically lost their partners; two have lost male lovers, one a female. In another story, a young man named Charicles is killed in an accident while riding a horse given to him by his lover, Clinias. A servant of Charicles' family rushes to tell Clinias of his lover's death, after which Clinias and the father of Charicles weep together over his funeral bier. In the *Amatorius* of Plutarch, the mother of a handsome youth who is being courted by both males and females leaves the decision of whether he should marry to his older cousin, "the most responsible of his lovers." It's important to note that the homosexual loves portrayed in these romances are not just affectations of the upper classes, but are experienced equally by members of all classes.[100]

Sexual relationships between women, while not as common, also appear in literature of the period. The relative rarity of references to lesbian love in Roman society should not be taken as an indication of the infrequency of homosexual love among Roman women. As in the case with classical Greece, most writers were men, and so depictions of sexual love are almost always seen from the male standpoint, whether it is the pursuit of young men or women. Though sparse, there are enough references to female homosexuality in the literature produced in the first several centuries of the Empire to suggest that, like male homosexuality, it was a common occurrence, and not an exceptional situation. In Petronius' *Satyricon*, the banquet scene in the house of Trimalchio includes a description of two of the wives, Fortunata and Scintilla, "giggling, slightly tipsy, and smooching together while talking about their domestic business, or about their husbands who amused themselves outside the house and neglected them."[101] There are also references to homosexual love among women in the works of Martial and Juvenal, though those two writers, reflecting typical Roman male chauvinism, regarded female homosexuality as an affront to male sexual privilege. *"Hic ubi vir non est, ut sit adulterium,"* writes Martial in his first satire: "Where no man is, there is adultery."[102] Ovid takes a similarly negative attitude, when in his *Metamorphoses* he has a woman who has fallen in love with another women lament the unnatural quality of her love.[103]

Writers in the Greek-speaking eastern Empire seemed less judgmental. In the *Dialogues of the Courtesans,* by the second-century A.D. writer, Lucian of Samosata, the reader follows a conversation between two women, Leaena and Clonarium, about a sexual affair Leaena was having with a woman named Megilla, who had apparently fallen in love with and seduced Leaena. Leaena seems somewhat embarrassed about it, though she was at the time still living with Megilla, who was also married to another woman from Corinth. Clonarium seems fascinated, and tries to pry as many details as she can about these affairs from her friend.[104] In another work of the period, the *Babyloniaca* of Iamblichus, love between two women is depicted in purely romantic terms. Contained within the longer action of the novel is a subplot about the passionate love of Berenice, queen of Egypt for "the beautiful Mesopotamia." In the story, Mesopotamia is kidnapped from Berenice by the villain Garmos, who wants to kill her. But one of Berenice's female servants, Zobaras, "having drunk from the spring of love, and seized with a passion for Mesopotamia," rescued her and returned her to Berenice, who married Mesopotamia, and then went to war against Garmos "on her account."[105]

As the references to the marriages between women mentioned in these stories suggest, formal marriages between same-sex couples were not uncommon among Romans during the empire. Nero's marriage to two of his male lovers has already been described. The Emperor Elagabulus, who ruled in the early third century A.D., married an athlete from Smyrna named Zoticus.[106] But same-sex marriages were not just limited to emperors. Martial and Juvenal both casually refer to ceremonies involving ordinary citizens. In one such ceremony, Martial describes "the bearded Callistratus" marrying "the rugged Afer," complete with dowry and legal arrangements. Juvenal depicted the wedding of two male friends of his as completely commonplace: "I have a ceremony to attend tomorrow morning in the Quirinal valley." "What sort of ceremony?" he is asked. "Oh, nothing special: a friend is marrying another man, and a small group is attending." He goes on to describe the dowry, the legal ceremony, and the banquet.[107] Though Juvenal saw these marriages as symptomatic of what he saw as a decline in Roman morals, his complaints about the casual acceptance such same-sex unions received among his contemporaries is itself testimony to their frequency.[108] According to John Boswell the legal arrangements for same-sex unions included the use of a kind of adoption, collateral adoption, to unite the partners legally. Under such an arrangement a man would adopt another man, making him his legal "brother" which bestowed on him inheritance rights under the law to the man's property.[109]

Rather than the unrestrained sexual promiscuity that many today associate with the Roman Empire, the popular literature of the period reveals the same interest in romantic love and committed relationships among Roman writers and their audiences as among people in our own time. The only difference between the two societies in this regard is that to the Romans such a committed and emotionally fulfilling sexual relationship could be had just as easily with a member of the same sex as the opposite sex. This is not to say that all Romans were completely bisexual, totally indifferent to the gender of their partners, though many apparently were. There is evidence among the Romans of the same variability in sexual preference and orientation that can be seen among other human societies. Nor does it mean that they were indifferent to the importance of marriage. All the evidence seems to show that marriage and the family were as highly valued among Romans of the empire as among modern Western societies. But, unlike the modern West, there was at the same time, running as a counterpoint to the institution of heterosexual marriage, the constant presence of same-sex sexual expression, as a feature of youth, an option for the unmarried, and a means of emotional and sexual gratification for aristocrats in arranged marriages.[110]

9

Ambisexuality in Ancient Rome: The Christianized Empire and the Foundations of Western Homophobia

By the middle of the third century A.D., the Roman Empire, that only a century earlier had seemed in its power and glory destined to last forever, was showing serious signs of deterioration. The disasters and upheavals that occurred in this period set in motion social and political changes that were to have an enormous impact on the character of not only imperial government, but of Roman culture and society, changes that would eventually lead to a profound transformation in, first, moral attitudes to homosexuality, and then, ultimately, its legality under imperial law.

The reign of Antoninus Pius (A.D. 138–161), who succeeded Hadrian, had seen the Roman Empire at the peak of its magnificence and power. It was a time of unprecedented peace and prosperity for its citizens, a period when both the economy and the vast government bureaucracy functioned effectively, when harmony marked the relations between the emperor and the Senate, and only raids and rebellions in far off borderlands marred the otherwise sublime picture of earthly tranquility that prevailed under the *Pax Romana*. But under Antoninus' successor, Marcus Aurelius, threats to the empire's borders, brought by Germanic tribes along the Danube, and from the Parthian Empire in the east, were much more serious and required sustained military campaigns by the emperor to restore the security of the frontiers.

Upon the death of Marcus Aurelius in 180, his 19-year-old son, Commodus, assumed the throne. A conceited, erratic and intemperate young man, Commodus, unlike his father, had little interest in the affairs of state, devoting himself instead to sensual pleasures. Serious matters of governance were turned over by Commodus to his favorites, whose unscrupulous ambitions and consequent intrigues resulted in plots, brutal murders, treason trials and general disarray in the top levels of the government. Commodus was finally assassinated in 192, but his death did not restore the imperial government to harmony. He was succeeded by the prefect of the city of Rome, who himself was assassinated by the Praetorian Guard after only three months on the throne. The Praetorians then installed as emperor a former general, who apparently got the job because of all the candidates he had promised them the largest *donativum*, a bonus given to each soldier upon the accession of a new emperor. This development provoked the anger of the provincial armies, several of whom appointed one of their own generals as emperor, thus leading to four years of civil war between competing claimants to the throne and their armies. Finally, in 197, Septimus Severus, leader of the army of the Danube, prevailed and established himself as emperor.

This convulsive period brought to the surface one of the major flaws in imperial government, the absence of an orderly process of succession, and the increasing influence of the military in politics. The lack of any effective solution to this problem led to nearly a century of political instability and intermittent civil war, with competing factions of the army assassinating emperors in order to install their own claimants to the throne, who were in turn challenged by usurpers supported by their own armies. Indeed, of the 38 emperors who ruled in the century between the death of Marcus Aurelius in 180 and the ascension of Diocletian in 284, only four died of natural causes. The frequency of military rebellion and consequent civil strife had reached such a level by the mid-third century that in the 50 years between 235 and 284 thirty different emperors held the throne, an average of one every 20 months, and of the thirty, all but three were assassinated.

With the frequent military revolts, imperial assassinations and consequent civil warfare severely disrupting imperial governance, the frontiers were left vulnerable and became subject to repeated barbarian invasions, which wreaked havoc throughout the empire for several decades in the mid-third century. The invasions precipitated serious economic decline throughout much of the empire, with many regions ravaged and many important cities sacked or destroyed. Commerce was frequently brought to a halt by incursions of barbarians, who caused many trade routes to be impassable. Plague, brought back by the armies from the East, spread throughout Europe between 250 and 270 with devastating results. The deterioration of social order encouraged gangs of bandits who roamed the countryside, attacking villages and country villas, while pirates disrupted commercial traffic at sea. The disorders and calamities of the period may have resulted in the deaths of as much as one third of the population, and much of the empire was left impoverished.

The economic crisis among the populace was exacerbated by military requisitions and ever increasing taxation required for the support of the army. The collection of the military taxes was overseen by brutal and frequently larcenous noncommissioned officers, just one element of an intrusive military presence that had transformed the late empire into a harsh military dictatorship. By 270, Roman generals, in no small part due to the increasing militarization of imperial government, were finally able to exert the forces necessary to stem the tide against the barbarians. However, this victory was reached at the cost of the transformation of Roman government from a somewhat liberal state, where personal freedoms were only impinged on to the extent that commerce and public order were protected and imperial authority respected, to a totalitarian state which intruded into many areas of the lives of citizens.

Mystic Cults, Christianity and Sexual Asceticism

In response to the uncertainty and bleakness of life in these tumultuous times, many Romans sought escape in mysticism and inward-turning religious cults, many of them imported from the East. It was in this period, too, that Christianity, which had spread relatively slowly in the first two centuries of the empire, and mostly in the East, began to make significant inroads in the West. It is easy to see that the apocalyptic brand of Christianity being promoted by Christian preachers of the period, which predicted the imminent destruction of the world, would have had great appeal to third century Romans. The apocalyptic Christian vision provided a ready explanation for the disorders and calamities they saw around them, while the promise of everlasting salvation would have given comfort to ordinary Romans, who felt abandoned by traditional Roman deities.

Concurrent with the growing popularity of religions and mystic cults was the increasing influence of ascetic philosophies, which emphasized withdrawal from the world, and looked askance at sensual pleasures. The most widely influential philosophical school of Greco-Roman times was Stoicism, which developed in Athens in the third century B.C., a similar period of political upheaval and social instability. Stoicism held that a sublime order underlay all of nature, and that, despite the appearance of disorder and chaos in the world, the ultimate character of the universe was rational. In the decades after Athens had lost its independence to Philip of Macedon and his successors, its people found themselves no longer free citizens, but subjects of foreign occupiers. In this period of great social and political disorder, when the traditional Greek view of an orderly world presided over by Olympian gods no longer seemed meaningful, Stoicism provided a way of thinking which allowed a peaceful accommodation with a seemingly chaotic and uncertain world by orienting oneself to the rational and ordered reality underlying the universe. Therefore, in the conduct of his life, a man could emulate the calm and rationality of the universe through acceptance of the events of life with a detached and tranquil mind. In order to achieve this detachment, Stoics believed a man should not be controlled by his passions, but by his reason, and thus many Stoics were wary of sexual pleasure, some even preaching that sex for reasons other than to have children should be avoided.

Stoicism first gained popularity among the Romans during the first century B.C., another period of political instability. Among Stoicism's most prominent Roman exponents were the jurist and statesman Cicero, the philosopher Seneca, who served as Nero's tutor; as well as the philosophers Epicetus, a freed slave, and Musonius Rufus, who had many followers among the Roman upper class. By the end of the second century, basic Stoic concepts were familiar to most educated Romans, among them the emperor Marcus Aurelius, whose *Meditations*, a series of reflections on duty and courage in the face of the vicissitudes and challenges of life, is regarded as a classic, and is still read today.

In their effort to discern a natural order in the universe that could provide a basis for the governance of human lives, Stoics often looked to the patterns they saw in nature for guidance. Since the role of sex among animals in nature appeared to them to be the perpetuation of the species, it seemed to follow that procreation must be the purpose of human sexuality. Hence, Stoics defined any sexual activity other than that specifically directed toward the production of children to be not in accordance with "nature." Musonius Rufus held that sex with one's wife simply for the purpose of affection or pleasure was unnatural, as was heterosexual intercourse using contraception, as well as homosexual behavior.[1] It should be emphasized, though, that the distinction that the Stoics drew between natural and unnatural behavior was a theoretical ideal, not a moral absolute. Moreover, when the Stoics described behavior as unnatural, they were not labeling it as a corruption or aberration of nature, but as something that is man-made or artificial. Seneca categorized as "unnatural" a whole host of activities that few today would regard as immoral, including swimming in heated pools, keeping plants indoors in pots, trying to maintain a youthful appearance, and drinking wine on an empty stomach.[2]

In regard to sexuality, most Stoics were more concerned with detachment and self-control, that is, not allowing one's passion to control behavior, and were not specifically hostile to sexual relations. Many prominent Stoics were known for homosexual relationships, including Zeno, the founder of Stoicism, the statesman Cicero, who kept a male concubine, and the philosopher Seneca, whom Dio Cassius claimed introduced Nero to homosexuality.[3] Indeed, Zeno said that one's sexual partner should be chosen without regard to gender: "Do not make invidious comparisons between loving youths and loving women"; "You make distinctions about love objects? I do not." Despite this admonition, Zeno himself was said to have had sexual relationships only with males.[4] The Roman Stoic Epicetus looked upon homosexual and heterosexual desire as equivalents, and encouraged his students to avoid judging people on their sexual tastes.[5]

The Stoic concept of the natural purpose of sexuality was shared by other philosophies of the period, and was an outgrowth of the same Greek quest to understand the nature of the universe that propelled their advances in astronomy, mathematics and the natural sciences. But the belief that non-procreative sex is unnatural, which was derived from an assessment of animal sexuality in apparent ignorance of the widespread homosexual behavior among many species, is no more accurate an understanding of nature than the assertion of the Greek astronomer Ptolemy, that the earth was the center of the universe, and that the sun, planet and stars revolved around the earth in crystal spheres. Like Ptolemy's concept of an earth-centered universe, the Stoic belief in the unnaturalness of non-procreative sex was based on a limited knowledge of nature. And like Ptolemaic astronomy, which was not challenged until the observations of Galileo in the Renaissance, the concept of the reproductive purpose of sex dominated thinking in the area of sexual morality well into the modern era.

Nonetheless, the concept of the naturalness of procreative heterosexual activity, in contrast to the supposed unnaturalness of homosexual behavior, nicely complemented traditional Roman thinking about marriage and the family, which had undergone a resurgence under Augustus. In order to restore the strength of Roman society and recover from population losses after decades of civil war, Augustus had launched a campaign promoting family life and traditional Roman values. Attitudes toward marriage and family life were also influenced by the growing popularity of Stoic concepts in the early Empire. As a result, moralists of the period were preaching that one must marry not only to provide new citizens for the Empire, the traditional Roman view, and the thrust of the Augustan campaign, but now because the divine order of the universe required propagation of the human race.[6] During the first several centuries of the empire, many members of the middle class, disdainful of the excesses of the wealthy, comforted themselves with the moral superiority they felt from their devotion to traditional Roman family values, which contrasted so sharply in their minds with the debauchery of their social superiors.

The increasing skepticism toward sexual pleasure and homosexual practices in the second century was reinforced by medical theorists, who maintained that sexual activity was a danger to health. Soranus, a prominent physician of the period, wrote that sexual intercourse is damaging, that a man's body was weakened by every emission of semen. According to Soranus, men who controlled their impulses were bigger and stronger than their promiscuous compatriots, and the way to regain one's vigor and strength was through sexual abstinence.[7] Thus, by the end of the second century, a more restrictive view of sexuality was gaining influence in the Roman world, an attitude shaped by philosophical concepts, proponents of traditional values, and the beliefs of medical theorists about the debilitating effects of sex.

Negativity toward sexuality reached a new and unprecedented level in the third century with the emergence of Neo-Platonism, an anti-material and anti-sexual school of philosophy that reflected the profound pessimism toward the physical world that was felt by many educated Romans in the bleak third century. Not to be confused with the philosophy of Plato, Neo-Platonism was similar to Manichaeism, Gnosticism and other dualistic religious cults of the day which viewed the universe as divided between good and evil, spirit and material. Neo-Platonists held that the soul is a spiritual being trapped in the physical body at the lowest plane of material being, and viewed the body and sensual pleasure as impediments to the evolution of the soul. The purity of the soul, they believed, was polluted by the evil of sexual desire. According to Plotinus, the school's most prominent proponent, "the purifying virtues which turn a man from sensuality were higher than social virtues which only restrained lust to meet social needs." Hence, he urged abstinence from all sensual pleasures, including sexual intercourse.[8] Plotinus, accordingly, disapproved of homosexuality as a "straying from perfection," though he at least admitted that it arose from "natural principles."[9] The negative view of sexuality taught by Neo-Platonism echoed the extreme anti-sexual asceticism of Gnosticism, Manichaeism and other dualistic sects, some of whose proponents were so hostile to sex that they condemned marriage and even practiced self-castration.[10]

The Ascetic Influence on Early Christian Doctrine

The theoretical frameworks of sexuality espoused by the ascetic philosophies had a profound influence on the development of the thinking of the early Christian Fathers. The writings of Saint Paul, a Greek-educated Jew, show a strong Stoic influence. His discussion of nature and the concept of natural law in I Corinthians could have been written by one of the Stoic philosophers. Paul's argument in the epistle, in fact, is nearly identical to concepts that appear in the *Manual* of the Roman Stoic, Epicetus.[11] The close similarity between the moral precepts of Seneca and Paul in some areas caused later Christian leaders, including Saint Jerome, to claim that Saint Paul and Seneca conducted a literary correspondence with each other.[12] The thoroughness with which some Christians had absorbed Stoic concepts is illustrated in the writings of the influential third-century Christian leader Saint Clement of Alexandria, who pronounced that "to have sex for any purpose other than to produce children is to violate nature," as if "nature" were a moral code.[13] Indeed, elsewhere Clement copies verbatim the precepts on marriage of the pagan Stoic Musonius Rufus without citing their true author.[14]

The extreme hostility to sex that characterized Neo-Platonism and the dualistic sects was also reflected in the teachings of early Christian leaders. Saint Augustine, the most influential of the early Father, of the Church, was heavily influenced by Neo-Platonism, particularly the writings of Plotnius, whose negative judgment on sex is evident in Augustine's close association of sexual pleasure with sin.[15] Nearly all the early church Fathers, including Jerome, Ambrose and Gregory of Nyssa, praised chastity and regarded sex with barely concealed revulsion. Some Christian leaders, like the theologian Origen, followed the example of the more extreme of the dualist sects and castrated themselves to avoid the contamination of sex. A second-century text, the apocryphal *Acts of the Apostles*, held that even married couples should abstain from sex, while another text, the *Acts of Paul and Thecla,* taught that only virgins could be resurrected. In the early church in Syria, only the unmarried could be baptized, and one theologian, Eustathius of Sebastia, preached that married people could not gain salvation. The second century theologian Tatian taught that marriage was corruption, and that since sexual intercourse had been invented by the Devil, anyone who attempted to be married and remain Christian was attempting to serve two masters. Another second century writer, Julius Cassianus, whose works were quoted by Jerome and Clement of Alexandria, taught that the mission of Jesus in coming into the world was to save men from copulating. The degree to which the anti-sexual attitudes of pagan and dualistic philosophies had become assimilated into the thinking of early Christian leaders is seen in the teachings of Athanasius, the fourth-century patriarch of Alexandria, and a Doctor of the Church, who stated that "the appreciation of virginity and chastity was the supreme revelation and blessing brought into the world by Jesus," an attitude toward sex that is found nowhere in the Gospels.[16] In fact, in their zeal to promote their anti-sexual morality within the church, early Christian leaders were not above distorting the teachings of Scripture to meet their ends. As the 19th-century moral historian W.E.H. Lecky remarked, "The Fathers laid down a distinct proposition that pious frauds were justifiable, and even laudable; and if they had not laid this down, they would nevertheless have practiced them as a necessary consequence of their doctrine of exclusive salvation. Immediately all ecclesiastical literature became tainted with a spirit of the most unblushing mendacity."[17]*

Third- and fourth-century Christian leaders were particularly influenced by the treatment of Stoic and Platonic concepts in the writings of the Hellenistic Jewish philosopher Philo Judaeus, also known as Philo of Alexandria, who melded the Stoic concept of a natural order with the moral absolutism of Mosaic Law. Philo was one of a number of Jewish writers who reacted to the dominance of the Greco-Roman culture of their times by asserting their native Hebrew world view within the framework of Greek philosophy. The saturation of the lands around the Eastern Mediterranean with Greek culture and customs that came with Alexander's conquests was met with great resistance by many Jews, who clung tenaciously to their ancestral traditions. The attempt of Greek rulers to impose Greek religious traditions on the Jews in Palestine in the second century B.C. stirred up an intense hatred for Greek culture among many devout Jews. Though a number of educated Jews in the years to follow became thoroughly Hellenized and had great admiration for the work of the Greek philosophers, many continued to resent the inundation of their land with Greek moral and cultural values that conflicted with their own religious beliefs. As we saw in Chapter 4, devout Jews particularly detested the Greeks' homosexual customs, which they regarded as indisputable proof of the idolatry of the Greeks.[18]

Philo Judaeus, the most prominent of the Hellenistic Jewish writers, revered the philosophy of Plato and in his writings applied Greek philosophical methods to an explanation of Hebrew tradition. While the Stoics and other Greeks postulated conceptions of a cosmic order, deviations from which would be "not of nature," that is, man-made or artificial, Philo and other Hellenistic Jews translated the Stoic concept of "natural order" as "God's order" as interpreted through Jewish Law, deviations from which were both unnatural and sinful. Therefore, idolatry and sexual impurity were evidence of the same condition, deviation from God's natural order. In the view of the Hellenistic Jewish writers, then, if it is not in the Law, it is unnatural; if it is unnatural, it is evil.[19]

Hebrew tradition had long regarded the sin of Sodom not as homosexuality, but as an amalgam of every evil objectionable to the beliefs of devout Jews, be it pride, cruelty, inhospitality, adultery or idolatry. As the Jews became more exposed to Hellenistic society, which surrounded and dominated them, their association of the wickedness of Sodom was transferred to what was, in their eyes, the distinguishing characteristic of Hellenistic Greek tradition — homosexuality. In his writings, Philo expanded the application of the Stoic concept of nature and natural law onto sexual morality as defined in Hebrew tradition, linking the "unnatural" homosexual acts that the Jews associated with the hated Greek traditions with the destruction of Sodom.[20] Philo wrote that the men of Sodom engaged in a debauchery that defied

---

*In a footnote in his book, Lecky relates a response to this provocative statement by Cardinal Newman: "The Greek Fathers thought that, when there was a justa causa, an untruth need not be a lie. St. Augustine took another view, though with great misgiving, and, whether he is rightly interpreted or not, is the doctor of the great and common view that all untruths are lies, and that there can be no just cause of untruth.... Now, as to the just cause, the Greek Fathers make them such as these—self-defense, charity, zeal for God's honor, and the like." Lecky counters that "It is plain enough that this last would include all of what are commonly termed pious frauds."

"the law of nature.... Not only in their mad lust for women did they violate the marriage of their neighbors, but also men mounted males without respect for nature.... For not only did they emasculate their bodies by luxury and voluptuousness, but they worked a further degeneration in their souls and ... were corrupting the whole of mankind."[21] Philo's condemnation of homosexual behavior went well beyond the enforcement of Hebrew sexual and ritual norms that was the basis of the disapproval of male homosexuality in Leviticus. By labeling the sin of the Sodomites a violation of nature which provoked the horrific wrath of God, Philo established the precedent for viewing men who commit homosexual acts as a threat to society itself.

Because rabbinical tradition had no interest in the kind of logical discourse practiced by the Greek philosophers, Philo's work, ironically, was never widely accepted in Judaic thought. Philo's writings, with their Stoic formulations on sexuality and their linkage of homosexuality with the sin of Sodom, were, however, embraced with enthusiasm by Christian leaders in the third and fourth centuries, who welcomed the intellectual respectability Philo brought to Old Testament moral absolutes by expressing them within the rational framework of Greek philosophy. Saint Jerome even listed the Jewish thinker Philo Judaeus among the Fathers of the Church.

The emergence of anti-sexual asceticism as a prominent feature of Christian teaching in the third and fourth centuries had the effect of solidifying a negative view of homosexual practices in the thinking of Christian moralists. But it was a judgment on homosexuality that, contrary to popular belief, was far from universal among Christians up to that point. Some of the Christian dualist sects, for example, accepted homosexual relationships while discouraging heterosexual marriage. The sects believed the Apocalypse was imminent and so denounced heterosexual relations because they thought it immoral to bring another soul into the material world, but accepted homosexual behavior because same-sex relations could produce no offspring. Roman sources also depict Christians of the early Empire as "given to every form of sexual indulgence — including homosexual acts."[22] In fact, the widespread belief among Christians today that there has been monolithic opposition to homosexuality among Christians since its earliest beginnings is a myth. Moreover, a close reading of the Gospels suggests that, if anything, Christ showed a positive attitude toward homosexual love.

Jesus and Homosexuality

Given the vehemence with which later Christian authorities condemned homosexual acts, the absence of any disapproval of homosexuality in the Gospels is, indeed, curious. Christ was not reticent about other moral issues that stirred him, and he would certainly have been aware of the homosexual practices of the Hellenistic Greeks and Romans living around and among the Jews in Palestine. There are, in fact, several passages in the Gospels in which Jesus appeared to have an opportunity to speak out against homosexual practices if he was so inclined, but did not.

Chapter 5, verses 5 to 13, of the Gospel of Matthew relates the story of Jesus and the Roman centurion who came to him, "beseeching him, saying, 'Lord, my servant lies at home sick of the palsy, grievously tormented.'" Jesus replied that he would go to the servant and heal him. But the centurion responded in his famous declaration of faith, "Lord, I am not worthy that thou should come under my roof: but speak the word only, and my servant shall be healed." When Jesus heard this he exclaimed, "Verily I say unto you, I have not found so great faith, no, not in Israel." He turned to the centurion and said, "Go thy way; and as thou hast believed, so be it done unto thee," and, according to the text, the servant was cured the same day.

Some scholars have remarked that it would have been unusual for a battle-hardened Roman officer to have been so disturbed by the illness of an ordinary servant that he would seek help from a figure who was, from his perspective, a foreign cult leader, normally looked down upon by the Romans. They have argued that the centurion's apparent deep concern arose because that servant was his male lover. Homosexual relationships, after all, were commonplace in the Greco-Roman world of the time of Christ, and such a relationship is the kind that would be expected of a Roman soldier posted in a region far from his home. The Greek word translated as "servant" in the passage is *pais*, which could mean "servant." However, its far more common usage was as the term used universally in the Greek world for the younger male lover of an adult male. In fact, *pais* is the root of *pederasty—pais, paid*, "boy," and *erasthai*, "to love." A similar usage occurs in French, where *garçon*, can mean "waiter" or "busboy," but most commonly means "boy." The argument that the writer of the Gospel meant to indicate the beloved of the centurion with the use of *pais* is strengthened by the evidence of the centurion's emotional attachment to the youth, made apparent by his going to the extent of "beseeching" help from a man he would regard as a foreign cultist.

The emotional attachment of the centurion to the *pais* is underscored in a recounting of the same episode in Luke, Chapter 7:1–10, where the centurion's servant is described as "dear to him" in the King James Version and his "favorite" in the Jerusalem Bible translation. Instead of *pais* to denote the servant, the Greek manuscript of the passage in Luke uses *doulos*, slave, which in the context of a relationship with a Roman would also have a strong sexual connotation. Given that the custom of Roman men having sexual relationships with slave-concubines was, by that time, a centuries-old tradition, it would have been quite normal, and even inevitable, for a Roman centurion in a foreign post to have a male slave-concubine for sexual companionship. The Roman historian Procopius used the very same term, *douloi*, "slaves," to describe the young male lovers of Germanic warriors he encountered.[23]

There can be little doubt, then, that these two passages depict Jesus as having a direct encounter with a man in a homosexual relationship. If Jesus shared the contempt for homosexuality found among contemporary Hellenistic Jews like Philo or that would have been expected from the Pharisees, it would have been inconceivable that his encounter with the centurion would have occurred without at least an admonition to the centurion about his relationship with his pais, just as Jesus had done in the episode with the prostitute Mary Magdalene. That Jesus reacted with compassion rather than judgmental scorn is strong evidence that Jesus did not share the concern of his fellow Jews with homosexual practices.

It is also of interest at this point to note that some historians, as well as several historic figures, including King James I of England and Christopher Marlowe, have claimed that Jesus himself had a homosexual relationship with his disciple John. King James, in defending his decision to bestow on his male lover, George Villiers, the title of Earl of Buckingham, told parliamentarians, "Christ had his John, and I have my George."* The king was referring to the description of the relationship between Jesus and John in the Gospel of John, in which the youthful John is described four times in the Gospel as the disciple "whom Jesus loved."[24]

The king's complete statement to the parliamentarians is

   I, James, am neither a god nor an angel, but a man like any other. Therefore I act like a man and confess to loving those dear to me more than other men. You may be sure that I love the Earl of Buckingham more than anyone else, and more than you who are here assembled. I wish to speak in my own behalf and not to have it thought to be a defect, for Jesus Christ did the same, and therefore I cannot be blamed. Christ had his John, and I have my George. [Rictor Norton, "Queen James and His Courtiers," in Gay History and Literature, *Essays by Rictor Norton, http://www.infopt.demon.co.uk/jamesi.htm].*

It was John who laid his head on Jesus' breast at the Last Supper, and it was John about whom Jesus said to his mother from the Cross, "Woman, behold thy son." The inference in these passages of a close, passionate bond between them is undeniable.

Saint Jerome, evidently recognizing the sexual implication of the Gospel's description of the relationship between Jesus and John, argued that "Jesus loved John the most because he was youthful and virginal," by which he apparently intended to dispel any suggestions of a sexual element in the relationship. However, as John Boswell has observed, given the universal assumption in the ancient Mediterranean world that older men would regard "youthful, virginal" males as attractive sex objects, Jerome's argument is hardly persuasive, and, in fact, could have been taken by some of his contemporaries as arguing the opposite.[25] Saint Aelred of Rievaulx, a 12th-century Cistercian abbot and adviser to Henry II of England, also took note of the special intimacy between Jesus and John, which he called a "heavenly marriage." Saint Aelred, who in a letter acknowledged his own homosexual loves in his youth, expressed in his treatise *De Spirituali Amitia* an idealized vision of passionate love, invoking the relationship between Jesus and John as an example. Reminiscent of Plato's description of love in his *Symposium*, Saint Aelred described carnal love as a pathway to a higher, spiritual relationship in which the lovers would find union with themselves and with God.[26] "And lest this sort of sacred love should seem improper to anyone, Jesus himself, in everything like us, patient and compassionate with us in every matter, transfigured it through the expression of his own love: for he allowed one, not all, to recline on his breast as a sign of his special love... a more intimate love, that he should be called the 'disciple whom Jesus loved.'"[27]

A passage in the Gospel of John relating the story of Jesus raising Lazarus from the dead has also been cited as possibly indicating a sexual relationship between Jesus and Lazarus. In John 11:1–4 the sisters of Lazarus, Mary and Martha, send word to Jesus of their brother's illness: "Lord, the man you love is ill." But Jesus delayed his departure for two days before going to Judea, and when he finally arrived in Bethany to see Lazarus he was told by Mary that Lazarus had been in the tomb for four days. Seeing Mary's tears, "Jesus said in great pain, with a sigh that came straight from the heart, 'Where have you put him?' They said, 'Lord, come and see.' Jesus wept, and the Jews said, 'See how much he loved him'" (John 11:35–37). The characterization of Lazarus by the sisters as "The man you love" and the deep sorrow Jesus displays when hearing of Lazarus' death would be consistent with the existence of a sexual relationship between the two.

In an early Christian text, the Secret Gospel of Mark, there is another version of the story in which a sexual relationship between Jesus and the youth he raised from the dead is more strongly implied. The existence of the Secret Gospel of Mark is known only through a reference to it and excerpts from it included in a letter of Saint Clement of Alexandria in which he criticized the interpretation of the text by the Carpocratians, a prominent second century Christian sect. Scriptural scholars have concluded from the information in Clement's letter that the Secret Gospel of Mark is an earlier version of the Gospel of Mark as it now appears in the New Testament, the present version being an abridged version of the lengthier earlier work. The excerpts of the lost gospel quoted by Clement in his letter are, in fact, the only portions of the text that are known to survive. In his letter Clement specifically stated that the passages he quoted were authentic excerpts from an earlier, authentic version of the Gospel of Mark. He even indicates where in the final version of Mark the passages he quotes should be placed. Clement then goes on in his letter to state that certain other passages quoted by the Carpocratians are falsifications.[28]

One of the excerpts, which Clement says is authentic and which would appear immediately after Mark 10:34, relates an earlier version of the story of Jesus raising from death a unnamed youth, whom the later Gospel of John names as Lazarus. In the excerpt, Jesus had just arrived in Bethany when a woman approached Jesus and prostrated herself before him saying, "Son of David, have mercy on me." The disciples of Jesus at that point rebuked her, which angered Jesus. He then went with her to the garden where the tomb was, "and straight away, a great cry was heard from the tomb." Going to the tomb, Jesus rolled the stone from the door away and went into the tomb where he came to where the youth lay.

> He stretched forth his hand and raised him, seizing his hand. But the youth, looking upon him, loved him and began to beseech him that he might be with him. And going out of the tomb they came into the house of the youth, for he was rich. And after six days Jesus told him what to do and in the evening the youth comes to him, wearing a linen cloth over his naked body. And he remained with him that night.

The passage goes on to state that Jesus introduced him to the mysteries of the Kingdom of God.[29]

Conventional interpretation of the excerpt would no doubt explain the passage where the youth "looking upon him, loved him and began to beseech him that he might be with him," as expressing the desire to become a disciple of Jesus. But the passage two sentences later, where the youth came to Jesus almost completely naked, save for a single piece of linen covering him — the equivalent of wrapping a towel around the waist after a shower — and then spending the night with him, strongly suggests that the youth's love for Jesus was not merely spiritual: "and in the evening the youth comes to him, wearing a linen cloth over his naked body. And he remained with him that night." Later in his letter Clement quotes another excerpt from the Secret Gospel which refers to the same young man as "the youth whom Jesus loved" which underscores the presence of a singular bond between Jesus and the youth.

While the suggestion that Jesus had a homosexual relationship with John, Lazarus or the unnamed youth raised from the dead would be regarded as blasphemous by most devout Christians, there are other factors besides the references in the Gospel which support the plausibility of such a relationship. To begin with, relationships between adult men and younger males were as common as heterosexual marriage in the Greco-Roman world in which Christ lived. Jesus would have been exposed to them many times in his life, as he most likely was in his encounter with the Roman centurion. We know, further, that after the conquest of Palestine by the Greeks under Alexander, a large number of Jews, according to the Book of Maccabees, abandoned the sexual proscriptions of Mosaic Law and engaged in the "sexual impurities" of the Gentile conquerors.[30] The assumption that there was universal observance of the prohibition in Leviticus against homosexual behavior among Jews in the time of Christ is unfounded.

To seek intimate companionship with another is one of the most basic of instincts, yet Jesus never married, which was unusual for a Jew at that time. A normal option for unmarried men in the period when Jesus lived was a homosexual relationship, unless, of course, engaging in one was prohibited by one's religion. However, the episode with the Roman centurion and his *pais*, and the total absence of any hint of disapproval of homosexuality in the Gospels shows that Jesus seemed unconcerned about the prohibition against homosexual acts in Jewish Law. This would not have been unusual for a Nazarene, as Jesus was, since the people of Nazareth had a reputation for not following the Law (John 1:46).

There would have been nothing unusual, then, in a charismatic, unmarried man like Jesus, in the prime of his life, and in that time and place, having a sexual relationship with a younger male like John, who according to Christian tradition was exceptionally good looking. The implausibility of such a relationship to Christians stems solely from the incongruity to them of associating Jesus with a practice they believe to be one of the most heinous of sins.

However, if one removes the assumption that homosexual practices are sinful, it would be hard to argue that a sexual relationship between Jesus and John was not plausible, given the description of their relationship in the Gospel of John and the longstanding homosexual traditions of the Greco-Roman culture that had inundated Palestine in the time of Christ.

The Origins of Christian Condemnation of Same-Sex Love

With no obvious indication of disapproval of homosexuality in the Gospels, many assume that Christian condemnation of homosexuality had its origins in the disapproval of homosexual behavior in Jewish law, a disapproval that was supposedly exemplified in the destruction of Sodom and Gomorrah by God. However, as we saw in Chapter 4, the popular understanding that homosexuality was the sin for which God punished Sodom and Gomorrah is incorrect. As to the assumption that Christian disapproval of homosexual acts derived from Hebrew scripture, one of the principal elements of the teachings of Saint Paul was that the New Covenant that Christ brought to the world replaced the Covenant of the Israelites with God, which encompassed Mosaic Law.* The Gospels according to Paul therefore represent a liberation from Mosaic Law. Accordingly, Gentile converts in the early church were excused from obeying the myriad proscriptions of Jewish Law, which include among the provisions on circumcision, dress and diet the prohibition against male homosexual behavior in Leviticus. As we saw in Chapter 4, a man taking the passive role in sex with another man ("lying the lyings of a woman") was condemned as idolatrous (*to-ebah*) as part of a campaign to rid Hebrew worship and cultural practices of goddess worship and other foreign elements. Jewish converts to Christianity who still regarded themselves as Jewish — many of them viewing the teachings of Christ as being a new development in Judaism — often continued to observe Jewish Law. However, it would have been nonsensical for newly baptized Greek and Roman converts to be freed from the requirements of Mosaic Law with the exception of one narrow provision on homosexual behavior that rejected centuries of their own sexual traditions.

If Christians, according to Saint Paul, are freed from the obligations of Jewish Law and by implication its injunction against homosexual behavior, and since a disapproval of homosexuality is absent from the Gospels, the question remains as to the source of the emphatic condemnation of homosexual acts that became woven into Christian tradition. While the sharp hostility to sex that the early Christian thinkers acquired from pagan asceticism in the third and fourth centuries certainly left its impact on Christian doctrine, the concerns of the ascetics were directed at sex in general, and not specifically to homosexuality. So we cannot look solely to the influence of pagan philosophies on Christian thinking for an explanation of the strident disapproval of homosexual behavior in Christian sexual morality.

Though Saint Paul is the apostle whose arguments and efforts persuaded the early church to excuse Gentile converts from the obligations of Jewish Law, it is, ironically, Paul's own intensely neurotic reaction to sexuality that set the tone for the anti-sexual, anti-homosexual developments in Christian doctrine that came to the fore in the third and fourth centuries.

---

*The word testament *derives from the Greek word for covenant; hence, New Testament = New Covenant.*

Saint Paul, Sex and Neurosis

Saint Paul was born with the name Saul into a prosperous Jewish family not in Palestine, but in Tarsus, a Greek city in Anatolia, modern Turkey. His father was a Roman citizen, a right that the young Saul inherited, and it is thought that it was for this reason that he took the name Paul — Paulus in Latin. Paul had a traditional Jewish education which would have entailed the study of Mosaic Law and Hebrew tradition. Since an emphasis in education during that time was the work of the Greek philosophers, Paul would have had a general understanding of the main currents of Greek thought, including Stoicism. He very likely would also have been exposed to the works of the Hellenistic Jewish writers, including Philo, who lived in the same period, but was a generation older than Paul and came to prominence during Paul's early years. As mentioned earlier, Paul's writings show a strong Stoic influence, but they also show the same melding of Stoic concepts and Jewish morality found in Philo's treatment of Stoicism. Therefore it seems likely that Paul's moral views were shaped in part by his experience with the works of Philo Judaeus and other Hellenistic Jewish writers.

Saint Paul is universally regarded as the single most influential figure in the development of early Christianity besides Christ himself. He is credited with development of the Christian doctrine of divine grace and salvation, and his letters comprise one of the largest portions of the New Testament — more than a quarter of the entire New Testament, and two thirds of the material outside of the Gospels. While his Epistles contain passages of matchless beauty, a distinctive feature of his writings, absent from that of the other apostles, is a clearly articulated abhorrence of sex.

In a passage that foreshadows the anti-sexual Christian ascetics of the third and fourth centuries, Paul writes, "Do not gratify the desires of the flesh. For the desires of the flesh are against the Spirit, and the desires of the Spirit are against the flesh."[31] For Paul, a principal purpose of sexual relations in marriage was to stave off temptations from Satan because of lack of self-control.[32] He writes, "it is better to marry than be aflame with passion," though earlier in the same letter he seems to preclude even that "it is well for a man not to touch a woman."[33]

In his writings, in fact, Paul displays the self-loathing and torment of a man in conflict with his desires, and seems to regard his sexual urges as a scourge, "a thorn in the flesh," as he says. The Episcopal bishop and theologian John Shelby Spong described Paul's torment as a "war within himself,"[34] made evident in Paul's own words:

> The Law ... is spiritual, but I am unspiritual. I have been sold as a slave to sin. I cannot understand my own behavior.... I do not do what I want, but I do the very thing I hate.... So I find it to be a law that when I want to do right, evil lies close at hand. For I delight in the law of God, in my inmost self, but I see in my *members* another law at war with the law of my mind and making me captive to the law of sin which dwells in my *members*. Wretched man that I am! ... Who will deliver me from this body of death?"[35]

Though until recent decades the topic would have been unthinkable in church circles, a number of theologians have recently put forward the argument that the source of Saint Paul's torment was his efforts to repress strong homosexual desires, that he was a repressed homosexual. The facts of Paul's life would support such a conclusion. If Paul, indeed, harbored strong homosexual desires, his training in Jewish Law would have engendered grave self-doubts and repulsion for his bodily urges. His exposure to Philo and the other Hellenistic Jewish writers, with their linkage of the Law with natural order, and behavior outside the Law with the unnatural and evil, would have reinforced his negative feelings toward his body.

Spending much of his life among Greeks and Romans, Paul would have frequently observed men in homosexual relationships, which in continually reminding him of his own sexual urges would have aggravated his inner conflict. Because the Law was seen as the means of controlling man's sinful nature, Paul would have regarded a strict observance of the Law as the means of controlling unholy passions such as his own. As a young man, Paul became a devotee of the Law as a member of the Pharisee sect, the biblical fundamentalists of the day, which demanded the strictest adherence to the letter of the Law. Because of his psychological dependence on the Law to check his own impure desires, Paul would have felt personally threatened by the subversion of Mosaic authority that he saw in the early followers of Christ, a reaction that would explain the zealousness of his persecution of the early Christians in Palestine before his conversion.

As a Pharisee, Paul would have been expected to get married, but he never married, which, as in the case of Jesus was unusual for a Jew in that period, especially one, like Paul, so devoted to the Law. Bishop Spong observed that throughout his life, Paul "seemed incapable of relating to women in general, except to derogate them."[36] His later life, instead, was marked by a series of close friendships with younger men, especially Timothy. After a consideration of these circumstances of Paul's life, Bishop Spong concludes, "the war that went on between what he desired with his mind and what he desired with his body, his drivenness to a legalistic religion of control, his fear when that system was threatened, his attitude toward women, his refusal to seek marriage as an outlet for his passion — nothing else accounts for this data as well as the possibility that Paul was a gay male."[37]

As we saw in the Introductory Chapter, empirical research has demonstrated that the level of homophobic dread or hatred in males correlates closely with the level of homosexual responsiveness in the individuals. The deep seated hostility to homosexuality found in the research subjects is a product of psychological defense mechanisms arising from the conflict between strict anti-homosexual moral conditioning and homosexual responsiveness within the individuals. Such a conflict breeds loathing for one's self, which the mind's defense system redirects to others exhibiting the same trait. In Saint Paul we see the classic archetype of the neurotic, self-hating homophobe, obsessed with his own wicked nature and with repugnance for other people exhibiting that same sexual nature.

With this in mind it is easy to see that the negativity that Paul brought to sex in general and homosexuality in particular was driven by loathing for his own sexual nature, brought on by indoctrination in early life into a very strict heterosexually oriented morality. Because of his conflicted sexual nature, Paul could never be comfortable with any sexual activity in himself or others. He could approve of sex only in the confines of heterosexual marriage, and then apparently chiefly for the purpose of avoiding "the temptation of Satan."

Because Paul believed that the Gospels of Christ brought liberation from the obligations of Mosaic Law, which by implication would excuse converts from the prohibition against male homosexuality in Leviticus, it would seem that the disapproval of homosexuality that Paul expressed in his Epistle to the Romans could not be based on Jewish Law or the Hebrew tradition. And since as earlier noted there is no disapproval of homosexuality in the Gospels, the question remains as to the rational basis for Paul's position. In Romans 1:26–27, Paul writes: "Even their women exchanged natural relations for unnatural ones. In the same way the men also abandoned natural relations with women and were inflamed with lust for one another." In these verses, which are strikingly similar in language and tone to passages of Philo Judeaus condemning homosexuality, Paul describes the homosexual acts not as violations of the Law, but as behavior he views as unnatural.

We can therefore see that Paul's stated disapproval of homosexual acts is based neither on Mosaic Law nor the teachings of Christ. Rather, his negative judgment on homosexuality rests solely on his notion of what was natural, an understanding of nature and "the law of nature" that resulted from the synthesis of the Stoic intellectual concept of a natural order with Hebrew Law that was espoused by Philo Judaeus and the other Hellenistic Jewish thinkers. Even though Paul believed that the New Testament freed Christians from the obligations of Mosaic Law, which would include the condemnation of homosexual acts in Leviticus, he appears to have accepted the negative moral judgment on acts seen as "unnatural" or "against nature" that was advocated by Philo Judaeus.

It has been argued that Paul's negative attitude to sex in general — "the desires of the flesh are against the Spirit" — could have been influenced by experience with the Essenes, a monastic Jewish sect of the period that preached celibacy and asceticism, or the anti-material, dualist leanings in the works of some Greek philosophers. However, the ascetic life led by the Essenes was actually the result of an obsessively rigid devotion to the dietary and purification regulations of Mosaic Law, a devotion that went far beyond the strictness of even the Pharisees, and had little in common with the spiritual concepts taught by Paul. The Essenes' ascetic lifestyle, in fact, was denounced by Paul, who said that one should not delight in false humility and let oneself be governed by human regulations, a reference to the Essenes' devotion to Mosaic Law.[38] And whether or not Paul was influenced by the dualist anti-materialism in the works of some Greek philosophers, purely intellectual beliefs rooted in the assertions of pagan philosophers would not explain the degree of visceral loathing Paul displayed in discussing sex. The special intensity of Paul's negative reaction to sex can best be explained by a deep and painful psychological conflict of the sort that would arise from strong sexual and emotional feelings that are diametrically opposed by one's moral convictions.

Alfred Kinsey remarked, in discussing attempts to deny or repress normal sexual needs because of moral beliefs, "It is difficult to imagine anything better calculated to do permanent damage to the personality of an individual."[39] The self-loathing exhibited by Saint Paul because of his "thorn in the flesh" is a perfect example of this. The recent sexual research that directly correlates the kind of homophobic disturbance displayed by Paul to latent homosexual responsiveness strongly suggests that one of the principal factors underlying the unusual vehemence of the ascetic Christian hostility to homosexual acts that developed in the third and fourth centuries was the psychological conflict within the early Christian moralists between their beliefs and their own innate sexual feelings. Saint Augustine himself provides an example of this in the disgust he expressed in his writings for a homosexual relationship he experienced as a youth. Saint Paul is unfortunately only the earliest prominent example of the sexual neurosis that was to become endemic in European society as Western civilization developed, encumbered by a vision of human sexuality straitjacketed by the confining intellectual concepts of late Hellenistic philosophy and its outmoded understanding of nature.

The Continuity of Homosexuality
Among Christians After Paul

But it is also clear that sexual asceticism and disapproval of homosexuality were by no means widespread among early Christians. To the contrary, according to Roman writers of the early Empire, including Tacitus and Pliny the Younger, the early Christians in general were known for sexual laxness and homosexuality.[40] While some may question the motivation and credibility of these pagan critics of Christianity in their claims about the sexual behavior of early disciples, a surely unimpeachable source of evidence about the sexual practices of early Christians can be found in the writings of the revered church Father, Saint John Chrysostom. In one of his letters, Chrysostom complains bitterly about the widespread homosexuality among both the laity and the leadership of the Christian church in Antioch, and in doing so essentially confirms the testimony of Tacitus and Pliny:

> What then is this evil? ... Not only are the laws established [by man] overthrown but even those of nature herself.... So the extremity of this outrage causes lewdness with women, which had been intolerable, to seem so no longer. Indeed ... there is some danger that womankind will become in the future unnecessary with young men instead fulfilling all the needs women used to. And this is not even the worst, which is that this outrage is perpetrated with the utmost openness, and lawlessness has become law.... But seemingly rational humans, the beneficiaries of godly learning, those who instruct others in what should and should not be done, those who have heard the Scriptures brought down from heaven — these do not consort with prostitutes as fearlessly as they do with young men.[41]

While providing strong testimony on the prevalence of homosexual practices among Christians in Antioch, Chrysostom in this passage illustrates the same visceral disgust for same-sex relations found in Saint Paul's writings. Elsewhere Chrysostom describes male homosexuality as "monstrous," "Satanical," "detestable," and "execrable," and labels those praising Greek-style love as "even worse than murderers."[42] The neurotic abhorrence that Chrysostom displayed to homosexuality was typical of the attitudes of those Christians heavily influenced by the sexual asceticism of the Stoics and Neo-Platonists. Indeed, the very vocal and frequently histrionic opposition to homosexuality displayed by some of the Christian leaders supports the impression that there was uniform opposition to homosexuality in the early church, an impression that is still being promoted by conservative Christian bodies.

However, the reaction displayed by Chrysostom and other ascetic Christian leaders to homosexuality was far from universal among early Christians. For example, a prominent Christian contemporary of Chrysostom, the poet and teacher Ausonius, showed quite a different attitude toward homosexual love. One of the first contributors to Latin Christian literature, Ausonius had in his personal library works of homosexual literature that even contemporary Romans would have found shocking. Fond of witty epigrams, Ausonius delighted himself with his translation from the Greek of a ribald riddle of Strato about four sex acts being performed by three men at the same time.* At the same time, Ausonius was carrying on a passionate relationship with a former pupil, Paulinus, bishop of Nola in Italy. In one letter to Paulinus, he writes, "As long as I am held within this prison body, in whatever world I am found, I shall hold you fast, grafted onto my being, ... Everywhere you shall be with me, I will see with my heart, and embrace you with my loving spirit." Commenting on their relationship, John Boswell has written that "their friendship can scarcely be called anything but passionate.... It was certainly a relationship involving *eros* in the Greek sense. No one seems to have considered the attraction 'unnatural,' nor did Saint Paulinus's ardent love for a man trouble his conscience."[43] Far from it, Paulinus, a man later elevated by the church to sainthood, wrote back: "Wherever in heaven our Father shall direct me, there also shall I bear you in my heart. Nor will that end ... release me from your love."[44]

Despite the ascendancy of advocates of sexual asceticism among the leadership of the church, homosexuality remained a common practice during the Late Empire, even in heavily Christianized areas. In addition to the testimony of Saint John Chrysostom about the

---

John Boswell's translation: "Count as three all those on a bed, of whom two are active. And two are passive ... the one in the middle performs doubly, pleasing in the back and being pleased in the front" (Boswell [1980], page 132, n.38).

widespread homosexuality among Christians in fourth-century Antioch, the Christian historian Salvian reported in the period that homosexuality was rampant among Christians in Carthage, in North Africa, a region which had so many Christians that bishoprics were numbered in the dozens.[45] Among Coptic Christians in Egypt, it was even not uncommon for a man to invoke a spell to get God's assistance in winning the love of another male. In one such spell, the lover prays:

> I adjure you by your powers ... and places where you dwell ... that you must take his heart and his mind; you must dominate his entire body.... He must seek me from town to town, from city to city, from field to field ... until he comes to me and subjects himself under my feet ... until I satisfy with him the desire of my heart and the demand of my soul, with pleasant desire and love unending.[46]

Saint Augustine, a native of North Africa, and the son of a Christian mother, wrote in his *Confessions* of his own homosexual relationship in his youth with a male friend. He wrote that when his friend died he was so devastated that the pain of it drove him to God: "For I felt that my soul and his were one soul in two bodies, and therefore life was a horror to me, since I did not want to live as a half." Augustine then turned to the dualistic Manichaean religion, but disillusioned with that, embraced Neo-Platonism, with its highly negative view of sexual relations, a mentality he later brought to his extremely influential writings on Christian moral philosophy. And so he came to bitterly regret the sexual aspect of his youthful love relationship: "Thus I contaminated the spring of friendship with the dirt of lust and darkened its brightness with the blackness of desire."[47] Though Augustine's Neo-Platonist vision of sexual desire as an evil pollution of the soul was to be immensely influential on church thinking on sexual morality, it is evident that there was considerable variance in attitudes toward homosexuality among early Christians of the empire, with many indulging in it, but with a very vocal minority strongly opposed.

Despite the apparent indifference of many of the early Christians to the ascetic arguments of Stoicism and the Neo-Platonism against non-procreative sexuality and homosexuality, the essential elements of those philosophies, including a pronounced anti-sexual bias, became assimilated into the developing dogma of the growing Christian church, so much so that the moral arguments of early Christian theologians became indistinguishable from the writings of the more severe of the ascetic pagan philosophers. But, as the historian Paul Veyne has observed, there was a major difference between the two in the consequences for the individual. The ascetic precepts of the Stoics and Neo-Platonists were philosophical ideals that free individuals could aspire to or not, depending on how persuasive they found the arguments. However, those same precepts as incorporated into Christian dogma became moral absolutes and preconditions for a salvation that the church felt was its mission to bring to all men, whether they were persuaded or not.[48] And so as the church grew in size and influence in the third and fourth centuries, an obsessive and neurotic hostility to sex and homosexuality became a central feature of the moral teaching of its most influential leaders.

The Theocracy of the Late Empire

After nearly a century of political and military anarchy, orderly government was finally restored to the Roman Empire under Diocletian, an Illyrian general who came to power in 284. Like most of his 3rd century predecessors, whose accession to power was the result of murder, intrigue and the heavy hand of the military, Diocletian was acclaimed emperor by his troops after the mysterious death of Numerian, the brother and co-emperor of the emperor

Carnius. At first, Diocletian shared power with Carnius, but after the latter's assassination by a group of soldiers Diocletian became sole ruler of the empire. Not wanting to share the fate of so many of his murdered predecessors, Diocletian set about the process of ending the influence of the military in political matters and creating a new and stable mechanism for orderly succession.

Recognizing the difficulty of effectively overseeing the administration of so large a realm as the empire, Diocletian appointed another general, Maximian, as co-emperor, to govern in the West from Milan, while Diocletian supervised the eastern empire from his capital at Nicomedia in western Anatolia. He then appointed a junior co-ruler for himself and Maximian, so that in effect there were four co-emperors, an arrangement that's been referred to as the tetrarchy. Under this system, Diocletian hoped that an orderly succession would be achieved through the elevation of each of the junior co-rulers upon the retirement of the two co-emperors. Each of the co-emperors were given armies and a sector to oversee, though Diocletian retained ultimate power, reserving to himself the authority to enact new laws and make political appointments.

Believing his rise to power was divinely ordained, Diocletian declared his kinship with the god Jupiter, and required those approaching him to prostrate themselves on the ground, as was the practice in oriental monarchies. It is also likely that Diocletian felt that creating an aura of divinity would further discourage potential assassins. Like Oriental rulers, Diocletian surrounded himself with a level of pomp and ceremony that would have brought scorn and resentment from earlier Republican-minded Romans, who traditionally had been suspicious of strong, king-like rulers. But Diocletian was not merely an Oriental-style despot. He also instituted wide-ranging reforms and reorganized the government, subdividing the provinces to make administration more manageable, but also to prevent the formation of local power centers that might threaten the authority of the emperor. By the beginning of the fourth-century, most of the empire had been restored to stability and prosperity, though its citizens were now living under an increasingly autocratic and oppressive dictatorship that bore more resemblance to the royal theocracies of Persia and Egypt than to earlier Roman governments. And with the establishment of an imperial government bureaucracy at his court in the Eastern Empire, Diocletian laid the foundation for the later Byzantine Empire, while hastening the decline of the city of Rome and the western provinces, which even then had not fully recovered from the devastations wrought by the civil wars and barbarian invasions of the third century.

While Diocletian is credited with reviving the strength and power of the Late Empire, he is probably better known for a violent campaign of persecution against the Christians, which he launched near the end of his rule. Christians had long been suspect to traditional Romans and the imperial government, because, in their worship of a God who transcended national boundaries, they claimed allegiance to no state. Further, the growth of an organization that denied the religious basis of imperial authority, and refused to sacrifice to state gods, was an increasing cause for concern for the co-emperors, not to mention the imprudence and provocation of the Christians in building a church directly across from Diocletian's palace in Nicomedia. In 303–304 a series of edicts was issued ordering the demolition of churches, seizure of sacred books, jailing of the clergy, and a sentence of death for those refusing to sacrifice to the Roman gods. The persecutions were particularly violent in the Eastern Empire, but didn't succeed in stamping out the new religion, and the persecutions died out by 312, leaving the Christian Church largely intact.

In 305, Diocletian decided to retire, and so he and his co-emperor Maximian abdicated —the latter quite unwillingly—allowing the ascension of their two junior co-rulers, who then appointed two new junior co-rulers under them. But the new tetrarchy did not last long. One of the co-emperors died the next year, and the armies of Gaul and Britain, without regard to Diocletian's plan of succession in the tetrarchic system, proclaimed Constantine, the son of the deceased co-emperor, as the new co-emperor. The son of Maximian then had himself proclaimed emperor in Rome. To add to the confusion, an usurper in the North African provinces also proclaimed himself emperor, with the result that there were then seven emperors. After some years of the inevitable civil wars, all but two of the competing co-emperors had been winnowed out: Constantine and Licinius, who had become one of the co-emperors at the time of the elevation of Constantine. The two co-emperors shared power, not always peacefully, for the next decade, until 324 when war broke out between the camps of the two emperors and Licinius was defeated and executed, leaving Constantine sole ruler of the empire.

Constantine the Great, as he has been called ever since, is one of those few historic figures who truly changed the course of history. Constantine was a brilliant military leader, who, in addition to his successes in the various civil wars, also led imperial armies in victories over the Franks, the Sarmatians, and the Goths. As an emperor, he ranked with Rome's greatest, in his administrative reforms, the establishment of a new currency that was to endure for centuries and revolutionary innovations in the organization of the military. Another signal achievement was his founding of the city of Constantinople, later capital of the Byzantine Empire, and for many centuries one of the greatest cities of the world. But Constantine's greatest significance is in the pivotal role he played in almost single-handedly transforming the pagan empire into a Christian state, not only embracing the Christian religion, but, in closely associating the church hierarchy with the government apparatus, laying the foundations for the Byzantine government to follow, and the ruling establishment of Medieval Europe.

Constantine's rise to power has always been closely associated with his conversion to Christianity, and, indeed, the emperor himself credited his success to the Christian God. According to an account by Eusebius, during one of the battles of succession, Constantine saw a vision of the Christian symbol for Christ, a monogram of the Greek letters chi and rho, in the sky with the legend, "In this sign, conquer." After seeing the vision, Constantine ordered the symbol painted onto the shields of his soldiers, and his army easily routed the opposing forces, prompting the emperor to embrace the Christian God he felt had led him to victory. After assuming power, Constantine not only legalized Christianity, but actively promoted the new religion, building numerous churches, donating state property to the church, and issuing laws granting the church and its clergy financial and legal privileges and immunity from civic obligations. Constantine's involvement in the new religion went well beyond spiritual devotion: he inserted himself into church matters ranging from the appointing of bishops to theological disputes, and even convened the Council of Nicea, the first ecumenical council of the church, which he presided over and dominated.

In 324, Constantine founded and built the city of Constantinople, sited on the banks of the Bosporus, between the Mediterranean and the Black Sea, as a specifically Christian city, complete with a magnificent basilica, still standing today. The move of the administrative capital of the empire to this site in Anatolia, chosen for its strategic and economic importance, close to the Danube and Euphrates frontiers, and at the juncture of important sea and land trading routes, underscored the degree to which the economic and political center of gravity of the empire had shifted to the East, and contributed further to the decline of Rome and the Western Empire.

After Constantine's death in 337, the promotion of Christianity by the government continued, amid an increasing association of the imperial government with the church's ruling establishment. Theodosius I (379–395) was even less hesitant than Constantine in inserting himself into church matters. In 380, in response to a bitter doctrinal dispute, Theodosius, without consulting the church leadership, issued an edict declaring that the Nicene Creed, a statement of faith issued under Constantine's earlier Council of Nicea, was to be binding on all subjects, an act that in effect outlawed the practice of any form of Christianity other than that approved by the emperor, as well as all other religions. It is noteworthy that this standard of faith for a true "Catholic Christian," a term that also appears here for the first time in an imperial document issued under Theodosius, was mandated not by the church, but by the emperor. Theodosius then convened a second ecumenical council of the church, the Council of Constantinople, to secure church sanction for his actions. Theodosius went on to prohibit pagan sacrifices and the visiting of temples, and in 392 completely forbade the worship of pagan gods.

As under Constantine, the church hierarchy enjoyed a privileged position in society. Bishops were given special civic insignia to wear, served as official ambassadors for the emperor, and the patriarch (archbishop) of Constantinople enjoyed rank at court above all civil officials. Church censures of heretics were enforced by civil penalties, and at least one heretic, Priscillian, was executed by the state. So closely had the political and church establishments become intertwined that many Christians thought of the church and empire as synonymous, as is illustrated in the writings of Saint Ambrose, bishop of Milan, who uses the terms "Roman" and "Christian" interchangeably. Thus, by the end of the fourth-century, the Christian church, which barely a century earlier was viewed with suspicion as a subversive and dangerous threat to the empire, had become a central pillar of the imperial establishment. Not only that, standards of Christian orthodoxy were even being enforced by the state. The pagan theocracy established by Diocletian had been replaced by a Christian theocracy, presided over by the emperor in Constantinople. But by this time, the empire was Roman in name only.

Anti-Homosexual Laws of the Late Empire

With the arrival of the Christian Church as a force in government, it was probably inevitable that the attitudes and beliefs of church leaders, many of whom subscribed to the severe anti-sexual asceticism promoted by the more extreme pagan philosophers, would be reflected in imperial policy. And indeed, during the Late Empire, Christian emperors issued a series of statutes, at first apparently aimed at homosexual prostitutes and passive homosexuals, but eventually encompassing all homosexual acts and even punishing them with the death penalty.

The first such law was issued in 342 under the sons of Constantine, the co-emperors Constans and Constantius, and because of its odd and ambiguous language has given rise to a great deal of debate among scholars as to what was intended by it. The text opens with a reference to the target of its penalty: "When a man 'marries,' [and is] about to offer [himself] to man in a womanly fashion ..., what does he wish, when sex has lost its significance; when the crime is one which it is not profitable to know, when Venus is changed into another form? ... We order the statutes to arise, the laws to be armed with an avenging sword, that those infamous persons ... may be subjected to exquisite punishment."[49] The curious use of the Latin verb *nubere*, which means "to marry," has prompted one scholar to argue the law was a prohibition against same-sex marriages.[50] Other scholars have suggested that "it was enacted in a spirit of mocking complacency,"[51] or that it was facetious.[52] Though there is evidence for same-sex marriages being carried out during the empire, especially among the upper classes, there is no indication that these ceremonies met with much disapproval, and so it would seem odd that civil authorities would be so disturbed by them that they would seek to severely penalize them.[53] Because *nubere* could also be used to indicate a man giving himself sexually to another man, as would a woman in marriage, other scholars have contended that the law was directed against passive homosexuals.[54]

But there are other problems: the law invokes the enforcement of existing statutes — "we order the statutes to arise"— but the only laws existing at that time that had anything to do with homosexuality were those enacted during the Republic prohibiting the seduction of the minor son of a Roman citizen, which clearly would not apply in this case. Finally, there is the puzzle of an anti-homosexual law being enacted under an emperor, Constans, who, according to the historian Aurelius Victor, was himself a homosexual in his private life,[55] who was said to pick his bodyguards more for their beauty than their competence,[56] and who had a reputation for scandalous behavior with "handsome barbarian hostages."[57] Though the imperial government had been thoroughly Christianized under Constans' father, Constantine, it is clear that the anti-sexual asceticism among Christian leaders had not yet had any influence there: Constantine himself was reported by the historian Ammianus Marcellinus to have indulged himself with the *spadones*, young males who were castrated in adolescence, so they would retain their sexual capacity, while retaining their youthful beauty into adulthood.[58] So it is plausible that a homosexually inclined emperor, as Constans clearly was, might enact the law as a mocking gesture to prudish moralists of the time, as some scholars have suggested, or as an attempt to placate a public scandalized by his own outrageous sexual behavior, as another scholar has argued.[59] But in any event, most scholars are agreed that the law, if it was serious, had absolutely no effect, because there is no evidence for its enforcement.

A second anti-homosexual law was issued fifty years later, in 390, under Theodosius, and was addressed to the vicar of the city of Rome:

> We cannot tolerate the city of Rome, mother of all virtues, being stained any longer by the contamination of male effeminacy, nor can we allow that agrarian strength, which comes down from the founders, to be softly broken by the people, thus heaping shame on the centuries of our founders.... [You] will therefore punish among revenging flames ... all those who have given themselves up to the infamy of condemning their manly body, transformed into a feminine one, to bear practices reserved for the other sex ... carried forth from male brothels ... and that he who basely abandons his own sex cannot aspire to that of another without undergoing the supreme punishment."[60]

Invoking, here, the old myth of the supposed heterosexual purity of the noble farmers of early Rome, the directive orders the punishment of men who have condemned "their manly body ... to bear practices reserved for the other sex," passive homosexuals. But the reference to carrying them "forth from male brothels" seems to indicate that it is male prostitutes who are being targeted by the law. And the penalty? To undergo the "supreme punishment," that is, death, in "revenging flames," a brutal sentence imposed by this Christian emperor that we cannot imagine being endorsed by Christ himself.

The law appears again in the Theodosian Code, a compilation of laws enacted after 312 that was published in 438 under Theodosius' grandson, the Emperor Theodosius II. But in this second iteration of the law, the reference to male brothels is dropped, suggesting a general prohibition against passive homosexuality. This would have been consistent with traditional Roman attitudes that frowned on the passive male, but at the same time approved of the active male's role in a homosexual act as a sign of virility. Whether the law was directed against male prostitutes or passive homosexuality seems immaterial, since, according to the Byzantine historian Evagrius, the centuries old tax on male prostitution was still being collected by the imperial treasury at the beginning of the sixth-century, more than a century after the Theodosian law's adoption, suggesting that the law, like the earlier legislation enacted under Constans, could not have been seriously intended or enforced. In any case, it seems to have had little effect on curbing homosexual practices.[61]

Theodosius I was the last of the emperors who ruled a united Eastern and Western Empire. After his death, the western provinces became subject to repeated barbarian invasions until 410, when the Visigothic chieftain Alaric conquered Rome itself, and pillaged it for three days, bringing to an end an era of Western history. Successive invasions and counter-measures continued, and by the mid-century Germanic chieftains were de facto rulers, controlling the West through puppet emperors. Finally, in 476 the Germanic Chieftain Odoacer deposed the last of the emperors, and the fall of the Western Empire was complete.

The Eastern Empire, on the other hand, with its more easily defended frontiers and its stronger government structure, easily withstood the period of the invasions. In fact, under Justinian, who ruled for nearly 40 years in the mid-sixth-century, imperial forces recovered sections of Italy and North Africa that had fallen to the barbarians. While the remains of the Western Empire was divided into a number of warring Germanic kingdoms, the Eastern Empire continued its evolution as a theocratic state, so that by the end of Justinian's reign the character and temper of the government and society had moved so far away from its Greco-Roman origins that historians define that period as the beginning of the Byzantine Empire.

Not the least of these changes was the continued transformation of society, under Justinian's strong direction, into a thoroughly Christianized community, so highly regulated in matters of personal conduct and religious observance that it came to resemble a monastic state. Indeed, under Justinian, the association of church hierarchy with the imperial government that began under Constantine became total. Justinian's government enacted legislation regulating almost every aspect of Christian life — conversion and Baptism, administration of the sacraments, and the proper conduct of the laity. Justinian even issued rules regulating the size of churches and monasteries, and standards for the clergy to follow. On the other hand, by the late sixth-century, many functions hitherto carried out by civic and imperial officials had been taken over by the bishops or the Patriarch — the collection of taxes, administration of justice, regulation of commerce, dispensing of charity, negotiations with barbarians, and even the recruitment of soldiers. The result of these developments was that by the early seventh-century the typical Byzantine city had been transformed into what was essentially a religious community under ecclesiastical rule.

The Code of Justinian

It is within the context of this nearly total assimilation of church and state that two anti-homosexual articles of law that were issued under Justinian should be viewed. The two laws are contained within the Code of Justinian, a monumental compilation of laws that was at first intended to build on the Theodosian Code, but that was later extended under Justinian to encompass all of Roman jurisprudence from the time of Hadrian. Because Roman law, as set out in the Code of Justinian, was looked to in later periods as a model for law codes throughout Europe, its provisions on homosexuality carried special authority, and set the standard in terms of tone and the severity of punishment of homosexual acts for much of European history.[62] But the anti-homosexual provisions included within the Justinian Code are not a part of the compilation of legal statutes and precedents from the great corpus of Roman law, the majesty of which was one of the great contributions of Roman civilization, but in fact represent the insertion of an ascetic Christian sexual morality that repudiated a thousand years of Roman legal, social and cultural tradition.[63]

The first provision, published in 538, was directed against sinners who the authorities feared would provoke the punishment of God on their cities, that is, those who commit homosexual acts and blasphemers. The inclusion of blasphemers in this imperial legislation is telling — there can be no better illustration of the extent of the confluence of church and state than in an imperial edict punishing the violators of a commandment of Moses. Indeed, the language of the provisions reads like they could have been written by one of the ascetic church Fathers:

> since certain men, seized by diabolical incitement, practice among themselves the most disgraceful lusts, and act contrary to nature: we enjoin them to take to heart the fear of God and the judgment to come ... so that they may not be visited by the just wrath of God on account of these impious acts, with the result that cities perish with all their inhabitants.... For because of such crimes, there are famines, earthquakes, and pestilences.... But if after this our admonition any are found persisting in such offences, first, they render themselves unworthy of the mercy of God, and then they are subjected to the punishment enjoined by the law. For we order the most illustrious prefect of the capital to arrest those who persist in the aforesaid ... and to inflict on them the extreme punishments, so that the city and the state may not come to harm by reason of such wicked deeds.[64]

The second article, published in 544, restricts its attention to homosexual acts, and, in its language and references to scripture and penitence, bears more resemblance to an Episcopal letter than a legal provision:

> Though we stand always in need of the kindness and goodness of God, yet is this specially the case at this time, when in various ways we have provoked him to anger on account of the multitude of our sins.... We speak of the defilement of males, which some men sacrilegiously and impiously dare to attempt, perpetrating vile acts with other men.... For, instructed by the Holy Scripture, we know that God brought a just judgment upon those who lived in Sodom, on account of this very madness of intercourse, so that to this very day that land burns with inextinguishable fire. By this God teaches us, in order that by means of legislation we may avert such an untoward fate.... Wherefore it behooves all who desire to fear God to abstain from conduct so base and criminal that we do not find it committed even by brute beasts. But as for those who have been consumed by this kind of disease, let them ... also duly to penance, and fall down before God, and renounce their plague in confession to the blessed Patriarch.... Next, we proclaim to all who are conscious that they have committed any such sin, that unless they desist and, renouncing it before the blessed Patriarch, take care for their salvation ... they will bring upon themselves severer penalties ... lest if we are negligent we arouse God's anger against us."[65]

Aside from the overtly religious language and tone, which did not appear in the earlier anti-homosexual legislation, there are other major differences that distinguish Justinian's provisions from the laws of Constans and Theodosius. First, the law describes as its target those "men, seized by diabolical incitement, [who] practice among themselves the most disgraceful lusts, and act contrary to nature," and speaks of a defilement, "which some men sacrilegiously and impiously dare to attempt, perpetrating vile acts with other men." There is no mention here of a passively homosexual male, who offered his body as though it were a woman's. The laws, then, are specifying any male involved in a homosexual act, whether in the active or the passive role, as being the intended target. And so the Justinian laws, for the first time in Roman history, penalized not just passive homosexuals, but also the male who sexually conquered another male, an act that for nearly a thousand years had been regarded as measure of virility for Roman males.

A striking aspect of the two laws is the repeated statement that the laws were being enacted not out of concern for the souls of the sinners, or to uphold standards of public morals, but out of fear that the sins of homosexuals would bring God's punishment onto the empire's cities, as the text says occurred in the biblical story of Sodom and Gomorrah. The linkage in the laws between homosexuality and the destruction of Sodom was one of the first appearances of such an association in Western culture and was to become a precedent in later periods for justification for extreme sanctions against homosexual behavior. Though citing concerns for the safety of its cities from God's fury as a rationale for a criminal penalty may seem to modern readers an example of superstitious paranoia, it was common practice among Christians, pagans and Jews in the ancient world to blame catastrophes on divine wrath. The Hebrew prophets, in fact, repeatedly predicted the destruction of Israel by God because of the Israelites' sins. In the case of the Justinian legislation, the fears may have been prompted by recent experience. In 525 a series of natural catastrophes visited regions of the eastern empire, with earthquakes and floods destroying a number of cities, including Edessa and Corinth, while a devastating fire ravaged the city of Antioch. The second law, of 544, was published only one year after a great plague swept through Constantinople.[66]

The two anti-homosexual provisions of the Code of Justinian can be seen, then, not as statements of traditional Roman family-oriented moral values, nor even as a reflection of Roman attitudes to homosexuality, which they in fact repudiate, at least in regard to the active male role. They are, rather, expressions of a peculiarly religious late imperial culture, complete with the sort of superstitious paranoia cloaked in well intentioned righteousness that was to be such a prominent feature of the Christian religion in the later European Middle Ages.

But it is also evident that the enactment of the Justinian anti-homosexual legislation was not simply the case of a devotedly Christian sovereign concerned about the well-being of his subjects. Inasmuch as there is no reliable evidence that any of the imperial laws against homosexuality were uniformly enforced, it seems that the principal use made of the legislation was as a tool with which to persecute political enemies, or as a pretense to seize property from wealthy opponents. Procopius of Caesarea, considered the most reliable historian of the day,[67] wrote that Justinian and his empress, Theodora, used the law as a pretext against his political opponents, or those "possessed of great wealth, or who happened to have done something else which offended the rulers."[68] The great historian Edward Gibbon, in his *History of the Decline and Fall of the Roman Empire*, cited "the avarice of Justinian" in administering the law, and labeled him a "venal" prince "who sold without shame his judgments and his laws."[69] Though Gibbon himself was hostile to "unmanly lust," he regarded the Justinian legislation as a perversion of justice, "the cruelty of which, can scarcely be excused by the purity of his motives." Gibbon, noting that "the impure manners of Greece still prevailed in the cities," wrote that the provisions were enacted "in defiance of every principle of justice." As carried out by Justinian, he wrote, homosexuality "became the crime of those to whom no crime could be imputed."[70]

Procopius related the unfortunate fate of one such victim, a young man of an opposing political faction, named Diogenes, who had made uncomplimentary remarks about Theodora. According to Procopius, the empress "could find nothing worse to charge Diogenes with than homosexual affairs," which, as John Boswell has observed, implied that most people of the day would have regarded homosexuality as at worst a peccadillo.[71] Despite the outcry of "the whole populace" who had attempted to intervene for the young man, Theodora then had Diogenes "indicted as a homosexual, forcibly removed from the church in which he had taken refuge, hideously tortured, and then castrated without benefit of trial."[72] Procopius relates that Theodora then tried to have another political opponent convicted on the same charge, but was unsuccessful, because of the many prominent people who came to his aid. After the judge refused to try the case, despite Theodora's bribing the witnesses, the entire city cele-brated in his honor.[73]

The anti-homosexual statutes of Justinian, because of their association, through their inclusion in the Code of Justinian, with the great and august body of Roman jurisprudence, were looked to as a model and justification for anti-homosexual laws for much of European history. But the fact that these laws, used as prototypes for laws to enforce public morality, were mainly employed by their authors, not in defense of any elevated moral standards, but for the most squalid of purposes — greed, avarice, and petty vengeance — raises questions about the motivations behind their enactment, and the seriousness with which they were intended, especially since there is no credible evidence that they were enforced other than against polit-ical enemies.

Conclusion

The two chapters on the Roman civilization complete the survey of homosexual tradi-tions among the peoples of the ancient Western world. The universal appearance and accept-ance of homosexual practices among the peoples of the ancient Middle East, the Mediterranean Basin, and among the early Indo-Europeans illustrates the degree to which homosexuality was an ever-present aspect of human sexuality before the imposition of the anti-homosexual religious attitudes that has characterized much of Western culture since.

The male-oriented Roman sexual tradition had, except for safeguards to protect the sex-ual honor of underage males, young girls and married women, essentially an "anything goes" attitude, in which the fulfillment of a man's sexual needs was felt to be as wholesome and natural an activity as eating a meal to nurture the body, especially if the man kept to the active role, though during the empire even that proviso seems to have been relaxed. Hence, homo-sexuality was accepted by most Romans "as a natural and inevitable part of a man's sexual life."[74] Indeed, from the earliest days of the Roman Republic the ability to sexually conquer other males as well as females was regarded as a mark of virility among Roman men, which is itself a testament to the Roman belief that it was perfectly natural for men to view other males as potential sexual objects.

It is noteworthy that there were no social traditions in Rome of the kind that existed in classical Athens and Sparta that actively promoted homosexuality, and that Romans who kept male slave-concubines or who pursued free born youth could just as easily have pursued females. The fact that so many Roman men apparently preferred males to women, who were equally available, underscores the persistence among all societies of a strong homosexual com-ponent in human sexuality.

The disapproval of homosexuality that began to emerge among some quarters during the empire, and that finally manifested itself in anti-homosexual legislation in the Late Empire, was entirely due to the influence of man-made concepts, chiefly the sexual asceticism of Sto-icism and Neo-Platonism that, in turn, became incorporated by an influential core of asce-tic Christian leaders into the dogma of the growing Christian church. That ascetic Christian leaders were instrumental in the imposition of anti-homosexual attitudes is demonstrated by the fact that the anti-homosexual laws did not begin to appear until after the imperial gov-ernment was Christianized in the fourth-century. The Christian influence on the anti-homo-sexual legislation is clearly evident in the religious language, scriptural references, and the admonition to penance in the two Justinian laws, which incorporate a judgment on the role of the active male in homosexuality that was entirely foreign to a thousand years of Roman tradition. Though there's no evidence that the anti-homosexual attitudes of the Christian ascetics were shared by many in the population even after the imperial government was Christianized, the ascetic sexual morality promoted by church leaders and the corresponding anti-homosexual legislation enacted by the Christian emperors laid the foundations for the sexual repression and homophobia that was to become dominant in the West in the European Middle Ages.

10

A Regal Love: The Ancient Tradition of Same-Sex Love in China

In the early second millennium B.C., as the old civilizations of Mesopotamia and Egypt were reaching the apex of their power and influence, and as the movements of Indo-Europeans into Anatolia and the Aegean were laying the seeds for the later development of Western civilization, another high civilization was beginning to emerge four thousand miles to the east along the Valley of the Yellow River in China. This distance, and the high mountains and inhospitable desert that separated it from its Middle Eastern contemporaries, insured that the culture that was rapidly growing from the Neolithic farming villages of northeastern China would retain a distinctive character, little affected by external forces. By the middle of the second millennium, a high civilization had taken form under the Shang dynasty that was similar in some ways to those of the ancient Middle East—for example, in the use of war chariots by a warrior aristocracy who ruled over a farming peasantry. But the pottery and other art objects produced under the Shang showed no resemblance to similar artifacts from Babylon or Egypt, and already display in this early period the distinctive forms and motifs that would distinguish Chinese culture all throughout the history of Chinese civilization down to the present day. In a similar way, the social organization that was established in that period— a half-divine emperor presiding over a layered society of courtiers and nobles, artisans and merchants, all depending on the economic production of peasant family farmers at the bottom—was to endure, almost unchanged, into the 20th century.

Because of the family-oriented philosophy of Confucianism, which ordered Chinese society for over two millennia, it is often assumed that homosexual behavior was not known to the Chinese, and in fact was traditionally disapproved by Chinese society. Contemporary Chinese, whether on the mainland or in Taiwan, and citizens of Chinese descent in countries around the world, uniformly believe that homosexuality was foreign to traditional Chinese culture, and that its occurrence in modern Chinese society is solely due to influences from the decadent West. This is yet another modern assumption about sexuality which is demonstrably false. In fact, it is especially ironic since China, alone among world cultures, has an unbroken documented history of homosexuality covering nearly three thousand years of its history, from the early Zhou dynasty until the 20th century. Throughout the long history of Chinese civilization, from the earliest periods to modern times, homosexual loves have been a highly visible feature of Chinese society, even at times influencing the course of Chinese political history.*

Until the publication of Bret Hinsch's Passion of the Cut Sleeve *in 1990, which was the first Western scholarly work to examine China's long homosexual tradition, little was known in the West about the unusually rich history of same-sex love throughout Chinese history. R.H. Van Gulik's* Sexual Life in Ancient China *provides a comprehensive study*

Early travelers to China frequently commented on the pervasive homosexuality they witnessed there. A ninth-century traveler, describing his impressions of the Chinese, wrote that "the popularity of 'the abominable vice of sodomy' was an unforgivable flaw in an otherwise admirable society."[1] Matteo Ricci, a Jesuit missionary who visited Peking in 1583, deplored the widespread homosexual prostitution he encountered in that city: "There are public streets full of boys got up like prostitutes. And there are people who buy these boys and teach them to play music, sing and dance. And then … these miserable men are initiated into this terrible vice."[2]

Another sixteenth-century visitor, Galeote Pereira, reported homosexuality to be common among all social classes: "The greatest fault we do find [among the Chinese] is sodomy, a vice very common in the meaner sort, and nothing strange among the best." The missionary Gaspar de Cruz was very explicit in his disapproval of Chinese homosexuality. Calling China a "new Sodom," he predicted that God would send earthquakes, floods and other disasters to punish the Chinese for their tolerance of the "filthy abomination, which is that they are so given to the accursed sin of unnatural vice, which is in no wise reproved among them."[3]

Modern Westerners would no doubt be surprised to learn of the prominence of homosexuality in China's social history, but before the introduction of Western sexual values and taboos by missionaries and other Western visitors in the 18th and 19th centuries, educated Chinese throughout Chinese history were well aware of a long tradition of homosexual loves extending back to the earliest dynasties. As early as the time of the Northern Qi dynasty in the sixth century A.D., Chinese writers were making references to the role of homosexual favorites in the court life of emperors going back as far as the Xia (2205–1766 B.C.) and Shang (1766–1122 B.C.) dynasties.[4] In a discussion of this ancient tradition of same-sex love, an eighteenth-century writer, Zhao Yi, also noted the prominence of homosexual loves in the courts as far back as the Xia and Shang dynasties, and went on to cite the names of numerous lovers and imperial favorites of the Zhou (1122–221 B.C.) and Han (206 B.C.-A.D. 220) dynasties.[5]

Homosexual Favorites in the Courts of the Zhou

Since our knowledge of the Xia dynasty relies solely on legend, and the art of writing came into use only under the late Shang dynasty, there is no historical evidence from which we can gain an understanding of sexual practices of those early Bronze Age dynasties. It was only under the Zhou dynasty, which lasted nearly a thousand years, from the twelfth century to the third century B.C., that a literature appeared sufficient to allow us to get a picture of the character of ancient Chinese homosexual customs, and the role that same-sex love played in early Chinese society. And since the literature that survives from that early period deals almost exclusively with the lives and affairs of the imperial court and the aristocracy, our understanding of the social role of homosexuality among the ancient Chinese is restricted primarily to the part it played among the upper classes.

A principal source of information on social life during the Zhou dynasty is found in histories compiled by court historians to record the lives and accomplishments of the rulers. Included among the recitation of royal deeds, names of wives and assorted political gossip in

(footnote continued) *of Chinese marriage customs, concubinage and female prostitution, but only scattered coverage of Chinese homosexual traditions. Because of the paucity of published scholarship on the Chinese homosexual tradition, this chapter relies primarily on Hinsch's work, with supplementation of others where noted.*

these histories are accounts of the love of the emperors for male favorites. Some of the dynastic histories, in fact, include whole sections devoted to the biographies of the homosexual lovers of the emperors. These royal companions seemed to have provided the emperors with the kind of intimate friendship and companionship not possible with a harem of wives and concubines or with courtiers. While love between male peers is not unknown in the histories of Chinese court society, the homosexual relationships described in the dynastic histories and other early literature are between a sovereign or lord and a younger male lover of a lower social status. In fact, for more than two thousand years of imperial history these hierarchical relationships were a prominent fixture of life in the imperial courts and among the aristocracy.

The frequency of married men maintaining sexual relationships with male companions was ironically partly due to the central role of marriage and the family in Chinese society. Marriage among the Chinese, as among many other peoples, from indigenous tribal peoples to the Roman aristocracy, was usually undertaken not for romantic reasons, but to link two clans or family lineages. For the aristocracy, political power and privilege depended on their hereditary line, and on alliances forged through marriage. Similarly, for rural villagers or the growing class of city-dwelling commoners, whatever political influence they had or favors they could obtain depended on family ties and the kinship-based traditions of clan rule. Therefore, marriage was a fundamental requirement for participation in the network of family, social and political ties that bound ancient Chinese society together.[6] However, as long as a man satisfied his familial obligations through marriage, he was free to pursue whatever sexual relationships he desired outside of marriage.

To the Chinese the sexual act was considered a part of the natural order, and as a result was never looked upon as sinful or attended by the feelings of guilt so common in the West.[7] And since most marriages, especially among the upper class, were devoid of romance, a man would naturally look elsewhere to meet his sexual and emotional needs. As among the Roman upper class, then, it was not uncommon to find a married man keeping a mistress or male lover, an arrangement that ancient Chinese society freely accepted as part of the necessities of life. The emperors, too, almost without exception throughout the four thousand years of imperial history, found intimate companionship with male lovers while at the same time maintaining wives and harems of concubines.

Homosexual Love Under the Zhou

One of the most famous of the homosexual figures of the Zhou Dynasty was a young man named Mizi Xia who became the beloved of Duke Ling, the ruler of the feudal state of Wei in the late sixth-century B.C. The story of Mizi Xia, later recounted in a philosophical text, *Han Fei Zi,* had a tremendous hold on Chinese of later periods, so much so that his name became synonymous with homosexual love, much like the association of the name of Ganymede, the Trojan youth loved by Zeus, with homosexuality in the Middle Ages and Renaissance.

As related by the text's author, Han Fei, the state of Wei had a law under which anyone who used the ruler's carriage without permission would be punished by having his feet amputated. When Mizi Xia, the young lover of Duke Ling, learned that his mother had become ill, he forged an order from the duke allowing him to use the carriage, and went to see his mother. When the ruler heard about what happened, instead of punishing his beloved, he praised him for risking punishment to go see his sick mother. On another occasion, Mizi Xia was walking with the duke in an orchard, when he picked a peach and bit into it. He thought it was delicious, so he offered the remaining half to the duke for him to enjoy. The duke exclaimed, "How sincere is your love for me! You forgot your own appetite and think only of giving me good things to eat!'" After some years had passed, and Mizi Xia's youthful good looks were fading, he found that the duke's passion for him had waned. One day he was accused by a jealous courtier of some crime against the ruler. Turning on Mizi Xia, the ruler growled, "After all, he once stole my carriage, and another time he gave me a half-eaten peach to eat!" And so Mizi Xia's tragic fate was sealed. Han Fei explained that Mizi Xia was behaving no differently from the way he had in the past, but that the difference in circumstances was only "because the ruler's love had turned to hate," with the passing of Mizi Xia's youthful beauty. So, Han Fei, cautions, "if you gain a ruler's love, your wisdom will be appreciated and you will enjoy his favor as well; but if he hates you, not only will your wisdom be rejected, but you will be regarded as a criminal and thrust aside." Han Fei's sympathetic portrayal of Mizi Xia reflects the favorable view of homosexual love under the Zhou dynasty. References to the story of Mizi Xia and his tragic story appear throughout Chinese literary history, showing a conscious awareness among Chinese of later periods of a tradition of same-sex love from the earliest times. In subsequent centuries, Mizi Xia's name and the incident of the "half-eaten peach" became commonly used as terms for same-sex love.[8]

Hinsch notes that in relating the story Han Fei took the homosexual nature of the relationship between the two as a given and not requiring special mention, probably reflecting the frequency of same-sex relationships in his time. In fact, Han Fei describes Mizi Xia and the duke not in terms of their sexual orientation, but in terms of their relationship, which he describes with the word *chong*, which, according to Bret Hirsch, denotes a hierarchical relationship of regular patronage, or favor, bestowed by a superior on a man who happened to be a sexual partner.[9] The Chinese, then, didn't describe individuals according to their sexual orientation, as in the modern West, but, like the ancient Greeks, in terms of the relationship they had with another — seemingly taking the presence of same-sex eroticism for granted. Having no analogous term for "homosexual," the Chinese would refer to same-sex passion with euphemistic phrases, like "the love of Mizi Xia," or "the love of the half-eaten peach," expressions that were used down through Chinese history until the twentieth-century, when Western terms for homosexuality began to appear in Chinese culture.

Additional evidence of the familiarity of same-sex love in Chinese courts of the Zhou is found in several incidents reported by ancient writers of court officials making sexual overtures to rulers. Such presumptuous behavior by an underling toward a sovereign would have been an unusual breach of courtly etiquette, and so worthy of mention by chroniclers of the period. One story is related in a philosophical work of the writer Yanzi, *Spring and Autumn Annals of Master Yan*, which tells of the desire of a court official for the handsome Duke Jing, ruler of the powerful state of Qi. The official would gaze at the ruler, enraptured by his good looks. Seeing the man, a minor official, staring at him, the duke was annoyed and asked his courtiers to find out why the man was staring at him. The minor official replied, "If I speak I will die, but if I do not speak, I will also die — I was stealing a glance at the beautiful duke." Hearing this, the duke was angered at the presumptuousness of the official, declaring, "He lusted after me. Kill him." But the philosopher Yanzi, one of the duke's advisors, intervened, reminding the duke that to resist desire is not in accordance with the Way, that it would bring bad luck to reject it, and so the duke relented. In fact, the duke forgave the official and promoted him, making him a retainer of the ducal bath, a position of highest trust and intimacy. Hinsch explains that by gazing suggestively at the duke, the lowly official was acting as the aggressive partner in initiating a relationship, and, in effect, challenging the duke's social standing. Because of the enormous disparity in the social status of the two, such impertinent behavior demanded the maximum penalty according to Chinese tradition. But after hearing Yanzi's wise advice, Duke Jing forgave the official, and then even promoted him, making him a retainer of the ducal bath.[10]

Another story from the period tells of the love of a court official for a handsome ruler of the state of Chu, in southern China. The shy official, Zhuang Xin, burned with love for his lord, Xiang Cheng, and finally approached him, "May I hold your hand?" The lord, startled by the provocative request, said nothing. In desperation, Zhuang Xin then told his lord the story of another ruler, who was similarly loved in secret by his boatman, who sang: "What a fine day is this, that I share a boat with you, my prince! Unworthy that I'd be so desired, when have I ever felt such shame? My heart's perplexed to no end, that I've come to know you, my prince! There are trees in the mountain, and branches on trees. I yearn to please you, *and you do not know.*" Charmed by the song of his boatman, the prince accepted his love. After Zhuang Xin finished relating this story to Lord Xiang Cheng, the ruler took Zhuang Xin's hand and accepted his love, too.[11]

Because of his subservient status, Zhuang Xin was restrained from making the first moves in seeking a sexual relationship with his lord, and so when he awkwardly asked for the lord's hand, the ruler was understandably indignant. But after hearing the story that Zhuang Xin related, which subtly but effectively conveyed Zhuang Xin's predicament, the lord was moved to accept his love. Zhuang Xin's turning to the story of the prince and his boatman is another illustration of the conscious awareness of the ancient Chinese of a tradition of same-sex love, a tradition in which Zhuang Xin could not only place his love for his ruler, but in which he could find a useful story to help him communicate the dilemma of the unrequited love he felt for his ruler. The sympathy and tenderness with which Zhuang Xin's predicament is related by the writer further underscores the positive view accorded homosexual love under the Zhou.

Probably the most romantic example of homosexual love from the Zhou period is found in the story of the love of another ruler of feudal Chu, Wang Zhongxian, for a beautiful young scholar named Pan Zhang. Hearing of Pan Zhang's scholarly reputation, Wang Zhongxian went to him to request his writings. According to the story, the two fell in love at first sight and were "as affectionate as husband and wife, sharing the same coverlet and pillow with unbounded intimacy for one another." When they died, they were buried together on a mountain side. Soon afterwards a tree with long sinuous branches began to grow in their grave. In time the branches intertwined with each other, as if embracing. The people thought the embracing of the branches was a miracle, and in time the tree was called the "Shared Pillow Tree."[12]

This strikingly romantic example shows that under the Zhou dynasty homosexual love was not limited to extramarital affairs entered into for the divertissement of the ruling class, but could take the form of the sort of all-consuming passionate love between males that was celebrated in the epics of the ancient Greeks or the sagas of the Norse. The burial of the two lovers together, in fact, recalls the Indo-European custom of warrior-lovers being buried in the same grave. The intertwining branches of the tree that grew above their grave — considered an auspicious omen in Chinese religion — is also a frequently used motif in Chinese poetry to denote devotion between heterosexual lovers, and its use here is a further indication of the positive view of homosexual love among the ancient Chinese, a love that in this story was framed as a direct parallel to heterosexual love.[13]

Though the story of Pan Zhang and Wang Zhongxian demonstrates an awareness among the ancient Chinese of exclusive and permanent homosexual unions, such affairs did not displace the role of heterosexual marriage, which remained a central institution of ancient Chinese society, crucial for commoners because of the importance of progeny for economic survival, and necessary to the aristocracy for the continuance of hereditary privilege and political influence. But these stories show that at the same time homosexual relationships existed side by side with heterosexual marriage, most notably as a complement to the official but often passionless marriages of the landed aristocracy.

The ubiquity of homosexual favorites in the courts of Zhou China is illustrated by their frequent mention by writers of the period. A constant presence in court life and in the inner circle of the ruler, homosexual favorites inevitably became involved in politics and the exercise of power, serving as court officials or ministers of state, or deploying their influence for or against particular political factions. Their involvement in politics could stir resentment against them, as in the case of the Marquis Shen, the young lover of King Wen of Chu, who, when the king lay dying of a grave illness, was sent by the king into exile to a friendly neighboring kingdom so that he would be protected from jealous reprisals after his royal protector was dead. That it was common in the Zhou period for male lovers of rulers to be promoted to the rank of powerful officials or state ministers is illustrated in a humorous anecdote from the seventh-century B.C. During a visit by Prince Chonger of the northern state of Jin to the Duke of Cao, the duke heard that the prince had double ribs. Curious about this unusual anatomical condition, the duke drilled a hole through the wall of the prince's chambers so that the duke and his wife might be able to observe Prince Chonger in his bath and so view the double ribs. But when they peered in upon Prince Chonger in his bath, they were greeted with the unexpected sight of Prince Chonger having sexual intercourse with two male retainers. At this sight, the duke's wife dryly remarked that Prince Chonger's retainers seemed capable of becoming ministers of state. Though meant as a humorous dig at the social-climbing of many male favorites, the remark wouldn't have had any meaning or humor unless it was commonly known that court officials and ministers often acquired their positions through homosexual relationships with powerful superiors.[14]

In fact, the phenomenon was widespread enough that manuals on statecraft frequently included advice to inexperienced rulers to be wary of such relationships. In one such text, dating from the late Zhou, the writer warns rulers of the sort of corrupting practices that could endanger his rule and his country:

> If you dare to have constant dancing in your palaces, and drunken singing in your chambers.... If you dare to set your hearts on wealth and women, and abandon yourselves to wandering about or hunting — that is called the way of dissipation. If you dare to despise sage words, to resist the loyal and upright, to put far from you the aged and virtuous, and instead pursue sexual intimacies with youths — that is called the way of disorder.... If the prince of a country is addicted to these, his state will surely come to ruin.[15]

Another late Zhou text is even more specific about the threat of the influence of homosexual nepotism on a country's ruler.

> Rulers employ their relatives, or men who happen to be ... pleasant-featured and attractive.... If men such as these are given the task of ordering the state, then this is simply to entrust the state to men who are neither wise nor intelligent, and anyone knows that this will lead to ruin. Moreover, the rulers and high officials trust a man's mental abilities because they love his appearance, and love him without bothering to examine his knowledge. As a result a man who is incapable of taking charge of a hundred persons is assigned to a post in charge of a thousand.... Why do the rulers do this? Because if they assign a man they like to such a post, he will receive an exalted title and a generous stipend. Hence they employ the man simply because they love his looks.[16]

So prevalent was the role of homosexual favorites in court politics in the late Zhou that a Machiavellian political handbook of the Han dynasty included in a discussion of Zhou period political tactics the use of a male sexual favorite to bring down an enemy. In the example cited, a powerful baron, Duke Xian, wished to attack the neighboring state of Yu, but was wary of its formidable ruler, Gong Zhiqi. An adviser quoted a line from a philosophical work, *The Book of Zhou*, which said, "A beautiful lad can ruin an older head," and told the duke to "send the king a comely boy" with secret instructions to spread disinformation among the enemy's subjects. Such a beautiful youth was found, and sent to the court of Gong Zhiqi who, as predicted, fell for the youth who then was in a position to carry out the disinformation plan. After this was done, Duke Xian attacked Yu and easily conquered it. It should be noted that the aphorism quoted here, "a beautiful lad can ruin an older head," does not imply disapproval of homosexuality. The complete passage that the Han text quoted from *The Book of Zhou* reads, "A beautiful lad can ruin an older head; a beautiful woman can tangle a tongue." So the text actually is not a comment on homosexuality, but is a warning on how sex in general can blind men with lust and hobble their judgment. And to the Chinese of the Zhou, the temptations of sex included the allure of attractive young males as well as beautiful young women.[17]

The concerns of Chinese moralists about the corrupting influence of homosexual favorites in politics were not based on academic theorizing. In one case, the influence of an over-reaching male favorite on a ruler nearly plunged the country into civil war. Duke Huan, the ruler of the feudal state of Song, was passionately in love with an official of the court, Ziang Dui, and made him a military commander. But Xiang Dui seriously over-stepped the bounds of courtly etiquette when he persuaded the duke to favor him over the duke's own son. "At that time, the duke's son, Tuo, had four white horses. Xiang Dui wanted them," and so he used his influence on the ruler to get them. "And so the duke took them ... and gave them to him. The duke's son was furious, and had his followers pursue Xiang Dui, who was afraid and wanted to flee." To avoid further deterioration of the social order, the duke allowed his son to mete his vengeance on the social upstart. And so "closed the gates," preventing his beloved from fleeing, "and wept for [Xiang Dui] until his eyes were bruised."[18]

A rare glimpse of homosexual love outside the confines of the Zhou royal courts is found in *The Classic of Odes*, the earliest surviving collection of Chinese poetry, which provides insight into the lives and feelings of people outside the elegant courts. The work is a compilation of popular songs and poetry, many of which are believed to date from long before the collection was assembled in the seventh-century B.C. In contrast to the stylized verses of court poets, the poems of *The Classic of Odes* reflect the day-to-day reality of ordinary farmers and soldiers—the prospect of famine, the dangers of war, but also the passion and sorrow of love. And it is clear from the poems in this anthology that social attitudes under the Zhou fully accepted love and intimacy between men, to the extent that the open and effusive expression of affection between men was common.[19]

In one verse, the poet writes: "There is a beautiful man, clear, bright, and handsome. Unexpectedly we meet, fitting my desire." Another poet describes the unabashed admiration between two athletic noblemen: "How splendid he was! Yes, he met me between the hills of Nao. Our chariots side by side we chased two boars.... How strong he was! Yes, he met me on the road at Nao. Side by side we chased two stags.... How magnificent he was! Yes, he meet met on the south slopes of Nao. Side by side we chased two wolves. He bowed to me and said 'that was good.'" In another work, the poet expresses the affectionate and intimate companionship between two masculine warriors:

> How can you say that you have no clothes? I will share mine with you. The king raises his army, we put in order our dagger axes and lances; I will have the same enemies as you. How can you say that you have no clothes? I will share my trousers with you. The king raises his army, we put in

order our *mao* lances and *ji* lances. Together with you I will start on the expedition. How can you say that you have no clothes? I will share my skirts with you. The king raises his army; we put in order our mail-coats and sharp weapons; together with you I will march.

Instances of sexual love between masculine peers, of a sort suggested by these examples, frequently appeared in the literature of later periods.[20]

The anecdotes that have come down to us about the homosexual favorites of rulers of the Zhou period, which come from all the regions of China, make clear that same-sex love was a widespread feature of the lives of the ancient Zhou aristocracy. The examples mentioned here are mentioned by the writers only in passing, in the context of broader philosophical or political discussions, suggesting that such loves were taken for granted, and were viewed as natural part of life's experience, worthy of comment only when the relationships figured in a larger issue of philosophical concern or controversy. The only warnings we see from moralists concerning homosexual love come not from the nature of the sexuality involved, but where such relationships negatively influence political decisions.

Han Dynasty

By the fifth century B.C., the power of the Zhou dynasty had declined to the point where they were rulers in name only, with powerful regional barons vying with each other for military and political dominance. After several more centuries of almost constant warfare between competing feudal states, the ruthless Shi Huang Ti, ruler of the western Ch'in state, emerged in 221 B.C. as the supreme ruler of all of China, bringing the Chinese feudal states under a strong, unified rule for the first time. The new Ch'in emperor quickly moved to consolidate his rule, replacing the traditional feudal ruling courts with an imperial administrative apparatus run from the emperor's court and enforced by the imperial army. A unified law code was imposed throughout the country, and, to facilitate military control over the vast empire, a network of roads and fortifications, including the massive structure that became the Great Wall, were built throughout the country. The effect of these undertakings was to establish a unified political structure throughout the country, and to inculcate a sense of national identity among the residents of what had been more than a dozen far flung feudal states stretching over an area nearly as large as Europe. Fittingly, the nation of China has ever since taken its name from the Ch'in emperor.

But the stability that Shi Huang Ti's conquests brought to China was short-lived. When he died in 210 B.C., after only 11 years on the throne, he left a spectacular tomb complete with a life-sized terra cotta army of over four thousand soldiers, but violence and intrigue within his family prevented the establishment of an enduring dynasty. His legitimate heir was forced to commit suicide by his usurping brother, who only ruled four years before a mutiny broke out in the army. The rebellion was quickly joined by some of the old feudal barons, eager to reclaim their titles. After the second emperor was killed by one of his ministers, the last surviving Ch'in prince surrendered to a rebel leader in 206 B.C. Power was thereupon claimed by Liu Pang, one of the rebel princes, who proclaimed himself emperor in 202 B.C., establishing a dynasty that came to be known as the Western Han.

Though the organization of the Chinese state had undergone an enormous transformation during this period, the visibility of homosexuality among the ruling elite remained the same under the Han as it had been under the Zhou.[21] In fact, so prominent was the role of the homosexual favorites of the Han emperors in court life that the official histories of the emperors included entire chapters devoted to the biographies of the male lovers of the rulers.

One of the official historians, Sima Qian, made note of the influence of these sexual companions of the monarchs, and the long history of this sexual tradition, in the introduction to his chapter on their biographies:

> Those who served the ruler and succeeded in delighting his ears and eyes, those who caught their lord's fancy and won his favor and intimacy, did not so only through the power of lust and love; each had certain abilities in which he excelled. Thus, I made The Biographies of the Emperors' Male Favorites.... It is not women alone who can use their looks to attract the eyes of the ruler; courtiers and eunuchs can play at that game as well. Many were the men of ancient times who gained favor this way.[22]

In his history of the Roman Empire, Edward Gibbon noted that all but one of the first fourteen emperors were known for their homosexual loves. The same could be said for the ten emperors of the Western Han, who ruled from 206 B.C. to A.D. 1, all of whom have been identified by ancient Chinese historians with one or more homosexual lovers. The first Han emperor, Liu Pang, usually known by his title Gaozu, set the precedent for rewarding official positions to attractive males willing to employ their sexual abilities, a custom taken up by his son, Emperor Hui. According to Sima Qian, "When the Han arose, Emperor Gaozu, for all his coarseness and blunt manners, was won by the charms of a young man named Ji, and Emperor Hui had a boy favorite named Hong. Neither Ji nor Hong had any particular talent or ability; both won prominence simply by their looks and graces. Day and night they were by the ruler's side, and all the high ministers were obliged to apply to them when they wished to speak to the emperor." As Sima Qian observed, these favorites accrued enormous influence by virtue of the special intimacy they shared with the sovereign, especially since they could chose what ministers or officials could have access to the inner sanctums of the imperial court. When Gaozu was succeeded by his son, Hui, his "boys were clad like officials, with gold-pheasant caps and gem-studded girdles; they powdered and rouged their faces, and were constantly in the emperor's bedchamber."[23]

There are many more examples in the official histories of the Han of young men from humble origins who rose to positions of exalted rank and influence because of their intimate relationships with the emperor. One such favorite was Deng Tong, a peasant from a rural province, employed in the palace grounds as a boatman, whose uniform included a yellow cap. As related in Sima Qian's history, one night Emperor Wen, the third of the Han monarchs, "dreamed that he was trying to climb to Heaven but could not seem to make his way up. Just then a yellow-capped boatman boosted him from behind, and he was able to reach Heaven. When the emperor turned around to look at the man, he noticed that the seam of the boatman's robe was split in the back, just below the sash." When the emperor awoke from his dream, he went to the lake to search for the man who had boosted him up in his dream. "There he saw Deng Tong, who happened to have a tear in the back of his robe exactly like that of the man in the dream." When the emperor found that the man's surname was Deng, a word which means "ascend," and that his personal name was Tong, which means "reach," he took that as confirming Deng Tong as being the yellow-capped boatman of his dream. The emperor brought Deng Tong into his household, where the young man was given ever-increasing favors and honors, eventually assuming a position comparable to that of "official concubine" of the emperor.

Deng Tong responded to his newly privileged position with tact and grace, and "as a result, the emperor showered him with gifts until his fortunes mounted to tens of billions of cash and he had been promoted to the post of superior lord." Unlike other favorites of Emperor Wen, whose knowledge or skills endeared them to the emperor, "Deng Tong does not seem to have had any special talent" other than that of "entertaining the emperor," wrote Sima Qian.

Because of his intimate relationship with the emperor, Deng Tong, wittingly or unwittingly, had an inordinate influence on court politics. Any sudden shift in the political currents swirling around the emperor could make him vulnerable to retribution by resentful ministers. At one point, the imperial chancellor sought for political reasons to take revenge on Deng Tong, who was only saved from being beheaded by a last-minute intervention by the emperor.[24]

The degree to which a sexual relationship with the emperor could enhance the social position of a favorite is illustrated in an incident that occurred when Emperor Wen was suffering from a tumor. Deng Tong "made it his duty to keep it sucked clean of infection. The emperor was feeling depressed by his illness, and, apropos of nothing in particular, asked Deng Tong, 'In all the empire, who do you think loves me most?' 'Surely no one loves Your Majesty more than the heir apparent,'" replied Deng Tong, referring to the emperor's son, who was to become Emperor Jing. "Later, when the heir apparent came to inquire how his father was, the emperor made him suck the tumor." The emperor's son complied, but clearly found the task distasteful. When he later learned that Deng Tong had been performing that service for the emperor, which in effect implied that the two of them were on the same level in their relationship to the emperor, he was filled with shame, and forever afterward bore a grudge toward Deng Tong. When Emperor Wen eventually died, and Jing assumed the throne, he carried out his revenge on Deng Tong, who was stripped of his position and possessions, leaving him impoverished for the rest of his life. The story of Deng Tong and his downfall is a striking example of how a commoner could advance through a sexual relationship with the emperor to the level of being essentially a rival with the crown prince for the monarch's affections. It also underscores the fragility of the favorite's position, being entirely dependent on the patronage and favor of the ruler, and vulnerable to threats from both the imperial bureaucracy and the emperor's own family.

But becoming the emperor's lover could also bestow lasting privilege on not only the young man, but on his family as well. The official histories cite many examples of families being raised to wealth and nobility as a result of the sexual relationship of one of their sons with the ruler. When Emperor Wen's son assumed the throne as Emperor Jing he, too, had a favorite beloved, Zhou Ren, who, like Deng Tong, seemingly had no talents, other than in pleasing the emperor with "secret games" played in the imperial bed chambers. Emperor Jing showered Zhou Ren and his family with wealth and aristocratic titles, which were passed down to his children, allowing his family to rise to the ranks of hereditary nobility. As illustrated by the case of Zhou Ren, many of the favorites were actively bisexual, and, in addition to homosexual relationships with the emperor, often had wives and children of their own.

The historians of the Han also make clear that the male lovers of the rulers were not feminine effetes who played a consort role comparable to that of a woman. For that they had their wives. Rather, the emperors' favorites shared a distinctly masculine comradeship with the ruler, frequently accompanying them in hunting and even, in some cases, battle. One example was Han Yan, the favorite of Emperor Wu, who succeeded Emperor Jing in 140 B.C. Emperor Wu, himself, is regarded by traditional historians as "a quintessentially masculine emperor," whose name itself means "martial." Indeed, Emperor Wu devoted his lengthy rule to conquering and subjugating neighboring non–Chinese peoples. He met Han Yan, the illegitimate grandson of a marquis, when they were both young and studying writing together. According to the account of the Han historian, Sima Qian, during their studies,

> the two grew very fond of each other. Later, after the emperor was appointed heir apparent, he became more and more friendly with Yan. Yan was skillful at riding and archery ... was well versed in the fighting techniques of the barbarians, and therefore, after the emperor came to the throne ... he treated Yan with even greater respect and honor. Yan had soon advanced to the rank

of superior lord and received as many gifts from the ruler as Deng Tong had in his days of honor. At this time, Yan was constantly by the emperor's side, day and night.

Emperor Wu shared with his lover, Han Yan, an enthusiasm for the stereotypically masculine pastimes of riding, archery and warfare, and in this regard the two of them epitomized the masculine virtues prized by the Chinese aristocracy since the time of the Shang warrior-rulers.[25] Other imperial favorites were also noted for their masculine character. A later historian singled out Ji Sengzhen, a lover of one of the Northern Qi rulers, for his masculine good looks and stylishness, "combining martial valor with a rakish bearing."[26]

As among the Zhou, homosexual lovers were not an exclusive feature of the imperial bed chambers, but were pursued by other figures in Han imperial society. One such example was Huo Guang, a powerful general who served under the Han Emperor Xuan. General Huo Guang, though he was married, nonetheless kept an exceptionally attractive male lover named Feng Zidu, whom he was so fond of that he included him in all his official activities. Though sharing the reins of power with a sexual favorite was certainly not unprecedented in the Han court, the thought of a sexual favorite being "trusted with a general's power ... provoked laughter in the wine shops of foreigners," in the words of one Chinese historian. This example also illustrates the acceptance by Chinese wives of their husbands' male favorites, who were viewed not as rivals, but a necessary part of the natural order. Indeed, after General Huo Guang's death, his widow, Xian Guang, who had her own sexual designs on Feng Zidu, entered into an affair with him, where it was reported that they "roamed playfully throughout the house together."[27]

Literature of the Han also contains some references to cases of love between women, in contexts that suggest they were not isolated instances. According to the Dutch scholar R.H. van Gulik, female homosexuality was widespread in the Zhou and Han periods.[28] However, as in Greece and Rome, literature was produced by men for a male audience, and so the lives of women were of little interest other than in their relationship to men, and thus, except for an occasional mention, little written about. The Han writer Ying Shao remarked on homosexual relationships among women in the emperor's household: "When palace women attach themselves as husband and wife it is called *dui shi*. They are intensely jealous of each other."[29] That there was a term, *dui shi*, for two women in a sexual relationship shows that the phenomenon must have been common enough under the Han to acquire a recognizable name. The *Records of the Han*, and other works also write of lesbian relationships, noting them among servants of the empress, and among slave girls. However, other than these incidental references, writing about sexual matters focused exclusively on men.

The Love of Emperor Ai and the End of the Western Han

The most famous of the homosexual lovers of the Han emperors was a young man named Dong Xian, the beloved of Emperor Ai, the tenth ruler of the Han dynasty. Like the effusive displays of affection of the Roman Emperor Hadrian for his beloved Antinous, which captured the imagination of the Roman people, the intensity of Emperor Ai's love for Dong Xian, and the extravagant expression of it, was a cause of wonder for the Chinese public. The emperor was so fond of Dong Xian that he even tried to have him made his successor. Emperor Ai was probably exclusively homosexual: according to the Han historian, Ban Gu, "By nature Emperor Ai did not care for women."[30] But, like favorites before him, Dong Xian was evidently bisexual — he had several wives and children, a situation which did not apparently interfere with his relationship with the emperor. Indeed, Emperor Ai bestowed great wealth and numerous honors on Dong Xian and his family. Dong Xian was made an official of the court, and both he and his father were given the aristocratic rank of marquis, with lands to go with it. Dong Xian was even given the singular honor of being entrusted with the erection of the emperor's tomb, a responsibility of the greatest official and ritual gravity.

The level and number of offices and honors bestowed upon Dong Xian by Emperor Ai was remarkable, even by the standards of the largesse showered upon imperial favorites. An indication of the power achieved by Dong Xian in the imperial government was that at one point he was able to block an important land reform proposal, a measure that would have cut into the income of large rural landowners, such as he had become. But it goes without saying that the offices and titles bestowed on Dong Xian by Emperor Ai had little to do with his qualifications, and much more to do with his good looks and his talents in pleasing the emperor. Once, when a visiting Mongol chieftain was being entertained at a feast, he marveled at the incongruous youth of so high an official. The emperor explained that Dong Xian was a great sage, and that was why he had achieved so much at so young an age. At this, the chieftain congratulated the emperor on having such a wise man in his court. Of course, the real reason for Dong Xian's achievements had nothing to do with intellect or wisdom, but was almost entirely due to his physical allure to the emperor. And, indeed, Dong Xian was certainly quite aware that his position rested on his physical appeal, and so put a lot of care into his dress and appearance. This, in turn, spawned a competition of sartorial elegance among other male courtiers, who, according to a contemporary account "competed to ornament themselves as seductive beauties" in order to catch the attention of the emperor.[31]

The love of Emperor Ai for Dong Xian figures in one of the most famous incidents in the history of the Chinese homosexual tradition. As described by an anonymous Chinese historian: "Emperor Ai was sleeping in the daytime with Dong Xian stretched out across his sleeve. When the emperor wanted to get up, Dong Xian was still asleep. Because he did not want to disturb him, the emperor cut off his own sleeve and got up. His love and thoughtfulness went this far!" That the title of the history from which this passage is taken is titled, *Duanxiu pian*, "Collection of the Cut Sleeve," is an indication of the power that the image of the mighty emperor going out of his way to avoid waking his sleeping lover had for subsequent generations. Seeing the cut sleeve as signifying the tenderness of Emperor Ai's love for Dong Xian, males in the court took to the fashion of cutting off one of their sleeves, in tribute to the devotion between Emperor Ai and Dong Xian. To Chinese of later periods, the image came to be taken more generally as a symbol of male homosexual love. And so, like the episode of Mizi Xia offering his royal lover a half-eaten peach, the incident of the cut sleeve entered the language of Chinese of later ages as a euphemism for homosexual love and devotion.[32]

Toward the end of his life, Emperor Ai, who, with no sons of his own, lacked a designated heir, decided to make Dong Xian his successor and openly announced his desire to do so. In justification, he even invoked ancient mythical precedents, but was met with strong opposition from the imperial counselors. Nonetheless, on his deathbed, in A.D. 9, the emperor turned over the imperial seals to Dong Xian, and declared him the new emperor. Lacking legitimacy of his own, and with many political enemies ready to move against him, Dong Xian was forced to commit suicide. With the throne in the hands of a usurper, Emperor Ai's failed attempt to turn over his office to his homosexual lover brought the line of Western Han emperors to an end.

Homosexuality in the Literature of Post-Han China

After several unsuccessful attempts at political and social reform, the new ruler, Wang Mang, found himself confronting repeated insurrections and increasing civil disorder. Finally, in A.D. 25, Wang Mang himself was assassinated, and a member of the Liu family seized the throne, restoring the rule of the Han dynasty — called now the Eastern Han because its capital Lo-Yang lay several hundred miles to the east of the old Han capital in Ch'ang-an. After a half a century of strong imperial rule, the dynasty gradually came under the influence of court factions and the families of the imperial consorts, with the result that royal succession was manipulated to favor the interests of a family or faction. The consequent weakness of the emperors is illustrated by the fact that eight of the 12 Eastern Han rulers came to the throne as infants or young children, and a number of them were murdered to make way for another family's candidate. With a succession of weak emperors, and with imperial governance hampered by increasing corruption and the intervention of powerful families, the empire in the late second century fell victim to invasions on a number of fronts. Insurrections and rebellions added to the chaos, until 221, when Ts'ao P'ei, the son of one of the rebel chiefs, accepted the abdication of the last of the Han emperors, and took the throne, though his forces controlled only the northern part of the country. Competing rulers set themselves up as emperors, one in Shu in the Southwest, and another in Wu province in the Southeast, resulting in what has been called the period of the Three Kingdoms.

These civil divisions presaged several more centuries of weak emperors, short lived dynasties and frequent civil war and domestic unrest — a period referred to by historians as the Six Dynasties. The political instability did not come to an end until the establishment, in the early seventh-century, of the powerful and illustrious Tang dynasty which ushered in a long period of peace and prosperity in China. Under the Tang, who ruled from the early seventh to the tenth-century, and the Song Dynasty, who reigned from the middle of the tenth-century to the late 13th-century, China's culture reached new heights of richness and sophistication. The increasing production of literature during this period, from the end of the Han through the splendor of the Tang and Song dynasties, provides abundant evidence of the continued pervasiveness of homosexual love relationships among Chinese men.

Throughout the long period of political instability and intermittent warfare that followed the downfall of the Han, homosexuality continued to be a prominent feature of life in the imperial court, regardless of which dynasty was in power at the time. But the literature produced during this period provides evidence that homosexuality was also highly visible among elements of society beyond the courts, and that in addition to the extensive official histories of the lives and loves of the imperial ruling class, less formal works now provided descriptions of the loves of minor officials, poets, scholars and other men of lesser rank. Thus, it was not uncommon in literature of the time to see frank declarations of love for other men by writers, poets and philosophers, and a body of love poetry was even produced, that in its passionate treatment of homosexual love, rivaled the work of the lyric poets of the Greeks and Romans. Surveying the extensive evidence of homosexuality in the post–Han period, R.H. Van Gulik, a historian of Chinese sexual practices, cited the late third century "as a high point in the openness of male homosexuality."[33]

An example of Tang literature that testifies not only to the continued presence of homosexuality in the centuries following the Han, but the apparent broad social acceptance of it as a commonplace aspect of sexuality is a work of the early 9th-century poet Bo Xingjian. In "The Poetical Essay on the Supreme Joy of the Sexual Union of Yin and Yang and Heaven and Earth," Bo Xingjian attempts to set out a description of all the varied facets of human sexuality and their place in the cosmos. Included among such topics as the cosmic significance of sex, the onset of puberty, instructions for the wedding night, sexual etiquette in the royal bedchamber, the sex lives of peasants, sex in Buddhist monasteries, and even a catalog of famous ugly women, is a section on homosexuality. In it Bo Xingjian recalls the long tradition of the "cut sleeve" and mentions some of the famous homosexual lovers of ancient times, from the Zhou dynasty Lord Long Yang and his beloved Mizi Xia, "who shared a peach with his lord," to the Han Emperors Gaozu and his lover Jiru, and Emperor Wu and his lover Han Yan.[34] The neutral and non-judgmental tone of Bo Xingjian's treatment of homosexual love, and his use of the euphemisms "cut sleeve" and "half-eaten peach," as well as the brief allusions to famous homosexual lovers of the past, assume a familiarity on the part of the reader with the long historical tradition of homosexual love in China, and further testifies to an awareness and acceptance by post–Han Chinese of homosexuality as an aspect of the sexual "cosmos."

The pervasiveness of homosexuality during these centuries was remarked on by a Song dynasty historian, who wrote that from the third century onward, homosexuality "flourished considerably and was as extensive as attraction to women. All of the gentlemen and officials esteemed it. All men in the realm followed this fashion to the extent that husbands and wives were estranged. Resentful unmarried women became jealous." Other writers describe men so enamored of the love of other men that they would flee at the sight of a woman.[35] A contemporary poet captured the predicament of a woman in such an atmosphere, worrying about whether the man she loves will reject her in preference for a boy: "She dawdles, not daring to move closer, afraid he might compare her with leftover peach," alluding here to the term, "half-eaten peach," used as a reference to homosexual love since Mizi Xia, a thousand years earlier, had offered one to his Zhou dynasty royal lover.

As in earlier times, dynastic historians included chapters on the male lovers of the emperors in their official histories. The custom persisted until the end of the Song Dynasty in the 13th-century, by which time the bureaucratic organization of government authority had eliminated opportunities for influence of the imperial favorites, and, hence, their interest to historians. But the continued prevalence of the tradition of emperors taking homosexual lovers up to that time is attested by the great number of biographies of male favorites that have survived in the official histories — one dynastic history alone contains biographies of forty imperial lovers.[36]

To account for the inclusion of biographies of imperial favorites in the official histories, some of the historians offered various explanations that provide a glimpse into the thinking of the early Chinese on the phenomenon of homosexuality. Some of the historians cited the precedent of tradition as the reason for devoting sections to royal favorites, showing again a continued awareness of what was by that time a long tradition of homosexual love in Chinese culture. But another historian saw the presence of homosexual lovers of the ruler as part of the larger natural order: "When there are celestial portents, there will certainly be people acting accordingly. When there is the star of favored officials, they will be arrayed beside the imperial throne."[37] Several historians cited concerns about the influence sexual favorites had on emperors and the disruptive effect they could have on orderly government, and used the histories of these favorites as a warning to future rulers of the undesirable effects of letting young lovers have too much power. These historians were not making judgments on the morality of homosexuality, per se, but were merely including it as among the influences and distractions — luxurious palaces, pearly pools with jade bridges and frolicking fish, flowery halls full of delights, cited by one historian — that could corrupt an undisciplined ruler. But regardless of their feelings about homosexuality, the official historians of the period were unanimous in their recognition of the ubiquity of the practices. One historian commented on "how widespread favoritism was at the end of the Qi," while another remarked in his history that "everyone at the court" desired such homosexual relationships. Another historian, after reciting a long list of famous imperial lovers, asked rhetorically how such a widespread practice could possibly be avoided.[38] The author of the *History of the Song* concluded that "it was unavoidable that there would be favorites at the courts of rulers," and that even enlightened rulers had them.[39]

Like the favorites of Zhou and Han rulers, the lovers of the emperors of the period came from all walks of life, and they and their families were typically enriched through their relationships with the ruler. Because of the frequent warfare during these centuries, many of the favorites were soldiers or military officers who caught the emperor's attention while on campaigns. Some were scholars or government officials, while others were famed for their skill in battle or fine horsemanship, and one favorite "soothed the ruler with beautiful lute music." Another royal lover, according to the official historian, was well known for his erotic skills, which, he wrote, were said to match those of his mother, herself a royal concubine.[40]

But the literature produced during this post–Han period demonstrates that homosexuality was an aspect of the lives of many men of the times, and was not confined to court or aristocratic circles. One such work from the fifth century, a compendium of anecdotes, famous remarks, witty tales, and gossip about the notable figures of the day even includes a section describing the renowned male beauties of the day. The inclusion of a chapter on male beauty underscores the degree to which males of the period were viewed as potential sex objects by other men, and shows that the physical and sexual attractiveness of certain men was a frequent topic of conversation among other males. The appreciation of male sexual attractiveness could even find its way into day-to-day affairs of the bureaucracy, as when an official might compliment the sexual appeal of a superior in order to win favor. Once, Huan Wen, a powerful grand marshal in the fourth-century court of the Eastern Jin, asked a subordinate what he thought of the looks of Prince Sima Yu, the court chancellor and one of the famous male beauties of the day. The subordinate replied that the prince, playing an important role in the government, was "naturally majestic like a divine ruler. But Your Excellency, too, is the *object of all men's gaze.*"

That a minor bureaucrat would routinely include a reference to the erotic appeal of a superior in his flattering remarks demonstrates not only the open acceptance and practice of male homosexuality among the Chinese in the post–Han centuries, but that sexual appeal to other men was a subject of discussion and even a concern for men of the age. Indeed, as we have seen, a sexually attractive physical appearance could be instrumental in advancing a man's career. As a consequence, men devoted great attention to their personal appearance, using oils to dress their hair, and powders to lighten their complexion — lighter skin being associated with the wealthy upper classes, in contrast to the darker skin of peasants who labored in the sun. Thus, an attractive man might be described as, as one writer put it, with a "face like congealed ointment," and eyes, "like dotted lacquer; this is a man from among the gods and immortals." The third-century Emperor Wen of Wei once was so enthralled by the extremely light skin of one male beauty that he was convinced he used facial powder. To test his theory, the emperor offered the young man "some hot soup and dumplings. After he had eaten it, he broke into a profuse sweat, and with his scarlet robe was wiping his face, but his complexion became whiter than ever." The use of facial powders by men was so prevalent during the period that the trade in facial powders became very profitable, and was even made a state monopoly at one point. One contemporary writer thus summed up the male ideal as "oiled hair, powdered face, and small gleaming buttocks," the last point leaving no doubt that erotic appeal was paramount.[41]

References to homosexual relationships and the love lives of men outside the ranks of the court and the nobility are also found in the literature of the period. One text of the time mentions a sexual relationship between a well-known poet and a male companion who are described as "sworn brothers." "Pan Yue and Xiahou Zhan both had handsome faces and enjoyed going about together. Contemporaries called them the 'linked jade disks,'" a popular expression of the time for couples in a sexual relationship.[42]

Another homosexual relationship described in the literature of the time was between Yu Xin, a prominent sixth-century writer, and Wang Shao, who eventually became a powerful government official. As described by the historian, "When Wang Shao was young, he was beautiful, and Yu Xin opened up his home to him and loved him. They had the joy of the cut sleeve. Wang Shao relied on Yu Xin for clothing and food, and Yu Xin gave him everything. Wang Shao received guests, and was also Yu Xin's wine server." This was obviously the case of young beauty "kept" by an older man, who provided for his needs in return for his sexual companionship — an arrangement somewhat akin to that of a patron and a concubine, though the text also states that despite the quasi-commercial character of the relationship there was nonetheless genuine love in the relationship, "the joy of the cut sleeve." Later in life, Wang Shao was appointed to the powerful position of censor of the western provincial city of Yingzhou. Once, when Yu Xin had an occasion to travel to the west, he stopped in to see him, but

> Wang Shao greeted Yu Xin very weakly. Sitting together, Wang Shao's affection for him decreased. He had Yu Xin enter the feast and seated him beside his couch. Yu Xin looked like a widower. Yu Xin could bear this no longer. Having drunk too freely, he jumped directly on Wang Shao's couch and repeatedly trampled and kicked his food. Looking directly at Wang Shao he said, 'Today your appearance seems very strange compared to your former one!' Guests filled the hall. Wang Shao was extremely embarrassed.

Though it was common for good-looking young men to be taken as lovers by prominent older men in return for favors and advancement — indeed, it was a venerable imperial tradition — Wang Shao was nevertheless embarrassed, as a high government official, to be confronted with evidence of his youthful sexual servitude in the person of his former patron. But it should be noted, too, that Wang Shao's earlier subservient relationship with Yu Xin had no negative effect on his career, an illustration of the lack of concern of Chinese society for sexual passivity in men.

Another prominent homosexual couple mentioned in post–Han literature was the third-century scholar Xi Kang, considered one of the great intellectual forces of the age, and his lover, Ruan Ji, a renowned poet in his own right, who wrote a lengthy poem memorializing the famous homosexual lovers of the Zhou and Han periods. Aside from his formidable intellect, Xi Kang was also known for his good looks, tall in stature, and "with an imposing facial expression," he "never added any adornment or polish, yet had the grace of a dragon and the beauty of a phoenix."

Xi Kang and his lover figure in an amusing anecdote that recalls the story of the Zhou dynasty duke who drilled a hole through the bed chambers of a noble guest, where he and his wife observed him in sexual intercourse with his male retainers. Xi Kang and Ruan Ji had become close friends with a noble, Shan Tao, who held them in such high regard that their friendship was described as "stronger than metal and as fragrant as orchids." An account of the story was given in the *Shih-shuo-hsin-yu*, a collection of stories and anecdotes by Liu I-ch'ing. "Shan T'ao's wife discovered that her husband's affection for those two was different from an ordinary friendship, and asked him about it. Her husband said, 'Those two are the only persons I consider as my real friends.'" Shan T'ao's wife then recalled the old Zhou story of the duke and his wife who spied on their guest in bed, and she asked her husband if she could do the same. Shan Tao assented, and so the next time Xi Kang and Ruan Ji came to visit, she cut a hole in the wall of their bed chamber and spent the whole night watching them. When at dawn she finally returned to bed with her husband, he asked her what she thought of the two men. Evidently impressed with the sexual prowess she had seen the men demonstrate, she replied, "Your own ability is in no way comparable to theirs," and added dryly that if he was going to compete with them, it would have to be on an intellectual level.[43]

From this little vignette of third-century China, we can see that not only were homosexual relationships an accepted part of life during the period, discussed with not the slightest hint of disapproval in literary works of the time, but that the educated elite were completely aware of homosexual figures and anecdotes of earlier periods in Chinese history. This is further testament to the atmosphere of non-judgmental acceptance and appreciation of homosexuality as an aspect of human sexuality that prevailed in the centuries between the Han and the rise of the Tang dynasty.

Homosexuality in Poetry

As among the ancient Greeks, some of the most beautiful poetry of the time was a celebration of the passion of homosexual love. But unlike the comparable poetry of the Greek poets, in which the visceral character of the love is often on the surface, the poetry of the Chinese is more circumspect with regard to erotic feelings, which are conveyed with suggestive hints, while sensuous imagery is used to evoke an atmosphere of romance and passionate excitement. An example of this delicate sensibility can be found in the work of Ruan Ji, lover of Xi Kang and one of the most prominent poets of the day: "Roving glances gave rise to beautiful seductions; speech and laughter expelled fragrance. Hand in hand they shared love's rapture, sharing coverlets and bedclothes."[44]

In a poem written by the sixth-century Emperor Jianwen to a boy favorite, we see another example of the indirect treatment of sexual love with the use of suggestive imagery, here invoking the sights and sounds of the bedchamber, and the barest of suggestions of sexual contact to portray a sense of erotic passion: "Our feather curtains are filled with morning fragrance, within pearl blinds I hear the distant drops of an evening water clock....Our curtained bed is inlaid with ivory....When you touch your pants, I lightly blush."[45]

Another example, from the fourth-century poet, Zhang Hanbian, uses similarly lyrical language, but this time to dress up the somewhat tawdry subject of male prostitution, in this ode to his beloved Zhou Xiaoshi: "The actor Zhou elegantly wanders, the youthful boy is young and delicate, fifteen years old. Like the eastern sun, fragrant skin, vermillion cosmetics, simple disposition mixes with notoriety. Your head turns — I kiss you, lotus and hibiscus."[46] In this poem we see an early linkage of prostitution with acting, an association that would become more pronounced in later centuries, and would, in fact, persist in Chinese theater until modern times.

Prostitution was almost certainly a presence in Chinese cities from the earliest periods, a custom that emerged, as in other cultures, with the rise of cities and social classes. And given the evident lack of taboos toward homosexuality in Chinese society, from the Shang dynasty forward, it can be assumed that both male and female prostitution was as prevalent in early China as it was in contemporary societies in the Middle East and Mediterranean region.

Though the language of the poem paints a romantic picture of the elegant and delicate boy prostitute — perhaps reflecting the poet's own one-sided perspective as the client — we can assume that the reality of the boy's existence was not nearly as glamorous.

Another poem, by the sixth-century poet Liu Zun, provides a more realistic view of the conditions under which such a male prostitute must work, dependant on his only asset, his looks, and on the capricious favor of his patrons: "How pitiful the young boy Zhou is. Barely smiling, he plucks orchids professionally. Fresh skin paler than powdered whiteness, Mouth and face like pink peach blossoms, He hugs his catapult near Diaoling, And casts his rod east of Lotusleaves.... From an early age he knew the pain of scorn, Withholding his words; ashamed to speak." Unlike the boy prostitute of the earlier poem, who was compared to "lotus and hibiscus," and who lived a life of "extravagance and festiveness," surrounded by "the leisurely and beautiful," the later poem portrays the difficult life of a youth, forced by poverty or social conditions to seek his living, "barely smiling," "plucking orchids professionally," and having to "cast his rod" seeking clients. "Lucky to be chosen" for lowly sexual servitude, he "knew the pain of scorn," for his status, and so was "ashamed to speak." As if that wasn't enough, his position is not secure, for "new faces stream through the palace."[47] In contrast to the sorry lot of the young male prostitute, whose fate depended on the whims of his patron, many young favorites seemingly held the upper hand in their relationships with older lovers. The Tang poet Li Qi drew on an incident involving the fifth-century General Ji Long's love for a singing boy named Zheng Yingtao to dwell on the sad condition of wives cast aside because of the favor shown a boy lover by a husband.

While these poems attest to the frequency of class-structured or hierarchical relationships between an older male patron and a younger, passive partner, other literature of the period makes clear that relationships between peers seemed to be just as common. An example is seen in a Tang dynasty poem written by the poet Bo Juyi, who was also a minor government official, recalling the nights spent with a dear friend, another official: "We are fond of the moon, and nights sleep side by side; we love the mountains and on clear days view together." In another poem, he remembers a cold winter night they spent together: "Mist and moon intense piercing cold. About to lie down, I warm the remnant last of the wine; we face before the lamp and drink. Drawing up the green silk coverlets, placing our pillows side by side; like spending more than a hundred nights, to sleep together with you here."[48]

Poems such as these, expressing deep love and affection between male friends, often with erotic overtones, had their antecedents as early as the ancient Zhou dynasty poetic anthology, *Classic of Odes*, and were taken up by early post–Han literary figures, such as Xi Kang and Ruan Ji. But by the Tang they had become a major literary preoccupation of the educated class of scholars and government officials, so much so that expressing one's affection for a friend through such poetry came to be seen as the mark of a cultivated gentleman.[49]

Homoeroticism in Popular Prose

The Tang dynasty also saw the first great profusion of Chinese prose literature, which quickly grew in popularity. The every day situations involving ordinary people that are described in the stories, which often include bawdy themes, provide additional evidence of the widespread presence of homosexuality well outside the effete and sophisticated confines of the imperial courts. Unlike poetry, whose conventions demanded circumspection with regards to sexual matters, prose literature was often quite open in its portrayal of erotic themes, as is illustrated in this excerpt from an early story: "When Wu Sansi saw his beloved's pure whiteness, he was immediately aroused. That night Wu summoned him so they could sleep together. Wu played in the 'rear courtyard' until his desire was completely satisfied."[50] Here we see the expression "rear courtyard" as a reference to anal intercourse, an illustration of the openness with which sexual relations were treated in Tang prose stories.

Another example of prose from the period is something of a morality tale, depicting the prodigal life of the son of a wealthy family who squandered his inheritance on luxuries and gambling and ended up on the street.

> Then one day a band of rogues came. Because of his exceptional good looks he was repeatedly sodomized. He grew accustomed to this "coupling of skins" and at last found his place as a street boy. He indiscriminately associated with Buddhist and Taoist monks, robbers and thieves, and was a beloved to all of them. Day and night men excitedly played in his real courtyard. One could hang a bushel of grain from his erect penis and it would still not go down! It looked like the shaft of a miller's wheel, and could be used to beat a drum loudly enough to alarm people. Because of this, two of the rogues fought one another over him."[51]

Whereas in earlier periods, going back to the Zhou dynasty, homosexual love was usually presented in the loftiest of romantic terms, as an expression of society's elite, and treated in the dynastic histories and in poetry in sensitive and discreet language, we now see homosexuality being depicted among society's lowliest members, and described with a coarse and vulgar humor. The narrative portrays a social climate under the Tang in which virtually all men, even among the lowest class, seemed to have been just as eager to avail themselves of homosexual opportunities as heterosexual opportunities, especially if they involved good-looking young men. The "rogues" who set upon the handsome young man were surely not a band of homosexuals, but were undoubtedly meant by the writer to signify the kind of ruffians who might just as well have taken advantage of a young woman in a similar situation. The sexual attraction of the rogues for the beautiful youth shows that for many men of the period homosexuality was a very real option for sexual release. And the fascination of the men with the young man's penis makes clear that these men were not seeking sex with him as a substitute for sex with a female, as is sometimes argued about "opportunistic" homosexuality, but were pursuing him because of his distinctively masculine sexual appeal.

It is also interesting to note the reference in the story to the homosexual proclivities of Taoist and Buddhist monks, a topic alluded to in Bo Xingjian's catalogue of the various aspects of human sexuality in his "Poetical Essay."[52] Westerners are accustomed to thinking of monks as celibate ascetics who have sublimated their sexuality to the devotion to God. However, Eastern religions in general have a much more positive view of sexuality, and don't assume the inherent conflict between sexuality and spirituality that exists in Western religion, and which underlies the rationale for celibacy among priests and monastics in the West. Taoism and Buddhism were mostly positive toward sex — certain aspects of Taoism actually encouraged sexual relations — and the two religions were neutral, for the most part, on homosexuality. In later periods, some Buddhist moralists did disapprove of homosexuality, but this was a reflection of the influence of ascetic Indian sects on some Chinese Buddhists, and was not a trait of Buddhism, per se. In fact, according to Japanese folk tradition, homosexual love was brought to Japan by the founder of one of the two principal branches of Buddhism in Japan, the Buddhist monk Kobo Daishi, the most revered of Japanese saints, who, it was said, learned the practice while studying Buddhism in China. Some Buddhists and Taoists saw physical beauty as a manifestation of the divine and so regarded sexual love as entirely consistent with spiritual devotion.

While Taoist and Buddhist monks did renounce worldly possession, and were forbidden from marrying, their vows did not preclude homosexual practices. To the contrary, some monks pointed to their homosexuality as proof that they were abstaining from sex with women. Given their attitudes toward sexuality, then, the reputation for homosexuality that both Taoist and Buddhist monks had among the Chinese of the Tang, Song and later periods is not surprising. Indeed, homosexuality was reported to be common in monasteries throughout eastern Asia, from Central Tibet to Japan, for many centuries.

Homosexuality in Popular Humor

Another source of information on popular attitudes toward homosexuality is humor. Just as a large percentage of popular humor in cultures around the world includes sexual elements, so, too, the collections of jokes and humorous stories from the Tang, Song and other periods of Chinese history contain a fair share of jokes involving homosexuality. As the story above suggests, monks and priests were the butt of a lot of jokes. In one such example a priest seduced a young disciple, who became very aroused so that he developed an erection. When the priest entered him from behind, the youth reached such arousal that semen started oozing out of his penis. At that point the priest reached around and, grabbing the penis, exclaimed, "Oh Amida Buddha, it's pierced all the way through," thinking that it was his own penis he had grabbed.[53] Aside from the humor, the joke shows that the Chinese recognized that a male could experience pleasure to the point of orgasm by being sexually penetrated, as occurred with the young disciple. Another joke plays upon the reputation monks had for having insatiable sexual appetites. A monk and a disciple had journeyed to a patron's house, and upon arrival at the door, they saw that the disciple's belt had come loose, which caused some papers he was carrying under his garment to fall out. "It looks as though you have no bottom," joked the priest. "If I hadn't," replied the disciple, "you wouldn't be able to exist for a single day!"[54]

Other groups stereotyped in humor for their homosexual reputations were students and government officials. In one example, a young man was taking a river journey on a boat at night. While he was lying on the deck sleeping, another passenger pressed close to him and penetrated his anus. Shocked, the young man asked him what he was doing. Someone else replied, "Oh, he likes to do it that way," to which the young man replied, "I thought the only ones who liked to do it that way were students!" In a joke mocking the hidebound conformance to rules and customs of government bureaucrats, an official travels to a provincial town on an inspection tour. Though he was very austere and strict in his behavior, when it came time to go to bed he ordered a subordinate to get in bed with him. The young man asked the official whether he wanted to be fellated or to do it another way. The official asked what the local custom was concerning this, and when the subordinate replied that it was mutual fellation, the official stiffly replied that they should do it strictly in accordance to custom. An indication of the strong the association of government bureaucrats with homosexuality is that in many humorous stories a man who likes sex with other men is jokingly referred to as a "petty official."[55]

The prevalence of homosexuality among males before marriage is suggested in another joke. A man and woman went to bed on their wedding, whereas the man immediately grabbed on to his wife's buttocks, attempting to have anal sex with her. "You're doing it the wrong way," exclaimed his wife. "But I've been doing it that way since I was very young—what's wrong with that?" he answered. "Well, I've been doing it since I was very young, too, and it wasn't that way," she replied. This joke, contrasting the worldly-wise wife with her heterosexually inexperienced husband, who apparently up to that time has had sex only with other males, recalls one of the sexual satires of the Roman poet Martial. In that poem, Martial remarks about a similar husband-to-be, whose sexual experience had been limited to slave boys, that heterosexual relations is *ignortum opus,* "unfamiliar work."

There are also humorous stories that depict men continuing homosexual relationships even after marriage. In one story a young wife, after seeing her husband's affairs with other men, runs to her mother complaining of being cuckolded by her husband — a term normally used to refer to the husband whose wife is being romanced by another man. Another story tells of a man who arranges a wife for his young lover. "And having done this, he moved freely within the family circle and didn't avoid anyone. One day he was just entering the bedroom when the wife's mother chanced to visit, so she asked her daughter, 'Which relative is he?' 'He's my husband's husband,' the wife replied."[56] The prose stories and humorous collections produced under the late Tang and continuing under the Song depict a social climate in which homosexuality is viewed as just another feature of day-to-day human relations, an aspect of sexuality that played a role in the lives of many ordinary men, and that was particularly associated with government officials, monks, students and the unmarried, but also not unusual even among married men.

In addition to the proliferation of popular prose stories, scientific and medical texts and manuals also began to be produced under the Song. Further evidence of how commonplace male homosexuality must have been among all ranks of society in this period is the inclusion in medical texts of descriptions of the effects of copulation on the anus, such as in this example from the thirteenth-century *The Washing Away of Wrongs,* the oldest known forensic manual in the world: "Examine the anus in question for broadness and looseness. A lack of tightness and construction is the condition resulting from sodomy over an extended period." Legal authorities, too, would routinely order the examination of the bodies of male robbery victims, to look for signs of anal rape.[57]

Homosexual Prostitution in the Cities and a Moral Backlash

As the Tang dynasty gave way in the tenth-century to three centuries of Song dynasty rule, the rapid urbanization of Chinese society spawned an explosion of prostitution in the cities. Female prostitution, long a feature of Chinese urban life, also reached unprecedented levels during the Song.[58] Class-structured homosexuality, in which a wealthy or powerful man had the option of meeting his sexual needs outside of marriage through a relationship with a younger male, usually of a lower class, had been a feature of Chinese society since the earliest dynasties. But the increasing number middle-class merchants, artisans and craftsmen who were filling the growing cities could not afford the full time upkeep of a boyfriend as could the upper class and the royalty. The availability of male prostitutes, thus, provided middle-class men who were so inclined with the opportunity to have their homoerotic needs satisfied without the expense of maintaining the lifestyle of a full time favorite. The popularity of both male and female prostitution in the cities was described by an early Song dynasty writer, Tao Gu, in his *Records of the Extraordinary,* which noted the activity of the many male brothels, euphemistically called the "Misty Moon Workshops." "Everywhere people single out Nanhai for its Misty Moon Workshops, a term referring to customs of esteeming lewdness. Nowadays in the capital those who sell themselves number more than ten thousand. As to the men who offer their own bodies for sale, they enter and leave places shamelessly. And so prostitution extends to the hive of alley and lanes, not limited to the Misty Moon Workshops themselves." The general climate of openness to homosexuality under the Song was remarked on by another contemporary writer in his comments on the pleasure loving atmosphere of the time: "Clothing, drink and food were all they desired. Boys and girls were all they lived for."[59]

Given the conspicuous growth of male prostitution in the period and the increasing moral looseness of life in the burgeoning cities, it was probably inevitable that there would be a backlash among Chinese moralists. By the ninth century a movement to revive the tenets of the family-oriented philosophy of Confucius had begun to gain influence. Combining elements of Buddhist and Taoist thought, this reformulation and extension of Confucian thought, known as Neo-Confucianism, emphasized spiritual cultivation in the individual as the basis of order in the state. But unlike classical Confucianism, which was neutral with regards to homosexuality, or Taoist thought, which was amenable to personal gratification, Neo-Confucianism advocated a strict family-oriented morality that emphasized sexual asceticism.

In a striking parallel to Stoicism, which taught that one could rise above the chaos of the world by aligning oneself with the natural order underlying the universe, adherents of Neo-Confucianism maintained that a man's development required the deep cultivation of moral consciousness, which was ultimately achieved through an inner experience of feeling at one with universal principles. An early proponent of the movement, the Tang philosopher Han Yu, like the Stoics, stressed moderation of feelings and condemned unbridled passion, which, he said, led to extramarital sexual relations. The Song philosopher Zhu Xi continued this theme in his writings, with such statements as, "A man with passions has no strength, whereas a man of strength will not yield to passions," an assertion that could have been lifted straight from a second century Roman Stoic text. While the Neo-Confucians did not directly address homosexuality, their linkage of morality with sexual asceticism, and a consequent disapproval of extramarital relations, contributed to a growing intolerance of male prostitution which developed under the Song. Finally, in the early 12th century, a law was promulgated which punished men who became prostitutes, the first such law in Chinese history.[61]

However, like the late Roman laws which penalized male prostitution, the Chinese law doesn't appear to have been enforced. A thirteenth-century author noted the case of a particularly flamboyant male prostitute and complained that even in his case the authorities failed to enforce the law:

> Wu practiced this custom [of prostitution] to an extreme.... He applied cosmetics, dressed opulently, had beautiful needle-like fingers, and spoke in a voice like that of a woman. Wu was always imploring others for sex. His nicknames were "Shaman"* and "Actor's Costume." Officials accused him of unmanliness and ordered an investigation of his degenerate practices. Nothing could have been more blatant than this, yet still they did not resurrect the old prohibitions.

It would be a mistake to infer from this passage that there was significant disapproval of homosexuality or male prostitution during the late Song. Numerous sources under the Song and during later periods continue to testify to a widespread and well-entrenched system of male prostitution. Indeed, according to Chao I, an 18th century scholar cited by Van Gulik, the late Song period "marked the heyday of male homosexuality." The absence of attempts to enforce the law is very likely a result of the Chinese government's traditional reluctance to interfere in personal sexual matters.[61]

Given the reports of 19th- and 20th-century ethnographers of transvestite shamans among rural Asian populations in regions from Korea to Southeast Asia, vestiges of a tradition that, like the berdache tradition of the Native American tribes, was very probably thousands of years old, it seems likely that the prostitute's nickname derived from popular familiarity with homosexual shamans in rural 13th-century China.

Continuing the Tradition Under
the Yuan and Ming Dynasties

By the time Marco Polo reached the court of the Mongol Emperor Kublai Khan in 1275, Chinese civilization had been at the peak of its sophistication for hundreds of years. The invasion of China by the Mongols in the early 13th-century that was begun under Ghengis Khan, and which culminated in the establishment of Ghengis' grandson Kublai Khan as emperor, brought the Song dynasty to an end. Though at first the Mongol rulers retained the austere, military lifestyle of their nomadic forebears, they were quickly softened by the richness of the culture they found in China, which at that time was centuries ahead of the West in development.

The ingenuity and creativity of the Chinese in this period brought revolutionary advances in many areas of human endeavor, from the economic to the scientific to the cultural. Commerce and trade were transformed by the invention of the abacus which enabled rapid and accurate calculations, and the development of an advanced monetary system which facilitated trade in commodities and manufactured goods across vast regions. Coal, which Marco Polo referred to as "black stones" in his written account of his travels, was used in vast quantities in applications from home heating to industrial production, and minerals such iron, tin, lead, silver and gold were produced in large amounts. Irrigation and sewage systems supported the growth of large cities, some of which grew to over a million in population, the largest in the world at that time. Medical advances included the development of such specialized fields as acupuncture, obstetrics, dentistry, laryngology, ophthalmology and treatments for rheumatism and paralysis. Scientific investigations flourished, and the development of movable-type printing spurred the spread of literacy. In addition to the explosion of popular prose literature that began under the Song dynasty, histories, collected scholarly works, and encyclopedias were produced in large numbers. The cultural sophistication of the times extended to life in the cities, where the inhabitants could take advantage of such amenities as teahouses, wine shops, catering services, and could take in the entertainment of puppet shows, storytellers, and performing arts of all sorts, as well as acrobats, jugglers, wrestlers, sword swallowers, snake charmers, fireworks, and gambling. The upper classes enjoyed such divertissements as music, painting, poetry, as well as intricate games, pets, calligraphy, and other tasteful hobbies.

While some strains of Islamic teachings of the period frowned on homosexuality, there is no evidence that the Mongols shared that aspect of their Muslim faith. Quite the opposite: according to one Western visitor, the Mongols were "addicted to Sodomy or Buggerie," and another source described sodomy as nearly universal among the Uzbek Khans. Thus, the ascension of the Mongol emperors over China doesn't appear to have had any influence on the attitudes to homosexuality among the Chinese. At any rate, the Yuan dynasty set up by Kublai Khan began to lose control over China only a few decades after his death, and after a period of insurrection and rebellion that gradually spread across China, the Mongol rulers were replaced in 1368 by a new dynasty of rulers, the Ming.

During the period of the Ming dynasty, China was at the apex of its power and influence. Under the Ming, Chinese rule extended into Korea on the east, Uzbekistan on the west, and down into Vietnam and Burma in the south. During this period, too, regular contact with the West began, and Chinese goods, ranging from luxurious silks to porcelain began to be imported into Europe in large quantities. Production of vernacular literature, stories and novels continued to increase, and gives us further insights into the interplay of homosexuality in the lives of ordinary Chinese people. Of course, the emperors continued to have their homosexual favorites, as they had for ages past, but with the administration of government now in the hands of a professional bureaucracy, imperial favorites had little or no influence in the course of government, and thus were of little interest to the court historians who no longer included them in the imperial biographies. Instead of the lives of the court aristocracy which had been the principal focus of the literature of earlier periods, stories and novels of the Ming deal with the lives and loves of ordinary Chinese — shopkeepers, soldiers, poets and minor officials — and provide us with a view of a society in which homosexual loves existed side by side with the social obligations of heterosexual marriage.

Though some moral handbooks of the day continued to disapprove of homosexuality, it is plain that this was not a widely held view. The lack of seriousness with which moral proscriptions on homosexuality were regarded is illustrated in a scene in a humorous Ming story in which the judge of hell is to decide on the punishment to be given to four recently deceased men who were guilty of various sins. The sinners include a young man guilty of frequenting female prostitutes, a man who used fragrant woods in building his house in violation of regulations on sensuality, a man who liked to sing, as well as a man who liked to indulge in homosexuality. To equate homosexuality with such trivial "sins" as singing or using fragrant woods, as the author does, shows that it was considered a minor transgression, if that, and at any rate no worse than consorting with prostitutes, which, as we have seen, only came under disapproval with the revival of family-oriented morality under the Neo-Confucians. Indeed, the author chose the sins in the story precisely because of their relative triviality in order to mock the moral prudery of the ascetic Buddhist and Neo-Confucian preachers. The punishments chosen for these "sins" are just as ludicrous: they were all to be reincarnated as flying creatures — a butterfly, a swallow, an oriole, and for the man guilty of homosexuality, a bee, "with sucking mouth and stinging tail."[62]

The commonplace pursuit of homosexual relationships alongside heterosexual marriage during the Ming dynasty is illustrated in a story of Li Yu, one of the most widely read authors of the period. The story, "The House of Gathered Refinements," depicts two well educated young men who refuse to take the official examinations to enter the bureaucracy "because of the vulgarity of using learning to pursue a career." Instead they opened a boutique where they could indulge their refined tastes in books, flowers, incense and antiques. Though the two young men, Jin and Liu, were both married, they took in a beautiful youth as a lover, whom they shared, or as the story put it, "the two friends shared a single Long Yang." Long Yang was a euphemism for homosexual love taken from the name of a lover of a ruler of the ancient Zhou dynasty, and its use is comparable to the use in Renaissance Europe of the name of Zeus' youthful lover, Ganymede, to denote a younger lover. While Jin and Liu went home at night to their families, the youth, Quan, slept at the shop. Jin and Liu "each took turns accompanying him for one night. Under the pretense of 'guarding the shop,' in fact, they enjoyed the flowers of the rear courtyard."[63]

Because of their sophisticated tastes and witty conversation, the shop became a great success among the educated and powerful of the day, all of whom, the story notes, "had the desires of Long Yang." Among those attracted to the shop was "a powerful and corrupt official, Yan Shifan," who immediately took an interest in the beautiful Quan. But Quan had no desire to reciprocate Yan Shifan's interest and wished to remain with his two lovers. "He is not a male prostitute for accompanying officials," Jin and Liu insisted, evidently alluding to another commonplace practice. Yan then ordered Quan to appear before him, and attempted to hire him as a "favorite," but still Quan refused. Growing ever more lustful toward the youth, Yan locked Quan in his quarters for several nights, but Quan repeatedly resisted his advances. Finally Yan had no option but to let him go, but then planned vengeance for this commoner's rejection of him. He went to another powerful official named Sha and told him of Quan's sophisticated familiarity with books and antiques, and told him he should castrate the youth and take him on as a personal servant. Sha invited the youth to see him, and served him drugged wine. After Quan passed out, Sha had his servants perform the operation on the unconscious Quan. "First they undressed him, grasped Quan's penis and scrotum, gently sliced them off, and tossed them on the floor where the dog scampered over to gobble them up." Waking from his sleep, Quan discovered what they had done, and vowed revenge for the violence done to him. A short while after Quan assumed his duties as Sha's servant, Sha died, and Quan was taken into the imperial court as a retainer. When Quan told the emperor what Yan Shifan had done to him, the outraged emperor had Yan beheaded. Quan received final retribution by using Yan's skull as a urinal, saying, "You cut off my testicles, I got rid of your head — the high is exchanged for the low."[64]

In this story we see the variety of sexual relationships that could be observed during Ming China. The relationship of the married Jin and Liu with Quan, while based on deep affection, was typical of the sort of class structured hierarchical homosexual relationships that were a feature of Chinese society from the earliest dynasties. But there was an added feature in the relationship of Jin and Liu with each other, which is implied in the story in the narrator's comment on how completely "three people acted as one," suggesting that theirs was a ménage à trois, in which the sexual bonds existed between the older men as well as between them and their younger lover. Yet at the same time Jin and Liu remained devoted to their heterosexual marriages, a state to which Quan also aspired himself, at least before his castration. Finally there was the coercive relations Yan Shifan sought with Quan, a type of sexual relationship brought about by the exercise of class privileges and intimidation that, unfortunately, was also none to infrequent during the long history the Chinese.[65]

The type of coercive relationship that could be attempted by the wealthy and powerful with young men of a lower class is illustrated in another Ming story, which tells of a young actor who becomes the lover of an older man. However their happy relationship is interrupted by a wealthy villain who kidnaps the beautiful youth and takes him into his household. The young actor refuses to submit to the villain's approaches, and commits suicide to escape him. The youth's spirit then returns from the afterlife to his former lover, takes revenge on the loathsome kidnapper, and returns in peace to the spirit world.

Homosexual relationships between upper-class men and good-looking lower-class males weren't necessarily forced or unpleasant for the younger man. In the Ming novel *The Golden Lotus*, considered a masterpiece of erotic fiction, the wealthy Ximen Qing, after pursuing sex in innumerable ways with his wife and concubines and still finding himself unsatisfied, turns his attention to one of his servants, a handsome youth, Shutong, who responds, "I will do your bidding in all things." As a result of satisfying his master's sexual appetites, Shutong rises in position and influence in the household. But eventually he is forced to run away, after one of his female rivals finds him making love with another of the women of the house.[66] The sexual role that the servant Shutong finds himself in is reminiscent of the customs in ancient Rome where good looking males among the household servants were often employed for sexual use, as is the bisexuality apparent in both the master of the house and Shutong.

But unlike the Romans, the Ming Chinese had no qualms about sexual passivity in a masculine male, as occurred in another Ming story, the *Chronicle of Chivalric Love*. The story relates the comradely love between two men, one of whom had earned a reputation as a valiant soldier. One night after drinking heavily the two of them went to bed. After the soldier, Zhang had fallen asleep, his companion, Zhong, proceeded to sexually penetrate him. "In his drunken dream state, Zhang felt he was no longer in control of his body.... It felt like a sting, but didn't sting. He wanted to take it into himself, but wasn't able.... So buried in sleep he was that he didn't seem to know whether his body was a man's or a woman's." After this, the two of them became devoted lovers. When Zhang had to return to his duty as a soldier, he went into battle and again showed his valor on the battlefield. When Zhang returned to his lover after the battle, they joyously embraced together in a passionate ecstasy:

> Zhong became slow and gentle, giving tight thrusts and cautious pulls. In a short while waves of passion gushed forth from Zhang's cave of sin and sprayed out like jade mist. The waves of passion, rich and milky, flowed against the current and, wending past his coccyx, wetted the bamboo mat below. The waves of passion, frothing and surging, first streamed forth along the length of Zhong's member, then soaked downward along his body."[67]

It is notable that in this story of masculine passion the two men were peers of equal status, rather than the hierarchical pairing of unequals so common in the Chinese homosexual tradition.

Homosexual Marriages in Fujian

The works of several Ming writers deal with a Chinese sexual tradition that recalls another facet of Roman homosexuality—same-sex marriages. These homosexual marriages were particularly prominent in the southern province of Fujian, a region renowned for centuries in China for its homosexual traditions. The men of Fujian, according to the Ming writer Shen Defu, "are extremely fond of male beauty. No matter if rich or poor, handsome or ugly, they all find a companion of their own status ... they love each other and at the age of thirty they are still together, sleeping in the same bed like husband and wife.... Such passion can be so deep that it is not uncommon that two lovers, finding it impossible to continue their relationship, tie themselves up together and drown themselves."[68] Another Ming author, Li Yu, also wrote of the prominence of homosexual love in Fujian, writing that it was "the region foremost in passion for men." According to the anonymous historian of *Duanxiu Pian,* the men of Fujian "look at the young and handsome and remember them. They do not discuss literature and art, but instead notice new patronages (love relationships)." When officials retired in Fujian, it was the custom "for several young and handsome youths to come to his retirement party." The festivities would last for several days during which "favors would be continuous," that is, sexual liaisons were frequent. Though such a sexually licentious scene would have been appalling to the ascetic Neo–Confucians of the day, the youths were not criticized for their behavior. On the contrary, "these youths would find themselves recommended for important positions by the recipients of their charms."[69] A Dutch soldier, Hans Putnams, who visited Fujian in the early 17th century, confirmed the prevalence of male homosexuality in Fujian, complaining that men of the region were "filthy pederasts."[70]

A story of the popular Ming writer Li Yu provides a detailed view of the traditions surrounding same-sex marriages in Fujian. The story concerns Jifang, a brilliant and unusually handsome young scholar, a type that would have been considered the romantic ideal. According to Li Yu, in his youth, Jifang, "had been a catamite of extraordinary gifts, and many older friends gathered about him, dallying with him all day, vying for his favor .... The sight of him also made women boiling hot, but the sight of them turned him to ice." In fact, Jifang had such a well-developed dislike of women that he went on in the story to outline it in detail. Nonetheless, he bowed to social convention and married a woman and fulfilled his social duty by having a son with her. Tragically, his wife died during the childbirth, leaving Jifang to raise his young son by himself.

Some time later, after a series of natural disasters, the men of the area were ordered to attend special ceremonies in a temple in an attempt to placate the local deity. During their time in the temple grounds, the men decided to hold a beauty contest, to see which of the young men was the most alluring. That the men would use the occasion of religious ceremonies, called to propitiate the gods after a natural disaster, to have a contest with such obvious homosexual implications is a dramatic illustration of how different the Chinese attitudes to sex and religion were from those of their European contemporaries. In that very same period Europeans were blaming homosexual activity as *the cause* of natural disasters, and were burning men at the stake for homosexual acts.

The winner of the beauty contest was a fourteen-year-old youth named Ruiji, whose extraordinary good looks so captivated the young widower Jifang that on the spot he decided he wanted to marry the youth. At this point the writer, Li Yu, inserts a brief note about the local wedding customs, apparently for non–Fujianese readers. "In Fujian the southern custom is the same as that for women. One tries to discern a youth for whom this is the first marriage. If he is a virgin, men are willing to pay a large bride price." Li Yu explains that the male-male marriage customs even include marriage ceremonies. "They do not skip the three cups of tea or the six wedding rituals — it is just like a proper marriage with a formal wedding." Then, in accordance with custom, Jifang went to the youth's father to ask for his son's hand in marriage, and because, as the Li Yu explains, the bride price for a male youth in Fujian can be very high — especially if he is extremely beautiful — Jifang was forced to sell all of his land in order to come up with the amount needed. [71]

After the marriage ceremonies Jifang and Ruiji settled down in a household where Jifang showed exceptional devotion to his beloved. But Jifang's happiness was clouded by the thought that under Chinese tradition Ruiji will some day have to find a wife and get married. Ruiji, out of gratitude for the love Jifang had shown for him, decided to do away with the source of Jifang's worries: "Better to cut if off and put an end to all the trouble it's going to cause me."[72] And so Ruiji went and had himself castrated.

Even after this sacrifice of Ruiji, the couple's happiness didn't last long. Other men in the area, jealous of Jifang for monopolizing the beautiful Ruiji, went to the local prefect, complaining that Ruiji's castration was against the law. The prefect, also jealous of Ruiji, ordered Jifang flogged for unlawfully castrating Ruiji, a violation of Confucian precepts on fertility. Ruiji then explained to the prefect that he had himself castrated, out of gratitude for Jifang's devotion. At this the prefect ordered Ruiji flogged for the self-mutilation, but when Ruiji disrobed in preparation for the punishment — and the gathering crowd rushed forward to catch a glimpse of his beautiful flesh — Jifang could bear it no longer and pleaded with the prefect to allow him to be beaten in Ruiji's place. Jifang then took Ruiji's place, and was beaten so severely that he was mortally wounded. On his deathbed Jifang told Ruiji that the men of the area brought this terrible calamity on them because they coveted him, and were jealous of the happiness the two of them had enjoyed. Jifang warned Ruiji that after his death the men would plot over him, and so told him that he should flee the area and take his young son away and raise him for him. Ruiji dutifully carried out his lover's deathbed wishes, moved to a different region, and went to work in a shoe shop so he could support them, and see to the child's education.

While the story is mainly a tale celebrating the extraordinary devotion of the two lovers, the homosexual marriage which provides the context of the story provides a view of a custom that seems to have been commonplace among men in Fujian throughout the Ming dynasty and the Ching dynasty that followed. More details about the same-sex marriage customs in Fujian are provided by Shen Defu. According to Shen Defu, the relationships were typically between an older male, referred to as the *quixiong*, "adoptive older brother," and a youth, *qidi*, "adoptive younger brother." The fraternal terms and the characterization of the relationship as one of adoption is similar to the legal arrangements used in some same-sex Roman marriages After the marriage ceremony, the younger partner would move in with his older lover's family, where he would be treated as a son-in-law. During the marriage relationship, which could last as long as twenty years, the older lover was entirely responsible for his lover's upkeep. When the inevitable time came for the younger partner to yield to social obligation and get married to raise a family, it was the older lover who would pay the bride price necessary to acquire a suitable bride for his beloved. The varied details of the same-sex marriage customs provided by Ming writers — the use of a formal ceremony to mark the marriage, the special terms for older and younger partner, the acceptance of the younger partner into the older lover's family, the expectations of the older partner for the upkeep of his lover and in his role in the acquisition of a bride for the younger man — attest to a long established tradition. Indeed, in Fujian there was even a deity who was the patron of homosexual marriages, to whom the men of the region dedicated sacrifices.[73]

The information we have on homosexual life in Fujian — the all-male retirement parties featuring overt homosexual liaisons, the conspicuous role of homosexual relations in promoting a young man's career, the cultic rites involving all men, elaborate same-sex marriage customs, and even a patron god of same-sex marriages — point to not only an open acceptance of homosexuality as a common feature of male sexuality, but to a level of participation of the men of the region in homosexual relationships on a scale comparable to the societies of classical Greece and Rome.

Lesbian Love in Ming Literature

The popular novels written under the Ming dynasty give us information on another aspect of sexuality that was shared with the Greeks and Romans — same-sex love among women. Literature from earlier periods contained occasional instances of eroticism between women, but because of the male-oriented nature of earlier works, discussions of sexuality that didn't include men were rare. The increased attention given by Ming writers to stories of love between women may in part be due to a greater openness toward sexual matters under the Ming. Another factor may be that with the great proliferation of vernacular literature and the growing literacy of the population, the material explored by writers continued to expand, as compared to earlier periods, so that where lesbian relationships might have been implied in the past, Ming writers would depict that aspect of sexuality in much more detail.

In the novel *Flower Shadows on a Window Blind*, two young girls just coming of age begin to discover their awakening sexuality, first teaching each other kissing lip to lip and tongue to tongue, but soon begin to explore more. When they hear a couple in an adjoining room making love, they get in bed with each other, and mimic the lovemaking they had heard others talk about. The girls' involvement with each other is portrayed by the writer as a natural part of growing up.[74] In a play of the widely read Ming author Li Yu, *Pitying the Fragrant Companion*, a married woman is in love with a younger, unmarried woman. The older woman prays that she would be turned into a man so she could marry the younger woman. When that miracle fails to occur, she takes to wearing men's clothes and marries the younger girl. No sooner were they married than they were separated. Finally, the older woman convinces her husband to take the younger woman in as his concubine, which he agrees to, to the delight of all three of them, who then share a ménage à trois.[75] Suggestions of an easy acceptance of lesbianism among the Chinese are also found in descriptions of sexual acts in literary works that sometimes describe the involvement of two woman and a man, such as in the following passage:

> Lady Precious Yin and Mistress White Jade lay on top of each other, their legs entwined so that their jade gates (vaginas) pressed together. They then moved in a rubbing and jerking fashion against each other like fishes gobbling flies or water plants from the surface. As they became more excited, the "mouths" widen, and choosing his position carefully, Great Lord Yang thrusts between them with his jade root (penis). They moved in unison until all three shared the ultimate simultaneously."[76]

The works of Ming writers mention lesbianism among Buddhist and Taoist nuns, a confirmation of long-held popular suspicions.

Ming literature also detailed the variety of ways in which women could find sexual satisfaction with each other. Aside from rubbing the genitals together, referred to as "grinding the bean curd" by the Chinese, women might also engage in cunnilingus, manual stimulation of the genital area and the use of sex toys. Olisboi, a device like a dildo made of wood, ivory or plant fibers, were quite common, many of them with double heads which would allow simultaneous vaginal penetration by both partners. Women could also place hollow metal balls inside their vaginas to increase sexual sensations.

Marriage relationships between women were not uncommon in some regions. In a typical relationship, two women, one designated the "husband" and the other the "wife," would formalize their union in a ceremony in which they would exchange gifts, as was the practice in normal heterosexual marriage ceremonies. At the conclusion of the ritual the female friends of the couple who witnessed the ceremony would join them in a feast. The two married women sometimes adopted female children, who were then entitled to inherit property from the parents of the couple. These lesbian marriages, called "Golden Orchid Associations," were particularly common in Guangdong province, which lay on the eastern border of Fujian province, the center of the male-male marriage tradition.

Evidence from Ming literature, then, shows that homosexuality among women was very likely just as frequent among women as among men during the period. Given the lack of prohibitions against homosexuality from the earliest dynasties, it seems probable that same-sex love would have been as common among women as it had been among men down through the course of Chinese history, even though the orientation of the literature around the lives of men caused it to be rarely mentioned before the time of the Ming.

Qing Dynasty

Under the Ming Dynasty's nearly three hundred years of rule, China had enjoyed several prolonged periods of stability and prosperity. During these peaceful times, scholarship flourished, great libraries were founded, the science of medicine advanced, and art and literature reached ever new heights of sophistication. However, beginning in the 16th-century, under a succession of weak emperors, exploited by powerful ministers, the central government began to deteriorate, a situation that was exacerbated by partisan strife in the vast bureaucracy. The government was further weakened by a lengthy campaign to push back a Japanese invasion of the kingdom of Korea, a Chinese vassal and protectorate. As a result, during the early 17th century, the Ming found it increasingly difficult to beat back a series of invasions by the Manchu. Originally a dynasty of far eastern Manchuria, the Manchu by the late 16th-century had gradually taken control over all of Manchuria and had occupied at various times

Chinese territory down to the suburbs of Beijing. Finally, in 1644, the Manchu, ostensibly coming to the aid of the Ming ruler to help oust a local rebel who had captured the capital at Beijing, seized the throne for themselves, bringing Ming rule to an end and setting up the Qing Dynasty, who then reigned until the 20th century.

The first acts of the new Manchu emperor were to restore order and tighten moral standards after nearly a century of declining moral standards that had accompanied the political disorder. The Manchus brought with them a somewhat austere attitude to sexuality, a reflection of their rural, agrarian background, and sought to restore order to society by re-establishing the age-old Confucian norms, which emphasized a family-oriented sexuality morality. Whereas the Ming period was an era of individual self-expression, under the Qing the pendulum swung back to stricter conformance with moral constraints.

As part of efforts to restore traditional moral standards, the first of the Manchu rulers, known as the Kangxi emperor, turned his attention to homosexual practices, especially acts of violence or exploitation. The emperor first tried to bring a halt to the more exploitative practices of the period, such as the purchase of boys from their families in the south for the purpose of employing them as prostitutes in the northern cities, a frequent occurrence. He also promulgated several new laws dealing with different kinds of homosexual rape, with varying penalties depending on the age of the victim, the degree of violence used in the assault and other considerations. In a society in which male homosexuality was a common phenomenon, it was inevitable that male-male rape would be a recurring problem, and indeed literature of the day includes numerous references to homosexual rapes. There is no doubt that the Kangxi emperor himself had a clear distaste for homosexuality: he even had three male favorites of his son executed when he discovered his son's sexual involvement with them.[77] He also put into law a provision punishing consensual homosexual relations, the first in Chinese history, though the punishment, a month in jail and 100 blows, was extremely mild compared to punishments handed down in the West at that time, and was light even compared to the punishment for other sexual offenses in Chinese law. Considering the lenience of the punishment, it is likely that the law was less a judgment on the morality of homosexuality than it was an attempt at promoting a family-oriented sexual morality, after decades of social chaos under the late Ming.

In any event, it is clear that the anti-homosexual law, like those of the late Roman Empire, was never seriously enforced, because abundant evidence survives in the literature of the period and in the reports of foreign visitors that testifies to the prevalence of homosexual practices throughout the fabric of Chinese life under Manchu rule. The Manchu emperors themselves, finding the seductions of the sophisticated Chinese civilization too hard to resist, gradually abandoned their rustic outlook, and consequently some of them even began keeping male favorites. The ubiquity of homosexuality in government and court life under the Qing was remarked on by Sir John Barrow, a late eighteenth-century visitor, who complained that "the commission of this detestable and unnatural act is attended with so little sense of shame, or feelings of delicacy, that many of the first officers of the state seemed to make no hesitation in publicly avowing it. Each of these officers is constantly attended by his pipe-bearer, who is generally a handsome boy, from fourteen to eighteen years of age, and is always well dressed." Another report which appeared in a Western journal in 1835 expressed similar disgust at "this abominable practice, which exists to a great extent, in almost every part of the empire, and particularly in the very officers of the 'shepherds of the people,' the guardians of the morals of the celestial empire."[78]

The pervasiveness of the male homosexual aesthete in upper class Chinese society was also noted by a writer during the rule of the Kangzi emperor himself, who wrote that "it is considered in bad taste not to keep elegant man servants on one's household staff, and undesirable not to have singing boys around when inviting guests for dinner." Writers of the day were steeped in the details of the long tradition of homosexual love in literary and court life. The great Qing literary master Zhao Yi demonstrated his familiarity with this history by listing men from ancient times known for their homosexual loves. His list went back as far as the Shang Dynasty (1766 B.C.), and enumerated many of the well known lovers and favorites of the Zhou and Han dynasties (approximately 1200 B.C. to A.D. 200). In referring to homosexual love, writers still used the ancient euphemisms for homosexual love, such as "followers of Dong Xian," or those with the "passion of the cut sleeve."[79]

In the art of the period, the reticence and discretion in regards to sex that was observed in earlier periods was abandoned, with the result that erotic art was produced showing both hetero- and homosexual intercourse. An early British embassy official was shocked to come across a marble statue in the Imperial Palace depicting two youths engaged, as he put it, "in the vice of the Greeks."[80] In another example, a painting depicting a man and women engaging in copulation shows a second man inserting his erect penis into the rear of the first man. Like some of the erotic art from classical Greece and Rome, the artists distinguished between the active and passive partner in homosexual intercourse by rendering the passive partner in lighter tones.

In the popular literature produced under the Manchu, homosexual love is shown alongside heterosexual love as a feature of the lives of individuals from all walks of life, across all social strata. In one of the most famous novels of the period, Cao Xueqin's *Dream of the Red Chamber*, a humorous passage depicts a drunken page boy stumbling around propositioning the other young male servants, while at the same time in another room the master of the house is involved in an adulterous heterosexual tryst. In the garden of the house, a young woman named Parfumee comes across a girlfriend burning offerings and finds that her friend was mourning the death of another young woman who had been her lover. Parfumee herself had her own sexual relationships with other young women in the household. In another scene, a boorish young man named Xue Pan crudely propositions a handsome young actor, on the popular assumption that actors are generally sexually available. Instead of the easy liaison he was expecting, Xue Pan is severely beaten by the young man, Liu Xianglian, who turns out to be a young Chinese aristocrat who was acting because of falling on hard times. The actor is not offended by the suggestion implicit in the proposition that he would engage in homosexual activity, but by the insult implied to someone of his stature submitting to one so crude. Throughout the novel, the author uses the character of Xue Pan as a comic foil to the sophistication and grace of his wealthy cousin, the protagonist, Baoyu, a handsome young aristocrat, who in another scene displays subtlety and wit in cleverly seducing another young male actor. Jealous of Baoyu, the loutish Xue Pan tells Baoyu's father of his son's relationship with a commoner of the most despised social class which further strains the already difficult relationship between Baoyu and his prudish father.[81]

Another passage finds Baoyu with his dearest friend, Qin Zhong, at a school, where what the author calls "the passion of Lord Long Yang" runs rampant. Both Baoyu and Qin Zhong are themselves enticed by a charming pair of students. Qin Zhong is later embarrassed when a classmate gleefully tells the other students that he found Qin Zhong with one of the pair "in the rear courtyard, kissing each other and feeling asses as plain as anything." While the other students have assumed that Baoyu and his friend Qin Zhong are lovers, the author provides only tantalizing hints about the extent of their friendship. A telling incident occurred when Baoyu discovers Qin Zhong making love to a young novitiate nun. Without making a sound, Baoyu rushed in, surprising them in the act. "Suddenly, in less time than it takes to tell, a third person bore down upon them from above and held them fast. The intruder made no sound, and for some moments the other two lay underneath his weight, half dead with fright. Then there was a sputter of suppressed laughter, and they knew that it was Baoyu." While the girl left in mortified haste, Qin Zhong implored Baoyu to keep his illicit meeting with the girl a secret. To which Baoyu cryptically replied, "Wait until we are both in bed and I'll settle accounts with you then!" The author then coyly added, "As for the 'settling of accounts' that Baoyu had proposed to Qin Zhong, we have not been able to ascertain exactly what form this took; and as we would not for the world be guilty of fabrication, we must allow the matter to remain a mystery."[82]

Fiction under the Qing dynasty also frequently featured humorous or ribald vignettes dealing with the relations between wealthy upper class men and the male prostitutes with whom they dallied. One such scene appears in *Dream of the Red Chamber*, where a gambling party is depicted attended by Baoyu's cousin, Xue Pan, and several other of Baoyu's more debased relatives, accompanied by a number of young male servants, "all pages of fifteen or under. There was also a pair of male prostitutes, powdered, overdressed youths of seventeen or eighteen." The two prostitutes fawned over the older males, plying them with drink and affection, but they don't attempt to conceal the fact that their interest in the men was purely mercenary. When the fortunes of one of the gamblers took a turn for the worse, the two youths abandoned him and directed their attentions to the player who was then winning. The drunken loser loudly complained that they were ungrateful, and were forgetting his past favors to them, to which they cheerily replied: "Don't be angry with us, dear old friend. We are only children. We have to do what we are told. Our teacher always tells us ... the person who at any moment has the most money is the one you must be nice to." At this, another guest coarsely interjected, "He's only lost a bit of money, hasn't he? He hasn't lost his prick!" at which the revelers burst into raucous laughter.[83]

Despite the early attempts of the Qing rulers to regulate prostitution, young male prostitutes, who by the Qing had acquired the nickname of "rabbits," were widely available throughout Manchu China, especially in the northern cities. There were prostitutes who catered to all social classes, from aristocrats and scholars to common laborers, working their trade in venues that ranged from the most elegant mansions to the tawdry stalls of the public baths. The sheer numbers of male prostitutes in the cities of the period is suggested by an account of a Western visitor to the coastal city of Tianjin in 1860 who wrote of the 35 male brothels in that city, housing as many as 800 young males, all "trained for pederastic prostitution."[84]

The most elite of the male prostitutes were actors, a profession that had a strong association with prostitution at least since the time of the Jin Dynasty (A.D. 265–420). Scholars have offered various reasons for the strong connection between acting and prostitution. In the acting schools, a youth's handsome appearance was cultivated as much as his talents, making the theaters a natural source of attractive young males trained in getting the most out of their looks. Further, since females were forbidden to participate in the theater, young males would play female roles on stage, and often carried that role into their off-stage life, making them naturally receptive to the advances of theater patrons. Another obvious factor is the extra income a poorly paid young actor would receive from prostitution. Finally, the theater was outside the family-oriented world contemplated by Confucian ethical norms, and so the actors would have been regarded as "fair game" to the theater patrons out looking for a night's entertainment. The works of numerous authors over many centuries make clear that the Chinese public universally regarded all actors to be homosexually inclined and readily available for sex.

Many of the actors came from the south, and as young boys had been purchased from their parents under a multi-year contract with the acting school under which the teacher would be paid for the schooling out of earnings the youth received for prostitution. In their lessons, the boys were trained in the erotic arts as well as in stagecraft. As described by one observer, they were taught to "speak and walk in the most charming manner and to use their eyes with great efficacy." To enhance their looks, they applied a special broth to their faces, had a special diet, and rubbed ointments on their bodies at night. Consequently, according to another description, if an actor, "has a clean, white complexion, and is unusually good looking, it is safe to assume that he has other skills unknown to outsiders."[85]

In order to prepare the students for anal intercourse, according to the writer, We Shan Shen, the boys sat in the acting class on benches fitted with round wooden pegs which each student would insert into his anus to stretch it. The benches in the rear, on which the newest students sat, had smaller pegs, with the pegs growing progressively larger as the student advanced in his studies. When at last he was ready to be graduated, he was "initiated" into anal intercourse, which, according to tradition, would be with his teacher.[86] Sometimes the training of a prostitute could be brutal, as in a story in the early Qing collection, *Hairpins Beneath His Cap,* in which a 16-year-old student, Li Youxian, is tied up and raped until the sensation of being penetrated became pleasurable.[87]

While for centuries young male actors were universally assumed to be homosexual prostitutes, and so looked on by moralists as spreaders of moral degeneracy, not all of the encounters between the actors and their patrons were of the tawdry commercial variety. Relations of love and tenderness between an actor and his patron were not unknown, and in fact some of those involved in these relationships went on to become devoted lovers for life. The great 19th-century erotic novel by Chen Sen, *Precious Mirror of Ranking Flowers,* was inspired by one such relationship, which occurred between a prominent eighteenth-century official, Bi Yuan (1730–1797), renowned as a politician and scholar, and a prominent actor, Li Guiguan. After years living the life of an actor/prostitute Li Guiguan welcomed the attention of Bi Yuan, and saw in his love for him a way to escape the life of the stage. The two exchanged vows of fidelity and lived the rest of their lives together in a relationship that was regarded by Bi Yuan's friends as a marriage.[88]

In some instances the situation between actor and patron was reversed, where it was the young actor pursuing the patron. One such case was described by the eighteenth-century poet Yuan Mei in his account of his first meeting with a desirable young actor, Xu Yunting:

All the Hanlin scholars were crazy about him .... I was young and good looking, but I was so poorly dressed that I did not think Yunting could possibly regard me as worth cultivating. But I noticed on one occasion that he often glanced my way and smiled, quite with the air of indicating that he had taken a fancy to me. I hardly dared to believe this, and did not try to get into touch with him. However, very early next day I heard a knock at my door. There he was, and we were soon on the most affectionate terms.[89]

Another 19th-century novel, *A Mirror of Theatrical Life,* a work set in the world of the theater, and based in part on actual personalities of the period, also dwelt on the interplay of patrons and actors. Of course, many of the relationships were purely mercenary and base, as would be expected between actor/prostitutes and their vulgar patrons. But here, too, relationships are described between officials and actors which reach an elevated level of passionate romance. According to the scholar Lu Hsun, "The whole novel is filled with tender and romantic sentiments, the only difference [from heterosexual romances] being that the 'beauties' are young men."[90]

By the mid-nineteenth-century the continual condemnation of homosexuality by Western missionaries, who had been working in China for several centuries, began to have an effect on social attitudes to same-sex love. The anti-homosexual attitudes of Christian preachers and other Western visitors served to reinforce the anti-homosexual leanings of Neo-Confucianists and prudish government officials, so that an atmosphere of disapproval of homosexual love began to spread across Chinese society. Thus, we have a character in *Precious Mirror of Ranking Flowers* lament the new intolerance: "I do not comprehend why it is acceptable for a man to love a woman, but is unacceptable for a man to love a man. Passion is passion whether to a man or a woman. To love a woman but not a man is lust and not passion. To lust is to forget passion. If one treasures passion, he is not lewd."[91]

The growing cloud of intolerance to same-sex love that was overtaking the country, then, lends a wistful cast to an eloquent encomium to the ideal of homosexual love given by another character in the novel, an expression of sentiment that seems to sum up the elevated view of male beauty and same-sex passion that ran through Chinese literature from the earliest dynasties:

> Across tens of thousands of miles of territory, through five thousand years of history, nothing and nobody is better than a male favorite.... Elegant flowers, beautiful women, a shining moon, rare books, grand paintings — these beautiful things are liked by everyone. However, these beautiful things are not all combined. Male favorites are like elegant flowers and not grass or trees; they are like beautiful women who do not need make-up; they are like a shining moon or tender cloud, yet can be touched and played with; they are like rare books and grand paintings, and yet they can talk and converse.... The loss of a favorite cannot be compensated for by any beauty in history. The gain of a favorite makes the loss of any beauty of the past a small matter."[92]

By the late 19th century, the power of the Qing rulers had seriously deteriorated as a result of the combined effects of social unrest brought about by the ever widening economic inequality, the disasters of the Boxer rebellion, defeat in the Sino-Japanese war, machinations of the military leadership and, not least, the sheer ineptitude of the imperial court in confronting the challenges brought by the presence of Western colonial powers in East Asia. The last Qing emperor finally abdicated in 1912, leaving no heir, with all power now residing in the new republican government of Sun Yat-sen. With the demise of the four thousand year old imperial government, the increasing dominance of Western moral attitudes, and the introduction of Western practices into government, the military, business and education, many age-old customs and beliefs of the Chinese cultural tradition fell by the wayside. Thus, as China moved into the 20th century, homosexuality came to be widely disapproved in Chinese society, while the ancient and rich history of same-sex love in China was completely forgotten by the Chinese public.

Conclusion

The literature produced since the Chinese acquired the art of writing under the late Shang dynasty provides a detailed picture of a continual and vibrant tradition of homosexual love. The documentary evidence of this long tradition, over three thousand years of Chinese literary history, is unprecedented among societies of the world, and provides additional proof of the natural prevalence of homosexual behavior in societies where, as C.E. Tripp puts it, "it is merely approved."[93] Given the unusually well documented tradition over such a vast period of time, it is no small irony that Chinese today uniformly deny the existence of a tradition of homosexuality in China's past. This fact is a testament to the power of the heterosexual mindset that that pervades Western cultures and that was imported into non-Western societies as they came under the political and economic influence of America and the European powers, becoming westernized in the process.

The patterns of homosexual relationships and role of homosexuality in Chinese society as revealed in its long literary history are strikingly similar to those found in ancient Rome, where a man was free to pursue sexual satisfaction outside marriage as long as his family obligations were met. The widespread occurrence among both the Chinese and the ancient Romans of homosexuality among youth who later went on to marriage, and among married men strongly suggests that, absent the sort of strict moral taboos present in the West, this sort of bisexuality, which appears to be a product of the natural character of male sexuality, would be a widespread practice among males. Sexual relationships that were found among Chinese and ancient Roman women, before or to supplement a marital relationship, suggest that these, too, are a natural aspect of the sexuality of females. The presence among both societies of hierarchical or status ordered relationships among males underscores as well the universally strong tendency of males to form such relationships. And the clear evidence of individuals throughout Chinese history who would have been exclusively homosexual were it not for the obligation to marry attests to the variability in the degree of sexual orientation of individuals that is, again, a trait shared with people in cultures around the world. The sexual customs and practices displayed by the Chinese over their history, then, are consistent with those found in other societies throughout the world, and give additional testimony to the universal presence of this facet of human sexuality among the peoples of the world.

Since homosexuality was found to be so common in China, one might suppose that homosexuality could be found in other Asian countries, since those societies share a similar religious history, largely devoid of the fierce hostility to same-sex love found in the West. Indeed, the hierarchical homosexuality among males found to be so prevalent in China was also reported by ethnographers to be quite common in 17th-century Siam and in 19th-century Indo-China.[94] Homosexuality was also reported to be a normal feature of youth in Korea before the modern era.[95] And among the Japanese, another venerable homosexual tradition can be found that dates back almost to the origins of Japanese culture, itself. The same-sex practices in Japan, and particularly the homosexual customs of the Samurai knights, which bear a fascinating similarity to the homosexual tradition of the ancient Greeks, will be explored in the next chapter.

11

Monks and Warriors: A Thousand Years of Noble Love in Japan

In 804, amid the splendor of the Tang Dynasty at its peak, a young Japanese aristocrat arrived in Chang-an, the Tang capital. A member of one of early Japan's most illustrious noble families, Kukai had not journeyed to China as a government emissary, but rather to study under Hui-kuo, a great master of Indian esoteric Buddhism. Kukai immediately became the favorite disciple of the old master, who told Kukai that he had long expected him as one alone among his students capable of receiving his special esoteric knowledge. The next year, when the master was dying, he honored Kukai by anointing him as his successor, and from his deathbed transmitted the esoteric knowledge to him. Kukai then returned to Japan and, under the emperor's auspices, began spreading the teachings of esoteric Buddhism. Soon he had scores of followers, and in 816 he built a monastery and temple on Mount Koya, in central Japan. The Mount Koya monastery became the center of what was to become one of the two principal branches of Buddhism in Japan, *Shingon*. Because of his seminal work in the development of Buddhism in Japan, Kukai, or Kobo Daishi, as he became known to later generations, is today one of Japan's most revered saints, with a stature somewhat analogous to the place of Saint Paul among Christians. But according to Japanese folk tradition this great saint introduced another venerable tradition to Japan — same-sex love — which he was said to have learned while studying in China.

Though it is now a little-known aspect of their history, homosexuality played a major role in Japanese social institutions for over a thousand years. Homosexual relationships between Buddhist monks and novice students were not only a major feature of monastery life for many centuries, but the aesthetic and spiritual appreciation of the beauty of the monks' youthful lovers, who were regarded in early times as incarnations of the "Divine Child," became inextricably bound up with the beliefs and traditions of monastic Buddhism in Japan. Among the Samurai knights and their squire protégés, the mores of homosexual love became intertwined with the knightly code of honor in a tradition that rivaled the idealism of the warrior-lovers of ancient Greece.

Today, if this long heritage of same-sex love is mentioned by Japanese writers or historians at all, it is in expressions of dismay at a peculiar vice of the *ancien régime*, an ancient dishonor best forgotten, or a sign of the lack of moral development of early Japanese society.[1] As a consequence, this long-running tradition is virtually unknown among modern day Japanese. Like contemporary Chinese, today's Japanese regard homosexuality in their society as an imported Western phenomenon alien to traditional Japanese culture, when in fact the suppression of this ancient homosexual tradition is, ironically, *the result* of the westernization of Japanese culture. Just as the adoption of Western clothing and architectural styles led to a virtual abandonment of traditional Japanese architecture and dress in much of the country, the importing of Western sexual attitudes has caused the Japanese to regard this once hallowed tradition as "a deficiency or sexual anomaly."[2] As a result, the carnal nature of love among monks and their apprentices is denied, the tradition of passionate love of knight for squire that inspired the samurai in battle is omitted in popular samurai films, and homosexual elements have been cleansed from other cultural traditions, such as the *noh* theater, an ancient art form imbued with a homosexual aesthetic, which loses much of its meaning when shorn of its same-sex content.

The Jesuits Confront an Oriental Sexual Tradition

Early missionaries to Japan were well aware of widespread homosexuality among the Japanese. The Jesuit Saint Francis Xavier, who arrived in 1549, was appalled by the homosexuality he witnessed and the casual acceptance it received even in the monasteries.

> There are monks who love the sin abhorred by nature; they admit it themselves; they never deny it…. Nobody, neither man nor woman, young nor old, regards this sin as abnormal or abominable; this sin is well known among the monks, and is even a widespread custom amongst them …. The monks lodge many young sons of samurai within their monastery, and commit this crime with these boys whom they teach reading and writing. The public, even if it does not find it desirable, does not at all consider it outrageous, for it has been the custom for a long time already.

In 1550, visiting a large Zen monastery while en route to Kyoto, Xavier again found rampant homosexuality: "Amongst them the abominable vice against nature is so popular that they practice it without any feeling of shame. They have many young boys with whom they commit wicked deeds."

It was not just among the monks that the Jesuits found the sin of Sodom, but among the samurai warriors and their daimyo lords as well. As described by the Jesuit Alessandro Valegnani in 1579,

> The first evil we see among them is indulgence in sins of the flesh; this we always find among pagans …. The gravest of their sins is the most depraved of carnal desires, so that we may not name it. The young men and their partners, not thinking it serious, do not hide it. They even honor each other for it and speak openly of it…. In ancient Japan, I have been told, such a sin did not exist, and all lived in peace under the rule of a single king. But five or six centuries ago, an evil monk put forward the pernicious doctrine nowadays so widespread.

Valegnani went on to blame the nearly constant warfare of the Japanese feudal period on the sodomy of the Samurai knights: "What followed were incessant revolt and destruction until our own day. They have been struck by the sword of divine justice, and their crime has been punished."[3]

Of course the "evil monk" Valegnani referred to in this passage was the great Japanese saint, Kobo Daishi. By the time of the arrival of the missionaries in Japan, the legend attributing the founding of same-sex love to Kobo Daishi had been well established for centuries. But it is clear that the claim of the old folk tradition about Kobo Daishi and the origins of Japanese homosexuality is simply a myth. Aside from the fact that a tendency to homosexuality seems to be a universal human trait, found among societies the world over, with no reason that Japanese society should be an exception, there are references in the oldest Japanese literary sources to homosexual love relationships well before the time of Kobo Daishi.

The *Nihon Shoki*, the "Japanese Chronicles," compiled in 720, includes a story dating from the 3rd century concerning a mysterious darkness that had come over the land after two

Shinto priests, who, the story assumes, were homosexual lovers, were buried together in the same tomb. It was apparently a sin against the natural order for Shinto priests of different temples to be buried together. The resulting darkness was only dispelled when the Empress Jingu, who had discovered the cause of the strange phenomenon, had the priests reburied in separate graves, in separate locations. That the supernatural darkness was caused, according to the story, not by the homosexual relationship of the two priests, but because of the violation of ritual that occurred when priests of two different temples were buried together, suggests a familiarity with homosexual relationships during that early period, as well as a lack of moral concern for such homosexuality among the people of the time.[4]

The burial of two inseparable male friends in the same grave appears in another early work, *Shoku Nihon Gi*, "The Origin of Things in Japan." According to the story, the passionate love of the two men for each other was so intense that when one of them died, the other, unable to bear the grief, committed suicide and was buried in the same grave as his lover.[5] The same work also includes an account of a scandal involving a prince during the reign of Emperor Koken (A.D. 757), half a century before Kobo Daishi was supposed to have introduced homosexuality to Japan. The work relates a meeting of ministers called to discuss the "disorderly behavior" of the prince, whom they discovered had had sexual relations with a boy-servant before the mourning period for the previous emperor had ended. The writer's account makes clear that the offensive behavior of the prince was not that he engaged in homosexual relations with a servant, but that the sexual relations occurred during a time when the demands of ritual prohibited all sexual relations. Hence, the homosexual relationship, itself, between the prince and his servant was not of concern, and in fact it's likely that such relationships were as commonplace among the Japanese aristocrats of the period as they were among their counterparts in 8th-century China.[6]

It is beyond doubt, then, that homosexuality was a familiar aspect of Japanese life long before Kobo Daishi took his journey to study in China. It is most probable that the folk tradition crediting Kobo Daishi with the founding of homosexuality in Japan developed because of the conspicuous presence of a homosexual tradition in Buddhist monastery life from the earliest years of Buddhism in Japan. Because the people had for so long associated one with the other, it seems natural that the origins of homosexual customs in the country would become associated in the popular mind with the historic figure most famous for the spread of Buddhism in the country. Japanese folk tradition makes other claims of dubious accuracy about Kobo Daishi, such as his inventing *Kana*, the phonetic writing system used in Japan,[7] so it doesn't seem odd that he would be credited with another tradition long associated with the monasteries. In any event, by the time of the arrival of the Spanish missionaries, Kobo Daishi had become so strongly linked to homosexuality that his name had become synonymous with male homosexuality. In fact, a monastery text, containing instructions on the "mysteries of loving boys" was titled *Kobo Daishi's Book*.[8]

In contradiction of claims that the monks' affection for their disciples was entirely chaste, the text provides graphic proof of the sexual nature of the monks' interest in their students. The first part explains the hand signals students use to make their feelings known to the monks. The second section explores in greater detail how to determine a student's readiness for sex, offering advice on "how to recognize boys who are ready to be penetrated and how to prepare those who are not." The former are boys who display the quality of *nasake*, empathy for the sexual and emotional needs of the priest. But regardless of the boy's development, "no matter how lacking in sensitivity to the mysteries of love an acolyte may be, he can be made yours if you approach him right." In the case of such students, the book advises: "Stroke his penis, massage his chest, and then gradually move your hand to the area of his ass. By then he'll be ready for you to strip off his robe and seduce him without a word." The final section provides an astonishing illustration of how closely homosexual love was associated with spiritual practices in Japanese monastic Buddhism — instructions on anal copulation in a variety of Tantric meditative postures.[9]

Understanding just how homosexuality became enmeshed with Buddhist worship in early Japan requires an appreciation of the enormous difference between the way sex is regarded in religions of the East and in those of the West, and how the view of sex in Eastern religions harmonizes with the thrust of Buddhist mysticism. In some respects, the treatment of sex in Eastern religions is the exact opposite of the approach to sexuality in Christian doctrine. This is especially so in the rigidly anti-sexual attitudes, discussed in Chapter 9, that Augustine and some of the other Church Fathers borrowed from pagan Neo-Platonist philosophy and incorporated into Christian moral teachings. This negativity toward sex — which has at times approached the level of mass hysteria — has profoundly shaped Christian teachings on sexuality from late Roman times to the present.

In contrast, Buddhism and the religions of the East regard the natural world as a reflection of the beauty of the transcendent Divine. In the view of the *Shingon* Buddhism, and the mysticism of the Indian Buddhist sects from which it was derived, the entire universe is seen as the body of the Supreme Buddha, and hence the carnal expression of the physical body is nothing less than the play of the Divine in the physical world. The body and its needs and urges are not condemned or mistrusted, but respected as part of the universe of Divine creation. Indeed, under Japanese esoteric Buddhism and the Vajrayana Buddhism of India from which it stemmed, the sex act itself was seen as holy. This conception of sensual carnality as a reflection of the in-dwelling divinity is summarized a passage in the Rishu-kyo sutra, a Japanese version of an Indian text much admired by Kobo Daishi: "To say that voluptuousness is pure is a truth of the state of Bodhisattva (the manifest Buddha). To say that desire is pure is a truth of the state of Bodhisattva ... to say that physical pleasure is pure is a truth of the state of Bodhisattva.... And why? It is because all dharmas, all creatures, are in essence pure."[10] The appreciation by a monk of the sensual beauty of a youthful novice, then, was not far removed from an appreciation of the mystical beauty of the transcendent Buddha. And thus, in this perspective even homosexual copulation could be elevated to the level of spiritual devotion.

The worship of the transcendent Buddha through the appreciation of the beauty of a youthful student comports closely with another aesthetic preoccupation of the Japanese, the transitory beauty of cherry blossoms, fated to wither and blow away almost as soon as they appear. The contemplation of the brief display of the blossoms, which embody for the Japanese the impermanent beauty of the physical world, evokes for the Japanese the sense of pathos that attends the ephemeral universe. This, in turn, brings one to a realization of one of the essential truths of Buddhism, the temporality of life, and the sorrow that comes from attachment to earthly things. Accordingly, the 17th-century Japanese author Ihara Saikaku wrote of "a boy in the bloom of youth.... His blossom of youth falls cruelly to the ground.... Loving a boy can be likened to a dream that we are not given time to have."[11]

Love in the Monasteries

It is not known precisely how the tradition of love between monks and their young disciples got its start — it may simply have been a natural consequence of housing young teenaged male students in close quarters with celibate monks in a society with an absence of moral qualms about sexual relations between males. As in China, Buddhist monks were required to abstain from heterosexual marriage, but there were no rules prohibiting homosexual relations. However, several legendary episodes from the early days of Japanese Buddhism suggest a very early link between homosexuality and worship in Buddhist monasteries.

These early legends involve another figure prominent in the spread of Buddhism in the country, Saicho, founder of the second principal branch of Japanese Buddhism, *Tendai*. According to one of the legends, Saicho, who was living as a hermit on Mount Hiei, was walking in the forest one day when he came upon a beautiful, angelic boy. "Who are you, mysterious boy?" Saicho asked. The boy responded, "I am really the Divine Child who rules the world. I am the god of Dosei, also known as the *deva* of Nissho, the god of Yugyo or the Master Juzen. I assure you that your prayers will be answered." Saicho at once prostrated himself and worshiped the child, "Oh, my master Juzen, I offer you all my devotion. This mountain is truly sacred and fortunate." And on that very spot Saicho founded a monastery and temple, which became the center of *Tendai* Buddhism. In another story, Saicho was sailing in the Sea of Japan when a fierce storm arose, imperiling the boat and all on it. He went into prayer, and in that instant a beautiful, angelic boy appeared on the waves who identified himself as "Father of the *Tendai* teachings," and quieted the storm.[12]

According to the Japanese scholar Jun'Ichi Iwata, these legends are mythical representations of a very old Japanese cult under which it was believed that "the gods appear incarnate in the form of angelic boys."[13] The association of beautiful boys with the "incarnate gods," then, provided for the monks a spiritual framework in which to place the natural appreciation that they felt for the sensual beauty of the younger males, who, in the years following the establishment of the *Shingon* and *Tendai* sects, were sent by the nobility to the monasteries for their education. The monks would have been naturally sexually drawn to the good-looking, well-mannered boys in their midst, and, according to Iwata, because the boys were viewed as "gods incarnate," they were also objects of "worship and spiritual admiration." Because the beliefs of Japanese esoteric Buddhism actually encouraged the fulfillment of sexual desires, and given the absence of negativity toward homosexuality in the period, there would have been nothing to prevent the conflation of sexual love for the boys in the minds of the monks with a spiritual veneration of the Buddha which they saw manifesting in the boys' beauty. Hence the love of boys, or *chigo*, became an integral part of worship in the monasteries, a tradition that continued for many centuries. An indication of the preoccupation with the love of the *chigo* in the monasteries of Medieval Japan is found in the *Tendai* maxim, *Ichi chigo ni sanno*, "*Chigo* first, devotion to god* second," which, of course, would be regarded as the most heinous of blasphemies under Christian doctrine, but in fact underscores the union of spirituality and sensuality that occurs in Japanese mystical Buddhism.[14]

Homosexual Love in Early Literature

During the centuries following the establishment of the two great schools of Japanese Buddhism there was an explosion of culture centered on the imperial capital of Kyoto. The literature that resulted provides a view into the sexual practices of the period, including homosexuality. Since most of the stories produced at first dealt with the lives of the courtiers and their courtesans, and include a great number of stories of heterosexual romance, little can be gleaned about life in the monasteries. There is, however, a story containing a homosexual

*Referring to the patron god of the Tendai monastery on Mount Hiei.

episode in the most famous collection of the period, *The Tale of Genji*. In a story about Lord Genji and his preoccupation with an unyielding lady he desired, he finds himself rebuffed yet again and so consoles himself by making love to her handsome younger brother. "Well, you at least must not abandon me. Genji pulled the boy down besides him. The boy was delighted, such were Genji's youthful charms. Genji for his part, or so one is informed, found the boy more attractive than his chilly sister."[15] The story relates this homosexual incident in a non-judgmental, matter-of-fact way, as if it were a perfectly natural and understandable response to the situation in which Lord Genji found himself. This little anecdote, in a collection of stories of heterosexual intrigue written by a woman, is another bit of evidence suggesting a familiarity and acceptance of homosexual love between males among the social elite of early Japan. In another work of the period, *Ise Monogatari*, "Tale of Ise," a poem recounts the feelings of a man yearning for the company of a male friend traveling in a distant region: "I cannot believe that you are far away, for I can never forget you. And thus your face is always before me."[16]

Evidence of the familiarity of the Japanese aristocracy of the period with homosexuality is also found in diaries of courtiers from the 11th-century and onward. One such aristocrat, Fujiwara Yorinaga, wrote of a night in 1148 when he took a young male dancer to bed with him. "Tonight I took Yosimasa to bed, and really went wild. It was especially satisfying." The diaries also include accounts of emperors involved in homosexual relationships. The dalliance of the 11th-century emperor Shirakawa with a beautiful boy he retained for sexual purposes was mentioned in several court diaries, as was the relationship of the early 12th-century emperor Toba with a youth he kept. Another diary recorded the love of the 12th-century emperor Go-Shirakaw for a young man of the powerful Fujiwara family, Fujiwara Nobuyori, who was appointed to several high imperial positions as a result of the sexual relationship.[17]

By the tenth century and onward, collections of prose and poetry, including love poems written by monks to boys, were being produced in the many flourishing monasteries of Shingon and Tendai Buddhism.[18] Manuscripts from the period include many stories and poems which provide examples of the cult of boy love among the monks. A story from Ninna-ji, the headquarters monastery of Shingon Buddhism, which we are told is based on historical fact, relates the poignant story of the love of the lord-abbot, a member of the emperor's family, for a beautiful chigo. Senju was a sweet, affectionate youth whose flute playing and singing delighted the abbot. It came to pass that a second chigo, who had just joined the monastery, caught the lord abbot's fancy. The second youth, Mikawa also had musical talents, and excelled in playing the *koto* (a Japanese stringed instrument), but was also a gifted poet. When Senju saw that the abbot began to direct all his affections to Mikawa, he felt dishonored, and so stayed away from the abbot's presence. One day, when the abbot was entertaining friends at a small dinner, he noticed Senju's absence, and remembering his love for him, sent a servant to look for him. But Senju resisted the abbot's call, and only relented after the lord demanded that he come. Senju went before the abbot, who wanted to hear him sing. Senju then sang a sad and wistful song: "What shall I do? I am abandoned even by the innumerable ancient Buddhas. Among the innumerable paradises I find none where I may be reborn." Moved to tears by Senju's song, the abbot took Senju into his arms and carried him straight away to his bed chamber. The incident was the subject of much discussion throughout the monastery that night. The next day the abbot found a poem left for him by Mikawa, lamenting the transience of human feeling and announcing his departure from the monastery.[19]

A 14th-century manuscript kept among the treasures of the Buddhist monastery of Daigo-ji contains a charming illustrated story, also purported to be true, of the devotion of a beautiful chigo for an old and revered monk, famous for his virtue. The monk was attended to by a number of chigo favorites, but he loved one beautiful boy above all, with whom he often slept. "But already old, all he could manage was 'to rub his arrow between two hills'; penetration was out of the question." Longing for his master to penetrate him, the chigo carefully prepared himself the next evening. First he had his servant, a youth like himself, "work with his fingers" on his anus. Next the chigo had his servant insert a dildo into his ass. By this time the servant, sexually excited by this intimate contact with the beautiful chigo, started to masturbate, saying he couldn't help himself. The chigo then told the servant, "Smear on the oil," and "then screw me with your full five sun (six inches)." An illustration accompanying the story shows the young servant doing just that. Finally, the servant put a heater under the chigo's ass to warm it for the old monk. When the old master called for his beloved to join him in bed, they at last found that his preparation was perfect — the old man was able to penetrate the beautiful chigo with ease.[20]

A striking testament to the prevalence of homosexuality in the monasteries can be found in a set of written vows recorded by a 36-year old monk in the early 13th-century cited by the historian Gary P. Leupp:

• Having already fucked ninety-five males, I will not behave wantonly with more than one hundred [meaning he would stop with one hundred].
• I will not keep and cherish any boys except Ryuo-maru.
• I will not keep older boys in my own bedroom.
• Among the older and middle boys, I will not keep and cherish any as their *nenja*.

In discussing this remarkable written record, Leupp noted that the monk's evident commitment to Ryuo-maru did not apparently bar him from sexual relations with five more males. Leupp added that the vows also contained a fascinating proviso, "that these vows are limited to the present lifetime and do not apply to future incarnations."[21]

In another story of the 14th-century, we see an example of the continued association of beautiful chigo with the Divine. The story tells of a monk, Keikai, who lived during the 12th-century at the monastery on Mount Hiei, the center of Tendai Buddhism. Seeking help with his studies, Keikai traveled to a temple to pray to Kannon Bosatsu, the version of the manifest Buddha most worshipped in Japan. One night while sleeping he dreamed of an unusually beautiful chigo, and awoke with great feelings of love for the youth of his dream. While on his way back to Mount Hiei, Keikai passed another monastery, Mii-dera, and was surprised and delighted to catch sight of a beautiful youth, fifteen or sixteen years old, in the monastery grounds who looked like the boy of his dream. Keikai inquired about the youth and was told that his name was Umewaka, and that his father was a minister of the emperor. Keikai arranged to spend the night at the monastery, and sent Umewaka a love poem. Keikai was thrilled when he received a poem in reply. Later that night Keikai was invited to the youth's rooms, and spent a blissful evening with his beloved chigo.

The next day Keikai continued his journey back to Mount Hiei. Umewaka, in the meantime, whose passions had been awakened by his night with Keikai, longed to be with his lover again, and so left Mii-dera to follow him to Mount Hiei. While en route, Umekawa was attacked by robbers, and taken prisoner. When the monks of Mii-dera realized Umekawa was missing, they accused the monks of Mount Hiei of kidnapping him, and sent out a call for 2,000 warrior-monks. After the monks of Mount Hiei heard about this, they attacked Mii-dera first, and a fierce battle ensued, during which the buildings of the monastery were set on fire. Umekawa, in the meantime, had been rescued from his imprisonment by an old man and returned to Mii-dera during the midst of the battle. When he saw the burned buildings and learned what happened he said, "The fault is mine! I cannot live any longer," and killed himself.

Keikai was deeply grieved by the death of his beautiful beloved, and so after attending to his burial he left the monastery at Mount Hiei and took up the life of a hermit. Back at Mii-dera, the monks, while asleep one night in the only building to survive the fires, dreamed that the patron deity of their temple had received the patron deity of Mount Hiei as a friend. The monks cried out to their patron deity, asking why they had undergone the disaster of the destruction of their monastery and the death of Umekawa. The deity replied: "Good and evil are not always the same for men as they are in the law of the Buddha. This catastrophe has been the occasion of the true conversion of Keikai. He will become a religious of great virtue. His name will outlive him." And then the deity revealed that Umekawa was none other than the manifestation of Kannon Bosatsu, who had incarnated as the beautiful chigo to enable the spiritual enlightenment of Keikai.[22] It is interesting to note that, as in Plato's *Symposium*, where homosexual love is described as a stepping off point for spiritual development, here, too, the homosexual love for a chigo is the stimulus for spiritual transformation.

The Spread of Idealistic Homosexuality Outside the Monasteries

From the time Kobo Daishi began spreading the teachings of esoteric Buddhism under the auspices of the emperor, and throughout the growth and development of Shingon and Tendai Buddhism in the following centuries, their monasteries continued to be closely linked with the emperor, his court and the aristocracy. The emperor and the members of the aristocracy donated funds for the building of opulent monasteries, and frequently visited them both for devotional reasons and to attend ceremonies and rituals. The lavish ceremonies often featured singing and dancing by the beautifully dressed chigo, who were much admired by many of the homosexually inclined courtiers and aristocrats, who used the occasion of their visits to woo the more beautiful boys.[23]

The links between monasteries and the imperial court became even closer in the 11th-century as a result of a peculiar development of court politics under which the emperor ostensibly abdicated, or "retired," in favor of a successor, but continued to exercise decisive influence over government policy. Under this system, known as "the cloistered emperors," the retired emperor took vows, became a Buddhist priest and moved into a monastery, but at the same time continued to wield the power of the emperor from behind the throne of what was for all intents and purposes a figurehead ruler. This system continued for nearly three centuries, during which time large numbers of aristocrats followed the emperor's example, took vows and likewise moved into monasteries. Rather than embracing the ascetic life, however, the aristocrats brought with them their extravagant lifestyle and continued their involvement in politics and worldly affairs, with the result that the monasteries became centers of political intrigue, and, in essence, extensions of the world of the court. By this time, it had became the norm for imperial princes and the sons of the aristocracy and government officials to be sent for their education to the monasteries, where most of the higher posts in the Shingon and Tendai monasteries were already being held by members of the imperial family or aristocrats. With the arrival of the cloistered emperors and the court aristocracy in the monasteries, the world of the monasteries and the court, which had been closely linked since the days of Kobo Daishi, seemed to blend seamlessly.

One result of intersection of these two worlds was that some of the ideals associated with the love of chigo in the monasteries began to rub off on the courtiers. Homosexual relations between courtiers and aristocrats with younger males of lesser social status had long been a familiar part of court life, just as it had been among the Chinese aristocracy. But with the influence of the cult of the chigo from the monasteries, a new, more elevated kind of homosexual relationship began to be seen in the court and among the aristocracy, in which a noble or aristocrat would take as a lover a younger male of the same social class in a relationship where there was now an expectation of betterment for the beloved in a spiritual and educational, as well as material sense. The handsome favorites of powerful nobles and officials might still be given lands or other favors, as before, but as among the ancient Athenians, the younger lovers were now regarded as protégés of their older lovers, who were expected to look after their social development and political education.

The Rise of the Samurai and the Shogunate

In the meantime, lesser members and relations of the aristocracy, frustrated by their lack of opportunities in the court or government ministries, started to take government posts in the provinces where they settled, acquired estates, and began to establish local power bases of their own. Natural competition among them resulted in frequent disputes and armed skirmishes, and as a result they began to raise private armies to protect their interests. The spread of this phenomenon led to a situation where these provincial barons, with their armies to back them up, might erupt into fighting over even minor disagreements. This environment forced a continual effort to hone warrior skills among what was quickly developing into a professional warrior caste — the samurai, a corps of highly trained and dedicated warriors analogous to the knighthood of Medieval Europe. As the samurai developed, they acquired a highly idealistic code of chivalry, similar in some respects to the chivalrous code of the European knighthood, that demanded "rectitude, justice, courage, endurance, and absolute readiness to die for duty."[24] According to Inazo Nitobe in *Bushido, the Soul of Japan,* these virtues were inculcated in the samurai from childhood onward with a kind of Spartan insistence. "To rush into the thick of battle and be slain in it, is easy enough, and a common churl is equal to that task; but to live when it is right to live, and to die only when it is right to die — that is true courage."[25] The samurai ideal was a life of simplicity lived in service to the nation and emperor. Reaching a number of over two million at their peak, the samurai enjoyed an elite status in Japanese society and were excused from paying taxes by the shogun and emperor.

Over time the more powerful among the samurai knights established a presence near the capital, serving as a sort of military police, supposedly looking after the interests of the emperor. Cultivating relationships with the powerful aristocratic families to whom some of them were related, these samurai lords gradually acquired standing of their own in the court. Thus, in a short span of time, the samurai, with the clout that came with their military capabilities and familial ties to members of the court aristocracy, emerged from the provinces as a powerful force on the national stage, and began to play a decisive role in political and military conflict.

By the end of the 11th century, two clans had emerged as preeminent among the ranks of the samurai. When disputes developed between the cloistered emperor and the sitting emperor in the early 12th century, resulting in a division of the royal family into two camps, each faction turned to one of the two rival samurai clans for armed support. By mid-century the disputes broke into open fighting, leading to several decades of intermittent civil war between the forces of the two powerful clans. In 1185, one of the two samurai clans, the

Minamotos, led by Minamoto Yoritomo, completed the destruction of the forces of their samurai rivals, along with the banishment of the mighty Fujiwara family, the most powerful of the old aristocratic families, whose members had controlled the line of imperial succession for over three centuries. With the military capability of their rivals destroyed, Yoritomo appointed military governors for all the provinces and began building a government apparatus independent of the court bureaucracy — a tribunal for keeping his samurai vassals in line, a secretariat for government administration, and the beginnings of a court system.

Four years later, in 1189, Yoritomo's army crushed the remaining resistance of the once all-powerful Fujiwara family, an event which finalized the stunning transfer of political power that was occurring within Japan, from the old court aristocracy which had ruled Japan for centuries, to the new samurai barons. In 1192 the emperor gave Yoritomo the title of *seii tai shogun*, "barbarian-destroying generalissimo," the highest rank a warrior could attain in Medieval Japan. The title, shortened to *shogun*, would be held by all of Yoritomo's successors, who, as the military leaders of the country, were the de facto rulers of Japan. The rule of the shoguns, and the government organization that grew from Yoritomo's military government, the *bakufu*, was to endure for nearly seven centuries, from the creation of the Shogunate in 1192 to the restoration of imperial power in 1867.

The Noble Love of the Samurai

With the power of the emperor overshadowed by the military might of the bakufu under the first shogun, Minamoto Yoritomo, Japan entered a feudal period in which power and authority rested not in the emperor, but on the vassal relationships between the shogun and his military governors, or *daimyo*s, and between the daimyo and their local vassals — all of it depending on the loyalty and warrior skills of their samurai knights. As among the knighthood of Medieval Europe and the warrior societies of earlier periods, the world of the samurai was a world of men, oriented around masculine values and military prowess, and organized by ties of loyalty to one's lord and comrades. Such all-male societies, where martial valor, masculine accomplishment and the male physique are glorified, are naturally conducive to strong emotional ties among men.

As the samurai rose in prominence and established their power in the Imperial court in the 11th and 12th centuries, many of them also embraced the homosexual customs that had spread from the monasteries to the court. As boys, many of the samurai had been sent to the monasteries for their education where they would have participated in the idealized love relationships with the monks.[26] It should not be surprising, then, that as the military government of the shogun developed in the 13th and 14th centuries the idealistic homosexuality of the monks found a particularly fertile ground in the manly world of samurai knights. In this masculine society, women were looked down upon, viewed by many of the knights as mere "holes to be borrowed" for carrying the children of warriors. The attitude of many of the Samurai could be summed up, "women are for breeding, but boys are for pleasure."[27]* In fact, for the first several hundred years of Samurai rule, it was felt that only love between men was deemed worthy of a true warrior.[28] In the following centuries the practice of love between the samurai knights and their protégés or squires, at first loosely modeled on the pattern of

---

*It is interesting to note the number of warrior societies in which the same, exact attitude is found. In addition to the Samurai, the sentiment was most famously a trait of the ancient Greeks. However, it is also found among aboriginal groups as varied as Melanesian peoples, (among the Sambia of New Guinea studied by Gilbert Herdt, sex with youths is pleasurable "play," whereas sex with women is "work"), and tribal groups in Africa (among the Ubangi males of the Congo women were said to exist for procreation, and adolescent males for pleasure).

love in the monasteries, developed into a rich tradition of noble love, with its own etiquette, ideals and standards of honor, which in its idealism and refined sensibilities rivaled the homosexual customs of the ancient Greeks.

Unlike the monks and their chigo, though, whose ages could range from 12 to 16 or 17, the samurai knights had a distinct preference for older youth. Perhaps because of the rigors of life among the samurai — the intensely physical training, living in camps, the frequent travel on horseback, the possibility of military action, all of which could have been difficult for a boy in early adolescence — the youths they loved were anywhere from the mid-or late teens to even the early twenties. This difference in age of the beloved is reflected in the terms used to describe them. While the monks referred to their love-objects as *chigo*, which literally means "young child," the protégé-lovers of the knights were called *wakashu*, literally "young man," derived from *waka*, "young," and *shu*, "men."[29]

Though it is likely that no small part of the chigo's appeal to the monks and court aristocrats was the androgynous beauty of the boys, it is clear that the attractiveness of the wakashu for the samurai was in their masculine good looks, "sufficient to draw women as well as men."[30] In contrast to the tone of sweetness and delicacy that surrounded the love of chigo in the monasteries, the environment in which the samurai courted their lovers reflected the temperament of warriors: "Rough and brawny," according to the 17th-century writer, Ihara Saikaku. "Men swaggered when they spoke. They preferred big, muscular boys, and bore cuts on their bodies as a sign of male love. This spirit reached even to boy actors, all of whom brandished swords."[31]

The spiritual and idealistic underpinnings of the tradition of the samurai's love for their wakashu is seen in the term they used to describe the custom, *shudo*, which is the shortened form of *wakashu-do*, that is, "the way" of young men, *do* being the Japanese variant of the Chinese *Tao*, used also in the term *Shinto* (*Shin-do*), "the way of the gods."[32] According to Watanabe, for the samurai, the attractiveness of a wakashu resided not in his appearance, but in his soul.[33] This is a striking parallel to the way the Dorian Greeks described an attractive youth, *agathos*, meaning beautiful in a virtuous or noble sense, in contrast to the term *kalos*, beautiful in a sensual way, used by the Athenians.

As among the Greeks, the relationships between the samurai knights and their squires were infused with an idealism in which romance and valor in battle were closely linked. The writer of a commentary on the civil wars of the 15th and 16th centuries remarked on how "many strong and courageous warriors emerged from among the [warriors'] male sex partners," while another writer commented on how "most of those who storm onto the battlefield, warding off the enemy and accompanying their lords to the end, are the lords' male sex partners."[34] The greatest honor the lover of a samurai could achieve was to fall in battle in order to save the life of his master. Accounts of samurai battles include numerous instances of such "love-inspired valor," where wakashu heroically died in the service of their samurai lovers.[35]

One such heroic death was described by the Jesuit missionary Father Louis Frois, in his account of the overthrow of the 13th shogun, Ashikaga Yoshiteru, who was killed in an attack in his castle by the army of one of his generals. According to Father Frois, the shogun's squire, Odachidono, the son of a distinguished nobleman, "fought so valiantly and with such intrepid spirit that all the rebels started to shout out that he should not be killed, but that he should be taken alive. Nonetheless, seeing his master die, and believing it a great dishonor to survive him, the youth threw away his sword, and pulling out his dagger, he cut open his throat and then his belly. Finally he killed himself by lying down flat with the dagger in his belly."[36]

In addition to his service to his knight as squire or page, the youth was also expected to submit to the lover sexually, "serving as the sheath (receptacle) for his mentor's sword (phallus),"[37] and not just to satisfy his master. There is evidence that the Medieval Japanese shared with the ancient Greeks and other peoples the widespread ancient superstition about a man's virtuous qualities and masculine skills passing into a younger male during intercourse. Indeed, there are hints that early Japanese society may have featured sexual initiation rites comparable to those found among the Melanesian warrior tribes and the ancient Indo-European warriors. During the *gen-puku* rite, an ancient coming of age ritual that was practiced as early at the 7th century, a ceremonial headdress would be placed on the youth's head by an older male, his "*eboshi*-father," who would then serve as the youth's mentor, role model and guardian. In the villages of early Japan, the youth would then move into a young men's house until the time for his marriage, a striking parallel to both Melanesian rites and the initiation rituals of the early Indo-European warriors.[38]

Sexual submission of the youth to his older lover also had a spiritual dimension under Buddhist teachings, and was a demonstration of the youth's virtue. Sensitivity to his master's feelings, and responding to his desires and needs were considered evidence of the youth's *nasake*, compassion, one of Buddhism's most valued virtues, through which he would demonstrate his worthiness for his master's love.[39] According to Ihara in his 1643,"Record of Heartfelt Friends," for a handsome wakashu to refuse to give himself to those desiring him was to be "like a flower with no fragrance. Not to give himself to a suitable male lover was shameful and carried the risk of physical deformity in the next incarnation."[40]

But it's also clear that the young men did not consider this sexual service an onerous duty. Writers of the period without exception portray the youth's sexual submission to the knight as a pleasurable and emotionally satisfying experience. In erotic drawings of the period, young men being penetrated by older men are frequently shown with erections, and even ejaculating, obvious signs of sexual arousal.[41] The wakashu are also described as deeply touched by love letters from suitors, and even "taking the initiative in offering themselves to men who attract them."[42]

In return for the wakashu's service and sexual submission, the older lover, or *nenja*, had an obligation to tend to the youth's education, provide emotional support, guide his social development and serve as a role model during his apprenticeship as a warrior. Of primary importance, though, was the training of the youth in the warrior arts, because "it is only in this way that the *shudo* (way of youths) becomes *bushido* (way of warriors), according to a seventeenth-century commentator.[43] Therefore, under the supervision of his nenja, the wakashu underwent intensive training in swordsmanship, archery and horsemanship. For his part, "the boy was expected to be worthy of his lover by being a good student of samurai manhood. Together, they vowed to uphold the manly virtues of the samurai class: to be loyal, steadfast, and honorable in their actions." The two lovers would frequently signify the seriousness with which they undertook this oath by cutting a mark on their arms or legs, or cutting off a part of their fingers. Together, the two lovers, master and student, formed a spiritual whole, in which the youth's response to his older lover's desire constituted "a form of the Buddhist spiritual experience of mutability (*mujo*)."[44]

The moral obligation of a wakashu to demonstrate nasake by alleviating the suffering (sexual desire) of an older man by sexually submitting to him did not stop with his lover, but applied to other men who might have passionately fallen for the young man. This sort of demonstration of compassion by the youth was not without risk. If his lover were to learn of such a tryst, it could lead to the youth's death. Ihara Saikaku, though, wrote of cases where the older lover forgave his lover when he saw that he was simply responding with compassion to the suffering of another man.[45] In his stories Ihara never hesitated to deride the moral failings of others, particularly Buddhist monks, but he invariably depicted the wakashu's actions in such cases not as a result of the youth's lust, but "motivated by duty to alleviate suffering, sacrificing his own interests, even breaking his vows in order to share his body with those burning with desire for it." The extraordinary moral dilemma in which a youth could find himself through devotion to nasake is captured in a poignant passage of one of Ihara's stories when a wakashu admits to his daimyo, "A certain man has fallen in love with me. If I refuse him, I betray my honor as a follower *shudo* (the way of the love of youths). If I act freely, it means breaking my lord's laws and is tantamount to rejecting your longstanding benevolence toward me. Please kill me so that I may escape this quandary."[46]

Unlike classical Athens, the norms for the ages of the older and younger lovers were not hard and fast. In one of his stories, Ihara wrote of a young man who continued as younger lover to his older lover even after his coming of age ceremony. To the Japanese of the period, the ages of the partners were less important than the wakashu's willingness to subordinate to the nenja. "So long as one partner took the role of 'man' and the other the role of 'boy,'" the relationships were accepted.[47] In several stories in his *Nanshoku Okagami* (Great Mirror of Boy–Love), Ihara depicts nenja-wakashu relationships between youth of the same age. In another story are two old men, still lovers in their sixties, "two old cherry trees still in bloom," with the sixty-year-old playing the nenja role to his sixty-three-year-old wakashu.[48]

When the young man finally came of age, the long lock of hair worn on the forehead signifying his youthful status was cut, and he began to wear the short-sleeved tunic of adult men and sometimes even changed his name. While the period of his training and service as a squire was over, the lovers usually continued as intimate friends "sacrificing their interests in a mutual fashion and helping each other all their lives."[49] Even after they married, the bonds between the two would continue. In another of Ihara's stories, a character comments, "Homosexual love should be quite different from ordinary love between man and woman; this is why a prince, even when he has married a beautiful princess, cannot forget his pages. A woman is a creature without any importance whatsoever, while sincere homosexual love is true love."[50]

Homosexual Protégés of the Shoguns

By the fourteenth-century, homosexual loves had become a prominent feature of the military rule of the shoguns. Minamoto Yoritomo, the first shogun, began the tradition with his own favorite, whom he made an officer of the imperial guard.[51] With the Ashikaga shoguns, who came to power in the early 14th century, homosexual love relationships with younger protégés became a firmly entrenched tradition among the shoguns and principal samurai lords. Gary Leupp has remarked that the list of shoguns and daimyo involved in sexual relationships with male lovers "reads like a Who's Who of military history." Leupp listed 26 prominent shoguns and warlords from the 14th to the 18th century linked in documents with male lovers.[52]

As the homosexual tradition among the samurai rulers developed, a relationship of a youth with an illustrious noble or samurai became a common path to social advancement. Shoguns frequently bestowed on their lovers titles, positions in the government and land. Daimyo and prominent samurai knights followed the example of the shoguns and also kept lover protégés who would be given secure positions in the ruling hierarchy in return for their service. Because of the social advancement and wealth that could come with a relationship with powerful lords or knights, samurai families with teenaged sons went to great pains to interest suitable samurai knights or lords in their sons, even to the point of preparing their sons for anal intercourse. To prepare a youth for love making with a knight, his parents would have him relax and then insert a smooth wooden dildo-like instrument into his rectum to stretch it and help him adjust to penetration. It is hard to imagine a more graphic example of the enormous divide in attitudes toward sex between the Medieval Japanese and the Western society, where parents would be horrified at the thought of their sons being involved in such a pederastic relationship, not to mention actually preparing their sons for anal penetration.[53]

As occurred with some of the Chinese rulers, the favors lavished by shoguns and samurai lords on their lovers sometimes led to unfortunate results. The fourteenth-century shogun, Ashikaga Yoshimochi fell in love with a young samurai of a distinguished samurai clan, Akamatsu Mochisada, whose family played a major role in the battles that brought the Ashikaga shoguns to power. According to a fifteenth-century account, Mochisada, described as very beautiful, was given three provinces "through the homosexual favors of the lord."[54] An arrogant young man, Mochisada flaunted his new status and "conducted himself in such an arbitrary manner that he committed injustices." Akamatsu Mitsusuke, the head of the Akamatsu clan, regarded Mochisada's actions as a dishonor to the clan, and to uphold the clan's honor called a council of lords and brought charges against the young man. Unable to deny his guilt, Mochisada was ordered to kill himself by his lover, the shogun, Ashikaga Yoshimochi, who himself was bound by duty to order the punishment. Grieving the loss of his lover, the shogun fell ill and was said to have died full of hatred for Akamatsu Mitsusuke for his role in the death of Mochisada.[55]

Mochisada's son, Akamatsu Sadamura, in turn became the lover of the sixth Ashikaga shogun, Yoshinori, who was Yoshimochi's younger brother. Yoshinori, was even more extravagant than his brother in the favors he bestowed on the young Sadamura. According to an account from the period, Sadamura "received homosexual favors the like of which will not anywhere be found." The shogun decided that he wanted Sadamura to become the chief of his clan, the Akamatsu, and so sent a secret message to him telling him to take over three provinces belonging to the Akamatsu clan head, the same Akamatsu Mitsusuke who had brought charges against Sadamura's father, Mochisada. When Mitsusuke got wind of the plot, he was naturally greatly angered, and so he invited the shogun to his palace one evening on the pretext putting on a banquet to honor him and murdered him.[56]

Not many years later, another Ashikaga shogun granted favors to a younger lover, also a member of the Akamatsu clan, which had even more disastrous consequences. (One would think that by this point an Ashikagi shogun would be wary of romantic involvement with another member of the Akamatsu clan.) After the death of the shogun Yoshinori at the hands of Akamatsu Mitsusuke, warlords loyal to the Ashikaga family went to battle to punish Mitsusuke, and as a result an Akamatsu fiefdom was given to Yamana Sozen, one of the most powerful of the samurai lords. At the urging of the head of the rival Hosokawa clan, the shogun, Ashikaga Yoshimasa took on as a lover, Akamatsu Norinao, the handsome nephew of Akamatsu Mitsusuke. In love with the beautiful young man, the shogun granted him permission to retake the Akamatsu fiefdom given to Yamana Sozen. When Yamana heard of this, he assumed it was a plot of the rival Hosokawa clan, and attacked the castle of Norinao, who killed himself in the ensuing battle. In the aftermath of Norinao's death, tensions between the Yamana and Hosokawa clans rose to the point where war broke out. The fighting, called the Onin Civil War, lasted ten years and when it gradually died down, with neither the Yamana or Hosokawa clans prevailing, the Ashikaga capital at Kyoto lay in ruins.[57]

The Civil Wars of the Sengoku Period

During the entire period the shogun, Ashikaga Yoshimasa, paid little heed to the fighting between the Yamana and Hosokawa clans, and was instead preoccupied with cultural activities and with plans for building a pavilion to rival the famous Golden Pavilion in Kyoto, built by his grandfather. The fighting and the shogun's passivity to it contributed to a weakening of centralized authority, and encouraged daimyos and feudal lords throughout the country to assert greater authority in their provinces. While the power and influence of many daimyos increased, the positions of others eroded, leading to their overthrow by ambitious vassals sometimes allied with groups of disgruntled peasants. The general political instability led to more armed conflict between rival factions, with the result that warfare raged on and off throughout the country for the next century and a half, a period known as the Sengoku, or Warring States, period (1478–1605).

The constant civil warfare of the Sengoku period, with the inevitable emphasis on military valor and warrior ethos, saw the full flowering of the noble love and idealism of *shudo*. Later Japanese historians mark the period as the point when the idealistic homosexual love of the shudo tradition became universal among the samurai class. By the late fifteenth-century, shudo had come to be regarded as a longstanding tradition of the samurai that must be preserved. In a 1482 commentary on shudo, Ijiri Chusuke, argued,

> In our empire of Japan this way flourished from the time of the great master Kobo.... In the world of the nobles and the warriors, lovers would swear perfect and eternal love relying on no more than their mutual good will. Whether their partners were noble or common, rich or poor, was absolutely of no importance.... In all these case they were greatly moved by the spirit of this way. This way must be truly respected, and it must never be permitted to disappear.[58]

Written histories of the many battles of the Sengoku period include a number of accounts of the heroism and valor inspired by love between knight and squire. It was in this period, too, that a ship carrying Portuguese Jesuit missionaries led by Francis Xavier was blown off course on its way to China and landed in Japan, resulting in the first Western accounts, mentioned earlier in the chapter, of "the abominable vice against nature" that flourished among the Japanese.

In the mid-sixteenth-century, a powerful regional daimyo, Oda Nobunaga, took control of Kyoto and, displaying a genius for military strategy, prevailed against the other daimyo lords and started gradually unifying the country. By distributing fiefdoms to his vassals and granting continuing privileges to powerful local landowners, temples and monasteries, Nobunaga managed to pacify large regions of the country while preventing the rise of potential regional rivals. Nobunaga's rule was cut short, however, by the treachery of one of his commanders who led a rebellion against him. Surrounded by his enemies, Nobunaga was forced to commit suicide. Nobunaga's death, with his handsome young lover, Mori Ranmaru, fighting till death beside him, provided one of the great romantic images of the noble love of the samurai of that era, an episode recounted in later histories, featured in works of fiction, and depicted in art — and now even featured in a video game.*

Nobunaga was succeeded by the most powerful of his daimyo vassals, Toyotomi Hideyoshi, who continued Nobunaga's unification strategies, which further diminished the power of regional barons. After a reckless attempt by Hideyoshi to invade Korea in 1597, which resulted in his death, Tokugawa Ieyasu emerged as his successor after defeating rival

---

*PlayStation 2, Samurai Warriors, *though of course the game provides no hint of the nature of the bond between Mori Ranmaru and Oda Nobunaga.*

daimyo lords at the climactic battle of Sekigahara. Having achieved unquestioned military supremacy over the country, Ieyasu built on the centralized power structure begun by Nobunaga and Hideyoshi and established the Edo bakufu, more commonly known as the Tokugawa shogunate, which lasted until the Meiji restoration in 1867, when the last Tokugawa shogun yielded power to the emperor.

The Tokugawa Shogunate

The political stability and peace which the unified rule of the Tokugawa shoguns brought to the country led to an extended period of economic growth and prosperity. The economic expansion was further stimulated by intensive building projects, both to rebuild the cities after a century and a half of destructive warfare, and to strengthen the military defenses of the shogun and his principal daimyo retainers and vassals. The rebuilding and related commercial activities spurred increased trade to cope with the demand for materials, while the need for craftsmen, artisans and laborers led to rapid growth in the cities. By the early 17th century a growing class of city-dwelling merchants and craftsmen was emerging alongside the samurai who themselves were being transformed from a warrior class to political and civic administrators.

With the continuing peace of the period, the importance of the samurai warriors as the basis for political power began to diminish. At the same time, the shogun needed to ensure that the hundreds of thousands of idled samurai could not be mobilized by a disgruntled daimyo to threaten his rule. In order to keep an eye on restive daimyos and their vassals, as well as their thousands of samurai knights, the shogun required that all the daimyo and principal vassals maintain residences in the shogun's capital, Edo (modern Tokyo) for part of the year. As a result, tens of thousands of samurai were garrisoned in the capital at any point in the year. With their exposure to the samurai living alongside them in the cities, it became fashionable for the growing middle class to take up the customs and practices of their samurai superiors. Craftsmen and merchants began cultivating the warrior arts of the samurai — judo, kyodo and kendo, for example — not for military training, but as a sport or spiritual discipline. Along with military arts, the urban middle class began to emulate the tradition of shudo, as well, but instead of aristocratic youths aspiring to warrior nobility, their love objects were more often found in brothels or in theaters. The idealism of the shudo tradition remained largely a devotion of the samurai class.

The economic growth and political stability of the Tokugawa period also encouraged a proliferation of art and literature. In the thirteenth and fourteenth centuries the Ashikaga shoguns as well as many of the daimyos and samurai lords had begun to build grand and elegant castles and temples, and began a long tradition of artistic patronage that led to an unusually rich profusion of painting, exquisitely decorated lacquered woods, ceramics and finely embroidered fabrics. With the peace and prosperity of the Tokugawa period, the cultural development accelerated. The growth of a city-dwelling bourgeoisie expanded the market for decorative objects and provided a growing audience for theater and popular literature. The closing decades of the prosperous 17th century saw the cultural flowering in the resurgent cities reach such a level of splendor and richness that the period is considered a golden age of Japanese civilization, known since as the Genroku period.

Homosexual Love in Tokugawa Literature

As an expression of the culture of the times, the literature of the period frequently featured homosexual love, now often called *nanshoku*, male love, which frequently focused on the beauty of the wakashu and his devotion to the ideals and valor of the shudo tradition. The prevalence of male homosexuality among both the samurai and the commoners of the period and the extent to which homosexual love and the sentiments of shudo shaped the lives of the people are illustrated particularly in the stories of Ihara Saikaku. Ihara's works rank among the great literature of Japan and were very popular during his lifetime. His stories reflect the perspective and experiences of the ordinary samurai and the urban middle class of craftsmen and shop keepers of 17th-century Tokugawa Japan. A recurring theme is nanshoku, which was becoming widespread among the commoners of the cities and towns. In his stories, Ihara lays out a romantic ideal for homosexual love among the samurai and urban middle class based on the loyalty and selfless devotion of shudo.

Ihara's "The Love of the Two Enemies" is a tragic story that demonstrates the extremes of self-sacrifice that the samurai ideals of loyalty and honor could demand. The story relates the love of a samurai for a young man who one day learns from his mother that his lover was the man who had some time in the past killed his samurai father. The mother insists that her son fulfill the samurai code of honor and avenge his father's death. The son is torn in two by his dilemma, but in the end does not resist his mother's demand. When he next saw his lover he tells him what he had learned. "I know that you could not act in any other way and that you did so on the orders of your master. But as the son of a samurai, I cannot overlook it. Truly, I am infinitely sorry to kill you and my distress is overwhelming." His lover took the accusation calmly. He acknowledges that he, indeed, was the murderer of the young man's father, and said that he had no idea that he had fallen in love with the son of the man he had killed. "Yes, I am your father's murderer, but it would be pleasant for me to die at your hand." The samurai put aside his sword and bent over to offer his neck to the young man. But the son said that instead they should fight with the same weapons.

Just then, the young man's mother, who had been eavesdropping on their conversation from another room, burst in and interrupted them. "I admire both of you. You are truly men of honor." She begged them to make love to each other one more time and to enjoy their last evening together. The two young men then spent the evening together, drank some wine to commemorate their last night with each other, and then went and got into bed lying side by side. The next morning, the mother went into their room to wake them and found the two lying together in silence. She called them to wake them, but got no reply. She then pulled off the blanket and saw that the younger one had run his friend through the heart with a sword, impaling himself with it as it came out of his lover's body. When the mother saw the two bleeding corpses she sat down in meditation, and then killed herself, so she, too, would not be found unworthy of such a love.[59]

A story from Ihara's collection, *Five Women Who Loved Love,* provides an illustration of how the homosexual preoccupation of young men of the time was taken for granted. During the Tokugawa period a typical progression for males was for a youth to be the lover of an older man in his twenties or thirties, and then when he came of age to be the lover of another youth, and then eventually getting married to have a family. Ihara's "Gengobei, the Mountain of Love" tells the story of a handsome man who still at 26 had yet to have sex with a woman, having instead been in a long-term relationship with a wakashu. During this time, a pretty girl named O-Man, had fallen in love with Gengobei, and kept sending him letters telling him how much she loved him, but could not succeed in interesting him in her. After

Gengobei's young lover died unexpectedly, the grieving Gengobei set out on a pilgrimage. Hearing this news, O-Man cut her hair like a boy, and dressed herself up to look like the perfect young wakashu. Following Gengobei on his pilgrimage she succeeded in attracting his attention and getting him into bed. When together in bed he discovered she was not a wakashu, but a woman, she opened her heart to him "with such a sincere confession of love" that he was moved, and accepted her love, and later married her. It's likely that Ihara's reader would have found great humor in this variation on the usual progression of a young man from nanshoku to heterosexual marriage.[60]

The ambisexual norm of the period is seen in another of Ihara's works, *The Man Who Loved Love*. The stories in the collection relate the life of a lusty rake, Yonosuke, a Don Juan of sorts, who appears meant to be seen as a vulgar version of the courtly lover Prince Genji in the tenth-century classic, *The Tale of Genji*. In one of the stories which depicts Yonosuke in his youth, his unusual sexual prowess is illustrated by the young Yonosuke surprising and confusing a young samurai by turning the tables and aggressively trying to seduce and penetrate him, which the story suggests he accomplished. While most of Yonosuke's sexual conquests related in the book were heterosexual, the diary he kept shows that by his 54th year he had seduced 3,742 women, but also 725 young men.[61]

The noble obligation of a wakashu to demonstrate *nasake*, compassion, and to give of himself to relieve the suffering of others is depicted in an account recorded in 1653 about the most beautiful of the lovers of Hashiba Hidetsugu, who served as regent under the powerful warlord Toyotomi Hideyoshi, the successor of Oda Nobunaga during the last years of the Sengoku period just prior to the establishment of the Tokugawa shogunate. Recorded some sixty years after the events were to have taken place, its accuracy in all details is doubtful. However, the poignant drama of the story beautifully conveys the romance and idealism with which homosexual love was regarded in the literature of the early Tokugawa shogunate.

The beauty of the regent's page, Fuwa Bansaku, stood out even among the many handsome youths Hidetsuga had brought to his court, and when Hidetsuga traveled, Bansaku received as much attention as his master. Because of his extraordinary good looks, the regent wanted Bansaku always at his side. One day, while traveling away from Hidetsuga's castle, Bansaku noticed a samurai on the side of the road at Fukakusa, a village on the road to Kyoto. Though they had not met, the young samurai greeted Bansaku as he passed on horseback. Bansaku paid the incident little notice since he was accustomed to the admiration of strangers greeting him in his travels. The next time Bansaku accompanied the regent on the road to Kyoto, the samurai was at the same spot, gazing at the beautiful page. Returning the samurai's greeting, Bansaku this time looked intently at the samurai, who caught his gaze without a blink. Passing the samurai, Bansaku looked back at him a second time and their eyes met again for a few moments as the procession went on. Later, back at the castle, Bansaku could not help thinking about the samurai and wondering what was in his heart. Was he not in the service of some lord? How could he be there at Fukakusa waiting for him to pass?

The next time the regent had to travel, Bansaku again accompanied him at his side. When the procession drew near to Fukakusa, Bansaku slowed his horse down to a walk and looked around, his heart beating fast. There again was the young samurai, standing by the side of the road. Bansaku greeted him first, and the samurai returned the greeting, gazing inquiringly into his eyes. Bansaku saw that the samurai had tears in his eyes, and bowed slightly to him as he passed. Every time after that when Bansaku accompanied the regent on the road past Fukakusa, the young samurai was there to gaze at him and greet him. By this time it was clear to Bansaku what was moving the samurai. But he wanted to know why the samurai was always at Fukakusa, and not in the service of a lord. To get the answer to his questions, the next time the procession passed Fukakusa, Bansaku had his servant remain behind and follow the samurai to find out where he lived. When the servant returned later that day he told Bansaku that at first the samurai refused to divulge his true identity, but when the servant mentioned that he had been sent by Bansaku, the samurai tearfully opened up and told him his story.

The samurai had until recently been in the service of a great lord of Kyushu (the southernmost island of Japan, a great distance from Kyoto). The samurai told the servant that he had traveled with his lord on a mission to the capital at Kyoto, which is how he found himself standing beside the road at Fukakusa when the Regent Hidetsuga's procession passed by. Seeing the beautiful page at the regent's side, the samurai was overcome with the youth's beauty and fell immediately in love with him. After that he could not get the image of the beautiful page out of his mind. He felt that if he could never fulfill his desire to love him, he could at least see his beloved's beautiful face and so ease his passion. He then asked his master for permission to leave his service and began his solitary life in Fukakusa, waiting every day for the chance to see the beautiful youth pass by again.

When Bansaku heard the story from his servant, his heart melted. He could not disregard the passion of the young samurai, even if it meant disloyalty to his lord. This samurai, he thought, has given everything up for him, and only lives for the hope of seeing him pass by. At first, Bansaku felt he would return the samurai's love because of duty, nasake. But the more he thought about it, the more he was moved by the samurai's singular devotion. He thought of the joy of being loved by such a man. "His good appearance, his burning eyes, he is a true samurai," Bansaku thought.

A couple of days later a messenger of Bansaku arrived at the samurai's lodging in Fukakusa with a letter. The samurai read it over and over again, weeping tears of joy. Not long after, the regent decided he wanted to go out on a hunt. Bansaku was to accompany him, as usual, but this time the young page dressed himself more magnificently than usual, and all that day onlookers remarked on the radiant beauty of the youth. At the end of the day when the party was about to return to the castle, Bansaku suddenly fell ill, complaining of pain in his stomach. The regent was anxious because of his favorite's sudden illness, and had him taken to a nearby temple where they left him in a private room with a doctor and some servants. A little later that evening, Bansaku appeared to recover suddenly, and feeling refreshed he organized a little feast to celebrate his recovery. When night came, all but Bansaku had fallen asleep, drunk.

Quickly gathering his cloak, Bansaku crept out of the room without a sound and made his way to Fukakusa. There leaning against the side of the bridge he saw a dark figure and called out. The young samurai stepped out of the shadow so Bansaku could see him. Bansaku dropped his cloak and the two of them approached each other. Without speaking a word, they understood each other perfectly. Embracing one another, the samurai reveled in the scent of Bansaku and the precious incense the young man used.

In the meantime, the regent back in his castle was worried about his favorite's condition, and so he sent an aide to check on him. The regent's attendant rode on horseback as fast as he could. When he approached the bridge at Fukakusa he immediately noticed the scent of Bansaku's perfume and recognized it. Dismounting from his horse, he walked over to the bridge and called out to the two figures he saw in the shadows. "Bansaku, it is I, Ueda Mondonosho, sent by our master. I think I know why you are there. But I will report to our master in such a way that all will be well for you." With that he mounted his horse and rode quickly back to the castle. Listening to the words of the regent's aid, Bansaku was moved to tears of relief. He told the samurai that he would always love him, but because of his bond to his master it would be impossible for them to see each other. He begged the samurai to instead take his linen undergarment as a consolation and as a memento. Taking it off, he gave it to the samurai who, noticing the exquisite scent of Bansaku on it, fell into tears.

The two spent the night together, and when dawn approached Bansaku quickly hurried back to the temple. True to his word, the regent's aid kept his silence about what he had observed, and the love between Regent Hidetsuga and Bansaku continued as ever. After the departure of Bansaku, the samurai realized that he had achieved his greatest desire in life, and, so, with nothing else to live for, he killed himself by running his sword through his belly and throwing himself into a nearby lake. When the locals discovered the body later, they saw the linen undergarment the man was wearing and remarked how it was like that worn by a page to a great lord. Word of the incident came to Bansaku, who recognizing that it was his samurai lover's body, secretly arranged for the body to be buried with honors in a nearby temple cemetery.

According to the written account, a few years later when the regent had a falling out with the warlord Toyotomi Hideyoshi and was forced to commit suicide, Hidetsuga called his three most beloved pages to join him in *hari-kiri*. Before their deaths, Hidetsuga asked the three what they were thinking. Bansaku tearfully confessed to Hidetsuga about his affair with the young samurai, and asked his forgiveness. The account says that Hidetsuga, himself, was moved to tears by the passionate torment of the young samurai and agreed to forgive Bansaku for his act of nasake toward the samurai.[62]

Homosexuality and Japanese Theater

Along with popular literature, the early years of the Tokugawa period saw the development and proliferation throughout the country of Japan's distinctive theater, noh and kabuki. Though modern productions of traditional Japanese theater contain no hints of the prevalent homosexuality of the period in which the theater developed, the plays of noh and kabuki theater were no different from the other literature of the times in their frequent portrayal of homosexual love.

The theater of Medieval Japan began under the patronage of the great monasteries and temples, which sponsored performances during religious festivals somewhat akin to the mystery plays of Medieval Europe. However, like Chinese theater in the same period, the theater evolved into a center for popular entertainment, where samurai would gather, get drunk and seek sexual trysts with the young actors who as in China also served as male prostitutes. However, during the rule of the 14th-century shogun Ashikaga Yoshimitsu, the work of the actor Kan'ami and his son, Fujiwaka, transformed what was degenerating into a vulgar divertissement into an elegant and elevated art form. The shogun greatly admired the performances of Kan'ami, and invited him to establish a theater at his court. Yoshimitsu was particularly enamored of Kan'ami's beautiful son, Fujiwaki, and took him on as a lover in the shudo tradition. Under the auspices and support of the shogun, Fujiwaka, known today as Zeami, was given free rein to develop his art, which quickly revealed an unusual artistic genius. By the time of his death, in the mid–15th century, Zeami had written and produced 40 plays and twenty-one books of theory that laid the foundation for what became the Noh Theater.[63]

As a reflection of the society of its time, noh plays frequently featured homosexual themes. In fact, the historian Tsuneo Watanabe says that it is impossible to appreciate certain plays without an understanding of the homosexual tradition of the monks and samurai of the period, which is usually lost in performances of the plays in modern times. An example is the play,

"Kaguetsu," which tells the story of a samurai who became a monk after the disappearance of his only child. Visiting Kyoto on a pilgrimage, the monk sees a *kasshiki*, a young male popular entertainer who doubles as a prostitute, performing a juggling act in front of a temple. The monk soon learns that the handsome kasshiki, who went by the name Kaguetsu, is his own son. Kaguetsu, through dance, relates the story of how he was kidnapped by a group of mountain hermits, dressed as *tengu*, legendary mountain creatures dressed grotesquely with long noses and wings, who passed the boy among them as a sex object. Escaping from them the youth earned a living as a juggler and prostitute. At the conclusion of the story Kaguetsu joined his father and accompanied him on the rest of his pilgrimage. Watanabe says that this play is frequently performed in modern times without any allusions to the homosexual connotations in the story, without which much of the tragic pathos of the story is lost.[64]

As noh theater developed in the 15th and 16th centuries, traveling companies brought the theater from the cities to the towns of the provinces, where it was embraced by the merchants and craftsmen of the commoner class. The commoners in the theater audiences, like their counterparts in the cities, also began to emulate the homosexual traditions of the samurai and vied with each other in pursuing the young actors who traveled with the companies. Instead of the idealized tradition of shudo, though, the sexual relationships of actors with commoners were mostly of a commercial character. So during the period when the noble idealism of shudo was reaching its zenith among the samurai, a less elevated homosexual tradition was beginning to spread among the growing population of bourgeoisie in the newly developing cities and towns.

The flavor of the sexual atmosphere in a provincial town during the period can be gleaned from a *kyogen* play, a kind of short farcical comedy put on between noh plays. In the play, called "The Old Warriors," a beautiful, aristocratic chigo accompanied by a servant arrives at an inn in a provincial town. Word of the youth's stunning looks quickly makes its way around the town, with the result that a number of the local *wakashu*, the young men of the town, gather at the inn to see the chigo, eventually persuading the innkeeper to let them join the chigo in his room for a feast. As the feast is about to begin an older man arrives and demands to be let in to see the chigo, "so as to comfort his old age." The man is rebuffed by the innkeeper, who said the room is already too full, and so the older man goes off in a huff to get his friends, who return with him with weapons. Just as a fight between the wakashu and the older men is about to erupt, the young men, following a plan of the chigo's servant, jump into the arms of the older men and start kissing and embracing them. The older men find themselves, to their surprise, "*waka-zoku*-philes," lovers of wakashu, rather than "*shonin*-philes," lovers of boys. Watanabe notes that the little farce illustrates a popular understanding that there were different kinds of homosexual loves, *waka-zoku*, the love of older adolescents or young men, and *shonin*, a term for the love of a chigo, adolescents seventeen years of age or under.[65]

During the growing prosperity that accompanied the peace and political stability of the early years of the Tokugawa shogunate a new form of theater not tied to the monasteries and temples began to take root and develop *kabuki*. Beginning among the women's dance companies which performed on stages built up along the Kamo River in central Kyoto, kabuki from the outset had no pretensions to the elevated intentions of noh, drawing its material from everyday life rather than the classics or legends. Acted without masks, a great attraction of the plays was the physical appeal of the performers, especially the young girls who played the parts of young males as well as female roles. The great popularity of the early kabuki plays, often featuring overtly erotic themes, attracted legions of male customers. Because of the female prostitution and consequent sexual notoriety that soon grew up around kabuki, in 1629 the authorities issued a decree prohibiting the appearance of women on stage. As a result, the roles of both male and female parts began to be played by wakashu.

If the authorities thought that banning women on stage would bolster public morals, they were mistaken. To the contrary, the appearance of young men dressed prettily as pages or young women created a sensation. Attendance at the plays skyrocketed, with scores of townsmen joining the samurai ogling the young actors. A commentary written in 1658 described the scene: "They have produced a theater called *wakashu kabuki* in which the dancers are young men. Many men were so enchanted by their charms that they ended up swearing their eternal love and becoming ill by seriously wounding their arms."[66] The mention of men "wounding their arms" is a reference to the samurai custom of two lovers cutting their arms to mix their blood as a sign of union. An incident recounted by Jini'chi Iwata tells of a samurai, just arrived from the provinces, who attended a performance and was so enthralled with the beauty of a wakashu actor that he climbed up on to the stage, cut off his ear with his sword and handed it to the young man as a sign of everlasting devotion.[67] Another contemporary account noted the financial toll that the riotous lifestyle began to have on the theater patrons: "They got young men to sing and dance, and there were many rich men who were so carried away that they spen[t] mad sums on them and ended up in ruins." But even in describing such tawdry degeneracy the writer could not avoid the Japanese fondness for poetic allusion: "Their property disappeared as a thin covering of snow melts away beneath the rays of the spring sun."[68]

Finally, in 1652, in response to the moral dissipation surrounding the theater, the wakashu kabuki itself was banned. The actors were required by the edict to cut off the long lock of hair on the forehead that was the distinguishing trait of a youth, and as related in *Edo meisho ki*, "Beautiful Places in Edo," the theater-goers, "finding that their beautiful *wakashu* were no longer *wakashu*, [they] wept tears of blood."[69] The actors, however, were not about to let government regulation interfere with their lucrative side business. By covering their foreheads with a kerchief, called a *yaro*, to disguise the loss of their forelocks, and by the use of makeup and other techniques, the actors managed to make themselves as erotically appealing as ever and so ensured their continuing roles as homosexual love objects. With the actors wearing their kerchiefs, or yaro, the wakashu kabuki became yaro kabuki, the form in which it has come down to modern times. Without the forelock, the actors had to work harder to bring off the feminine role, which led to the development of the *oyama*, a specialist in women's roles. With the curtailment of the erotic displays of the young wakashu actors, kabuki began its development from what was essentially a lewd and vulgar burlesque to an authentic art form in itself.

While the new regulations had a restraining effect on the overtly erotic content of the performances, they had no effect on the brisk off-stage sexual trade of the young male actors. Called *tobiko*, "fly boys," their numbers grew rapidly to meet the demands of the growing urban population enjoying the prosperity of Tokugawa Japan. The fly boys of the theater were quickly joined by other, full-time male prostitutes, called *kagema*, who worked in tea houses and in brothels, known as *kagemajaya*, which sprang up quickly in the theater districts. The fly boys and the kagema were immensely popular among the merchant class and cultural sophisticates of the day, who practiced a debauched form of *nanshoku*, wining and dining the young men in a caricature of the noble love of the samurai. The young kabuki stars were much in demand among wealthy patrons who competed with each other for the privilege of purchasing their services. The more beautiful actors even had devoted followings and were celebrated like the Hollywood stars of today.

The Golden Age of Nanshoku

The rise of a middle class with money to spend and leisure time to fill, the exposure of commoners to the sexual traditions of their samurai superiors, now rubbing shoulders with many of them because of their large presence in the cities, and the dispersion of theater with its accompanying actor prostitutes throughout the country all contributed to the rapid spread of nanshoku as a social custom through all segments of Japanese society. The garrisoning of thousands of samurai in the cities in the early 17th century was itself a contributing force in the spread of nanshoku, not just because of the example the samurai ruling class set for the commoners with their preoccupation with male love. The introduction of the thousands of samurai into the cities greatly exacerbated the ratio of men to women, which by limiting sexual options for young males would have naturally encouraged the spread of nanshoku among middle-class men. During the mid–18th century the ratio of men to women in Edo reached as high as 170 males for every 100 women.[70]

As illustrated in the popular literature of the period, homosexual love by the time of the Genroku period had become widely established in the lives of the men of all walks of life. In sharp contrast to modern Western society, there was a widespread understanding during the centuries of Tokugawa rule that "all males are potentially vulnerable to the attractions of their own sex. Among young men, in particular, a passion for boys or other youths was regarded as normal."[71] Another reflection of how nanshoku had become engrained in social traditions is in the frequent use of "brotherhood" contracts, written agreements akin to a marriage agreement that spells out the obligations of "older brother" and "younger brother" in a relationship. One such contract alludes to the prevalence of ambisexuality among the men of the time. The contract prohibits the "older brother" from having sex with a woman during the relationship. On this stipulation, Leupp remarked, "the very fact that such clauses were considered necessary indicates that bisexuality was common but that some 'younger brothers' resented sharing their partners with women."[72]

Though the experience of most of the urban middle class with the more edifying elements of the shudo tradition was mostly limited to what they read in literature, there remained among the samurai a conviction about the necessity of shudo in inculcating virtue and character in young men. In a work of 1653, *Inu Tsurezure,* the author writes: "It is natural for a samurai to make every effort to excel with pen and sword. Beyond that, what is important to us is not ever to forget, even to our last moment, the spirit of *shudo.* If we should forget it, it will not be possible for us to maintain the decencies, nor gentleness of speech, nor the refinements of polite behavior."[73]

With the widespread prevalence of nanshoku throughout the country, and the celebration of the noble sentiments of shudo in art and literature, the first two centuries of the Tokugawa Shogunate have been called the Golden Age of Nanshoku.[74] The *bakufu* government instituted occasional campaigns in an attempt to rein in the excesses of nanshoku, especially as practiced in and around the theater world. Nonetheless, male prostitution continued to flourish, and homosexual love endured as a prominent feature of the lives of the shoguns and the samurai aristocracy.

Notwithstanding the moral tone and sexual restraint they tried to establish during the period, the Tokugawa shoguns were well known for their devotion to nanshoku. The first Tokugawa shogun, Ieyasu, despite his thirteen wives and concubines and the seventeen children he produced, was also known for his fondness for young men. The third shogun, Iemetsu, displayed a marked preference for males all his life.[75] The fifth Tokugawa shogun, Tsunayoshi who presided over the cultural brilliance of the Genroku period, was especially preoccupied with his wakashu, even considering the standards of the time. According to the *Sanno gaiki*, Tsunayoshi's biography, the shogun pursued sexual relationships with more than one hundred young men, some of whom were procured for him by a special officer he appointed in 1693 for that purpose.[76] The *Sanno gaiki* adds that Tsunayoshi's passion for the young men was irrespective of social origins or rank. "If they were handsome, he appointed them attendants."[77]

Many of his wakashu were kept as concubines in the women's quarters along with his wives and female concubines. Several dozen, however, were housed in a special dormitory in the palace of Tsunayoshi's court chamberlain, himself a former lover of the shogun. There they lived regulated lives, with their schedule, meals, studies and travels to Tsunayoshi's palace and back all carefully managed.[78] Some of Tsunayoshi's lovers gained appointments to high office as a result of their relationships with the shogun. Some progressed from page all the way up to the rank of daimyo. In fact, the *Sanno Gaiki* listed nineteen different daimyos who rose to their positions through sexual relationships with the shogun. One young man in particular, Yanagisawa Yoshiyasu, who was noted for his intelligence, education and administrative abilities, rose to become the most powerful of the shogun's ministers. By the time of his death Yoshiyasu had become a great daimyo with enormous wealth and property. Other boys who sexually pleased the shogun received regular stipends and lesser noble ranks. However, as was the case with lovers of Chinese rulers, acquiring such a position had its risks. Wakashu who at some point displeased the shogun, some with ranks as high as daimyo, were stripped of their positions and sent into exile.[79] Many of the daimyo and samurai lords shared the Tokugawa shogun's interest in young men, who likewise could advance in rank and wealth as a result of the relationships.

Comparisons Between Tokugawa Japan and Classical Athens

Like the culture of classical Athens during its golden age, homosexual love was an aspect of life of the times that was featured in literature and art, and was subject to the restraint of social traditions and civil law. As was also the case in classical Athens, the mores of homosexual love, which had developed in the context of military education of the nobility, evolved into a set of ideals and traditions that were widely admired and aspired to, if not closely adhered to by the bulk of the population.

While the ideals and practices of shudo among the samurai, and the sexual customs and attitudes of Tokugawa society that evolved from shudo, are remarkably similar in many ways to the pederastic tradition of classical Greece, there are notable differences between the two traditions, especially in regard to the rigidity of the customs. For much of the classical era in Greece, for example, it was considered dishonorable, if not downright immoral, for an adult male to take the passive role in sex with another male. In contrast, the Japanese in the Tokugawa period appear to have had little concern about a male, regardless of age, taking the receptive role in sex, as long as the dominating partner was deemed worthy. Indeed, as we saw earlier, taking the passive role with a superior was thought to be beneficial, since there was a belief that the noble qualities of the superior would be passed to the passive partner during intercourse.[80]

Nor was the passive role in anal sex considered an unpleasant duty, as some ancient Greek writers claimed. To the contrary, taking the passive role in intercourse was widely understood as being deeply pleasurable. A sex manual of the day, the *Shikido kinpisho*, in a section on masturbation, instructs the reader to increase his pleasure by masturbating his penis with one hand while inserting the middle finger of his other hand into his anus. The manual explains that the reason for that is because the sexual energy of the body collects in the lower parts. Literature of the period also often included jokes about the desire of males of all ages to take the receptive role in intercourse.[81] Absent from Tokugawa literature is any hint of the social disapproval or ridicule felt for men taking the passive role or even overtly seeking penetration by other males, an attitude frequently expressed in classical Greece, especially in the comedies of Aristophanes.[82]

Gary Leupp notes that the passive role could even be taken by a social superior to the active partner, provided a rationale for placing the relationship in the framework of older lover-younger beloved existed. The third Tokugawa shogun, Iemetsu, reportedly played the receptive role to an "older brother," Sakabae Gozaemon, who was a personal attendant in his household. The shogun had known Gozaemon, four years older than him, since childhood, and was sexually attracted to him. When they developed a sexual relationship, Iemetsu, sixteen at the time, took the role of "younger brother" to his twenty-year-old personal attendant.[83]

Another notable distinction between the tradition of shudo and the sexual mores of classical Athens was that the wakashu could be the one who initiated the relationship. According to *Hagakure* (Hidden by Leaves), a samurai manual written by Yamamoto Tsunetomo in the early 1700s, "A young man should test an older man for at least five years, and if he is assured of that person's intentions, then he too should request the relationship.... If the younger man can devote himself and get into the situation for five or six years then it will not be unsuitable."[84]

A commentary on sexuality of the period, *Wakashu no haru*, provides a gradation of sorts on the desirability of young males at different ages of their development, a direct parallel to a similar ranking of adolescents at various ages provided by the classical Greek writer, Strato. From age eleven to fourteen, the boy was a "blossoming flower"; from 15 to 18 "flourishing flower"; 19 to 22 "falling flower." According to another writer the age of a suitable younger partner for an adult male could be very broad, from the age of seven to twenty-five, since during this time the boy would develop from child to adult.[85] While these works suggest that boys could be regarded as sex objects at what would be, by modern standards, a very young age, the Japanese exhibited no qualms about a boy beginning a sexual life while still very young. Perhaps because of the general recognition that sex was one of the gifts of life, to be freely enjoyed by all, Tokugawa society appeared to have been unconcerned with protecting even young teenagers from the sexual advances of their elders, as long as the intentions were honorable and the younger male was well treated. Indeed, sexual relationship between teenaged males and older males were considered desirable. In one of his stories, Ihara comments that "a youth with no male lover is like a maiden without a betrothed."[86]

As noted earlier, the shudo tradition had no hard-and-fast rules on the upper age limits of the partners, as was the case in classical Athens, as long as one played the noble mentor role. Nor were young men who continued in a relationship with an older samurai well into adulthood stigmatized, as was the tragic poet Agathon, who was ridiculed by Aristophanes for his continuing relationship with his erastes, Pausanius. In fact, while it was typical for young men to progress from insertee role with an older man, to lover of a younger man and then to marriage, Tokugawa society seemed not to care whether the progression in fact occurred or whether a man remained a devotee of nanshoku his whole life.[87] The moral quality of a homosexual relationship, then, did not depend on such social rules, but on the character of the relationship. The devotion of a samurai in patiently courting a younger man would have been seen as reflecting the highest ideals of shudo, while a merchant spending a fortune because of his infatuation with an actor prostitute might have been seen as contemptible debauchery.[88]

It seems inevitable in a cultured society where homosexual love flourishes alongside heterosexual love that at some point a debate would be held on the merits of each respective way. In the Greek classical period such a debate appeared in several works, Lucian's *Amores*, Plutarch's *Amatorius*, and the *Greek Anthology*. A similar debate on which of the two ways of love was superior is contained in an anonymous work of the mid–17th century, *Denbu mongatari* (The Boor's Tale), though that debate ends with a draw. On the other hand, the 18th-century poet Hiraga Gennai wrote that because the love of youths and the love of women were both forces or nature, there was no point in debating which was better: "Cold and hot seasons, day and night come in turn. No one can control how the spring blossoms or autumn leaves fall. So how can anyone criticize either the way or Men or the Way of Women?"[89]

Western Influence and the Decline of Shudo

Since their first appearance in Japan in the mid–16th-century, Christian missionaries never hesitated to denounce the homosexual traditions of the country. The Jesuits had great success at first in converting the peasants and samurai aristocracy of southern Japan during the rule of Oda Nobunaga, who protected them for political rather than spiritual reasons. The missionaries, however, were expelled barely 50 years after their arrival by Nobunaga's successor, Toyotomi Hideyoshi, who resented the destruction of many Buddhist temples and monasteries by the Christians. Nonetheless, the condemnation of Japan's native homosexual traditions by the Jesuit missionaries in the 16th century and the continued denunciations by the missionaries and Western traders who regularly visited Japan over the next several centuries gave support to conservative Japanese moralists who disapproved of the customs.

The moral stature of the nanshoku tradition began a steady decline in the early 18th century because of the increasing commercialization of homosexual activity in the world of the theater and the kagema prostitutes. As the importance of the samurai as a military force and a basis for power gradually diminished over the peaceful years of the Tokugawa rule, the military ethos that gave focus to the idealism of shudo likewise lost its potency. With the gradual decline of the prestige of shudo and the concurrent growth in prostitution, the image of nanshoku among mainstream Japanese began to lose its association with masculine ideals and selfless nobility, and instead was more and more identified with the moral dissipation of the tawdry urban entertainment districts and their increasingly effeminate male prostitutes. By the early 19th century, the cumulative effect of the continual criticism of Japan's homosexual customs by Westerners combined with the increasing disrepute of the commercialized nanshoku in the cities began to erode support for the ancient traditions of same-sex love among many Japanese.

The authorities had made attempts in 1716 and 1787 to curb the excesses of both male and female prostitution in the cities, which rather than eliminating it mainly caused the practitioners to use more discretion in promoting their trade, in effect lowering its profile in the cities, if not its frequency. Another period of reform began in 1841 with the authorities assailing "commercial sex, 'lewd' art and literature, and extravagance in general." While the measures forced the closure of brothels and teahouses, forbad theater-owners from forcing their actors into prostitution and restricted kabuki theaters to a district on the outskirts of Edo, the reforms again were unsuccessful in completely eradicating prostitution, but rather forced the male prostitutes underground, plying their trade as "tailors and incense peddlers."[90]

The final assault on the centuries-old traditions of shudo came with the rapid westernization that followed the Meiji Restoration, which marked the end of the bakufu government of the shoguns. The Meiji Restoration was instigated when the daimyo governors of two provinces, Satsuma and Chosu, formed an alliance against the shogun in favor of the restoration of power in the emperor. The two daimyo were not particularly devoted to the emperor. Rather, they envisioned an imperial government similar to that of the pre-bakafu period, when most of the power rested in a handful of powerful ministers, themselves and a few allies, with the emperor a mere figurehead.

Under pressure from the Satsuma-Chosu alliance, the shogun, Tokugawa Yoshinobu, on November 9, 1867, formally put his services "at the emperor's disposal," resigning his office ten days later. Despite his formal relinquishment of the reins of government to the Emperor Meiji, Yoshinobu held on to most of his power. The following January, samurai forces of the daimyos of Satsuma and Chosu attacked the forces of the shogun and defeated them, whereby the emperor stripped the shogun of his remaining power. The daimyo of Satsuma and Chosu and their allies quickly formed a government, ostensibly serving the wishes of the emperor, but in fact governing as an oligarchy. The Meiji government then launched a vigorous campaign to catch up with the industrial West and to assert Japan's place among the world's military powers.

With the opening to the West, rapid industrialization and consequent westernization that accompanied the Meiji Restoration in 1867, the government recognized that the continued visibility of widespread homosexuality in Japanese society was a liability in their attempt to present Japan to the West as a modern industrial power. As a result, in 1873 a law was enacted prohibiting same-sex relations, and imprisoning for 90 days anyone caught practicing homosexuality. Perhaps because homosexual traditions were so deeply entrenched in Japanese society, especially among some quarters of the military, it was inevitable that the effort to expunge homosexuality from the country would meet with resistance. Indeed, there is considerable irony in the fact that a large part of the samurai forces that were responsible for finally defeating the bakufu army and installing the oligarchy in power were from the province of Satsuma, a region renowned among the Japanese for its Spartan-like martial spirit and devotion to shudo.[91] With the samurai from Satsuma and Chosu forming the heart of the new Japanese army, homosexuality remained a widespread custom in the military under the Meiji government. The anti-sodomy law of 1873 was, in fact, repealed in 1883 and replaced with a much milder law against "indecent assault," the sexual seduction of someone of either sex under the age of 16.

Despite the efforts of the government, then, nanshoku continued as a very visible feature in the lives of some segments of Japanese society. In the late 1890s homosexuality was so widespread among university students that it became a concern of the press, which by that point was thoroughly westernized. An article in the *Japan Daily Mail* of September 2, 1896, displayed the heavy influence of Western moral attitudes as it deplored widespread homosexuality among students: "Among certain students ... activities whose victims are young boys rather than young girls are now in fashion. We would not wish to draw attention to conduct *so abominable*, but as it is happening, it would be useless to close one's eyes to it." An article in the *Eastern World* in February 1898 complains that "Male homosexuality ... is so widespread among the students of Tokyo that adolescent boys cannot go out at night." Another journal, *Mancho-ho*, in May 1899 demanded legal measures to stop "habitual conduct of such bestiality amongst the future lawyers, officers and teachers of Japan."[92]

The continued visibility of male homosexuality in the military even into the early 20th century was commented on by a European observer in 1910.

> In peace as in war, the Japanese soldier marches arm in arm with the friend with whom he is in an intimate relation.... Many officers have told me of scenes where a soldier in love with another had fought at the risk of his own life, rushing willingly to the deadly spot. This is not simply due to the warrior spirit and contempt for death characteristic of the Japanese soldier, but also to their passion for another soldier."[93]

The German anthropologist Ferdinand Karsch-Haack similarly remarked on the role of love-inspired valor in the Japanese victory in the Russo-Japanese War of 1904–1905: "Comrade-love is still — as a legacy from the Samurai — much favored in both the Japanese army and navy.... it has contributed not a little to the marvelous results of their late war with Russia."[94]

The love-inspired valor among the Japanese soldiers in the Russo-Japanese War that was commended by these European observers was, however, the last vestige of the once hallowed tradition of shudo in Japan. With the continued transformation of the country from a feudal agricultural society into a modern industrial state, and the rapid adoption of Western systems of education, business management, and styles of dress and entertainment, the noble tradition of same-sex love that for a thousand years had inspired spiritual devotion in the monasteries and military valor on the battlefields was quickly forgotten. A contemporary writer, Tahuro Inagaki, sadly reflected on the passing of shudo: "Without our noticing it this cultural tradition has been lost to us.... When we were schoolboys we often heard of an affair in which two students had quarreled on account of a beautiful young boy and had ended by drawing knives.... But since the new era of Taisho (1912–1926) we no longer hear of this kind of thing. The *shudo* which had clung on to life has now reached its end.[95]

Conclusion

In considering the venerable homosexual traditions of China and Japan one cannot fail to notice the remarkable similarity of those two traditions to the sexual traditions of the two great civilizations of the Western classical age, Greece and Rome. While specific details of the traditions are of course quite different, the patterns in which the ambisexual nature of human sexuality manifested in the customs of the two great Oriental cultures nonetheless show striking parallels to the customs of ancient Greece and Rome.

Like the traditions of Rome, the Chinese tradition allowed even married men to engage in same-sex relationships as a complement to their marital relationships. Like Rome, however, which disapproved of adult citizens taking the passive role in sexual relationships, the Chinese tradition frowned on a male taking the passive role in a relationship with one of his own class. Hence while the Roman tradition approved of married men having same-sex lovers, the passive partner had to be either a slave-concubine or a non–Roman. Likewise, under the Chinese tradition, because of the status issue, the passive partner was generally a male of a lower social class. Another parallel between the Chinese tradition and that of ancient Rome is that in both cases same-sex relationships could be formalized in a marriage ceremony. Under the Roman Empire the partners, be they two men or two women, would sometimes use Roman adoption laws to effect a legal union, under which the partner would have inheritance rights. The same-sex marriage tradition in southern China appears to have been more elaborate, having its own ceremonies and an expectation that the older partner would be obligated to look after the younger partner's future, for example, finding a suitable bride and providing the bride price. In contrast, to the Roman and Chinese traditions, the idealized loves of a monk for a chigo, or of a samurai knight for a squire apprentice, were, like the educational relationships between Greek men and youths, regarded as suitable for two males of the same class since in both cases it was believed that the younger, passive partner benefited from the relationship with the older male.

The overall pattern, though, of all four cultures is of a recognition by each society of the possibility of same-sex relationships as a feature of youth and as an adjunct to the marriage relationship. While relations among women in all four societies are not well documented, due to the patriarchal character of all four cultures, we do have enough information to see that same-sex relationships between women, though sometimes puzzling or distasteful to the men of each society, provided a parallel option where a woman could find intimate companionship with another woman in her youth or as a complement to her marital relationship.

The manifestation of this ambisexual pattern among all four of these great civilizations is a testament to the persistence of homosexuality as a deeply engrained trait of human sexuality and to the harmonious accommodation of each of the four societies to the ambisexual nature of the human sexual drive.

12

Homosexual Love
in the World of Islam

And round about them will serve boys of perpetual freshness: if thou seest them, thou wouldst think them scattered pearls.

Qur-an LXXVI:19

There is in Paradise a market wherein there will be no buying or selling, but will consist of men and women. When a man desires a beauty, he will have intercourse with them.

Al Hadis, Vol. 4, p. 172, No. 34[1]

Many in the West would no doubt find it surprising that the vision of Paradise in Islamic scripture includes among the varied delights awaiting blessed souls in the afterlife boys "of perpetual freshness ... like scattered pearls," as the quotation from the Qur-an above indicates. Lest it be thought that the boys are merely to look at, the excerpt quoted above from *Al Hadis*, a collection of sayings attributed to the Prophet, promises that a man who "desires a beauty" can have intercourse with his choice of not just beautiful women, but beautiful men as well. The idea of homosexual love as one of the promised pleasures of Paradise may seem doubly surprising to Westerners given the heated condemnations of homosexuality by puritanical Sunni imans and Iranian mullahs, and the well publicized trials in some Islamic countries in recent times of men accused of homosexual acts. After all, as Islamic scholars would be quick to note, there are also passages in the Qur-an that seem to strongly disapprove of homosexuality, such as "Would ye really approach men in your lusts rather than Women? Nay, ye are a people grossly ignorant!" (Qur-an XXVII: 55). This puzzling juxtaposition, however, is an example of a long-running contradiction in the Islamic world concerning love between members of the same sex. Throughout the history of Islam a long and varied tradition of same-sex love, complete with a rich body of homosexual love poetry and literature, has co-existed with a religious tradition whose spiritual leaders have routinely taught that homosexuality is immoral under Islamic tradition. Even today, when homosexual practices are against the law in nearly every Islamic country, a vast majority of Muslim men continue to participate in same-sex relationships at some point in their lives. The explanation for this contradiction lies in how the teachings of one of the world's great religions has accommodated the inherent ambisexuality of the human race, and the homosexual expression that Islamic culture has long regarded as an inevitable feature of human nature.

Ironically, the conservative sexual mores that are associated today with Islam in the Arab world, particularly in Saudi Arabia, are not a reflection of longstanding popular attitudes in Islamic countries, but are a result of Western influences introduced in the colonial era. According to the Arabic scholar As'ad AbuKhalil, the well-known sexual conservatism of modern Saudi Arabia is due more to Victorian Puritanism than to Islamic mores. It is quite inaccurate to attribute prevailing sexual mores in present-day Arab society to Islam. Originally, Islam did not have the same harsh Biblical judgment about homosexuality as Christianity. Homophobia, as an ideology of hostility toward people who are homosexual, was produced by the Christian West. Homophobic influences in Arab cultures are relatively new, and many were introduced ... from Western sources.[2]

The negative moral judgment on homosexuality found in much of the Arab world in recent times, which some have attributed to a deep-rooted hostility to same-sex love in the scriptures of Islam, is, like the modern-day attitudes to homosexuality in China and Japan, another import from the West.

Notwithstanding the Western origins of recent homophobic attitudes found in some elements of the Islamic world, the Islamic religious and legal tradition does in fact include a well-documented hostility to same-sex love. In addition to verses in the Qur-an,[3] the oral teachings assembled in *Al Hadis* contain, along with the references to beautiful men in Paradise for a man to have intercourse with, a number of harsh condemnations of same-sex love. According to sayings in *Al Hadis*, the Prophet feared that his people would fall in to the lustful ways of the "people of Lot," a reference to the inhabitants of the biblical city of Sodom. Therefore, both the active and passive partner in a homosexual act between males must be killed. Another provision states that "the man who sodomizes another" will "on the Day of Resurrection be regarded as more reprehensible than carrion." In another, it is said that the passionate kissing of an adolescent will lead a man to punishment in Hell. Other provisions of Islamic law prescribe burning alive as the penalty for homosexual practices, throwing such an offender from the top of a minaret, and stoning to death as a punishment for a passive homosexual. However, the Islamic scholar Charles Pellat, after listing and summarizing these and numerous other provisions of Islamic law concludes, "The legal provisions set out above are thus to a large extent theoretical, since homosexual relations have always been tolerated."[4] Even under the Iranian theocracy of the mullahs, who executed men for homosexuality by the hundreds in their early years in power, the authorities turn a blind eye to rampant homosexuality in the religious schools, traditional centers of male homosexual love.[5] The persistence of widespread same-sex love throughout the Islamic world from its earliest centuries to the modern day, despite the disapproval of homosexual acts in the Islamic legal tradition, is a powerful testament to the strength of this trait as an aspect of human sexuality.

Historical Reports of Homosexuality in Muslim Lands

Homosexuality in the Islamic world has long been known to Europeans from the early Middle Ages onward through reports brought back by travelers. Lurid descriptions of widespread homosexual practices of the Muslims in the Holy Land were, in fact, a principal element used in Christian propaganda attempting to rouse the Christians of Europe for the Crusades.[6] The thirteenth-century Dominican friar William of Adam wrote of the homosexuality he witnessed in Egypt: "These Saracens, forgetting human dignity, go so far that men live with each other in the same way that men and women live together in our own land." He added that Jews in Egypt "follow the example" of the Egyptians and pursue homosexual relationships with youths.[7] In the 16th century Leo Africanus wrote of the availability of young male prostitutes in Fez, Morocco, and of men living with youths in hostelries. Another sixteenth-century report commented that the public baths in Turkey had such a reputation for lesbian relations that husbands refused to let their wives go to them.[8] An English visitor to Alexandria, Egypt, in the 1680s wrote of his shock when he heard soldiers openly bragging about screwing boys.[9]

With the development of European colonialism in 18th and 19th centuries many more reports of the "sodomitical" habits of the Muslims came back to Europe. A British traveler, James Silk Buckingham, journeying through Mesopotamia in 1817, wrote in disgust of his seeing "boys publicly exhibited and set apart for the purposes of depravity not to be named." Buckingham was later was shocked to discover that the "amour" that his guide and translator spoke of with great feeling was not the daughter, but the son, of an elderly man they met on their way.[10] Visiting Turkey in 1819, Lord Byron described the public baths there as "marble palaces of sherbet and sodomy."[11] The great French novelist Gustave Flaubert, visiting Cairo in 1850, wrote about his discovery of the Egyptian's open acceptance of homosexuality. "Here is it quite accepted. One admits one's sodomy, and it is spoken of at table in the hotel."[12]

Sir Richard Burton, the 19th-century British soldier and explorer, scandalized the Victorian world with his translations of sexually candid literature from the exotic East. In an essay he appended to his ten-volume translation of *Arabian Nights* which he published in 1885 Burton laid out in detail the homosexual customs in the Islamic world from Morocco to the Punjab, a geographic area he described as a "Sotadic Zone," in which the vice of Sodom was widespread. In Morocco, Burton wrote, "the Moors proper are notable sodomites; Moslems, even of saintly houses, are permitted openly to keep catamites.... Vice prevails throughout the old regencies of Algiers, Tunis and Tripoli and all the cities of the South Mediterranean seaboard." Moving eastward, "we reach Egypt, that classical region of all abominations." Burton mentions that when Napoleon's army was in Egypt, one of Bonaparte's aides, Pierre Jaubert, wrote in a letter that the Arabs and the Mamlukes do to their prisoners what Socrates did to Alcibiades — a reference to the philosopher's famous homosexual love for his student.* Moving eastward again, Burton says of the Druze of Syria "'unnatural propensities are very common amongst them" and then "the whole of Asia Minor and Mesopotamia now occupied by the 'unspeakable Turk,' a race of born pederasts." In Persia, Burton says, "the corruption is now bred in the bone. It begins in boyhood," and then tells of the 17th-century traveler and Persian scholar Jean Chardin writing "that houses of male prostitution were common in Persia whilst those of women were unknown." Burton adds that "the same is the case in the present day and the boys are prepared with extreme care by diet, baths, depilation, unguents and a host of artists in cosmetics." As a final note on the Persians, Burton relates a favorite punishment meted on strangers caught in the harems: "strip and throw them and expose them to the embraces of the grooms and Negro slaves." Concluding his tour of the Sotadic Zone, Burton writes that "the cities of Afghanistan and Sind are thoroughly saturated with Persian vice," that "each caravan is accompanied by a number of boys and lads" for sexual partners, and that "the Sikhs and the Moslems of the Punjab are much addicted to Le Vice."[13]

Though British colonial rule replaced that of the Ottomans in the Middle East in the early 20th century, and the French were ruling much of North Africa, the indigenous homosexual customs of the Islamic world continued as before. In fact, sexual researchers in the early and mid–20th century estimated that homosexual activity outnumbered heterosexual activity in much of the Arab world.[14] In the period between the First and Second World Wars, North African cities, particularly in Morocco, became tourist destinations for Western homosexuals looking for respite from the severe repression of contemporary Western culture. The rise of Islamic fundamentalist leaders in much of the Arab world and the consequent empha-

---

*"*Les Arabes et les Mamelouks ont traité quelques-uns de nos prisonniers comme Socrate traitait, dit-on, Alcibiade. Il fallait périr ou y passer.*"

sis in many countries on strict adherence to Islamic moral tenets has not affected the frequency of homosexual activity among Muslims, only its social visibility.

Sexual Attitudes in the First Centuries of Islam

Mohammed began his preaching in the early 7th century in his native Mecca, at that time a trading town near the Arabian coast of the Red Sea. By the time of the death of Mohammed all of the tribes of the Arabian Peninsula had been united under the new faith. Within 30 years of his death the caliphs who succeeded him as leaders of the movement had expanded the territory of the believers north and eastward to include Palestine, Syria, Persia and present-day Afghanistan and Pakistan, and westward through Egypt as far as Tripoli. Under the Umayyad dynasty, which came to power in 661, the territory of Islam expanded further, until it reached from Spain and Morocco on the Atlantic, to the borders of India and the Himalayan foothills on the east.

The sexual morality taught by Mohammed and his immediate successors showed a very positive attitude to sex in general, a sharp contrast to the anti-sexual morality that the Christian Church was at the same time trying with little success to enforce on the newly converted Germanic tribes of Europe.[15] While Christian teaching looked upon sex and sensuality as permeated with sin, Mohammed and his followers regarded sex as a positive force in life, and felt that sexual intercourse was good for a man's health. Mohammed's native Arab Bedouin culture was especially male centered when it came to sexual morality, and in that respect the attitudes and sexual mores that developed in Islam were very similar to those of the Romans and Germanic tribes. A man was allowed multiple wives or concubines, if he could afford to keep them, while on the other hand women's sexuality was tightly restricted. Women were regarded as property of their husbands and fathers, and hence heterosexual activity outside of marriage was also strongly disapproved. Women were socially segregated from males, and were forbidden to appear in public alone. Even more than under Christian sexual mores, Islamic sexual tradition placed a great emphasis on the sexual modesty of women, who were required to drape themselves almost completely when in public. In later times, the demands for modesty were extended to males, who were forbidden to display their genitals in any way, which led to the tradition of robes or loose fitting trousers worn by devout Muslim men down to the mid–20th century.

While a negative judgment on homosexuality is clear in Islamic scripture, no passages in the Qur-an directly condemn homosexuality, nor are any punishments for homosexual acts clearly specified.[16] The conflicting passages on homosexual love in Islamic scripture — promising boys and beautiful men in Paradise on the one hand while on the other declaring that those who practice same-sex love are immoral — have driven the ambiguity found in Islamic attitudes to homosexuality. Because of the social mores that encouraged polygamy and concubinage, while severely punishing adultery and fornication, heterosexual outlets for young men were effectively eliminated. Hence, the circumstances of Muslim society strongly encouraged homosexuality, especially among young men.

The sexual mores of Islam in its first century of expansion discouraged homosexuality, reflecting the sexual conservatism of the tribal Bedouin culture of Mohammed and his immediate successors. In later times Muslim jurists continued to base their rulings on the anti-homosexual passages in the Qur-an and Al Hadis. However, actual social attitudes to same-sex love loosened considerably under the Abbasid dynasty which came to power in A.D. 750. The Abbasids ruled the Muslim world with the sole exception of Muslim Spain until their power declined and they were finally overthrown by Mongol invaders in the 13th century. Muslim Spain remained largely under the more conservative Umayyad dynasty, based in Córdoba, until the return of Christian rule in the Middle Ages. The cultural distance of the Abbasids, who ruled from a luxurious palace in Baghdad, from the Bedouin origins of Mohammed and the first caliphs was no doubt a contributing cause to the relaxation of attitudes to same-sex love. Another influential factor was most likely the predominance of homosexual customs in many of the lands conquered by the Muslims. As we've seen in earlier chapters, the homosexual customs of the societies in the Middle East and the Mediterranean Basin were deeply engrained traditions that extended continuously back to the earliest stirrings of human civilization. Given the tight restrictions on heterosexual outlets under Islamic law, the accommodation of Islamic tradition to the human homosexual potential that was apparent from the time of the Abbasid dynasty onward was most probably an inevitable development if social harmony was to be maintained.

The pattern of sexual customs that came to dominate Muslim societies from the 8th century onward, then, was of tightly controlled heterosexual relationships surrounding the male family head, complemented by widespread homosexuality among young unmarried men, among women in their segregated world, and as an outlet even for married men. It has been argued that homosexuality that occurs where the sexes are segregated or where heterosexual outlets are not available is not real homosexuality, but is "situational" or artificial. In the past writers have pointed to prisons or the military as artificial environments and argued that the same-sex relationships that occur in such situations are aberrations for the normal "heterosexual" individuals involved in them, and that such behavior would disappear when the individuals re-entered a heterosexual environment. The sexually segregated Islamic society would seem to be a prime example of such an environment.

However, such sexually-segregated groupings, where heterosexual opportunities are restricted to dominant males, leaving the remaining males no outlet except for homosexuality, and where segregated females engage in homosexual relations with each other, is a very common pattern in nature. As shown in Chapter 1, such a pattern is found among many species, such as gazelles, giraffes and elephants. The pattern is also found among whales and dolphins, and among some primate species, such as gorillas. Arguing that homosexuality among individuals in sexually segregated societies is due to the unnaturalness of the same-sex environment displays a profound ignorance of the way sexual and reproductive patterns have manifested in nature. The sexually segregated Muslim society, in fact, seems a nearly perfect example of the sort of natural sexual regulation that appears among many animal species, where heterosexual couplings are restricted primarily to mature individuals capable of providing the parenting necessary for the healthy growth of the offspring.* Given the predominance of this pattern among social animal species, it does not seem coincidental that the same pattern manifested nearly universally, albeit with considerable variance, among the indigenous tribal cultures surveyed in Chapter 2. The ambisexuality of Islamic societies, therefore, clearly visible from the time of the Abbasids onward, is not only consistent with sexual patterns found among many other societies around the world, but seems an inevitable product of human sexual nature.

---

*Saying that the sexual segregation of Muslim society is a perfect example of natural sexual patterns is not to endorse the subordination and subjugation of women that has characterized traditional Muslim societies.

Same-sex Love in Islamic Literature

Testifying to the persistence of widespread homosexuality from the early centuries of Islam onward is an unusually rich and varied body of homosexual love poetry. Collections of poetry were produced in abundance under both the Abbasid rulers in the East and the Umayyad dynasty in Spain, called Andalusia, by the Muslims. The Umayyad rulers retained the moral conservatism of the Arabian tribes, and consequently the writings of Islamic jurists under the Umayyads are uniformly harsh in dealing with homosexuality. At the same time a vibrant tradition of homoerotic love poetry developed, but because of overt disapproval of same-sex love the poet in many cases wrote of the desired boy as an indescribably beautiful yet unattainable object. In this respect, the love poetry in Umayyad Spain bears some similarity to the poetry of the Troubadours, who wrote passionate paeans praising the beauty of the lady of the castle, at the same time lamenting their love that would remain unrequited. Many of the poets who longed for the love of a beautiful boy consoled themselves with a saying from Al Hadis attributed to the Prophet that "He who loves and remains chaste and conceals his secret and dies, dies a martyr." Hence, in Islamic Spain, the figure of a man suffering in secret because of his love for a handsome youth became a frequent theme among poets. One of the most distinguished jurists of 9th-century Spain, Ibn Daud, was also a prolific poet. In his *Book of the Flower* Ibn Daud acknowledged that passionate love between males was possible, and in fact dedicated the book to a male lover, Muhammad ibn Jami. According to accounts of his life, Ibn Daud's love for Muhammad ibn Jami was never consummated: he died a "martyr of love."[17]

Despite the official disapproval of same-sex love in Muslim Spain, there is no doubt that homosexuality was widely practiced. Given the uniform judgment of the Islamic jurists that same-sex love was improper, public displays of love between men would have been rash and an affront to Islam, and so discretion was the rule in same-sex affairs under the Umayyads. Despite Islamic scruples homosexual loves were even widespread among the Islamic leaders, as in the case of Ibn al-Farra, a scholar and teacher of the Qur-an who addressed love poems to his students. In one of his poems, he wrote, seemingly facetiously, of a man who took his young lover to court for spurning his advances — the judge ruled in favor of the plaintiff.[18]

An intensely passionate affair between the eleventh-century caliph, al-Mutamid, himself a great poet, for another poet ended in tragedy. When he was 13 years old, al-Mutamid's father, the reigning caliph, made his son the Emir of Seville, and appointed Ibn Ammar, also a noted poet, who was then 22 years old, as his vizier, a position akin to chief counselor or chief minister. The young al-Mutamid fell in love with Ibn Ammar, and one night after enjoying wine and poetry with him, al-Mutamid declared, "Tonight you will sleep with me on the same pillow!"[19] Because al-Mutamid's father disapproved of the relationship, he sent Ibn Ammar into exile to separate the two. When al-Mutamid succeeded his father, however, he recalled Ibn Ammar, with whom he could not bear to be parted, "even for an hour, day or night," and appointed him to positions of high military and political rank.[20] According to a story told about their love, one night when al-Mutamid and Ibn Ammar were sleeping together Ibn Ammar dreamed that al-Mutamid would kill him, and so fled in fear from al-Mutamid's chambers. The young caliph tried to soothe him and assured Ibn Ammar that such a thing would never happen. Not long afterwards, the two men got into a furious quarrel. Al-Mutamid, who was known for his generosity and justness, pardoned him, but "then, when Ibn Ammar boasted too triumphantly of his reprieve" the young caliph "fell into a rage and hacked him to death with his own hands." After Ibn Ammar's death, al-Mutamid grieved him bitterly "as long ago Alexander had wept for Hephestion, and gave him a sumptuous funeral."[21]

One of the greatest of the Islamic poets of Spain, and considered one of the greatest of all Medieval poets, was a tall, blond and blue-eyed bohemian, Ibn Quzman. Writing in the early 12th century, when the Umayyads had been overthrown, but an anti-homosexual attitude was still being professed by Islamic moralists, Ibn Quzman led a rakish life, far removed from the courtly manners of many of the earlier poets, and has been called an Islamic counterpart of François Villon. Like the Troubadours, with whom he's often compared, Ibn Quzman wrote poems in praise of "wine, adultery and sodomy," and enjoyed mocking the prudish Islamic moralists: "What do you say about a beloved, when he and you, without anyone else, are alone, and the house door is locked?"[22]

Literature under the more liberal Abassid dynasty, based in their sumptuous capital of Baghdad, displays few attempts to disguise the erotic interests of the writers. One of the most prominent figures in Arabic literature, and considered one of its greatest classical poets, was Abu Nuwas, born in the mid–8th century of mixed Arabic and Persian parentage. Abu Nuwas was not his given name, but a nickname, "Father of the Locks," a reference to the long locks of hair which hung down to his shoulders. Sold by his mother to a shopkeeper when he was only a child, Abu Nuwas worked in his owner's grocery business in Basra for several years. When he was a young adolescent his beauty and intelligence attracted the attention of his handsome cousin, Walibah ibn al-Hubab, a well known poet of the day, known for his blond hair. Al-Hubab purchased the youth's freedom from the shopkeeper and took him to live with him, and soon they became lovers. Al-Hubab mentored the young Abu Nuwas and taught him grammar, the Qur-an, theology and poetry. Later, Abu Nuwas continued his studies under Khalaf al-Ahmar, a master of pre–Islamic poetry, and according to Arab tradition he then spent a year living among Bedouin tribes so he could master the nuances of pure Arabic.

After migrating to Baghdad with al-Hubab, Abu Nuwas was soon renowned for his witty verse and ribald lyrics. Contrary to convention, his poetry did not deal with traditional Bedouin themes, but celebrated life in the city, and the joys of wine drinking, homosexual love, and lewd humor. In a verse that sums up his poetic philosophy, Abu Nuwas writes, "I delight in what the Book forbids, and flee what is allowed." The poetry of Abu Nuwas is filled with mockery and satire, often poking fun at sexual passivity in men and the sexual looseness of women. Typical of the poet's irreverence, which often shocked Arab society, were the verses about masturbation he included in some of his poems in which he judges it inferior to loving boys, but preferable by far to marriage. He had little patience for hypocrisy either, "Away with hypocrisy ... discreet debauchery means little to me. I want to enjoy everything in broad daylight."[23]

A story related by the 13th-century Arab poet Ahmad al-Tifashi about Abu Nuwas illustrates the poet's impudent personality. One day the brother of an acquaintance named Badr was walking in Baghdad with his young sons and met Abu Nuwas coming by on a horse but didn't recognize him, though the poet clearly recognized him. Abu Nuwas called out to Badr, but though Badr finally recognized his face, he could not remember the poet's name. "I'm Abu Nuwas," exclaimed the poet. Badr finally remembered the affair he had with the poet years before. Abu Nuwas asked Badr, "Who are these young boys you have with you?" Badr responded that they were his children. "Allah, be praised!" shouted Abu Nuwas. "And just think, you almost had sons by me back when we were together," Abu Nuwas said. "Go away and may Allah strike you down," shouted Badr. "Facts are facts," said Abu Nuwas as he rode away laughing.[24]

When Harun al-Rashid ascended the throne as the fifth Abbasid caliph, Abu Nuwas quickly became a court favorite. Harun al-Rashid ruled the Abbasid Empire at the zenith of its power and prestige, and under his patronage science and the arts flourished. A great classic of Arabic literature, the *Thousand and One Nights*, was written under al-Rashid, and the prominence of Abu Nuwas in the court and in Baghdad society is illustrated by his being included in several of the stories of the collection. In one such story, Abu Nuwas sets out to find a suitable youth with whom to spend the night, but instead comes across three handsome and beardless youths whom he then propositions: "Steer ye with your steps to none but me who has a mine of luxury," and then he describes the fabulous wines and meats he has to offer them. The three young men agree to go home with Abu Nuwas, who then can't decide which of them had the handsomest face and shapeliest form. Going from one to the other, Abu Nuwas continues drinking, and gets progressively drunker and drunker until his revelry is interrupted by the caliph who in his displeasure appoints Abu Nuwas as judge of pimps and panderers. To the caliph's chagrin, Abu Nuwas was not upset by his appointment, but rejoiced. When he appeared unrepentant in the ruler's court the next morning, the caliph ordered him stripped of his clothes and a saddle put on his back, and led him to the harem where he expected the women to make fun of the poet. But Abu Nuwas made so many jokes about his punishment that the caliph was finally unable to carry through the sentence.[25]

In time, Abu Nuwas' satiric poetry and his notorious outings in the wine bars got him in trouble with the caliph who, because of his role as Defender of the Faith, was obliged to maintain an air of propriety in the court. When the Barmakis, a powerful court family whose over-reaching had estranged the caliph, were crushed and exiled, Abu Nuwas wrote an elegy for them, as some of them had been his patrons. Al-Rashid was enraged by the brazenness of the poet, and Abu Nuwas had to flee, ending up in Egypt. After al-Rashid died, his successor, the 22-year-old Muhammad al-Amin, who also shared the poet's taste for wine and boys, welcomed Abu Nuwas back to the court, and for a while the two were inseparable companions. However, the poet's wild living and irreverence for the sensibilities of proper Islamic society would put him in jail or in exile several more times before his death in 814. Despite the reputation he had in his lifetime as an irreverent carouser and pursuer of boys, Abu Nuwas is remembered as a giant of Arabic literature, and as a poet who influenced writers as diverse as the 11th-century Persian poet, mathematician and philosopher Omar Khayyám and the great 14th-century mystic poet, Hafez.[26]

Homosexual love poetry also came from some of the most revered religious figures of Medieval Islam. In fact, some of the poets most known for religious devotion and mysticism were also capable of lyrics of unusual coarseness and lewdness. The great 13th-century mystical poet Rumi, who wrote rapturous verses praising the transcendent Divinity, also penned lewd verses about male prostitutes. In one poem he writes about a clever young hustler whose newfound affluence amazed his rivals who remembered him in his poverty. "Why are you so astonished," the poet said. Why shouldn't he have riches, seeing that the Royal Mint is there in his baggy britches!"[27] The 14th-century Persian mystic and poet Hafez accompanied his mystical poetry with poetic commentary on the boys he loved. In one such work, Hafez paints an evocative picture of the erotic atmosphere of the bed chamber, "With locks disheveled, flushed in a sweet drunkenness, his shirt torn open, a song on his lips, and wine-cup in hand. With eyes looking for trouble, lips softly complaining. So at midnight last night he came and sat at my pillow. He bent his head down to my ear, and in a voice full of sadness he said: 'Oh, my old lover, are you asleep?'"[28] It's also interesting to note that in contrast to the writings of Christian mystics, who have used the analogy of a heterosexual relationship to describe the relationship between God and the individual soul, Muslim mystics, almost without exception, use the analogy of a homosexual relationship between the soul and the beloved Godhead.[29]

One of the most famous of the Islamic poets was the 13th-century Sufi mystic Sa'di. In his poetry, Sa'di continuously dwelt on the theme of the beauty of adolescent males, as witnesses on earth to the beauty of God, or the object of his unending passion. While in his mystical poetry he used the love of boys as a metaphor for the union of the soul with God, his verses on his own love life are earthy and profane and offer cynical ruminations on the joys and tribulations of loving boys.[30] He wrote of one youth, "He, the down of whose cheek drinks the water of immortality, whoever looks at his sugar lips eats sweetmeats." When Sa'di found a habit of the youth's irritating, he sent the young man away, but then regretted it. He writes, "I lost the time of union, and man is ignorant of the value of delightful life before adversity. Return. Slay me. For to die in thy presence is sweeter than to live after thee." Some time later the beautiful youth returned, but his beard was now full and Sa'di was no longer interested in him. In another poem Sa'di wrote of the impetuousness and aloofness of such youths: "When a beardless youth is beautiful and sweet, his speech is bitter, his temper hasty." But when he is older and his beard is full, then he comes back and "seeks affection."[31]

Sa'di's taste for youth whose beards are first growing was shared by many other poets. In fact, according to John Boswell, "poems about the physical allure of a young man's first beard constitute an entire genre of Arabic poetry."[32] But unlike Sa'di, other poets found young men with fuller beards just as attractive. A poem of the 12th-century Andalusian poet Sara of Santarem illustrates the fascination of Islamic men for the growth of beard on a youth: "See, his beard is sprouting yet, beauty's fringes delicate; delicately through my heart, passion's thrilling raptures dart."[33] In another poem, Sara writes, "with the sprouting beard his loveliness merely grew subtler, finer, and my love for him followed suit. For us, the beard was not some vile darkness creeping cross his cheeks, but only a trickling down of the beautiful blackness of his eyes.[34]

The 14th-century Egyptian Sufi mystic and naturalist Muhammad al-Nawaji bin Hasan bin Ali bin Othman had such a reputation for piety that he had a nickname, Shams al-Din, or Sun of Religion. As a young man he studied Islamic law under the master al-Damiri, and later taught al-Hadis and Islamic law at the religious colleges of Cairo and led Sufi mystic prayer sessions. His religious devotion, however did not preclude a constant preoccupation with beautiful young males, a love explored in many of his poems. Al-Nawaji writes in one poem that in his burning desire to possess one young man, a "young male gazelle," he has spent his life to no purpose. So he asks the youth "What will put out the fire that you have lit in me?" The young man answers, "My lips."[35]

The most famous work of Islamic literature after the Qur-an is certainly the *Thousand and One Nights,* the collection of tales that includes the well-known stories of "Aladdin," "Ali Baba and the Forty Thieves," and "The Seven Voyages of Sinbad the Sailor." The book starts with the story of Shahryar, a Persian king, who finds that his new bride, whom he thought to be a virgin, had been unfaithful. Declaring that all women are unfaithful, he had her executed. He then married a succession of virgins, and then executed each one after his first night with them. After this goes on for a while, the king's vizier cannot find any more virgins to wed the king. But Scheherazade, the vizier's daughter, offers herself as the next bride and her father reluctantly agrees. On the night of their marriage, Scheherazade tells the king a story, but does not tell him the ending, which forces the king to keep her alive so he can hear the end of it. The next night Scheherazade finishes the previous night's story and then tells the king a new story but doesn't end it. The king is forced to keep Scheherazade alive another night. Scheherazade continues in the same pattern each night for 1,001 nights. The stories in the collection are, then, the stories told by Scheherazade to the king each night.

Reflecting the sexual customs of the day, the *Thousand and One Nights* features a number of stories with homosexual themes. Even in the stories featuring heterosexual loves, though, there are continuous references to young men or male slaves whose beauty is "as bright as the sun," or adolescents and young men "whose delectable good looks are celebrated by everyone."[36] The stories are not simple fairy tales, but often show the breath of life from the ecstatic joy of two friends uniting in love to a sordid murder brought about through the public humiliation of a homosexual lover. In the latter case, from "The Story of the Magic Book," a sheik was trying to explain how it came about that he killed a young man whose body the police had just discovered. The sheik said that he had killed the young man in a fit of jealousy. His friend, he said, didn't hesitate to take his money, but he was unfaithful. The sheik then names the buffoons his friend had slept with, and it turns out that nearly every one on the street, even the street cleaner and the cobbler, was boasting of having slept with his friend. So, the sheik said, "the world went black" before his eyes, and he killed his ungrateful friend. When the caliph heard the story he was so moved that he didn't punish the sheik but pardoned him instead.

Another story, "The Story of Princess Zuleika," includes an allusion to the promise of boys in Paradise, mentioned in the passages in the Qur-an cited at the beginning of the chapter. In the story, a vizier approaches a handsome boy in the street, a student from Damascus, and praises his beauty and begs him to accompany him back to the palace to meet the king, "who likes handsome faces." When the youth agrees, the vizier gazes at him, admiring the good looks and elegance of the young man, and exclaimed, "By Allah! If all the young men of Damascus are like you, that city is a region of Paradise, and the sky over Damascus is Paradise itself."[37]

Lesbian love is also featured in the collection in "The Story of the Baibars and the Captains of Police," in which a woman tells one of the captains without any embarrassment of the love she feels for a younger girl. She then asked the captain to help her get rid of her friend's father. "Between her and me," she says, "what happens has happened. And that is a mystery of love." The woman goes on to say that "Between her and me a passionate pact has been concluded," and that "she burns for me with equal ardor. Never will she marry and never will a man touch her." The police captain utters no words of disapproval, but is somewhat amazed to find himself the procurer of one woman for another. Still, he ponders what "these two gazelles with no penis" can do together."[38]

As the works of the Islamic writers make clear, the most predominant relationship pattern among males is the love of an older man for a youth or young man. These loves are often pursued by men who show a distinctive homosexual inclination, but they are also just as frequently described by writers who praise the love of women as much as they delight in the love of boys. In fact, it was and still is universally assumed in the Islamic world that all men were susceptible to the beauty of young males, just as it was understood that many men would pursue sexual relationships with them. In this regard, the 12th-century Islamic jurist Ibn al-Gauzi wrote: "He who claims that he experiences no desire [when looking at beautiful boys or youth] is a liar, and if we could believe him, he would be an animal, not a human being."[39] The 11th-century Persian prince Kai Ka'us ibn Iskandar even advised his son not to restrict his sexual interests to one sex only, but to indulge in both males and females. In his "Mirror for Princes," a work he wrote as a guide for his eldest son, he instructed his son: "As between women and youths do not confine your inclinations to either sex; thus you may find enjoyment from both kinds without either of the two becoming inimical to you. Further, if, as I have said, excessive copulation is harmful, complete abstention also has its dangers. When you do it, let it be in accordance with appetite and not as a matter of course."[40]

Same-Sex Love in Muslim India

The Umayyad push eastward from Persia brought Islam to the borders of India by the 8th century. In the following two centuries successive Islamic invasions were able to penetrate into the northern subcontinent, but none were successful in retaining territory until the 10th-century sultan Mahmud of Ghazni, the son and grandson of Mamluke-slaves, conquered Ghazni, a region of present-day Afghanistan, and established the Ghazni Empire in the territories of present-day Afghanistan and Pakistan. In the early 13th century a Mamluke ex-slave took over the remains of the Ghazni Empire and established the first of a series of sultanates based in Dehli from which Islamic rule then spread over large portions of the subcontinent. Along with their faith, the Islamic rulers brought their homosexual customs, and as a result homosexual loves figured in the lives of some of the most prominent of the Islamic rulers of India.

The love between the first Islamic ruler in the Indian subcontinent, Sultan Mahmud of Ghazni, and his slave Malik Ayaz was such that it became an Islamic legend. Poets praising the power of love looked to Sultan Mahmud as a prime example the man who, because of the power of his love, becomes "a slave to his slave." Malik Ayaz became the embodiment of the ideal beloved, and a model for purity in Sufi literature. According to a famous anecdote about the two, the sultan one day asked Ayaz whether he knew of any king greater and more powerful than he was. Ayaz replied, "Yes, I am a greater king than you." Surprised by the answer, the sultan asked Ayaz for proof. "Because even though you are a king, your heart rules you, and this slave is the king of your heart." Another anecdote about Sultan Mahmud was included by the great Persian poet Sa'di in his collection of verses, *Bustan*: "Some one found fault with the king of Ghazani, saying, 'Ayaz, his favorite slave, possesses no beauty. It is strange that a nightingale should love a rose that has neither color nor perfume.' This was told to Mahmud, who said, "My love, O sir, is for virtue, not for form or stature."[41] Later, Sultan Mahmud appointed Ayaz as the sultan of Lahore, and under his slave's rule the city, which had been destroyed by repeated battles, was rebuilt and became a center for culture and education, renowned for its poetry.

One of the greatest poets of Muslim India was Amir Khusro, born in 1253 in northern India during the reign of the Mamluke sultanate. Khusro was regarded as a master of the Ghazal, a form of love poetry featuring expressions of love and separation, and the sense of powerless of the lover to resist his feelings yet unable to attain his beloved. The theme of unattainable passion is evident in a brief excerpt of one of Khusro's Ghazals describing the effect of a beautiful youth on his would-be lovers. "I wonder what was the place where I was last night. All around me were half-slaughtered victims of love, tossing about in agony. There was a nymph-like beloved with cypress-like form and tulip-like face, ruthlessly playing havoc with the hearts of the lovers."

Homosexuality continues to be prevalent among the Muslims of India, Pakistan and Afghanistan down to the present day. The widespread homosexuality of Islamic India, a contrast to the more restrained sexual mores of Hindu India, came as a shock to the British when they discovered the customs during their colonial rule. When, in 1845, Sir Charles Napier conquered and annexed Sindh, the region around Karachi in modern-day Pakistan, his forces discovered a number of male brothels featuring boys and eunuchs. Napier assigned Richard Burton to investigate, and his investigation led him to a wider study of homosexuality in India and the Middle East, which he documented in his "Terminal Essay" that he appended to his translation of *One Thousand and One Nights*, quoted earlier in the chapter.

According to Burton, "the cities of Afghanistan and Sindh are thoroughly saturated with

Persian vice," as are the men of Kashmir as well as "the Sikhs and the Moslems of the Punjab."[42] Burton notes that Afghani caravans "always include boys to accompany the men," a tradition that appears to extend down to the present day in Pakistan and Afghanistan. A 1994 report from Karachi said that truck drivers, like earlier camel drivers, "always have younger boys" with them.[43] In the remote, mountainous areas of Pakistan prominent Swat men traditionally kept several *bedagh*, younger men who specialized in playing the passive sexual role. Despite the availability of female prostitutes, many men considered the most satisfying form of intercourse to be that with a bedagh. Even though homosexuality has declined among Western-educated Swat men in recent times, the first sexual experience of most young men is usually with a bedagh or with one of their peers playing the receptive role, and adult men still frequently keep younger male lovers.[44]

Sexual attitudes among Hindus have been historically more conservative than among the Muslims, though with wide variation from the extreme sexual asceticism of some sects, to the active encouragement of sexual activity among Tantric sects. It was, after all, the Vajrayana Buddhism of India transmitted to China from which Kobo Daishi, the Japanese saint, derived his teaching that sensual carnality is a reflection of the in-dwelling divinity. Some of the earliest Buddhist texts, dating from at least the third century B.C., look upon homosexuality as an ordinary part of life, and other Buddhist writings contain references to homosexual activity among the monks in the monasteries. The fifth-century A.D. Indian teacher Vatsyayana, who wrote the *Kama Sutra*, a religious text, devoted an entire chapter to instructions to a masseur for administering oral sex on a male. A tenth-century temple of Visvanatha contains bas relief carvings depicting the approaches made by a monk to a layman, who greets him respectfully while allowing his penis to be felt. A 12th-century temple features a bas relief showing a monk administering oral sex on a prince.[45] A relic of the ancient worship of the mother goddess also survives in India, in the *Hirjas,* a sect of transvestite passive homosexuals, whose ceremonies venerate Sakti, the Hindu name for the goddess.

In modern times, the Hindu middle class uniformly disapproves of homosexuality, and in fact, same-sex love is rarely even acknowledged. This attitude does not derive from traditional Hindu teachings, however, but developed with the advent of British colonial rule. In fact, as sexual attitudes in Great Britain relaxed in the late 20th century, the Hindu middle class has stubbornly held on to the Victorian attitudes imported by the British colonial rulers.

The Mamlukes: A Homosexual Warrior Caste

By the beginning of the 9th century fractures were beginning to develop in the far-flung empire of the Abbasid caliphs reigning in Baghdad. Local governors and emirs were growing more autonomous and were establishing dynasties, which weakened the central authority of the caliph in Baghdad and tended to divert military manpower and revenues away from the caliph to the local emirs for their own purposes. In addition, with the army dependent on recruits from across the Islamic world, the caliphs were faced with increasing difficulty in retaining the loyalty of all the army units, many of whose soldiers felt stronger ties to their local tribes or sheiks than they felt for the ruler in distant Baghdad. In the early 9th century, the Abbasid Caliph al-Ma'mun addressed this problem by establishing an army composed completely of Turkish and Slavic slaves, which owed loyalties to no one but the caliph.

Known as the Mamlukes, the soldiers were purchased as slaves when they were children or young adolescents, either from impoverished families or from slave-traders who had kidnapped them. They were mostly Georgians and Circassians from the Caucasus and the region north of the Black Sea, and hence were not Arabic or Persian. As a unique military body, with no ethnic or tribal connection to the people of the Abbasid Empire, the caliph was assured of their loyalty. When the boys or young adolescent first entered the force they were given rigorous military training, including extensive training in archery and horsemanship. The Mamlukes lived and worked within their garrisons and kept company among themselves.

Even with the Mamluke force, though, Abbasid fortunes continued to sink after the 9th century, with many regions of the former empire under the rule of independent emirs and sultans, most of whom had also procured Mamluke forces. In the 12th century, the Mamlukes serving under Saladin, at that time vizier of the Emir of Syria, Nur ad-Din, successfully defended Egypt from incursions of the Crusader Kingdom of Jerusalem. After Nur al-Din's death, Saladin succeeded him and united both Egypt and Syria under his rule, founding the Ayyubid dynasty. The Mamlukes forces under Saladin then defeated the Crusaders and reconquered Jerusalem. After Saladin's death, his sons began fighting over the division of Saladin's empire, and to help themselves in the conflict with their brothers, each tried to build as powerful a Mamluke force as possible. Eventually Saladin's brother, al-Adil, succeeded in defeating each of his nephews, and incorporated the Mamluke forces of each of them into his own. When Al-Adil died, the process was repeated, with his sons fighting among themselves for control of the empire, until one of the sons, al-Kamil, succeeded in defeating the rest. The process was repeated yet again after al-Kamil's death. In the meantime, Mamluke were becoming more and more powerful as a force behind the rule of the Ayyubids.

In 1249 King Louis IX of France, leading a Crusader army, attacked Egypt and captured Damietta, a town at the intersection of the Mediterranean and the Nile River. After the death of the Ayyubid sultan at the time, As-Salih, his son ruled briefly, but he was murdered by his mother, who took over the rule, and then with Mamluke backing attacked the French forces and defeated them. Taking too long in their retreat, the French forces were overrun and King Louis himself was captured, and only released after paying a huge ransom. Because of religious pressure for a male leader, As-Salih's wife was forced to marry Aybak, the Mamluke leader. Aybak, however, was assassinated shortly afterward while in his bath, and in the ensuing power struggle the Mamluke vice-regent, Qutuz, assumed power. Qutuz consolidated his hold on power and established a dynasty of Mamlukes which would rule Egypt and Syria until the 16th century.

The rule of the Mamlukes was unique in a number of remarkable ways, not the least of which was that each leader had started as a slave, purchased usually from the region around the Caucasian Mountains in South-Central Asia. Mamluke, in fact, means "one owned" or "white slave" in the Arabic parlance of Iraq, where the institution originated.[46] Castration was not considered conducive to military success, and so it was never performed on slave-recruits. A strong current of homoeroticism ran throughout Mamluke customs, and they had a strong preference for boys from the Caucasus, particularly Circassians, who were famous for their good looks. Evidently owing to the selectivity of their purchasers, the Mamlukes as a group were universally regarded as exceptionally good-looking men. The Mamlukes usually didn't grow beards until they had moved up in the ranks, and so their youthful good looks were not obscured by grown beards. Western travelers who encountered them often commented on their striking physical attractiveness. A visitor in the late 18th century commented that the Mamlukes of Egypt "are in general distinguished by the grace and beauty of their persons." A 19th-century traveler visiting Iraq described the Mamluke bodyguards in the palace of the pasha in Mosul, as "extremely handsome, and all of them young and superbly dressed."[47]

The cohesion of the Mamlukes as a military ruling class, and their unswerving loyalty to the reigning Mamluke sultan, were achieved to a great extent by the fact that each recruit was removed from his family and transported a great distance from his home region into a nation of people totally alien to him and his upbringing. The ties of the recruits with their families were completely broken and replaced with ties of loyalty with the Mamluke "family." Indeed, family relationships were consciously emulated among the Mamlukes, with each recruit referred to as the "son" of his purchaser or master, who in turn was referred to as the youth's "father," with the boy's comrades referred to as his brothers. The recruits were not housed all in one section of the citadel, but were divided among the military units, living in special sections of each unit's barracks reserved for the cadets. Close bonds were encouraged between the cadets and Mamlukes of each unit, and socializing was exclusively among them members of their own unit, with the result that members of other units were regarded as outsiders, and not a member of the unit's "family." The strong kinship-like ties between the members of the unit were regarded as instrumental to the Mamlukes' military cohesion on the field of battle.[48]

The slave status of the cadets should not be taken as an indicator of their social status, however. They were selected and purchased specifically to be raised as warriors, leaders and rulers. "They were to pride themselves on the fact that they were selected for special training, and to be the beneficiary of their master, whom they would succeed." They were inculcated with the sense that they were a superior class to their Arab subjects, and so therefore intermixing with the local Arab society was strongly discouraged. They owed their loyalties not to any local family or tribe or country, but only to their "master, trainer, and benefactor, the man who bought them and gave them everything."[49]

The segregation of the Mamlukes from the native population is regarded as an additional factor in the effectiveness of the Mamlukes rule. Most Mamlukes had disdain for the native Arab culture of Syria and Egypt, and Mamlukes who had been purchased when they were adolescents couldn't even speak the language. Maintaining separation between the Mamlukes and the native population was also done to protect them. Coming from a region geographically distant from the lands they ruled, the Mamlukes had little immunity to native strains of diseases, and periodic outbreaks of common diseases would kill or incapacitate large numbers of them. With their purchase and years of military training they were valuable investments, and protecting their health was of paramount importance.

The cadets were given rigorous military training in archery, the use of the lance and battle axe, and in horsemanship. Because of the allure of the young slave-recruits to the Mamluke soldiers, eunuchs were placed in charge of the training of the youths to keep their seduction by the adult Mamlukes under control. Nonetheless, scholars take it as a given that pederastic relationships between the slave-cadets and adult Mamluke warriors was common practice.[50] An indication of the general sexual preferences of the Mamlukes is that though they were permitted to marry, it is evident that few did. According to the Englishman W.G. Browne, who visited Egypt in the 1790s, Mamlukes "seldom marry till they acquire some office. It is worthy of remark that though the Mamlukes in general be strong and personable men, yet the few who marry very seldom have children.... Of eighteen Beys, whose history I particularly knew, only two had any children living."[51]

After the youths had completed their training and had joined the Mamluke forces, they were technically freed from their slave status, but without exception they remained loyal to their Mamluke masters as before. When he graduated from training, each Mamluke was given a salary and assignment, and if he was skilled and dedicated, it was possible for him to advance to a high rank, since the Mamluke organization was governed by strict system of meritocracy. If a Mamluke married, he continued to live in the citadel with the rest of the Mamlukes, and if he had children, they were raised there as well. The sons of Mamlukes were, however, prevented by the rules from becoming Mamlukes themselves. When a Mamluke died, his property, his wife and his children became the property of the Mamlukes. The Mamlukes, who were, in effect, the ruling nobility of Egypt and Syria, were in essence "life" peers because their status could not be inherited by their children. Because no son of a Mamluke could ever become a Mamluke, and because property could not be passed down to progeny, the possibility of ruling dynasties was eliminated, and the problems of nepotism were avoided.[52]

That the Mamlukes' unique system of rule was a great success there is no doubt. The Mamlukes defeated the last of the Crusaders in the Holy Land, recaptured Cyprus from the Christians, and were responsible for the first serious defeat of the Mongols, who had overthrown and executed the last of the Abbasid caliphs. When the Mongols carried their invasion into Syria, they were routed by a Mamluke force at Ain Jalut in 1260. Thereafter the Mamlukes ruled the Middle East from Syria to Egypt until the 16th century, when they found that their cavalry charges and skills in personal combat were no match for the rifles of the Ottomans. Even after their defeat, though, the Mamlukes continued as governors of Egypt, keeping their own army, and had won back a measure of self-rule by the 18th century. Their rule in Egypt continued until 1798 when they were defeated by Napoleon Bonaparte's forces in the French invasion of Egypt.

The historian Paul Hardman argues that the unusual character of the Mamluke system is an undeniable factor of their success: "What we have here is a unique phenomenon in history: young boys were purchased, then trained to be the companions and the eventual heirs of a master who truly cared for them. They in turn devoted themselves to the master, and all his endeavors, with a remarkable degree of loyalty." According to Hardman, the sexual and affectionate bonds between slave and master, and between Mamluke soldiers, were an important element of their success. Furthermore, the extraordinary coherence and continuity of the Mamluke system would not have been possible were it not for the affectionate bonds "between master and the boy who he would educate to succeed him. It was a strategy for governing, and for living, in the context of a culture which accepted homosexuality as a natural part of human existence."[53]

The Ottoman Slave-Elite

The Ottomans began their remarkable expansion with their founder Osman I, the emir of a tiny principality in Anatolia, who with the help of mercenaries and refugees fleeing the Mongols advance from the East took advantage of the collapsing Byzantine Empire in the late 13th century, routed Byzantine forces and established an empire that was to become a regional superpower for over six centuries. The Ottoman rulers maintained a ruling system similar to but more elaborate than that of the Mamlukes, under which slaves were bought and trained for military service, administrative management of the empire, and as sexual companions for the Ottoman sultans and other high officials. As in the case of the Mamlukes, many of the boys were purchased from Christian and sometimes Muslim families in the Caucasus, Georgia and in the Balkans.

The Christian families from whom the boys were purchased were eager to sell their sons for service to the Ottoman rulers not only for the cash it brought, but because the sons could in many cases look forward to a career in the ruling elite of the Ottoman empire. According to one historian, "The Georgians and Circassians, whose physical types were especially admired by the Turks, found the slave trade with Constantinople so profitable that they maintained slave farms to meet the demand. They not only regularly captured children for the purpose of selling them in the Turkish slave markets, but even reared their own children with this end in view."[54] In later periods, the slaves were also acquired by a "head tax" levied by the Ottomans on their provinces, which meant that as the empire grew boys would be sent from a broad area from the European provinces on the west to the Ottoman's Asian provinces on the east. Under the tax, each province was to supply a number of boys equal to one out of every forty boys in the total population of boys 14 to 18 years of age, though boys as young as 8 and as old as 20 could also be taken.[55]

When the boys arrived at the Ottoman palace in Constantinople they were held by the palace gate-keepers and then winnowed through a multi-tier selection process which separated out boys for military, governmental, administrative or sexual service to the Ottoman rulers. They were inspected and then selected for each type of training and career based on "bodily perfection, muscular strength and intellectual ability." Like specimens at a horse or dog show, the boys' bodies were examined to judge various attributes, and then separated into two groups. "The *sine qua non* of the sultan's service being physical beauty and bodily perfection, the most promising in every respect were set aside for palace service." The remaining boys, selected according to their strength and physical dexterity, were set aside for military service in the Janissary corps, an elite military unit that served as the sultan's palace guard and bodyguards and has been likened to the Praetorian Guard of the Roman emperors. Of the first division of boys, the finest of the group, "handsome boys, physically perfect and of marked intellectual promise" were sent for training as pages in the palaces of the sultans. The group selected to be student-pages was further divided to separate out the *crème de la crème*, the very finest, who were sent to the palace school of the Grand Seraglio (quarters of the harem).[56]

The fact that some of the boys were sent to be trained for service in the sultan's harem illustrates the extent to which the boys were regarded as sexual objects. A 17th-century French visitor, Paul Ricaut, wrote that they studied "Persian Novellaries [that] imbue them with a kind of Platonic love to each other." Ricaut remarked that since "the restraint and strictures of discipline makes them strangers to women, for want of converse with them, they burn in lust one towards another." But, Ricaut said, the passion was not only among themselves, but "persons of eminent degree in the seraglio become involved, watching out for their favorites, courting them with presents and services." Other reports from Europeans visiting Constantinople are unanimous in describing sodomy as rife within the ruling elite of the Ottoman Empire.[57] In fact, the historian Albert Lybyer observed that during the reign of the 16th-century sultan Suleiman the Magnificent "the visible court and retinue of the monarch was wholly ungraced by the presence of the fair sex; all great ceremonies and cavalcades were participated in by men alone." According to Lybyer, until the middle of Suleiman's reign, not a single woman resided in the "the entire vast palace where the sultan spent most of this time."[58]

The result of the division of boys by beauty, intelligence, muscular strength and physical dexterity and their subsequent training resulted in a ruling apparatus from foot soldier, to administrative officer, to governor, to vizier composed of a body of men whose loyalty would not be affected by ties to families or factions of the Ottoman subjects. As they entered service and worked their way up through the ranks, the men were given salaries and could acquire properties. Some boys, who had become favorites of their masters, might be given their masters' daughters in marriage or given a role in management of their masters' businesses or properties. A Croatian-born slave of Suleiman, a special favorite of the sultan, went on in life to have great wealth and power, and owned 17,000 slaves himself at the time of his death.[59]

Another favorite of Suleiman was a Greek-born slave, Ibrahim. When he entered the

Ottoman service as a boy he was sent because of his beauty for training in the palace school in Western Turkey. At the palace school he was befriended by Suleiman, a boy himself at the time, and they remained close companions until Ibrahim's death. When Suleiman became sultan, Ibrahim rose rapidly through the ranks, going from grand falconer and master of the pages to first officer of the Royal Bedchamber, provincial governor, vizier and ultimately grand vizier, the second most powerful position in the empire. According to one account, "they ate their meals together, went boating, and in times of war shared a tent — or even the same bed." During the heat of August when the sultan moved his court to the cooler climate of Adrianople, "he and Ibrahim spent days together engaged in falconry." Suleiman and Ibrahim even wore each other's clothes. The intimacy and depth of their relationship scandalized the Ottoman court, however, which considered it improper for the world's greatest emperor to show such favor to a mere slave.[60] After serving as grand vizier for 13 years, Ibrahim fell out of favor and was executed, ostensibly for awarding himself a title after a victory against the Persian Safavid empire, but more likely as a result of a scheme by Suleiman's wife. Suleiman immediately regretted the execution and loss of his friend, and spent a good part of the next 20 years in seclusion in his palace where he wrote poetry, often alluding to Ibrahim.[61]

Same-Sex Unions in Ottoman Europe

As the Ottoman Empire grew in power it continued to expand outward, and by the 15th-century the Ottomans had conquered much of Southeast Europe, including Greece, the Balkans, and the kingdom of Hungary, and even threatened the Hapsburg capital of Vienna. As a result of the Ottomans' rule in Southeastern Europe, which was not pushed back until the mid–19th century, Islamic influences were added to those of the Greeks, Romans and Slavs, producing the diverse ethnic, religious and cultural character of the Balkans today. With the push of the Ottomans up the Adriatic Coastline through the Balkans, it may have been inevitable that their tolerance of homosexuality would be reflected in the sexual practices of the people. We have seen that parents of adolescent sons in Bosnia and Croatia were eager to sell their boys for service to the Ottomans, and with the head-tax instituted in later times youths from throughout the Balkans would have joined boys from other regions of the empire chosen for service under the Ottoman rulers as palace pages, government administrators and Janissary soldiers.

In the late 18th and early 19th century the region of present-day Albania was overseen by the Ottoman Vizier Ali Pasha who kept a harem of 600 women, but according to a French diplomat, was "almost exclusively given up to the Socratic pleasures, and for this purpose keeps a seraglio of youths from whom he selects his confidants and even his principal officers." In the meantime, the Ottoman territory in Southwestern Greece was ruled by Ali's son, Veli, who shared "his father's appetite for money and for boys."[62] However, what is notable about sexual customs in the Balkans under the Ottomans is not the predilection of the rulers for beautiful youths, a custom that in the eastern Mediterranean Basin extended back at least 3,000 years, but the region's tradition of formalized same-sex unions, including ceremonies and religious rituals that may extend back in the history of the Balkans to Roman times or earlier.

In 1854 an Austrian diplomat, Johann Georg von Hahn, who had devoted himself to studying Albanian customs while serving there, published his *Albanische Studien* (Albanian Studies), in which he wrote of romantic sexual relationships between young men and younger adolescents. Hahn said that the Albanian males commonly married at about the age of 24 or

25, and that these homosexual relationships were considered normal for them before that age, though among some men they continued even after they had married a woman. In his study, Hahn related the following description provided to him by a Muslim Albanian about the customs:

> The lover's feeling for the boy is pure as sunshine. It places the beloved on the same pedestal as a saint. It is the highest and most exalted passion of which the human breast is capable. The sight of the beautiful youth awakens astonishment in the lover, and opens the door of his heart to the delight which the contemplation of this loveliness affords. Love takes possession of him so completely that all his thought and feeling goes out in it. If he finds himself in the presence of the beloved, he rests absorbed in gazing on him. Absent, he thinks of naught but him. If the beloved unexpectedly appears, he falls into confusion, changes color, turns alternately pale and red. His heart beats faster and impedes his breathing. He has ears and eyes only for the beloved. He shuns touching him with the hand, kisses him only on the forehead, sings his praise in verse, a woman's never.[63]

In discussing the Albanian customs, the early 20th-century psychologist Havelock Ellis noted that these relationships were reported by other researchers working in Albania, and that "while most prevalent among the Moslems, they are also found among the Christians, and receive the blessing of the priest in church. Jealousy is frequently aroused, the same writer remarks, and even murder may be committed on account of a boy." Another early 20th-century researcher, Paul Nacke, wrote that among Greek Orthodox Christians in the southern part of Albania, male homosexuality is a deeply engrained tradition.

> I have made inquiries among persons familiar with the country ... all confirmed Hahn's statements point for point. For handsome boys and youths, these Shqipetars [Albanians] cherish a truly enthusiastic love. The passion and mutual jealousy are so intense that even today they kill one another for the sake of a boy. Many instances of this kind were reported to me. In particular this love is supposed to flourish among the Moslems and even the Christians pay homage to this *amor masculus* (masculine love). It is further true that pacts of brotherhood, when they occur among Christians, are blessed by the papas (fathers) in church, both partners receiving the Eucharist.

Nacke added that his innkeeper, a Christian, had formed such a "pact of blood" with an Albanian Moslem. Nacke wrote that "each pricked the other in the finger and sucked out a drop of blood. Now each has to protect the other to the death."[64] A lexicon of sexual terms published by the German anthropologist F.R. Krauss in 1911 included two terms related to these homosexual unions, *buthar*, which literally means "butt-fucker," and *madzupi*, a term for such relationships.[65]

John Boswell created a storm of controversy in 1994 when he published a lengthy study of formalized same-sex unions, *Same-Sex Unions in Pre–Modern Europe*, which deals in part with Greek Orthodox liturgical ceremonies used in southeastern Europe to formalize and bless homosexual relationships. The Greek Orthodox ceremonies Boswell described presumably include the same Christian liturgies mentioned by Nacke, and confirmed by other contemporary scholars. According to Boswell, the customs were not restricted to Albania, but more generally widespread in the Balkan region and evidently longstanding. Boswell quoted from a lengthy account of Slavic rites for same-sex unions published by Alberto Fortis in 1774. Fortis wrote that the ceremonies could be used to unite two men together or two women. Fortis then provided a detailed description of a ceremony he witnessed which brought two women together in a church in a Dalmatian town. Boswell also cited a report indicating that religious ceremonies for same-sex unions were being performed in Montenegro as late as the 1920s.[66] The anthropologist Dinko Tomasic reported in a 1948 study that rites for pairs of men and women entering pacts of sworn brotherhood were still being conducted in churches in Montenegro, despite the disapproval of the orthodox priests "who considered the relationships vice-ridden and contrary to nature." Tomasic's sources make it clear that homosexual relationships and same-sex unions were still being fully accepted by society in rural areas of Montenegro in the mid–20th century.[67]

Sexual Attitudes in Contemporary Islamic Society

In recent times the same ambisexual patterns that characterized Muslim society from its earliest centuries continue to predominant in the Islamic world. Homosexual relationships, though rarely spoken of or acknowledged, are considered routine for adolescents and young unmarried adults. Heterosexual involvement rarely occurs before marriage, and even then many married Muslim men in Muslim countries continue to maintain close and intimate friendships with other males. Because same-sex relationships are a normal, if unspoken, part of life for many men and women throughout the Islamic world, especially in South and Southwest Asia and around the Mediterranean Basin, and have been for many centuries, many contemporary Muslims have a hard time comprehending the "gay rights" movement. According to Muslim social tradition, as long as individuals tend to family obligations, they are free to conduct whatever relationships they wish outside of their marriage.

Of course, Islamic law officially disapproves of homosexual relationships, but rules of evidence in Islamic law, which requires four eye-witnesses to the act, ironically make it very difficult, if not impossible, to carry out a prosecution of someone for a homosexual act carried out between consenting individuals in private. At the same time, penalties for false or unproven allegations are severe, and hence accusations against individuals for private sexual offenses are virtually non-existent. Therefore, even conservative Islamic religious authorities in a community could be aware of widespread homosexuality among the population, but would be unable to bring any prosecutions against anyone for homosexual acts as long as the activity remained private. Publicly flaunting homosexual behavior, on the other hand, would be considered an affront to Islam, and so would require action by the authorities for the sake of maintaining public morality.

Even devout Muslims in many cases have no qualms about participating in homosexual relationships. This is because the vision of human existence in Islamic teaching regards human nature as weak and prone to sin, while at the same time teaching that Allah is all merciful and always willing to forgive the transgressions of his people. Hence, in Muslim society no human being is expected to be perfect, and because God's mercy is always there to excuse sexual behavior outside the norms of Islamic law, giving in to homosexual desire is regarded as a normal aspect of human nature.

Another factor that works against enforcement of anti-homosexual provisions in Islamic countries is that in Muslim society it is and has been considered bad form to call attention to any kind of non-conformity or aberration, social or sexual. As a result, facts plain to everyone are nonetheless ignored because of the social convention against publicly acknowledging them. This has led to sexual attitudes in which people feel free to do whatever they want in private as long as it is never acknowledged in public. A masculine married man in a conservative Islamic country could, therefore, meet an attractive male in a coffee shop, go home with him and take the passive role in anal intercourse — a fact that would bring him shame and dishonor in his community were the act to become known — without any effect on his masculine self-image or his public reputation because his partner would be restricted by the unspoken taboo against divulging in public sexual acts that take place in private.[68]

The prevailing attitude was summed up by a Kuwaiti-born Palestinian, Trig Tarazi, in an interview with the journalist Rex Wockner: "The Arab world is very much into the family unit and men must fulfill their family role. But as long as they do that, they are free to do whatever they want and this is not questioned. And since nobody talks about homosexuality, they don't have to fear somebody is going to say this, or even think this about them." Because of the freedom to satisfy their homosexual desires in private, many Muslim men do not see the point of the activism of the very small minority in Arab countries of those who consider themselves "gay" in the Western sense. "The rest of the men (those who don't claim gay identity) are very comfortable," says Tarazi. "They think it's the best of all possible worlds. Since nobody recognized homosexuality as even existing, they can get away with things we cannot get away with here. But if you start talking about homosexuality [in public] they get very uncomfortable."[69]

Conclusion

In the previous two chapters, we surveyed the sexual customs of the Chinese and Japanese civilizations and saw many similarities — some of them striking — to the sexual traditions of ancient Greece and Rome. While the Chinese and Japanese cultures have two of the longest and best documented traditions of same-sex love of all the world's civilizations, it is ironic that their homosexual traditions are all but unknown to modern day Japanese and Chinese, a circumstance caused by the wholesale importation of Western customs and values in the early 20th century. The long and equally well-documented history of homosexual love in the Islamic world — not as long as the Chinese tradition, but going back slightly farther than the Japanese — is, on the other hand, a tradition that has been regarded with some pride by many Muslims, though the overt expression of same-sex passion has been more restrained, especially so in recent times as a result of the influence of the Victorian sexual prudery of the British Colonialists.

Aside from the specifics of social customs and mores regarding public discussion or display of sexual expression in each society, the three civilizations demonstrate a remarkable uniformity in the patterns in which sexual behavior has manifested in their societies. Each of the three societies has been traditionally built around a strong family-centered system, where individuals are married in their 20s, supplemented by widespread homosexuality among adolescents, unmarried young adults, and even as an alternative for married men and women. In all three societies extramarital heterosexual relations, with the exception of female prostitution, have been traditionally strongly discouraged, a custom that continues in the Islamic world today, though it has loosened somewhat in modern-day China and Japan. The relaxation of traditional strictures against extramarital heterosexual relations in the latter countries came with the introduction in the early 20th century of Western moral values that at the same time were responsible for abruptly ending the age-old homosexual traditions of those societies. Leaving aside the changes in the 20th century because of the influence of Western European moral values, however, the strong similarities in the patterns of sexual customs of China, Japan and Islam underscore the persistence of the ambisexual character of human sexuality in human societies.

PART III: SEXUAL
NEUROSIS IN WESTERN SOCIETY

As a result of the survey of sexual activity in the animal world, a review of sexual customs among indigenous tribal peoples, and a consideration of the beneficial role that homosexual behavior seems to play among human societies, we saw in Part I that homosexuality is an inherent aspect of human sexuality, and that there can be little doubt that the human species inherited its ambisexual character from millions of years of evolutionary development of mammals. To answer the question as to whether the widespread homosexual traditions found among the vast majority of pre–Westernized indigenous tribal cultures are properly representative of human sexuality, we looked in Part II at sexual practices in all the world's major civilizations, and saw that the general patterns of sexual expression found among tribal societies are repeated over and over again among the great civilizations of human history. As observed in the Introductory chapter, it is evident that the human species is an ambisexual species, and has been one for a very long time.

If that's the case, why is it that the understanding of human sexuality in modern Western society is so different? In Part III we will follow the development of the attitudes to same-sex love in the West, from its wide acceptance in Greco-Roman times through its transformation into a sin so heinous that its very name was uttered in fear. Picking up the historical narrative in Chapter 13 with the fall of Rome in the West we will take a close look at the sexual customs and attitudes of the post–Roman European population, and will see that the strict anti-homosexual, "family values" sexual morality thought by traditional moralists to have been the norm since the beginning of time was a preoccupation of only conservative moralists in the church up until the High Middle Ages. The sexual attitudes and practices of the European population, on the other hand, up to that time displayed the same ambisexual patterns found in other societies around the world.

In Chapter 14 we will see the triumph of the anti-sexual moralists in the church and the peculiar confluence of historical forces that led to the, at times, brutal enforcement of the church's severe and ascetic sexual moral code throughout Western Christiandom. The hostility of the church to sex, and in particular to homosexuality, resulted in a seven century struggle to impose the church's narrow definition of sexuality on the ambisexual human nature with, as we shall see in Chapter 15, very inconsistent results. Finally, in Chapter 16, the widespread sexual neurosis and social problems in modern society resulting from the attempt of Western sexual morality to force human sexuality to conform to an artificial and simplistic vision of sex will be briefly surveyed.

13

Medieval Europe: Sexual Tolerance in the Age of Chivalry

> The deepest of worldly emotions in this period is the love of man for man, the mutual love of warriors who die together fighting against odds.... These male affections were themselves lover-like. In their intensity, their willful exclusion of other values, in their uncertainty, they provided an exercise of the spirit not wholly unlike that which later ages have found in "love."[1]

With these words C.S. Lewis was commenting on the love depicted between knights in the early French epic, *Chanson de Roland* (Song of Roland). Lewis, a devout Anglican, of course, hastened to assure the reader that the love and devotion that the text portrays between the knights was a love "wholly free from the taint that hangs about 'friendship' in the ancient world."[2] In the passage, Lewis was expounding on the intense affection this great Medieval epic describes between the hero, Roland, and the singular friend the poem describes as "his companion fast," "the man he loves so tenderly," and whom the hero, himself, addresses as, "My Olivier, my chosen one."[3] Even though Roland is betrothed to a noble woman at home in France, he rarely thinks of her. Olivier is first in Roland's thoughts, Lewis writes. "The figure of the betrothed is shadowy compared with that of the friend, Olivier."[4]

Lewis himself described the affection between the knights in the epic as "lover-like," and having "an intensity which our tradition is loath to allow except to sexual love."[5] Yet he and most scholars who have examined the *Song of Roland* and other literary accounts of the lives of Medieval knights have projected onto the affectionate bonds between knightly companions a virtuous chastity very much at odds with the evidence from the period. Like many traditional scholars, Lewis, a distinguished scholar of Medieval literature, though better known as the author of the *Chronicles of Narnia,* viewed the knighthood through the lens of an idealized conception of knightly honor and virtue, a heterosexual ideal popularized by 19th-century romantic novels such as Sir Walter Scott's *Ivanhoe.* According to the historian Johan Huizinga, such a vision was a conceit widespread in the late Middle Ages, belied by the accounts of knightly ways by late Medieval chroniclers who write "of covetousness, of cruelty, of cool calculation, of well-understood self-interest."[6]

As explained by the military historian Christon Archer, our image of the Medieval knight has been largely shaped by stories such as those of King Arthur and his knights, the songs of the troubadours, and the poets of courtly love who "handed down a romantic, lyrical glorification of knighthood and chivalry. The literary image of the knight errant, the romantic appeal of knighthood in flower, the formation of chivalric orders, the flattering portraits of the courtly life of the nobility, and the heroic descriptions of tournaments have dominated our perception of the age of chivalry."[7] This romantic conception of the knighthood has little basis in fact, however, but was an invention of late Medieval writers who evoked the noble gallantry and Christian virtues of a fictional chivalry to gloss over the unedifying realities of life in the late Middle Ages.[8] In reality, Archer says, knighthood resembled more a gang of "robber barons whose function was closer to that of a brigand than to that of the valiant protector of honor and fair maidens."[9] The British historian F.J.C. Hearnshaw gives a similar description of the behavior of the knights on their way to liberate the Holy Land, calling them "a horde of sanctified savages, whose abominations scandalized even the Byzantines and whose ferocities horrified the very Turks themselves."[10] In their camps "shameless profligacy, and scandalous debauchery—the old and deep-grained vices of the unregenerate feudal knighthood—were displayed in profusion."[11]

And as for the image of the knight as exemplifying the Christian heterosexual ideal, commentators from the period present quite a different picture of the chivalrous world of the knights. "Like from the flames of Sodom!" is how one 12th-century clergyman, Ordericus Vitalis, described a young knight of his acquaintance returning from knightly company in the service of the Earl of Chester.[12] Other contemporary writers left similar accounts that leave little doubt about the "depraved habits" of the knighthood,[13] and chroniclers of the times took homosexuality among the knighthood as a given.[14]

The longstanding supposition, found in scholarly writings and popular culture alike, that the knights of the European Middle Ages were exemplars of Christian moral ideals and paragons of heterosexual manliness, "free from the taint" of the kind of passionate sexual bonds found among warriors of the ancient world, is another of the hoary old myths surrounding sex that we in the modern West have inherited. And it wasn't just among the knighthood that Medieval sexual behavior veered from the heterosexual norm that is assumed in academic works, popular novels and films on the Middle Ages. Though many of the clergy of the early Middle Ages were married, the clergy in general were widely regarded as prone to homosexuality. Numerous examples of love letters and love poetry written by monks and nuns that survive from the period seem to confirm that perception. Nor was a proclivity to homosexuality restricted to same-sex communities, like those of the knighthood and in the monasteries and convents. The 12th-century monk Bernard of Cluny wrote that people indulging in open and unabashed homosexual relations "are as numerous as grains of barley, as many as the shells of the sea, or the sands of the shore." All of Europe, he lamented, was "awash" with them, from the cities to the countryside. Another clergyman complained that, "the entire universe—alas—is addicted to this sordid practice."[15]

Western Europe in the Post-Roman Period

As Europe passed through the upheavals following the collapse of the Roman Empire in the West, and Christianity emerged as the central pillar of the nascent European culture growing in the ruins of Roman civilization, the widespread fear and loathing of homosexuality that later developed in Europe had still not appeared. Despite the fervent and continuing efforts of a small, vocal minority of ascetic anti-sexual clergy, the early Middle Ages was a period of relative sexual tolerance, in which the ambisexual nature of human sexuality revealed itself throughout society, demonstrating the same patterns found among other cultures in the world. It is true that the anti-sexual morality promoted by Augustine, Jerome and other third- and fourth-century Christian theologians (examined in Chapter 9) found vigorous support among some elements of the leadership of the Christian church. However, there was still no unified church campaign against homosexuality, or any effort to single it out as an offense graver than other sexual sins, like adultery and fornication.

The Medieval period is known for its harsh and brutal enforcement of religious and sexual conformity and the persecution of witches, Jews and "sodomists," but that development came only in the late Middle Ages. The ascetic sexual morality that developed in the Christian church in the late Roman period found few adherents among the population of Western Europe even hundreds of years after the fall of Rome. In fact, the church would have no success at all in imposing its anti-sexual morality on the Western European population until it could turn to the centralized secular enforcement authorities that came with the emergence of powerful nation-states in the High Middle Ages.

Indeed, in the immediate post–Roman period there wasn't even a unified Christian Church in the West. Most of the Germanic tribes settling in Western Europe were Arian Christians, having been converted by Arian missionaries sent from Constantinople in the fourth-century when Arianism enjoyed a large following in the Eastern Empire. Their conquered subjects, like most Christians of the Empire, adhered to the Nicene Creed, laid down as the standard for Roman Christians by Emperor Theodosius I in the late 4th century. With two entirely separate churches operating side-by-side in the newly established Germanic kingdoms, a uniform set of moral teachings to guide European Christians was, of course, impossible. It wasn't until the early 8th century, when the Arian kingdoms were either defeated by Nicene neighbors or voluntarily converted to Nicene Catholicism, that a unified church in the West was achieved. But even then, the anti-sexual moralists in the church had little influence on public attitudes and behavior.

In looking at the sexual beliefs and behavior of the people of early Medieval Europe, it's important to keep in mind the makeup and sexual attitudes of the population of Western Europe in the post–Roman period. While much of Western Europe and the British Isles were under Celtic control in the centuries before the time of Julius Caesar, the expansion of the Roman Republic into Empire, begun by Caesar's conquest of Gaul (modern France) and continued by his successors, led to an infusion of Romans, Greeks and settlers from other areas of the Empire into Western Europe in the first several centuries of Christianity. The population of Western Europe outside of Italy prior to the massive influx of Germanic tribes, then, was a largely Celtic base, supplemented by Romans, Greeks and people from other reaches of the Empire. As we saw in earlier chapters, same-sex relations were common among the Celts and widespread among the Romans, and continued among many despite the proliferation of anti-sexual asceticism and dualistic philosophies in the late Empire.[16] In the absence of contrary evidence, it can be safely assumed that even with the conversion of most of the population to Christianity, and then the successive barbarian invasions, plagues and social disruption, some portion of the surviving Roman population of Western Europe at the time of the Germanic migrations would have retained much of the sexual tolerance and general ambisexuality of earlier times. The Christian historian and moralist Salvian, writing in the mid–5th century during the height of the barbarian invasions, confirmed as much in Book VII of his treatise, *De Gubernatione Dei (The Government of God)*, where he complained at length about the licentiousness, both heterosexual and homosexual, of the people of southern Gaul, Spain and North Africa.[17]

The Germanic tribes who inundated Western Europe in the fifth and sixth centuries brought with them attitudes and social customs that appear to have been little different from those of the Celts or Romans in the area of sex and homosexual relations. Like other peoples of the ancient world, the Germanic tribes were known for their homosexual customs which were documented in accounts of Roman writers. The first-century A.D. Roman rhetorician and teacher Quintilian cited the Germans' high regard for homosexual love in one of his oratorical works. In the late 4th century, Ammianus Marcellinus wrote of homosexual customs among the Taifali, a Germanic tribe related to the Goths, which involved formal homosexual relationships between warriors and young men undergoing initiation and military training. Clovis, king of the Salian branch of the Franks in the late 5th century, acknowledged his own homosexual relationships in his earlier life at the time of his baptism. The sixth-century historian Procopius described homosexual relationships very similar to the homosexual initiation of the Taifali among warriors and young initiates of one of the Frankish tribes, the Heruli.

An incident related by Procopius, that occurred during the time of the Vandals' capture of Rome is also highly revealing of the Germanic attitude to male homosexuality. In the episode, discussed in Chapter 5, the Vandals sent 300 of their sexually attractive young men as homosexual bait, offering them as "house slaves" for Roman patricians, who, falling for the trick, took them into their houses, after which the young men murdered their hosts. With the city caught off guard, the Vandals easily captured the city. Such a scenario would seem highly unlikely if the Vandals had contempt for homosexuality, as claimed by Salvian in his writings.*

We also saw in Chapter Five that among early Scandinavian warriors sexual relationships between warrior peers, called blood brothers, were formalized with a "blood brothers" ritual, and that such blood brother relationships were a significant enough element of early Norse society that they were enshrined in one of the Sagas. Archeological evidence indicates that such peer relationships may have dated back as far as 2000 B.C., to the time of the arrival of the first Indo-Europeans in Northern Europe. In view of this evidence it would be hard to argue, as some have, that the Germanic peoples were unaware of male homosexuality, were opposed to it, or, indeed, had any native reservations about it at all when practiced within social norms.[18]

Germanic Laws

The Vandals, Visigoths, Ostrogoths, Lombards and Franks who settled in Western Europe shared with one another a common Germanic heritage, which included a well-developed legal tradition. Germanic tribal laws had a primary emphasis on protection of property rights. In line with that concern, laws relating to sex chiefly dealt with protecting a husband's rights vis-à-vis his wife and virgin daughters, who were, in effect, treated as property under the Germanic legal tradition. The monetary value attached to women under Germanic law is illustrated by the fines imposed in laws of the Ripuarian Franks, which set a penalty of 600 *solidi* for the killing of a female between puberty and the age of 40. A fine of 600 solidi would have been equivalent to the value of 50 male horses or 300 cattle, an enormous sum for the times, and because of that provisions were included in the laws allowing the payment over three generations.[19]

Because of the high monetary value attached to a woman, the most prominent sexual crime was adultery — adultery of the wife, not the husband. The laws allowed males the right

---

*Since the time of Tacitus, Roman writers critical of the morals of their fellow Romans had used the supposed rustic purity of the Germanic tribes to highlight the debauchery of the Romans of their times. In excoriating the sexual laxness and homosexuality of the Christians of Carthage, Salvian held up the supposed "chastity" of their Vandal conquerors as a moral example.

to punish physically, including killing if caught in the act, any male who sexually violated their wives. Because of the dowry or bride price they could expect from their daughters' engagement, the virginity of their daughters also had a property value. Accordingly, a father or male guardian had the right to administer physical punishment on any male caught having sex with a virgin daughter. In common with Roman attitudes, the men were free to engage in whatever sexual activity they wished before or outside of marriage as long as they didn't violate another man's wife or virgin daughters. Conspicuous by their absence in the German tribal laws are laws of any kind punishing homosexual acts.[20]

By the late 8th century local law codes had been adopted throughout most of Western Europe. Though the various codes included provisions on a wide variety of sexual matters, including adultery, rape, incest, illegitimacy, marriage and fornication, the codes, like the tribal laws on which they are based, are notably silent on homosexual acts.[21] The only exception is the law code enacted under the Visigoths in Spain. The condemnation of homosexual acts in the Visigothic code has been used to claim that the Germanic peoples disapproved of homosexual practices,[22] but it indicates nothing of the sort. Rather than a statement of the Visigoths' attitudes to same-sex relations, the inclusion of the anti-homosexual provisions in the Visigothic law code was instead a product of the inordinate influence of the Catholic Church in the rule of the Visigothic kings.

Migrating into Spain after they were routed and expelled from their French kingdom by the Franks, the Visigoths were vastly outnumbered by the native population of Spain and were unable to ever establish an effective government administration. Instead, they depended almost entirely on the Roman Catholic Church for administration of justice, the collection of taxes and other government functions. The Visigoths even converted from Arian Christianity to Roman Catholicism in order to ensure the support of the church. The laws enacted under the Visigoths, therefore, reflected the heavy influence of church authorities and included provisions punishing homosexual acts that in language and tone seem to be lifted straight from the Code of Justinian. The church-influenced law code resulted in what the historian Vern Bullough called an "intolerant royal orthodoxy" that intruded deeply into the lives of the people. The resulting oppressive atmosphere further estranged the rulers from their subjects, and ultimately was a contributing factor to the ease with which the Moors conquered Spain.[23]

Outside of the quasi-theocratic kingdom of Visigothic Spain the law codes enacted in Europe in the centuries following the fall of Rome were almost entirely devoid of Christian influence. Instead, they retained most of the elements of Germanic law as it evolved from the Germans' pagan, tribal heritage. While some of their laws on sexual matters paralleled Christian teachings — for example, laws on adultery, rape and incest — they on the other hand permitted other activities — polygamy, divorce and the keeping of concubines — that would have been unimaginable in a thoroughly Christianized state. Despite their conversion to Christianity and ostensible embrace of Christian dogma, then, the Germans, particularly the Franks, were Christian in name only for several centuries after their conversion. As a result, their sense of morality continued to reflect their pagan roots as a tribal people of warriors.[24] Indeed, many aspects of the Germans' pagan heritage continued into the Middle Ages, including phallic pillars that were still being erected outside of churches in Northern Europe as late as the 12th century,[25] and rites involving male transvestism that suggest some continuity of the fertility cults of pre–Christian times.[26] Some parts of Scandinavia, in fact, were not even Christianized until the 12th century. In an illustration of the survival of Germanic or pre–Christian beliefs and cults well into the Christian era in Europe, a provision punishing the swallowing of semen for the purposes of magic, a practice found in rituals among Neolithic tribal peoples in recent times,* was included in a manual for confessors written in the late seventh-century by Archbishop Theodore of Canterbury.[27] The persistence of the practice of pre–Christian pagan rites in western Europe even as late as the 9th century was condemned by the Synod of Paris which met in 829.[28]

Historians have long taken the fact that post–Roman Europe was Christianized as proof that a general hostility to homosexual practices reigned in Europe from the fall of Rome onward. For example, the historian and moral philosopher Edward Westermarck wrote that throughout the Middle Ages, "Christian lawgivers thought that nothing but a painful death in the flames" could atone for homosexual acts.[29] Yet all the evidence suggests that the Germanic peoples remained uninterested and unconcerned with Christian moral teachings on sex for hundreds of years after their conversion to Christianity. In 744, nearly three centuries after the fall of Rome, Saint Boniface wrote in a letter that the Anglo-Saxons in England were "living a shameful life, despising lawful marriages, committing adultery and lusting after the fashion of the people of Sodom."[30] Even though converted to Christianity, the Germanic peoples held on to a vision of sexual morality, as Vern Bullough observed, that found nothing wrong in the expression of "open and frank sexuality" as long as sexual behavior did not violate another man's property rights. Indeed, there was a widespread belief among Europeans of the period that sexual continence was unhealthy, and doctors even prescribed more intercourse for some of their ailing patients.[31] As Christianity became well established in early Medieval Europe, therefore, Christian moralists found themselves preaching to a people stubbornly holding onto sexual attitudes diametrically opposed to the anti-sexual asceticism at the root of Christian sexual morality.[32]

Carolingian Laws and Forgeries

With the church firmly entrenched as a social institution amid the developing Germanic states, it was probably inevitable that the anti-homosexual convictions of the ascetic Christian moralists would be reflected in laws at some point. And so, in the late eighth century a series of enactments under Charlemagne, which cited the ongoing practice of homosexuality among monks, declared sodomy between monks as "sexual sins," along with fornication with animals and engaging in incestuous marriages.[33] Rather than legal punishment, however, the provisions called on the perpetrators to perform penance, which in itself betrays the ecclesiastical origins of the enactments. Such a penalty would have been inconceivable under a Frankish monarch if the offenses were considered truly serious.

In the century after the death of Charlemagne, moral zealots in the church succeeded in inserting much harsher penalties for homosexual acts into secular law, though they had to resort to legal forgeries to achieve their end. The traumas Europe experienced in 828 from the Moors' conquest of Spain and the onset of the Viking invasions provided a biblical context in which advocates of sexual asceticism could argue for severe measures to punish sexual transgressors. The Synod of Paris, meeting in 829, was quick to blame the twin catastrophes of the fall of Spain and the onslaught of the Vikings on the sins of the people, invoking the example of God's destruction of Sodom and Gomorrah for their sins. The Synod cited in particular sodomy, bestiality and the continued practice of pagan religion by the people, and warned that Europe would suffer the same consequences because of sinners unless the Carolingian monarchs took action against them.[34] But the Frankish rulers remained uninterested

*See Chapter 2 on customs of Melanesian tribes.

in serious enforcement of Christian sexual moral tenets and no such royal enactments were forthcoming. However, the work of clerical forgers saw to it that the failure of secular law to sufficiently punish sexual sinners was addressed.

Beginning in the late 8th century and continuing through the ninth, an assortment of unscrupulous churchmen took advantage of the disorganization of Carolingian legal records and concocted a series of forgeries of royal documents which advanced the interests of the church in a number of areas. The most notorious of the forgeries, the *Pseudo-Isidorian Decretals*, which included the infamous "Donation of Constantine," gave the pope dominion over all of Western Europe, turned over huge tracts of land to the church, and declared that anyone who accused a bishop of a crime would suffer eternal damnation, among other measures. The forged decretals were used by the papacy to claim vast secular authority for over six centuries until the forgeries were unmasked in the Renaissance.

Another set of forgeries, called the *False Capitularies* of Benedict Levita (Benedict the Deacon), are thought to be the product of the same group that produced the *Pseudo-Isidorian Decretals*, and include additional measures to elevate the position and power of the church under Carolingian law. Mixed in with some genuine Carolingian laws is a hodgepodge of Bavarian and Visigothic laws, ecclesiastical texts, a letter of Saint Boniface, Biblical texts, as well as provisions taken directly from the Theodosian Code and the Code of Justinian. Two of the capitularies quote verbatim from the proclamations of the Synod of Paris and statutes in the Code of Justinian to label homosexuality as a continued threat to the survival of the kingdom and the church, again citing the destruction of Sodom and Gomorrah in the Old Testament. A third capitulary, interpreting the Arab conquest of Spain as God's punishment for the acts of sinners, cites Roman law in calling for the burning of those guilty of homosexual acts.[35] Such a punishment for sodomy was radically harsher than any penalty prescribed for homosexual acts or any other sexual sin up to that point in post–Roman Europe, and was of a severity that would not be seen again for three centuries. Rather than being a reflection of contemporary church attitudes towards homosexuality, it was instead the product of an obsession with sexual purity among a small but growing number of anti-sexual moralists among the clergy whose persistent efforts would begin to bear fruit only in the 12th and 13th centuries.

The forged capitularies have also been cited as evidence of uniform condemnation of homosexual practices during the early Middle Ages by secular authorities.[36] However, even though the clerical forgers were successful in inserting penalties for homosexual acts into Carolingian law, there is no evidence that the provisions were enforced, or even taken seriously by anyone outside the church. Rather than being a reflection of any general concern in the population that sodomists would bring divine wrath upon them, the forgeries appear to have been created to try to incite such fears in a largely indifferent population, as the historian David Greenberg has observed.[37] Nonetheless, because of the prestige of Carolingian law, the forgeries had a significant influence on legislation covering sexual offenses in later periods, and created a precedent in Western European law for equating those engaging in homosexual acts as a threat to society.

Sexual Catalogues in the Penitentials

A body of documents that is much more accurate than the forged capitularies in revealing the attitude of the early Medieval church to homosexuality and other sexual sins are the numerous handbooks for confessors, called penitentials. Written from the sixth through the

12th century, their use originated in the Celtic Church in Ireland and spread first to England and then, later to France, Germany and Italy. The penitentials were used to advise priests hearing confessions on the relative gravity of various sins and on the penances, usually a period of fasting, to prescribe for remission of those sins. As such they are detailed compendiums of sinful acts ranging from swearing, drunkenness, gluttony, avarice, anger, pride, lying and stealing to the sexual sins of fornication, adultery, incest, bestiality, masturbation and homosexual acts. By listing the various sexual offenses and the varying degrees of gravity assigned to each one, the penitentials give us a good understanding of the attitude of the early Medieval church to sexuality in general and the relative gravity of homosexual offenses compared to other sexual sins. But as catalogues of sexual sins they are also useful in providing a picture of the sexual practices of the period. Because of the detail the penitentials provide on the various sexual acts a priest might have to deal with in hearing a penitent's confession, they are regarded as among the most valuable sources of evidence on both the sexual moral teachings of the church and the actual sexual behavior of the people of the early Middle Ages in Europe.[38]

As we saw in Chapter Nine, the moral attitudes to sex that developed in the early Christian Church were not rooted in the Gospels or Jewish Law, but originated primarily in the restricted notion of natural law derived by Saint Paul and subsequent Christian leaders from Stoic and late Hellenistic Jewish philosophy. The church's natural law-based notion of sexual morality was then elaborated with the strident anti-sexual asceticism derived by Saint Augustine from dualist philosophy and pagan Neo-Platonism. The sexual morality that the church sought to impose on the Christians of post–Roman Europe was therefore based on a general aversion to sex and a belief that sex was intrinsically opposed to spirituality. Because of the equation of sex with sin and chastity with virtue, sexual expression was tolerated only insofar as it was practiced specifically in order to produce a child. As crisply summed up by the historian Rattray Taylor, the church's attitude was based "quite simply upon the conviction that the sexual act was to be avoided like the plague, except for the bare minimum necessary to keep the race in existence. Even when performed for this purpose, it remained a regrettable necessity."[39] The teachings of the ascetic Christian moralists, therefore, condemned not only non-procreative sexual acts such as adultery, fornication, intercourse using birth control, heterosexual anal sex, oral sex, homosexuality, masturbation and bestiality, but even a man having sexual relations with his wife out of love rather than for the specific purposes of conception. In reflecting the church's ascetic sexual vision, the penitentials took aim at any sexual act other than coitus between a man and his wife, in the missionary position, for the specific purpose of having a child. Homosexual acts were not singled out as particularly heinous sins, but were included along with the other non-procreative sexual acts.

As manuals to advise priests in confession, the penitentials list the great variety of sins a confessor was expected to encounter, and in many cases go into further detail on the circumstances of a particular act so that its gravity can be determined and appropriate penance given. In some cases, the descriptions of sexual sins seemed to have verged on the pornographic, such as those in the 10th-century penitential of Burchard of Worms which, according to the noted Medieval scholar Pierre J. Payer, feature "startlingly vivid descriptions of various homosexual practices."[40] In the area of sexual offenses, the penitentials amount to a kind of early Medieval Kinsey Report, providing a catalogue of sexual acts of every imaginable type, heterosexual, homosexual, solitary or with animals. They further specify differing penances depending on the type of act performed; the age of the sinner; whether the partner was under the age of 20; whether one or the other was married; whether one was a member of the clergy, and if so, what rank; whether it was a first time offense, a habitual act, or an act performed under coercion; whether ejaculation occurred; whether it was oral, anal or interfemoral (intercourse between the partner's legs); whether fondling and kissing were involved; and if between women whether a "device" was used. Indeed, as the historian Allen J. Frantzen has remarked, "There appear to have been no details of sexual experience that confessors did not inquire about."[41] So thoroughly do the penitentials document the sexual practices of the time that the prudish 19th-century historian Charles Plummer labeled them "a deplorable feature of the Medieval church. Evil deeds, the imagination of which may perhaps have dimly floated through our minds in our darkest moments, are here tabulated and reduced to a system."[42]

The variety of homosexual practices described in the penitentials is illustrated in a listing of homosexual acts that typically appear in seventh- and eighth-century Anglo-Saxon penitentials: man with man, once; man with man, often; man with man, over 20; performing sodomy; taking the passive role in sodomy; habitual sodomy; non-habitual sodomy; sex with a boy, first time; sex with a boy, repeated; interfemoral intercourse; boys with boys; boy having interfemoral sex with a boy; boy having sex with an older boy; oral sex; brother having sex with brother; interfemoral sex with a cleric; sodomy by a bishop; sodomy by a priest; by a deacon; by a subdeacon; woman with woman; nun with nun; nun with nun with device. An example of the detail provided by the penitentials is found in a section "On the Sinful Playing of Boys," in the seventh-century Penitential of Cummean, which includes gradations of penances for: kissing between boys; kissing between boys licentiously but without ejaculation; kissing between boys licentiously with ejaculation or embrace; engaging in masturbation with another boy once; engaging in masturbation with another boy repeatedly; boys engaging in interfemoral intercourse, once; boys engaging in interfemoral intercourse repeatedly; a boy "misusing" a small boy under 10 years of age; a boy under ten consenting to sex with an older boy; oral sex between boys; and so forth.[43]

Frantzen has also pointed to the use in the Anglo-Saxon penitentials of the term *baedlings* to indicate a male who only took the passive, that is, feminine role with another male.[44] Such a distinction would show that males identified as exclusively passive homosexual were common enough that the culture had a name for them. Having a term to distinguish such passive males from other males also underscores the variability in sexual orientation and preferences among individuals that has been universally observed in societies around the world.

The large variety of homosexual acts recorded in the penitentials demonstrates that the clergy was quite familiar with homosexual practices among the faithful, which suggests that homosexual acts were encountered by priests hearing confessions with some frequency. Indeed, a notable feature of the penitentials is the recognition that sex between members of the same sex can take a variety of forms, of which sodomy, that is, anal intercourse, is only one. Such a distinction did not appear in the works of earlier church writings.[45] In contrast, patristic writers of the early church seem to have regarded homosexuality as one undifferentiated evil, and wrote of it as if viewing it with horror from a distance.

Because there was still no uniform Christian canon on sexual morality in the early Middle Ages, and would not be until the 13th century,* there was wide variation between penitentials in the degree of gravity and, hence, the penances assigned for each homosexual offense. Most of the penitentials assigned a gradation of increasing severity starting with the relatively minor offenses of kissing and masturbation, followed by interfemoral intercourse, oral sex and then, gravest of all, anal sex. Likewise, a clergyman would be assigned a greater penance for a particular act than a layman, a man a greater penance than a youth, and a nun a greater

The first official collection of church cannons is the Decretalia Gregorii Noni or Liber Extra, of Pope Gregory IX, issued in 1234.

penance than a lay woman. But between penitentials there was considerable variation in the penances assigned for the same act. For example, the *Penitential of Finnian* prescribed a penance of three years fasting for anal sex performed by a man, whereas the *Old Irish Penitential* assigned a penance of two years for the same act. The *Penitential of Columbian* called for a penance of ten years for the act in one place, and seven years in another passage.[46] On the other hand, the *Penitential of Bede* assigns a penance of four to seven years for the same act, depending on circumstances, Cummean's, seven years, and Ecgbert's, one to fourteen years.[47]

It is important to appreciate that in most cases the penances assigned for homosexual acts were paralleled by equal penances for heterosexual offenses. For example, Cummean's penitential specifies a penance of seven years' fasting for men engaging in homosexual sodomy, and the same penance for heterosexual adultery. Regino of Prum, author of an influential penitential collection of the late 9th century, called for three years' penance for anal intercourse, whether homosexual or heterosexual, and also three years' penance for heterosexual adultery. As David Greenberg notes, the basis for disapproval of homosexual acts according to church teaching of the period was that they were not procreative, and as such homosexuality was seen merely a subsidiary category of non-reproductive sex. The penitential authors did not treat those guilty of homosexual acts as "monsters" nor fulminate against them with references to Sodom and Gomorrah, calling them threats to society, but treated them as they did other members of the community of the faithful. They had sinned, but with contrition and the performance of penance for their sins, they would be restored to grace.[48] It's also notable that the descriptions of homosexual acts in the penitentials are almost entirely devoid of the histrionic vituperation found in references to homosexuality in the writings of early Christian leaders like Paul, John Chrysostom, Augustine and Jerome. It is evident that most of the early Medieval clergy were much more comfortable with the thought of homosexual acts than the early Christian leaders, whose visceral disgust for homosexuality, apparent in their writings, undoubtedly reflected psychological conflicts between the severe ascetic standards they preached and their own sexual urges.

The penitentials unquestionably demonstrate that there was a uniform judgment within the church of the early Middle Ages that homosexual acts were sinful. At the same time it is also clear that homosexual acts were considered no worse than heterosexual sins. While the attitude of the church is clear, there is scant evidence that the church was successful in persuading the population of early Medieval Europe of the seriousness of any sexual sins, heterosexual or homosexual. Despite the inclusion of penances for homosexual acts in the penitentials, their impact on the general population was very probably limited because of the fact that few people in the early Middle Ages went to confession in the first place. Despite a church campaign in the sixth and seventh centuries to get the faithful to go to confession, very few went on a regular basis, and many waited until they were about to die before seeking absolution for their sins. For those who did make it to confession, the penances assigned for sexual acts may not have had the desired remedial effect because the assigned penances were often commuted. Most of the penitentials allowed for fulfilling the penance through other methods, such as the giving of a certain amount of alms, or the recitation of the Lord's Prayer a specified number of times, and so it is unlikely that many were completely carried out as specified.[49]

While there is no doubt that the church consistently disapproved of homosexual acts as part of its general condemnation of all non-procreative sexual practices, it found itself unable to enforce its moral code to any great extent among the population. The actual reality was most likely that expressed by one 11th-century monk, "Pious books tell one story and men's lives and habits another."[50] Indeed, the church could not even enforce its sexual morality among its own clergy.

Feudal Society and Sexual Morality

We have seen that the stubborn persistence of Germanic tribal sexual customs and attitudes was a major obstacle to the Christian church in its efforts to impose its strict code of sexual morality among the people of early Medieval Europe. Another factor that prevented effective enforcement of the Christian sexual code, and that would have undermined enforcement of any laws on sexual morality that might have been enacted even if the church had been able to get secular rulers to focus on it, was a gradual fragmentation of political authority that culminated in the proliferation of feudal fiefdoms. Because Germanic law revolved around the concept of private property, German rulers saw the state as their own personal property, to be divided upon their death among their sons. Charlemagne would have divided his realm among his three sons, but two of them died early, leaving the empire intact under his remaining son, Louis the Pious. With the latter's death in 840 the tradition resumed, with the result that the Carolingian states were divided, first, among the heirs of the Frankish monarchs, and then among princes, nobles, their sons, and so on.

Further contributing to political division was the practice by rulers of awarding tracts of land to their knights in return for fealty and service. Faced with the threat of the Moors in Spain and the Vikings from the North, the Frankish rulers began the custom when they found themselves without sufficient armies of their own to counter the menace, and so traded allotments of lands in return for the service of their knights. The knight's claim to the land, or tenure, was based on his military service to the lord, and as the system developed, the standard for service was usually 40 days a year for each fief granted to a knight. A vassal of significant rank and holdings might owe multiple 40 day units of a knight's service, corresponding to multiple tracts of land, which the vassal could satisfy through the service of his own knights. The tenure for the land would pass to the knight's son, who when he became a knight would continue to fulfill the obligation of military service to the Feudal lord. As a result of the division of lands among heirs, and the further proliferation of fiefdoms granted to vassals and knights of land holders, the vast Carolingian Empire created by Charlemagne in the early 8th century, that stretched from Spain, to northern Italy, to the North Sea and to the frontiers of eastern Europe, had by the end of the 10th century fragmented into over a thousand separate fiefdoms.

Central authority was further weakened by wars of succession among heirs of the Carolingian monarchs and the upheavals caused by the invasion of the Norsemen. As a result, power on the local level fell by default to powerful local barons. Local feudal lords were supported by their own vassals and knights, and the peasants at the bottom who worked the lands and provided food and rent in return for protection. With the fragmentation of authority to the local level, the effect of royal laws and decrees diminished, while the power of feudal lords, more capable of controlling their local vassals, knights and peasants than any distant monarch, correspondingly increased. At the same time, with local jurisdictions organized around an ever-vigilant and well-armed military aristocracy, the people felt better protected and so had less incentive to pay heed to Christian preachers who raised the specter of death and destruction for those who ignored the strict sexual morality promoted by the church.[51]

By the 11th century the powerful noble families, recognizing the erosion of their power and position resulting from the division of lands through inheritance, had instituted primogeniture, the practice whereby only the eldest son would inherit the family's estate. By the end of the 12th century the practice had become universal throughout Europe. While the institution of primogeniture halted further division of lands and authority, the reversal of the fragmentation of political power that came with the proliferation of Feudal fiefdoms required several more centuries before European Feudalism was effectively ended.

The lack of any effective means of enforcing a uniform sexual code across Europe on top of the centuries-long resistance of the Germanic European population to Christian sexual teaching resulted in a long period of relative sexual tolerance among the population that persisted, despite the increasingly strident denunciations of contemporary sexual practices by conservative Christian moralists, throughout most of the High Middle Ages. With little incentive to conform to the strict and confining sexual code promoted by the church, the European people continued to hold on to the sexual attitudes and customs of their Germanic tribal ancestors. Against this backdrop it could be expected that homosexuality would have manifested as a feature of the lives of the people, particularly in the military society of the knighthood and the same-sex communities of the monasteries and convents.

Love and Affection Between Warriors

As noted earlier, the Roman historian Ammianus Marcellinus, in the late 4th century, wrote of homosexual relationships between Germanic warriors and youths undergoing warrior initiation among the Taifali, one of the Gothic tribes. Procopius reported similar homosexual relationships among warriors and young warrior initiates among one of the Frankish tribes, the Heruli, in the mid–6th century, at a time when the Franks had already established their kingdom in post–Roman Gaul, present-day France. While there is no documentary evidence on whether this deeply engrained Indo-European tradition continued among the warriors as the Germanic kingdoms developed in post–Roman Europe, we have no reason to believe that it did not continue in some form. Indeed, the same factors that have contributed to homosexuality among other military societies were equally present among the elite warriors of the Frankish kingdoms — an all-male world with a status apart from the rest of the population, the idealization of masculine prowess and achievement, and ties of affection sealed by blood shed in battle. Therefore, in view of 1) the strict Germanic laws protecting the virginity of young unmarried women, which would have tightly restricted the availability of suitable females, 2) the ongoing resistance of the Germanic peoples to Christian sexual moral teachings, 3) the existence of established homosexual traditions among Germanic warriors that persisted even into post–Roman Europe, and 4) what is now known about the homosexual potential in adolescents and young adults, it is reasonable to assume that same-sex relations would have be a frequent feature in the lives of early Medieval warriors.

However, because nearly all the literature produced in Europe until the High Middle Ages was written by the clergy, many of whom, as we've seen, were opposed to any sexual expression at all outside the bare minimum necessary for procreation, the information we have that would shed light on the sexual practices of the warriors in post–Roman Europe is meager. Nonetheless, between the references we have to the lifestyles of warriors in clerical writings, and the literature that began to appear in greater quantities in the High Middle Ages, we are able to glean enough details to form a picture of the nature of relations between warriors as Feudal Europe emerged from the tribal kingdoms of the early Middle Ages and culminated in the Age of Chivalry in the 11th and 12th centuries.

Some indication of the sexual relationships between warriors in the early Medieval period can be seen in the secular literature that survives from the period. In Chapter 5 we saw how homosexual bonds between warriors, called blood brothers, were documented in one of the Scandinavian sagas, which were passed down through oral tradition in the early Middle Ages and set to writing in the 12th-century. John Boswell cites a humorous exchange in another saga, the *Saga of Harald Hardradr*, that underscores the easy familiarity of warriors with homosexuality. In the passage, Halli, a favorite of King Harald, is admiring the king's axe. "Have you seen a better axe?" Harald asks. "I don't think so," says Halli. "Will you let yourself be sodomized for the axe?" asks the king. No, Halli impudently replies, "It seems to me that you should rather dispose of the axe in the same way that you acquired it." As Boswell observes, "This casual banter regarding homosexual relations inserted into a popular epic indicates that they were a familiar matter of little consequence, even if the whole exchange is entirely facetious."[52] The general lack of hostility of the warrior aristocracy to homosexuality in the early Middle Ages can be seen in an incident in which Hugh Capet, ruler of France in the 10th century and founder of the Capetian royal dynasty, came across two men caressing each other in a corner of a church and apparently thought little of it. He took no action against them.[53]

The historian Allen Frantzen has called attention to a remarkably direct allusion to homosexual love-making that appears in an unusual translation of one of Saint Augustine's *Soliloquies* attributed to Alfred the Great, Anglo-Saxon king of England in the 9th century. Frantzen notes that the king's translations were unconventional in that "Alfred often added to and changed the meaning of his presumed Latin original." Augustine's text is a hypothetical dialogue between Augustine and "Reason" on the degrees of loving "Wisdom." The point made by Reason is that it is best to love Wisdom directly, not through the interpretations of others, like touching something with a gloved hand. But in making the analogy, Alfred chooses to use the astounding example of a man making love to another man.

> How do you not know that for each of those men who greatly loves another man, it pleases him better to stroke and kiss the other man on the bare body than where there are clothes between? I now see that you love Wisdom very much and that you so wish to see and feel him naked that you do not want any cloth between you. But he will seldom reveal himself so openly to any man. In those times when he will reveal any limb so bare, then he reveals it to very few men. But I do not know how you can grasp him with gloved hands. You must also place your bare body against him, if you will touch him.[54]

It is inconceivable that King Alfred would use such an analogy in translating a religious text if same-sex love were not a well-known and acceptable mode of love in Anglo-Saxon England.

The use of a homosexual analogy by Alfred to translate a text of Saint Augustine, as bizarre as it may seem to modern readers, is entirely consistent with what we know of the sexual attitudes and customs of Germanic warriors. As we saw earlier in the chapter, the Germanic warrior class had a distinct lack of interest in Christian sexual moral teachings, throughout the early Middle Ages, even in the face of regular admonishments by Christian clergy. Furthermore, a distinctive feature of the Germanic warrior class, from their tribal period onward, was the bonds of affection that traditionally existed between the ruler and his warriors, and among the warriors themselves, which in many cases may have included overtly sexual ties.

In very early times, the tribal king was accompanied by a select number of warrior-companions who functioned as bodyguards. Sworn to be faithful to the king and to protect him, even to death, they were called *hirdh* by the Scandinavian tribes and *truste* by the Franks. The close personal ties were strengthened by experience together in battle, so that their bonds to the king became like ties of blood. They served the king and shared his meals, hence were his personal companions — from the Latin, *cum panis*, "one having bread with."[55] A similar role in Anglo-Saxon culture was the *thane*. Thanes were warrior-protectors of the king, who figure as beloved warrior companions of King Hrothgar in the early Anglo-Saxon epic *Beowulf*. In that epic, love between lord and warriors is mentioned repeatedly — the words "love" and "beloved" are used more than two dozen times to refer to feelings between the warriors and their lord. The king says of Beowulf, "I shall heartily love as mine own, my son," and addresses him as "love of mine" and "my loved one." When Beowulf is departing to return to his homeland, the epic says of Hrothgar's feelings for him, "safe in his soul a secret longing, locked in his mind, for that loved man burned in his blood." Beowulf tells the king that to win more of his love he would gladly come back to fight for him: "If ever on earth I am able to win me more of thy love, O lord of men, aught anew, than I now have done, for work of war I am willing still!"[56]

By the time of pre–Conquest England, the role of the thane had developed into that of a noble, with a rank just below that of an earl, while the expressions of affection of earlier times, born out of personal companionship and camaraderie in battle, continued in the rituals of allegiance between lord and vassal. In some cases such affectionate expressions may have been more symbolic than substantive, such as when incorporated into gestures of allegiance between a sovereign and powerful landed nobles between whom relations were frequently strained. However, truly heart-felt affection continued to characterize the relations of warriors to their own feudal lord and among themselves as the Feudal period developed, and in fact were to become a critical element in cementing the web of allegiances upon which the feudal power structure was built.

The Emergence of the Knighthood

Warriors on horseback had been a feature of the military arsenal of the Germanic tribes from their earliest days in Western Europe. Though Frankish armies for a period in the 5th and 6th centuries had employed infantry supplemented by an elite warrior cavalry, by the 9th century the armored warrior mounted on horseback came to dominate military engagements in Northern and Western Europe. Indeed, it was the return of Charlemagne to the exclusive use of mounted warriors that enabled his far-flung conquests and the establishment of his empire. Because of the cost, not only of the armor, but of the several horses, their feed, handlers and related accoutrements required to maintain mounted warriors at readiness, their ranks were necessarily filled only by sons of the families of the warrior aristocracy. In addition to the considerable expense involved, the years of training necessary to hone the multiple martial skills required of a mounted armored warrior resulted in the development of a caste of full time, professional soldiers.

The term *miles*, from the Latin for soldier, originally had applied to any common foot soldier, but by the end of the 10th century and the development of the war-fighting prowess of the mounted armored soldier, *miles* began to be exclusively applied to the mounted warrior, and came to signify an elite social status. With the development of Feudalism, many of them had been awarded fiefs in return for their service, and so *miles* also implied a landholding rank. The Anglo-Saxon word *knight*, which originally referred to a youth, or young adult between adolescence and marriage-age, by 1100 began to be applied to the miles in England, while in France, the mounted warriors were called *chevalier* (later, cavalier), from *cheval*, horse — an association that because of the expense always denoted prestige and status. From *chevalier* comes "chivalry," which came to represent the institution of knighthood and the associated knightly virtues of honor, courage and devotion to duty.

Many of the knights were attached to the estates of the great hereditary nobles, some of whose positions traced back to Carolingian times. These great lords had a constant need of armed warriors, to look after their interests, keep their peasants in line, and to fight for them in their incessant disputes with neighboring nobles. Knights of lesser means — and there were thousands — were more than willing to accept the offer of money, horses, armor, board and association with some great aristocratic line in return for military service to a powerful noble.[57] A knight who performed well might be awarded tenure to a manor of his own, on which he could establish his own line, as a vassal to the great lord. A feudal lord could also acquire the service of knights by taking charge of the education and training of sons of suitable parentage, providing them with room, board, training, and, when the training was complete, bestowing on them a horse, sword and suit of armor, the hugely expensive essentials of life for a knight.

The base of activity for the knights was the castle where they gathered to perform their required service. The knights also assembled at the castle if needed to uphold the peace or respond to a threat to the castle lord. The lord of the castle was the master of his knights, in peace as in war, with authority over them that was "familial," according to the historian Georges Duby, like that of a father. The castle community of knights, squires and other retainers in service of the lord of a castle in Norman England and France was called a *familia*, Latin for family or household. This "family" relationship between the knight and the castle lord was formalized when the youth came of age and "pledged his body" to the lord, a pledge "sealed by the giving and receiving of hands, signifying the gift of oneself, and by a kiss, a sign of peace and token of reciprocal loyalty." According to Duby, the "rites sealed a kind of bargain, and between the parties to the contract there grew up bonds that could easily be confused with the bonds of kinship." Indeed, in copies of decrees issued by feudal lords that survive from the period, names of knights were often intermingled indiscriminately with names of blood relatives of the lord.[58]

In this military family, the feudal lord treated his knights as he would his own sons, or sons-in-law. He fed and housed them, sometimes awarded tracts of land to them if their service warranted it and he was rich enough, reined them in if discipline was needed, and served as mediator if disputes arose among them. As part of their duties, the knights assisted in the administration and oversight of the "familial" property, which included keeping the peasants on the lands of the castle lord in line. This would be accomplished through regular tours of the lord's dominion, called cavalcades, in which the knights would show off their armed might in a menacing display consciously intended to intimidate the peasants and townspeople.[59]

Exceptionally close personal bonds between the young male and his master and between the youths in training were established from the time a young boy began his training for the knighthood. A boy of the warrior class being preparing for knighthood would typically be sent, sometimes as early as the age of seven, to the castle of a relative or some other patron, or, if his father was a vassal to a lord, to that of his father's lord. There he would serve as a page to the lord of the castle, performing duties around the castle, practice archery and swordsmanship, learn hunting in the forest, listen to tales of heroes like Arthur, Charlemagne, Roland and Perceval, and absorb the atmosphere of warriors, a world "of cavalcades, of stables, of armories, of hunts, of ambushes and manly sports."[60]

In the castle he would join the company of other boys of his caste in training, which involved strenuous physical exercises as well as training in the warrior arts. Running, swimming, wrestling and especially horseback-riding — critical to success in battle — were constantly practiced. At the age of 14 each boy would be attached as a squire to a knight for military training. The word *squire* is derived from the Old French *escuier*, or *écuyer* in modern French, which in turn was derived from the Latin word *scutarius*, which means "shield bearer," the same role carried out by the youthful beloved of a warrior among the Dorian aristocrats of ancient Greece, and the lover-apprentices of the warriors of the African Azande. The squire looked after the knight's horses, cleaned the stable, polished his armor and maintained his weapons. The knight supervised his squire's development, taught him the use of the lance and the mace, and trained him in the difficult skills of mounted combat. The youth's rigorous physical training also continued, and so he would practice wielding the battle-axe for long periods, so he could do so without fatigue, as well as running, scaling walls, jumping over ditches, and vaulting onto a horse — all in full armor. Equally important was mastering horsemanship, because of the vital necessity for the fine control of the horse for crucial maneuverability in battle.

Living in close quarters with his peers and the knight, a deep emotional attachment usually developed between a youth in training and his peers and with his knightly master, while a strong father-son bond grew between the youth and the lord of the castle. As noted in Chapter 3, psychologists and sexual researchers have long recognized that homosexual responsiveness is a normal aspect of puberty. The all-male world of the youth in knightly training, where masculine attributes and the male physique were idealized, would have been a particularly conducive for the growth of homosexual feelings and attachments. The natural inclination of young adolescents to seek role models, which can often lead to the infatuation of a youth for an admired older male, would have further encouraged strong emotional attachments between a squire and his knight. In such an atmosphere, where suitable female sex objects were almost non-existent, and at a time of life when sex hormones were at their peak, it would hardly have required encouragement for overt homosexual love relationships to have sprouted and flourished. This was a time, it must be remembered, when the church lacked any means of enforcing its ascetic sexual morality other than through florid denunciations of disapproved sexual activity. And of all the segments of society, the knighthood, as we shall see, was the least inclined to pay heed to the moral objections of conservative clergy.*

There are indications that homosexuality may have been common among the women of the castles, as well. Duby writes that "moralists were obsessed with thoughts of the guilty pleasures which, they had no doubt, women enjoyed in the gynecaeum either alone or in conjunction with other women." According to the early 12th-century biography of Saint Godelieve, women were "constantly vulnerable to the pricks of desire, against which there is no defense, and that they usually satisfy these desires through homosexuality."[61]

The lord of the castle, for his part, took a keen interest in his young charges, observing their growth, and sizing up their qualities of courage, honesty and fortitude, which could not be faked at such an early age, and upon which his life could one day depend. When the youth came of age and finished his training, usually by the age of 20 or 21, he became a knight in

---

*Nineteenth-century writers, who propagated the fictional image of the knight as a chivalrous ladies' man, imagined that the castles were filled with eligible young ladies for whom the young knights-in-training would become enraptured. An example is Thomas Bulfinch's introduction to his chapter on King Arthur and his Knights. "The same castle in which they received their education was usually thronged with young persons of the other sex, and the page was encouraged, at a very early age, to select some lady of the court as the mistress of his heart, to whom he was taught to refer all his sentiments, words, and actions. The service of his mistress was the glory and occupation of a knight, and her smiles, bestowed at once by affection and gratitude, were held out as the recompense of his well-directed valor" (Thomas Bulfinch, The Age of Chivalry, Chapter 1, Introduction). As the work of Georges Duby and others cited in this chapter has shown, such an image is pure fiction. These naïve impressions seem to have been based on fanciful projections from the romances and courtly literature of the late Middle Ages. That literature was written at a time when chivalry, in its pure form, no longer existed and when strenuous efforts were being made throughout society to suppress the open homosexuality that was widespread until the mid–13th century.

a dubbing ceremony, a vestige from the earliest days of tribal warriors. The word *dubbing* is derived from the Frankish word *duban*, which means "to strike." A youth completing training would be told to kneel and then his foster father or master, or the lord under whom he trained would strike him hard on the shoulder, to test his resistance and strength. In earlier times it was a rite of passage, "proof that the young man could hold his own in battle and kill to protect his clan."[62] Along with the dubbing, the newly created knight was usually given a horse, sword and suit of armor by his biological father, foster father, patron or the lord of the castle.

The newly dubbed knight then entered the ranks of young men called by contemporary chroniclers *juventus*, "youth," a status that began with a young man's dubbing ceremony, and ended, if he survived long enough, when he married and became a father. The *juventus* made up the greatest proportion of the total population of knights, and because of that, their character, behavior and adventures came to define the knighthood as a whole. The period of "youth" of these knights, as described in the literature of the times, was a period of impatience, turbulence and instability, says Duby. Always about to depart for some distant goal, or on the way to some destination, the knightly youth is on the move, "in quest of prize and adventure," or "to conquer for reward or honor."[63] By the end of the 11th century, with the institution of primogeniture taking hold, the ranks of young knights wandering the countryside began to swell. These were the younger sons who were excluded from the family patrimony by primogeniture, whose best hope for fortune and lands of their own was to be found on the road.

The newly created knights did not remain around the castle of their patrons for long. The next phase of their development, considered part of their "education" in the early Feudal period, was for them to go off into the world, accompanied by a band of young knights like themselves, to seek fame and fortune in the tournaments, and perhaps, if lucky, a suitable bride, that is, one with lands and a sizable dowry. When he was still very young, or newly dubbed, the young knight was assigned a mentor by his father or patron, usually an older, experienced knight, who was to accompany him on his adventures, look after him, and try as best he could to keep the young knight's enthusiasms from getting him in trouble.

An example of these arrangements is provided by Lambert of Ardres, chronicler of the family of one of the great Norman lords, Baldwin, Count of Guines. The count's son, Arnold of Ardres, was sent as a child to the castle of his father's lord, Philip, Count of Flanders, "to be brought up in good manners and instructed in the office of knighthood." In the castle of Flanders, young Arnold distinguished himself, "by his good looks and by his prowess in every military exercise."[64] When he was ready to be knighted, his father arranged a grand ceremony, and Arnold, along with four "fast friends" was knighted. Immediately afterward, Arnold, not wanting "to stay in his own country in idleness and without martial diversion" was anxious to get off on the road, "in search of tournaments and glory."[65] His father and the Count of Flanders, the master of the castle and his father's lord, arranged a suitable mentor, and young Arnold and his bosom companions were soon off looking for adventure.[66]

These companies were often formed immediately after the dubbing ceremony by the young men who had just been knighted. These were inseparable companions, who "loved each other like brothers," according to the chroniclers, and who would remain together their whole lives, unless one of them went as far as marriage and fatherhood.[67] The *maisnie*, or "household," as they were referred to in contemporary accounts, were typically formed around a leader, sometimes an established knight, but more often another "youth" like themselves, who would "retain" the young knights, giving them money and arms, and who led them in their adventures. The leader was frequently the newly dubbed son of the noble who was the lord of the fathers of the other newly dubbed knights, so that the group comprised the next generation of lord and vassals — tied together by not by the demands of political or military expediency, but by genuine affection and love.[68] The affections and attachments of these bonds would last a lifetime, and could even influence their future loyalties amid the constantly shifting political allegiances of monarchs, powerful barons and their feudal vassals.

Newly dubbed, outfitted with horses and armor, eager for battle and riches, and accompanied by lifetime friends, "a gang of children," Duby says, thus, "reached maturity and left the great seigneurial roof together, led by the heir who had just acceded to the knightly estate."[69] Life in one of these armed "gangs" of youths was spent in pursuit of pleasure, adventure and profit. The leader often squandered great sums of money on a lavish lifestyle featuring rich foods and wine, entertainment from minstrels, and horses, dogs and games. They wandered the countryside in search of excitement and advancement through knightly exploits, whether it was in battle or in one of the numerous tournaments in which they could showcase their knightly skills. The tournaments, while great social occasions full of colorful divertissements from miming and minstrels to puppets and games, all accompanied by generous quantities of wine and food, were at the same time serious affairs for the young knights. The tournament put the young knight on the world stage, and was an opportunity for him to advance his position through the display of superior skill. More importantly, it was also an opportunity to acquire the means to sustain the expensive knightly life. A knight who prevailed over an opponent by dismounting him with his lance could take his valuable warhorse, and even take the bested knight captive until ransom was paid. But this opportunity for gain also carried the risk of defeat, and loss of a horse, at a minimum, if the knight was dismounted himself.

Because of the effects of primogeniture, the numbers of young landless knights wandering the countryside seeking their fortune was constantly growing. These restless companies, whose main business was fighting in tournaments or battle, provided military manpower for expeditions near and far. Ordericus Vitalis wrote of a company of Norman knights providing reinforcements for a military campaign being waged by the Duke of Salerno in southern Italy, nearly a thousand miles away from their homes.[70] Duby, in fact, maintains that it was this surplus of armed warriors, constantly looking for action and reward, that formed the "spearhead of feudal aggression," and whose availability made possible and sustained the Crusades.

Roaming the countryside in knightly company also had its perils. Aside from the risk of serious injury or death in military engagements, which were frequent, the riotous lifestyle carried with it dangers as well. Many of the references to the knightly "youth" in contemporary accounts are of their violent deaths or injuries suffered during their escapades — death from injuries sustained in a tournaments, dying from wounds after being speared during an exercise, dying in hunting accidents, dying in drunken duels, dying from falls from horses while drunk. Perhaps owing to the hazards of a young knight's life, the average life span of a male of noble blood in 11th and 12th-century France and England was only 30 years.[71]

Manly Love in a Manly World

According to Duby, "morals were far from strict" among these youthful gangs. It was the lifestyle of just such a company of young knights that so appalled the conservative cleric Ordericus Vitalis that he invoked the flames of Sodom to describe their habits, as noted at the beginning of the chapter.[72] Ordericus Vitalis, whom John Boswell said "seems to have been obsessed with homosexuality," claimed it was rife among the Norman knighthood.[73] In fact, clerical literature of the day uniformly characterizes the knighthood as devoted to "the vice of Sodom."[74] Saint Anselm, 11th-century archbishop of Canterbury, thought that homosexuality was "rampant in the English and Norman courts," and was reported to have lectured King William II (William Rufus), son of William the Conqueror, about his sexual habits and the reputation he was acquiring in the kingdom, that "by no means befitted the dignity of a king."[75] The 12th-century clergyman Walther of Châtillon wrote that that this "crime" was a "habit" among the aristocracy, and that young knights learned it when they "went to France to study."[76]

Sexual bonds established while in training in the castles may well have continued among "bosom friends" in knightly company. Younger sons, especially, those for whom wives and property were not available, might remain in these groups for as long as 20 years, from the time they entered training at the age of 11 or 12, until the age of 30 or longer if they were unable to find a suitable bride. Unable to develop any enduring relationships with females, and restricted by custom to long-term companionship with each other, it may have been inevitable that they would turn to each other for intimate companionship and sexual fulfillment. As the sexual historian Vern Bullough has observed, "Under such conditions, though ultimately the eligible male would marry, if only because social convention demanded he do so, homosexuality, or at least bisexuality, was encouraged."[77] To assume, as many historians have, that unmarried knights in these companies would remain chaste and devoted to Christian chastity would be naïve, to say the least, considering all that we now know about the long-standing sexual attitudes of the Germanic warrior class and the lifestyles of the aristocratic "youth."

Of course, prostitutes were available, as in any historical period, and the young knights may have taken advantage of young peasant girls, where available. Wealthy sons who could afford concubines sometimes kept them, as well. But such relations with the opposite sex were more utilitarian than substantive, indulged in for sexual release rather than to meet their needs for intimate companionship. After all, Duby remarks, "This is a masculine world, and in it only males count."[78] In this manly world, so vividly featured in the *Song of Roland*, discussed in the beginning of the chapter, men love only men. "Of reverence for women," C.S. Lewis wrote, "there is hardly a hint. The center of gravity is elsewhere," in the "happy fidelities" among knights. When the poet finally does bring in a mention of the noble woman to whom Roland is betrothed, Lewis says that in doing so, he is "filling up chinks, dragging in for our delectation the most marginal interests after those of primary importance had their due."[79]

The Song of Roland is a very early example of a genre of literature known as the *chanson de geste*, epic poems that celebrated the heroic feats of a great hero, which predate by a century the literature of courtly love. The poem depicts a battle that occurred in 778 when Charlemagne's forces were on their way home from an inconclusive campaign in Spain. In the battle, a company of warriors, bringing up the rear guard, was trapped by Basque warriors in a mountain pass at Roncesvalles and slaughtered. Among the dead was a young noble, "Hruodland, Warden of the Breton Marshes." The historic facts of the events are not known and much debated, though there is consensus that whatever it was that happened represented Charlemagne's worst defeat ever — whether it was the loss of the "rear guard" or of his entire army is not known.[80] Perhaps because of the magnitude of the losses, a legend soon grew up around the battle, exalting the courage and devotion to duty of the trapped warriors led by Hruodland, or Roland, as his name is recorded in the written poem. During the Battle of Hastings in 1066, some of King William's men were said to have sung a song about Roland, and sometime around the mid–12th century the legend was set to writing by an Anglo-Norman poet. Though the story is set in the late 8th century, the written poem was a product of its time, the High Middle Ages, and so it is thought to be true to the customs and sentiments of 12th-century Feudal Europe. The audience for the poem would have been the feudal courts, and hence the passionate love and devotion that is depicted between warriors in the epic would have been intended to reflect the actual attitudes and interests of 12th-century knights.[81]

William Marshal

Another example of the chanson de geste, and an extraordinary source of information about the life and world of the Medieval knight, is the *Chanson de Guillaume le Maréchal*, a great epic poem that recounts the life of William Marshal, a renowned knight in his day, about whom King Philip Augustus of France said, "I have never seen a better knight than he in all my life."[82] The poem was commissioned by Marshal's son and heir, who wanted a record of his father's accomplishments, partly to protect Marshal's reputation against distortions by past political opponents. Drawing on the testimony of those who knew him, and very likely a partially written history maintained by one of his closest friends, the poem traces Marshal's life from his humble origins as the younger son of a minor noble in Norman England through his knighthood and rise through the feudal society of England and France, to his becoming a powerful earl and intimate of kings, with fiefdoms in France, England, Wales and Ireland.

Georges Duby, considered one of the greatest Medieval historians of the 20th century, has called the *Chanson de Guillaume le Maréchal* an unusually valuable historical document because, rare among surviving Medieval documents, it is not a product of the "clerical intelligentsia," but of the secular feudal world. As such, Duby says, "what is given us is infinitely precious: the memory of chivalry in an almost pure state, about which, without this evidence, we should know virtually nothing." The anonymous author, called Jean le Trouvère (troubadour) in the poem, showed himself to be a conscientious historian, says Duby, who drew on "sources that, without him, would have remained inaccessible to us, for they are located on the secular side of thirteenth-century culture." Faithfully recording the events of Marshal's life, Duby says the author produced what amounts to "the personal memoirs of a knight contemporary with Eleanor of Aquitaine and of Philip Augustus."[83] Along with a wealth of details about knighthood and chivalry, the poem, even more so than *Chanson de Roland*, makes clear the degree to which sexual bonds were frequently a dimension of the affection between knights, attachments that could sway allegiances even many years after the youthful affairs in which they were formed.

The poem starts with a physical description of Marshal — well-made, upright in his person, fine hands, strong of stature, with brown hair — quite within the norm for Anglo-Norman knights. The poem also adds that Marshal's *enfourchure* — his crotch — was "very large."[84] This reference to Marshal's genital development — astonishing by modern standards — speaks volumes about the way men regarded each other in the chivalrous period. It is probably not immaterial to note at this point that male mammals routinely size up each other by sniffing each other's genitals, and it could be expected that such a behavioral trait would be among those traits inherited by humans from their animal ancestors. After all, sexual researchers and psychologists have long understood — as discussed in Chapter 3 — that males from early childhood up through adolescents display an instinctive interest in the genitals of other boys and men, though in modern Western society it is normally repressed as the boys grow up. The fact that the ancient Sumerian *Epic of Gilgamesh* also includes an approving reference to the hero's "large phallus" seems to show that, outside the homophobic confines of modern Western society, it has been widely understood that men often view other men in a sexual dimension — or, at a minimum, find their genital development of interest.

As a youth, William Marshal entered knightly training in the household of a Norman lord, William, Count of Tancarville, his father's cousin and chamberlain of the English king. According to the poem, Marshal vied with the other knight-apprentices to win the love of this foster-father, soon becoming the lord's favorite. The young Marshal thrived in the household and in time became the squire of Tancarville's chamberlain, the highest official among the retainers in the castle. In 1167, after eight years of training, William was knighted. Leaving the castle soon afterwards, as was the custom, William immediately made his way to the tournaments, in a company headed by his former knightly master, Tancarville's chamberlain. In the competitions, William showed unusual ability from the start, quickly earned a reputation as skilled fighter, and began accumulating riches from his winnings to go with his reputation.

In the tournaments the newly dubbed knight was given an opportunity to demonstrate his valor and skill before stands full of spectators. According to the popular image we have of these events, the spectators would include dozens of fine ladies, for whom the knights would vie in competition, especially if one of the ladies favored a knight by dropping her handkerchief or sleeve. However, the descriptions of the events in the *chanson*, which devotes considerable space to Marshal's competition in dozens of tournaments, and is filled with copious details of the events, only mentions women in two of them. In those cases their appearance is brief, and "on the margins of the action." Concludes Duby, "The story of William Marshal suggests that women, in those days, did not attend the tournaments so often as is presumed."[85] At a particularly grand tournament, the spectators are joined by the wife of the sponsor, a countess and an elegant, beautiful woman, who came escorted by her ladies and maidens, "all elegant, courteous, and in fine array." At the sight of her, the knights break ranks and vie for her attention, "drawn by this lure." But, Duby says, "Let us consider more closely what role is assigned to women. They are present in order to excite the warriors to great valor. Under their gaze, the fighting will be all the more ardent; the war, or the simulacrum of war, then assumes the guise of a competition of males, one of those biological mechanisms."[86]

Toward the end of his first year as a knight, Marshal crossed over the Channel from Normandy to return to the area of his birth in the South of England, where he took up service to his maternal uncle, Patrick, Earl of Salisbury. Soon after Marshal's arrival, the earl was entrusted by Henry II to protect his wife, Eleanor of Aquitaine, on a trip back to her homeland to deal with some rebellious vassals. While in Aquitaine their party was attacked by some of the rebels and his uncle, the earl, was killed. William's valor in responding to the attackers was such that he won the gratitude and esteem of Queen Eleanor and her husband, the king.[87] Two years later, King Henry set up the up the *maisnie*, or "household" of knightly companions for his son, Henry the Younger, who was then 15 years of age and not yet a knight. The king asked William to take his son under his care, see to his knightly training, and serve as his mentor until he came of age. Though he had only been knighted three years before, William thus found himself at the age of 25 the knightly "master" to the heir to the English throne.[88]

According to the *chanson*, a deep love soon developed between William and his royal charge. In fact, so great was their affection for each other and the favors bequeathed on Marshal as a result of it that as time passed some of the other nobles in the young prince's household grew jealous of William's relationship with Henry. To try to dislodge Marshal from the prince's affections the courtiers concocted a scheme to spread a rumor that William was sleeping with the prince's wife, Margaret, the daughter of the French king, whom the younger Henry had wed in a politically inspired marriage. To make sure Henry heard the rumor, and to maintain distance from the affair to avoid the prince's wrath — and that of William — the conspirators decided to use as a messenger a close relative of the prince, his young page, Raoul Farci, Henry's cousin. Henry, the poem says, felt a great love for his young page, who apparently also shared his bed. The conspirators proceeded to get the page drunk, told him that William was sleeping with Henry's wife, and sent him off to the prince's chambers, where, as expected, he babbled to Henry about the supposed betrayal by the knight he loved so much. William had heard the rumor, too, but since under the circumstances to publicly defend himself could only bring dishonor to the prince's reputation, William remained silent. Feeling deeply betrayed, the poem says the prince "turned his back on William and spoke to him no longer. He withdrew his love from him," the worst of punishments, says Duby.[89]

Feeling that there was no alternative, William left Henry's court alone. A great tournament was just then getting underway, and William decided to compete in it, to get back to doing what he did best. Seeing Prince Henry's maisnie arrive to participate, William, without saying a word, fell in with them to compete under the prince's colors. Displaying his formidable skills, William won numerous matches, in the course of which he deftly prevented the prince's capture by opponents three times. Though the prince's company was cheered to see William there, Henry would not acknowledge William's presence. The next week, William heard that King Henry II was going to hold a plenary court on Christmas, and decided to go there and plead his case in front of the king, Henry the Younger, and all the prominent nobles of England. When the day came, William went in front of the king and the assembled nobles and challenged his accusers to trial by combat, and even offered to have a finger cut off his hand to handicap him to make it harder for him. None of the accusers would speak up, and young Henry would have no part of it. William, seeing that was the case, told the assembled court that, having his rights denied, he would seek a better life elsewhere. William then departed the realm. But barely two weeks had passed before Prince Henry, who had in the meantime "rid himself of his wife," sent messengers to William "begging him to return." As Duby says, "Nothing keeps him from loving William, who remains, as it happens, indispensable. He loves him once more. With an indulgence that is astonishing to our eyes."[90]

A striking aspect of the way the episode is related in the poem is that the prince's wife in the supposed adultery is never spoken of at all. Margaret is never confronted with the allegation, as one might expect, either in public or in private, nor is her presence in the castle even directly acknowledged. According to Duby, "Men's business, a matter of shame and of honor, of virile love (need I constrain myself to speak of mere friendship?). Let me repeat: only men are said to love each other in a narrative from which women are almost entirely absent."[91]

Duby, in fact, sees in the episode as related in the chanson a rare, factual example of the courtly love made famous by the troubadours, who were coming to prominence in Marshal's lifetime. The songs of the troubadours celebrate the passionate love of a knight for the wife of a lord, an adulterous love whose romance and intensity stood in contrast to the sterility of many of the politically arranged marriages common to the feudal nobility. In the noble houses of 12th-century Europe, Duby says, "the presumption of adultery is latent.... All the young knights lay siege to the lord's wife. This is the sport of courtesy. It adds spice to the permanent competition of which the court is the site. All are rivals." In this competition, Marshal may, in fact, have enjoyed the suspicion that he had conquered the lady. But were the knights in rivalry for the lady of the castle? Such has been our presumption. But as Duby points out,

"This is a masculine world, and in it only males count."[92] Duby poses the real question at the heart of the competition: "Who will win the lady's love — in order to attract the lord's to himself?"[93] So, according to Duby, the entire affair turned on love: the love of men among themselves. "We are beginning to discover," Duby writes, "that love *a la courtoise* ... the love that the knights devoted to the chosen lady, may have masked the essential — or rather projected into the realm of sport the inverted image of the essential: amorous exchanges between warriors."[94] Just as in the tournaments, where the lady serves as a symbol to spur the competition among men, so, in the relations between men, the lady of the castle is the fulcrum around which the competition for love among men revolves.

Throughout his life, according to the chanson, Marshal was never without a knightly companion with whom he was tied in love. We've seen the love relationship between Marshal and Henry the Younger. Later, Marshal had a squire, Henry Fitzgerald, with whom, according to the chanson, he was bound in love. After Fitzgerald was knighted and went on in his career, he remained a member of Marshal's household, his maisnie. But the deepest and most lasting love in Marshal's life was a young knight born in the same countryside as William, John D'Erley. Their relationship began when D'Erley was a teen, and Marshal, then in his early 40s, took him on as a squire. The chanson makes clear that their love never waned, and, in fact, they remained companions for 31 years until the earl's death in 1219. The poem refers to D'Erley as William's *bon amour*, a description that should remove any doubt about the physical character of their relationship. D'Erley was his constant companion, functioning as his "alter ego" and closest confidant. Indeed, the text of the poem says that D'Erley put his own funds, from estates he had inherited in Berkshire, toward the composition of the chanson, so that the quality of the knight he loved so dearly could be commemorated.[95]

As Marshal's career advanced, his role in Anglo-Norman politics became more prominent. Through his relationship with Henry the Younger, and service to the prince's father, Henry II, Marshal gradually accumulated honors and lands. In gratitude to Marshal, Henry II gave him as a wife the widow of the Earl of Pembroke, a marriage that brought with it the title of earl, second only to that of the king in the feudal pecking order, and vast estates to go with it. As a powerful baron, Marshal became an important figure in the endless struggles for lands and power between the English and French kings and their powerful nobles.

Under the chivalric system, a knight's first loyalty was to members of his household, his maisnie, and to his immediate lord, who could be vassal to a powerful count, who in turn could then be a vassal to an earl or the king. Thus the king's power depended on the strength of the allegiances of his vassals to him, the loyalties of subsidiary vassals to the king's vassals, and on down to the elementary basis of feudal power, the allegiance of the knights at the bottom to members of their knightly household and to their immediate lord. In the case of a knight with multiple titles and holdings, who could be lord to subsidiary vassals and at the same time a vassal several times over to powerful barons or kings, the exercise of allegiance in times of conflict could be very complicated.

The role of the ties of friendship born out of love among knights in knightly company came to the fore at a critical point in Marshal's life when he was thrust into conflict between his loyalty to the English king and allegiances that bound him as vassal to the French king through lands he held in Normandy. When John Lackland, younger son of Henry II, assumed the throne on the death of his older brother, Richard the Lion Heart, his machinations quickly put him in conflict with the French king, Philip Augustus. John was technically a vassal of Philip through his title, Count of Poitou, in Normandy, but John estranged himself from the barons in Poitou when he ruthlessly eliminated his nephew, Arthur of Britany, whom many thought the rightful claimant to the throne. John then defied Philip by his marriage to Isobel of Angouleme, who was already engaged to one of Philip's vassals. As John's feudal lord, Philip summoned him to his court to answer the charges, but John refused to appear. In response, Philip confiscated John's lands in Normandy and sent his army there to expel John's retainers. This, of course, enraged John who then prepared for a war against Philip to regain his inheritance.

In the course of his war preparations, John insisted that all his barons renounce any allegiances any of them had to Philip through lands they held in France. Marshal, who had earlier gotten John's permission to swear his allegiance as vassal to Philip in order to safeguard his holdings in Normandy, refused to do so. Marshal was here asserting one of the fundamental feudal loyalties, that to his family and lineage.

To renounce his allegiance to Philip could lead to the forfeiture of his Normandy holdings, which he felt obliged to safeguard for his son's inheritance. In response, John denied giving Marshal permission to pledge fealty to Philip for his lands, accused him of treason, and called him to judgment before his barons. But none of the assembled barons would side with either John or William, which left John and William facing each other alone, with only their closest associates as their sides. With Marshal stood only John D'Erley, his bon amour, and Henry Fitzgerald, his former squire. Duby notes that when feudal allegiances break down in such a conflict, only the "domestic bonds" hold fast, that is, the bonds of a knight and his company or household.

John then called for his barons to vote to confiscate William's lands. Only one baron stepped forward to defend Marshal: Baldwin, Count of Béthune, who had been one of Marshal's companions in knightly company in the days of their knightly wanderings. Baldwin, in defending Marshal, put his own standing in jeopardy, and could have forfeited his lands, as well, if the king had prevailed. As Duby observes, "But here again it is the closest friendship that enters into play, the camaraderie of combat and, perhaps, much more if, reading between the lines, we suspect that there is also involved, scrupulously muffled, that love which men bear each other in the knightly companies." Addressing the barons, Baldwin says, "Be still, it is neither you nor me to judge in court a knight of the earl's quality," to which the king could offer no rejoinder. Finding himself unable to summon the feudal allegiances to prevail in his conflict with William, John could do nothing else.[96]

In the next several years, the arrogance and high-handed maneuvering of King John continued to undermine his power and the loyalty of his barons. In a footnote to King John's downfall, we can see yet another example of the power of "that love which men bear each other in knightly company" to affect feudal allegiances. In 1215, the barons reached the breaking point in tolerating King John's treachery and brutality and were in open revolt. While Marshal himself, 70 years old at the time, took no role in the revolt against the king, his own son and heir, William, sided with King John's bastard brother, William Longsword, "whom he loved like a brother," according to the poem, and who had joined the barons against his own kin.[97]

Richard the Lion Heart

As the *Chanson de Guillaume le Maréchal* and the other material thus far considered amply demonstrate, a large portion of the knights of the Age of Chivalry appears to have been more likely to feel passionate love for another knight than for a fair maiden in a castle. Such was also the case with the figure whom many see as the most prominent exemplar of the chivalrous age, and best known for his homosexuality as well, Richard I of England. The third son of Henry II, Richard is more commonly known as Richard the Lion Heart, *Coeur De Lion*, a nickname he earned because of his skill, courage and ferocity in battle. Richard's colorful and eventful career has been depicted in scores of novels, films and television shows, though few of them accurately portray his true sexual nature.

Inheriting through his mother, Eleanor of Aquitaine, the blood of the counts of Anjou, whom some think had a hereditary proclivity for sadism, Richard's life was marked by the ruthlessness with which he pursued his ambitions. At the young age of 17 he joined his older brothers in a revolt against his father, Henry II, and after a brief reconciliation continued to battle with his father over their inherited lands until Henry's death in 1189. In 1187, he allied with Philip II of France, later known as Philip Augustus, against his father. According to the 12th-century historian Roger of Hoveden, a passionate love developed between the 29-year-old Richard and Philip, then 22 years of age:

> Richard, duke of Aquitaine, the son of the king of England, remained with Philip, the King of France, who so honored him for so long that they ate every day at the same table and from the same dish, and at night their beds did not separate them. And the king of France loved him as his own soul; and they loved each other so much that the king of England was absolutely astonished at the passionate love between them and marveled at it.[98]

Philip evidently had a special fondness for Henry II's sons. Geoffrey, Duke of Brittany, Henry's second son, had earlier stayed with Philip at his court in Paris for extended periods, and had become such a part of Philip's life that he made Geoffrey an official in his court. When Geoffrey, at the age of 28, was killed during a tournament, Philip's grief at the funeral was such that his aides had to restrain him from throwing himself into Geoffrey's grave.[99]

In 1189 the forces of Richard and Philip defeated Henry II near Anjou in France, and the king died two days later, allowing Richard, Henry's oldest surviving son, to assume the throne of England. It wasn't until two years into his reign that Richard finally married, but his marriage to Berengaria of Navarre seemed to have been motivated primarily by his desire to acquire control of Navarre, a kingdom on the northeast coast of Spain, adjoining his mother's homeland in Aquitaine in southwest France. Richard wed Berengaria in 1191 on the island of Cyprus while en route to the Holy Land for a Crusade, and took her with him when he resumed his journey. However, it's not clear how long they remained together since they returned separately, with Richard in the company of a lover, Raife de Clermon, a young knight whom he had rescued from captivity by the Saracens.[100]

Roger of Hoveden wrote that in 1196 a hermit came to Richard and warned him, "Be thou mindful of the destruction of Sodom, and abstain from what is unlawful; for if thou dost not, a vengeance worthy of God shall overtake thee." Hoveden wrote that later that year, on Easter, "the Lord scourged him with a severe attack of illness" to get him to repent. Richard, he wrote, then confessed his sins, "and after receiving absolution, took back his wife, whom for along time he had not known, and putting away all illicit intercourse, he remained constant to his wife."[101]

It is not known whether Richard did in fact remain true to Berengaria, since he almost never saw her. When he died two years later of wounds suffered during the siege of a minor castle in Belgium, he had yet to father a child, a critical factor in cementing the union of two royal lines, as Richard had attempted with his marriage to Berengaria. Because of the failure to fulfill that elementary royal obligation, which in itself underscores Richard's distinct lack of interest in the opposite sex, some historians have questioned whether the marriage was ever consummated.[102] After Richard's death, Berengaria even had to sue the pope to be recognized as his heir.[103]

Homoerotic Love in Medieval Literature

Evidence of the popular appeal of passionate bonds between knights is found in one of the monuments of Medieval literature, a compilation of stories of Lancelot, the quest for the Holy Grail and the death of King Arthur that are contained in a rendition of the Arthurian romances called variously the *Lancelot-Grail*, the *Prose Lancelot*, or the *Lancelot Vulgate Cycle*. The *Lancelot-Grail* is the most elaborate and richly developed of the several versions of the Arthurian legends written during the Middle Ages, and was a primary source for Sir Thomas Malory's *Le Morte d'Arthur*. While the authorship is not definitively established, the cycle is believed to have been written by Cistercian monks between 1215 and 1235. Nearly half of the *Lancelot-Grail*, a section called "Lancelot Propre" (Lancelot Proper), is devoted to the story of Lancelot, his adventures with the Knights of the Round Table, and Lancelot's adulterous love for Queen Guinevere, wife of King Arthur.

In relating the story, the relationship of Lancelot and Guinevere is expanded to include another knight, Galehaut, "King of the Long Isles and Lord of Surluse," who enters the story as an invincible enemy of King Arthur, and whose forces seem destined to destroy Arthur and his knights. But when King Galehaut comes to wage war against Arthur, he ends up as a rival to Guinevere for the love of Lancelot. The love of Galehaut and Lancelot was prophesized, according to the legend, even before the birth of King Arthur by Merlin the Sorcerer, who foretold that a "wondrous dragon (Galehaut)," will come from the Distant Isles, constantly growing in power as he conquered more and more lands. When the dragon reaches Logres (a Celtic name for England) where Arthur's Camelot is located, the dragon's shadow "will be so vast that it will darken the whole realm." But Arthur's kingdom will not fall, "because a magnificent leopard (Lancelot) will hold the invader back…. Later there will be such love between the dragon and the leopard that they will feel they are one being, each unable to live without the other."[104]

In the battle brought by King Galehaut and his forces against King Arthur and his knights, Galehaut's forces nearly succeeded in defeating King Arthur and his knights were it not for the extraordinary feats of arms of a mysterious Black Knight who entered the battle at the last minute to help Arthur's forces. Watching the Black Knight against his own knights, Galehaut was struck with admiration for the valor and skills of the Black Knight, and wanted to meet that wonderful knight. When a break came in the fighting, Galehaut followed him off the field.

Riding up close beside him, Galehaut greeted him and praised him as the best knight there was and the man he wished to honor above all others. "I've come to ask you as a favor, come stay with me tonight." The Black Knight was taken aback by such an invitation from someone he didn't even know and asked Galehaut to identify himself. Finding that he was the powerful King Galehaut, who had almost conquered Arthur's forces, the knight exclaimed, "What? You are an enemy of Arthur and you ask me to stay with you? I'll never stay with you." But Galehaut persisted, "I would do more for you than you believe, and I have already begun. Again, I beg of you, for God's sake, stay with me tonight…. I wish to have your company tonight, and if I can have more of it, I'll take it." The Black Knight finally gave in to Galehaut's entreaties, and accompanied him to his camp. When they arrived, the knight wanted some assurance of Galehaut's word, and so asked him to pledge his safety in the presence of the two among his men he trusted most. Galehaut went into the camp and came to the two knights he considered most trustworthy. "Follow me and this very night you'll see the most powerful man in all the world," Galehaut told the men. But his men said, "What, my lord? Are you not the most powerful man in all the world?" No, Galehaut, answered. "But I will be this very night before I go to sleep."[105]

Galehaut's last response demands a comment: in the preceding narrative Galehaut had referred to the Black Knight as the most powerful man in the world because of the unrivaled mastery he had demonstrated in battle, which to the chivalrous knight meant everything. But when Galehaut tells his men, "But I will be [the most powerful man in the world] this very night before I go to sleep," there can be no doubt that Galehaut is suggesting that by conquering the young knight in love, he, Galehaut, will regain the status of the most powerful knight in the world. Since it has been established that the Black Knight is superior to all others in knightly prowess, could there be any way in which Galehaut could conquer him other than in love? It is difficult to see any other interpretation of Galehaut's remark to his men.

After this meeting, according to the story, a great love developed between Galehaut and the young knight, so that the two were "bound together not only by loyalty, but by an outspoken and specifically described passion."[106] At the knight's urging, and to honor his love for the young knight, Galehaut agreed to make peace with Arthur and pledged to serve under him. In the world of Medieval knights, in which ruthless ambition for power and glory were the rule, such an action would have been seen as an extraordinary sacrifice on the part of Galehaut — abandoning his own kingly status and ambitions out of love for the younger knight.

Galehaut soon learns that the still un-named knight is consumed with love for Queen Guinevere. Distressed by the anguish he sees in the friend he loves, Galehaut arranges a meeting between the Black Knight and Guinevere. Addressing the Queen, Galehaut said, "My lady, I ask that you give (the knight) your love, and that you take him as your knight forevermore, and become his loyal lady for all the days of your life, and you will have made him richer than if you had given him the whole world." In reply, Guinevere said, "In that case, I grant that he should be entirely mine and I entirely his."[107] At Galehaut's urging she then gave the Black Knight a deep and passionate kiss.

Up to that point, the story follows the image we have of courtly love — the passionate but adulterous yearning of a knight for the lady wed to his lord, which in this case was helped along by the knight's devoted friend. But here the story veers radically away from that stock image and adds a distinctly homoerotic dimension, true to the actual world of the knights as scholars are discovering, but totally unknown to modern readers. Galehaut then asked the queen for the knight's hand in companionship. Acknowledging Galehaut's passionate love for the younger knight, the queen replied, "Indeed, if you didn't have that, then you would have profited little by the great sacrifice you made for him." She then gave Lancelot to Galehaut "as in a marriage."[108] Guinevere took the knight's right hand and said, "Galehaut, I give you this knight forevermore, except for what I have previously had of him." And turning to the Black Knight, she said, "And you give your solemn word on this." And the knight then did what she asked. The queen then asked Galehaut if he knew who it was she gave him. When he replied that he did not, she told him that the young knight was none other than Lancelot of the Lake, the son of King Ban of Benoic. Galehaut was overjoyed to hear it, because he had heard that Lancelot was "the finest knight in the world."[109]

Galehaut then left Lancelot with the queen so that they could enjoy each other's company. When nightfall came, Galehaut rejoined them to walk back to their tents. When they were opposite Galehaut's camp, Lancelot excused himself and went into the camp, while Galehaut escorted Guinivere back to King Arthur. When Guinevere was about to retire for the night, Galehaut told her that he would rejoin Lancelot and "give him what comfort he could." The queen thanked him for that, saying, "He'll be so glad of your company." At that point, Galehaut took leave of the king, "and soon he and Lancelot were lying in one bed. They talked all night long of the joy they said was in their hearts."[110]

After Galehaut left the love triangle between the queen, Lancelot and Galehaut seemed to become a rectangle. As Galehaut was walking back to his camp, Guinevere stood in the window, musing on the pleasant events of the day, sure that her discretion had kept the romance between her and Lancelot secret. As she was standing there in her thoughts, one of her ladies, Blaye, crept up to her and remarked with a sigh, "Ah, four.... Wouldn't that be a welcome number, my lady?" "Why, what do you mean" the queen responded. Blaye confided that she had seen Guinevere together with Lancelot and Galehaut when she kissed Lancelot, and added, "I thought of four when I saw the three of you in the meadow — you, Galehaut and a certain knight who loves you more than anything else in the world." Guinevere exclaimed that she could keep no secrets from Blaye, but then continued, "I still don't understand your remark about four." Blaye explained that when Lancelot's duties take him away from her, which would be often, "at least he can speak of his love to Galehaut. But you will be all alone, with no one to share your secret, unless we make a company of four." Guinevere was moved by Blaye's feelings for her, and the two continued to talk for a while, and then the queen insisted that Blaye share her bed that night. After that the queen and her lady retired to Guinevere's tent for the night, where they may have shared with each other the sexual comfort that church moralists were convinced that women enjoyed with each other in the women's quarters.[111]

Later in the story, when Lancelot goes on a mission to rescue Gawain from capture by Arthur's treacherous half-sister Morgan le Fay, Galehaut is sent a message by le Fay saying that Lancelot was killed. Hearing the false report, Galehaut is plunged into grief, and dies ten days later. After Lancelot returns, he has Galhaut buried in a grand tomb, and when Lancelot is himself killed at a later point in the story, his body is laid to rest besides Galehaut's in the same tomb. The burial of Galehaut and Lancelot together in the same tomb is yet another example of warrior-lovers buried together in the stories and practices of Indo-European groups. We have seen that the practice of burying warrior lovers together among the Scandinavian warriors may date back as far as 2000 B.C. Other Indo-European warrior pairs buried together include Achilles and Patroclus; the Greek warrior hero Epaminondas who was buried with his lover Caphisodorus; a pair mentioned in Plato, Philolaus, a great statesman of Thebes, and Diocles, a famous Olympic athlete; as well as the two knights who were the heroes of the Medieval stories of Amis and Amille. In Petronius' *Satyricon*, the two anti-heroes, Encolpius and Giton, tie themselves together during a shipwreck so that they will be buried together if they die. We've also seen examples of male lovers being buried together in ancient China and among the Samurai of feudal Japan, showing that the custom was relatively widespread in past periods. The burial of Lancelot and Galehaut in the same tomb underscores the passionate character of the love portrayed between the two in the legend, and indicates that a sexual bond between the two was clearly intended by the authors of the Vulgate-Lancelot.

While Lancelot is clearly depicted as bisexual, as a large portion of the knighthood undoubtedly was, a distinctly homosexual orientation in Galehaut is well developed in the story. The figure of Galehaut, in fact, has been called "one of the great homoerotic portraits of Medieval literature," a tragic portrayal of passionate love and self-sacrifice.[112] Perhaps owing to the virulent homophobic atmosphere that enveloped Europe in the 14th and 15th centuries, the relationship of Galehaut and Lancelot is omitted in later treatments of the legends. In Malory's *Le Morte d'Arthur*, written in the 15th century, for example, Galehaut, a formidable figure in *Lancelot-Grail*, is mentioned only peripherally.*

---

*Yet even in the version Malory produced in the homophobic 15th century, the intense love that could occur between knights makes its appearance, though in the background to the action. In the tale of "The Fair Maid of Astolat" in

That such homosexual love should play a central role in a cornerstone of Medieval literature amply demonstrates that passionate love between knights, as we saw in the early Medieval epics and in the chanson celebrating the life of William Marshal, had a continuing popular appeal as late as the 13th century, even as the church was rapidly taking steps to eradicate same-sex love from European Christian society.

Stories of Love Between Men in Popular Literature

In addition to the great works of literature, stories of loving devotion between men were also found in works of popular literature that circulated throughout the Middle Ages. A 10th-century story tells of the extraordinary love between two young men, Lantfrid and Cobbo, about whom the story says, "The two were as one." When Cobbo was about to return to his homeland, Lantfrid was "desolate," and so asked if he could go along with him. Cobbo urged him to stay behind. Cobbo then, to test Lantfrid's love, asked Lantfrid to give him the wife Lantfrid had just acquired (the text says purchased), "so that he might enjoy her embrace" on his trip. Lantfrid happily agreed, and said, "Let it never be said that I have held back anything which I possess." Cobbo then sailed off with Lantfrid's wife, but when he had gotten out of sight, turned around and sailed back, and gave Lantfrid back his wife, "untouched." In relating the story, John Boswell observed, "it is hard to imagine a marriage begun under such circumstances mattering much to Lantfrid. Clearly his affection for Cobbo is the primary emotional focus of his life."[113]

A series of stories about the extraordinary devotion between two knights, Amis and Amile, enjoyed immense popularity all across Europe in the 12th century. The stories were originally written in Latin, but were quickly translated into most of the vernacular languages of Medieval Europe. The two knights not only loved each other, but looked so much alike that one could substitute for the other in tournaments. In the stories the knights find themselves constantly being separated from each other through mishaps and misfortune in which their love for each other is frequently tested. Nonetheless, they always manage to find each other for ecstatic reunions, however brief, before the next misadventure begins. On one occasion, when they had been separated for two years, they finally met. "They lighted down from their horses, and embraced and kissed each other, and gave thanks to God that they were found. And they swore fealty and friendship and fellowship perpetual, the one to the other, on the sword of Amile, wherein were relics."[114]

In a particularly poignant story that illustrates the extremes to which the pair would go for each other, Amis takes Amile's place for him in a tournament, "saved his life from a traitor, and won for him the King's daughter" as a wife. Not long afterward, Amis was struck with leprosy, and was brought to the house where Amile and his royal bride were living. See-

---

(footnote continued) *Part VII of the work, after Lancelot is injured in a tournament, he asks Sir Lavain, a young knight who was Lancelot's companion at the time, to pull out the head of a spear that had pierced his side. Afraid that doing so would cause Lancelot to die of loss of blood, Sir Lavain refuses, to which Lancelot responds, "I tell you, if you love me, pull it out." Later Sir Lavain compared his passionate love for Sir Lancelot to that of his sister, the fair maid of the title, who was dying out of unrequited love for Lancelot. Deeply distressed at the anguish of the lady, whom he would not wed, Lancelot thought it best to depart her castle, and asked his young companion, Sir Lavain, what he was going to do. "Sir, what should I do," said Sir Lavain, "but follow you, if you would have me." And then after Lancelot remarked to the lady's father on his daughter's qualities, Lavain turned to his father. "Father," said Sir Lavain, "I dare make good she is a clean maiden.... But she is like me, for since I saw first my lord Sir Lancelot, I could never leave him." (Emphasis added.) (Translation after Malory: the Mort Darthur, D.S. Brewer, ed., York Medieval Texts, Chicago: Northwestern University Press, 1968, pages 54–67.)*

ing Amis's condition, Amile and his bride were "sore grieved, and they brought him in and placed him on a fair bed, and put all that they had at his service." One night when Amis and Amile were sleeping in the same room, the Angel Raphael came to Amis. The angel told him that he was "a fellow of the citizens of heaven" and that he was Raphael, an angel of the Lord, who had come to tell him of a medicine that would heal him in answer to his prayers.

The angel said: "Thou shalt tell to Amile thy fellow, that he slay his two children and wash thee in blood, and thence thou shalt get the healing of thy body." Amis was horrified when he heard what the angel said, and resolved not to tell Amile. But Amile had heard the angel's voice and insisted that he tell him what the angel had said. When Amile heard, "he was sorely grieved. But at last determined in his mind not even to spare his children for the sake of his friend, and going secretly to their chamber he slew them, and with some of their blood washed Amis who immediately was healed." Amile then dressed Amis in his best clothes and the two of them went to church to give thanks. There they met Amile's wife who, not knowing what had happened to her children, rejoiced with them. When they got home, Amile went up to the children's room, and found them playing in bed with only a red thread around their necks to mark what had been done. The two knights were killed in battle not long afterward, fighting side by side, "for even as God had joined them together by good accord in their life-days, so in their death they were not sundered." The story adds that a miracle then occurred, "when they were buried apart from each other, the two coffins leapt together in the night and were found side by side in the morning."[115]

Also popular in the Middle Ages were stories of paired military saints. John Boswell examined in detail the proliferation in the Byzantine world of saints paired together, typically pairs of Christian soldiers who had been martyred for refusing to persecute Christians or renounce their faith in the late Roman Empire. Two of the most famous are Saints Serge and Bacchus, fourth-century Roman soldiers of high standing, friends of the emperor and described as devoted lovers. Refusing to renounce their Christian faith, they were brutally martyred by the emperor. Images of them together were widely popular in the Eastern church from early Byzantine times through the 14th century. Severus of Antioch in the 6th century said they should be always mentioned together because "we should not separate in speech those who were joined in life." In a tenth-century manuscript describing their lives, Serge is described as the "sweet companion and lover" to Bacchus.[116] Another pair of military saints popular in the Middle Ages was a pair of soldiers, both named Theodore, one a foot-soldier, one a general. The two are frequently depicted in paintings with arms around each other, or tenderly embracing each other.[117]

Boswell's assertion that these paired saints were all homosexual lovers stirred enormous controversy among Eastern Orthodox Catholics who insisted their relationships were chaste. But one has to wonder how relationships between men, who are characterized as passionately devoted to each other, who are described as "joined in life," and who were depicted as tenderly embracing each other would not include a physical dimension. Other pairs of military saints with followings in Western Europe during the Middle Ages include Saints Demetrius and George, Saint Maurice and the martyrs of the Theban legion, and Saints Eustace and Sebastian. Considering what we are learning about sexual attachments among the knights, it does not seem coincidental that the lives of these passionately devoted saintly pairs were all used as themes of sermons by the chaplain to Hugh of Chester's knightly household.[118]

Medieval Same-Sex Unions

The material examined in this chapter on the world of the Medieval knights amply illustrates that passionate friendships between males, which we can be certain in most cases would have involved sexual relations, were a common occurrence in the Middle Ages among the warrior class. In a social atmosphere in which two men would find it possible to form long-lasting sexual bonds, it could be expected that some men would want to have their relationships formalized with some sort of ceremony. We've already seen how love bonds among Scandinavian warriors were formalized through a blood-brothers' ritual, and that these rituals appear to have been a feature of early Scandinavian society for many centuries. We also have evidence of formal unions between men from two other regions of Medieval Europe, Germany and Celtic Ireland.

A sexual union with strong similarities to those of the blood-brother relationships among Scandinavian warriors was described in a story about two knights in the *Gesta Romanorum*, a hugely popular collection of stories compiled in 13th-century Germany that supplied material for later writers from Boccaccio to Shakespeare. In the story, two knights "love each other" so much that they want to form a union so strong that afterward neither would "divorce" the other, either "in prosperity or adversity, and "whatever either one earned would be shared equally with the other." They then engage in a ritual in which each drank a small amount of the other's blood, after which they live their lives in the same house.[119]

A strikingly similar ceremony for joining two men in a sexual union, which also involved the drinking of blood, was described by the clerical writer Gerald of Wales in the late 12th century as occurring among pairs of men in Ireland. But unlike the Scandinavian ceremony or the ritual described in the *Gesta Romanorum*, the Irish same-sex union also involved blessing in a Christian church.

> First they are united in pacts of kinship; then they carry each other three times around the church. Then, entering the church, before the altar, in the presence of the relics of saints and with many oaths, and finally with a celebration of the Mass and the prayers of priests, they are permanently united as if in some marriage. At the end, as further confirmation of the friendship and a conclusion to the proceedings, each drinks the other's blood, which is willingly shed for this. This, however, they retain from the rites of pagans, who customarily use blood in the sealing of oaths.

In commenting on the ceremony, John Boswell, observed that the "description of the ceremony as a wedding, conducted by a priest in church and accompanied by the Eucharist, is unmistakable."[120]

That such a same-sex ceremony would be allowed in a church in 12th-century Ireland suggests that the disapproval of homosexual activity included in 7th- and 8th-century Irish penitentials was either forgotten by the 12th century, or frequently ignored. Indeed, a great quantity of literature and letters that survive from the Middle Ages provides plentiful evidence that the well-documented disapproval of homosexuality in church manuals of the early Middle Ages was not only widely disregarded, but that homosexual loves may have been as common among the clergy as among the knighthood.

Same-Sex Love Among Monks and Nuns

Given what is known about the inherent homosexual capability in humans, especially among adolescents and young adults, it should not be surprising to find that homosexuality appears to have been a frequent occurrence in the same-sex communities of the monasteries and convents of the Middle Ages. Church leaders had long been aware of the potential for homosexuality among cloistered clergy, and seem to have understood that every individual was susceptible to the lure of homosexual attraction. Saint Basil, in the late 6th century, included warnings to monks on avoiding sexual temptation in his *Renunciation of the Secular World*: "If thou art young in either body or mind, shun the companionship of other young men and avoid them as thou wouldst a flame. For through them the enemy has kindled the desires of many and then handed them over to eternal fire, hurling them into the vile pit of the five cities under the pretense of spiritual love." Basil goes on to advise choosing a seat at meals far from other young men. And if some young man were to speak to the monk, "lest perhaps by gazing at his face thou receive a seed of desire sown by the enemy and reap sheaves of corruption and ruin, it is best to reply to him with your eyes fixed firmly upon the ground."[121]

Church authorities went to great pains to prevent the development of sexual love among monks. Among other measures, the Council of Tours, in the 6th century, required that monasteries enforce a rule that two monks must not share a bed, a common practice among the laity throughout Europe in the Middle Ages.[122] Monks were not allowed to be alone, the abbot slept in the midst of the monks, and lights were kept burning all night long. As George Duby remarked, "The needs of community took second place in this regard, owing to an unarticulated but obsessive fear of homosexuality."[123] In some cases, the measures were extreme. The rules of the Bavarian monastery at Hirchau in the 10th century forbade boys from speaking with each other, exchanging signs or smiles or having any kind of familiarity, even seeing each other's faces. An older monk was assigned to chaperone them at all times, including supervising their visits to the latrine. Saint Bonaventure included in his regulations for young novices rules against sleeping on one's back or in "any other lewd manner," that is, naked, with hands on the body, the buttocks protruding or without sufficient covering.[124]

Were all these precautions effective in preventing homosexuality in the monasteries? Evidently not. The continued necessity for maintaining the rules from the 6th century onward suggests that the monastic leadership found that the problem they were exerting great efforts to avoid was a continuing issue. The detailed provisions in the penitentials about sex between monks and between nuns also show that homosexual activity among the clergy must have been encountered by priests hearing confessions with some frequency. The listing of clergy involved — priests and nuns, deacons, subdeacons, bishops — demonstrate that homosexuality was found among clergy of every rank. The clerical activists responsible for the enactments issued under Charlemagne that denounced sodomy among monks were surely acting on their own observations of homosexual liaisons in the monasteries. One of the enactments, in fact, cites homosexual practices in the monasteries as a reason for the necessity of such a provision. But while some church leaders of the period were keenly focused on the elimination of homosexual love among the clergy, other prominent churchmen seemed to have a more lenient view of same-sex love, some apparently in Charlemagne's own circle.

Alcuin, the great scholar, poet, educator, counselor to Charlemagne and abbot of the great monastery at Tours, denounced adultery, incest and other heterosexual sins in his writings, but avoided any comment on homosexuality. Some of Alcuin's letters to friends, on the other hand, contain a markedly homoerotic character. It is true that correspondence between friends of the times often contained florid expressions of affection, but a letter of Alcuin to one friend, cited by John Boswell, uses language that could hardly be more erotic: "I think of your love and friendship with such sweet memories ... that I long for that lovely time when I may be able to clutch the neck of your sweetness with the fingers of my desires. Alas, if only it were granted to me ... to be transported to you, how I would sink into your embraces, ...

how much would I cover, with tightly pressed lips, not only your eyes, ears and mouth, but also your every finger and toe, not once but many a time."[125]

A tolerant attitude to same-sex love is revealed in another letter Alcuin wrote to a young man — renowned throughout England for his beauty, according to Boswell — whom Alcuin addresses as "sweetest son, brother and friend." In the letter Alcuin gently scolds the young man for an apparent homosexual indiscretion that had come to his attention when he heard "everyone giggling in public" about it. Alcuin's reproach was not because the young man had committed a homosexual act, but because the manner in which it was carried it out was "puerile, unbecoming to a scholar and apt to lead to a bad reputation." In his late life Alcuin wrote that he regretted the "sins of his youth," which seems an admission that at least some of his passionate friendships may have been consummated in bed.[126]

Boswell notes other examples of passionate love expressed in letters of monks and abbots of the early Middle Ages. The early ninth-century theologian Walafrid Strabo, in a letter to a friend, referred to their relationship as, "two lovers, divided in body, but linked in the spirit by one love."[127] With the cultural renaissance that came with the revival of cities in the late 10th and the 11th centuries, the volume of clerical writings expressing same-sex love for another cleric soared. One of the most prominent clergymen of the 11th-century, Anselm, archbishop of Canterbury, dedicated himself to the ideal of monastic celibacy, yet was engaged in a series of deeply emotional attachments with other members of the clergy. Born in Italy in 1034, Anselm was educated at the Abbey of Bec in Normandy, renowned for its learning, and headed at the time by Lanfranc, one of most formidable intellects of the day. Lanfranc himself was known for his passionate friendships with young monks, and according to Boswell, Anselm developed "an extraordinarily emotional relationship" with the older monk.[128]

According to one of Anselm's biographers, "love and friendship had been the dominant feature of his early and middle years."[129] His letters are filled with expressions of the most intimate kind of love. To one friend, Anselm writes,

> How could I forget you? Can a man forget one who is placed like a seal upon his heart? In your silence I know that you love me; and you also, when I say nothing, you know that I love you. Go into the secret place of my heart, look there at your love for me, and you shall see mine for you.... You knew how much I love you, but I knew it not. He who has separated us has alone instructed me how dear to me you were. No, I knew not before the experience of your absence how sweet it was to have you, how bitter to have you not.

In another letter, Anselm writes, "My eyes ardently desire to behold you; my arms expand to embrace you; my lips sigh for your kisses; all the life that remains to me is consumed with waiting for you.... the less I can enjoy your presence, the more the desire of that pleasure burns in the soul of your friend."[130]

Whether Anselm's loves were ever consummated in bed is not known. However, Anselm seems to have been well aware that his feelings of love for his friends were sexual. In old age he wrote of the torment caused him by his sexual passion in words reminiscent of those used by Saint Paul in Romans when he wrote of his "thorn in the flesh."[131] Because of Anselm's reputation as a theologian and the founder of Christian scholasticism, some of his biographers have been loath to see a carnal element in his friendships. Richard W. Southern said Anselm's love for his friends was a spiritual love "nourished by an incorporeal ideal."[132] One of the most prominent recent scholars of Anselm's works, on the other hand, has written that it would be appropriate to view Anselm's loves as rising from homosexual feelings.[133]

While there is no doubt that Anselm was troubled about his homosexual desires, it is clear that other clergymen of the day had no reservations at all about engaging in active and undisguised homosexual relationships. At the other extreme from Anselm were churchmen, including some of the highest ranking clerics of the day, whose blatant pursuit of homosexual relationships scandalized conservative moralists among the clergy. Ivo of Chartres, a contemporary of Anselm who became bishop of Chartres in 1090, complained bitterly in a letter to Pope Urban II about a certain promiscuous youth named Jean being made the bishop of Orléans despite his reputation for sexual looseness and the fact that he was underage. Jean's sexual affairs had brought him such notoriety, in fact, that he had gained the nickname Flora, after a well-known local courtesan, and had become the subject of a number of lewd street songs. In an attempt to head off Jean's elevation to bishop, Ivo had previously sent samples of the lurid lyrics of the songs to the archbishop of Lyons, the papal legate, but to no avail. The installation of Jean as bishop of Orléans had been arranged by Jean's then lover, Raoul II, Archbishop of Tours, who had obligingly crowned Philip I King of France on Christmas Day in defiance of a papal interdict placed on Philip for "immoral behavior." In exchange for the favor, Philip agreed to arrange a bishopric for Jean, who it so happens had also been a previous lover of the king. Philip, himself, had boasted of the affair to Ivo.[134]

Oddly, Ivo's objections seem to have had less to do with Jean's sexual activities than his youth. The principal concern expressed by Ivo in his letter was that the inexperienced Jean would be a puppet of Archbishop Raoul, in effect giving the latter two bishoprics. Archbishop Raoul had previously antagonized Urban II by siding with King Philip in a dispute against the papal legate, yet the pope refused to interfere with Ralph's installation of Jean as bishop of Orléans. John Boswell has noted that the lack of action against Ralph and Jean by the papacy was not an indication of indifference to the morals of the clergy. Not long after Jean's investiture, Urban II's successor, Paschal II, directly intervened to remove another French bishop for adultery, while leaving Ralph and Jean, whose sexual relationship was well known in ecclesiastical circles, in their positions. And despite the circumstances of his elevation to the post, Jean went on to serve ably and effectively and retired with honors nearly 40 years later.[135]

Passionate sexual affairs appear to have also been commonplace among nuns. As we saw earlier, provisions on sexual relations between nuns were included in many of the penitentials, an indication that church authorities had long been aware of lesbian love in the convents. An example of the kind of passionate love that may have frequently occurred behind convent walls is found in a love letter with a decidedly erotic cast that survives in a 12th-century manuscript from a monastery in Tegernsee in Bavaria. In the letter, an anonymous nun writes to another: "I am weighed down with grief, for I find nothing I would compare to your love which was sweeter than milk and honey.... it is you I have chosen for my heart, I love you above all else, you alone are my love and desire. Like a turtledove who has lost her mate, and stands forever on the barren branch, so I grieve ceaselessly until I enjoy your love again." Another letter, which Boswell cites as perhaps the outstanding example of medieval lesbian literature, tenderly expresses the pain of separation of two lovers, evident in a short excerpt: "When I recall the kisses you gave me, and how with tender words you caressed my little breasts, I want to die, because I cannot see you. What can I, so wretched, do? Where can I, so miserable, turn? ... As long as the world stands you shall never be removed from the core of my being. What more can I say? Come home, sweet love! Prolong your trip no longer; know that I can bear your absence no longer."[136]

Another example of the expression of passionate love between clergy is the heart-felt lament on the death of a beloved companion written by one of the most eminent churchmen of the Middle Ages, Saint Bernard of Clairvaux, the great Cisterian abbot and a Doctor of the Church: "Flow, flow my tears, so eager to flow! He who prevented your flowing is here no more! It is not he who is dead; it is I who now live only to die. Why, O why have we loved, and why have we lost each other."[137] Perhaps the most eloquent exponent of passionate friendships in the monasteries was another great Cistercian abbot, Saint Aelred of Rievaulx, an advisor to Henry II and a protégé of Saint Bernard. Known principally for his "Life of Saint Edward, King and Confessor," Aelred also left two treatises on love, "Spiritual Friendship" and "The Mirror of Love," the latter written for Saint Bernard. In his treatises Aelred developed a conception of Christian friendship with an emphasis on affection that laid out a vision of human love as a pathway to spiritual love — a striking parallel to Plato's concept of spiritual love described in his *Symposium*. Alfred's belief in the interrelationship of friendship and spiritual love is succinctly summed up in his statement that "he who abides in friendship abides in God and God in him."[138]

Most historians now accept that Aelred was homosexual.* Aelred himself was very open about his sexual feelings: "While I was still a schoolboy, the charm of my friends greatly captivated me, so that among the foibles and failings with which that age is fraught, my mind surrendered itself completely to emotion and devoted itself to love. Nothing seemed sweeter or nicer or more worthwhile than to love and be loved." In his later life he expressed some regret at his youthful passions when, he said, "a cloud of desire arose from the lower drives of the flesh and the gushing spring of adolescence," and "the sweetness of love and the impurity of lust combined to take advantage of the inexperience of my youth." In what seems a frank admission of homosexual relations when he was a youth, Aelred wrote to his sister that in the period of their youth, she held on to her virtue and he lost his.[139]

When Aelred entered the monastic life he apparently accepted a vow of celibacy, though he continued to have intensely emotional relationships with other monks. He fell in love with another monk named Simon, and was devoted to him until Simon's death. In his grief Aelred wrote a heartfelt paean to their love "without whom he cold hardly be said to live." Aware that others in the monastery might see the intensity of his grief for Simon as indication of a sexual relationship, Aelred wrote, "But some may judge by my tears that my love was too carnal. Let them think what they wish.... Others see what is done outwardly. They cannot perceive what I suffer inwardly." Aelred later developed a relationship with a younger monk about whom he wrote: "He was the refuge of my spirit, the sweet solace of my griefs, whose heart of love received me when fatigued from labors, whose counsel refreshed me when plunged in sadness and grief.... Was it not a foretaste of blessedness thus to love and thus to be loved?"[140]

Aelred's acceptance of a physical, or sensuous, aspect of love is in sharp contrast to the moral writings of the early church Fathers, which often depicted physical sensuousness as tantamount to the lure of Satan. According to Aelred, physical beauty could be a "completely legitimate inspiration of love, as long as it did not obscure a vicious character."[141] Aelred's conception of physical beauty as an inspiration for spiritual growth and development is paralleled by the philosophy of another prominent clergyman of the 12th century, Abbott Suger of Saint-Denis, a French contemporary of Aelred. Suger, an advisor to Louis VII of France, is considered one of the most influential artistic figures of the Middle Ages for his work in developing the Gothic style, which he cultivated in his rebuilding of the Abbey at Saint-Denis near Paris. Suger believed that man can only come to understand the absolute beauty of God through the effect of precious and beautiful things on our senses. "The dull mind rises to truth through that which is material," a revolutionary idea in the Medieval world.[142]

This appreciation of the pleasures of the senses was a distinguishing feature of much of the literary and artistic output of the High Middle Ages which burst forth amid the prosperity of the 12th century "like a Russian spring," in the words of Kenneth Clark, after the cultural barrenness of the "Dark Ages." A greater appreciation of *la douceur de vivre,* the sweetness

---

*Indeed, he is the patron saint of Integrity, a gay and lesbian organization of the Episcopal church of the United States.

of life, was expressed in the pursuit of greater refinement of living in dress and manners, and in the arts through the development of tapestries, secular music and poetry. At the same time, a rediscovery of the Greek and Roman classics injected new life and an appreciation of temporal beauty into the intellectual life of the period.

One of the most well-known examples of the secular and profane direction of literature of the High Middle Ages is *Carmina Burana*, a collection of poems dating from the early 13th century which became famous in recent times because of the use of 24 of the poems by Carl Orff in his oratorio of the same name.* The poems are thought to be the work of the Goliards, young clergymen, mostly students at the universities of France, Germany, Italy and England, who delighted in satirizing the church and its institutions. One of the poems relates a dialogue between two young clergymen who are lovers, who are arguing over the decision of one of them to become a monk and dedicate himself to God in hopes of being cured of a sickness. His lover is horrified and begs him not to do so, and argues against it, saying if he entered a monastery they would never see each other again. Finally the first lover relents and resolves never to become a monk.[143]

This openness to the enjoyment of the senses, a love of beauty for its own sake rather than as a stepping stone to spiritual fulfillment, and the sensual influence of the Greek and Roman classics is all reflected in the love poetry of some of the most prominent clergymen of the early 12th century. Marbod of Rennes, master of the School of Chartres and Bishop of Rennes, went well beyond Aelred's passionate expressions of friendship and praises the beauty of young men he sought in frankly erotic terms: "A rare face, perfectly hued ... flame red offerings of full lips... that spectacular youth whose beauty is my fire." To a youth who spurned his attention: "This vision of a face, radiant and full of beauty, kindled with the torch of love the heart of whoever beheld him. But this boy, so lovely and appealing, a torment to all who looked upon him.... Surely he is wicked, cruel and wicked, who by the viciousness of his character denies the beauty of his body.... This flesh so fair, so milky, so flawless, so healthy, so lovely, so glowing, so soft."[144]

A positive attitude to homosexual love is also evident in the works of prominent churchmen who showed no interest, themselves, in same-sex love. Hildebert of Lavardin, bishop of Mans and later archbishop of Tours, referred to the widespread homosexuality of the time in one of his poems, "no way of life escapes it." In another poem, Hildebert said that calling homosexual love a sin "is a mistake" and that the "council of heaven" has erred in doing so.[145] The renowned 12th century scholar, Peter Abelard, famous for his sexual relationship with his student, the beautiful Héloïse, included in one of his works a poem recounting the love of David for Jonathan in language that poignantly and sympathetically evokes the passionate love between the two Biblical heroes.

> More than a brother to me, Jonathan, one in soul with me.... How gladly would I die and be buried with you! Since love may do nothing greater than this, and since to live after you is to die forever: half a soul is not enough for life.... I should have rendered either of friendship's dues: to share the triumph or suffer the defeat; either to rescue you or to fall with you, shedding for you that life which you so often saved, so that even death would join rather than part us.[146]

Another student of Peter Abelard, a clergyman known as Hilary the Englishman, frequently alluded to the Greek and Roman mythical figures associated with love in his poetry. To one youth, "The moment I saw you, Cupid struck me." Like Marbod, he had his fair share of complaints about beautiful but unyielding young men: "Beautiful and singular youth, kindly

---

Some parts of the oratorio have even penetrated popular culture: the opening chorus was used in the film The Omen *and its sequels, and European rock bands have performed arrangements of excerpts from the work.*

inspect, I implore you, these writings which are sent by your admirer…. As a patient I demand a doctor, holding out my hands in supplication. You alone have the only medication…. Oh, how I wish you wanted money!" To another, "Gold haired, fair of face, with a small white neck, soft spoken and gentle — but why do I praise these singly? Everything about you is beautiful and lovely; you have no imperfection, except that such fairness has no business devoting itself to chastity." Hilary then makes clear the erotic dimension of his love for the youth, by comparing him to the mythical Ganymede, the legendary son of the king of Troy who because of his beauty was carried off by Zeus to live with him among the other gods: "Believe me, if those former days of Jove (Roman variant of Zeus) should return, his handservant would no longer be Ganymede, but you, carried off to heaven; by day the sweet cup, and by night your sweeter kisses you would administer to Jove. You are the common desire of lasses and lads; they sigh for you and hope for you, because they know you are unique."[147]

Such poetry was the product of a highly literate clerical culture that abounded especially in the cities, universities and cathedral schools of the 12th century. The writers were often individuals of considerable rank, and their same-sex love poetry constitutes only a small part of their output, most of which was devoted to normal religious or theological issues.[148] Nonetheless, there is evidence that much of this erotic poetry was circulated and widely read within these circles, an indication that clergymen with homosexual preferences were abundantly scattered throughout the cities and educational institutions, and were also aware of others of their own interests.[149] The universities, especially the University of Paris, had by the end of the 12th century acquired a reputation for being centers of homosexual activity.[150] References to thriving homosexual brothels in Chartres, Orléans and Paris made in some of the poetry provide evidence that the numbers of males actively seeking sex with other males was sufficient to support a lively sexual trade in the cities.[151]

The literate clergymen of the High Middle Ages were well aware of the homosexuality depicted in classical literature and myths, and may have looked to such classical sources for validation of their own homosexual desires in the face of increasingly strident denunciations of homosexual relations by the ascetic sexual moralists in the church. Ganymede, in fact, became both a symbol for same-sex love in the writings of homosexually inclined clergy, and a term for someone with pronounced or exclusively homosexual preferences. References to Ganymede not only appear in literature of the period, but a sculpture depicting the youth being abducted by Zeus, in the form of an eagle, was even incorporated into the capital of a column of the Abbey church of Sainte-Marie-Madeleine, in Vézelay, France.

The most prominent piece of literature of the Middle Ages featuring the mythical Ganymede is a lengthy anonymous poem, the "Debate of Ganymede and Helen," that was widely popular during the period, and which survives in manuscripts found throughout Europe. Like similar poetic debates written by Plutarch and Lucian of Samosata in the late classical period, the poem relates a debate between Ganymede and Helen on the merits of loving boys versus loving women. Helen starts the debate by repeating the standard arguments — homosexual love is unnatural, it does not produce offspring and it is against the law of scripture. Further, she says, such love is not real love, it does not affect the heart; a man is only motivated by lust and all that motivates the boy is money. Ganymede's arguments, in response, are irreverent and glib, but the poet was obviously enjoying himself in penning them. The gods invented boy-love, he said, and in testament to its superiority, the most imminent men of the day practice it, princes, nobles, bishops and priests — including those who dictate morality for others. And as for procreation, let older men propagate, Ganymede says, youth is for pleasure. And of money? "The fragrance of profit is pleasing," no one turns down money, he says.[152]

If these examples do not make it clear that a deep current of eroticism ran through the loves and friendships of the Medieval clergy, the vivid denunciations of sodomy among the clergy in the writings of a fierce proponent of clerical celibacy, Saint Peter Damian, should remove any doubt that homosexual relationships were a frequent occurrence among the priests and nuns of the 11th and 12th centuries. Damian was not alone in complaining of homosexuality among the clergy. Alexander of Roes wrote that sodomy was a vice prominent among the French clergy. The Italian Cardinal Henry of Susa also wrote that sodomy was widely practiced by the clergy.[153] The 12th-century satirical poet Walter Mapes said the Cistercian order as a whole was addicted to sodomy with the exception of Saint Bernard of Clairvaux. Mapes recounts a humorous tale, perhaps apocryphal, that he says proves Saint Bernard's virtue. Bernard was called to Burgundy by a prominent noble who told him his son was sick and asked him if he could cure him. Bernard had the youth brought to a private room and after everyone had left the room, Bernard lay on top of the boy and prayed. Soon afterwards, the youth's illness left him. According to Mapes: "He was indeed the most unhappy of monks, for I have never heard of a monk who had lain on top of a boy and who did not immediately rise after him."[154]

Clerical homosexuality was a particular preoccupation of Peter Damian, who in his *Liber Gomorrhianus* (Book of Gomorrah) decried what he called an "abominable and terribly shameful vice" that had taken root among the clergy. Damian campaigned relentlessly for the church to crack down on widespread homosexuality among the clergy, and bitterly complained about the leniency of the church authorities towards sexual activity among the clergy. But when Damian presented his great compendium of clerical vice to the Pope Leo IX he could get no response from the pope other than a "polite acknowledgment, assuring him that he had demonstrated himself to be an enemy of carnal pollution." One of Leo's immediate successors, Pope Alexander II, actually took the book from Peter on the pretext of wanting to make a copy of it, locked it in his safe and refused to return it, infuriating Damian.[155]

While Peter Damian was unsuccessful in achieving the reforms he wanted in his own lifetime, his vociferous campaigns within the church protesting the sex lives of the clergy had an impact, and encouraged other ascetic clergymen to take up the battle. The scattered complaints of the ascetic moralists among the clergy about the sexual behavior not only of the clergy, but of society in general, which had been heard since the early days of the Frankish kingdoms, gathered in momentum in the 11th and 12th centuries, just as the cultural expression of same-sex love was reaching its peak. By the end of the 12th century the denunciations of contemporary sexual practices by anti-sexual moralists reached a crescendo. Combined with the strenuous efforts of the church to enforce celibacy among the clergy begun in the late 11th century, the work of the ascetic moralists was to have an enormous impact on the attitudes of secular officials and society to homosexuality by the end of the 13th century. The far-reaching and unexpected effects of the church's efforts to control the sexuality of its clergy, which led to profound changes in European society and laid the foundations for the sexual neurosis that plagues modern society, will be examined in the next chapter.

14

Medieval Europe: The Propagation of Neurosis

> There is one evil, an evil above all other evils, that I am aware is always with me, that grievously and piteously lacerates and afflicts my soul. It was with me from the cradle, it grew with me in childhood, in adolescence, in my youth it always stuck to me, and it does not desert me even now that my limbs are failing because of my old age. This evil is sexual desire, carnal delight, the storm of lust that has smashed and battered my unhappy soul, emptied it of all strength, and left it weak and empty.[1]

Late in life Saint Anselm of Canterbury anguished in these words over the sexual drive that, despite a lifetime of devotion to God, stubbornly refused to release him even in old age. In writing these words Anselm could have been speaking for many of the other Medieval clergymen who devoted themselves to the church's strict anti-sexual moral teachings—a moral code that demonized their own sexual natures. The roots of psychological disturbance or neurosis are easy to see in the sincere dedication of these devout clergymen to an ascetic sexual ideal that not only required them to suppress a fundamental human instinct, but taught them that an aspect of their innermost selves was evil. The conflict between their beliefs, on the one hand, and the urges of their bodies, on the other, set in motion a psychological struggle that was, in fact, a classic example of neurosis as defined in a standard psychoanalytic reference work, *The Psychoanalytic Theory of Neurosis* by Otto Fenichel: "First, a defense of the ego against an instinct, then a conflict between the instinct striving for discharge and the defensive forces of the ego, then a state of damming up, and finally the neurotic symptoms which are distorted discharges as a consequence of the state of damming up."[2]

Such a conflict would appear to be particularly acute in the case of a person conditioned by religious indoctrination to be repelled by sex, one of the most basic of instinctual drives. If the urges were homosexual, the psychological stress would be even greater. The "neurotic symptoms" produced in individuals with such an internal conflict typically take the form of reaction formation, a psychological defense in which the negativity they feel toward the intolerable characteristic is directed to others who display the same loathed characteristic. In the case of the men in the Adams study discussed in the Introduction, the level of the hostility they displayed to homosexuality was directly proportional to the strength of the homosexual responsiveness recorded within each of them.

A clergyman of the Middle Ages devoted to the teachings of the church and dedicated to Christian sexual morality would have early in his life disciplined himself to force back, or suppress, any unwanted sexual thoughts or urges that intruded into his consciousness. However, the sexual energy that produced the sexual thoughts did not just go away with his efforts to avoid such thoughts, but continued as a subconscious irritant, and because of the nature of biological processes would continue to build up behind the "dam" the clergyman created to avoid them. The psychic tension created by this "damming up" of sexual impulses would make the clergyman especially sensitive to sexual behavior, or even intimations of sexual behavior, among the people around him. Observing others involved in sexual behavior, or even the thought of it, would cause visceral and emotional discomfort in the clergyman. As a result, any time the clergyman would have to consciously deal with the topic of sexual behavior or sexual morality his thought processes and the expression of the topic would be, as Fenichel says, "distorted as a consequence of the state of damming up" and the psychological discomfort the subject caused him.

Putting it another way, because of the distorted lens through which such a clergyman perceived sex, and because of his own emotional discomfort with it, he could never deal with the subject truly rationally or dispassionately. Hence the references we see to sexual behavior in the writings of the morally conservative clergy of the Middle Ages are in almost all cases couched in histrionic and super-heated hyperbole. Likewise, the visceral disgust conservative clergy felt for those practicing homosexuality is plainly evident in the description Ordericus Vitalis provides of the young nobles of the court of William Rufus: the "effeminate predominated everywhere and reveled without restraint, while filthy catamites, fit only to perish in the flames, abandoned themselves shamefully to the foulest practices of Sodom."[3]

Where individuals are conditioned to believe that the evil of illicit sexual acts will lead to ferocious punishment by God — in the form of the destruction of war, for example, or the devastation of the plague — the knowledge that many people were engaging in all kinds of illicit sexual activity could create significant paranoia in the individual. In fact, psychological research in the last century has found that the attempt to repress unwanted homosexual desires, even among people with a healthy heterosexual drive, can also have a powerfully corrosive effect on mental health. Sigmund Freud found that severe paranoia in one of his patients functioned as a psychological defense to repressed homoerotic desires, and that a key factor in driving the patient's paranoid delusions was his conflict over repressed homosexual feelings. The connection Freud posited between repressed homosexual feelings and paranoia has since been validated in a number of research studies.[4] Freud's finding that paranoia can develop as a defense against homosexual feelings would explain the frequent linkage of denunciations of homosexual behavior by church moralists with dire warnings predicting imminent catastrophes and destruction because of sodomists in the population. To such a person, keeping the evil of sex in check to ward off the punishment of the Almighty becomes an urgent imperative fraught with anxiety.*

During the early Middle Ages the influence of the sexual ascetics among the clergy on popular sexual morality was limited by such factors as the fragmentation of authority, the resistance of secular rulers to the interference of the church in the domestic affairs of their countries, and the apparent disinterest of much of the clergy in strict enforcement of the church's sexual morality. As the Middle Ages progressed, however, the conservative clergy began to get the upper hand in their struggle to enforce their rigid sexual code on the people of Europe. The moral crusade of the sexual ascetics gained momentum when the church embarked on a campaign to reform the morals of the clergy, an initiative undertaken in response to

---

*We saw a similar paranoid dynamic in Chapter 4 in the rigid sexual code the Aaronite priesthood attempted to impose on the Israelites after the traumas of the destruction of the Northern Kingdom and the Babylonian invasion and exile, both of which the priests blamed on the sinfulness of the Hebrews; in Chapter 9, in the harsh provisions punishing homosexual acts in the Code of Justinian that were enacted, according to the statutes, to protect the citizens from divine retribution for the sins of a few; and in Chapter 13, where because of fear of further raids of the Norsemen and the threat of the Muslims in Spain, the ninth-century church leaders who were gathered at the Synod of Paris exhorted the Frankish monarchs to act against heterosexual fornication and homosexual practices lest further catastrophes be inflicted on the people of Christian Europe by a vengeful God.

increasing attacks on the church for corruption. With the church on the defensive because of the deplorable morals of many of the clergy, the sexual ascetics came to dominate church thinking and policy with regard to sexual morality. As a result, what James Brundage, an authority on Medieval sexual regulation, calls a "fear and loathing of sex," already widespread among the clerical reformers, became a general trait of the church leadership by the 12th century.[5]

A centerpiece of the reform movement was a prohibition against marriage among the clergy, many of whom had families. Though the clerical reform movement would require a lengthy campaign over several centuries before its goals had been accomplished, the effective elimination of healthy sexual outlets for members of the clergy that came with the enforcement of clerical celibacy would have the effect of replicating the neurotic reactions to sex of the moral reformers among the newly celibate clergy. The psychological consequences of the attempts of the moral leadership of the church to live within its own anti-sexual moral code were to have profound and long-lasting effects on European society.

The Anti-Sexual Reformers

A common characteristic of the clerical reformers who began assembling the ecclesiastical opinions, penitentials, patristic writings, and the edicts and decrees of church councils into the first collections of canon law was an undisguised horror of sexual activity. The philosophical roots of the anti-sexual theology of the ascetic moralists was based on Augustine's view that sexual pleasure was sinful, a concept Augustine had derived from his experience with the dualism of Manichaeism and Neo-Platonism, discussed in Chapter 9. Because in Augustine's view, sexual desire bound a soul to the world, it was a barrier to the attainment of salvation, and hence an evil in itself. The ascetic reformers, therefore, were convinced that to achieve salvation it was necessary to be freed from the evil of sex. They not only took a vow of chastity, but strove to eliminate even sexual thoughts from their minds.

The "neurotic symptoms" produced by the "damming up" of their sexual drives were readily apparent in the preoccupation that many of the conservative clergy displayed with the sexual morals of Medieval society and in the visceral disgust with which they described sex in their writings. The 11th-century clerical reformer Saint Peter Damian is the most prominent example of the sexually obsessed clergy, but there were many others among prominent reformers and church leaders, including Burchard of Worms, Guibert of Nogent, Honorius of Autun, Pope Leo IX, Pope Gregory IX, Alain of Lille, and Gratian, the 12th-century Bolognese monk and legal scholar called the "father of canon law."

According to Brundage, the reformers as a group "considered sex and other pleasurable experiences tainted by evil and a potent source of sin. They were not merely suspicious of sex, but hostile to any sexual activity at all, save for marital relations undertaken expressly and consciously to conceive a child." In their zeal for sexual purity, the reformers went beyond even the asceticism of the early church Fathers, and were determined to limit marital sex to the absolute minimum, and on penalizing extra-marital sex as harshly as possible.[6]

The 11th-century theologian Guibert of Nogent, abbot of a Benedictine monastery in Normandy, was "obsessed with the filthiness of sex" according to Brundage. In his writings Guibert frequently dwelt on the ever present pollution of sex. "We are burdened and doomed ... by sexual fantasies that spring unbidden to our minds, even in sleep; sordid desires subvert our efforts to attain chastity and plunge us into ever deeper despair…. It taints and befouls every living person. Even when death finally delivers us from the grasp of lust, it is likely to pitch us into hell." Bishop Burchard of Worms, author of one of the first canonical collections, described sexual desire as a condition that degrades the soul and causes "inconsiderateness, shiftiness of the eyes, hatred of God's commandments, attachment to worldly things, misery in this life and despair for the future."[7] The reforming Pope Leo IX called homosexual acts "filthy," "obscene," and an "execrable vice."[8] The 12th-century theologian Alain of Lille speaks of homosexual love-making as "unspeakable and monstrous acts," and a "vicious perversion." He writes that the human race "perverts the rules of love by a practice of extreme and abnormal irregularity" and that "such a great body of foul men roam and riot along the breadth of the whole earth" that the "world is endangered by the almost universal fire of impure love."[9] According to Pope Gregory IX, sodomists "are abominable persons — despised by the world, dreaded by the council of heaven ... more unclean than animals, more vicious than almost anything alive, who have lost their reason and destroyed the kindness of nature, who are deprived of interior light."[10] Albert the Great, the 13th-century scientist, Aristotelian scholar and a doctor of the church, departed from the rational in his writings on same-sex activity; he wrote that sodomy starts in a "burning frenzy," that sodomists are distinguished by their foulness, a stench that even rises to heaven, and that sodomy is addictive and contagious, rapidly spreading from one person to another.[11] Even Saint Aelred of Rievaulx, one of the Middle Ages' most liberal voices among the clergy with regard to same-sex love, in late life came to regard his sexual drive as a "horrible stench" within him.[12]

Brundage remarks that Gratian, in his writings on canon law, regarded sexual pleasure in general as a "disturbing element in human life" that turned Christians away from the goal of salvation and that should be avoided altogether. To Gratian sexual pleasure was "an instrument that the devil regularly employed to entice souls into hell."[13] In this, Gratian and the other anti-sexual reformers were taking their lead from Pope Gregory the Great who in the sixth-century declared that "There can be no sexual pleasure without sin."[14] Church moralists were particularly outraged by anal or oral sexual pleasure, described by Gratian as "extraordinary sensual pleasure"— though one might wonder how a celibate monk would know of such things.[15]

Men and women who married simply because they were attracted to each other had committed fornication in Gratian's eyes. The harsh attitudes to marital sex enunciated by Gratian and the other reformers were not new, however. Saint Jerome, the fifth-century church Father, said a man who loved his wife too passionately had committed adultery, a dictum reasserted by the 12th century theologian Peter Lombard, in his treatise *De excusatione coitus*: "for a man to love his wife too ardently is a sin worse than adultery."[16] The fourth-century bishop and monk Eustathius of Sebastia, one of the signatories of the Council of Nicea, went even further, preaching that married people could not gain salvation at all.[17]

Sexual intercourse within marriage was permitted only in what the moralists deemed the "natural" position, with the woman on her back and the man above her, face to face, referred to in recent times as the "missionary position." Intercourse in any other position, heterosexual or homosexual, was categorized by Gratian as "sodomy" and a "sin against nature," among the most serious of crimes, on a par with "murder, forgery, arson, sacrilege and heresy." Then, according to Gratian, married couples were allowed sexual intercourse under only three conditions: 1) for the explicit purpose of conceiving a child; 2) to prevent the temptation of marital infidelity; and 3) to yield to the unrelenting demands — most likely sinful — of their partner. Even then the sexual intercourse could not be performed in the daytime, had to be in the "missionary position," could not be performed on Sundays, Wednesdays or Fridays — removing the equivalent of five months of the year — and was not to be performed during Lent or any other forbidden times, which removed another three months from the period when intercourse could be performed.[18] All other sexual activity was categorically condemned.

The sexual historian G. Rattray Taylor observes that "it was not actually the sexual act which was damnable, but the pleasure derived from it — and this pleasure remained damnable even when the act was performed for the purpose of procreation." To assist the couple in their performance of intercourse with as little pleasure as possible, therefore, a device, *chemise cagoule*, was invented, a heavy nightshirt with a hole strategically placed to allow the husband to impregnate his wife with as little bodily contact as possible.[19]

Heterosexual sins were ranked by Gratian according to the level of their indecency: "The evil of adultery is greater than that of fornication, but still greater is that of incest; for it is worse to sleep with one's mother than with the wife of another. Worst of all, however, is everything that takes place against nature, for example, when a man wishes to use a part of his wife's body that is not permitted for such use." The "unnatural intercourse" Gratian refers to includes coitus interruptus and any kind of contraception. "Those who procure the poisons of infertility are fornicators, not spouses," Gratian writes. Under Gratian's logic, which was incorporated into canon law, contraception was worse than incest with one's mother or adultery with another man's wife.[20]

Lay men and women greeted the new rules with disbelief, and could not understand how intercourse with one's legal spouse could be a sin. Nor could they comprehend how sexual relations between unmarried men and women — which seemed natural and inevitable to most people — would be sinful, much less a violation of the greatest gravity. Indeed, common law marriage, under which a man and a woman simply moved in with each other and lived as a couple without ceremony, church blessing or legal sanction, was the rule in Europe until the 15th century. Nonetheless, the tenets of sexual morality codified by Gratian were an accurate reflection of the moral thinking of not just the sexual reformers, but of the entire church leadership from the beginnings of the 12th century onward. Gratian's assembled work, referred to as the *Decretum,* became, in fact, the standard textbook on canon law, and was still in use by church legal scholars as late as the early 20th century.[21] Under the anti-sexual reformers the church clamped on a tight and restraining harness even in the previously sanctioned sexual relations of the marriage bed.

Rattray Taylor remarks that we should not get the impression that the detailed code of sexual morality produced by the church in the 11th and 12th centuries was arrived at by church moral theorists through a detached and business-like logical methodology. Rather, Taylor says, the true picture was of a number of individual figures like Burchard of Worms, Peter Damian, Gratian, Peter Lombard and other reformers "tormented by the virtual certainty of damnation for all who so much as thought of sexual pleasure, desperately striving to build dams against the rising tides of sensuality in a frantic, desperate attempt to save people from the results of their own folly. Never mind the justifications; never mind the cruelty and injustice, if only this frightful disaster can be prevented." Taylor says that "only real desperation" can explain the ruthlessness with which church moralists routinely falsified and distorted passages of Scripture in order to find justifications for the church's draconian and anti-sexual morality, a moral code for which no basis exists in the Bible.[22]

The "real desperation" of the ascetic clergy to be free of the evil of sex and the world and achieve salvation drove many of the clergy to extremes of self-abuse, and led to a significant degree of neurosis. In a study of psychological disorders among the ascetic clergy of the Middle Ages, the psychiatrist Alfred Gallinek underscores the psychological costs that resulted from rigid devotion to their anti-worldly ideology: "Only by means of a tremendous repression was it possible to achieve the ascetic ideal." Most of those who devoted themselves to sublimating their sex drive "did so at the expense of their mental equilibrium," Gallinek says. "The renunciation not only of sex activity, but also of sexual dreams and the very existence of such urges, built up colossal feelings of guilt.... Instincts and desires, conscious or unconscious, were identified without hesitation with all things earthly ... and thus with the devil. Suppression was the goal and path of Salvation.... A great emotional stress was the result of this situation."[23] The self-negation attempted by some of the clergy was extreme. As Gallinek observes, the physical world was a hindrance for the soul, the clergy believed, and so "the more tortured the body, the more disassociated the soul from this pain racked body."[24]

We can get a picture of the kind of torture to which the ascetic clergy subjected themselves from the autobiography of a German monk, Henry Suso, who, writing of himself in the third person, described the means he took to subdue his bodily urges: "He wore for a long time a hair shirt and an iron chain, until the blood ran from him, so that he was obliged to leave them off." To defeat his carnal urges,

> he secretly caused an undergarment to be made for him; and in the undergarment he had strips of leather fixed, into which a hundred and fifty brass nails, pointed and filed sharp, were driven, and the points of the nails were always turned towards the flesh. He had this garment made very tight and so arranged as to go around him and fasten in front, in order that it might fit the closer to his body, and the pointed nails might be driven into his flesh.... He would sometimes, as he lay thus in bonds, and oppressed with toil, and tormented also by noxious insects, cry aloud and give way to a fretfulness and twist round and round in agony, as a worm does when run through by a pointed needle.

The abuse Henry suffered led him to frequent hallucinations in which he had visions of heavenly youths coming to comfort him and give him joy.[25]

The effects of the earnest efforts of the clergy to repress their bodily urges manifested among nuns in the form of delusions that they were visited in the night by a supernatural being called an Incubus with whom they had intercourse. Modern psychologists recognize the phenomena as fantasies born of severe sexual repression. Even some Medieval writers understood the connection between the repressed sexuality of the victims and their fantasies, noting that "Incubi infest cloisters." The church, however, took them seriously and declared that they were demons in human shape and sent exorcists to convents having outbreaks of such fantasies to cast them out.[26] Sexual fantasies also figured in the visions of the writings of Christian mystics during the period. Mechthild of Magdeburg, a 13th-century Cistercian nun, wrote in overtly erotic language that she was tormented by her passionate love for the Savior, and wrote that all virgins should "follow the most charming of all, the eighteen-year-old Jesus" to win his embraces. In one of her mystical works, *Dialogue between Love and the Soul,* she wrote, "Tell my Beloved that His chamber is prepared, and that I am sick with love for Him." In another passage she wrote, "Then He took the soul into His divine arms and placing His fatherly hand on her bosom, He looked into her face and kissed her well."[27] The 14th-century Dominican nun Christine Ebner imagined that she had conceived a child by Jesus, and cut a cross into the skin over her heart and tore it off. In other cases, the psychological reaction of nuns to their sexual drives was, like Henry Suso, very negative. Christina of St. Trond, a 13th-century German nun, also known as Christina the Astonishing, went to great lengths to defeat her carnal urges, including laying herself in a hot oven, having herself put on a rack, having herself hung from a gallows like a corpse, and having herself partially buried.[28] After her death she was beatified by the Catholic Church and is now, fittingly, the patroness of lunatics, madness, mental disorders, mental handicaps, mental health professionals, mental illness, mentally ill people, psychiatrists and therapists.

The figure most responsible for ratcheting up the church's obsession with the evil of sex, however, was Peter Damian, the 11th-century Benedictine monk, who through his own self-abasement became the model and inspiration for legions of ascetic monks and nuns like Henry Suso and Christina of St. Trond in the battle against their physical bodies.

Saint Peter Damian's Obsession with Clerical Sex

Peter Damian's obsession with the sexual morals of the clergy, particularly homosexuality, was a passion that drove his lifelong campaign for the enforcement of celibacy among the clergy. He went so far as to detail his charges in a lengthy dissertation describing the moral depravity of his fellow clergymen, his *Liber Gomorrhianus* (Book of Gomorrah), mentioned briefly in the previous chapter. Damian himself seems to have been a textbook example of a sexual neurotic. The Medieval historian Michael Goodich called him "a classic case of the abandoned and brutalized child whose early privations drove him to puritanical extremes later in life."[29]

Peter was born around 1007 in Ravenna, Italy, into a poor family, without a father. Peter's biographer, the 12th-century Italian bishop John of Lodi, wrote that his mother was so depressed after his birth that she refused to nurse him. Rescued from near death by a priest's concubine, he was soon after taken in by an older brother and his abusive wife who treated the small child cruelly and used him "as a slave" according to John of Lodi. When he was 12 another brother took over care of him and, unlike his older brother, treated him with care and compassion. But by that time the psychological damage had already been done and was to have a lasting impact.

The sense of identity that young children develop reflects very closely their early environment and the way they are treated. The harsh conditions and abusive treatment Damian suffered in his early childhood would have left him with a highly negative self-image, a deep sense of unworthiness and shame, and severely critical of himself. Not surprisingly, Damian pursued a lifestyle of self-degradation and self-denial, subjecting himself to constant mortification in an effort to cleanse himself of the impurities with which he was convinced he was infected. In a desperate prayer to the Blessed Virgin, he summed up his wretched condition himself, "Oh my glorious mother, mirror of virginal purity and standard of all virtue, how have I, wretched and unhappy creature, offended you by the filthy putridness of my flesh, and have violated the chastity of my body, of which you are the mother and author."[30]

The self-abasement and denial to which he subjected himself for the rest of his life was a natural consequence of the abuse and severe deprivations of his childhood. Yet John of Lodi, Damian's biographer, regarded Peter's self-degradation as a sign of saintly virtue, and took special note of the "vile foods, fasts, bare feet, abstinence, and isolation, both spiritual and physical, that filled his life." Because of the influence Peter was to have in his later life, his lifestyle of self-abasement and denial, traceable directly to the abuse and privations of his childhood, was to become the model for monastic life and "the religious ideal" for the next several centuries.[31]

On the other hand, Damian's intense phobia of sex, which he shared with the other moral reformers, does not seem to have been directly caused by the problems of his childhood. Guibert of Nogent, whose writings on sex nearly equal Damian's in virulence, was the son of Norman nobility, raised in the aristocratic style and evidently well cared for by his mother, according to his autobiographical writings. Ordericus Vitalis, another clergymen obsessed with sexual morality, was the son of a prosperous Anglo-Norman clergyman, who was awarded a church as a benefice for his service to the Earl of Shrewsbury. The well-documented abhorrence of each of the three men to sex seems primarily due to their common devotion to the church's strict anti-sexual moral code.

When he was in his early teens Peter entered a monastery to study for holy orders where his aversion to sex apparently took root quickly. His biographer describes how in his teens Peter "was subjected to sharp carnal pains at night. He would then immediately rise from his bed, undress and plunge naked into cold water until his limbs were thoroughly frozen. Then he would get out, say several psalms, by which time the 'noxious heat' that had afflicted him would have receded." Peter's horror of what were apparently sexual dreams, a commonplace of adolescence, calls to mind Kinsey's remark about the attempt to suppress normal sexual needs because of moral reasons: "It is difficult to imagine anything better calculated to do permanent damage to the personality of an individual."[32]

Goodich remarked that the particular venom with which Damian later addressed homosexuality among the clergy suggests a "personal experience of traumatic impact,"[33] perhaps an unwelcome homosexual seduction while a teen in the monastery. The findings from the Adams study, discussed in the Introduction, suggest that Peter's very high level of hostility to homosexuality would correlate to a very high level of homosexual responsiveness. Whatever the cause, Damian seemed incapable of writing about sex with any but the most lurid and deprecatory language. In Damian's mind, sex was a "violation, sacrilege, profanation, contagion, or corruption. Sex is never the product of love, only of animal lust." Damian's hatred of sex extended even to loathing of the human body, which he called "hideous putrefaction and filth," and consumed by lust.[34] Even to readers with only a casual familiarity with psychology, Damian's writings would come across as those of someone with a seriously disturbed view of physical life. Yet as clerical reform progressed in the 12th and 13th centuries, Peter Damian's attitude to sex was to set the tone for the writings on sexual morality of the church's most influential moral leaders.

Damian was so outraged by the practice of homosexuality among the clergy that he took the trouble to set down his complaint in his *Liber Gomorrhianus,* a 50-page discourse that is, in fact, the only extended work of literature on homosexuality that survives from the Middle Ages. In his book, Peter describes the types of homosexual acts committed by priests and directs a passionate argument to the offending clergy in an attempt to persuade them to repent their ways. In the opening preface of the work, here translated by the Canadian scholar Pierre Payer, Peter evokes the specter of divine punishment on not only the perpetrators, but society in general, for the clergy's sins: "A certain abominable and terribly shameful vice has grown up in our region. Unless the hand of severe punishment resists as soon as possible, there is certainly a danger that the sword of divine anger will be used savagely against it to the ruin of many." He then apologizes for having to even write about such an evil: "Alas! it is shameful to speak of, shameful to suggest such foul disgrace to sacred ears! But if the doctor shrinks in horror from infected wounds, who will take the trouble to apply the cauter? If the one who is to heal becomes nauseated, who will lead sick hearts back to health? Vice against nature creeps in like a cancer and even touches the order of consecrated men…. It rages like a bloodthirsty beast in the midst of the sheepfold of Christ."[35]

Damian then relates the sexual techniques used by the priests — solitary masturbation, mutual masturbation, interfemoral intercourse, and, most dreadful of all, anal intercourse — and describes the ascending order of seriousness, from masturbation to anal intercourse. "The devil's artful fraud devises these degrees of failing into ruin such that the higher the level the unfortunate soul reaches in them, the deeper it sinks in the depths of hell's pit."[36] Damian goes on to rage against priests who avoid severe penances by confessing the sin to a priest with whom they were having sex — "the impure confesses to the impure the wickedness they have committed together" — and then against priests who seduce young men to whom they should be ministering the Gospel.[37]

Turning to address himself to the clergy who sin in these ways, Damian tries at length to convince them of the enormity of the sin they are committing:

> Truly, this vice is never to be compared with any other vice because it surpasses the enormity of all vices. Indeed, this vice is the death of bodies, the destruction of souls. It pollutes the flesh; it extinguishes the light of the mind. It evicts the Holy Spirit from the temple of the human hear; it introduces the devil who incites to lust.... It defiles everything, stains everything, pollutes everything. And as for itself, it permits nothing pure, nothing clean, nothing other than filth.[38]

Damian tries to get the sinning priest to see the cloud of evil surrounding him: "Consider, O miserable one, how much darkness weighs on your soul; notice what thick, dark blindness engulfs you. Does the fury of lust impel you to the male sex? Has the madness of lust incited you to your own kind, that is, male on male? ... Does a ram leap on a ram, maddened with the heat for sexual union? In fact, a stallion feeds calmly and peacefully with a stallion in one stall and when he sees a mare the sense of lust is immediately unleashed."[39] Damian even courted with heresy when he suggested that sacraments performed by priests who commit homosexual acts were not valid, that "God is loath to receive sacraments from the hands of the impure."[40]

Despite Peter Damian's heartfelt efforts, it's likely that few, if any, of the clergy he addresses so passionately ever read his words. When Peter presented the book to Pope Leo IX, the pope agreed with Peter on the gravity of the problem of homosexual behavior among the clergy, but resisted his demands to begin a crackdown on clerical homosexuality. The pope reminded Peter that justice should always be tempered with mercy and that harsh punishments should be reserved for most severe cases.[41] The mild reaction of Leo IX, a man in the forefront of the reform movement, to Peter's demands for actions against clerical homosexuality has been taken by several historians as confirmation that strong feelings against homosexuality and a sense of urgency in dealing with it were not widespread within the church in the 11th century, even among the ranks of prominent reformers.[42] Boswell observes that the apparent disinterest of the early Medieval church in attacking homosexual practices among the clergy is evident in the fact that to back up his arguments Peter could cite no more recent ecclesiastical enactment than the Council of Ancyra of 314.[43] While there is no question that same-sex relations continued to be regarded as a serious sin, the leading reformers with the exception of Damian were at first far more concerned with other problems among the clergy — clerical marriage, the appointment of church officials by secular rulers, the purchase of church offices, and the scandalous enrichment of many clergymen through the indiscriminate sale of indulgences, a practice whereby the church granted remission of temporal punishment for sins.

It is striking to note in this regard that one of most influential theological and moral texts of the Middle Ages contains not a single mention of homosexual acts. The *Libri Quatuor Sententiarum*, or the *Four Books of Sentences,* by the 12th-century theologian Peter Lombard, was so highly regarded that it became the standard church text on theology until the 16th century and commentaries on the text became one of the most widespread philosophical genres among scholars. In fact, while Gratian is regarded as the "Father of Canon Law," Peter Lombard has been called the "Master of Dogmatic Theology."[44] In the book, Peter notes the gravity of adultery and discusses the different types of unnatural sex which he defines as fornication, the illicit seduction of a virgin female, adultery, incest and rape. Peter incorporates and embellishes many of Gratian's provisions on heterosexual sins, as in his addition to Gratian's condemnation of a woman who uses contraception as a fornicator: "She is her husband's harlot, and he an adulterer with his own wife."[45] Remarkably, Peter makes not a single reference to sodomy.[46] It does not seem possible that Peter Lombard could have been ignorant of homosexuality in general or homosexual relationships among the clergy, since he spent nearly his entire adult life in Paris, a city renowned in the High Middle Ages as a center of homosexual love. Moreover, the Cathedral School of Notre Dame, where Peter was a professor of theology, and the University of Paris, where he doubtless had many friends, were the homes of many of the literate clergy among whom the homosexual verse and love poetry discussed in the previous chapter circulated.

Nonetheless, Peter Damian had a number of sympathizers among the church leadership for his campaign for sexual purity among the clergy. Though the *Liber Gomorrhianus* did not have the impact that Peter had hoped, it was the first in a long line of tracts that were to come in the next century targeting the sexual practices of the clergy. In fact, a friend of Damian and a supporter of his moral campaign, Hildebrand, soon to become Pope Gregory VII, appears to have interceded with Pope Alexander II to retrieve the *Liber Gomorrhianus* for Peter after the pope had locked it up in his safe.[47]

The Gregorian Reforms

The elevation of Damian's friend Hildebrand to the papacy in 1073 as Pope Gregory VII was a turning point in the long-standing struggle of the anti-sexual moralists to enforce the church's strict sexual moral code among the people of Europe. Gregory was a vigorous leader whose tireless efforts consolidated and significantly advanced the work of church reform. The reform movement was chiefly focused on restoring the moral authority of the church and asserting its primacy in religious and moral matters. However, two elements of reform, the enforcement of celibacy among the clergy, and the assertion of the church as the embodiment of an all-inclusive Christian society led by the pope as God's representative on earth, would each in its own way significantly contribute to the harsh and repressive atmosphere that was to envelop Europe by the 14th century.

The foundation for the vast changes that were to take place was started under the papacy of Gregory's predecessor, Leo IX, who had begun his career as a reformer when he was bishop of Toul in Lorraine. Upon his elevation to the papacy, Leo IX called to Rome many of the men he had worked with in his reforms, a group that included Hildebrand, himself. Leo's chief goal was to raise the moral standards of the church by eliminating what he saw as its chief problems: clerical marriage; simony, the practice of purchasing offices of the church; and lay investiture, a long-established process whereby secular rulers exercised the power to appoint bishops and other church officials.

As a first step in achieving these ends, Leo felt that it was vital that the authority of the church in spiritual and moral matters be definitively established, and that the church assume the central role in all aspects of Christian life. A central principle followed by Leo in his reforms was the assertion that the pope was the successor to Saint Peter, an axiom that the Medieval legal scholar Walter Ullmann called an "ecclesiastical expression for papal monarchy."[48] While the effects of Leo's efforts were not outwardly visible at first, he laid the foundation for strengthening the role of the pope as unquestioned leader of the church by overseeing the organization of an administrative apparatus for governing the church from Rome, and taking steps to subordinate bishops, who had hitherto been operating mostly autonomously, under the direction of his administrative structure in Rome and the authority of papal legates he sent to major European capitals to look after the pope's interests. The work of the reformers under Leo's direction laid the groundwork for the implementation by Gregory VII of a unified leadership structure under the pope with which Gregory and his papal successors could wield the church's power to try to bring the Christians of Europe into line with the church's vision of a Christian society.

Even more so than Leo, Gregory was committed to establishing and asserting the primacy of the church in human affairs. In Gregory's view, the church was founded by God and charged with the mission of uniting all of humankind into a single community ruled by divine law. As a divine institution established by God, the church had a natural authority over the secular state, Gregory believed, and the pope, as head of the church, was God's regent, acting in God's name. Therefore, disobedience to the pope was, in effect, disobedience to God, and brought with it exclusion from Christian society. Under Gregory's leadership the church hierarchy was reorganized, with clear and unquestioned lines of authority descending from the pope, at the top, while the papacy, itself, underwent a dramatic transformation from what had been a somewhat parochial Roman institution into an international power. An early success in asserting of the primacy of the pope as the moral leader of Christendom was the spectacle of the Holy Roman Emperor, who only a generation earlier had the power to appoint even the popes, having to cross the Alps to beg absolution from the pope, as Henry IV did after being excommunicated by Gregory VII. While Gregory VII was the victor in his famous confrontation with Henry IV over lay investiture, the realization of his goal of bringing all the secular rulers of Europe under the absolute moral authority of the pope was to be an often contentious battle.

The efforts to assert the superiority of the church's moral leadership to that of the secular rulers of Europe were undermined, in the first place, by the deplorable morals of much of the clergy, from cardinals and bishops on down to local parish priests. Simony, the purchase of church positions, was widespread, and in a way easy to understand since holding a church office could be a very lucrative position if skillfully exploited. Bishops, abbots and local pastors often oversaw vast landholdings from which they derived income from rent and the taxes they levied on the residents. Priests often served as local officials and so collected taxes and other fees, a significant percentage of which many of them would pocket as commissions. Many bishops were essentially feudal lords and levied their own taxes and fees on their subjects, over and above the profits they received from church lands in their control. Priests could also increase their income by padding the fees they charged for basic liturgical services, such as officiating at funerals. Some clergymen fleeced parishioners and pilgrims through the sale of fake relics by passing off animal bones and scraps of cloth as those of some saint or even of Christ himself.[49] The most notorious of the corrupt practices was the retailing of indulgences by clergymen, who offered gullible sinners the prospect of escaping eternal damnation in Hell in exchange for a few pieces of gold. The high living and ostentatious display of wealth by many clergymen was, naturally, bitterly resented by the peasants and townspeople who suffered from the greed of the clergy.

While many of the peasants and townspeople of Europe were keenly aware of the avariciousness of many of the clergy, the clerical reformers believed that the chief problems in the church were the interference of secular rulers in church affairs and clerical marriage. The reformers felt that they could make no progress against the former until they had eliminated a practice that in their minds seriously diluted the moral authority of the clergy, clerical marriage. On the other hand, because many bishops and priestly offices were being filled through appointments of secular rulers, the church had little control over most of them. This meant that enforcing celibacy among the clergy would be a difficult task until the church could take back control over ecclesiastical appointments. Nonetheless, the ascetic moralists like Peter

Damian were determined to eliminate marriage among the clergy and pressed the issue within the church.

Church leaders as far back as Pope Leo I in the 5th century had decreed celibacy as the standard for the clergy, but enforcement of the rule since that time was essentially non-existent outside the monasteries. Many priests were married and had families, while others maintained concubines, mistresses or same-sex lovers. In some areas of Europe, the local population was scandalized by the sexual lifestyles of the clergy, and some of the laity even stopped attending services conducted by married priests. In other areas, though, the people considered it the norm.[50] To the ascetic moralists like Peter Damian, a priest "who engaged in the sordid delights of the bedchamber sullied himself and the sacred mysteries." As Damian saw it, when such a priest, even one legitimately married, engaged in intercourse with his wife he contaminated himself with the impurity of sex, and thus polluted any liturgical action he performed, even the words that he spoke.[51] Damian and the reformers attributed the source of this pollution to lust: without lust there would be no sex and sex, according to Damian, was "sacrilege, profanation, contagion, and corruption."

As if the priests' lawful sexual relations with their wives weren't enough of a problem, the reformers insisted that married priests were incapable of devoting themselves fully to carrying out their sacred duties because of the distractions of home and family. According to Damian, married priests desecrated their high calling "when they lived as married men, amid the reek and screams of sniveling brats, side by side with a smirking, randy wife, bedeviled by daily temptations to unclean thoughts, words and deeds."[52] Mired in the swamp of this lewd corruption, the reformers believed, married priests blackened their sacred trust with the sordid filth of carnal pollution.

As energized as the ascetic reformers were against married priests, there was another dimension to the problem which seems to have been of greater concern to the church leadership. In the Feudal period, it had long been the custom for men to pass their positions and property on to their sons. In the case of bishops and priests, who often viewed church property as their own, church offices and property frequently passed from father to son. Clerical dynasties were, in fact, common in many regions of Europe in the 11th century. If the sons didn't care to pursue a career in the church, they would often view the church property passed on by their fathers as their inheritance and put it to other uses. As a result of the spread of the customs of Feudal inheritance among the married clergy, the church was losing an enormous amount of property and wealth. When Gregory VII realized the magnitude of the losses, he concluded that the only way to stop them was to forbid the clergy from marrying. Though the agitation of the sexual ascetics for moral reform of the clergy pushed the issue of clerical marriage to the forefront, the enormous loss of church property appears to have been the deciding factor that set the campaign to ban clerical marriage in motion.[53]

The Campaign to Abolish Clerical Marriage

Marriage by members of the clergy, theoretically forbidden since the 5th century, was singled out for condemnation in statutes passed by the Council of Mainz presided over by Pope Leo IX in 1054. Gregory VII, however, made the abolition of clerical marriage a major goal of his papacy and continually browbeat bishops at annual councils to enforce the ban on marriage among clerics. Within a year of assuming the papacy, Gregory presented a detailed statute at a synod of bishops he called in Rome that seemed to be an all-out assault on any kind of sexual relationships by clergymen. Gregory's statute forbade non-celibate priests from officiating at mass, prohibited clergy who were still married from having any sexual intercourse at all, and required that married clergy who did not immediately separate from their wives be defrocked.[54] Not content to leave enforcement of the ban solely to the bishops, Gregory enlisted support from secular rulers, even including Henry IV. In response to the decrees from Rome, local councils issued orders enforcing and publicizing the ban in their regions, and Gregory continued to press bishops at annual synods to take action against the great numbers of clergymen who remained in their marriages.

Resistance to the church's efforts to abolish clerical marriage and enforce celibacy among the clergy was fierce and widespread. Defiance of the ban, in fact, would persist for nearly two centuries before it was established with finality across Europe. In Italy pitched battles were fought between soldiers of the bishops and those of the families of the priests. When the archbishop of Rouen announced to clergymen assembled in the cathedral that they would be required to forsake their wives and concubines and begin a life of celibacy, they "rioted, attacked the soldiers of the archbishop and fought to drive them out of the cathedral." Italian bishops refused to issue the ban for fear of their lives after the bishop of Brescia was nearly killed.[55] In 1077, Gregory VII wrote in a letter to the bishop of Paris that an ardent proponent of clerical celibacy "had been burnt alive" by the enraged clergy of Cambrai in northern France. The bishop of Paris, himself, was driven out of his cathedral "with jeers and blows" by outraged clergy when he tried to announce the ban. He finally had to take refuge with the royal family to escape from the clergy's wrath.[56]

Overlooked by the zealous moral reformers in their campaign to abolish clerical marriage was the plight of the wives and children of married clergy. Women, some of them daughters or granddaughters of bishops or priests, who had entered into marriage with clergymen in good faith, found themselves thrown out of their homes, stripped of their social position, subject to public scorn, and accused of lechery and immorality. Children of clergymen were declared illegitimate, denied any inheritance and cast into an uncertain future. The children of the clergy, despised as the "cursed seed of their fathers' lust," became, as Brundage observed, "the innocent victims of high-minded idealists such as Peter Damian, Gregory VII and other reform leaders."[57]

Not all of the opposition to the assault on clerical marriage was violent. Lambert of Hersfeld wrote that the reformers' campaign for clerical celibacy was "madness," and contrary to the teachings of Scripture. The Anglo-Norman writer known as Anonymous of York vehemently denounced the ban, arguing in favor of the rights of priests to marry, and holding that both natural justice and canon law directed that the rights and legitimacy of sons of clergymen be protected.[58] The North Italian Bishop Ulric of Imola passionately argued in a written tract that marriage was a "natural right," and warned that banning clerical marriage could lead clergymen to homosexual relationships.[59] The contemporary historian Henry of Huntingdon wrote that the ban was controversial among the church hierarchy, and also noted the fear among some churchmen that prohibiting marriage to the clergy could drive some of the clergy to homosexual acts. Huntingdon wrote: "The prohibition seems quite proper to some, but dangerous to others; for in their attempt at purity many [priests] might fall into disgusting filth, to the great shame of the name of Christian."[60]

Bishop Ulric's reasoning against the ban was condemned by the Synod of Rome of 1079, under the leadership of Gregory VII, while the arguments of other opponents were dismissed as irrelevant.[61] With the anti-sexual reformers long established in control of the policy machinery of the church the outcome was never in doubt. By the early 12th century the requirement for clerical celibacy was the unquestioned doctrine of the church, though it would take well into the 13th century before the campaign would achieve success. Successive church conclaves had to reiterate the decrees against attending mass presided over by married clergy, the First Lateran Council in 1123, the Second in 1139, and again at the Fourth Lateran Council in 1215 under Pope Innocent III.[62]

For the first century of the campaign, the fire of the reformers was directed solely at priests in heterosexual relationships. This inevitably led to some backlash by the married clergy against bishops or other church officials in open homosexual relationships. The well-known love affair discussed in the preceding chapter between Archbishop Raoul of Tours with Jean of Orléans, the young man nicknamed Flora by contemporaries for his sexual reputation, whom Raoul had installed as Bishop of Orléans, occurred during the midst of the church campaign against clerical marriage. The resentment of married clergymen to church authorities, ordering them to give up their wives and families while at the same time maintaining relationships involving the "sin against nature," would have naturally focused hostile attention on homosexuality among the clergy. John Boswell remarked that "There is indeed some evidence that accusations of homosexuality against prelates attempting to enforce clerical celibacy may have taken on the aspect of a smear campaign in the thirteenth-century, and a defensive reaction against such charges could be partly responsible for the increasing severity of the church."[63] Whether acting out of defensiveness or pressed to action by the ascetic moralists, the church leadership belatedly took up Peter Damian's call to action and began moving aggressively against homosexuality among members of the clergy as the 12th century progressed.

Targeting Sodomites

The Council of London of 1102, called by King Henry I at the urging of Anselm of Canterbury to address moral problems of the clergy, principally clerical marriage, followed the example of recent councils and issued decrees condemning marriage among the clergy and as a punitive measure "declared that wives of priests were the property of the bishop."[64] But the council also required that "those who commit the shameful sin of sodomy, and especially those who of their own free will take pleasure in doing so, were [to be] condemned by a weighty anathema until by penitence and confession they should show themselves worthy of absolution." The council directed that any clergyman found guilty of sodomy be stripped of his priestly rank, and that a layman "should be deprived of his legal status and dignity in the whole realm of England."[65]

Anselm had previously raised "the matter of sodomy" with Henry's predecessor, William Rufus, and urged the king to call a council lest the entire country "become like Sodom itself," but received no support from the king.[66] As motivated as Anselm seems to have been to act against homosexuality in the clergy and among the public, he at the same time seemed to have been ambivalent about the matter. Anselm directed his archdeacon in a letter to ensure that when confessors dealt with those confessing the sin they take into consideration the circumstances, since "this sin has hitherto been so public that hardly anyone is embarrassed by it, and many have therefore fallen into it because they were unaware of its seriousness."[67] At Anselm's urging, the council issued a decree directing that the public be informed of the gravity of homosexual acts, and that in the future they should confess sodomy as a sin.[68]

Oddly, the council's enactments on homosexuality were apparently never published. Anselm deferred their publication at first, claiming that they needed more careful drafting and some revision before publication, but John Boswell cites evidence that the provisions were never actually published. Boswell suggests that Anselm's failure to publish the council's enactments could have been because he was mindful of Leo IX's decree forbidding extreme measures in dealing with homosexuality among the clergy. In addition, Boswell says, Anselm may also have had personal reservations about publishing them. Anselm's many passionate love letters to his male friends seem to indicate that his reluctance to take strong action could have been motivated by his own self-interest. Anglican Bishop Michael Doe has argued that Anselm's refusal to publish the council's edicts can be seen as further evidence of Anselm's homosexual orientation.[69]

Anselm's inaction may also have reflected sympathy for fellow clerics with sentiments similar to his own. Similarly, Boswell suggests that the lack of action against homosexuality among the clergy by the church up until the 12th century may have been likewise due to clergymen reluctant to punishing others like themselves.[70] Accusations against church officials for homosexuality up until the 13th century were, in fact, frequently ignored.[71] It is not known whether any pronouncements were communicated to the laity after the council about the gravity of homosexual acts. Several years after the end of the council, an unidentified prelate wrote to Anselm complaining that even after the London council, "sodomites remained unmolested."[72]

Ironically, the church's furious campaign against clerical marriage may have had the effect of increasing the number of clergy involved in same-sex relationships, as Henry of Huntingdon and Bishop Ulric of Imola had predicted. Researchers have long recognized that males in environments where they were deprived of sexual opportunities with females frequently turn to their own sex for release.[73] An increase in the visibility of homosexuality among clergy during the 12th century could also have been a result of an enormous increase in the sheer number of monks due to the explosion of new monastic orders founded during the century.[74] Outside the monasteries, local parish priests who could not dare establish a relationship with a female would have found it easier to find sexual companionship with another clergyman or layman whose company would not have attracted the kind of attention that would have fallen on a relationship with a woman.

By the late 12th century the reformers' attention began to be focused more and more on homosexuality among the clergy. To the dismay of some reformers, the first ecumenical councils called to advance the Gregorian reforms continued to place primary emphasis on clerical marriage and other heterosexual sins, such as incest and consanguineous marriages, ignoring homosexual practices completely.[75] The 12th-century theologian Peter Cantor vehemently attacked homosexual love, saying it was not just a violation of chastity, but an offense on a par with murder as one of two sins that "cry out to heaven for vengeance." Referring to the destruction of Sodom and Gomorrah, Peter wrote, "Why is it that what the Lord punished severely the church leaves untouched?" Perhaps in response to the complaints of reformers like Peter Cantor, but also reflecting what John Boswell called a growing intolerance in European society for non-conformity, the Third Lateran Council of 1179 included sanctions against those guilty of homosexuality among sanctions it imposed against heretics, moneylenders, Jews, Muslims, mercenaries and others.[76] Along with penalties for priests who failed to "expel" their wives, or "without clear and necessary cause" visited nunneries too often, it ordered the removal from office and confinement in a monastery for any clergyman "involved in that incontinence which is against nature." But the council also, the first time by an ecumenical council, officially condemned homosexuality among the laity which up to that point had been mostly ignored by the church leadership: "If a layman, he shall suffer excommunication and be cast out from the company of the faithful."[77]

Motivations for Reform

In considering the intensifying efforts of the church to control not just the sexuality of the clergy and the laity, but also conformance to church doctrine, it is important to appreciate both the neurotic reactions of the increasingly celibate clergy to their own sexuality and the threats the church perceived to its power and position as the unquestioned moral authority of Europe. The psychological stress suffered by the clergy because of their efforts to suppress their sexual instinct would have required release in some direction, and an aggressive campaign to extirpate sexual nonconformity among others would have provided an effective outlet.

The social historian David Greenberg was the first scholar to point to the role played by psychological conflicts within the clergy caused by the repression of their sexual drives in the ferocity of the church's campaign to control the sexuality of Medieval society. As Greenberg explains,

> The more the church suppressed priestly marriage and concubinage, the stronger must have been the homosexual drive it aroused within its ranks. The organizational suppression of sexuality, made more effective by the strengthening of monastic discipline, would have prevented many priests from giving expression to their homosexual impulses. As official pronouncements insisted on the incompatibility of homosexuality with clerical status, it would have been psychologically risky for priests to acknowledge their own homosexual desires even to themselves.[78]

As we saw at the beginning of this chapter, the drives the clergymen were attempting to suppress did not just disappear, but continued in the subconscious, building up behind the "dam" they created and releasing in what Otto Fenichel called "distorted discharges" usually manifested as the psychological defense of reaction formation. Seeing others with the loathed desires and acting on them, as Greenberg observed, "places the repression from one's own consciousness in jeopardy, and thus evokes the punitive reaction ... fueled by the energy of the repressed impulse."[79] With the increasingly effective enforcement of clerical celibacy, the numbers of clergymen strenuously suppressing their sexual impulses multiplied rapidly from the small but vocal minority of moral ascetics of the early Middle Ages to a majority of the clergy by the early 13th century. When one then multiplies the "neurotic discharges" resulting from the buildup of repressed sexual energy in each clergyman by the tens of thousands, and then channels that energy via an increasingly disciplined church organization into aggressive elimination of sexual nonconformity, real or imagined, the result would explain the highly repressive social atmosphere that developed in 13th-century Europe. As summarized by Greenberg,

> fear and loathing of homosexuality developed in the Middle Ages as a psychological defense mechanism against the inner conflict created by the imposition of clerical celibacy and the rigid repression of all sexual expression. The irrational and at times hysterical tone in which homosexuality was discussed in the late Middle Ages can thus be understood as a manifestation of reaction formation and projection originating in organizationally inducted psychological conflict.[80]

The paranoia that Freud and later researchers found was engendered by repressed homosexual feelings would only have added to the intensity of the vitriolic attacks by the sexually repressed clergy on sexual non-conformists.

The histrionic and super-heated denunciations of homosexuality in the writings of Peter Damian, Ordericus Vitalis and Guibert of Nogent became the norm among both the clergy and secular authorities by the mid–13th century. But the fear and loathing of sex among the clergy also heavily influenced church moral doctrine on sex as it was laid down and incorporated into canon law. The highly negative view of sex that shaped church sexual doctrine can be seen in the writings of one of the most influential theologians of the day, William of Auvergne, who was for several decades professor of philosophy at the University of Paris before being installed in 1228 as bishop of Paris. William was one of the first to combine Christian theology with Aristotelian philosophy and because of that his works are considered among the founding works of Christian scholastic philosophy. In his writings, William bases his moral arguments on what was by then the standard definition of "natural" sexual relations, intercourse between a husband and wife performed in the "missionary position" with the specific intent of conceiving a child. All other sexual expression was "unnatural," defined as any release of a man's seed outside a proper vessel (which would not explain how lesbian relations would be unnatural). To William, every form of "unnatural lust" was a sacrilege, since it shows lack of respect for the sacred, and the sinner is, therefore, "similar to a pig who wallows in and even eats his own filth." An example of how the Christian scholastics employed logic to lead to what to us would seem absurd conclusions is William's argument that masturbation is a greater evil than incest. According to William "the crime becomes more severe the closer one is to the person with whom it is committed," and the reason masturbation is worse is that one is closer to one's self than one's mother.[81]

Like many of his contemporary theologians, William held that sodomy is doubly evil because the man who wastes his seed outside its proper vessel is not only offending God by committing an unnatural act, but is committing murder. Thus, he says, the sin is so great that "the air is corrupted by the mere mention of it," and that even the Devil is embarrassed by it. According to William the sin is so heinous, in fact, that "preachers dare not name it, referring instead to the 'unmentionable vice,'" one of the first documented uses of that famous expression. William adds that sodomy is one of the sins that caused the Deluge in the Old Testament, thereby labeling those engaging in homosexual acts as "the destroyers of mankind."[82]

A good example of the shroud of sin the 13th-century moralists cast around sex is the way they dealt with nocturnal emissions, a natural process whereby the male body eliminates an excessive build up of semen. Even though the process is completely involuntary, occurring when the person is sleeping, the scholastic theologians held that it was still sinful, since it fit the definition of "unnatural" sexual acts, those where a man's seed is released outside a proper vessel. However, if the nocturnal emission was not preceded by lewd thoughts the night before, the act was only a venial sin. If licentious thoughts occurred the night before, it was a mortal sin. In all cases, penance was to be performed the following morning.[83]

Between the mid–12th century and the papacy of Gregory IX in the mid–13th century, the moral writings and collections begun by Regino of Prüm, Burchard of Worms, Ivo of Chartres and Gratian, all of whom displayed a "fear and loathing" of sex, were revised and supplemented by church legal scholars under papal direction and incorporating the more recent theological developments of the Christian scholastics. A final compilation and revision commissioned by Pope Gregory IX, known as the *Liber Extra*, was promulgated in 1234 and established as the official doctrine and law of the church. Thus, the anti-sexual moral writings of the ascetic moralists, developed in copious detail in the penitentials, council decrees, collections of the early canonists, and supplemented by the moral prescriptions and formulae of the scholastic philosophers was codified and published, providing a unified corpus of sexual moral doctrine that could be enforced throughout Christendom. The dammed-up sexual energies among the rapidly growing ranks of sexually repressed clergy provided the impetus for enforcement.

Threats to Church Primacy

Another factor in the growing intensity of church efforts to seek rigid enforcement of its doctrine was the threats to its primacy that it saw in the conquest of the Holy Land by Muslims, growing heretical movements, and European monarchs who were centralizing power and authority in their kingdoms at the expense of church interests. The underlying principle of the Gregorian reforms was Gregory's vision of the church as the unifying force of Christian society, directed by the pope, God's regent on earth. Deviance from the church's conception of Christian morality and Christian social order were not only sins against God, but in the church's eyes they represented threats to the church's sense of legitimacy which the leadership felt should be defended at all costs. By the end of the 12th century Gregory's vision of the church as the center of God's society on earth was being seriously tested. The manner in which the papacy faced those challenges and the mechanism of doctrinal enforcement that would be put in place in the 13th century set the mold for the papacy as it was known for centuries afterwards, and in the end was to have a profound impact on the character of European society.

In the late 11th century and throughout the 12th century serious threats to the church's self-appointed role as the prime arbiter of Christian moral and social order had arisen on several fronts. The Muslim conquest of the Holy Land and occupation of Christianity's most sacred shrines was not only regarded by the church leadership as sacrilegious, but as a threat to Christian society itself. In a perfect illustration of the degree to which sexual deviance was becoming identified in the minds of the church leadership with threats to the church's primacy, exhortations under Urban II to rouse popular support for the First Crusade focused not on the religious imperatives of freeing the Holy Land from the heathen infidels, but on allegations of atrocious and despicable violations of Christian sexual morality. According to one inflammatory tract disseminated to support the crusade, the Saracens not only raped Christian virgins and mothers but forced the mothers to sing obscene songs while being made to watch the violation of their daughters. The missive then goes on, "But what next? We pass on to worse yet. They have degraded by sodomizing them men of every age and rank: boys, adolescents, young men, old men, nobles, servants and, what is worse and more wicked, clerics and monks, and even — alas and for shame! something which from the beginning of time has never been spoken of or heard of— bishops! They have already killed one bishop with this nefarious sin."[84] Even worse than the rape of a virgin girl, according to the church leaders, was a sexual assault on one of their own.

The First Crusade, launched by Urban II, was successful in recapturing Jerusalem and establishing a Christian presence in the Holy Land. However, later crusades were not as successful, some were outright disasters, and by the end of the 12th century the Holy Land was back in Muslim hands. In the meanwhile, preachers and church leaders steadily stoked the fears of the European population with tales of gruesome violence and depraved sexual outrages by the Muslims, so that by the 13th century the "sodomitical" Muslims were being seen as a greater and greater threat to Europe. The thirteenth-century theologian Jacques de Vitry charged that the prophet Mohammed "popularized the vice of sodomy among his people, who sexually abuse not only both genders, but even animals.... Sunk, dead and buried in the filth of obscene desire, pursuing like animals the lusts of the flesh, they can resist no vices but are miserably enslaved to and ruled by carnal passions."[85] Another clergyman, William of Adam, claimed that sordid Christians cooperated in these atrocities by beautifying and selling innocent Christian youths into sexual slavery to the Muslims: "Feeding them with sumptuous meals and delicate beverages to make them pinker and rosier and more voluptuous, and then more alluring and apt to satisfy the lust of the Saracens. And when the libidinous, vile, and wicked men — the Saracens — corrupters of human nature, see the boys, they immediately burn with lust for them and, like mad dogs, race to buy the boys for themselves ... so that they can have their evil way with them." The Muslims were, therefore, not only a threat to Christian adults, but to their children as well.[86]

In Europe, especially serious challenges to the church's role as supreme arbiter of Christian doctrine came from a spate of heretical movements. Some of the heretical groups had large followings and even dominated entire regions of Europe, as the Cathars had by the 12th-century in southern France, northern Italy and the Rhineland. Saint Bernard of Clairvaux, sent by the papacy into France to try to convince the people to rejoin the church remarked that part of the reason for the popularity of the Cathars was the massive corruption of the church and a lack of piety and enthusiasm for pastoral duties among the clergy.[87] The dualist beliefs of the Cathars were similar to the Manicheans of early Christianity, and in rejecting marriage some accepted homosexuality as a valid form of sexual expression. A similar dualist heresy, the Bogomils, originated in Bulgaria in the 10th century and spread from there into Western Europe. Like the Cathars, the Bogomils tolerated homosexual practices, and, in fact, it is from their name, or some think their origination in Bulgaria, that the word *buggery* is derived. Another prominent movement was the Waldensians, founded in 1177 by a wealthy French merchant, Peter Waldo, who renounced his position, gave away his wealth, and preached a simple Christian lifestyle that emphasized charitable works and disregarded the church's complex theologically-based moral doctrines. Aside from a repudiation of church doctrine, the heretical movements had removed whole regions of Europe from church control, depriving it of revenue and undermining its broader authority. The continued existence of the heretical movements, therefore, could not be tolerated if the church was to realize its vision of a unified Christian society overseen by the pope.

Because of the acceptance of homosexuality by some of the heretical movements, heretics in general were branded sodomists and vice versa. Hence, extermination of sexual nonconformity of any kind became intertwined with the church's fierce campaigns to crush heretical movements. Those who disagreed with the church's rigid sexual code, therefore, were doubly damned by the church, as sodomists and as heretics. And because deviance from the church's vision of Christian moral and social order was, to church leaders, defiance of God and a grievous sin which could provoke the horrific punishment of God on all of society, the reaction of the church to differences of opinion over doctrinal issues combined a revulsion for those who embodied the sexuality they loathed and not a little paranoia over the possibility of mass punishment by God for the sins of sodomists and heretics.

Finally, as the 13th century opened, the church was faced with newly assertive monarchs in Europe. Richard the Lion Heart in England, Philip Augustus in France and Henry VI in Germany were in the process of throwing off the restraints of feudalism and were seeking to centralize power in their kingdoms and increase their revenue, often at the church's expense. The secular monarchs rejected the church's claims to sole jurisdiction over moral matters, and insisted that the authority they had from God over their people gave them dominion over matters of morality within their kingdoms as well. Competition over authority between these kingdoms and the papacy contributed to the intensification of the authoritarian atmosphere when each side, in order to claim jurisdiction over their subjects' lives enacted numerous laws prohibiting and regulating various activities. The effect in the 13th century was a deluge of new laws and regulations that increased the pressure on non-conformity, while the strengthened power resulting from the centralizing of authority in the secular nation-states provided new and effective avenues of enforcement not possible with the fragmentation of authority under the Feudal system of the early Middle Ages.

Coming when the church was still struggling to eliminate the interference of secular rulers in church appointments and policies, the growing power of the centralized monarchies represented a new threat to church autonomy and authority. As the 13th century opened, therefore, the specter of the Saracens in the Holy Land, mounting criticism of the church for corruption, the growing number of heretical movements threatening the authority of the papacy, and the challenges of the growing power of the centralized monarchies of Europe led to a sense of defensiveness and paranoia among church leaders, and a determination to assert church authority in imposing spiritual order on European society.[88]

The Fourth Lateran Council

Under Pope Innocent III, who was elected pope in 1198, a renewed and more aggressive campaign to enforce conformity to church doctrines and policies was implemented. Innocent III was an able and energetic leader who shared Gregory VII's beliefs in the absolute primacy of the church and used his papacy to aggressively pursue the goals of Gregorian reform, which had been neglected under his immediate predecessors. One of his theological works, *On the Miserable Condition of Man*, written before he assumed the papacy, placed him squarely in line with the ascetic moralists on theological and moral philosophy. Innocent III made clear his belief in the superiority of papal power to secular authority by inserting himself repeatedly into the political disputes among secular rulers. Before he died he had obtained the feudal homage of seven European monarchs, including Philip II of France, John of England, Peter II of Aragon and the Holy Roman Emperor Frederick II, whose election the pope had helped arrange.

The pope was not satisfied with the progress that had been made in instituting celibacy among the clergy and was determined to strictly enforce clerical celibacy and to crush heretical movements. The Fourth Lateran Council, convened by Innocent III in 1215 brought one of the largest ever assemblages of church leaders to Rome, including four hundred and twelve bishops, nine hundred abbots and priors, and even 71 patriarchs from the Eastern church. In opening the council, Innocent announced himself "ready to drink the chalice of the Passion for the defense of the Catholic faith," to save and protect the Holy Land, and establish "the liberty of the church" from the interference of secular rulers. The pope then presented to the council drafts of 70 decrees he had already prepared that proclaimed the primacy of the papacy, resolved outstanding questions of doctrine, set up an office of enforcement which soon became the Office of the Inquisition, required Jews to wear special identifying dress, launched a new crusade to restore the Holy Land to Christian rule, and established new restrictions on the behavior of the clergy including a restatement of the demand for celibacy. The assembled prelates could do little more than approve the 70 decrees, which nonetheless obtained for Innocent the unquestioned backing he sought from the assembled leadership for his agenda.[89] Though he died only two years after the conclusion of the council, the end result of the initiatives undertaken by Innocent III was the creation by the late 13th century of a religious tyranny overseen by the papacy, and enforced not only by the Inquisition, but by the newly organized mendicant orders, who made it their business to seek out and punish sexual nonconformists, intellectual dissidents or anyone else who fell outside of the papacy's vision of a Christian society ruled by God's law as dictated by the pope.

A number of the decrees provided new tools to the church for the enforcement of church moral doctrine. Canon 3 set up an administrative office for the investigation, trial and punishment of heretics. The same canon specified that the new administrative office — formally promulgated as the Papal Inquisition in 1231 under Pope Gregory IX — was also to be used to investigate and prosecute sexual offenders, including adulterers, bigamists and sodomists. The canon further required that convicted laymen were to have their property confiscated and then be given over to civil authorities for punishment. Members of the clergy were to be first expelled from their orders and then handed over to secular authorities for punishment.[90] Inviting secular authorities to enact punishments that could be applied to the clergy, over whom the church had long and jealously claimed jurisdiction, was an indication of the gravity with which the church leadership was now viewing sexual activity among the clergy. In fact, by the mid–13th century a number of states had asserted themselves into church governance by enacting laws against strictly clerical crimes, such as clerical marriage and even the conspicuous display of wealth.[91]

Responding to charges that the church hierarchy was too lenient or had been negligent in acting against homosexuality among the clergy, the council also imposed penalties, including physical punishment, on bishops or other officials who failed to vigorously act against clerical sodomy. The council further required secular rulers to expel convicted heretics from their land, and if a ruler refused to do so, the pope would then declare the oaths of fealty of the ruler's vassals to be dissolved. Archbishops and bishops were also ordered to appoint three men "of good reputation" for every parish under their authority to be responsible for identifying heretics or any other individuals whose "life and habits differ from the normal way of living of Christians." To ensure that the faithful were aware of the threat to their souls of illicit sexual behavior, the council instituted a requirement that all Christians confess their sins to a priest at least once a year. The priests in turn were instructed to inquire into every aspect of any sexual act mentioned by penitent and to make sure they understood the gravity of each act.[92]

By the end of the 13th century what the historian Michael Goodich called "this net of prohibitions and investigative procedures" had expanded throughout Europe and was pulling in heretics as well as anyone accused of sexual nonconformity. As Goodich observed, "an efficient mechanism for the persecution of religious, sexual and sometimes even political opposition to Rome was thus created; and the state was called upon to fulfill its obligations to guarantee Catholic doctrine."[93]

Instruments of Repression

Taking up the lead of Pope Innocent III and Lateran IV, local councils and synods began issuing decrees against "the crime against nature" in increasingly harsh rhetoric, and broadened the decrees to include clergy and laity alike. The Synod of Angers meeting in 1216 declared that homosexuality was worse than adultery, because "it turned men into monsters." The Cistercians, who in 1221 began expelling monks for sodomy, in 1279 ordered all monasteries to build prisons for the incarceration of sodomites, thieves, arsonists, forgers, and murderers. By the mid–13th century, English bishops were issuing regulations requiring priests to "seek out and punish sodomites."[94] Local preachers across Europe seemed preoccupied with carnal sin throughout the 13th century, fulminating not only against sodomites, but against adulterers and fornicators as well.[95]

The Dominican Order, founded in 1216, was in the forefront of the hunt for heretics and sodomists. Dissatisfied with the effectiveness of prosecution of heretics by the bishops' courts, Pope Gregory IX turned the operation of the Inquisition over to the Dominicans, and by 1255 Dominicans were conducting inquisitions in all the countries of Central and Western Europe.[96] The tenacity of the Dominicans in pursuing enforcement of sexual and doctrinal conformity earned them the nickname *Domini canes*, "Hounds of God." To assist the Inquisitors in their work, Pope Innocent IV issued a bull in 1252 authorizing the use of torture to extract confessions from accused sodomists or heretics, an authorization that was reaffirmed in decrees of Pope Alexander IV in 1259 and Pope Clement IV in 1265.[97]

Secular authorities were quick to take up the call of the church to action. By the 13th-century the widespread sexual neurosis among the clergy that came with enforcement of clerical celibacy was rapidly spreading among the laity, and provided a similar neurotic impetus to drive the increasingly barbaric enforcement measures being enacted by civil authorities. With the widespread denunciation and prosecution of any type of sexual nonconformance, which would include prohibited heterosexual as well as homosexual offenses, the lay population of Europe would have begun to experience the same psychological stresses that were driving the sexual neuroses of the celibate clergy. While involvement in homosexual relationships was relatively widespread in Europe only a century earlier, the steady stream of invective preached against sodomists by clergymen, not to mention the over-heated propaganda against the sodomitical Muslims, would have begun to significantly affect popular sexual attitudes to same-sex love by the beginning of the 13th century. Among laymen with a significant homosexual component, the anxiety and consequent urge to act out against sodomists would be significant. It's also likely that laymen who had committed homosexual acts themselves would be anxious to prosecute or implicate others for sodomy to deflect attention from themselves. Because most people are capable of homosexual responsiveness to one degree or other, it was inevitable that the demonizing of homosexual eroticism by the church would lead to some amount of psychological conflict among a large portion of the laity. Even a momentary sexual stimulus, such as might occur in an older man coming across a particularly attractive male youth, could be cause for anxiety.

Furthermore, with the church now demanding severe restrictions on heterosexual activity, the devout or even superstitious layman would have also been subject to considerable anxiety over sex. For even a person of primary heterosexual orientation, the tightly restricted bounds of acceptable sexual behavior — allowing only a passionless, mechanistic performance of the sex act in the missionary position for the explicit purpose of producing a child — provided ample potential for guilt and spiritual paranoia. The church's condemnation of masturbation as among the worst of sins — a greater evil than fornication according to Aquinas — would have by itself been enough to engender significant guilt and anxiety in most of the lay population. In the superstitious atmosphere of Medieval Europe, the declaration of the church that people would burn forever in Hellfire just for having sex was sure to unnerve a lot of people and fuel paranoia caused by repression of their sexual instincts.

It seems inevitable, therefore, that neurotic anxieties, paranoia and the psychological defense mechanism of reaction formation, similar to what was found among the celibate clergy, would have been a growing force among the lay population of Europe and would have been a significant factor in propelling the ferocity of secular persecution of sodomists and other nonconformists that had gained momentum by the late 13th century. As the psychiatrist Alfred Gallinek observes, "The suppression of evil ... and the resulting repression and projection particularly of the sex urge, led to the witch hunts of the late Middle ages with all their sadism."[98]

The willingness of some personality types to condone or even take part in violence or brutality against other groups of people even when doing so conflicts with their stated moral values has been shown by psychological research to be closely linked with adherence to a strictly authoritarian religious or ideological world view. Such an outlook divides the world into good people like themselves, who believe what they believe, and everyone else, who are evil sinners in league with the Devil and intent on destroying the way of life of the good people. Eric Fromm remarked that such individuals find security by trading their freedom for the security of a powerful institution and a degree of devotion to the imperatives of that institution that can become masochistic. Other scholars have recognized the relationship between masochism and the authoritarian personality. The psychoanalyst S.L. Charme observes that "the masochist is willing to sacrifice all individual decisions, responsibility or interests and to find meaning, direction and protection by submitting to some larger power." Charme adds that this form of masochism is frequently found in authoritarian personalities involved in fascist organizations and religious movements.[99] According to another psychoanalyst, William Meissner, among authoritarian personalities sadistic tendencies may be found hand-in-hand with masochistic ones, often in the same personality.[100] Hence, authoritarian personality types are often willing to inflict barbaric punishment on people who they feel pose a threat to their institution or to society in general without the slightest moral qualm, and, in fact, usually derive a sense of righteous satisfaction in doing so.

The psychologist Bob Altemeyer, in researching the factors that make some people more susceptible than others to authoritarian movements, has identified a number of common traits among the authoritarian personality type: a willingness to uncritically trust people who tell them what they want to hear, a willingness to uncritically accept insufficient evidence that supports their beliefs, an inclination toward the "fundamentalist" or most prejudiced elements of their religion, a tendency to use religion to erase guilt over their acts and to maintain their self-righteousness, an inclination to volunteer to help the authorities persecute almost anyone, a tendency to view minorities of any kind with suspicion, and a blindness toward their own hypocrisy or personal failings. According to Altemeyer, the authoritarian personality types frequently grow up in environments where the world is viewed as a dangerous place, where it is taught that the Devil is out to trap people into sin, where morality is seen in black-and-white absolutes, and they nearly always exhibit a fear and loathing of homosexuals. When feeling threatened or provoked by an outside group or minority, the authoritarian types are quick to support brutal or violent means of eliminating the threat. The research has also found that authoritarian tendencies in a population, and the consequent incidence of people displaying these characteristics, increase proportionally to the level of perceived threat to the population.[101]

The factors that Altemeyer cites as conducive to the development of authoritarian personalities were all present in abundance in 13th-century Europe as the church accelerated its campaign for sexual and doctrinal conformity. With the intensified efforts of the church to impose its ascetic sexual doctrine on the people of Europe, hammered home by regular fulminations of the ascetic clergy in their sermons about punishment that would be meted on them in Hell because of sexual immorality, and the endless questioning and lecturing of penitents by confessors about their sexual behavior, the European masses were subjected to enormous levels of guilt and anxiety over their sexual lives. The increasingly frequent depiction of sodomists and heretics in the population as threats to society because of the punishment they could provoke on their community would also have significantly raised the level of fear of society and focused hostility on nonconformists. Any disaster or calamity, be it an earthquake, flood or outbreak of disease, would, of course, have aggravated the level of fear and paranoia of the people, and increased the chance of retribution on minorities or other nonconformists.

The psychological defenses and neurosis resulting from widespread sexual repression and the findings of psychological research on authoritarian behavior help explain the inhuman and barbaric violence that occurred in the late Middle Ages, sometimes on a massive scale, against not just sodomists, but heretics, Jews, lepers, gypsies or any other group unfortunate enough to not fit in with the church's narrow definition of Christian society. Such a mentality is evident in the brutal slaughter of tens of thousands of Cathars in southern France by the Albigensian crusaders sent by Innocent III to wipe out the heresy. To get the support of the nobles of northern France for the crusade, a papal decree promised them the lands confiscated from the Cathars and the nobles defending them, which resulted in a Medieval land rush among the northern nobles eager to enlarge their domains. In the assault on the Cathar town of Béziers, which was thought to have a population of about 200 Cathars among a much larger Catholic population, the papal legate and commander of the forces, Abbott Arnaud Amaury of the Cistercian monastery of Cîteaux was reported to have responded when asked how to distinguish the Carthars from the Catholics, "Kill them all. The Lord will recognize His own."[102] In the rampage the doors of the church of St. Mary Magdalene, where thousands of the inhabitants had taken refuge, were forced open and in the ensuing rampage 7,000 men, women and children were reportedly massacred. When the day was over, Abbott Arnaud sent a message to Innocent III, "Today your Holiness, twenty thousand citizens were put to the sword, regardless of rank, age, or sex."[103] In addition to the slaughter of heretics, barbarous violence was directed at other groups who were seen to pose a threat to the Christians of Europe, including Jews and gypsies. The conviction that leprosy was caused by sinning led to the burning of lepers, as occurred in Toulouse in 1320.[104]

In some cases, the people took matters into their own hands if they felt the church authorities were not sufficiently harsh in their enforcement of conformity. Guibert of Nogent described such an outcome in his account of the trial of two men accused of heresy in a French town. The bishop of Soissons was called in to officiate at the trial, but because no one could be found to testify to anything heretical the men said, it was decided that the two men would be subjected to a trial by ordeal in which they would be bound and thrown into a large tub of water. The first man floated like a log on the top, and so was acquitted. The second man sank, however, and so was imprisoned along with an onlooker who turned out to be a known heretic from another town. Guibert says that he and the bishop then went to report the matter to the Council of Beauvais to see what should be done with them. But in the meantime, the townspeople, fearful that the church would be too lax in dealing with the two men, broke into the jail, took the men out and burned them alive.[106]

Draconian civil legislation punishing sodomists and heretics and the formation of activist lay organizations charged with pursuing social nonconformists bear witness to the radically changed social attitudes to sex and social conformity that had overtaken Europe by the mid–13th century. Starting in the mid–13th century organized campaigns to root out heretics and sodomists were undertaken throughout Europe, often at the direction of the Inquisition. Under pressure from the Dominicans, officials of towns in northern Italy were required to take an oath to seek out and prosecute sodomists and heretics when they took office. Statues passed in Bologna in 1245 and 1267 created a municipal office to work with Inquisition to track down out and punish heretics and sodomists. In 1250 Bologna had passed a law requiring that convicted sodomists be exiled from the city. However, in 1259, at the Dominicans insistence, the law was changed to require that sodomists be punished by burning. Other cities followed suit in imposing death by burning for convicted heretics and sodomists.

A law passed in Orléans in 1260 required that a man "who has been proved to be a sodomite must lose his testicles, and if does it a second time, he must lose his member, and if he does it a third time, he must be burnt." A compilation of laws produced under King Louis IX, *Etablissements De Saint Louis*, dating from 1273, required that those found guilty of heresy or "bougrerie" be burned and their property given to the ruler. A French law enacted in 1283, *Coutumes de beauvaisis*, required that convicted sodomists forfeit their property and die by burning. A 1265 Spanish law, *Las Siete Partidas*, stated that "when one man desires to sin against nature with another ... both [were to] be castrated before the whole populace and on the third day after be hung by the legs until dead, and that their bodies never be taken down." The Spanish law also included language that was increasingly common in civil statutes on sodomy, a reference to the dangers that the community was exposed to because of sodomists: "for such crimes our Lord sent upon the land guilty of them famine, plague, catastrophe, and countless other calamities." The statute continues to state that the law was passed to prevent the "many evils" that occur in a land where sodomy is practiced.[106]

The campaign against sodomists also took on some aspects of a class conflict in some regions. In northern Italy, a populist, pro-papacy political party, the Guelphs, composed mostly of middle class tradesmen chaffing under the dominance of the old feudal aristocracy, began winning elections to local municipal positions in the mid–13th century. Strong supporters of the church reforms, the Guelphs were closely associated with the Dominicans, many of whom came from their ranks. In their zeal to defend conformity to church doctrine, the Dominicans exhorted the people to act against not only sodomists, but usurers and Jews. The middle class identified all three groups with the oppression they had suffered under the moneyed aristocracy, and saw in the move for moral reform the opportunity to right old wrongs. The populist anti-aristocratic Guelphs, therefore, were responsible for passing much of the harsh legislation punishing sodomy, which they had long associated with the old feudal aristocracy.[107]

Lay confraternities, founded to support the Dominicans in their work against non-conformists, also began to appear in local communities. A lay confraternity, Societe Beata Maria, Society of Blessed Mary, closely associated with the populist Guelphs, was formed in Bologna in the mid–12th century. Similar groups, also based in populist political movements, were founded at the same time in Mantua and Faenza. In a letter to the Bolognese confraternity written in 1255 to the group, the Dominican minister-general Humbert di Romanis commended them for the devotion to the Blessed Virgin, and urged them to be active in the fight against heresy and that "evil filth," sodomy. The officials of the local confraternities were, in essence, the local agents of the Inquisition, and candidates for the offices were first vetted and approved by the Inquisitor and his colleagues before they assumed their duties.[108] In 1265 legislation was enacted in Bologna that vested the Societe Beata Maria with the full authority to pursue heretics and sodomists and that required civil government bodies to cooperate with them in their investigations. To assist them in their work, some localities even awarded bounties to citizens who denounced heretics or sodomists to the confraternities. The *podestas*, or captains, of the confraternities were given complete authority to investigate, torture and punish suspects in any way they saw fit in order to rid the town of sodomists and heretics.[109]

By the end of the 13th century what Goodich calls "repressive, even barbaric, legislation against sexual offenders" had become the norm throughout Europe. An elaborate inquisitorial organization had been implemented across Europe, and in some areas local vigilante groups were deputized to seek out and identify heretics, sodomists or any other person whose "life and habits differ from the normal way of living of Christians," in the words of the Lateran IV decree. By the 14th century, legislation punishing non–conformists of any kind — sexual, religious, or social — routinely cited the threat of catastrophe to the town because of sinners in their midst as the reason for its enactment.

One does not need to have experienced life under a totalitarian state to appreciate the chilling atmosphere engendered by the church's rigid moral code, the spreading tentacles of the Inquisition and the network of laymen's groups deputized by the Inquisition, whose industry in rooting out heretics and sodomists was very likely spurred on as much by class hatred and the lure of bounties as by genuine religious devotion. The defeat of a country in battle or a natural catastrophe would lead to heightened demands from the both the clergy and the populace for measures to attack heretics and sodomists whose presence they felt threatened their safety. When one third of Florence was devastated by floods in 1333, contemporaries blamed the disaster on sodomists in the population.

When the Black Death hit Europe in the 1340s, the frightening virulence and rapid spread of the disease provoked widespread panic among the population, and was universally believed to have been caused by sodomists, heretics, Jews, usurers and other nonconformists in the population. Panicked vigilante groups in Northern Europe, blaming the epidemic on the Jews, conducted a systematic slaughter of Jews in Mainz, Cologne, Frankfurt and Brussels.[110] The devastations of the Black Plague, which decimated the European population in the mid–14th century, was deeply traumatic and brought paranoia among the population to a fever pitch. The continuing level of paranoia among the population in the late 14th and early 15th century is evident in the outbreaks of mass hysteria in Switzerland and Croatia among local populations who were convinced that servants of Satan were working among them. Under pressure from the fearful masses, local authorities began hunting down and prosecuting men, women, children and even animals accused of being in league with the Devil. Similar investigations of people engaged in the work of the Devil or witchcraft ensued throughout Europe. By the time the witch hunts had abated in the late 17th century an estimated 60,000 individuals had been executed for witchcraft.[111]

One of the more peculiar effects of the widespread imposition of the church's anti-sexual morality and the belief that physical life was tainted by sin was the rise of the flagellants, a movement of the Christian laity that practiced self-mortification for penance for their sins by parading in public, whipping themselves. The movement began in the Central Italian town of Perugia in 1259 when a devastating plague swept through the city causing a panic. People started a procession through the town, whipping themselves as penance for the sins they believed had brought the plague to the city. The mania quickly spread to include nearly all the inhabitants of Perugia. The flagellants marched through the town carrying crosses and banners and singing. Onlookers who would not join them were attacked and accused of being in league with the Devil. The movement then spread to the cities of northern Italy where processions involving as many as 10,000 marched through Bologna, Parma and Modena, whipping themselves and chanting as they marched. The pope outlawed the Italian movement, but it then spread to Austria and Germany. After a decline at the end of the 13th century, the flagellants returned in greater numbers after the outbreak of the Black Death in the 14th century when multiple movements erupted spontaneously across Northern Europe. In May 1348, in the midst of the epidemic, Pope Clement VI personally instituted flagellation sessions in response to the plague. However, the pope, apparently coming to realize the insanity of the movement, had a change of heart and in October 1349 issued a bull declaring that all flagellants were to be treated as heretics and their leaders punished severely.[112]

Prosecutions of Sodomists

The earliest record of an individual man being burned for sodomy was the case of a Belgian villager named John, a knife-maker by trade. He was arrested in 1292 and sentenced to death by the local lay judge for an act against nature, "detested by God," that he was alleged to have committed with another man. He was then taken and burned near the church of St. Peter in Ghent.[113] According to Venetian records, seven men were punished with death by burning for sodomy between 1338 and 1358, and another death by burning for sodomy was recorded in the same period in Chambery in southern France. It is not known exactly how many individuals may have been burned for sodomy because records of such cases are scarce. The lack of records doesn't necessarily indicate that the punishment was rare, however. In France, records of such cases were frequently burned with the sodomite because "the sin was so heinous that it should not be named." Sentences commonly stated that the guilty was to be "burned alive together with the records of his trial."[114]

There is no doubt that in some cases, the sentence would have been reduced, since some church leaders, even in the increasingly repressive atmosphere of the 13th-century church, still pushed for restraint in dealing with those accused of homosexuality. Writing in 1227, Pope Honorius III urged compassion and understanding in meting out punishment for those guilty of "that sin which should neither be named nor committed." In a letter to the Archbishop of Lund, the pope wrote, "Since divine mercy is greater than human perverseness and since it is better to count on the generosity of God than to despair because of the magnitude of a particular sin, we order you herewith to reprimand, exhort, and threaten such sinners and then to assign them, with patience and good judgment, a salutary penance, using modera-tion in its devising, so that neither does undue leniency prompt audacity to sin, nor does unreasonable severity inspire despair."[115] The measured response of Pope Honorius to those accused of homosexual practices had by the mid–13th century become the exception, how-ever. In an age marked by violence and superstition, it seems doubtful that the punishments written into the laws requiring sodomists to be burned, uniform across Europe by the 14th-century, would have rarely been invoked. We have already seen Guibert of Nogent's account of two men convicted of heresy and awaiting sentence from a bishop who were forcibly removed from a jail by an impatient mob of citizens and burned alive.

A first hand look at the work of the Inquisition is provided in the unusually detailed records left by a particularly industrious and efficient inquisitor, Jacques Fournier, later ele-vated to the papacy as Pope Benedict XII. After serving as abbot of a Cistercian monastery, where he was known for his learning as well as his severity, Fournier was installed in 1317 as bishop of Pamiers, a diocese in southwestern France that had been in the center of the Cathar heresy. The Cathars were all but wiped out after the horrendous slaughters of the Albigen-sian Crusade launched by Pope Innocent III in 1209, but in the late 13th century Catharism re-emerged in the area ruled by the Counts of Foix, at the time an independent principality. As a result the Inquisition set up shop in the region in the early 14th century.

When he became bishop of Pamiers, Fournier set up his own inquisitorial court, taking advantage of a ruling of the Council of Vienna in 1312 that stipulated that the powers of the local bishops be used to support the Dominican inquisitors. The Inquisition assigned the Dominican Friar Gaillard de Pomies to the office, but because of Fournier's formidable per-sonality and his prestige in the region Gaillard ended up serving as assistant to Fournier. The French historian Emmanuel LeRoy Ladurie describes Fournier as "a sort of compulsive Mai-gret, immune to both supplication and bribe, skillful at worming out the truth (at bringing the lambs forth, as his victims said), able in a few minutes to tell a heretic from a 'proper' Catholic—a very devil of an Inquisitor, according to the accused." At the direction of Fournier, a special prison was built to house the suspects brought before the Inquisition. Fournier, Ladurie says, was obsessive about detail, and participated in person in nearly all the proceed-ings of his inquisitorial court.[116] Because of his painstaking methods and concern with recording every detail, the records of Fournier's inquisitorial court constitute an especially valuable historical source.

While an effort to eradicate the remains of the Cathar heresy was the chief purpose of the Pamiers Inquisition, the investigation cast a wide net and drew in sodomists, adulterers, bigamists, lepers, Jews and many other nonconformists. Using the authority granted by recent popes, the investigators frequently used torture in extracting evidence from the suspects. Among the accused brought before the Inquisition was Arnaud of Verniolle, a 23-year-old Franciscan deacon living in the Pamiers village of Montaillou, who was charged with sodomy and heresy. The examination of Arnaud and of the witnesses called to testify against him brought forth a detailed description of a large network of young males in the village who had been sexual partners with Arnaud and with each other.[117]

Arnaud testified that his first homosexual encounter occurred when he was a young adolescent in school, and had to share a bed with another student, a 20-year-old named Arnaud Auriol, the son of a knight. Arnaud said that the fourth or fifth night he shared the bed with Auriol, the older student, thinking Arnaud was sleeping, began to embrace him and put his penis between Arnaud's legs and performed the sex act. Arnaud said Auriol continued to have sex with him for the next six weeks they shared the bed together. Later in his teens, Arnaud would have sex with both males and females. However, he said, in 1320, while he was in his late teens, "when they were burning the lepers, I was living in Toulouse. One day I 'did it' with a prostitute. And after I had perpetrated this sin, my face began to swell. I was terrified and thought I had caught leprosy; I thereupon swore that in future I would never sleep with a woman again." Henceforth, Arnaud had sex exclusively with other males.[118]

It is striking to note that during his entire sexual career Arnaud apparently never had any difficulty finding young males, mostly between the ages of 16 and 18, with whom to have sex. Some of his partners testified, perhaps to deflect blame from themselves, that Arnaud had forced them to have sex at knifepoint, which Arnaud categorically denied. One such youth was Guillaume Roux, who claimed Arnaud had lured him into his first sexual encounter with him by promising him a position in the church. Roux then testified that Arnaud suggested Roux accompany him to his rooms where he was going to show him a book which according to Arnaud said that sex between men was not as grave a sin as sex between a man and a woman. Roux then claimed that Arnaud threw him onto the ground and placed his penis between Roux's buttocks and ejaculated between his legs. Roux said that on another occasion he met Arnaud and went with him into a field where he claimed Arnaud "raped him at knifepoint." The next week Roux again accompanied Arnaud to his rooms where he was "raped" a third time. Obviously, if Guillaume Roux had not been willing to engage in sex with Arnaud, he would not have spent so much time with him or accompanied him to his rooms repeatedly. Indeed, Roux then testified that he had sex with Arnaud on several other occasions, in which the use of force by Arnaud was not mentioned. Arnaud de Verniolle was also not the first male to have sex with Guillaume Roux. According to the trial testimony Roux first had sex with a local aristocrat when the man seduced him as a child.[119]

Arnaud had sex with his partners in a variety of locations and in a variety of ways. On one occasion he screwed his partner unceremoniously on a dung heap. Other times he would take his partner to a cabin out in the countryside among the vineyards. According to the trial record Arnaud would have sex with his partners anally, from the front, from the rear and in other ways. On some occasions before engaging in the sex act, the partners would dress in tunics and wrestle and dance, and sometimes they undressed each other and lay together naked. The testimony in Arnaud's trial led to the discovery of an extensive social network of males who had sex with each other, which Goodich called "a veritable lavender underground," an indication that even in the early 14th century homosexual practices were still fairly wide-spread in rural localities. In fact, at one point in his trial Arnaud testified that "in Pamiers there are over a thousand people infected with sodomy."[120] Because Arnaud had claimed priestly duties and had actually performed a mass, he was tried for heresy, since he had not been ordained. Detecting and stamping out heresy was the stated goal of Fournier's inquisition, but it was Arnaud's extensive homosexual activity that determined his fate. After deliberating his case, the court sentenced Arnaud to imprisonment for life bound in shackles and a chain, with bread and water to eat.[121]

The most notorious case of prosecution for sodomy and heresy was the slanderous charges leveled by Philip IV of France against the Knights Templar, a military religious order that was organized in 1119 after the capture of Jerusalem in the First Crusade to protect the legions of pilgrims who traveled from Europe to visit the Holy Places in Palestine. With the patronage of Saint Bernard of Clairvaux, one of the most revered figures in the church at that time, the order was formally endorsed by the church at the Council of Troyes in 1129. Growing quickly in size and wealth, the order's knights were considered the finest fighting units in Europe, and admiration for their mission led to their receiving numerous and sizable donations and bequests from the wealthy of Europe. With an infrastructure of castles and garrisons across Europe and hostelries to shelter pilgrims on their way to and from the Holy Land, the Templars became, by the end of the 12th century, the largest and richest institution in Europe.

With the recapture of Jerusalem by the Saracens and a series of unsuccessful crusades in the 13th century the prestige of the Templars began to fade. Disunity among the Christian forces in the Holy Land was regarded as one of the causes of the lack of success, especially frequent disputes between the Templars and another military order, the Knights of Saint John of Jerusalem, know as the Hospitaliers. In 1306 Pope Clement V sought to have the Templars merged with the Hospitaliers and wrote letters to their leaders asking them to meet in France to discuss the matter. Jacques de Molay, grand master of the Templars, arrived in early 1307, ahead of the master of the Hospitaliers. While waiting for the other master to arrive, Clement decided to meet with de Molay to discuss charges brought by a former Templar knight concerning improper and heretical activities, allegedly involving homosexual rites, that occurred during initiation of knights joining the Templars. After meeting with de Molay, Clement concluded that the charges were of no substance. However, Philip IV, who had heard of the charges from the pope, and who was deeply indebted to the Templars, decided to use the spurious charges to attack the Templars. Under French law, those found of guilty of serious charges were required to surrender their property to the state. Philip IV, with a greedy eye on the Templars' vast fortune, saw in the charges against the Templars an opportunity to rid himself of his debt to the Templars, and seize their wealth at the same time.

On Friday the 13th of October, 1307, Philip had Jacques de Molay and hundreds of other Templars arrested and accused of heresy and sodomy. Imprisoning them, Philip had them tortured until his men were able to extract confessions. After Philip threatened military action against the pope, Clement reluctantly agreed to dissolve the order. Using their forced confessions as proof, Philip in 1310 had several dozen Templars burned at the stake in Paris, and in 1314 de Molay and another Templar leader, Geoffrey de Charney, were burned at the stake. According to legend, when he was being taken to be burned, de Molay asked that he be tied in such a way that he could face the cathedral of Notre Dame and pray. Then, engulfed in flames, he cried out that he would soon be meeting Philip and Clement before God. The pope died the next month, and Philip was killed in a hunting accident later that year.

Conclusion

By the end of the Middle Ages the church had established itself as the absolute dictator of religious doctrine and morality in Europe. The official doctrine of the church set out an explanation for all aspects of human life, from sexual morality to the order of the cosmos. Challenges to its doctrinal authority or disagreements with its official canons were not tolerated and were treated as capital offenses. The extermination of non-conformists from Christian society continued in the prosecutions of heretics and sodomists whenever they were identified. The church's strict moral and doctrinal enforcement, its repeated strident condemnations of any deviant sexual expression — including non-conforming heterosexual acts and masturbation as well as homosexuality — and continual preaching about imminent disaster and destruction because of sinners in league with Satan resulted in a superstitious and fearful European population, constantly on the watch for the evils of Satan and suspicious of any social non-conformance or eccentricity.

To the people of Europe, life had become a perpetual battle against the forces of Satan which were intent on leading humankind into sin through every conceivable kind of trickery and deceit — and sex was Satan's biggest lure. After a centuries-long campaign, the church had succeeded in getting the stubbornly resistant people of Europe to see human life and sexuality the way the church saw it and to finally submit to the sexual morality preached by the ascetic church moralists. But as in the case of the conservative clergy of the early Middle Ages, the demonizing of sex and the rigid sexual repression resulted in a significant level of neurosis in the population which found expression in an obsession with sexual conformity and paranoia about the Devil. As the historian William A. Percy observes,

Subsumed under the crime against nature,' sodomy became invisible to the Christian mind, yet the object of a thousand fantasies. It was nowhere, yet everywhere threatened society with destruction. It was blotted out of the annals of the past, unrecorded in the present, forbidden to exist in the future. Trial records were burned along with culprits so no trace should remain. Yet, enveloped in the impenetrable darkness of ignorance and superstition, it existed silent and unseen. This shift from the explicit but not obsessive condemnation of earlier centuries to the frantic intolerance of homosexual expression has been a hallmark of Western civilization since the late 13th century.[122]

The historian G. Rattray Taylor has written that "Medieval Europe came to resemble a vast insane asylum" and observed a direct correlation between increasing church control over sexual behavior and neurosis in the population.[123] The neurotic reaction to sex of Saint Paul and the early church leaders reached full flower in the widespread sexual neurosis among the Christians of late Medieval Europe.

15

Authoritarian Religion versus Human Ambisexuality

By the end of the Middle Ages the church's centuries-long goal of bringing European society into accord with its vision of God's society on earth was being finally implemented, though most likely not in the way Gregory VII had first envisioned it. To bring European Christian life into conformance with church doctrine, the 13th-century church had established a vast inquisitorial network to identify anyone who stepped outside of the church's defined doctrine on faith and morals, deputized laymen's groups to hunt down and prosecute offenders, authorized torture to extract confessions from the accused, and pressured civil authorities to enact and carry out severe measures for punishing the guilty. The neurotic reactions to sex created by the church's fierce campaign to repress and demonize the sexual drive manifested in the writings and bizarre and self-abusive behavior of the celibate clergy, and was being replicated among the lay population. In the campaign to convince the faithful of the gravity of sexual offenses and heretical thinking, and of the horrific punishment that would befall European society because of its sodomites and heretics, the church succeeded in terrorizing the superstitious population of the late Middle Ages to the point where episodes of mass hysteria might erupt spontaneously without any apparent cause other than the conviction that servants of Satan were working among them.

An enormous source of fright for many people in the 14th and 15th centuries, and a mark of the success of the intense church campaign to demonize homosexuality, was the fear that the presence of sodomists would bring disaster and destruction of their communities, a concern frequently cited in laws and enactments of civil authorities during the period. The highest judicial body of 15th-century Venice, the Council of Ten, was so alarmed by the dangers to the republic it perceived because of sodomists in the population that it took over the responsibility to prosecute and execute sodomists. The Council of Ten had been established to prosecute only two categories of offenses, those which represented serious threats to the health and prosperity of the city: treason and counterfeiting — the latter a threat to the fiscal stability of the republic. Despite the fact that men were being burned alive for sodomy in Venice since the 14th century, the Council of Ten was still not satisfied with the zeal of the lower court charged with prosecuting sodomists, and complained that it was not "torturing men severely enough to obtain confessions."[1]

In 1418 the Council of Ten took over prosecutions for sodomy from the lower court, citing the danger of imminent destruction of the city because of sodomists in the population, and wondering how it was that God had not already sunk Venice's fleet because of the sodomists in the city. The council vowed to eradicate the vice "so that not only would no one presume to its practice but no one would even dare to mention it." The accused were subjected to severe torture to extract confessions and then burned between the Columns of Justice in the piazza between St. Mark's Square and the Grand Canal. From the year the Council of Ten took over jurisdiction of punishing sodomy, 1418, to the end of the century over four hundred men were prosecuted for the "nameless sin" and punished. The council even directed its wrath at children, whom it believed to be willing accomplices to the sin of sodomy, and so did not hesitate from torturing even young teen-agers. A 16-year-old boy accused of being an accomplice in sodomy had his genitals mutilated and was left with his arm so severely maimed that it had to be amputated.[2]

The council's action was a radical departure from the way in which the city had dealt previously with regulation of sexual conduct, and as such is a measure of the seriousness with which the city regarded the threat posed by sodomists. Not only was Venice renowned during the 15th century for its courtesans who operated under license from the city, but its punishment for serious heterosexual offenses was unusually lenient. For example, the sentence for rape, even of a female child, ranged from a couple of months to one or two years in prison.[3]

The savagery with which civil authorities in Venice and other European cities dealt with those accused of sodomy, out of all proportion to the treatment of those accused of any other sexual offenses, is a testament to the degree to which the church's campaign to enforce its repressive sexual code had warped the psyches of the population as Europe passed from the Late Middle Ages and entered the Renaissance. While the church had delegated prosecution and punishment of sodomists to secular governments, its own sexually neurotic clergy was in the forefront of whipping up passions against sodomists, and actively encouraging the kinds of barbaric treatment of sodomists on display in 15th-century Venice.

How it is possible for an individual dedicated to the teachings of Jesus Christ, who taught love and compassion for the sinner, to promote in good conscience the most cruel and inhumane treatment of a human being imaginable can only be explained by the ability of the authoritarian personality to compartmentalize his mind between his understanding of the Christian message, on the one hand, and how he serves those beliefs, on the other. As the research of Bob Altemeyer and others discussed in the previous chapter has found, a prime motivator in propelling the actions of authoritarian personality types is fear — fear of other groups as a threat to them, or fear that the evil activities of others will bring them great harm. We have also seen that the psychological conflicts caused by suppressing natural homosexual impulses manifests in disgust for one's sexual self — sometimes reaching severe levels as noted in the previous chapter — and an equally intense "fear and loathing" of people who display the abhorred sexuality. Where same-sex urges are strong, this suppression can even result in significant paranoia. When one considers the compounding effects of fear and paranoia when added to the visceral loathing of people personifying the detested sexuality, it becomes possible to understand the brutality and barbarism with which people accused of sodomy were treated in Western civilization from the 15th century up to modern times.

Despite the horrific punishments meted on sodomists and the widespread fear of the harm to society that could be caused by sodomists, however, it is clear that homosexuality continued to persist as a facet of sexual behavior among the people of Europe from the Middle Ages onward. Homosexuality was common among specific occupational groups in various periods, and in some historical eras it was practiced openly by a significant portion of society. The determining factor in the apparent prevalence or openness of homosexual practices in different places and times seems to be the degree of influence of authoritarian religion in those societies. The history of homosexuality in Western culture since the Middle Ages, then, is a reflection of the struggle between the efforts of proponents of authoritarian religion to restrict sexual expression to a narrowly defined norm and the stubbornly persistent ambisexual drive of the human species. In periods and localities where authoritarian religion still had influence, and among social groups most concerned with religious piety and sexual morality, the level of repression and prosecution of sodomists was vigorous. In periods when the forces or influences of authoritarian religion were in decline, or in cases where groups were isolated from the proponents of the authoritarian religion of the time, homosexuality was publicly visible and practiced by a significant segment of those groups.

Strict observance of sexual morality seems to have been a particular obsession of the urban tradesmen and merchants of the towns and cities of the late Middle Ages and early Renaissance, as we saw in the aggressive prosecution of sodomists by the merchants of 15th-century Venice and the role of the populist Guelphs in the enactment and enforcement of anti-sodomy legislation in the 13th century. This preoccupation with sexual morality was to be a continuing concern of the tradesmen and shopkeepers from whom the European middle class, the bourgeoisie, emerged in the late Middle Ages and Renaissance. In fact, from the time of the emergence of the bourgeois middle class to the present, the chief source of agitation for enforcement of sexual morality and of extermination of sodomy has been members of the middle class and its moral leaders—the burghers of 16th-century Protestant Germany and Switzerland, the urban bourgeoisie of late 17th- and early 18th-century France, the middle class of 18th-century Holland and London, the Victorian middle class of 19th-century England and northern Europe, and the exploding middle class of early and mid–20th-century America. The greatest levels of deviation from the heterosexual norm was found, as we shall see, in social segments outside the bourgeois middle class—the aristocracy and the artistic class, at one end, and on the other the legions of servants, apprentices, seamen, foot soldiers, and dispossessed youth. A common characteristic of all these groups is that they either felt the Christian condemnation of sodomy didn't apply to them, in the case of the aristocracy and some of the artists, or that they were outside the reach of the conservative moralists of the middle class, in the case of the latter.

The Persistence of Homosexual Love in Renaissance Italy

Throughout the 14th and 15th centuries, church preachers, convinced that sodomists were lurking everywhere within the population conniving to corrupt the innocent, continued to whip up public sentiments against the sin whose name could not be spoken. The Franciscan monk Saint Bernardino of Siena seems to have been obsessed with sodomy and gave regular sermons to the people of 15th-century Florence denouncing them for tolerating and even encouraging sodomy. "Wherever you hear sodomy mentioned," he said, "Each and every one of you spit on the ground and clean your mouth out well. Spit hard! Maybe the water of your spit will quench their fire." Bernardino went on to blame the city's sodomites as the cause of the plague and said they were "actively spreading their poison throughout the city."[4] Boys walking down the streets of Florence, he said, had a greater risk of being sexually assaulted than girls.[5] And parents, for their part, Bernardino claimed, liked to dress their boys up to make them as sexually appealing as possible, with a short doublet and "stockings with a tiny patch in front and another in back so they show a lot of flesh for the sodomites." Such boys parading around Florence in alluring clothes, Bernardino said, were a constant temptation to the men—Louis Crompton slyly suggests that we should take the saint's word on that point. And the boys' fathers, Bernardino said, even entertained their sons' lovers at home and prided themselves in the attention their sons received. Bernardino claimed that Florence and other Tuscan cities were so notorious for sodomy that Genoese authorities would not hire schoolmasters from the region.[6]

Crompton has remarked that Bernardino did not seem intent on reforming sodomists or getting them to repent; rather his goal was to exterminate them from society.[7] "To the fire!" exclaimed Bernardino in a sermon. "They are all sodomites! And you are in mortal sin if you try to help them!"[8] In a Lenten sermon, Bernardino compared Florence to a modern-day Sodom that was sure to be destroyed, and reminded his audience of the destruction of Sodom and Gomorrah. Bernardino seemed to delight in relating for his audience the gruesome details with which sodomists were executed in other cities. In Verona, he said a man was quartered and his limbs hung from the city gates. In another sermon he said he "saw a man tied to a column on high; and a barrel of pitch and brushwood and fire, and a wretch who made it all burn, and I saw many people standing round about to watch." Bernardino then compared the spectators to the "blessed spirits of paradise" who glorify in witnessing the justice of God. In his home city of Siena, he urged the city fathers to rid the city of sodomites, "even if they had to burn every male in the city."[9]

In 1490 the Dominican friar Girolamo Savonarola arrived in Florence and mounted a furious moral campaign in the city, preaching fiery sermons predicting the imminent destruction of the earth and the coming of the days of the Last Judgment. A deadly outbreak of a virulent form of syphilis in the city that coincided with his preaching added credibility to his fire-and-brimstone sermons. When the ruling Medici family were overthrown as a result of an invasion of Charles VIII of France, Savonarola found himself as head of a newly established democratic government, which the friar called a "Christian and religious republic." Savonarola demanded that the city government institute new laws against sodomites and "the cursed vice of sodomy, for which Florence is defamed throughout all of Italy.... I say make a law that is without mercy, that is, that such persons be stoned and burned."[10] At Savonarola's direction the punishment for sodomy was increased from fines to burning at the stake, and soon large numbers of citizens were accused and convicted of sodomy. In one of his sermons Savonarola urged the people, "Make a pretty fire, one or two or three, there in the square, of these sodomites ... make a fire that can be smelled in all of Italy."[11] Despite the friar's demands, however, city officials did not seem as anxious as Savonarola to see the men burned. In fact Savonarola's continued heated denunciations of Florentines for moral laxness began to earn him enemies, but he was undeterred. "Abandon, I tell you, your concubines and beardless youths. Abandon, I say, that unspeakable vice, abandon that abominable vice that has brought God's wrath upon you, or else: woe, woe to you!"[12]

In the spring of 1497 Savonarola and a group of followers mounted the famous Bonfire of the Vanities, which the preacher wanted to use to destroy the accouterments of vice and corruption. The friar sent his followers to each house in the city to collect the evidence of corruption — mirrors, cosmetics, fine clothing, lewd pictures, Greek and Roman classics, chess pieces and musical instruments along with a number of paintings of Renaissance artists — including even masterworks of Michelangelo and Botticelli. The assembled vanities were then set ablaze in a huge bonfire in a city piazza. But within a couple of months the Florentines had had enough of the preacher. In the midst of a sermon by Savonarola on the Feast of the Ascension groups of young males began to riot against the preacher, and were soon joined by hundreds of other Florentines fed up with Savonarola's theocratic republic. A city official was reported to have declared at the time, "Thank God, now we can sodomize!" The next month Savonarola was excommunicated by Pope Alexander VI, the corrupt Borgia pope who had been one of the main targets of Savonarola's moral campaigns. The city authorities then arrested Savonarola, tried him for heresy and treason, and the next year he was executed by hanging and burning. As his corpse was about to be put on fire, a man in the crowd grabbed a torch and lit the fire, exclaiming, "The one who wanted to burn me is now himself put to the flames!"[13]

As the reaction of the people of Florence to the moral hectoring of Savonarola shows, large numbers of people in some areas of Europe were still resistant to the stringent sexual code demanded by the church two centuries after the campaign for sexual purity was launched by Innocent III. In fact, Savonarola was correct when he said that Florence had a reputation for sodomy. The city's reputation for homosexuality was not just in Italy, but throughout Europe — so much so that a vernacular term for sodomists in Germany was the German word for Florentine, *Florenzer*.[14] For hundreds of years the city was known for the prevalence of homosexuality, among unmarried young men and married men as well. Unlike the rigid and efficient government of the Republic of Venice, Florence had been run by a council of city merchants, and then was dominated for most of the 15th century by the powerful Medici family, wealthy bankers and traders who generously promoted the artistic and cultural life of the city, an atmosphere that without doubt encouraged a level of sexual tolerance in the city that was unique in Europe.

With the campaign of the church to eradicate homosexuality from Europe, city officials were under constant pressure from religious leaders to enact and enforce measures to eliminate sodomy from the city. Crompton has remarked that unlike the authoritarian religious fervor operating in other regions of Europe at the time, and even with a healthy amount of religious sentiment in Florence, "something in the local culture kept it from running to excess."[15] Reflecting the ambivalence of the Florentine authorities, the severity of punishment and intensity of enforcement efforts swung back and forth from the issuance of mere fines, to castration and death. In 1365, when Florence was still recovering from the devastations of the Black Death, new legislation citing the fear of "divine wrath" on the city for sodomy reinstituted death by burning as a punishment. Adolescents under 18, however, were usually treated less harshly and could avoid punishment altogether if they agreed to testify against their lovers, though even young teen-agers could still be subjected to barbaric treatment. In 1365 a 15-year-old boy, Giovanni di Giovanni, "accused of relations with 'many men,' was paraded through the city on an ass, publicly castrated, and then branded with a red-hot iron 'in that part of his body where he permitted himself to be known in sodomitical practice.'"[16]

On the other hand, barely 40 years later, in 1404, two males, a 36-year-old man and his 17-year-old lover, were convicted of sodomy and instead of being burned to death were sentenced with a fine and exile. According to their trial record, it appears that the two had been involved in an intense love affair for two years, which was kept secret with the help of family and friends. The older man was quoted as saying that his love for the youth "meant more to him than his wife." The punishment imposed was a huge fine for the older man and exile for both, though later the fine was drastically reduced and the youth's sentence was remitted.[17] Summing up the implications of the broad range of laws and legal records of the period, the historian Michael Rocke observes that, "The wide-ranging norms contained in the laws of the fourteenth-century imply that homosexual activity was fairly common, for they suggest that male prostitution existed, that fathers sometimes promoted their sons' trysts, that innkeepers and property-owners often accommodated them, that people sang and wrote of sodomy's pleasures, and that any encounter between non-related men and boys could be suspect."[18]

In an effort to grapple with the continuing problem of sodomy in the city, the government of Florence in 1432 set up a special magistrate's office, called the Office of the Night, with a special charge to prosecute sodomists. As a result of an extensive examination of the well-kept records of the Office, Rocke has shown that an astounding percentage of the male population of Florence was implicated in sodomy between the years 1432, when the office was set up, and 1502, when it was disbanded. Drawing conclusions based on the percentage of cases resulting in convictions out of the total number of cases recorded between 1478 and 1502, Rocke says that it appears that as many as 17,000 men and boys were implicated in sodomy and investigated by the officers of the magistrate during the years the office was in operation.[19] Because the population of Florence was reduced by an estimated two thirds as a result of the Black Death in the 14th century, it was left with a relatively small population of about 40,000 during the period the office was doing its work. Of that total, the number of sexually active males would be not more than a quarter of the total, or 10,000 at any one time.* The fact that 17,000 men and boys out of a relatively small total population of sexually active men were investigated for sodomy during the 60 year run of the Office is dramatic evidence of the persistence of widespread homosexuality in Florence in the 15th century, during a time when the Florentines were regularly subjected to the anti-homosexual screed of preachers like Bernardino of Siena and Savonarola. As Rocke observes, "Sodomy was ostensibly the most dreaded and evil of sexual sins, and was among the most rigorously controlled of crimes, yet in the later 15th century the majority of local males at least once during their lifetimes were officially incriminated for engaging in homosexual relations."[20]

The continuing openness to homosexuality among the Florentines is illustrated in an anecdote related by the great master Michelangelo in a letter: a parent eager for the artist to take the man's son on as an apprentice coyly suggested that Michelangelo could have the boy "not only in my house, but also in my bed." Michelangelo did not accept the offer of "this consolation, not wanting to deprive" the father of it.[21] As a strategy to turn the males of the city from homosexuality, the city government even instituted municipal brothels and staffed them with prostitutes, an effort that Rocke said was "a resounding failure."[22] In the late 15th century, the city's Office of Decency had as many as 150 licensed female prostitutes under its direction. Creating and maintaining municipal brothels in an effort to turn males away from homosexuality was a strategy attempted in other areas of Europe during the period. According to the social historian J.L. Flandrin, "Every town in 15th-century France seems to have had a municipal brothel, usually built with public funds, regulated by the town council, and supposedly restricted to bachelors. The cost in municipal brothels was very cheap — about an eighth or tenth of a day's salary for a servant or journeyman."[23] The maintenance of municipal brothels for the specific purpose of luring men away from homosexual activity shows that by that time religious and civil authorities were so disturbed by the possibility of sodomy being practiced in their communities that they were willing to accept widespread extramarital heterosexual fornication if it could keep sodomy in check.

Elsewhere in Italy, despite the periodic anti-sexual campaigns of Dominican or Franciscan preachers, we can see during the Renaissance a measure of relaxation of social attitudes from the moral fervor of the late 13th century which produced the harsh anti-sodomy legislation of the Guelphs and the lay confraternities organized to help the Inquisition. A legacy of the prevalence of homosexuality in 15th- and 16th-century Italy can be found in the masterpieces of some of the greatest artists of the Renaissance, including Donatello, Botticelli, Michelangelo, Cellini, Leonardo da Vinci, Giovanni Bazzi and Caravaggio among many others. As Louis Crompton observes, "To experience the homoerotic side of this art, we do not need to study Italian or ferret out documents.... Few artifacts of the past reveal a homoerotic element at once so subtly pervasive and so accessible."[24]

While many of the masters were born in or worked in Florence, where their homosexual interests would have been easily tolerated, other masters spent either their entire lives or

*Assuming that approximately half of the population was male, and that half of the total city population would be under-age children, then no more than one quarter of the total would consist of sexually active males.

great length of time in other Italian cities, and appear to have had only occasional scrapes with the law because of their homosexual love lives. Caravaggio, whose work is known for its treatment of young adolescent males, and who was associated with young homosexual lovers his entire life, was born in Milan where he studied art, but spent his life working in Rome, Naples and Sicily. The master Giovanni Bazzi lived his professional life in Bernardino of Siena's home town, and was so notorious for his homosexuality that he went by the name Il Sodoma. Michelangelo started in Florence, but he spent a large part of his professional life in Rome where he produced some of his greatest masterpieces, including the frescoes of the Sistine Chapel. In fact, two of the popes Michelangelo is associated with are thought to have had their own homosexual affairs, including Sixtus IV, who was reputedly in love with his nephew, whom he made a cardinal at the age of 25, and Julius II, whom a contemporary writer claimed engaged in affairs with young men "without shame." Pope Leo X, according to rumors at the time, died while performing a sex act with a boy.[25]

While some segments of the Italian population clearly tolerated homosexuality, allowing many men to engage in same-sex love relationships, there was still the ever-present danger of the anti-sexual fanatics still to be found in the Roman church. While the popes of the early 16th century, Sixtus IV and Julius II, were urbane and pleasure-loving, for whom enforcement of the strict sexual morality of the church was a low priority, the mid-century saw the elevation to the papacy of Paul IV, an austere ascetic who revived the Inquisition and zealously pursued heretics and sexual non-conformists. Under Paul IV, according to one historian, "an actual reign of terror began, which filled all Rome with fear." A few years after Paul IV's death he was succeeded by Paul V, himself a former Inquisitor.[26]

Authoritarian Religion and Repression in Early Modern Europe

While the culturally rich and cosmopolitan atmosphere of Florence encouraged its citizens to ignore the strident sexual asceticism demanded by church, the religious atmosphere outside of Italy was far different. When the kingdoms of Aragon and Castile were united under Ferdinand and Isabella, and the monarchs in 1492 succeeded in conquering the last Moorish enclave in the kingdom of Granada, Spain was unified for the first time since the 8th century. The unified kingdom was a society of Catholics, Jews and Muslims who had co-existed peacefully in earlier times, but they had come to deeply distrust each other by the late 15th century. As a result of a wave of anti–Jewish persecutions fomented by church leaders in the late 14th century, great numbers of Jews converted to Christianity, which allowed them to escape persecution and enter some political offices. However, the newly converted Christians, called *conversos*, were disliked and distrusted by both the Catholics and the Jews, and in 1478 the monarch established the Spanish Inquisition for the purpose of detecting conversos whose conversion was insincere.

Before long, though, no resident of Spain felt safe from the Inquisition's reach. With the Inquisition, the monarch had a formidable prosecutorial organization with which it could insert itself into church affairs without the interference of the pope, rid the kingdom of distrusted minorities, and intimidate feudal nobles. Under the Spanish Inquisition, which operated from the late 15th century for three centuries, Spain saw a reign of some of the worst persecution of non-conformists Europe has ever seen. Its first Grand Inquisitor, and one of its most notorious leaders, the Dominican friar Tomas de Torquemada, instituted harsh rules of procedure for the court, ruthlessly enforced them and routinely employed torture to extract confessions.

In its zeal to prosecute non-conformity even Saint Ignatius Loyola and Saint Catherine of Avila were investigated, while books approved by the papacy were condemned. Over the course of its history an estimated 300,000 individuals were investigated, tried and sentenced by the inquisition for crimes ranging from heresy, "Lutheranism" and witchcraft to sodomy and bigamy.[27]

As would be expected, the harshly repressive environment in Spain created a populace fearful of sodomists and suspicious of strangers. Northern Europeans visiting in the 16th century put their lives at risk if they ventured into some areas of Spain without protection or apparent business. In one notorious incident in 1519, after a Franciscan priest preached a fiery sermon denouncing sodomy and blaming sodomists for an outbreak of the plague, an angry mob went out and hunted down four suspects who were summarily tried and burned at the stake. A fifth suspect they had rounded up turned out to be a member of the clergy and so was handed over to a church court for trial. When the ecclesiastical court gave the man a lesser penalty than burning, the mob seized the accused, strangled him and burned his body.[28]

As the authoritarian autocracy and its enforcement by the Spanish Inquisition was tightening its control over the people of Spain, the work of zealous religious reformers was creating a similarly oppressive religious atmosphere in Northern Europe. The Protestant Reformation began in the early 16th century in reaction to the corruption of the Catholic Church, particularly among its bishops and cardinals. Like the Gregorian reformers of the Middle Ages, the Protestant leadership believed that the church could be reformed only through the enforcement of a strict and exacting moral code. The movement's early leaders, Martin Luther in Germany and John Calvin in Switzerland, propounded a view of Christianity based heavily on the teachings of Saint Augustine, who in turn was heavily influenced by the anti-material, anti-sexual Neo-Platonism of the late Roman Empire (discussed in Chapter 9). According to Calvin, human life was deeply tainted by original sin, and because of this fallen state, people are incapable of following God's commandments. Only through divine intervention can people be turned from a state of sin to obedience to divine law. Like the moral theology of the early Christian Church, then, Protestant moral teaching was based on the assumption that the world and man's physical condition were irredeemably corrupted and that man's only hope for salvation lay in an austere and God-centered life. Because of this pessimistic view of man's condition, the early Protestant sects were uniformly negative to sexual indulgence, and preached a stern and austere lifestyle which, like the pronouncements of the early Medieval ascetic moralists, frowned on sexual pleasure and any form of worldly sensuality. The humanist and theologian Erasmus, who was living in Basel, Switzerland, during the rise of the Protestant Reformation, remarked in a letter about the fierce zealotry of the early Protestant reformers, writing, "I've seen them return from hearing a sermon as if inspired by an evil spirit. The faces of all showed a curious wrath and ferocity."[29]

Calvin established a strict authoritarian theocracy in Geneva which gave the clergy a voice in municipal actions, particularly with regard to enforcing theological and civil law among the people. The legal system imposed under Calvin included a stringent moral code for the city, and the Geneva authorities were particularly ruthless in prosecuting citizens for fornication, adultery, sodomy and witchcraft. The Calvinist government of Geneva soon became known throughout Europe for its zeal in prosecuting not only violations of civil law, but deviations from Calvin's religious teachings. With the formation of Calvin's Protestant theocracy, prosecutions for sexual offenses dramatically increased over the rate of prosecution in the previous century. Those guilty of fornication or adultery were publicly humiliated in public rituals while those convicted of sodomy were strangled and burned or drowned.[30] Men accused and tried for sodomy occupied positions across the social spectrum, including Pierre Canal, himself a Genevan official.[31]

As the Protestant movement spread to other regions of Northern Europe a similar zeal took hold of religious and civil authorities in prosecutions of sexual non-conformity. When religious conflict between Catholics and Protestants erupted in Belgium, the Protestants attacked Catholic monasteries as centers of sodomitical activity. In 1578 several Franciscan monks were convicted of sodomy and burned at the stake. In Ghent eight Franciscan and six Augustinian monks were similarly executed.[32]

Meanwhile in England, Henry VIII's dispute with the papacy and the removal of the English church from the control of the Church of Rome turned enforcement of moral offenses over to the state. Under Henry VIII the state now had assumed "the right to judge the sexual activities of its subjects and also to define what was 'natural' in terms of secular law." As Byrne Fone observes, "by politicizing and secularizing sodomy, Henry allowed English legal and popular opinion to construe sodomites themselves as enemies of the state, and sodomy as treason."[33] As in the case of the municipal governments in northern Italian cities in the mid–13th century, who seized the issue of the reform of sexual morals as a way to bring the corrupt feudal aristocracy to heel, the English parliament was populated with large numbers of anti-papist populists who resented the excesses of the English aristocracy and the Catholic Church, and used their power to legislate and enforce a strict code of sexual morality. Under Henry VIII and then Elizabeth I the death penalty was instituted for sodomy, a punishment that remained in English law until the late 19th century, when it was reduced to life imprisonment. Taking advantage of his legislation outlawing sodomy, the king used accusations of sodomy against monks as an excuse to close down and seize the wealth and property of the many Roman Catholic monasteries that had dotted the English countryside since the 11th century.[34]

In response to the spread of Protestantism in Europe, the Roman Catholic Church launched the Counter-Reformation, which took form under the stern and ascetic Pope Paul IV. Determined to end Protestantism, the pope followed an approach similar to that followed by Innocent III in the 13th century by embarking on a campaign to use the power of the church to strictly enforce canon law and prosecute heretics and moral offenders. To bring about enforcement of church doctrine, Paul IV revived the Inquisition. To restrict the dissemination of publications challenging the church's stands, the pope instituted a practice of censorship of prohibited books. In an effort to win back Protestant converts who had left the church in part because of the moral corruption of the clergy and church officials, Paul IV launched a vigorous campaign for moral reform, especially targeting sodomists among the clergy and in the laity. With the Protestant sects demanding conformance to a stringent moral code inspired by the anti-material and anti-sexual moral writings of Saint Augustine, and the Catholic Counter-Reformation launching a drive for enforcement of its own severe and repressive sexual morality, by the end of the 16th century all of Europe was under the jurisdiction of sternly authoritarian Protestant or Catholic governments, which promptly and harshly prosecuted and punished men or women accused of homosexual activity whenever they became known.

By the 17th century, after four centuries of religious preaching about the evil of sodomy and the dangers of sodomists to society, most of the population of Europe, especially the religiously devout or superstitious, were completely inculcated in the fear and loathing of homosexuality that in the early Middle Ages had been limited primarily to a small minority of clerical reformers. Indoctrinated in early life with the conviction that homosexual acts were a heinous crime and that homosexual urges were the work of the devil, the religiously devout European middle class commonly believed that homosexual sodomy was a crime against nature of such severity that to even name it seemed an act of impiety. The horror with which society reacted to sodomy is seen in the language of a sentencing judgment handed down by a Dutch court in 1730 against a sixteen-year-old boy who had engaged in homosexual relations with several wealthy men for whom he had worked as a servant boy. In sentencing the boy to be executed, the judgment referred to his crime as "the most horrible, yes unnatural sin of sodomy ... the mere thought of which makes one shudder and frightened."[35]

The Persistence of Ambisexuality in the Age of Homophobic Repression

The persecution and prosecution of men and women for homosexual acts in European history from the Renaissance to the modern age has been well documented in recent times and does not need to be recounted here.* Likewise, the histrionic and hyperbolic denunciations of "the sin whose name we dare not speak" uniformly spouted by religious moralists and civil authorities alike from the Middle Ages onward are familiar enough to the modern reader through the condemnations of homosexuality regularly heard today from conservative moralists from the Vatican to "family value" conservatives and television evangelists. Given the aggressive and unrelenting hostility of Western religious and government bodies to homosexuality since the Middle Ages, an animosity that has only abated in limited areas of the Western political world in recent decades, it is remarkable that homosexuality continued to persist among some groups in every Western country and in every age since the Middle Ages. The persistence of the homosexual drive of human sexuality in seeking expression under these harsh conditions is continued witness to the tenacity and durability of the ambisexual character of human nature.

Obviously a harshly repressive social atmosphere in which moral enforcement authorities are always on the alert to seize and prosecute homosexual offenders would require the homosexually inclined to take elaborate and creative precautions to keep their sexual activities hidden. Under such circumstances it is evident that a thriving homosexual subculture did develop in most major European cities at least from the period of the late Renaissance onward, networks that made it possible for not only exclusive homosexuals to conduct their sex lives, but which provided ambisexual youth and married men a homosexual alternative to meet their needs if they wished. Such an underground homosexual network was thriving in the cities of early 18th-century Holland under the noses of puritanical religious and government authorities until the sodomitical activities came to their attention through crimes of extortion committed by gangs of youths taking advantage of the middle-class homosexuals.

In Amsterdam, men looking for homosexual trysts would cruise the streets near the Town Hall and the financial exchange, and in the hallways of the Town Hall itself. The cruising men would recognize each through the use of codes, and would go to one of their homes or to an inn for their liaison — though court records show one pair who consummated their relations in the Town Hall itself. In the Hague, men cruised for each other in shady streets near the city park and would signal to each other through a wave of their handkerchiefs. A favorite

*The interested reader can find a detailed treatment of the subject in Kent Gerard and Gert Hekma, editors, Male Homosexuality in Renaissance and Enlightenment Europe (New York: Harrington Park Press, 1989); Byrne Fone, Homophobia: A History (New York: Metropolitan Books, 2000); and Chapters 9, 10, 11, 12 and 14 of Louis Crompton, Homosexuality and Civilization (Cambridge, Mass.: The Belknap Press of Harvard University, 2003), all of whom are cited in this chapter.

place for trysts was a local inn run by an innkeeper who himself was a member of the underground network. Similar inns hospitable to homosexuals steadily increased in number in Amsterdam, the Hague and in Utrecht in the first quarter of the 18th century. In the latter city, circles of homosexual friends developed around a number of middle class merchants. Among these groups long-term bonds sometimes developed between pairs of men, some of whom entered into formal relationships, such as a pair of young men who executed a "marriage contract" with each other that stipulated that neither of them would have sex with another male without first informing their partner.[36] In 1730 the government authorities were tipped off to the presence of these underground networks, and launched a major offensive to root out sodomy in the republic that used secret denunciations and torture to extract confessions. Before the campaign was over as many as a hundred men and boys had been convicted, put to death and the trial records burned with them.[37]

In 17th- and 18th-century England, prosecution of sodomy, and its resulting visibility, swung back and forth depending on the ascendancy of authoritarian moralists. In the early years of the break of the Church of England with Rome, sodomy and moral laxness were strongly associated with Roman Catholicism by populist anti–Catholic partisans. Henry VIII's daughter Queen Elizabeth I endorsed her father's stern anti-sodomy laws, but nevertheless an atmosphere of permissiveness pervaded her reign which saw thinly veiled homosexual love among her courtiers and a degree of moral laxness among the population. The relaxed atmosphere and greater levels of social tolerance of the Elizabethan era were very likely a contributing factor in the production of one of the greatest literary and intellectual outpourings in Western Civilization.[38] Showing that laxity in conformance to sexual morality is not an impediment to national greatness, the era also saw the laying of the foundations for Britain's later imperial dominance.

In Elizabethan England homosexuality was particularly associated with the theater world, the medium of several of the era's greatest geniuses. The works of several Elizabethan writers contain explicit references to homosexuality in the theater world, including Phillip Stubbs in *Anatomie of Abuses*, Edward Guilpin in *Skialetheia*, and Michael Drayton in *The Moone-Calfe*. The homosexuality of Christopher Marlowe, one of the greatest poets and dramatists of the era, is not in doubt. A contemporary of Shakespeare and considered in the top echelon of English-language dramatists, Marlowe's works were held in especially high esteem by his Elizabethan contemporaries, including Shakespeare himself. The bard's early plays show Marlowe's influence, and not only employed themes used by Marlowe but even quoted from one of his plays in one instance.*

Marlowe's *Edward II*, a play about the 14th-century homosexual English king murdered in a plot concocted by his wife and rebellious nobles, features homosexuality as a central theme. Direct references to male homosexuality are included in two other plays, *Dido, Queen of Carthage*, and *Hero and Leander*. In the latter play, Marlowe wrote of Leander, that "in his looks were all that men desire." When Leander swims in the sea, Triton the sea god becomes sexually aroused, "imagining that Ganymede, displeas'd ... the lusty god embrac'd him, call'd him love ... and steal a kiss ...upon his breast, his thighs, and every limb."[39] According to Richard Baines, an informer who testified against Marlowe in a trial, he heard Marlowe say that "all they that love not tobacco and boys were fools" and that "Saint John the Evangelist was bedfellow to Christ and leaned always in his bosom, that he used him as the sin-

---

Themes from Dido, Queen of Carthage *are found in* Antony and Cleopatra, *from* Edward II *in* Richard III, *and from* Dr. Faustus *in* Macbeth. Shakespeare's *As You Like It* quotes from Hero and Leander: *"Dead Shepherd, now I find thy saw of might, 'Who ever loved that loved not at first sight?'"*)

ners of Sodom." The playwright Thomas Kyd also reported that Marlowe had imputed homosexuality to Christ: "He would report Saint John to be Our Savior Christ's Alexis (the beloved of Corydon in a famous Eclogue of Virgil). I cover it with reverence and trembling that is that Christ did love him with an extraordinary love."[40] Even after Marlowe was stabbed to death in a mysterious brawl, his wild reputation continued. In a play put on by Cambridge University students in 1598, a character expresses admiration for his genius but horror for his lifestyle: "Pity it is that wit so ill should dwell, Wit lent from heaven, but vices sent from hell."[41]

Based on obvious references to a male love object in the Sonnets, homosexuality has also been attributed to William Shakespeare, or the writer who went by that name. However, because of Shakespeare's lofty status the claim has engendered great controversy. Crompton notes that an appendix to a 1944 edition of the Sonnets includes the opinions of no fewer than 40 different commentators on whether the Sonnets do or do not prove that the sentiments expressed by Shakespeare therein were based on homosexual love. As early as 1780 a critic, George Stevens, in writing about the Sonnets, wrote scornfully "It is impossible to read this fulsome panegyrick, addressed to a male object, without an equal mixture of disgust and indignation."[42]

When Queen Elizabeth died in 1603 she was succeeded by James I, whose court was particularly known for its moral laxity. There is little dispute that James I himself was primarily homosexual. Though he married Anne of Denmark and fathered seven children, he seldom saw the queen after the last was born. Throughout his life James was linked with a succession of male favorites, all of whom benefited — some spectacularly — from his affection. When James was 14 years old and reigning as King James VI of Scotland, he fell in love with Esmé Stewart, his father's French-born cousin and a handsome, elegant and charming man. In 1581 James made Stewart Earl of Lennox, and a year later Duke of Lennox. Because of the religious animosities at the time, the young king's making his French Catholic cousin the only duke in Scotland raised the ire of the Calvinist Scottish nobility, and within a year Stewart had been exiled to France. A few years later James shrewdly arranged the marriage of Lennox's sister to another companion, George Gordon, Earl of Huntley. The marriage provided justification for James to elevate Gordon to the position of Captain of the Guards, which allowed Huntley to station himself in the young king's bed at night as "body guard." In addition to Huntley, James had affairs with several other youthful nobles, including Alexander Lindsay, Lord Spynie, whom James nicknamed "Sandie" and appointed vice-chamberlain, and Francis Stewart Hepburn, Earl of Bothwell. On one occasion James caused a minor scandal when he casually kissed and embraced Bothwell in full view of the public.[43]

At the death of Elizabeth I in 1603 James was proclaimed king and was crowned King James I of England. The next major love of the king's life was another Scot, James Hay, a young man of noble birth who had spent time at the French court which gave him the grace and refinement in manners that James admired. Hay was quickly promoted, becoming first Viscount Doncaster and then Earl of Carlisle in short order. He proved his worth, though, by leading several successful diplomatic missions for James which he conducted with a high degree of skill and tact. Aside from his charm, his popularity in the court was assured by the extravagant feasts and entertainments he would stage — funded by the king. Desirous of marital unions to ease relations between his Scottish retainers and the English, in 1607 James arranged an English bride for Hay, and to overcome resistance by the lady's father, who didn't care for Scots, James gave the father a barony.[44]

With Hay married off, King James was in need of another companion and found one in Robert Carr, a handsome son of minor Scottish nobility who had started in the royal service at the age of 16 as a running-page, a boy who would run alongside the royal carriage. When James decided footmen were more dignified, Carr was sent back to Scotland. He soon returned to London, though, and in 1607 while the 20-year-old Carr was participating in a game of tilt, a kind of jousting match on horseback, he fell off his horse — some say conveniently — directly in front of the king's box, leaving him with a broken leg. Recognizing his good-looking former page, the king rushed on to the field, and to the astonishment of the assembled crowd cradled the young Carr in his arms. King James, then, personally supervised the young man's recovery, and visited his hospital room frequently.[45]

A great love that seems to have been genuine developed between the two, and Carr was appointed a gentleman of the Royal Bedchamber, later served as confidential secretary to the king, and eventually was made the earl of Somerset. Despite his rapid rise, Carr's devotion appeared to be genuine, and he never seems to have abused his influence with the king. When the king was afflicted with gout, Carr tended to his every need and stayed with him as he was nursed back to health. The king returned the devotion, and when Carr fell in love with Lady Frances Howard, the king arranged a munificent wedding for the couple and personally presided over it. Unfortunately, Lady Howard became implicated in the mysterious death of Sir Charles Overbury, an intimate friend of Carr's, and while Carr was never directly implicated other than as an unwitting accomplice, his career was nevertheless finished, and he ended his days banished to the countryside, where he died in near poverty.

Not long after Carr was married off to Lady Howard, James found another companion in George Villiers, the son of penniless rural gentry whom many called the most beautiful man in Europe. Introduced to the king in 1614 when Villiers was 22 years old, he was knighted the next year and made a gentleman of the Royal Bedchamber, a time when their first sexual encounter took place, according to love letters between the two. From that point his rapid rise through the peerage was spectacular. He was created baron Whaddon and viscount Villiers in 1616, earl of Buckingham in 1617 and then marquess of Buckingham in 1618. The attention and benefits bestowed on Villiers was so great that it became a cause of concern in the king's government, and in 1617 James found himself forced to defend his right to love men before the Privy Council. In the debate before the council, Sir John Oglander stated that "The King is wondrous passionate, a lover of his favourites beyond the love of men to women ... I never yet saw any fond husband make so much or so great dalliance over his beautiful spouse as I have seen King James over his favourites, especially Buckingham." The king's response, mentioned earlier in Chapter 9, compared his love for Buckingham with the love of Jesus for his disciple John: "I, James, am neither a god nor an angel, but a man like any other. Therefore I act like a man and confess to loving those dear to me more than other men. You may be sure that I love the Earl of Buckingham more than anyone else, and more than you who are here assembled. I wish to speak in my own behalf and not to have it thought to be a defect, for Jesus Christ did the same, and therefore I cannot be blamed. Christ had John, and I have George."[46] The king's homosexual love life was so well known in England at that time that a witty epigram making the rounds of London society went, *Rex fuit Elizabeth: nunc est regina Jacobus*, "Elizabeth was King: now James is Queen."[47]

During the height of the king's relationships with Carr and Villiers, the government of James continued to harshly enforce anti-sodomy laws, a hard line that Louis Crompton believes may have been an attempt to deflect criticism of his sexual lifestyle. In a book he wrote on kingship, James listed sodomy among those "horrible crimes which ye are bound in conscience never to forgive." In a letter to his chancellor, Lord Burleigh, in 1610, discussing pardons customarily issued at the conclusion of a session of parliament, James specifically excluded sodomites from the royal mercy.[48] For the obvious contradiction between the king's public stance on enforcement of sodomy and his equally public homosexual love life, the British jurist and philosopher Jeremy Bentham denounced James as a hypocrite.[49]

Not surprisingly, King James was perfectly comfortable with homosexual relationships among members of his court. Sir Francis Bacon, the brilliant scientist and philosopher, who is credited with formulating the principles of scientific induction, also served as the king's lord chancellor. The facts of Bacon's life have led several historians to believe he was primarily homosexual.[50] Bacon, also an intimate friend of Villiers, was married, but lavished affection on dozens of Welsh serving boys, many of whom slept with him in his bed, and some of whom were, unlike his wife, included in his will. Bacon's mother criticized him for his habit of sleeping with his servant boys, not because of the buggery involved, but because it was unbecoming for an aristocrat to sleep with a servant in the master bedroom of the house. She thought a lower-ranking bedroom would have been more appropriate.[51]

Notwithstanding the king's official hard line against sodomy, some level of popular tolerance, if not approval, of sodomy can be gauged from Jacobean literature of John Donne, Ben Jonson, Michael Drayton and Thomas Middleton, which satirized the ambisexual license among the young dandies of early 17th-century London. According to the British historian Alan Bray, the literature is "remarkably consistent: the sodomite is a young man-about-town, with his mistress on one arm and his 'catamite' on the other; he is indolent, extravagant and debauched."[52]

As the love relationship between King James and Villiers developed, the younger man quickly drew the king into a period of riotous living, frequent drunken feasts and "a fair amount of corruption and debauchery." The king's favors to Buckingham were so great that Villiers was able to enrich and ennoble his entire family all the way out to second cousins once removed, and crush anyone who got in his way. The historian Rictor Norton observes that at the same time, though, Buckingham brought about needed reform and greatly improved efficiency to the government, albeit with himself at the center, and that modern historians are increasingly recognizing that he probably eliminated much more court corruption than he engendered. Nonetheless, according to Norton, many of the courtiers were

> so eager to draw James's favor away from Buckingham, solely for motives of self-interest, that they began what was laughingly referred to as "the mustering of minions." Every day some aspiring Lord — notably Sir William Manson — would hire a troupe of handsome young ragamuffin boys, scrub their faces clean with curdled milk, curl their hair, powder them and perfume them, dress them in silk and lace, and lead them in dainty procession around the throne in order to seduce the King's favour.[53]

Delighted at first by this display, the king quickly realized that he was being made a fool of and had it stopped. The king was at last coming to his senses, and in 1618 the period of riotous debauchery ceased. His relationship with Villiers, though, continued to deepen, and when the king was against afflicted with gout, Villiers tended to him daily. In 1619 the king made Villiers lord high admiral, and in 1623 duke of Buckingham, which made Villiers at that time the most powerful man in England after James himself. Villiers was also well loved by the king's son and heir, Charles, and when James died in 1625 and his son ascended the throne as Charles I, Villiers remained on as a favorite of the king and continued his prominent role in government.

Charles I, who may have carried on some homosexual affairs in his youth, was less tolerant than his father of debauchery among his courtiers, and so a contemporary writes, "the fools, bawds, mimics and catamites of the former court grew out of fashion, and the nobility and courtiers who did not quite abandon their debaucheries, yet so reverenced the king as to retire into corners to practice them."[54] The 1631 prosecution for sodomy and execution of the Roman Catholic earl of Castlehaven, a prominent supporter of Charles I, was not, as it may have seemed, a reflection of Charles' attitudes to enforcement, but the result of a scheme by Castlehaven's powerful and well-connected wife and her friends, and was seen as an indirect attack on Charles for his perceived sympathies for Roman Catholics. Like the Castlehaven case, the few executions for sodomy that took place in England in the hundred years after the Buggery Act of 1533 all seem to have had an element of political motivation behind them.[55]

As the reign of Charles I continued, the strains between the parliament and the monarchy had frayed to such a point that the monarchy of Charles is now regarded as a thorough disaster. His reign ended with the English Civil War, his own execution, and the rule of the populist Puritans of Oliver Cromwell. Cromwell's government enforced an austere and sober public morality which resulted in the closing of theaters, alehouses, brothels and gambling establishments, while his Puritan followers made their way through Britain's churches and cathedrals destroying the stained glass windows and lopping the heads off of carved images and statues of saints — they thought the images of saints in the stained glass and statues to be sacrilegious. The English soon grew tired of the stern and prudish rule of Cromwell, and publicly rejoiced with the Restoration of the monarchy and the ascension to the throne of Charles II in 1660. Though King Charles II seems to have been strictly heterosexual, his dissolute personal life set the tone for his court, among whom the diarist Samuel Pepys wrote that homosexual liaisons were openly conducted with impunity.[56]

Departing from the moral revulsion found in much European writing since the late Middle Ages, the literature and drama of the Restoration portray sodomy as a subject of humor and satire. A play entitled *Sodomy or the Quintessence of Debauchery*, a farce written by the overtly homosexual Earl of Rochester was performed before the court of Charles II to much amusement.[57] A 1673 work ridiculing the metaphysical poet Andrew Marvell referred to him as an impotent homosexual. A popular tabloid in circulation during the reign of Charles II carried a story that claimed the pope had authorized his cardinals to engage in sodomy during the three hottest months of the year. Men in Restoration comedy were, like the "men-about-town" in Jacobean literature, portrayed as having both mistresses and young male boy friends.[58]

Throughout the 17th century, from the death of Elizabeth I, through the monarchies of King James and Charles I, the civil war, the Restoration and the reign of Charles II, sodomy remained a moral offense of the highest gravity and a crime on a par with murder and treason. Alan Bray has remarked that despite the fact that the dominant intellectual, legal and moral traditions uniformly condemned homosexuality in the harshest terms, the rate of prosecution was minimal, even though there was participation in homosexuality by a significant segment of English society throughout most of the century. Bray says that this should by no means be taken as tolerance, however. "It was rather a reluctance to recognize homosexual behavior, a sluggishness in accepting that what was being seen was indeed the fearful sin of sodomy."[59] Put another way, a large portion of the English population employed conscious denial to cope with the inevitable acting out of homosexual feelings or desires that are an inherent part of human sexual nature. As long as no one called attention to the true nature of the sexual activity that occurred, it could be ignored.

With the overthrow of the Catholic James II and the ascension of Protestant William III of Orange to the English throne in 1689, Roman Catholicism was relegated to the position of being a barely tolerated minority religion, while government power shifted dramatically from the crown to the Protestant middle class-dominated Parliament. These changes contributed to a tightening of public morals over the sporadically and unevenly enforced norms of the previous century. While the homosexual love life of James I was the subject of jokes — if it was mentioned at all — the same-sex loves of the bisexual William III were alluded to in coarse and caustic verses circulated by his political enemies in order to undermine the public's confidence in the king. In the newly hostile climate, the sodomite was pushed firmly into the closet, and as a result in 18th-century London an active homosexual underground or subculture began to develop. The centers of this underground were called molly houses, taverns somewhat comparable to modern gay bars, inconspicuous on the outside, but places where men could go and enjoy the company of others like them.

A description of a visit to one such establishment in 1725 was provided by Samuel Stevens, who is thought to have been spying on the establishment for the Societies for the Reformation of Manners, a prudish religious organization that, like organizations of the religious right in modern America, agitated for the prosecution of sodomists and prostitutes and the enforcement of the Sabbath. In a later trial of one of the house's occupants, Stevens says, "I found between 40 and 50 men making love to one another, as they called it. Sometimes they would sit in one another's lap, kissing in a lewd manner and using their hands indecently. Then they would get up, dance and make curtsies, and mimic the voices of women." In the trial of the proprietor of another such house, a police agent who investigated the scene testified about what he saw when he entered the establishment: "I found a company of men fiddling and dancing and singing bawdy songs, kissing and using their hands in a very unseemly manner.... In a large room there we found one a-fiddling and eight more a-dancing.... Then they sat in one another's lap, talked bawdy, and practiced a great many indecencies."[60]

The trial testimony of Stevens and the police agent was given at trials resulting from a series of raids on molly houses in 1725–1726, an enforcement campaign instigated by the Societies for the Reformation of Manners. Within a year or so of the 1726 trials, however, pressure relaxed, and life in the molly houses continued. Bray says that similar episodes of energetic enforcement had occurred in 1699 and 1707, and were to recur sporadically through the rest of the century.

Elsewhere in 17th- and 18th-century Europe a similar dichotomy continued between the laws on sodomy and actual practice, in most areas managed in a similar way, looking the other way if the perpetrators were in positions of prominence or influence, through denial of the obvious, or the kind of underground that developed in London and the cities of Holland. Sodomy "did not exist" in proper society, and because in most of society it had been driven under ground it was seldom prosecuted unless flagrant examples were discovered.

In 16th-century France, bloody conflicts erupted between the Huguenots and Catholics. The defensiveness of the Catholics for moral corruption ensured that the official government line on sodomy would be severe and strictly enforced. Hoping that enforcement of popular morality in France and the imposition of a work ethic would bring the religious conflicts to a halt, royal officials and the urban merchant bourgeoisie joined forces with the church to enact a strict moral code which reinforced prohibitions against sodomy and resulted in the banning of prostitution, nudity in art, immodest clothing and concubinage.[61] However, for members of the ruling aristocracy, it was another matter.

Henry III, who held the throne during the worst of France's religious conflicts, is considered to have been an able king, but was a man of wide contradictions. A courageous and gifted leader on the battlefield, he was a flamboyant queen in his private life who surrounded himself with dozens of prettified dandies — most with lofty aristocratic titles — who referred to each other by female epithets, and were known as the king's *mignons*, from the French adjective for "pretty," "adorable," or "endearing." The mignons were subdivided into *mignons d'état*, and *mignons de couchette* — the former were the young aristocrats who supported Henry politically, the latter his "bedroom favorites."[62] Well liked by his subjects, Henry's rule was nonetheless overwhelmed by the religious animosities that tore French society apart during the 16th century, and in the end the king was assassinated by a fanatical Dominican monk.

Henry III was succeeded by Henry of Navarre, who ruled as Henry IV, the first of the Bourbon line. Henry IV was resolutely heterosexual and had two of his courtiers burned at the stake as an example after they had engaged in sexual relations with two of his pages. Nonetheless, a contemporary writer noted that sodomy remained a continuing practice in the court, so much so that "it was best to keep one's hands in one's trousers."[63] After Henry IV was assassinated by a Catholic extremist, he was succeeded by his son, Louis XIII, whose sexual interest in other males is thought to explain the 20 year time span after his marriage that it took him to produce an heir, the future Louis XIV. In 1624, at the age of 23, Louis had the foresight to name Cardinal Richelieu as his chief adviser, and with the cardinal's assistance consolidated the rule of the monarchy over the troublesome nobility, brought the Huguenots into subservience to the crown, and made France the most powerful nation in Europe. Cardinal Richelieu's only concern with the king's love life was that his lovers be politically innocuous. Unlike Henry III, Louis XIII lacked any effeminate airs and was devoted to hunting and other manly pastimes. [64]

The first great love of Louis' life was Francois de Baradas, a handsome and athletic officer of the royal household. Of their relationship, a contemporary chronicler wrote that the king "loved Baradas violently; he was accused of committing a hundred filthy acts with him." Baradas apparently didn't know when he was ahead, and not content with the favors he had been granted, he became restless and when on a visit to Nantes he had sexual affairs with a couple of nobles. When Louis heard about it, he became jealous and decided he no longer loved the young officer. Next in line was Saint-Simon, a youth of far more tact and grace who remained with Louis for ten years and ended up as a duke. When Saint-Simon made the mistake of associating too closely with Richelieu's enemies, the cardinal had him banished. After Saint-Simon, Louis tried his luck with a lady, Madame d'Hautefort, but like her predecessor in the role, she couldn't resist involving herself in court politics on the side of the opposition to Richelieu. In response Richelieu craftily went about undermining Louis' trust in the lady and then ensured her departure by bringing in another young man for the king, the exceptionally handsome Marquis de Cinq Mars.[65]

With beautiful features, and elegantly dressed, Cinq Mars captivated the king, and lifted him out of a morose depression. Unfortunately for Louis, Cinq Mars was a spoiled aristocrat and the relationship was marked by a number of petulant quarrels, with the king sending a series of anguished letters to Richelieu complaining about their fights and the sleep he was losing over them. According to a courtier's account, a friend surprised Cinq Mars in his apartments one day when the young aristocrat was in the process of rubbing jasmine oil all over his body. "A moment after came a knock. It was the king. It would appear ... he was anointing himself for a contest." Cinq Mars met his downfall when he imprudently allied himself with a plot to assassinate Richelieu, and involved himself in secret negotiations with the Spanish, all of which was discovered by the cardinal. The king did not let his affection for Cinq Mars interfere with his duties as king, however, and had the young man beheaded for treason.[66]

Louis XIV, the Sun King, whose private life was spent with a lengthy series of mistresses who bore him 18 illegitimate children, ruthlessly enforced the sodomy laws during his long reign. Yet at the same time his court was occupied by some of the most flamboyant homosexuals in French history, and one of the most conspicuous of them all was the king's own brother, Philippe, Duc d'Orléans. The king's hostility to homosexuality was displayed in 1682 when he discovered the existence of a secret brotherhood composed of some of France's highest-ranking young aristocrats. The secret society modeled itself in a tongue-and-cheek way after a noble order, calling itself the La Sainte Congregation des Glorieux Pederasts (Sacred Fraternity of Glorious Pederasts), and devoted itself to the total avoidance of women — and a corresponding devotion to men. To identify themselves, the members carried around their necks under their shirts a cross with an emblem of a young man trampling a woman like a caricature of the familiar image of Saint Michael trampling the Devil. Among the members was Prince Louis de Vermandois, the king's 15-year-old illegitimate son, an exceptionally beautiful boy who had been legitimized and marked for high office. When the king caught wind of the group he quickly disbanded it and punished its members. Prince Louis was whipped in front of the king and exiled, along with another prince, two counts, two chevaliers, and a marquis.[67]

But as Crompton remarks, "these trials were nothing compared with what Louis had to bear at the bejeweled hands of his brother, Philippe d'Orléans." In early childhood, Philippe was dressed in girls' clothes by his mother because of his beauty, and all his life he had a fascination with women's dresses, jewels, perfumes, wigs, ribbons and high heels. Philippe's wife, Princess Elizabeth-Charlotte, daughter of the prince-elector of Palatine, tolerated her husband's tastes and love life, but kept her provincial relatives back in Germany fully informed of the promiscuous life at glamorous Versailles. Her letters, which cover a 50-year span and detail the love life of her husband and dozens of other men of rank, have been called "an encyclopedia of homosexuality."[68] In one of her letters describing her husband, she wrote that he "has the manners of a woman rather than those of a man. He likes to play, chat, eat well, dance and perform his toilet — in short, everything that women love .... Except in war, he could never be prevailed upon to mount a horse. The soldiers said of him that he was more afraid of the heat of the sun, or the black smoke of gunpowder, than he was of musket bullets."[69] Indeed, despite his extreme femininity, Philippe was regarded as a surprisingly effective warrior. In 1677 during war with Holland, Philippe was given credit for defeating the forces of William of Orange in the battle of Cassel.[70]

In 1688 Philippe had his *bon amour*, the handsome but impecunious Chevalier de Lorraine, installed in the grandest apartment in the Palais Royal, Philippe's residence in Paris. Lorraine remained in his elegant perch in the Palais Royal for the next 30 years, serving as a sort of "official mistress" and head of household to Philippe, all the while wheedling enormous amounts of money out of Philippe to pay for his mistresses, male lovers and extravagant lifestyle.[71] In a letter to her half-sister in which she is attempting to educate her on the sex life of Versailles, Princess Elizabeth-Charlotte wrote, "Anyone who would detest all who loved boys could not be friends with ... six persons here. There are all kinds of them. There are some of them who hate women like death and can only love men. Others love men and women ... others love only children of ten or eleven years, others youths from seventeen to twenty-five and these are the most numerous."[72] In another letter, she explained how those practicing sodomy justify their behavior given the condemnation of the practices in scripture:

> Those who give themselves up to this vice, which believing in Holy Scripture, imagine that it was only a sin when there were few people in the world, and that now the earth is populated it may be regarded as a divertissement. Among the common people, indeed, accusations of this kind are, so far as possible, avoided; but among persons of quality, it is publicly spoken of; it is considered a fine saying that since Sodom and Gomorrah, the Lord has punished no one for such offenses.[73]

The enthusiasm of the young aristocracy for homosexuality, despite the harsh laws punishing it, was evidently widely known in 18th-century France. A diarist writing in Paris in the middle of the century commented on the widespread homosexuality among young males of the aristocracy, writing that the "vice of the ass," which had been popular in France for a long time, was in his own time more in vogue than ever. "To the chagrin of the ladies of the court, the young lords devote themselves to it with a vengeance."[74]

Though the French court was filled with unceasing sexual indulgence, both heterosexual and homosexual, the standard for the middle class and the peasants was of unflinching conformity to the church's sexual moral code. The strict moral enforcement of 18th-century Paris necessitated an underground network, like that found in contemporary Holland and London. In fact, the same thriving homosexual subculture of Paris noted by writers in the mid–13th century was still going strong five centuries later, despite wars, plagues, and periodic campaigns by the authorities to stamp out the vice of Sodom. In the early 18th century under the reign of Louis XV the police of Paris began a systematic surveillance of those they knew to be involved in homosexual activity and their cruising and meeting places. More interested in maintaining public order than in enforcing religious morality, they generally only arrested individuals in cases where behavior outrageous to public decency was reported, or when offenses were committed which involved the corruption of minors, political intrigue or involvement in related crimes, such as kidnapping. In other words, where the participants used discretion and good judgment and did not involve minors, they were generally ignored. When in 1750 two young men, a 18-year-old and a 24-year-old, were caught in the performance of the act on a public street, the authorities were forced to act, and the pair were burned at the stake to set an example.[75]

A commander of the Paris police wrote in his *Memoires* that in 1725 the number of sodomites in Paris was estimated to be 20,000. Fifty-five years later a police commissioner showed friends "a large book in which were listed all the names of pederasts known to the police," a figure the commissioner put at 40,000 at the time. Another police official, expressing dismay at the apparent spread of open homosexuality from the nobility to the rest of society, wrote, "This vice, which used to be called the *beau vice* because it had only affected noblemen, men of wit and intelligence, or the Adonis, has become such a fashion that there is no order of society, from dukes on down to footmen, that is not infected."[76]

Male prostitution was so well developed as an institution in Paris that there were gradations for different classes of prostitutes, with their fees set accordingly. As described by the French write Honoré Mirabeau:

> Young people who consign themselves to the profession are carefully classified — so far do the regulatory systems extend. They are inspected. Those who can act as active and passive, who are handsome, ruddy, well built, filled out, are reserved for the great lords or get very good fees from bishops and financiers. Those who are deprived of their testicles — or in the terms of the profession who do not possess their 'weaver's weights' — but who give and receive, form the second class. They too are expensive, for women use them as well as men. Those who are so worn out that they are no longer capable of erection, though they have all the necessary organs of pleasures, set themselves down as pure passives and compose the third class.[77]

Homosexuality among women in 18th-century France was well documented, as well. Actresses and courtesans were commonly believed to be lesbians, and lesbianism among nuns in convents was frequently mentioned in plays and in novels, such as Diderot's *La Religieuse,* which dwells on lesbianism and sadism in a convent. Another writer, Pidauzet de Mairobert, in his *Apologie de la Secte Anandryne,* claimed that a lesbian organization similar to the La Sainte Congregation des Glorieux Pederasts (Sacred Fraternity of Glorious Pederasts) that so enraged Louis XIV had branches all over France and included many upper-class women.[78]

Sodomy at Sea

In the all-male world of the merchant fleets and navies of 17th- and 18th-century Europe sodomy, not surprisingly, was a common feature of the lives of the fleets' officers and seamen, even under the notoriously harsh military regimen of the British Royal Navy. When Winston Churchill was named first lord of the Admiralty just prior to World War I he was asked to name the traditions of the Royal Navy. "Rum, sodomy and the lash," he famously quipped.[79] A navy regulation instituted in 1627 required that "If any Person belonging to the Fleet shall commit Buggery or Sodomy, he shall be punished with Death." However, records of enforcement indicate that prosecutions were infrequent and occurred only in instances where the behavior of the accused was excessive or abusive, or when other crimes were present.[80] In the early 1900s a British naval official noted that "Homosexuality was rife…. In some services (the Austrian and French, for instance) nobody ever remarks about it, taking such a thing as a natural proceeding…. To my knowledge, sodomy is a regular thing on ships that go on long cruises. In the warships, I would say that the sailor preferred it."[81] While sexual activity among sailors declined in the 20th century with the advent of faster steamships which greatly shortened time at sea, in the fleets up until the end of the 19th century sodomy at sea was the norm.

The all-male conditions on board a navy or merchant ship in the 17th and 18th centuries, where the men and boys lived in close quarters with each other on voyages that could last two or three years, were naturally conducive to homosexuality. Furthermore, the type of men who chose a life in the merchant fleet or the navy very probably included a larger percentage of males more interested in their own sex than the opposite. If a young man had a real interest in women and a repulsion for sex with other males, it is very unlikely that he would choose a career at sea which would leave him no contact with women for years at a time. Young men with active heterosexual interests could, if they wanted, choose to serve aboard the large fleet of ships that served the coastal trade of England and the Continent, in which they were in port frequently, and rarely away from their homes for long periods.[82]

Most of the seamen in the Royal Navy during the 17th and early 18th centuries were volunteers, and because their service was by choice it is a reasonable assumption that they would be of the type of personality who most likely would not have greatly missed the company of women. However, during time of war, to meet the soaring demand for seamen, the Royal Navy began the practice of pressing young men into service, by sending naval units through England's towns and cities picking suitable young men off the streets for service. But even in cases where young men ended up in the navy against their will, and found themselves in an environment in which the only sexual outlet was with another male, it is unlikely that many would have resisted such a release, given what we know about the sex drives of young men, and the atmosphere of sexual tolerance of 17th-century England in which they grew up. Because of these various factors, there is little reason to believe that homosexuality would not have been at least as common among seamen among both the merchant and navy fleets of 17th- and early 18th-century Europe as among other all-male societies in history.

There is also evidence that a large portion of the population of boys and young men from whom seamen were drawn would have been individuals who already had homosexual experience. In 17th-century England numerous bands of youths composed of sons of poor families, orphans, runaways, seasonal workers or former apprentices roamed the countryside of England. Disparaging accounts of them by contemporary writers portrayed them as sinister gangs of miscreants with dissolute habits who were a threat to the survival of the nation. Characterizing gangs of 10- to 20-year-old unarmed males as a threat to the nation that was emerging as one of the most powerful nations in Europe was, of course, wild exaggeration. However, the charge of some of the writers that sodomy was a requirement for admission to their groups most likely had an element of truth to it since it would have been the only sexual outlet for the boys at an age when their sex drives were at their peak. This was during a time, it should be remembered, before the mostly middle-class parliament had gained control of the government and at a time when enforcement of sexual moral standards throughout the country was relatively lax. [83]

In their wanderings, the youthful gangs generally ended up in the Southeast coastal towns, where many joined the merchant fleet or the Royal Navy as cabin boys or seamen.[84] Because of the influx of young males into the coastal towns, and the regular intervals when ships were in port unloading or loading cargo or for repairs, there was often a sizable population of boys and young men hanging out in the streets of the sea ports looking for work or other divertissement, a number that could double during seasonal lulls in shipping. One late 17th-century observer complaining about them wrote: "The streets are crowded with boys intended for the sea service, who spend their time in open violation of decency, good order and morality. There are often fifteen hundred seamen and boys, who arrive from the whale fishery, and often double that number of unemployed sailors, who are left at leisure to exercise their dissolute manners."[85]

One of the most prominent aspects of the maritime world of the 17th and early 18th centuries, and a subject of numerous romantic novels and Hollywood movies, were the pirates and buccaneers who preyed on commercial traffic on the shipping lanes between Europe and colonial outposts, especially the treasure laden Spanish galleons carrying gold, silver and jewels from the New World to Spain. Men and boys of many nationalities found there way into the crews of pirate ships, though the largest segment of the pirates of the period were English, with the French and Dutch also providing sizable contingents. In the middle of the 17th century the English government realized that supporting and promoting pirate attacks on Spanish shipping would be a cheap way to wage war on the Spanish, and so authorized a number of pirates — referred to as buccaneers or privateers to distinguish them from other pirates — to attack Spanish shipping, under the condition that a portion of the booty went to the government. Francis Drake and Henry Morgan are two of the most famous buccaneers, and both made fortunes in their exploits and were knighted by Queen Elizabeth I on their return to England — Morgan was even made a member of Parliament. Even though they carried the backing of the English crown, buccaneers often operated without regard to the law and many could not refuse the chance to pick off attractive British vessels when they had the opportunity. The ships of the buccaneers were usually run by a loose democracy in which the captain was elected by the crew on the basis of his skills as a fighter and leader, and an organized system was followed to divide captured booty and to compensate mates who were wounded.

Contrary to the stock Hollywood image of the pirate captain as a rakish ladies' man, captains and crews with few exceptions avoided contact with women entirely, and instead carried on homosexual relationships with each other or with captured or purchased adolescent boys. According to officials of a favorite pirate haven, Port Royal, Jamaica, the town was "filled with sodomites."[86] The historian B.R. Burg, who examined the sexual practices of pirates and buccaneers, found that "when buccaneers had the opportunity for engagements with women prisoners, they were rarely taken, and in their relationships with members of the opposite sex, most pirates give every indication they were uncomfortable in the extreme.... When women were captured or otherwise present aboard ship, by far the greater number of pirates ignored the opportunities to use them sexually."[87] Blackbeard, who had a strict rule against women aboard his ship, was known to strangle women and unceremoniously pitch their bodies overboard. Stede Bonnet, called "the gentleman pirate," was reported to have said that escape from his shrewish wife was the reason he became a pirate. Reports of buccaneers availing themselves of the women natives of the Caribbean are almost non-existent, and on the infrequent occasions when buccaneers did get married, the marriages were nearly always unsuccessful. Likewise only a few reports of pirates carrying off women from plundered ships or towns for their sexual pleasure survive from the century long span of time in which buccaneers dominated the Caribbean.[88] On the other hand, when raiding coastal towns and villages buccaneers would sometimes bring back adolescent boys to join their crews — most in their mid-to late teens, though they sometimes kept boys as young as 10 or 12.[89]

If conditions on merchant ships and in the Royal Navy were conducive to homosexuality, the circumstances of life of buccaneers was even more so. Pirate life was a specific choice for the vast majority of them, who knew they would rarely see women, and who by their nature were among the least likely in society to care about religious attitudes to sex. A large portion of pirates had grown up in the dispossessed youth gangs of England or were runaways or adventurers who saw themselves as outsiders who had no place in proper European society and found a strong identity in the society and ways of their pirate companies.

Among pirates there was some variability in choice of companion, with some preferring adolescents or young men from the mid-teens to the early twenties, and others an adult peer. Relations with boys was particularly associated with captains, who often showed uncommon gentleness and care in their relationships, frequently ensuring that their young lovers got a share of the booty. Blackbeard was notorious for his cruelty to captives and crewmen alike, but he showed considerable tenderness in caring for the boy he kept. Another prominent buccaneer, William Dempier, was deeply in love with a boy he had acquired from another pirate. To purchase the boy, Dempier had to also purchase the boy's mother, which he did. Dempier became so attached to the boy that when the boy's mother died, the boy's mourning for her filled Dempier with grief. Some pirates rejected the sexual use of boys, not because they were opposed to pederasty, but because boys were frequently a source of conflict aboard ship. The shipboard rules enforced by the Welsh pirate Bartholomew Roberts, known today as Black Bart, forbade either boys or women aboard his ship. "No Boy or Woman to be allowed amongst them. If any Man were found seducing any of the latter Sex, and carry'd her to Sea, disguis'd, he was to suffer Death." Interestingly, Burg notes no penalty was mentioned for those smuggling boys aboard.[90]

Among buccaneers of the Caribbean a formalized sexual relationship called *matelotage* was also common. The term originated in a master-servant context, but quickly came to denote a recognized sexual bond between a buccaneer and a lover, who was called a *matelote*. The ship's surgeon on Henry Morgan's ship, Alexander Exquemelin, had started out as a matelote to a pirate himself, and later wrote of the relationship with fondness. When the notoriously cruel French buccaneer François l'Ollonais sacked and pillaged Maracaibo on the Venezuelan coast, he made certain that the booty was divided among not only the surviving crew, but that the portions of those killed went to their surviving matelote partners.

The relationships between pirates were often exceptionally intense attachments. When the French privateer Louis le Golif married a women in the buccaneer enclave on the island of Tortuga, his matelote, Pulverin, was deeply upset. Pulverin's first response was the solace of alcohol, but then he claimed the right to his partner's marriage bed, to which he was given access. Pulverin tried to live with the arrangement but still found himself unhappy with le Golif's wife and eventually got his revenge. Coming home early after a raid, the captain sent Pulverin on ahead to let his wife know he was coming. Pulverin arrived at the captain's house on Tortuga and found his wife engaged in sex with another man. Pulverin killed both le

Golif's wife and the interloper, and then disappeared. Captain le Golif later acquired another matelote, but never got over the loss of Pulverin.[91]

The intensity of attachments between pirates is also seen in an incident witnessed by the 17th-century buccaneer Richard Simpson. After a shipmate had gotten himself into an altercation with his captain, he was punished by being tied to a gang plank and being repeatedly doused with cold water. The man's partner was so distraught at his lover's treatment that he arranged for his release by agreeing to take his place and receive the second half of the punishment. The willingness of a buccaneer to go to extreme lengths for his partner was demonstrated in the case of the veteran buccaneer George Rounsivil who was sailing with a companion on a ship when it was driven by adverse winds onto rocks off of Green Key Island. With the ship beginning to break apart because of the rough seas, Rounsivil and five other men were able to launch the ship's boat and headed for shore. As they were paddling off, Rounsivil saw his partner standing on the poop deck shouting for him to come back and save him. "Rounsivil begg'd his companions to put back and take him in." But the men on the boat refused, saying that the rest of the men on the ship would try to get on the boat and they would all perish. Upon hearing this, Rounsivil "jump'd into the water and swam to the vessel and there perished with his friend since he could not save him."[92]

After examining the literature and documents from the 17th century on the lives and ways of buccaneers and pirates, Burg concluded that for many buccaneers, pairing with another male was an important part of life. "The unions between buccaneers often involved deep and abiding love and exhibited many of the traits usually associated with compatible heterosexual couples."[93]

Sodomy in the New World

When the Puritans were leaving England to sail across the Atlantic to build a new life in America where they could practice their "purified" religion free from interference, one of the reasons they gave — and gave frequently — for leaving England was to escape the punishment they were sure would be soon visited on England for the vice of Sodom. John Winthrop predicted that divine judgment on England was imminent, writing to his wife that a "heavy Scourge and Judgment" was coming soon. Carrying the analogy of the Old Testament story further, Winthrop compared the Puritans leaving England with the family of Lot who fled Sodom after the warning by the angels: "If the Lord seeth it will be good for us. He will provide a shelter and a hiding place for us and ours as Zoar for Lott." Another member of his congregation, Robert Ryece made a similar argument, writing that in England "where every place mourneth for want of Justice, where the crying sins go unpunished or unreproved.... and what so ever is evil is countenanced, even the least of these is enough, and enough to make haste out of Babylon, and to seek to die rather in the wilderness than still to dwell in Sodom." Another Puritan, Thomas Hooker, wrote that England had become "literally Babel and so consequently Egypt and Sodom," ready to be "abased and brought down to hell." In the minds of the Pilgrims, they were the "saving remnant" of humanity, embarking on a long and dangerous journey to save one small part of humanity from God's fearsome judgment."[94]

However, even as they sailed away from the Sodom of England toward the "New Israel," as they called it, they could still not rid themselves of the vice not to be named. In his account of the 1629 voyage of the *Talbot* carrying a load of Puritans on their way to the Plymouth Colony, the Rev. Francis Higgeson wrote they had caught five "beastly" boys in the act. "This day we examined 5 beastly sodomitical boys, which confessed their wickedness not to be named. The fact was so fowl we reserved them to be punished by the governor when we came to new England, who afterward sent them back ... to be punished in old England, as the crime deserved."[95]

Despite Winthrop's high hopes for his "city on a hill" the Pilgrims found that their long journey from England, the "New Sodom," had still not freed themselves from the nefarious sin with which they were so obsessed. William Bradford, governor of Plymouth Plantation in the mid–17th century, wrote in his history of the colony that

> And yet all this could not suppress ye breaking out of sundrie notorious sins, (as this year, besides other, gives us too many sad precedents and instances,) especially drunkenness and uncleanness; not only incontinence between persons unmarried, for which many both men & women have been punished sharply enough, but some married persons also. But that which is worse, even sodomie and bugerie, (things fearful to name,) have broke forth in this land, oftener then once. I say it may justly be marveled at, and cause us to fear & tremble at the consideration of our corrupt natures, which are so hardly bridled, subdued, & mortified.[96]

Bradford blamed the outbreak of sodomy in the colony on "our corrupt natures, which are so hardly bridled, subdued & mortified." The appearance of any homosexual behavior at all, much less "oftener then once," among the exclusively Puritan population, subjected as they were to heavy moral conditioning in their daily and weekly services, should be regarded as an indication of the continuing strength and persistence of the ambisexual nature of human sexuality, despite the best efforts of society.

Needless to say, the colonists who settled and populated the colonies up and down the coast of North America brought with them the same social attitudes toward same-sex love and the same harsh legal punishments for "the sin we dare not name" as prevailed in 17th- and 18th-century England, complete with the kind of torrid rhetoric regularly spouted about sodomy by moralists from the time of Peter Damian onward.[97] Because the Protestant settlers of the first colonies believed that all men were sinners, they understood that any man could commit sodomy. Young men, in particular, were suspect, and so some of the New England colonies, "to prevent sin and iniquity" prohibited young unmarried men from living alone or with each other, and required them instead to live as boarders or servants in homes of married couples with children.[98] Prosecutions for sodomy occurred, but were sporadic and infrequent, chiefly in aggravated instances, such as the prosecution of Richard Cornish, a ship's master in Jamestown in 1624 who was accused of forcibly raping a steward on his ship. In Cornish's case, whose offense occurred while he was intoxicated, the court that tried Richard Cornish consisted exclusively of landowners with large numbers of servants — the colonial ruling establishment. Katz remarked that the record of the Cornish trial suggests that "the execution of Richard Cornish was intricately involved with colonial class politics."[99]

Another man, William Plaine, executed in New Haven in 1624, was guilty of committing sodomy with two different men and also "corrupted a great part of the youth of Guilford by masturbation, which he had committed, and provoked others to the like above a hundred times." As if it wasn't bad enough that Plaine committed sodomy several times with different men and involved the youth of the town in his sinful deeds, he was blasphemous as well: "he did insinuated seeds of atheism, questioning whether there was a God," according to the account given by Governor Winthrop. "A monster in human shape," Winthrop wrote.[100] When violators were caught and prosecuted, the punishments were as cruel and inhumane as any dreamed up in the late Middle Ages. In 1646 a Negro living on Manhattan Island in New Netherlands was sentenced to be choked to death and then burned to ashes — a fairly standard punishment in Europe at the same time. The person on whom the act was perpetrated, a ten-year-old boy, who in Europe would have been punished more leniently, if at all, was ordered to be tied to a stake, faggots (wood) piled around him, and flogged "for justice sake."[101] The appalling inhumanity of such a sentence for a ten-year-old boy can only be explained by the callous zealotry of which proponents of authoritarian religion are capable.

As the colonies grew and prospered, and then rose up in revolt against the increasingly burdensome strictures and taxes demanded of them by the government of George III, the widespread fear and loathing of homosexuality engendered by the church in the Middle Ages continued to determine religious dogma on sexual morality and shape public laws, even among the foremost heirs of the Enlightenment among the men who formed the new American government. Thomas Jefferson, an inspired proponent of Enlightenment ideals, proposed to "reform" the law of Virginia on sodomy. His proposal? Replace the death sentence with castration if the accused was a male, and if a female "by cutting thro' the cartilage of her nose a hole of one half inch diameter at the least."[102]

As in the case in England and on the Continent, though, adherence with the religious prohibition against homosexuality was mainly a concern of the church-going mainstream middle class. But even among proper middle class society, homosexuality still persisted among some groups. A French lawyer and politician visiting Philadelphia in the 1790s — evidently an exemplar *par excellence* of the morally conservative French bourgeoisie — complained in shock in a letter about lesbian relations he observed among the teenaged daughters of the Philadelphia middle class. After deploring the "disregard on the part of some parents for the manner in which their daughters form relationships to which they, the parents, have not given their approval," he breathlessly added, "I am going to say something that is almost unbelievable. These women ... give themselves up at an early age to the enjoyment of themselves, and they are not at all strangers to being willing to seek unnatural pleasures with persons of their own sex."[103]

There is also evidence of the kind of homoerotic affection that seems to have characterized relationships among young nobles of the French aristocracy in the mid–18th century among the elite of the American Revolution. As several of George Washington's biographers have noted, during the revolution the commander-in-chief surrounded himself with a group of young officers in a close-knit circle that was marked by affectionate bonds of unusual intensity, a group Washington himself referred to as his "family."[104] The aides included Alexander Hamilton and John Laurens, whose letters to each other contain unreserved expressions of love, and Gilbert de Motier, the Marquis de Lafayette, who arrived from France at the age of 19 to help with the revolution, and joined Washington's retinue shortly thereafter. Washington was very fond of his young aides, especially Lafayette, had them by his side for several years of the war and would spend his evenings with them in his headquarters, trading stories with them while he cracked nuts by the fire.[105]

The specifics of Washington's own life have led to speculation about his own sexuality. Up until his marriage to Martha Custis, Washington had enjoyed only the company of men, and only infrequently attended church services. In his youth he was inordinately fond of an older neighbor, Lord Thomas Fairfax of Cameron, 6th Baron Fairfax, who owned enormous tracts of land in Northern Virginia near Washington's boyhood home. Washington lived with Lord Fairfax, who reciprocated Washington's affections, for long periods of his youth. As a young man in his early 20s, Washington worked as a land surveyor, which entailed spending great lengths of time in the wilderness with a close friend and colleague, Christopher Gist, surveying the lands of western Virginia and southern Pennsylvania as far west as Ohio.

In 1755 he and Gist were sent by the governor of Virginia to warn the French to leave Ohio, territory Virginia claimed, which meant a long journey through the Appalachian forests from Virginia to Fort le Boeuf near Lake Erie. On their way back to Virginia, Washington and Gist decided to attack Fort Duquesne overlooking the point where the Monongahela and Allegheny Rivers join to form the Ohio River — modern-day Pittsburgh. Their attack was successful, but after the French counter-attacked the Virginians had no choice but to surrender. Washington's gambit of seizing Fort Duquesne failed, but it did succeed in launching the French and Indian War — known as the Seven Years' War in Europe. During the war Washington served under General Braddock, and participated in Braddock's disastrous attack on Fort Duquesne. During the battle Washington displayed great heroism in rallying the troops and carrying the fight on after General Braddock and a number of his offers and men had fallen. The military physician tending to the wounded saw two horses shot from underneath Washington as he rode back and forth through the field of battle, heavily exposed, and wrote later that he expected to see Washington go down at any minute. When Washington returned to Virginia, the Virginia legislature honored him for his service with Braddock, and the governor put him in charge of the Virginia Militia. Serving as aide-de-camp to Washington was George Mercer, another wealthy planter's son, 23 at the time and a year younger than Washington.

In 1756 Washington, traveled to Boston to meet with Massachusetts Governor William Shirley, commander of British troops in North America, to negotiate on the command relationship of the Virginia militia to other colonial militias and the British army. On his trip, Washington was accompanied by Mercer, and a younger man, Robert Stewart, called a "favorite" of Washington and Lord Fairfax. Washington had special uniforms made for himself and his aides, and traveled in style, accompanied by three slaves and horses complete with livery uniforms. On their journey the trio lived it up, drinking, gambling, going to entertainments and shopping for themselves in Philadelphia, New York and Boston.[106] The trio apparently made quite an impression on the citizens of the northern colonies they encountered on their way. In his account of Washington's life, the 19th-century writer Washington Irving wrote that Philadelphia and New York at that time "were comparatively small, and the arrival of a party of young Southern officers attracted attention. The late disastrous battle was still the theme of every tongue, and the honorable way in which these young officers had acquitted themselves in it, made them objects of universal interest." Washington's companion on his first trip to the west, Christopher Gist, wrote to him that his name "is more talked of in Philadelphia than that of any other person in the army." According to Irving, "when we consider Washington's noble person and demeanor, his consummate horsemanship, the admirable horses he was accustomed to ride, and the aristocratic style of his equipments, we may imagine the effect produced by himself and his little cavalcade…. It is needless to say, their sojourn in each city was a continual fete."[107]

While Washington was being entertained in Philadelphia, New York and Boston, Indian allies of the French began attacking settlements and farm houses in the western part of Virginia. Some of Virginia's prudish citizens apparently took umbrage at Washington's living it up in the northern cities while the Indian "savages" were threatening the colony from the west. On September 3, 1756, the *Virginia Gazette* carried a blistering attack on Washington, complaining that Washington and his aides "give their Men an example of all Manner of Debauchery, Vice and Idleness." The writer then accused Washington of promoting his favorites, "raw novices and rakes, spendthrifts and bankrupts, who have never been used to command." Virtuous men who signed for service under Washington, the paper said, are "damped and mortified at the Sight of such Scenes of Vice, Extravagance and Oppression." The article then went on to compare Washington's escapades to the "debaucheries" of Alexander the Great, known even then for his homosexual love for his Persian boy, and said that the noble Romans had conquered "effeminate" peoples afflicted with the same weaknesses as Alexander. The truth of the charges cannot be proven, but such slanderous charges in a colonial paper against the commander of the colony's militia would probably have not been lodged if there was not a grain of truth to them. On the advice of friends, Washington decided not to respond, for fear of prolonging and exacerbating the affair.[108]

Up to the age of 27, Washington had sought only the company of men, and had lived for much of his majority in the wilderness, with only other men as company. As discussed later in the chapter, researchers have noted that homosexuality is often found among men working for long periods in remote areas, a condition that would apply to much of Washington's early life. A couple of years after the *Virginia Gazette* story, Washington married a wealthy widow, Martha Dandridge Custis, a choice of spouse that was strategically and financially beneficial to his career. Martha was from a wealthy landowning family, was a widow of another wealthy landowner, and the lands Martha Custis had inherited and controlled, combined with his own, would make Washington one of the richest men in Virginia. Though they raised the two children she had from her earlier marriage, the couple had no children of their own. Washington's biographers, seeking to explain the failure of the Father of the Country to produce any heirs during an age that placed a great value on the production of children, have speculated that an early bout of small pox may have left him sterile. Because of Washington's iconic status, few historians are willing to entertain the thought that Washington simply was not interested in women, other than the marriage required by the social conventions of his class.

Washington's love for the young Lafayette and his solicitous interest in him is another matter. A biographer of Washington, Marcus Cunliffe, wrote that "Washington opened his heart to Lafayette — there is a sprightliness in his correspondence with the Frenchman" not seen in his letters to others.[109] In one of his letters to Lafayette, the famously reserved Washington wrote, "I think myself happy in being linked with you in bonds of strictest friendship" and in response to an expression of love for him contained in a letter he received from Lafayette he wrote "of the happiness of my acquaintance with you." When Lafayette was called away on duty, the general made sure Lafayette's horse was well cared for, and wrote him that on his return he expected to embrace him "with all the warmth of an affectionate friend when you come to quarters, where a bed is prepared for you." When nightfall came during the Battle of Monmouth, Washington opened his coat and took Lafayette under his arm, and the two slept together through the night on the field. When Lafayette visited France in 1779 on leave, he wrote the general that he was homesick for the general. "Happy in our union, in the pleasure of living with you, I had taken such a habit of being inseparable from you, that I can't now get the use of absence and I am more and more afflicted of that distance which keeps me so far from my dearest friend." When Lafayette asked Washington to send him a picture of himself, he wrote that his request was something that "you may possibly laugh at and call woman-like."[110] Acceding to Lafayette's repeated request that he be given a command, Washington put him in charge of defending Virginia, where Lafayette played a role in the siege of Yorktown which led to the surrender of the British troops under Cornwallis. When Lafayette met Washington on the battlefield at Yorktown, the younger man embraced Washington and kissed him on his face from ear to ear several times.[111]

The young Alexander Hamilton seemed especially interested in his own sex and seems to have had a reputation as a flirt. Abigail Adams wrote to her husband to "beware of that sparrow cock. I have read his heart in his wicked eyes many a time. The very devil is in them. They are lasciviousness itself." John Adams replied that he had seen Hamilton's "debaucheries" first-hand, and wrote Abigail that he would keep clear of Hamilton's "puppyhood."[112] In a letter in 1780 to John Laurens, Hamilton described at length the beauty and charm of a captured British officer, Major John Andre, who was implicated in the plots of Benedict Arnold. John Laurens also had an eye for the beautiful male. In 1778 he wrote that he had found "a handsome young lad" who said he was an ensign in a British unit but had to flee because he had killed a man in a duel. But Lafayette apparently got to the young Englishman first, "Lafayette latched right on to him," Laurens said. Lafayette then wrote to the governor of New York saying that due to "the age of the gentleman and his being an enemy in our hands," he felt he should escort the young prisoner to Boston. General Washington, however, intervened, suspecting that the English youth was not a deserter, but a spy, and reported the incident to the War Board.[113]

Washington's circle of young aides were well educated, were versed in the Greek classics, were well aware of the homosexual loves of the ancient Greeks, and compared their loves for each other to the noble love exemplified by such Greek heroes as Damon and Pythias.[114] In camp during the war Hamilton kept a copy of Plutarch's *Lives*, and particularly admired the "Life of Lycurgus," the legendary leader of Sparta. Among notes Hamilton kept on the "Life of Lycurgus" is the notation, "Every lad had a lover or friend who take [*sic*] care of his education and shared in the praise or blame of his virtues or vices." In a letter to Hamilton, Laurens used the Greek phrase *kalos ka agathos*, a phrase used in fifth-century Greece and combining the Athenian term for beauty, *kalos*, which denotes physical or sensual beauty, with the Spartan term *agathos*, which means beauty in the spiritual sense of honor and valor. In commenting on the letter, the historian Charley Shively writes that *kalos ka agathos* was used in the 18th-century as a code word for homosexual love, a reference still understood in Greece to this day, Shively says.[115]

Even by the effusive standards of expressions of affection between men of the day, the letters from Hamilton to Laurens are remarkable in the depth of intimacy they display between the two men. In a 1779 letter to Laurens, Hamilton writes, "I wish, my Dear Laurens, it might be in my power, by action rather than words, to convince you that I love you. I shall only tell you that 'till you bade us Adieu, I hardly knew the value you had taught my heart to set upon you…. You should not have taken advantage of my sensibility to steal into my affections without my consent." In closing the letter Hamilton writes, "I have gratified my feelings, by lengthening out the only kind of intercourse now in my power with my friend. Adieu."[116] In a September 1780 letter to Laurens, who had been captured by the British and was asking for letters from the "family," Hamilton replies: "I have conveyed your reproof to the lads…. Writing or not writing to you, you know they love you and sympathize in all that concerns you." He closes with "My ravings are for your own bosom."[117]

Some remarkably frank letters between two young Southern friends referring to sexual relations between them show that homosexuality could occur without shame among sons of some of the most prominent families of early 19th-century America. The letters survived in the family library of one of the men, James H. Hammond, later governor and then United States senator from South Carolina. Hammond's friend and erstwhile bed partner was Thomas Jefferson Withers, later a newspaper editor and judge and one of the authors of the constitution of the Confederacy. In 1826 the two were young men, Hammond a 19-year-old and Withers 22 years old. Withers was studying law at South Carolina College at the time, and was recovering from an illness when he wrote to Hammond in response to an earlier letter from him.

After a brief introduction, Withers cuts to the chase and reveals what was on his mind:

> I feel some inclination to learn whether you yet sleep in your Shirt-tail, and whether you yet have the extravagant delight of poking and punching a writhing Bedfellow with your long fleshen pole — the exquisite touches of which I have often had the honor of feeling? … Sir, you roughen

the downy Slumbers of your Bedfellow—by such hostile—furious lunges as you are in the habit of making at him—when he is least prepared for defence against the crushing force of a Battering Ram.

Withers seems to have had fond memories of his experience as Bedfellow to Hammond because four months later he again brings up Hammond's "elongated protuberance," his "fleshen pole." In his commentary on the letters, Martin Duberman remarks that the tone of the letters shows not the slightest hint of concern about the morality of sexual involvement of the two young men. As Duberman observes, "The values and vocabulary of evangelical piety had not yet, in the 1820s, come to permeate American consciousness and discourse."[118]

Masculine Bonding on the Frontier

Away from the towns and cities of the Atlantic coast, in the woodland interior, trappers, hunters and explorers lived for months or years on end without seeing a woman—and probably even longer without seeing the inside of a church—with no company other than their male companions. At this point in the book it should be obvious to the reader that in situations where men are isolated from women, either in occupations of their choosing, or involuntarily, as in prisons, homosexuality readily manifests as a means of fulfilling the human need for intimate companionship and sexual release. The Kinsey study found that the highest incidence of homosexual activity that the researchers encountered among any single group was among males in isolated rural farm areas and geographically remote regions of the western United States. As the Kinsey report observes, "It is the type of homosexuality which was probably common among pioneers and outdoor men in general. Today is it found among ranchmen, cattle men, prospectors, lumbermen, and farming groups in general—among groups that are virile, physically active." These men, the report explains, are vigorous, masculine men whose attitude to sex is not based on moral philosophy but on their experience with life and nature. As the report notes, "These are men who have faced the rigors of nature in the wild. They live on realities and on a minimum of theory. Such a background breeds the attitude that sex is sex, irrespective of the nature of the partner with whom the relation is had."[119] The observations of the Kinsey team suggest that the passionate love between two cowboys depicted to great controversy in the movie *Brokeback Mountain* would have been the norm rather than the exception among the ruggedly masculine men whose efforts tamed the frontier and supported the westward expansion of the young United States.

A man who had worked as a logger in the early 1900s described his homosexual experiences in the camp as an understood part of the loggers' way of life. "Not one of us could be considered effeminate, neurotic or abnormal. Yet all but two engaged in homosexual activities.... The popular method, preferred by the majority, was sodomy, and it was in this logging camp that I was initiated into the discomforts, adjustments and ecstasies of this form of sexual activity." Later moving to work in the gold fields, he lived in a camp, where he said that of the 55 men in the camp, over half, conservatively, were having sex with one another. He said, "the brawny, ultra-masculine types invariably started out increasing their sociabilities, talking booze with them when dropping in on different buddies throughout the camp." He added that "two of the most masculine of the crew (a tram operator and a jackhammer man) soon started pairing off exclusively, moving into a cabin together." He said that the couple "was the envy of a number of us."[120]

In an interview the anthropologist Walter Williams conducted with an elderly woman in rural North Dakota, who had lived all her life on the farm her parents had homesteaded in 1890, Williams discussed male bachelor couples, and asked her if people thought that it was strange that the bachelors didn't marry but lived with each other. She replied, "Everybody had a 'do your own thing' attitude, so people respected each other's individual choice. There weren't that many women around, so it wasn't thought about if they didn't marry." When Williams asked the woman if she thought any of the bachelor couples may have been in homosexual relationships, she said, "People back then didn't talk about any kind of sex. So they wouldn't think anything of it." After reflecting on it, she added, "Now that I think about it, many of them probably were that way. We didn't talk about such things then. It was better than today, when everyone is paranoid about it."[121]

Popular literature of the early 19th century which featured stories of life on the frontier frequently portray an uninhibited exuberance in physical contact between men that suggests that the masculine frontiersmen were entirely free of the neurotic hang-ups about physical contact between males common among young men in modern Western society. A popular series that appeared in the 1830s and 1840s featuring stories of Davy Crockett's exploits had the handsome young hero often finding himself thrown into situations with clear sexual implications. In one of these "Almanacs," Crockett gives an account of a wrestling match he had with a stagecoach driver. Crockett starts out his story with him yelling to the stagecoach driver, "Take care how I lite on you." Then he says, "I jumped right down on the driver and he tore my trowsers right off me. I was driven almost distracted and should have been used up, but luckily there was a poker in the fire which I thrust down his throat, and by that means mastered him." In discussing the stories, Bryne Fone remarks that the homoerotic allusions in the tale were probably not coincidental. He adds that a frequently cited reason given by 19th-century preachers and moralists for avoiding masturbation and sexuality activity was that it depleted the energies of young men. Therefore to many of the stories' male readers, Crockett's saying he "should have been used up" could very likely have had a sexual connotation.[122]

If we read Crockett's account of the action keeping in mind the association of sexual activity with depletion of energy, the homoerotic subtext becomes blatant. Most obvious of the homoerotic allusions is the driver tearing Crockett's trowsers "right off" of him — which could be seen as a sexual act in itself, and in other settings might be the prelude to a sexual assault. That act drove Crockett almost to distraction — by which he presumably meant got him "all riled up," but which could also mean "aroused." The latter meaning would explain Crockett's next statement that he "should have been used up" by that, that is, he almost exhausted himself by nearly coming to an orgasm because of the excitement. The homosexual allusions in Crockett's response, thrusting a hot poker down the driver's throat to master him, leave little to the imagination, and would probably not have been lost on many of the young male readership of these and similar stories

The appeal of these stories to young men was no doubt a vicarious participation in the adventures of life on the untamed frontier and the manly exploits of heroes like Davy Crockett. But given the seemingly conscious attempt of the author to evoke a homosexual subtext in the stories, we may suspect that part of the appeal of the stories to the young male readers of the civilized, settled East Coast was life out in the wild, "with the boys," in a masculine world apart from women. The psychologist Fritz Klein, in developing his Klein Sexual Orientation Grid, recognized that conscious sexual desires or fantasies were insufficient to completely describe a person's sexual orientation. Klein found that that the sexual preference an individual has for social and emotional companionship and lifestyle preferences were equally important components of an individual's overall sexual orientation.[123] Masculine men who prefer the social and emotional company of other men, and who choose an occupation in an all-male environment isolated from women, not surprisingly as the Kinsey study found, frequently end up in homosexual relationships. In examining the literature of the 17th-century pirates and buccaneers, Burg pointed out that many of the buccaneers whose lives were documented showed a similar desire to seek adventure and fortune in a world apart from women, and found sexual and emotional fulfillment in a world of men.[124] The idealized adventures of life on the all-male frontier, then, allowed the male reader to vicariously live an extended childhood in an all male fantasy world where the romantic homosexual bonding common among pre-pubescent boys continues as an unspoken sexual backdrop to the close bonds between masculine men in the adventure stories.

In a comparable way James Fenimore Cooper's Leatherstocking Tales, a series of novels including *The Deerslayer* and *The Last of the Mohicans*, romanticized male bonding and established a stereotype of the white adventurer and his Indian companion that was emulated in countless dime store novels in the late 19th century and was the original prototype for the Lone Ranger and Tonto. The Leatherstocking Tales relate the continuing adventures of a white frontiersman, Nathaniel, or "Nattie," Bumpo, starting as a handsome 18-year-old in *The Deerslayer*, and his equally handsome Indian friend, Chingachgook, a chief of the Delaware tribe. The "two childless, womenless men, of opposite races" develop an unspoken but unmistakable erotic bond that ties them to each other for the next 40 years, which are related in the five novels of the series. Though never overtly sexual, the homoerotic core of their bond, noted by commentators from D.H. Lawrence to Leslie Fiedler, is repeatedly evoked in the novels, in terms of endearment they use for each other, in Bumpo's repeated delight in seeing the naked body of his friend striding through the forest, in their loving "intercourse," as the narrator frequently describes their close friendship, in their continually sharing food and lodging, and even, in the last book of the series, *The Last of the Mohicans*, in their adopting a child and raising him as their own.[125]

The Sex Life of Cowboys

A similar all-male world, away from women, where male bonds frame the emotional lives of the heroes is depicted in the literature of the Wild West. In the years after the American Civil War, novels relating the adventures of the settlers, cowboys and outlaws in the western U.S. territories exploded in popularity. Most of the dime store novels, which were generated in large quantities by writers capitalizing on the popularity of the genre, are no more than pulp fiction, but a few enduring classics emerged that are still read today. One of the most famous is Owen Wister's *The Virginian*, a novel set in the rough cattle country of Wyoming that deals with love and death against the backdrop of the struggle between cattle ranchers and rustlers.

The novel is related from the perspective of a narrator, a young greenhorn fresh from the East Coast on his way to visit a large cattle ranch in Wyoming Territory in the days before fences and when the herds were policed by ranch hands out in the great stretches of land where the cattle could find forage. When his train arrives at his destination stop, the narrator is immediately entranced by a young cow hand he sees lounging against a wall by the station,

> a slim young giant, more beautiful than pictures. His broad, soft hat was pushed back; a loose-knotted, dull-scarlet handkerchief sagged from his throat; and one casual thumb was hooked in the cartridge-belt that slanted across his hips. He had plainly come many miles from somewhere across the vast horizon, as the dust upon him showed.... But no dinginess of travel or shabbiness of attire could tarnish the splendor that radiated from his youth and strength.

Listening to the cowboy tease an older man about to be married, he thinks, "Had I been the bride, I should have taken the giant, dust and all." Watching the Virginian, the greenhorn thinks, "in his eye, in his face, in his step, in the whole man, there dominated a something potent to be felt, I should think, by man or woman."[126] When the greenhorn discovers that the "young giant" is the man sent from the ranch to meet him, he is thrilled. As the novel progresses, the narrator feels honored to find he is befriended by the young cowboy — the Virginian, as people called him — and the two develop a close and intimate bond of an emotional intensity and exclusivity most people would associate with sexual relationship.

Chris Packard, a scholar who has examined homoerotic bonds depicted in 19th-century action and adventure novels, remarked that many readers have overlooked the homosexual subtext in Wister's novel. To scholars who have doubted the intentional homosexual allusions in the novel, Packard points to a poem Wister wrote in 1893 musing on the constraints of polite society that require "fig leaves" to obscure facts "unfit and shocking" to the general public. "There are some things we say but must not hear; There are some things we do yet cannot know." In the concluding stanza, the poem resignedly admits, "Yes, I'm aware your daughter cannot read it.... Life's so indelicate, we have agreed it must be concealed by fig leaves and by hymns." In late 19th-century American society the principal subject avoided in polite conversation was sex, and sexual relations between men would, of course, be the kind of "things we do yet cannot know."[127]

A large number of humorous limericks that have survived from the Old West containing jocular references to sex between cowboys strongly imply an environment in which homosexual activity between cowboys is taken for granted. These lewd little poems were filled with jokes about the wild debauchery that could accompany drinking on a Saturday night, and feature barely concealed allusions to various homosexual acts.[128]

Wister's own admiration for the male body is illustrated in his account of a trip he made to the West in 1893, and his conversation with a young stagecoach driver who like him had been unsuccessful with women. "I sat beside the driver, whose name was Hunter, and he certainly was a jewel. He was handsome, and with that fascination that so many of his kind have."[129] Writing in a journal in 1885, Wister observed that "cowboys never live long enough to get old," and then remarked that "They're a queer episode in the history of this country. Purely nomadic, and leaving no posterity, for they don't marry. I'm told they're without any moral sense whatever."[130] When a 19th-century writer speaks of morality, we can be sure that in nearly all cases the reference is to sexual morality. Never marrying, and having no "moral sense whatever" would, obviously, leave open the option of sexual relations with other men, which as we have seen has been found by researchers to be common in isolated all-male societies.

If Wister intended to imply a sexual bond between the narrator and the cowboy he adores, and if as he writes in his poem that certain things "must be concealed," then one way such a relationship between the pair could be implied would be in the frequent remarks the narrator makes about the Virginian's good looks and handsome body. Observing the Virginian one day as they talked, the narrator's thoughts drifted to his friend's handsome allure, "He was still boyishly proud of his wild calling, and wore his leather straps and jingled his spurs with obvious pleasure. His tiger limberness and his beauty were rich with unabated youth."[131]

A sexual relationship would also be marked by intimate expressions of emotional support for each other and enough trust between the two to allow the sharing of the most intimate of feelings. Later in the novel such a moment arrives when the narrator learns that another cow hand named Steve, who had been the Virginian's partner, his sidekick and closest friend and confident, had become a rustler, a betrayal of the way of life the Virginian believed in. The Virginian and some other men from the ranch had hunted Steve and an accomplice down and hung the two from some cottonwood trees in a remote area of the ranch. Joining the Virginian just afterwards, the narrator sees that the Virginian was deeply grieved by Steve's outlaw life and emotionally upset by the frontier justice he and his men were forced to administer to Steve.

The Virginian says,

> You have a friend, and his ways are your ways. You travel together, you spree together confidentially, and you suit each other down to the ground. Then one day you find him putting his iron on another man's calf. You tell him fair and square those ways have never been your ways and ain't going to be your ways. Well, that does not change him any, for it seems he's disturbed over getting rich quick and being a big man in the Territory. And the years go on, until you are foreman of Judge Henry's ranch and he —,

the Virginian struggles with the words, "— is dangling back in the cottonwoods. What can he claim? Who made the choice? He cannot say, 'Here is my old friend that I would have stood by.' Can he say that?"

On the morning the men hanged Steve and the other, Steve engaged in light banter with the men doing their duty, but he refused to speak to the Virginian, his old sidekick, a silence that stung him to his quick and left him confused about whether he was doing the right thing. As they rode, the narrator tried to comfort him, suggesting that they brought their fate on them themselves. The Virginian went on, "Was it him I was deserting? Was not the deserting done by him the day I spoke my mind about stealing calves? .... The man I used to travel with is not the man back there. Same name, to be sure. And same body. But different in — and yet he had the memory! You can't never change your memory!" Saying that, the Virginian started sobbing a little, the first time the narrator had seen him cry. Pulling his horse up close, the narrator put his arm around his friend. "I had no sooner touched him than he was utterly overcome. 'I knew Steve awful well,' he said."[132]

The emotional intimacy between the two young men is depicted again when the Virginian invites the narrator to accompany him out into the wilderness to fish and camp at a remote site on the Snake River, another opportunity, Packard observes, for Wister to dwell on "the Virginian's large, wise, naked body, and the narrator's adoration of it." After an afternoon of fly fishing, the Virginian says, "Let's swim," since the fish aren't biting. "Forthwith we shook off our boots and dropped our few clothes and heedless of what fish we might now drive away, we went into the cool, slow, deep breadth of backwater which the bend makes just there. As he came up near me, shaking his head of black hair, the cow-puncher was smiling a little."[133] The two of them then climbed out of the river. "We dried off before the fire, without haste. To need no clothes is better than purple and fine linen." Then "we lay on our backs upon the buffalo hide to smoke and watch the Tetons grow more solemn, as the large stars opened out over the sky. 'I don't care if I never go home,' said I. The Virginian nodded, 'It gives all the peace o'being asleep with all the pleasure o'feeling the widest kind of awake,' said he. 'Yu-might say the whole year's strength flows hearty in every waggle of your thumb.'" The pleasure the two of them feel lying together on the buffalo hide, nude, after a year's absence is palpable. Packard notes that before meeting for the fishing trip, the two had been separated for an entire year, and that "since the partners are still naked at this point, it would be difficult to believe that their thumbs are the only appendages waggling with 'a whole year's strength' flowing through them."[134]

The life of the cowboy out on the open ranges of the West of the late 19th century was often dangerous, and because of the dangers and the great distances over which the ranch hands would be spread out, ranch foremen as a rule required that their men pair up for safety. A man's partner was called his sidekick, so called because the partners would ride close beside each other so that their knees touched as they rode. When a new hand joined the crew of a ranch, he was either assigned a partner or picked a partner himself, another cow hand like himself with whom a close emotional bond was usually developed. A man who worked as a cowboy in early 20th-century Arizona recalled that attraction for another cowboy "was at first rooted in admiration, infatuation, a sensed need of an ally, loneliness and yearning, but it regularly ripened into love." As they got to know each other, he said, their sexual relationship would slowly develop. "At first pairing they'd solace each other gingerly, and, as bashfulness waned, manually [i.e., mutual masturbation]. As trust in mutual good will matured, they'd graduate to the ecstatically comforting 69 [mutual oral sex].... Folk know not how cock-hungry men get."[135]

The deep feelings of attachment that grew between sidekicks is shown in a poem first published in 1915 by Charles Badger Clark, who had worked as a cow hand on ranches in South Dakota and Arizona in the early part of the century. One of Clark's poems, "Others," expresses the grieving of a cowboy whose partner had gone off to war and was killed.

> The daybreak comes so pure and still.
> He said that I was pure as dawn,
> That day we climbed to Signal Hill.
> Back there before the war came on.
>
> Across the gulch it glimmers white,
> The little house we plotted for.
> We would be sitting here tonight
> If he had never gone to war —
> The firelight and the cricket's cheep,
> My arm around his neck —
>
> And every day I ride to town
> The wide lands talk to me of him —
> The slopes with pine trees marching down,
> The spread-out prairies, blue and dim.
> He loved it for the freedom's sake
> Almost as he loved me.
> I let him go and fight to make
> Some other country free.[136]

Another poem of Clark, "The Lost Partner," in a similar way dwells on the feelings between two sidekicks, who "loved each other the way men do," "more than any woman's kiss could be."

> I ride alone and hate the boys I meet.
>   Today, some way, their laughin' hurts me so.
>
> I seem the only thing on earth that cares
>   'Cause Al ain't here no more!
> 'Twas just a stumblin' hawse, a tangled spur —
>   And, when I raised him up so limp and weak,
> One look before his eyes begun to blur
>   And then — the blood that wouldn't let 'im speak!
> And him so strong, and yet so quick he died,
>   And after year on year

When we had always trailed it side by side,
   He went — and left me here!

We loved each other in the way men do
   And never spoke about it, Al and me,
But we both knowed, and knowin' it so true
   Was more than any woman's kiss could be.
We knowed — and if the way was smooth or rough,
   The weather shine or pour,
While I had him the rest seemed good enough —
   But he ain't here no more!

The range is empty and the trails are blind,
   And I don't seem but half myself today.
I wait to hear him ridin' up behind
   And feel his knee rub mine the good old way
He's dead — and what that means no man kin tell.
   Some call it "gone before."
Where? I don't know, but God! I know so well
   That he ain't here no more! [137]

Homophobia in 20th-Century America

In the late 19th century a German-Hungarian journalist, Károly Mária Kertbeny, coined the word homosexual, by grafting the Latin *homo*, meaning "same," onto the Medieval Latin *sexualis*. The term was first used by Karl Ulrichs and other late 19th-century homosexual rights activists,[138] and by the turn of the 20th century, the term was finding acceptance among psychologists and sociologists and then gradually entered the mainstream. With the new term "homosexual," society had a word to describe people who deviated from what they considered "natural" and "moral" sexual behavior, a word which placed such people apart as a separate sub-species of the human race. Before the invention of the term, same-sex behavior was something people did, and was thought of as something that anyone could do. Even though it was recognized by many in Europe since post–Roman times that some people had marked preferences for their own sex, it was at the same time generally understood that same-sex behavior was something of which everyone was capable. Christian moralists acknowledged that each individual was capable of homosexual acts and frequently attributed the homosexual potential in every person to mankind's irredeemably corrupted nature.

As we saw in Chapter 3, psychologists, psychiatrists and sexual researchers, on the other hand, see it as an inherent aspect of human sexuality, and particularly a characteristic of childhood and early adolescence, though until the late 20th century most authorities regarded its manifestation in adults as a psychosexual disorder. In fact, Sigmund Freud said that "all human beings are capable of making a homosexual object-choice and have in fact made one in their unconscious." Freud added that the problem for research is not the existence of a homosexual component in each individual, but where people claim *exclusive heterosexuality*. "From the point of view of psycholo-analysis the exclusive sexual interest felt by men for women is also a problem that needs elucidating."[139] However, the development of the pseudo-scientific term, homosexual, made it possible for society to pretend that the only people who ever experienced homosexual feelings were "homosexuals" and provided the ego another defense with which to dam up the latent homosexual responsiveness that naturally occurs in each individual.

As the life on the open prairie faded into history with the rapid development of the West and the cowboy passed into American mythology, homosexual relations between men continued among groups isolated from mainstream society and in urban subcultures, as the Kinsey Report found. In the rapidly developing mass media of the 20th century—movies and radio in the 1920s and '30s, and then television in the 1950s—the only model for romantic affection allowed by the industry censors was the heterosexual norm. The homosexual nature of affectionate bonds between frontiersmen, pioneers and cowboys that Owen Wister was forced to conceal under a "fig leaf" of unspoken suggestion was even less tolerated in the action and adventure radio shows, movies, and television series.

The saturation of popular media with the heterosexual norm taught children at an early age that the only "normal" kind of love and affection allowed was between a man and a woman and that deviations from this accepted pattern were "queer" and "perverted." The new term, homosexual, and its use by scientific researchers, seemed to endorse the idea that people with a sexual preference for their own sex were different from the norm, that "normal" people were exclusively heterosexual—just like in the movies—and that anyone who sought sex with a member of their own sex was abnormal, sick, deviant and immoral. The adoption of the term in society in general made it possible to place a line in popular consciousness between "normal" heterosexual people, and unnatural and perverted "homosexual" people, with no gray area in between. Society had no category for a young unmarried man with a mixture of homosexual and heterosexual interests who happened to yield to temptation to engage in sexual relations with another male, perhaps while serving overseas in the military, and then moved on to heterosexual marriage. The coining of the term "homosexual" therefore inadvertently led to the emergence in popular culture of an artificial black-and-white distinction between "homosexual" people and everyone else.

As the 20th century progressed, the image of the homosexual as a social pariah or pathetic outcast was pounded in by the homophobic attitudes of the tough guy Hollywood heroes and the jokes of comedians targeting "queers" and "fruits." The depiction of Peter Lorre's sinister character in *The Maltese Falcon* as a homosexual was used in the film to develop his character's image as a creepy underworld deviant, but it also reinforced the message that "homos" were sleazy degenerates. Real men were tough, strong, assertive, like Sam Spade, didn't show emotion and decidedly didn't eat quiche. Women were supposed to be soft, fragile, sexy, emotional, nurturing, kind and always dependent on the man. These masculine and feminine stereotypes, in actuality distorted caricatures, became the models for adolescent boys and girls to emulate, role models constantly reinforced by the continued portrayal of them in movies, on television and in popular song.

When the Gay Liberation Movement was born in the Stonewall riot of 1969, the insistence of people with a primary homosexual orientation to have their rights respected started a gradual loosening of the homophobic attitudes and prejudice of modern Western society. Though a movement to promote the rights of bisexual people joined the homosexual rights movement a few years later, society still tended to view sexuality through the black and white distinction between heterosexual and homosexual. Because of the lingering stigmas attached to homosexuality, the vast majority of the masses of people who would place somewhere in the middle of the Kinsey scale have opted to restrict their sexual practices to the heterosexual norm. As the 20th century came to a close, therefore, the understanding and practice of sex in Western society was still ruled by the artificial norms of the heterosexual myth.

Conclusion

In this chapter, we looked at the effect on the sexual practices and social attitudes to sex of the rigid sexual morality that the church sought to impose on the people of Europe in the period since the Middle Ages. While the review of historical materials covering the actual sexual behavior of post–Medieval Europeans, as opposed to morally approved sexual behavior, is by no means exhaustive, it is readily apparent that sexual practices in Western society since the Middle Ages continued to display the same ambisexual character found in other societies around the world and down through history, even under the harsh constraints of Catholic and Protestant moral enforcement. We have also seen that in historical periods when Christian sexual morality was less rigidly enforced, and among groups isolated from or indifferent to Christian moral teachings that homosexuality readily manifests itself. As mentioned several times during the course of the book, the sexual researcher C.A. Tripp observed that in societies where homosexuality is merely approved it tends to be prevalent. After surveying the sexual customs of post–Medieval Western society we can add a corollary to Tripp's generalization: where anti-homosexual moral teaching is not rigidly enforced and authoritarian religion has diminished or little influence, homosexuality readily appears as an aspect of the sex lives of the people. During periods where the influence of moral authoritarians is pronounced, homosexuality, though driven underground, continued to be present.

The stubborn persistence of homosexual behavior among Europeans, even during the periods when enforcement of Christian sexual morality was at its most severe, is strong evidence of the indelible nature of this sexual trait among humans. The general pattern of sexual practices, then, of same-sex relationships as a feature of youth or unmarried adults, and as an outlet for married adults, all of which takes the pressure off of heterosexual coitus as a channel of sexual release, is perfectly consistent with the general pattern found among post–Roman and early Medieval Europeans, and every other society around the world from the earliest periods of human history.

From the Middle Ages up to the beginnings of the 20th century, enforcement of the rigid heterosexual norm and prosecution of homosexual deviance was performed primarily by religious and civil authorities. As the 20th century developed, the enforcement of the heterosexual standard by religion and government was substantially supplemented by the explosion of mass media, with its relentless promotion of the heterosexual norm as the only acceptable ideal for romantic love. Judging by the fact that homosexual behavior in the 20th century, outside of the isolated same-sex societies such as seamen, ranch hands and loggers, was until the last several decades of the century restricted to an urban underground subculture, the social enforcement of the heterosexual norm by the media seems to have been at least as effective as the rigidly theocratic government of 16th-century Calvinist Geneva and the Protestant middle-class societies of 18th-century Holland and England. With the relative relaxation of social tolerance toward same-sex relationships in contemporary Western society, the persistent promotion by the mass media of heterosexual romance as the only legitimate sexual option, with its implicit message that homosexuality is not normal, continues to have an enormous impact on society.

In the next and final chapter of the book we will look at the negative impact of the continued propagation of the heterosexual myth in Western society and the enormous social costs that are caused by the perpetuation of fear and ignorance of the human race's ambisexual sexual character.

Nature Out of Balance: Sexual Neurosis in Modern Society

Wherefore by their fruits ye shall know them.

Matt. 7:20

In the introductory chapter, a brief description was painted of the enormous stress that exists in modern society around homosexuality, and of the controversy and heated emotions that the subject arouses. The findings of the study performed by Henry Adams and his associates cited in that chapter provided strong empirical evidence that the visceral and emotional hostility to homosexuality exhibited by homophobic personalities correlates closely to the level of homosexual responsiveness within each individual. In other words, a neurotic fear and hatred of homosexuality has its roots in latent homosexuality within the individuals themselves. That hostility is understood by psychologists to be a result of a sharp conflict that exists within individuals with strongly anti-homosexual religious or moral beliefs and the inherent homosexual responsiveness that researchers have long recognized to be a facet of human sexuality. Such a conflict is an inevitable result of the continuing disconnect in Western society between the heterosexual model of sexuality demanded by Christian sexual morality and propagated by popular culture and the inherent ambisexuality of human nature.

The abundant homosexual behavior in the animal world, surveyed in Chapter 1, and the positive role it seems to play in the evolutionary success of many species should firmly end the argument on whether same-sex love is "natural." The review of sexual customs and patterns among indigenous tribal peoples in Chapter 2 made it clear that homosexuality was a pervasive facet of human sexuality, and a positive trait that diverted the sex drive away from heterosexual coitus for individual too young or otherwise incapable of providing the full-time focus and nurturing required to raise emotionally and psychologically healthy children. And the review of sexual practices and traditions among all the world's great civilizations in Part II made it clear that the pervasiveness of homosexual behavior among pre-westernized indigenous peoples and the positive role played by same-sex love in human societies was not restricted to "primitive," "heathen," and "uncivilized" aboriginal peoples. To the contrary, homosexuality and a recognized social role for homosexual relationships have been visibly present to some degree until recent times in every major civilization in the world going back to the beginnings of recorded history with the sole exception of post–Medieval European civilization.

The sexual traditions of the post–Medieval West are different only because of the successful efforts led by the church and civil authorities to impose by force on Western society an artificial concept of human sexual nature centered on the simplistic assertion that the sole "natural" purpose of the sexual drive is procreation. This erroneous assumption, based on an understanding of the natural world over 2,000 years old, has long been discarded by science, and overlooks the complexity of the natural system from which humans evolved. The psychological damage caused by the introduction by the early Christian Fathers of an anti-sexual, anti-homosexual moral code that sought to repress and deny a basic human instinctual drive is amply demonstrated by the manifestly neurotic reactions of the morally devout Medieval Christian clergy to their own sexual natures. The great success of the church in replicating its neurotic fear and loathing of sex among the European laity is illustrated by the transformation of the European public from a relatively easygoing and tolerant society in the early Middle Ages to a people so disturbed by sexual or religious nonconformity and paranoid about divine punishment that it systematically hunted down and viciously punished non-conformists, and could spontaneously erupt into mass hysteria over the mere thought of sinners among them.

Since the Middle Ages a key focus of Western religion has been sexual morality, especially so within such authoritarian religions as Roman Catholicism and Protestant fundamentalism. The central preoccupation of Western Christian religion with sex is illustrated by the fact that whenever Christian moralists have complained of moral decline or immoral behavior, their complaints have in nearly all cases been aimed at sexual behavior. The obsession with sexual behavior in Christian morality is all the more peculiar when one considers the fact that sexual morality is only briefly touched on in the teachings of Christ as related in the Gospels, as in the affirmation of the sanctity of marriage in the marriage at Cana, and in the encounter with Mary Magdalene, the prostitute, in which the emphasis in the account was not on the immorality of her prostitution, but on disapproval of the hypocrisy of her accusers. The absence of any condemnation of homosexuality at all in the Gospels underscores the degree to which the obsession with homosexuality in Christian moral teachings has radically diverged from the central thrust of the Christian message.

As observed in Chapter 15, the history of homosexuality since the late Middle Ages has been of the conflict between the forces and leaders of authoritarian religion and the ambisexual human nature seeking expression in same-sex behavior. In the 20th century, authoritarian religion was largely replaced by the mass media as the instrument of enforcement of the heterosexual myth. The powerful ability of movies, television, magazines and popular music to influence the way people think and behave has made the mass media an extremely effective means of inculcating the heterosexual norm in each new generation. As non–Western societies developed and became more and more exposed to Western media and popular culture, homosexual traditions in those societies, in most cases dating back thousands of years, have almost entirely disappeared and been replaced by an emphasis on heterosexual reproduction that has encouraged extramarital heterosexual promiscuity. However, despite the visible effects of the mass inculcation in the heterosexual norm in Western culture, which leads most people except those at the homosexual end of the Kinsey scale to choose an exclusive heterosexual lifestyle, the prevalence of homosexuality in non–Western societies around the world makes it clear that, unless the human species radically mutated in the years since Christian morality was forcibly imposed, people in Western culture have the same ambisexual character below the surface of their conscious heterosexual identities.

Despite the gradual rise in tolerance of sexual diversity in Western societies in the closing decades of the 20th century, the understanding of sexuality that dominates modern culture, obviously, continues to be shaped by the heterosexual myth. The artificial black-and-white distinction drawn in modern society between the "homosexual" and everyone else, with the implication that a person is either "straight" or "gay," obscures the actual continuum of orientation between homosexual and heterosexual that is readily apparent to sexologists and psychologists who have studied human sexuality.

This artificial distinction, which excludes the large percentage of people who would fall into the middle of the Kinsey scale, allows conservative religious groups to argue that homosexuals are only a very tiny deviant minority. If gays are a very tiny minority, it is easier for them to argue that homosexuality is an aberration, a disorder and a disease. However, because of the continuum of sexual orientation among humans, surveys that that attempt to determine the percentage of gay people in modern society are inherently misleading because they include only those respondents who identify themselves as gay. Nor do these surveys account for the many self-identified gay people who have had heterosexual experience, which includes a large percentage of the total gay population.[1] In classical Greece, imperial Rome, Medieval Baghdad and feudal Japan nearly all the men who pursued male lovers were either married at the time, or would move on to marriage later in their life. None of these men, who comprised a majority of men in their social classes, would have been included in any of the modern surveys counting individuals who identify themselves as gay. As a tool to help in understanding the role of homosexuality in human society, polls that attempt to measure the percentage of gay people in society are essentially irrelevant.

Therefore the problems in modern society caused by the clash of Western sexual morality with the ambisexual nature of human sexuality are not limited to the abusive treatment of gay men and lesbians that still occurs, but affect most of society to some degree since a large majority of the population fall somewhere between the exclusively heterosexual and homosexual extremes of the Kinsey scale.

Harm to Society Caused by the Heterosexual Myth

The psychological damage and fallout among the people of Western societies from the collision between the natural force of our ambisexual nature and the intensive and pervasive social and religious conditioning of the heterosexual norm in Western culture cannot be overstated. The issues discussed in this section are only a brief overview of the myriad ways in which the imposition of the artificial model of sexuality in Western culture has caused harm to individuals and society as a whole, but are provided to suggest to the reader the multiple dimensions of the damage caused to our society by the heterosexual myth.

We have seen the anguish and self-torture that members of the Medieval clergy subjected themselves to be cleansed of sexual desires, clearly homosexual in many cases. In the United States today the imposition of the heterosexual model as the only legitimate sexual standard has caused untold misery and harm to millions of teenagers coming to grips with their sexual drive; to the enormous number of gay and lesbian individuals victimized by anti-gay violence or hounded by self-doubt and self-hatred because of the social stigma of being gay; to adults on the homosexual side of the Kinsey scale who marry for moral reasons or for social approval; and to the children of those unhappy marriages.

Anxious Masculinity

One of the harmful effects of the heavy emphasis on the black and white divide between "heterosexual" and "homosexual" is that it leads people who see themselves as "heterosexual" to think that they are not supposed to have homosexual responsiveness. Therefore, when a young man, who may have a perfectly satisfying heterosexual sex life, finds his body responding sexually to another male, he is apt to think something is wrong with him, that he's not masculine enough. This kind of experience may be very common, considering the pervasiveness of the perception in modern society that one is either "straight" or "gay." This not only explains a lot of the homophobia found in today's society but it also helps explain the defensive pseudo-masculinity evident in the strutting machismo of a large number of American males that the psychologist Stephen Ducat calls "anxious masculinity." In studying this defensive masculinity and the role it plays in contemporary politics and popular culture, Ducat primarily focuses on the fear of many men of becoming "feminized."[2] However, the findings of Henry Adams' experiments, which correlated the level of homophobic defenses displayed by males with the level of their homosexual responsiveness, strongly suggests that Ducat's "anxious masculinity" is triggered by unwanted homosexual impulses as well, and that homosexual responsiveness in the men may be associated in their minds with feminization because of the cultural stereotype of gay men as effeminate. Ironically, the straight-gay divide is important to the homophobic male's psychological defenses against same-sex responsiveness because it allows him to think that he is not like "them." Ducat says that a homophobic male has less difficulty relating to a flaming drag queen — and in fact doesn't mind posing for photos with them — than initiatives like gay marriage which treat gay men and women more like everybody else.[3]

The uneasiness of males about their masculinity because of unwanted homosexual feelings has significantly contributed to sexist attitudes. Just as anxious males want to see "homosexuals" clearly defined as "not me," and are comfortable with them as long as they are effeminate and not Rock Hudson types, insecure males need to see the appearance and behavior of men and women tightly restricted to their traditional gender roles. Men are the breadwinners, tough and in charge. Women are the sex objects, and defer to men. As Ducat shows, this is why conservative men were obsessed with the presidential candidacy of Hillary Clinton — she was seen as a threat to their vision of the male/female dichotomy on which their sexual identities depend. Along with the rigidly defined male and female roles, such men need to see women as the sex object, and not men. Conservative men therefore want women to dress in a feminine, sexual way, with plenty of make-up, and always ready to run and get some coffee for the guys. As a result some women will routinely dress for the office in form-fitting attire and a display of cleavage that overtly advertises their sexuality. On the other hand, because the idea of other males as sex objects deeply disturbs anxious males — because of the need to repress their homosexual responsiveness — for a male to dress in a sexually appealing way for the office or anywhere else but a singles bar or disco has been taboo. Consequently, men have traditionally worn bland, sexually innocuous clothes that conceal their sexual persona. Accordingly, young straight males in the United States will never wear a Speedo or bikini-type swim suit at the beach, and feel the need to camouflage their sexuality in baggy shorts — they don't want to be seen as "gay." A main theme of Ducat's book, *The Wimp Factor*, in which he examines the phenomenon of anxious masculinity, is how conservative politicians have manipulated the fears anxious males have about their sexuality by branding liberals and their social concerns as effeminate and weak and casting the conservative right as the embodiment of masculine virtues and prowess.[4] A prime example of this was seen at the 2004 Republican National Convention where Arnold Schwarzenegger, a man who built his career on the projection of a distorted caricature of masculinity, charged that men who supported the decorated, battle-injured war hero John Kerry over the draft-avoiding, National Guard drop-out George Bush were "girlie-men."

Religious Paranoia

Freud found that severe paranoia in one of his patients originated as a psychological defense against strong, unwanted homosexual feelings and fantasies. One of Freud's most striking and original theories, the development of paranoia in an individual as a defense against homosexual urges or thoughts has been verified in a number of clinical studies and research experiments conducted from the 1930s to the early 1970s.[5] Because a significant level of homosexual responsiveness occurs in a fairly large percentage of the population, which would inevitably include a fair number with strongly anti-homosexual conditioning, it could be expected that some degree of paranoia arising as an anti-homosexual psychological defense would be occurring among some of those religious and social conservatives so affected. Paranoia is a term that has been overused and is often misused, but the irrational outbursts about the threat of homosexuals to the American way of life frequently heard from religious conservatives display a mentality that would be hard to describe any other way. A good example can be found in remarks made on the floor of a legislative chamber by member of a state legislature who says that the homosexual "agenda" is a bigger threat to America than Islamic terrorism, and that gays are trying to "infiltrate" government and "indoctrinate" children into their lifestyle:

> "The homosexual agenda is destroying this nation ... studies show that no society that has totally embraced homosexuality has lasted more than, you know, a few decades.... I honestly think it's the biggest threat, even in our nation. Even more so than terrorists, or Islam, okay ... they're going after, err, in schools, two year olds! You know why they're trying to get early childhood education? They want to get our young children into the government schools so they can indoctrinate them ... gays are infiltrating city capitals ... and it's spreading and it will destroy our young people and it will destroy this nation."[6]

If paranoia can develop as a defense against homosexual responsiveness, it seems inevitable that such paranoia would manifest among some of those individuals with strong anti-homosexual moral beliefs whose sexual orientation also happens to fall either in the center or on the homosexual end of the Kinsey scale. It's worth noting that research on the authoritarian personality type found that authoritarians, who are very often religious fundamentalists, and are nearly always homophobic, also typically have a somewhat paranoid view of domestic and world affairs.[7] If one adds paranoia to the animosity that can manifest from reaction formation in such a person, it's not hard to see how such a person could really believe that "the homosexual agenda is destroying this nation," that gays represent a greater threat than terrorism, that they are "infiltrating" government, and that they're trying to "indoctrinate" young people into their wicked ways. Most Americans strongly believe that all citizens are entitled to their own religious and moral beliefs. However, when the psychological conflict between moral beliefs and the inherent homosexual responsiveness within many people manifests among government policy makers, the result, in effect, can be government policy — domestic or foreign relations — born out of demonstrable neurosis. As in the case of the manipulation by politicians of the fears of anxious males discussed in the preceding section, candidates have been distracting voters and winning elections by stoking the paranoia of homosexually repressed religious and social conservatives about the supposedly encroaching homosexual threat.

The Effects of Homophobia on Teens

Because of the saturation of popular culture with the heterosexual standard, which teaches children at an early age that the only good, healthy and normal sexuality is heterosexual, postpubescent teens are subjected to enormous stress in dealing with the homosexual impulses that are common to adolescents. Most teens quickly learn to force their sexual attention to members of the opposite sex, but the irrepressible nature of the homosexual drive of adolescence is a cause of considerable self-doubt and self-hatred for a significant percentage of teens whose growing self-identity is fragile enough without the burden of dealing with unwanted homosexual impulses. Consequently teens mount a variety of defenses to convince themselves and their peers that they are "normal" and not gay. The Kinsey Report found that teen-aged males will go to great lengths to project a strong heterosexual identity, and noted that as males grow into adulthood they are "continuously on the defensive against reactions which might be interpreted as homosexual."[8] As a normal part of their developing identity, teenaged males and females consciously mimic male and female stereotypes which helps them feel and appear normal. But because of the anxiety arising from normal homosexual impulses such defensive behavior among teen-aged males often goes to the extreme, producing super-machismo bravado and ostentatious heterosexual displays, like leering at girls and other sexist, macho behavior.

According to the research sociologist Diane Elze, who studied the effects of homophobia among adolescents, many adolescent males seek to remove doubts about their heterosexual manhood by "laying" as many girls as possible. Elze said that teen-aged males usually deny that homophobia plays any role in their sexual decision-making, but she says that denial that is strongly disputed by the young women in study who have observed the heterosexual posturing of their teen-aged male peers at close range. According to one 17-year-old heterosexual girl, "Guys try to prove how manly they are by how much they score, how many girls they conquer. If they can brag about how many girls they've slept with, if they can score a lot, no one would ever think they are gay." Another girl told Elze, "If a guy goes out on a date with some girl, and his friends ask him if he scored last night, if he says no, they'd say stuff like, 'Oh, you're not good enough,' or "You must be a faggot.'" The defensiveness of adolescent males about their heterosexual image seems to be a contributing cause of date rape as well. An 18-year-old woman told Elze, "I have so many friends who have been date raped. I know someone who was raped in front of a male friend of hers, and he didn't do anything about it. She said he just looked away and allowed it to happen. I'm sure he was afraid of being called queer." A 17-year-old male who had come out as gay told Elze that before he came out he had sex with girls just show that he was normal: "I just fucked someone to prove that I was OK. I'd go to a party and go into a bedroom with someone, and I was OK."[9]

The pressures to show that they are straight also drive adolescent girls to have sex. A 16-year-old girl interviewed by Elze told her, "homophobia forces a lot of people to be sexually active. Even young people who know they're straight feel like they have to show it to prevent themselves from being called queer." Explaining the pressures on teens to be sexually active, another girl told Elze: "In the locker room we'd talk about how many of us were virgins, how this guy was in bed, what party you were going to that night, and who you were going to be with.... The thing to do was to go out and get laid." A 20-year-old Lesbian Elze talked to told her: "When I first noticed I was having these 'odd feelings' toward women, probably in seventh grade, I tried to hide them for a long time. By the time I was in high school, I was very sexually active with men. I'd have sex at parties just to prove I was straight."[10]

As Elze observes, the pressure to prove to their peers that they're "OK" puts the sexually active teen-agers at great risk of contracting AIDS or other sexually transmitted diseases. Each year 2.5 million teen-agers, or one out of six, is infected with either AIDS or another sexually transmitted disease. Moreover, only 24 percent of unmarried teenage females aged 15–19 use any form of birth control, and only 21 percent of that figure report regular condom use.[11] As a result of the lack of use of contraceptives, nearly 750,000 teenage women aged 15–19 become pregnant in the United States each year.[12]

For some adolescents, the pressures on them because of their sexuality are so painful that they end up killing themselves. Recent research has shown that youth in conflict over their sexuality seriously contemplate suicide at a rate 50 to 70 percent greater than their peers.[13] Social conservative activist groups are fond of disparaging a 1989 task force report of the U.S. Department of Health and Human Services that found that as many as 30 percent of youth who commit suicide each year do so because of conflicts over their sexuality.[14] However, other studies have shown even higher figures for teenagers who kill themselves because of their sexuality. A 1993 study reported that as many as 42 percent of teen suicides are related to anxieties over homosexuality,[15] while a 1995 study found that such troubled teens commit suicide at a rate two or three times higher than heterosexual youth.[16]

Because of the harsh social environment in which may gay men and women have grown up, which has resulted in a high degree of self-doubt and self-hatred among many of them, a disproportionate number of gay men and Lesbians develop serious problems with alcoholism and drug abuse. Studies conducted over the last two decades on alcoholism within the gay population have found that the rate of alcoholism among gay males over 30 is 50 percent or more higher than in the general population. Among lesbians over 26, the rate of alcoholism is three times the rate for women in the general population.[17]

Anti-Homosexual Violence

One of the most common psychological defenses employed by adolescents to manage their homosexual impulses and to project the desired heterosexual image, particularly among males, is active homophobia, acting out against anyone in their community perceived of as being gay. As the Adams study discussed in the Introduction illustrated, fear and loathing of homosexuals is a common response to homosexuality among people heavily indoctrinated in conservative sexual morality. The results of the study show that aggressive homophobia is in all cases linked with a significant level of homosexual responsiveness in the individual. For teens insecure in their identity because of unwanted homosexual feelings and anxious about their heterosexual image, overt hostility to gays or others even suspected of being queer, is *de rigueur*, and consequently homophobic language deriding "fags" and "queers" is a commonplace in high schools across America. The overt homophobia in high schools naturally makes life for teens with strong same-sex orientation even more stressful. A report of the National Gay and Lesbian Task Force found that 28 percent of high school students who identify themselves as gay, lesbian or transgenderal feel the need to drop out of school because they don't feel safe in school.[18]

While the gay-baiting and verbal abuse of gays and lesbians is probably as far as most adolescents will go in their homophobia, a significant number of young males find it necessary to prove their masculinity through violence against gays and lesbians. Crime statistics, in fact, show that the vast majority of assaults on lesbians and gay men are committed by males under 30, with teenage males accounting for one out of three crimes.[19] While anti-gay violence by teenaged males is fueled by a homophobic fear and loathing of homosexuality, such violence also in a perverse way helps the young males feel more normal. According to Gary David Comstock, a social ethicist who conducted research on anti-gay violence, teenaged males are seeking "high sex-role identification" which in their minds requires "recognizing and conforming to the cultural stereotype of masculinity."[20] Violence perpetrated against gays and lesbians can help the young males feel a positive identification with their male peers and more positively about themselves as well.[21]

That the "cultural stereotype of masculinity" as transmitted to adolescent males entails gay-bashing is in itself a sad statement of the kind of values Western Christian morality has produced. Anyone familiar with the gruesome history of religious and civil persecution of homosexuality since the Middle Ages can see where adolescents acquired this moral perspective. In the introductory chapter Gary Cochran, a former member of the Aryan Nation, was quoted in describing the attitude he had when he was with that hate group: "It was taught from the beginning that homosexuality was evil, that homosexuals were evil perverts, and there was no alternative but death." Some might claim that Cochran's coarse statement is that of an anti-social skinhead hate group, and not a reflection of traditional Christian moral teaching. However, one has only to read the letters and moral writings of church leaders and moral theologians from the 12th century onward to see hundreds of similarly violent pronouncements concerning homosexuals — which in many cases specify the kind of death they think the homosexuals deserve. Unfortunately, in a letter to American bishops that ostensibly was to intended to deplore violence against gays and lesbians, the Vatican showed that the same Medieval mentality was alive and well, albeit in more muted form, when it blunted its supposed disapproval of anti-gay violence by supplying the perpetrators of homophobic violence with grounds to feel justified in their actions, which some might interpret as an endorsement of sorts. According to the Vatican, "when civil legislation is introduced to protect behavior to which no one has any conceivable right," people should not be surprised when "irrational and violent reactions increase."[22]

Such "irrational and violent reactions" against homosexuality also occurred in a tragedy that took the lives of 17 young men who were killed because of hatred for homosexuality. But in this case, the homosexual hated by the killer was himself. The 17 young men were the victims of the grisly killing spree of Jeffrey Dahmer, the neurotic homosexual whose self-loathing fueled a macabre binge of sex, murder and cannibalism that ended with his arrest in July of 1991. In Dahmer's case the spectacularly "irrational and violent reactions" that led to the death of his victims were traced by a forensic psychiatrist appointed by the trial court to Dahmer's hatred for his own homosexuality which he acquired during his upbringing in a fundamentalist Christian family. Taught from an early age that homosexuality was wrong, Dahmer knew from the moment he realized his homosexual feelings that his sexual impulses were sinful, and because of that he was convinced that his family would never accept him if they knew about his sexuality. Matters were not helped by insecurities he developed as his parents' marriage broke apart and ended during his early adolescence. As he grew into an adult, the conflict he experienced between his sexuality and his religious indoctrination would have been particularly acute. In high school he was deeply traumatized by his homosexual feelings and the sense that something about him was wrong, a painful dilemma he dealt with by heavy drinking and isolation from his peers. As an adult the self-loathing he felt because of his homosexuality fueled a build up of aggressive anger that he then directed at his victims.

According to Dr. George Palermo, a nationally recognized forensic psychiatrist appointed by the trial judge to evaluate Dahmer, "Aggressive, hostile tendencies led to his murderous behavior. His sexual drives functioned as a channel through which destructive power was expressed." Dr. Palmer added, "I don't believe his behavior was sexually motivated. I believe Jeffrey Dahmer killed his victims because he hated homosexuality." As he concluded his testimony, Dr. Palermo said in summary that Dahmer's murders were caused by "pent up aggression within himself. He killed those men because he wanted to kill the source of his homosexual attraction to them. In killing them, he killed what he hated in himself."[23]

As the standard definition of neurosis discussed in Chapter 14 would put it, Dahmer's strict fundamentalist upbringing required a "defense of the ego against an instinct," his homosexual impulses, "then a conflict between the instinct striving for discharge," his homosexual desires seeking release, "and the defensive forces of the ego, then a state of damming up, and finally the neurotic symptoms," murder and sexual abuse of his victims abetted by his alcoholism, "which are distorted discharges as a consequence of the state of damming up." The psychological conflict that occurred within Dahmer between his fundamentalist Christian indoctrination and his homosexual impulses was no different than the conflict that occurred within the ascetic moralists of the Medieval church between their own sexual instincts and their beliefs. In the case of Saint Peter Damian, the negativity and hatred for himself—"filthy putridness" is how he referred to his body—was directed into abusive treatment of himself. Damian's neurotic self abuse served as an example that was emulated by other members of the clergy who strove for carnal purity through self-torture, such as Henry Suso and Christina of St. Trond. In the case of Saint Bernardino of Siena and Savonarola, the hatred for their repressed sexual natures was clearly directed, like Dahmer's, at homosexuality in others — in the persons of the sodomists they both wished to see burned alive.

As gruesome as the case of Jeffrey Dahmer was, that multiple tragedy represents only a fraction of the murders annually committed against people for their homosexuality. According to reports of the National Coalition of Anti-Violence Programs, which collects statistics from eleven population centers around the country representing 26 percent of the total U.S. population, 157 anti-gay murders were committed in the eleven reporting cities between 1998 and 2006. Extrapolating to a number representative of the total U.S. population yields a total of 604 murders, or approximately 67 per year, that targeted victims because of their sexuality.[24]

Marriages with a Gay Spouse

Another class of victims of the heterosexual myth dominating modern society is the large number of spouses and the families of men or women with a significant homosexual component who marry in order to appear normal, for moral reasons or because of family or social pressure. As the Kinsey research team was conducting their interviews of the 20,000 men studied in their research, they found that a large number of males were either married during the period of their homosexual activity or had engaged in homosexual relations with married men. Based on the data the team collected, the Kinsey Report estimated that 18–20 percent of the married men in the United States engage in sexual relations with another male at least once in their lives. The frequency of married men engaging in same-sex relationships outside their marriage is corroborated by the experience of many gay men, 70 percent of whom, according to recently collected statistics, have had sex with married men.[25]

The evidence surveyed in earlier chapters from societies around the world and down through history has shown that there is a broad variability in sexual orientation of individuals in society. As the Kinsey scale illustrates, a fairly large percentage of the total population has a significant level of same-sex responsiveness. That is, a sizable number of people occupy points from the mid-point to the homosexual end of the Kinsey scale. When these facts are considered against the backdrop of both the strong heterosexual conditioning of Western culture and the frequently fierce negativity with which same-sex love is viewed, it could be expected that a large number of people who in other times and places may have opted for a same-sex relationship would end up in a marriage and with children. While many other societies have recognized the homosexual side of human sexuality and have accepted same-sex relationships as a complement to marriage and family life, that has obviously not been the case in Western society since the Middle Ages.

Because of the stigma of homosexuality, and the expectations of Western tradition that married couples should find perfect happiness and satisfaction within their marriage, a spouse with a significant homosexual drive has no morally or socially acceptable alternative but to suppress their homosexual side and make do with whatever satisfaction, if any, they can derive from marital relations with his or her spouse. Christian sexual morality has held, and Catholic doctrine still does hold, that sexual pleasure in and of itself is sinful. However, psychologists and sexual researchers and the vast majority of people in Western societies have long recognized that a healthy sex life is an important part of the emotional framework that supports the ups and down of any relationship and the difficulties to be faced in raising children, putting food on the table and the other chores of maintaining family life.

Because of the nature of sexual preference, and the satisfactions that are gained in fulfilling the sexual drive in a healthy way, a spouse whose preference runs to their own sex who marries for moral reasons, social approval or family expectations enters into a long-term partnership that is inevitably going to be psychologically and emotionally difficult for both partners. The fact that 18 to 20 percent of married men in the sexually conservative mid–20th century time period of the Kinsey study found it necessary to seek sexual satisfaction outside of their marriage with other men suggests that a significant number of American marriages may be inherently flawed by the sexual incompatibility of the partners.

When emotional difficulties occur in a marriage and the partners' needs are not being adequately met, the parents' ability to provide the emotional nurturing and support that children require is seriously impaired. Some such marriages inevitably end in divorce, while partners in other similar marriages turn to alcohol or other unhealthy outlets to seek to get their needs met. When the ability of the parents to nurture their children is negatively affected, the children are left feeling emotionally abandoned and insecure and may themselves begin to act out in unhealthy ways because their needs are not being met. Therefore, to the list of victims of the heterosexual myth should be added the men and women who are spouses of primarily homosexual partners and the children of such flawed marriages who are denied the nurturing and care that only psychologically and emotionally healthy parents are capable of providing.

Nature Out of Balance

As the material presented in Parts I and II of this book has demonstrated, the inherent ambisexuality of human sexuality provided a relatively harmonious regulation of sexual activity, apparent in most non–Western societies, in which marriage was not entered into before the partners were mature enough and had the psychological and logistical capability of parenting children. The diversion of the sex drive into homosexual relationships among adolescents and unmarried adults provided a harmless sexual release and intimate companionship for individuals in those societies who for reasons of age or occupation were in no position to provide parenting for a child. In many of the societies where marriages are arranged between the families, the ability of the partners to find sexual satisfaction in a homosexual relationship that complemented that of their marriage without the risk of illegitimate offspring promoted a harmony and durability in the marriage that could have been threatened if one or both of the partners had found the sexual relationship with their "arranged" partner unfulfilling.

The changes that occurred among the indigenous tribal people of the Santa Cruz Islands of the Southwest Pacific as Westernization overtook their culture in the 1970s and 1980s illustrate in microcosm the imbalance in sexual expression that has occurred in Western society because of the imposition of the heterosexual norm. The anthropologist William Davenport, who studied the sexual practices of the islanders in the 1960s, found that among the natives of the islands homosexual relationships for adolescents and unmarried adults were the norm and were guided by long-standing traditions, and that heterosexual activity did not occur until the partners were in their mid–20s and had become married. When Davenport returned to the islands in the 1980s, he found that the pervasive same-sex traditions he studied were being replaced with extensive extramarital heterosexual permissiveness. As Davenport remarked on his return, there was a great deal of public indignation among the islanders about the extent of extramarital sex and the resulting children born out of wedlock, but he said that "both government and church, oddly, have worked hard and successfully against the application of severe sanctions against heterosexual offenses." He added that, "It is my impression that with this permissiveness toward extramarital heterosexual relations, there has been a distinct decline in peer same-sex relations."[26]

It is abundantly clear that the imposition of this heterosexual myth, a simplistic and rigidly defined model of sexuality, as the standard for all has engendered not a wholesome sexuality in the West, but an exaggerated emphasis on heterosexuality that throws out of balance a complex sexual harmony that has been long observed in many other world cultures. The stresses inherent in the struggle of many of the males who would fall into the middle of the Kinsey scale to mold their lives on the restricted heterosexual norm give rise to homophobic defenses on the one hand, and showy demonstrations of heterosexual interest on the other, contributing to the relegation of women as sex objects in contemporary society. The repression of homosexual impulses natural among adolescents incites homophobic paranoia and a need to act out heterosexually to prove that they are "normal."

The pressure for adolescents to conform to the heterosexual norm results in premature heterosexual development, conditioning them to a heterosexual identity well before they are physically, emotionally and psychologically capable of sustaining the enormous efforts required to raise and nurture a child. The epidemic of abortions and children born to unwed mothers testifies to the harm created in thwarting the natural deflection of the sex drive away from inappropriate heterosexual couplings. The experience of many societies throughout history has demonstrated that allowed free expression young people usually do not seek heterosexual fulfillment until they have matured and are ready to shoulder parenting duties, and will seek sexual companionship with their own sex until that time. Moral leaders hype chastity among the young, but Western history as well as a significant amount of research has demonstrated that sexual abstinence can do more harm than good. Human nature being what it is, it is inevitable that adolescents in a period of their lives when their sexual hormones are at their peak will seek sexual relationships, whether condoned by society or not.

As the pedophile scandal within the Roman Catholic clergy has demonstrated, the natural force of the sexual instinct is going to seek release one way or the other. The adult-youth relationship pattern the priests engaged in is ironically the single most common pattern of homosexuality among males in world cultures down through history, and has been shown to be very beneficial to the younger partner *under the right conditions*, as discussed in Chapter 3. However, the social environment in which they were conducted, and the absence of a culturally supportive context for the relationship, had the effect of creating enormous anxiety and guilt for the adolescents as they grew into maturity in a society that stigmatized the kind of relationships they innocently engaged in. The inappropriate direction in which the sexual interests of the pedophile priests was directed is a prime example of the "distorted discharges" that Otto Fenichel's definition of neurosis states occur as the result of the "damming up" of the instinct. The tragedies that have occurred in the lives of the pedophile victims, and in the lives of the priests themselves, is an inevitable consequence of the attempt to dam up a basic instinctual drive.

In the case of people with a primary same-sex orientation, the societal pressures on them to force themselves into a heterosexual lifestyle is like forcing square pegs into round holes. It causes tremendous suffering among those individuals for whom heterosexuality does not come naturally, leading to broken marriages, alcoholism and other emotional problems. Equally disturbing, it also harms the children of such neurotically stressed parents who are denied the nurturing and care only available from emotionally healthy and balanced people. Aside from the psychological harm resulting from imposing a heterosexual standard on people whose nature is incompatible with heterosexual marriage, the widespread intolerance of homosexuality that continues today has produced a ghettoized gay culture that encourages promiscuity and further stigmatizes gays in their minds and in the eyes of society.[27]

Hope for Our Species

It is hard to ignore the role that the abuse of religion has played in generating and enforcing the sexual neurosis that permeates our society today. As we saw in Chapters 4 and 9, condemnation of homosexuality is not rooted in an accurate reading of scripture, but in distortion and mistranslation of Hebrew scripture, and in the amalgam of pagan philosophical theories about sex and nature and the moral absolutism of the Old Testament that developed in the early Christian church.

If the authoritarian atmosphere created by the strengthening power of the Medieval church, the centralizing of authority in the newly powerful nation-states and the violent suppression of dissent and sexual non-conformity that accompanied these developments made possible the enforcement of sexual conformity in European society in the late Middle Ages, so the openness and free communication and thought of today's society may inevitably lead a reemergence of the natural homosexual complement to heterosexuality in our society — just as the availability of fax machines and open communications contributed to the collapse of communism in Europe. Under the ventilation of free inquiry and thought, the distortion of scriptural intent that seems obvious in current Christian sexual dogma would certainly become apparent to more Christians. Indeed, if Christian leaders are really interested in the primacy of love, as Christ taught, compassion might compel them to re-examine the supposed scriptural bases for their prejudice in view of the demonstrable harm done to both gay and straight people because of society's prejudice.

In several ways the heterosexual myth that emerged in the Middle Ages is similar to the Medieval view that the world is flat. It arose in an environment where much of what passed for knowledge was shaped by ignorance and superstition. It provided a comfortable, rational picture of what was familiar, and anything outside the margins was unthinkable and horrible. Captains who sailed too far from known waters risked mutiny from sailors who feared the ship would fall over the edge of the earth, just as men who fell in love with other men were branded heretics and burned at the stake. And like the "world is flat" theory, the heterosexual myth cannot survive objective scrutiny, from either a scientific, historical or scriptural perspective.

But the greatest hope for a restoration to sanity in the sexual life of our society comes from the nature of our species itself. Like the inevitable workings of time on the pyramids, society's attempt to thwart the true character of our natures must give way to the immutable flow of nature itself, renewing itself and emerging afresh, unsullied with each new generation born. Just as the pounding of the seas on a cliff gradually wear away the hardest rock, the sturdiest of human restrictions will fall away before the powerful tide of nature just being itself.

The Purpose of Sex

Men and women do not usually think of having children when they date, or even when they make love. In fact, considerable effort is often expended by heterosexual couples in today's world in trying to prevent conception of a child. The primary motivation driving people in seeking and dating another is the desire for loving and intimate companionship. As the Book of Genesis states it: "It is not good that a human remain alone. Every human has a need of a companion of his or her own kind!"[28] The aim of sexual desire, then, is for companionship, whether it be heterosexual or homosexual. The principal purpose of the erotic drive is to establish and maintain the physical bond that ties two partners together.[29] If the bond is heterosexual, the result, obviously, can be propagation of the species. If the bond is homosexual, the product is the economic, artistic and spiritual contribution to the quality of life and health of society as a whole that was recognized by Native American cultures in the role of the two-spirit (discussed in Chapter 2) and that was exalted by Plato in his dialogue on love, the *Symposium* (discussed in Chapter 7).

Because the desire for love and intimacy provides a tremendous incentive for young people to develop and improve themselves so that they can acquire an appropriate mate, the sex drive is also a powerful force in promoting general health and economic productivity in society. In a similar way the comfort and joy of a loving relationship provides powerful support for individuals in working toward goals and meeting life's challenges, whether they involve building a family or intangible contributions to society.

To say that the purpose of sex is solely to produce children, then, is a gross oversimplification of the role this powerful drive plays in human life. It would be more accurate to say that the purpose of this instinct is to drive physical life itself. Life means getting out there, doing things, creating and producing. And, for humans, creating sometimes means making intangible but important contributions to society's welfare, and it sometimes means the creation of new life. The sex drive, therefore, should be seen not only as a mechanism through which our species reproduces itself, but as a tremendous engine of human activity, providing incentive to grow and develop, spurring humans to seek companionship, powering the growth and maintenance of loving and mutually caring relationships, supporting creative and productive endeavors that contribute to the care and health of our society and, ultimately, under the right circumstances, bringing about that most beautiful miracle of life, the birth of a new human being. But saying that sex is only about producing offspring is to be blind to the complexities of our complex ambisexual nature, one of the most beautiful gifts nature has given us.

Chapter Notes

Introduction

1. *Random House History of the English Language*, Second Edition (New York: Random House, 2005).
2. *Bowers v. Hardwick*, 478 U.S. 186.
3. Ingrid Ricks, "Straight über alles," *The Advocate*, May 2, 1995, pages 35–37.
4. The actual quotation from Act III, Scene 2, of Shakespeare's *Hamlet* is "The lady doth protest too much, methinks." The line is spoken by Hamlet's mother about a character in a play Hamlet had performed for her and the king to test their reaction to a murder in the play that mimics circumstances that Hamlet thinks led to his father's death.
5. Henry E. Adams, Ph.D., Lester W. Wright, Jr., Ph.D., and Bethany A. Lohr, "Is Homophobia Associated with Homosexual Arousal?" *Journal of Abnormal Psychology*, vol. 105, no. 3 (1996), pages 440–445.
6. Alfred C. Kinsey, Wardell B. Pomeroy, and Clyde E. Martin, *Sexual Behavior in the Human Male* (Philadelphia: W.B. Saunders Company, 1948), page 639.
7. C.A. Tripp, *The Homosexual Matrix* (New York: McGraw-Hill, 1975), page 36.
8. G. Rattray Taylor, *Sex in History* (New York: Harper Torchbooks, 1970), page 19.

Chapter 1

1. Longus, *Daphnis and Chloe*, quoted in David F. Greenberg, *The Construction of Homosexuality* (Chicago: University of Chicago Press, 1988), page 209.
2. Alfred C. Kinsey, Wardell B. Pomeroy, Clyde E. Martin, and P.H. Gebhard, *Sexual Behavior in the Human Female* (Philadelphia: W.B. Saunders, 1953) page 448.
3. Clellan S. Ford and Frank A. Beach, *Patterns of Sexual Behavior* (Westport, Connecticut: Greenwood Press, 1951), page 142.
4. R.H. Denniston, "Ambisexuality in Animals," in Judd Marmor, editor, *Homosexual Behavior, A Modern Reappraisal* (New York: Basic Books, 1980), page 34.
5. *Ibid.*, page 32.
6. *Ibid.*, page 29, quoting Desmond Morris.
7. James D. Weinrich, *Sexual Landscapes* (New York: Charles Scribner's Sons, 1987), pages 283–285.
8. Denniston, pages 30–31.
9. Ford and Beach, pages 140–143.
10. Weinrich, pages 297–298.
11. John A.W. Kirsch and James D. Weinrich, "Homosexuality, Nature and Biology: Is Homosexuality Natural: Does It Matter?" in John C. Gonsiorek and James D. Weinrich, editors, *Homosexuality: Research Implications for Public Policy* (London: Sage Publications, 1991), pages 16–17.
12. Filmed on *Nature*, Public Broadcasting Service.
13. Denniston, page 34.
14. Wainwright Churchill, *Homosexual Behavior among Males* (New York, Hawthorn Books, 1967), pages 60–61.
15. Raymond De Becker, *The Other Side of Love* (New York: Grove Press, 1969) page 21.
16. Ford and Beach, page 143.
17. *Ibid.*, page 141.
18. C.A. Tripp, *The Homosexual Matrix* (New York: McGraw Hill, 1975), page 34.
19. Ford and Beach, pages 141–142.
20. Bruce Bagemihl, *Biological Exuberance: Animal Homosexuality and Natural Diversity* (New York: St. Martin's Press, 1999), page 406.
21. Denniston, page 34.
22. *Ibid.*
23. Bagemihl, page 406.
24. *Ibid.*, page 407.
25. Denniston, pages 34–35.
26. Bagemihl, pages 402–417.
27. *Ibid.*, pages 413–416.
28. *Ibid.*, page 392.
29. *Ibid.*, pages 397–400.
30. Denniston, page 38, quoting Desmond Morris.
31. Weinrich, pages 304–305.
32. Filmed on *Nature*, Public Broadcasting Service.
33. Bagemihl, pages 353–354.
34. Denniston, page 37.
35. A.F. McBride and D.O. Hebb, "Behavior of the Captive Bottlenose Dolphin, Tursiops Truncatus," *Journal of Comparative Physiological Psychology*, vol. 41 (1948).
36. Bagemihl, pages 342–347.
37. McBride and Hebb.
38. Bagemihl, pages 349–350.
39. Ford and Beach, 136.
40. Weinrich, page 299.
41. Ford and Beach, page 135.
42. *Ibid.*, page 134.
43. Kirsch and Weinrich, page 17.
44. Weinrich, pages 300–302.
45. Bagemihl, pages 302–313.
46. *Ibid.*, page 298.
47. Ford and Beach, 135–137.
48. Denniston, page 37.
49. Bagemihl, pages 280–282.
50. Thorkil Vanggaard, *Phallos, a Symbol and Its History in the Male World* (New York: International Universities Press, 1972), pages 73–74.
51. Lord Solly Zuckerman, *The Social Life of Monkeys and Apes* (London: Routledge & Kegan Paul, 1981), pages 229–230.
52. *Ibid.*, pages 248–249.
53. Frans B.M. de Waal, "Bonobo Sex and Society," *Scientific American*, vol. 272 (March 1995), page 82.
54. Adrienne L. Zihlman, John E. Cronin, Douglas L. Cramer, and Vincent M. Sarich, "Pygmy Chimpanzees as a Possible Prototype for the Common Ancestor of Humans, Chimpanzees and Gorillas," *Nature*, vol. 275 (26 October 1978), pages 744–745; de Waal, page 82.
55. Ben G. Blount, "Issues in Bonobo (Pan paniscus) Sexual Behavior," *American Anthropologist*, vol. 92 (1990), pages 705–706; de Waal, pages 84–86.
56. De Waal, pages 84–86.
57. De Waal, *Peacemaking among Primates* (Cambridge, Mass.: Harvard University Press, 1989), page 201.
58. Blount, pages 703–705.
59. De Waal, "Bonobo Sex," page

88; Blount considers the possibility, but is skeptical that whatever tension-reducing role sex played among early humans would have had a significant impact on the development of human sexual behavior.

60. Janet Mann, "Establishing Trust: Sociosexual Behaviour and the Development of Male-Male bonds among Indian Ocean Bottlenose Dolphin Calves," in P. Vasey and V. Sommers, editors, *Homosexual Behaviour in Animals: An Evolutionary Perspective* (London: Cambridge University Press, 2006), pages 107–130.

61. Volker Sommer and Paul L. Vasey, editors, *Homosexual Behaviour in Animals: An Evolutionary Perspective* (London: Cambridge University Press, 2006), contains studies from several dozen evolutionary biologists and ethnologists exploring these and other factors in the evolution of homosexual behavior among animals.

Chapter 2

1. Walter L. Williams, *The Spirit and the Flesh: Sexual Diversity in American Indian Culture* (Boston: Beacon Press, 1992), pages 136–137.

2. David F. Greenberg, *The Construction of Homosexuality* (Chicago: University of Chicago Press, 1988), pages 164–165.

3. C.A. Tripp, *The Homosexual Matrix* (New York: McGraw-Hill, 1975), page 42.

4. Francisco Guerra, *The Pre–Columbian Mind* (New York: Seminar Press, 1971), pages 70, 76.

5. Greenberg, page 164.

6. Williams, page 135.

7. Guerra, page 91.

8. Williams, pages 137–140.

9. Greenberg, page 165.

10. Williams, page 136.

11. Rictor Norton, *The Myth of the Modern Homosexual* (London: Cassell, 1997), page 31.

12. Guerra, pages 172–173.

13. Williams, pages 143–144.

14. *Ibid.*, pages 144–145.

15. Greenberg, pages 71.

16. Williams, pages 91, 120.

17. Greenberg, pages 68–71.

18. *Ibid.*, pages 69–70.

19. Claude Levi-Strauss, *A World on the Wane* (London: Hutchinson, 1961).

20. Williams, page 81.

21. *Ibid.*, page 59.

22. *Ibid.*, page 120.

23. *Ibid.*, page 46.

24. Mircea Eliade, quoted in Raymond de Becker, *The Other Face of Love* (New York: Grove Press, 1969), page 7.

25. Greenberg, pages 56–57;

Joseph Campbell, *Historical Atlas of World Mythology, Volume 1: The Way of the Animal Powers, Part 2: Mythologies of the Great Hunt* (New York: Harper & Row, 1988), page 174.

26. Williams, pages 141–142.

27. Gilbert H. Herdt, *Ritualized Homosexuality in Melanesia* (Los Angeles: University of California Press, 1984), page xix.

28. Greenberg, page 78.

29. Williams, page 13.

30. Greenberg, page 70n.

31. Williams, page 215.

32. *Ibid.*, page 13.

33. Greenberg, page 77.

34. Leslie L. Gambold, "Homosexuality and Lesbianism: Cross-Cultural Perspectives," in Vern Bullough, editor, *Human Sexuality, An Encyclopedia* (New York: Garland Publishing Company, 1994).

35. Wainwright Churchill, *Homosexual Behavior among Males: A Cross-Cultural and Cross-Species Investigation* (New York: Hawthorn Books, 1967), page 70.

36. Herdt, pages 73–74.

37. Merriam, quoted in Stephen O. Murray and Will Roscoe, *Boy-Wives and Female Husbands: Studies of African Homsexualities* (New York: St. Martin's Press, 1998), page xiii.

38. Churchill, page 71.

39. Kenneth E. Read, "The Nama Cult Recalled," in Herdt, page 216.

40. Clellan S. Ford, and Frank A. Beach, *Patterns of Sexual Behavior* (Westport, Conn.: Greenwood Press, 1951), page 129.

41. Greenberg, pages 81–88.

42. Jonathan Ned Katz, *Gay American History* (New York: Meridian, 1992), pages 288–293.

43. Katz, page 289.

44. *Ibid.*, pages 303–312.

45. Williams, page 92.

46. *Ibid.*

47. *Ibid.*, pages 168–169.

48. George Devereux, "Institutionalized Homosexuality of the Mohave Indians," *Human Biology*, vol. 9 (1937), pages 498–527.

49. Fred Voget, "American Indians," in Albert Ellis and Albert Abarbanel, editors, *The Encyclopedia of Sexual Behavior* (New York, Hawthorne Books, 1961), Vol 1., pp. 99–100.

50. Williams, pages 90–92.

51. Katz, pages 287–288.

52. Greenberg, pages 48–49.

53. Williams, page 18.

54. *Ibid.*, pages 18–21.

55. Devereux, page 501.

56. Williams, page 49.

57. *Ibid.*, page 63.

58. Greenberg, page 42.

59. Williams, page 234.

60. Greenberg, page 42.

61. *Ibid.*, page 49.

62. Williams, page 58

63. *Ibid.*, pages 55–57.

64. *Ibid.*, pages 68–69.

65. *Ibid.*, page 34.

66. *Ibid.*, pages 107–108.

67. *Ibid.*, pages 105–106.

68. *Ibid.*, pages 108–109.

69. *Ibid.*, pages 35–37.

70. Raymond de Becker, *The Other Face of Love* (New York: Grove Press, 1969), page 8, quoting Don C. Talayessva, *Sun Chief: Autobiography of a Hopi Indian*, ed. Leo W. Summons (New Haven, Conn.: Yale College, Institute of Human Relations, 1942).

71. DeBecker, page 7, quoting George Catlin, *Drawings and Notes on the Habits, Customs and Life of the North American Indian* (London: George Catlin, 1844).

72. Joseph Cambell, *The Masks of God: Primitive Mythology* (New York: Penguin Books, 1959), pages 282–283; Campbell, *Historical Atlas of World Mythology*, Vol. 1, Part 1, pages 75–76.

73. Campbell, *Historical Atlas*, Vol. 1, Part 2, pages 156, 164–165.

74. *Ibid.*, page 174.

75. Greenberg, page 58.

76. Bret Hinsch, *Passions of the Cut Sleeve: The Male Homosexual Tradition in China* (Berkeley: University of California Press, 1990), page 90.

77. Williams, page 255.

78. Greenberg, page 58.

79. Williams, pages 255–256.

80. *Ibid.*, page 258.

81. Greenberg, page 58.

82. Williams, page 256.

83. Stephen O. Murray, *Oceanic Homosexualities* (New York: Garland Publishing, 1992), page 399.

84. Greenberg, pages 117–118.

85. *Ibid.*, pages 58–68.

86. D. Michael Quinn, *Same-Sex Dynamics among Nineteenth-Century Americans* (Chicago: University of Illinois Press, 1996), page 38.

87. Stephen O. Murray, *Homosexualities* (Chicago: University of Chicago Press, 2000), page 97.

88. *Ibid.*

89. *Ibid.*, page 98.

90. Quinn, page 38.

91. *Ibid.*

92. Murray, *Homosexualities*, page 99, quoting 1990 correspondence from the historian Robert Morris.

93. Quinn, page 39.

94. *Ibid.*, pages 55–56n37.

95. Greenberg, pages 67–68; Ford and Beach, page 133.

96. W. Davenport, quoted in J.M. Carrier, "Homosexual Behavior in Cross-Cultural Perspective," in Judd Marmor, editor, *Homosexual Behavior, A Modern Reappraisal* (New York: Basic Books, 1980), page 119.

97. A. Bernard Deacon, *Malekula*

(London: Routledge Paul, 1934), page 261, quoted in Stephen O. Murray, "Female Homosexuality in Pacific Societies: Introduction," in Murray, *Oceanic Homosexualities,* pages 397–398.

98. Deacon, page 170, quoted in ibid., page 398.

99. Murray, "Female Homosexualitiy," page 358.

100. Greenberg, page 67.

101. Herdt, page 47.

102. Ford and Beach, page 132.

103. Murray, "Female Homosexualitiy," page 358.

104. T.N. Barker, "Some Features of Ai'i Society," Ph.D Dissertation, Laval University, 1975, quoted in Eric Schwimmer, "Male Couples in New Guinea," in Herdt, page 271.

105. Tobias Schneebaum, *Where the Spirits Dwell: An Odessey in the Jungle of New Guinea* (New York: Grove Press, 1989), page 42.

106. Schneebaum, page 195.

107. *Ibid.*, pages 193–196.

108. Greenberg, page 69.

109. Ford and Beach, page133.

110. Murray, *Oceanic Homosexualities,* page 399.

111. F.E. Williams, quoted in Herdt, page 21.

112. Herdt, pages 6–7.

113. Greenberg, page 39n70.

114. Raymond Kelly, quoted, in Carrier, pages 114–115

115. Herdt, *Guardians of the Flutes* (Chicago, University of Chicago Press, 1981), pages 251–254.

116. *Ibid.*, page 236.

117. Herdt, *Ritualized Homosexuality,* page 188.

118. *Ibid.*, page 176.

119. *Ibid.*, pages 189, 210 n7.

120. *Ibid.*, page 63.

121. Herdt, *Same Sex, Different Cultures* (New York: Westview Press, 1997), p. 85.

122. Herdt, *Ritualized Homosexuality,* page 27.

123. *Ibid.*, pages 63–64.

124. J. Van Baal, quoted in Carrier, page 115.

125. Schneebaum, pages 181–182.

126. Herdt, *Ritualized Homosexuality,* pages 24–28.

127. Schneebaum.

128. Weston La Barre, *Muelos: A Stone Age Superstition about Sexuality* (New York: Columbia University Press, 1984), pages 13–72.

129. Ibid; Bernard Sargent, *Homosexuality in Greek Myth* (Boston: Beacon Press, 1984), pages 1–4; Jan Bremmer, "An Enigmatic Indo-European Rite: Paederasty," *Arethusa,* vol. 13 (1980), pages 279–293.

130. Herdt, *Ritualized Homosexuality,* page 20.

131. *Ibid.*, pages 49–50.

132. Greenberg, page 35n.

133. Eric Schwimmer, "Male Couples in New Guinea," in Herdt, *Ritualized Homosexuality,* pages 259–268.

134. Herdt, *Ritualized Homosexuality,* pages 48–54.

135. *Ibid.*, pages 33, 53.

136. Greenberg, pages 35–36.

137. Arve Sorum, "Growth and Decay: Bedamini Notions of Sexuality," in Herdt, *Ritualized Homosexuality,* page 325.

138. Herdt, *Ritualized Homosexuality,* page 20.

139. Davenport, quoted in Murray, page 357.

140. Greenberg, page 36n57.

141. Herdt, *Ritualized Homosexuality,* page 5; Williams, page 278.

142. Edward Westermarck, *Ritual and Belief in Morocco* (London: Macmillan, 1926), quoted in Stephen O. Murray, "Some Nineteenth-Century Reports of Islamic Homosexualities," in Stephen O. Murray and Will Roscoe, editors, *Islamic Homosexualities, Culture, History and Literature* (New York: New York University Press, 1997), page 218.

143. E.E. Evans-Pritchard, "Sexual Inversion among the Azande," *American Anthropologist,* vol. 72 (1970), pages 1428–1431.

144. *Ibid.*, page 1430.

145. *Ibid.*, pages 1431–1432.

146. Wayne R. Dynes, "Homosexuality in Sub-Saharan Africa: An Unnecessary Question," *Gay Books Bulletin,* vol. 9 (1983), pages 20–21.

147. Greenberg, pages 66–71.

148. *Ibid.*, pages 68–69.

149. *Ibid.*, page 67.

150. Wayne R. Dynes, Introduction, in Dynes and Stephen Donaldson, editors, *Ethnographic Studies of Homosexuality* (New York: Garland Publishing, 1992), page xiii.

151. Greenberg, page 31.

152. DeBecker, page 6.

153. Ford and Beach, page 132.

154. Herdt, *Same Sex,* page 80.

155. Tripp, pages 68–69.

156. Greenberg, page 87.

157. *Ibid.*, page 79.

158. *Ibid.*, page 75–76.

159. *Ibid.*, page 81.

Chapter 3

1. C.A. Tripp, *The Homosexual Matrix* (New York: McGraw-Hill, 1975), page 68.

2. John A.W. Kirsch and James Eric Rodman, "The Natural History of Homosexuality," *Yale Scientific Magazine,* Winter 1977, page 7.

3. Sigmund Freud, "Bruchstuck einer Hysterie-Analyse," *Sammlung*

Kleiner Schriften zur Neurosenlehre (1909), quoted in Havelock Ellis, *Studies in the Psychology of Sex, Volume 1, Part 4, Sexual Inversion* (New York: Random House, 1942), page 80.

4. Otto Fenichel, *The Psychoanalytic Theory of Neurosis* (New York: Routledge & Kegan Paul, 1945), page 112; Ellis; on pages 80–81 Ellis summaries the similar views of other authorities in published studies from 1889 to 1912. See also Albert Moll, *The Sexual Life of a Child,* translated by Eden Paul (New York: Macmillan, 1919), pages 50ff.

5. Frank M. Richardson, *Mars without Venus: A Study of Some Homosexual Generals* (Edinburgh: William Blackwood, 1981), pages 6–30, 165–177; Frank Richardson, *Napoleon: Bisexual Emperor* (New York: Horizon Press, 1973), pages 79–80, 167–169.

6. Henry E. Adams, Lester W. Wright Jr., and Bethany A Lohr, "Is Homophobia Associated with Homosexual Arousal?" *Journal of Abnormal Psychology,* vol. 105, no. 3 (1996), pages 440–445.

7. Tripp, pages 82–83.

8. Walter L. Williams, *The Spirit and the Flesh: Sexual Diversity in American Indian Culture* (Boston: Beacon Press, 1992), page 91.

9. Tripp, page 41.

10. Stephen O. Murray, *Oceanic Homosexualities* (New York: Garland Publishing, 1992), page 357.

11. Tripp, page 81.

12. Fenichel, pages 335–336.

13. *Ibid.*, page 335.

14. Thorkil Vanggaard, *Phallos: A Symbol and Its History in the Male World* (New York: International Universities Press, 1972), page115.

15. These studies by Kurt Freund are described in James D. Weinrich, *Sexual Landscapes* (New York: Charles Scribner's Sons, 1987), Chapter 8.

16. Alfred C. Kinsey, Wardell B. Pomeroy, and Clyde E. Martin, *Sexual Behavior in the Human Male* (Philadelphia, W.B. Saunders Company, 1948), page 168.

17. Vanggaard, page 54.

18. Fenichel, page 334.

19. Tripp, page 81.

20. Vanggaard, pages 53–54.

21. Tripp, page 81.

22. Vanggaard, page 53; Tripp, pages 86–87.

23. Gilbert H. Herdt, *Ritualized Homosexuality in Melanesia* (Los Angeles: University of California Press, 1984), pages 62–63.

24. Vanggaard, pages 11–19.

25. Tripp, page 71.

26. Gilbet H. Herdt, *Guardians of the Flutes* (Chicago, University of Chicago Press, 1981), page 252n60.

27. Kinsey, et al. page 625.

28. *Ibid.* pages 625–626.
29. Wainwright Churchill, *Homosexual Behavior among Males* (New York: Hawthorn Books, 1967), page 58.
30. *Ibid.*, pages 610–666.
31. Francis Mark Mondimore, *A Natural History of Homsexuality* (Baltimore: Johns Hopkins University Press, 1996), page 89.
32. Fritz Klein, *The Bisexual Option* (Binghamton, N.Y.: Haworth Press, 1993).
33. The research is described in Mondimore, pages 136–141.
34. *Ibid.*, pages 141–146.
35. *Ibid.*, pages 122–128.
36. Edward O. Wilson, *On Human Nature* (Cambridge, Mass.: Harvard University Press, 1978), page 146.
37. *Ibid.*, pages 144–145; Kirsch and Rodman, pages 8–12.
38. David F. Greenberg, *The Construction of Homosexuality* (Chicago: University of Chicago Press, 1988), pages 36–37.
39. Herdt, *Ritualized Homosexuality,* page 57.
40. Bernard Sergent, *Homosexuality in Greek Myth*, translated by Arthur Goldhammer (Boston: Beacon Press, 1986), pages 1–4; Jan Bremmer, "An Enigmatic Indo-European Rite: Paederasty," *Arethusa*, vol. 13, no. 2 (1980), pages 279–293; Georges Dumezil, Preface to Sergent, pages vii–ix.
41. Weston La Barre, *Muelos: A Stone Age Superstition about Sexuality* (New York: Columbia University Press, 1984), page 35.

Chapter 4

1. Jaquetta Hawkes and Sir Leonard Woolley, *Prehistory and the Beginnings of Civilization* (New York: Harper & Row, 1963), page 218.
2. Joseph Campbell, *The Masks of God: Primitive Mythology* (New York: Penguin Books, 1969), page vii.
3. Hawkes and Woolley, page 242.
4. *Ibid.*, page 371.
5. Vern L. Bullough, *Sexual Variance in Society and History* (New York: John Wiley & Sons, 1976), page 55; David F. Greenberg, *The Construction of Homosexuality* (Chicago: University of Chicago Press, 1988), page 126.
6. Bullough, pages 54–55.
7. Greenberg, pages 124–126.
8. *Ibid.*, page 126.
9. Bullough, page 56.
10. *Ibid.*
11. Greenberg, page 127n.
12. *Ibid.*, pages 126–127.
13. Will Roscoe, "Precursors of Islamic Homosexualities," in Stephen O. Murray, editor, *Islamic Homosexualities* (New York: Garland Publishing), page 65.

14. Greenberg, page 97.
15. Hawkes and Woolley, pages 334–344; see also Marijas Gimbutas, *The Goddesses and Gods of Old Europe: Myths and Cult Images* (Berkeley: University of Califormia Press, 1982), pages 112–215.
16. Campbell, *Masks of God,* pages 36–37.
17. James Mellaart, *Catal Huyuk* (New York: McGraw-Hill, 1967), pages 23–24; see also Hawkes and Wooley, pages 218–227.
18. Hawkes and Woolley, pages 218–227; Campbell, *Masks of God,* pages 36–45.
19. Riane Eisler, *The Chalice and the Blade: Our History, Our Future* (San Francisco: Harper Collins, 1988), pages 56–58.
20. Gordon Rattray Taylor, "Historical and Mythological Aspects of Homosexuality," in Judd Marmor, editor, *Sexual Inversion: The Multiple Roots of Homosexuality* (New York: Basic Books, 1965), pages 148–149; Greenberg, 94–100.
21. Edwin M. Yamauchi, "Cultic Prostitution: A Case in Cultural Diffusion," in Harry A. Hoffner, Jr., editor, *Orient and Occident* (Neukirchen-Vluyn: Verlag Butzon & Bercker Kevelaer, 1973), pages 214–217.
22. Roscoe, pages 66–67.
23. Guerra, page 91.
24. Raymond de Becker, *The Other Face of Love* (New York: Grove Press, 1969), page 8, quoting Don C. Talayessva, *Sun Chief: Autobiography of a Hopi Indian*, ed. Leo W. Summons (New Haven: Yale College, Institute of Human Relations, 1942).
25. DeBecker, page 7, quoting Catlin.
26. Greenberg, page 101.
27. Yamauchi, page 214.
28. Greenberg, page 96.
29. Roscoe, page 67.
30. N. K. Sandars, *The Epic of Gilgamesh* (London: Penguin Books, 1972), pages 8, 13.
31. Anne Draffkorn Kilmer, "A Note on an Overlooked Word-Play in the Akkadian Gilgamesh," in G. Van Driel, T.J.H. Krispijn, M. Stol, and K.R. Veenhof, editors, *Zikir Sumim: Assyriological Studies Presented to F.R. Kraus on the Occasion of his Seventieth Birthday* (Leiden: E.J. Brill, 1982), page 129.
32. Sandars, page 30.
33. Translations, except where noted, from Alexander Heidel, *The Gilgamesh Epic and Old Testament Parallels* (Chicago: University of Chicago Press, 1971), pages 18–33.
34. Thorkild Jacobsen, "How Did Gilgamesh Oppress Uruk?" *Acta Orientalia*, vol. 8 (1929), page 70.

35. Kilmer, pages 128–129.
36. Sandars, pages 68–69.
37. Jacobsen, page 72.
38. Quoted in Martti Nissinen, *Homoeroticism in the Biblical World: A Historical Perspective*, translated by Kirsi Stjerna (Minneapolis, Minn.: Fortress Press, 1998), page 23.
39. George F. Held, "Parallels between the Gilgamesh Epic and Plato's Symposium," *Journal of Near Eastern Studies,* vol. 42 (1983), pages 133–137.
40. John Boswell, *Same-Sex Unions in Premodern Europe* (New York: Villard Books, 1994), page 128n.
41. Nissinen, pages 145n19, 23–24.
42. Greenberg, page 129.
43. De Becker, page 14.
44. Greenberg, pages 130–134.
45. De Becker, pages 14–15.
46. Bullough, *Sexual Variance,* pages 64–65.
47. *Ibid.*, page 65.
48. Some examples are Judges 19: 22–30; I Samuel 18:1–3; I Samuel 20: 30; II Samuel 1:26; Deuteronomy 23: 17; I Kings 14:24; II Kings 23:7.
49. Louis M. Epstein, *Sex Laws and Customs in Judaism* (New York: Bloch, 1948), pages 3–4. Oddly, Epstein goes on to claim that even though there is absolutely no record of disapproval of homosexual acts before the time of the exile, the Hebrews nonetheless always had disapproved of them. He bases this claim on the account in Genesis of the destruction of Sodom, and the story in Judges of the attempted rape of a male visitor to the town of Gibeah, which resulted in that town's destruction. In both cases, which are examined later in the chapter, ancient Hebrew tradition is unanimous that the evil which drew the punishment was not homosexuality, per se, but the brutish treatment of the visitors, which is even stated outright by the traveler's host in the account in Judges: "Seeing that this man has come into my house, do not do this vile thing." (Judges 19:22–30).
50. Tom Horner, *Jonathan Loved David: Homosexuality in Biblical Times* (Philadelphia: Westminster Press, 1978), pages 15–25.
51. Judges 3:2; Joshua 23:13; Exodus 23:29. See also Eisler, pages 58, 94–95.
52. Some examples: Joshua 6:21; 6:26; 7:24–26; 8:22–29; 11:6–17; 10: 10–11; 10:24–32; Judges 1:2–6; 1:17, 19; 1:25; 3:28–29; 4:15–16; 8:7, 16; 9:5; 12:6; 18:27; 20:35–48; 1 Samuel 11:11; 15:2–3; 15:7–8, 20; 22:18–19; 27:8–11; 30:17; 2 Samuel 8:2–4; 12:31.
53. Eisler, pages 43–45, 94–95.
54. *Ibid.*, page 93.
55. Christopher L.C.E. Witcombe, "Eve and the Identity of Women: Part 6, the Old Testament, Women &

Evil," paper presented at the seminar, Images of Women in Ancient Art, Sweetbriar College; online at http://witcombe.sbc.edu/eve-women/6womenevil.html.

56. Dennis Bratcher, "Speaking the Language of Canaan: The Old Testament and the Israelite Perception of the Physical World," paper presented at the Consultation on the Relationship between the Wesleyan Tradition and the Natural Sciences, Kansas City, Missouri, October 19, 1991.

57. Judges 2:11–13; 3:7; 6:25 et seq.; 10:6; I Samuel 8:4; 12:10.

58. Horner, page 64; Greenberg, pages 137–138.

59. Judges 2:13; 3:7, 6:25; 10:6; I Samuel 7:4; 12:10.

60. For example, Baal-Gad (Joshua 11:17; 12:7; 13:5); Baal-Hermon (Judges 3:3; I Chronicles 5:23; Baal-Meon (Numbers, 32:38; Ezekiel 25:9; I Chronicles 5:8).

61. I Kings 18:19.

62. Eisler, pages 87–88.

63. 2 Kings, 18:4.

64. Raphael Patai, *The Hebrew Goddess* (New York: Avon, 1978), pages 12–13, 48–50, quoted in Eisler, page 93.

65. Horner, *Jonathan Loved David*, page 64; Greenberg, pages 137–138; passages containing references to the *kadesh*, the male attendants, and *kadeshem*, the female attendants are I Kings 14.22–24, 15.12, 22.46; II Kings 23.7; Deuteronomy 23.17–18; Leviticus 18.3, 24–30, 20.23..

66. 2 Kings, 23, 7.

67. C.A. Tripp, *The Homosexual Matrix* (New York: McGraw-Hill, 1975), page 6.

68. Jeremiah 44:24–48.

69. 1 Kings 14:24; 15:12; 22:46; Deuteronomy 23:17–18; Leviticus 19:4.

70. Eisler, pages 44–45, 94–95.

71. Witcombe.

72. R.E. Friedman, *Who Wrote the Bible?* (San Francisco: HarperCollins, 1997).

73. Isaiah 6:13, 17:8, 27:9.

74. Witcombe.

75. 1 Kings 21:25.

76. 1 Kings 16:31–33

77. *Oxford English Dictionary.*

78. *American Heritage Dictionary.*

79. Norton, page 71; Greenberg, pages 139–141.

80. Greenberg, page 139–140.

81. For example, 1 Kings 14:23–24, where the Hebrew text uses the disapproving term *to-ebah*, meaning "idolatrous" or "ritually unclean," in reference to the activities of the *kadesh*. The derivation of the term is discussed later in the chapter.

82. Epstein, page 4.

83. In addition to the scriptural passages cited here, Greenberg, page 136n49, lists additional scriptural references to the sin of Sodom as inhospitality or cruelty to guests or travelers: Deuteronomy 29:23, 32:32; Isaiah 1:9–10, 3:9, 13:19; Jeremiah 23:14, 49:18, 50:40; Lamentations 4:6; Amos 4:11.

84. Luke 10:10–12.

85. Bullough, *Sexual Variance,* page 83; Bailey, pages 8–27 ; Robin Scroggs, *The New Testament and Homosexuality* (Philadelphia: Fortress Press, 1983), pages 85–98 ;

86. Judges 19:22–30.

87. 1 Samuel 16:12–23.

88. 1 Samuel 16:12–23.

89. 1 Samuel 18:1–4.

90. 1 Samuel 18:21.

91. 1 Samuel 18:5.

92. 1 Samuel 20:30–34.

93. 1 Samuel 20:40–42.

94. 2 Samuel 1:26.

95. Kilmer, page 130.

96. Boswell, *Same-Sex Unions,* page 135.

97. *Ibid.*

98. 2 Samuel, 9:1–13.

99. Horner, pages 31–32. For a detailed discussion with citations on the rendering of the passage in both the Septuagint and the Masoretic text by nearly two dozen scriptural scholars, see Bruce L. Gerig, "Saul's Sexual Insult and David's Losing it: Homosexuality and the Bible, Supplement," in *The Epistle: a Web Magazine for Christian Gay, Lesbian, Bisexual and Transgendral People,* at http://epistle.us/hbarticles/saulinsultdaveloseit1.html.

100. *Ibid.*

101. Boswell, *Same-Sex Unions,* pages 136–137.

102. Horner, page 28.

103. Quoted in Horner, page 39.

104. *Ibid.,* page 40.

105. Ruth 1:16–17.

106. Boswell, *Same-Sex Unions,* page 138n.

107. Greenberg, page 117.

108. Horner, page 20.

109. Daniel 1:9.

110. Greenberg, page 121.

111. Allen Edwardes, *The Jewel in the Lotus, A Historical Survey of the Sexual Culture of the East* (New York: Julian Press,1959), page 189.

112. Greenberg, page 122.

113. *Ibid.*

114. John Maxwell O'Brien, *Alexander the Great: The Invisible Enemy* (New York: Routledge, 1994), page 112.

115. Daniel 1:3.

116. *Odyssey,* 14:297, 15:449.

117. Joel 4:3. See discussion in Horner, page 68, for problems with some translations of this passage.

118. Greenberg, page 122n.

119. *Ibid.,* page 121n.

120. Ezra 7:26.

121. Epstein, page 7.

122. Testament of Patriarch Reuben, 1:21.

123. Epstein, page 7.

124. John Boswell, *Christianity, Social Tolerance and Homosexuality* (Chicago: University of Chicago Press, 1980), pages 100–102 ; Horner; Greenberg, pages 135–141; Rictor Norton, "Homophobia and the Ancient Hebrews," in Winston Leyland, editor, *Gay Roots: An Anthology of Gay History, Sex, Politics and Culture* (San Francisco: Gay Sunshine Press, 1993), pages 70–71.

125. Norton, page 71; other examples of *to-ebah* used to refer to idols or foreign worship are in Deuteronomy 7:25–26; 17:2–5; 13:12–15; 12:31; 18: 9–12.

126. Boswell, *Christianity,* page 100.

127. Victor Paul Furnish, "The Bible and Homosexuality: Reading the Texts in Context," in Jeffrey S. Siker, editor, *Homosexuality in the Church: Both Sides of the Debate* (Louisville, Ky.: Westminster John Knox Press, 1994), page 20.

128. Robert A. Di Vito, "Questions on the Construction of (Homo)sexuality: Same-Sex Relations in the Hebrew Bible," in Beattie Jung, Joseph Andrew Coray, editors, *Sexual Diversity and Catholicism: Toward the Development of Moral Theology,* Collegeville, Minnesota: the Liturgical Press, 2001, pages 114–116; Victor Paul Furnish, "The Bible and Homosexuality: Reading the Texts in Context," in Jeffrey S. Siker, editor, *Homosexuality in the Church: Both Sides of the Debate,* Louisville, Kentucky: Westminster John Knox Press, 1994, page 20. Saul M. Olyan similarly concludes that *miskebe issa* refers to taking the woman's role in copulation, which he refers to as "vaginal receptivity," but then inexplicably turns it around and argues that the verse condemns a man performing penetrative intercourse with another male; nor does Olyan address the sacred or cultic connotations of *zakar,* the male performing the act, which is amply illustrated in the scripture. Saul M. Olyan, "And with a Male You Shall Not Lie the Lying Down of a Woman: On the Meaning and Significance of Leviticus 18:22 and 20:13," *Journal of the History of Sexuality,* Volume 5 (1994), No. 2, pages 183–188. On the cultic connotations of *zakar,* see the detailed discussion, with extensive citations to the scripture, in Bruce L. Gerig, "Homosexuality and the Bible: the Levitical Ban: A Mysterious Puzzle," in *The*

Epistle: a Web Magazine for Christian Gay, Lesbian, Bisexual and Transgenderal People, at http://epistle.us/homobile.html and http://epistle.us/hb articles/zakhar2.html.

129. Epstein, pages 3–4.

130. Robin Scroggs, *The New Testament and Homosexuality* (Philadelphia: Fortress Press, 1983), pages 92–94. Texts quoted by Scroggs that condemn homosexual practices as idolatrous include the Letter of Aristeas, the Wisdom of Solomon, The Sibylline Oracles, and The Testaments of the Twelve Patriarchs.

131. Norton, page 71.

132. Bernard Bamberger, "Leviticus," in *The Torah: A Modern Commentary*, ed. by W.G. Plaut (New York: Union of American Hebrew Congregations, 1981), page 881; Norton, page 71.

133. 1 Maccabees, 14–15; 49.

134. Rictor Norton, *A History of Homophobia, Vol. 1: The Ancient Hebrews*, 15 April 2002, online at http://www.infopt.demon.co.uk/homophol.htm.

135. Quoted in Horner, page 84.

Chapter 5

1. Speech to the Asiatic Society, London, 1786.

2. Indo-European linguistic research summarized here is described in Gerhard Herm, *The Celts* (New York: St. Martin's Press, 1975), pages 71–77.

3. Riane Eisler, *The Chalice and the Blade* (New York: HarperCollins, 1988), page 47.

4. Herm, page 75.

5. Marija Gimbutas, "The Beginning of the Bronze Age in Europe and the Indo-Europeans: 3500–2500 B.C.," *Journal of Indo-European Studies*, vol. 1, no. 2 (1973).

6. *Ibid.*

7. Edgar C. Polome, *The Indo-Europeans in the Fourth and Third Millennia* (Ann Arbor: Karoma Publishers, 1982), pages 167–168.

8. Bernard Sergent, *Homosexuality in Greek Myth*, translated by Arthur Goldhammer (Boston: Beacon Press, 1986), page 1.

9. Jan Bremmer, "An Enigmatic Indo-European Rite: Paederasty," *Arethusa*, vol. 13. no. 2 (Fall 1980), pages 279–298; Sergent, pages 1–54; Thorkil Vanggaard, *Phallos: A Symbol and Its History in the Male World* (New York: International Universities Press, 1972); David F. Greenberg, *The Construction of Homosexuality* (Chicago: University of Chicago Press, 1988), page 243; Greenberg cites Lily Weiser-Aall, *Altgermanische Jung-*

lingsweihen und Mannerbunde (Buehl (Baden): Konkordia, 1927); Otto Hofler, *Kultische Geheimbunde der germanen* (Frankfurt am Main: M. Diesterwey, 1934); Jean Przyluski, "Les Confreries de Loups-Garous dan les Societes Indo-Europeens," *Revue de L'Histoire des Religion*, vol. 121 (1940), pages 128–145; Geo Widengren, *Der Feudalismus in alten Iran: Mannerbund, Gefolgswesen, Feudalismus in der Iranischen Gesselschaft im Hinblick auf die Indogermanischen Verhaltnisse* (Cologne: Westdeutscher Verlag, 1969).

10. Quoted in Herm, page 3.

11. Quoted in Weston La Barre, *Muelos: A Stone Age Superstition about Sexuality* (New York: Columbia University Press, 1984), page 16.

12. *Ibid.*, pages 16–17.

13. *Ibid.*, page 17.

14. Quoted in Herm, page 105.

15. La Barre, page 23.

16. *Ibid.*

17. *Ibid.*

18. Sergent, *Homosexuality*, pages 16–18.

19. Marija Gumbutas, *The Goddesses and Gods of Old Europe: Myths and Cult Images* (Berkeley: University of California Press, 1982), pages 216–217.

20. La Barre, pages 19–20.

21. Herm, page 3.

22. Vanggaard, pages 82–83.

23. Vanggaard, figures 15, 20, 21.

24. Bremmer, page 289. Procopius, *De Bello Gothico*, 6:xiv, 36

25. Bernard Sergent, *Homosexualité et initiation chez les peuples indo-européens* (Paris: Éditions Payot, 1996), pages 477–504; Sergent, *Homosexuality*, pages 8–15; Bremmer, pages 288–289; Greenberg, page 243.

26. Greenberg, pages 245–246.

27. *Ibid.*, pages 246–248.

28. Herm, page 4.

29. Aristotle, *Politics*, 2.9.7.

30. *Ibid.*, 2.6.6.

31. Quoted in Herm, page 57.

32. *Ibid.*, page 58.

33. *Ibid.*, page 58.

34. Greenberg, pages 111–112.

35. John Boswell, *Same-Sex Unions in Premodern Europe* (New York: Villard Books, 1994), page 94.

36. Vanggaard, page 119.

37. *Ibid.*, page 119.

38. Anne Ross, "Celtic and Northern Art," pp. 77–106 in Philip Rawson, editor, *Primitive Erotic Art* (New York, G.P. Putnam's Sons, 1973).

39. Vanggaard, page 121.

40. Greenberg, page 244.

41. Tobias Schneebaum, *Where the Spirits Dwell: An Odyssey in the Jungle of New Guinea* (New York: Grove Press, 1989), pages 193–196.

42. Vanggaard, page 121.

43. Greenberg, page 248n34, on the work of Gisela Bleibtreu-Ehrenberg.

44. *Ibid.*, pages 243–245.

45. *Ibid.*, page 245.

46. Jaquetta Hawkes and Sir Leonard Woolley, *Prehistory and the Beginnings of Civilization* (New York: Harper and Row, 1963), pages 334–344; Gimbutas, pages 112–215.

47. Greenberg, pages 245–247.

48. Vanggaard, pages 76–77.

49. Greenberg, page 249.

50. *Ibid.*

51. John Boswell, *Christianity, Social Tolerance, and Homosexuality* (Chicago: University of Chicago Press, 1980), page 70.

52. William Armstrong Percy III, *Pederasty and Pedagogy in Archaic Greece* (Chicago: University of Illinois Press, 1996), page 18.

53. V.R. Curtis, *Indo-European Origins* (New York: Peter Lang, 1989), pages 91–93, 120.

54. Paul D. Hardmann, *Homoaffectionalism: Male Bonding from Gilgamesh to the Present* (San Francisco: GLB Publishers, 1993), pages 22–27.

55. Raymond de Becker, *The Other Face of Love* (New York: Grove Press, 1969), page 18.

56. Hardmann, pages 22–23.

57. Boswell, *Christianity*, pages 20–21.

58. Greenberg, page 125n; Hardmann, pages 23–24.

59. Lise Manniche, "Some Aspects of Ancient Egytian Sexual Life," *Acta Orientalia*, vol. 38 (1977), pages 11–12.

60. Hardmann, page 24.

61. Greenberg, page 186.

62. Will Roscoe, "Precursors of Islamic Male Homosexualities," in Stephen O. Murray and Will Roscoe, editors, *Islamic Homosexualities: Culture, History, and Literature* (New York: New York University Press, 1997), page 79n6.

63. Curtis, pages 120–122.

64. *Ibid.*, pages 123–125 (Ayrans), 101–103 (Hyksos).

Chapter 6

1. Eric Bethe, "Die Dorische Knabenliebe: Ihre Ethik und Ihre Idee," *Rheinisches Museum fur Philologie* 62 (1907), pages 438–474.

2. Quoted in Percy, pages 32–33.

3. *Ibid.*, 29–30.

4. John Boswell, *Christianity, Social Tolerance, and Homosexuality* (Chicago: University of Chicago Press, 1980), pages 17–22.

5. Vern L. Bullough, *Homosexuality: A History* (New York: New American Library, 1979), page 53.

6. V.R. Curtis, *Indo-European*

Origins (New York: Peter Lang, 1988), page 60.

7. Robert Drews, *The Coming of the Greeks: Indo-European Conquests in the Aegean and the Near East* (Princeton, N.J.: Princeton University Press, 1988), pages 170–177.

8. *Ibid.*, page 194.

9. Jacquetta Hawkes, *The Atlas of Early Man* (New York: St. Martin's Press, 1976), pages 116–117.

10. Drews, page 179.

11. For example, Pelops and his father, Tantalus; Hyacinthus and Narcissus; see Bernard Sergent, *Homosexuality in Greek Myth,* translated by Arthur Goldhammer (Boston: Beacon Press, 1986), pages 74–75, 82.

12. Drews, pages 203–225.

13. David F. Greenberg, *The Construction of Homosexuality* (Chicago: University of Chicago Press, 1988), page 108n.

14. *Iliad*, IX:160–161

15. *Iliad,* IX:369–387.

16. *Iliad,* XVIII:23–35.

17. *Iliad,* XIX,:321–326.

18. Xenophon, *Symposium,* VIII: 31.

19. Sergent, page 250.

20. W.M. Clarke, "Achilles and Patroclus in Love," *Hermes* vol. 106 (1978), page 381.

21. Examples of those espousing this view include K.J. Dover, *Greek Homosexuality* (New York: Vintage Books, 1980), pages 197–198; David M. Halperin, *One Hundred Years of Homosexuality: And Other Essays on Greek Homosexuality* (New York: Routledge, 1990), pages 75–87; Eva C. Keuls, *The Reign of the Phallus* (Berkeley: University of California Press, 1985), page 287; Louis Crompton takes a middle view, "conceding a lover-like relation and yet provides no indication that this love took on an explicitly sexual form." Louis Crompton, *Homosexuality and Civilization* (Cambridge, Mass., and London: Belknap Press of Harvard University Press,2003), pages 3–6.

22. Hans Licht (pseudonym of Paul Brand), *Sexual Life in Ancient Greece* (London: Abbey Library, 1932), page 452, with reference to XIX: 193–194, 247; also Sergent, page 310n4, on the same.

23. Licht, page 451, in this regard cites *Odyssey* XXIV, 78; III, 109, XI, 467, XXIV, 15

24. Quoted in Greenberg, page 114.

25. Sergent, page 250.

26. Dover, "Greek Homosexuality and Initiation," page 54.

27. Clarke, pages 381–393.

28. Aeschines, *Against Timarchus,* 142.

29. Clarke, page 389.

30. *Iliad*, XVIII:81–82.

31. XVI:864.

32. XXIII:77–93.

33. IX:568.

34. XVI:97–100.

35. XXIV:128–131, emphasis added. See Clarke, pages 386–387.

36. XIX:321–326.

37. XIX:1–5.

38. XIX:319–321.

39. XIX:18–23.

40. XXIV:1–7.

41. XIX:338–341.

42. Clarke, pages 392–393.

43. See Chapter 4.

44. N.K. Sandars, *The Epic of Gilgamesh* (London: Penguin Books, 1972), page 95.

45. See Chapter 5.

46. John Boswell, *Same-Sex Unions in Premodern Europe* (New York: Villard Books, 1994), page 88.

47. Dante and Symonds quoted in Edward Carpenter, *Anthology of Friendship: Iolaus* (London: George Allen & Unwin, 1920), pages 68–69.

48. Quoted in Carpenter, page 68.

49. Aeschines, page 142; Plato, *The Symposium,* 179e.

50. Quoted in Boswell, *Same-Sex Unions,* page 60.

51. *Symposium,* 197e.

52. Keuls, page 72.

53. *Iliad,* V:325.

54. Clarke, page 383; Sergent, page 311n; Greenberg page 108n; Eve Cantarella, *Bisexuality in the Ancient World,* translated by Cormac O'Cuilleanain (New Haven: Yale University Press, 1992), page 11.

55. *Odyssey,* III:395–403.

56. *Odyssey,* IV:71.

57. *Odyssey,* IV:302–305.

58. XV:4–5, 44–45.

59. Clarke, 383.

60. Sergent, page 311n.

Chapter 7

1. K.J. Dover, *Greek Homosexuality* (New York: Vintage Books, 1980), page 195; H.A. Shapiro, "Courtship Scenes in Attic Vase-Painting," *American Journal of Archaeology,* vol. 85 (1981), page 141n58.

2. Unless otherwise noted, all quotations from the Lyric poets are from Cantarella, pages 13–14.

3. Quoted in Thorkil Vanggaard, *Phallos: A Symbol and Its History in the Male World* (New York: International Universities Press, 1972), page 66.

4. Bernard Sergent, *Homosexuality in Greek Myth,* translated by Arthur Goldhammer (Boston: Beacon Press, 1986), pages 1–4, 268–269.

5. See also David F. Greenberg, *The Construction of Homosexuality*

(Chicago: University of Chicago Press, 1988), pages 108–109.

6. Sergent, page 82.

7. *Ibid.*, page 85.

8. *Ibid.*, page 84.

9. Thomas Bulfinch, *Bullfinch's Mythology* (New York: Avenel Publishers, 1979), page 884.

10. Sergent, page 85.

11. *Ibid.*, page 8.

12. *Ibid.*, page 86.

13. *Ibid.*, pages 84–93.

14. *Ibid.*, page 88.

15. *Ibid.*, pages 64–67.

16. *Ibid.*, pages 62–64.

17. *Ibid.*, page 64.

18. *Ibid.*, pages 59–61.

19. *Ibid.*, pages 205–213.

20. *Ibid.*, page 141.

21. Raymond de Becker, *The Other Face of Love* (New York: Grove Press, 1969), page 36.

22. Sergent, page 149.

23. *Ibid.*, pages 143–145; Boswell, *Same-Sex Unions,* page 47n.

24. Sergent, page 143.

25. *Ibid.*, page 209.

26. *Ibid.*

27. *Ibid.*, page 212.

28. Greenberg, page 108

29. Quoted in Dover, *Greek Homosexuality,* pages 185–186.

30. *Ibid.*, page 185.

31. Quoted in Percy, page 33.

32. Quoted in Cantarella, page 5.

33. Greenberg, page 143.

34. Vanggaard, pages 45–46.

35. Aristotle, *Politics,* 1272a, 12, quoted in Percy, page 62.

36. Percy, pages 59–72.

37. Quoted in Boswell, *Same-Sex Unions,* page 56n.

38. *Odyssey,* X:277.

39. *Iliad,* II:671.

40. Quoted in Licht, page 420.

41. Jan Bremmer, "An Enigmatic Indo-European Rite: Paederasty," *Arethusa* vol. 13, no. 2 (1980), pages 279–298; Cantarella, page 6; Sergent, *Homosexuality,* page 1; Cantarella cites H. Jeanmaire, *Couroi et Couretes* (Lille, 1939); Louis Gernet, *The Anthropology of Ancient Greece,* translated by John Hamilton (Baltimore: Johns Hopkins University Press, 1981); A. Brelich, *Paides e Parthenoi* (Rome: Edizioni dell'Ateneo, 1969; P. Vidal-Naquet, *Le chasseur noir; formes de pensee et formes de societe dans le monde Grec* (Paris, 1981), page 151ff; H. Patzer, *Die Griechische Knabenlieb* (Wiesbaden: Franz Steiner, 1982; B. Lincoln, *Emerging from the Chrysalis* (Cambridge, Mass.: Harvard University Press, 1981); in addition, Sergent cites Jane Harrison, *Themis: A Study of the Social Origin of Greek Religion* (New Hyde Park, N.Y.: University Books, 1962); C. Pelekidis, *Histoire de l'ephebie attique, des origines a 3 lavant Jesus-Christ,* Paris, 1962.

42. Sergent, *Homosexuality;* Cantarella; Bremmer, "Enigmatic."

43. H.I. Marrou, *A History of Education in Antiquity,* translated by George Lamb (London: Sheed and Ward, 1956), page 27.

44. Sergent, *Homosexuality,* page 57.

45. Strabo, as quoted in Bremmer, "Enigmatic," pages 283–284.

46. Sergent, *Homosexuality,* pages 16–20; Bremmer, "Enigmatic," page 286.

47. Greenberg, page 108.

48. Bremmer, "Enigmatic," pages 285–289.

49. C.O. Mueller, *History and Antiquities of the Doric Race* (London: John Murray), Book IV, Chapter 4.

50. e.g. Vanggaard and Patzer.

51. Weston La Barre, *Muelos: A Stone Age Superstition about Sexuality* (New York: Columbia University Press, 1984), page 77.

52. Dover, *Greek Homosexuality,* page 195.

53. Vanggaard, page 24n.

54. La Barre, page 23.

55. Vern L. Bullough, *Sexual Variance in Society and History* (New York: John Wiley & Sons, 1976), page 100.

56. Vanggaard, page 59.

57. *Ibid.,* pages 61–62.

58. *Ibid.*

59. Plato, *Timeaus,* 91B; cf. 73F, 77D, 85B ff., 91A f.

60. Plato, *Symposium,* 208.

61. La Barre, page 77.

62. Mueller.

63. Quoted in Licht, page 415.

64. Bethe, quoted in Bremmer, page 283.

65. K.J. Dover, "Greek Homosexuality and Initiation," in K.J. Dover, editor, *The Greeks and Their Legacy: Collected Papers, Volume 2: Prose, Literature, History, Society, Transmission, Influence* (Oxford and New York: Basil Blackwell, 1988), page 118; see also Licht, page 415.

66. Dover, *Greek Homosexuality,* pages 185–193; Paul Cartledge, "The Politics of Spartan Pederasty," *Cambridge Philological Society, Proceedings,* vol. 27 (1981), pages 17–19.

67. Greenberg, page 107.

68. *Ibid.*

69. Jan N. Bremmer, "Adolescents, Symposion, and Pederasty," in Oswyn Murray, editor, *Sympotica: A Symposium on the Symposion* (Oxford: Clarendon Press, 1990), page 137.

70. Quoted in Cantarella, page 7.

71. Vanggaard, page 66.

72. *Ibid.,* page 37.

73. Cartledge, pages 21–22.

74. Dover, *Greek Homosexuality,* page 193.

75. Greenberg, page 107.

76. Cartledge, page 22.

77. Vanggaard, pages 34–36.

78. *Ibid.*

79. *Ibid.,* pages 37–39.

80. *Ibid.,* pages 34–36.

81. Aelian, quoted in Licht, page 442.

82. Vanggaard, page 40–41.

83. Licht, page 442.

84. Plato, *Symposium,* 178c, 178d.

85. Vanggaard, page 41.

86. Plutarch, *Life of Lycurgus,* 18.

87. Sergent, page 90.

88. Cantarella, page 78.

89. Sergent, page 90.

90. Cantarella, pages 82–83.

91. DeBecker, page 32.

92. *Ibid.*

93. Cantarella, page 79.

94. Quoted in DeBecker, pages 32–33.

95. Quoted in Cantarella, pages 79–80.

96. Cantarella, page 81.

97. Quoted in Cantarella, page 82.

98. *Ibid.*

99. Dover, *Greek Homosexuality,* page 173.

100. Licht, pages 314–317.

101. Reay Tannahill, *Sex in History* (Chelsea, Mich.: Scarborough House), 1992, pages 98–99.

102. Dover, *Greek Homosexuality,* pages 181–182.

103. Cartledge, pages 23–24; Greenberg, pages 106–108.

104. Bullough, *Sexual Variance,* page 99; Cantarella, pages 54–55.

105. Bremmer, "Adolescents," page 143.

106. Cantarella, page 16.

107. Bremmer, "Adolescents," page 143.

108. Shapiro, pages 137–138.

109. Bremmer, "Adolescents," page 142.

110. Dover, *Greek Homosexuality,* Shapiro, and Percy provide numerous examples.

111. Bremmer, "Adolescents," pages 135–137.

112. *Ibid.,* pages 137–139.

113. Elio Pellizer, *Outlines of a Morphology of Sympotic Entertainment,* in Oswyn Murray, editor, *Sympotica: A Symposium on the Symposion* (Oxford: Clarendon Press, 1990), pages 180–183; Bremmer, "Adolescents," pages 137–138.

114. Bremmer, "Adolescents," page 138.

115. *Ibid.,* pages 138–139.

116. Cantarella, page 40.

117. Quoted in Licht, page 418.

118. Cantarella, page 37.

119. *Ibid.*

120. *Ibid.,* page 38.

121. *Ibid.,* page 39.

122. Wayne R. Dynes, Introduction, in Wayne R. Dynes and Stephen Donaldson, *Homosexuality in the Ancient World* (New York and London: Garland Publishing, 1992), pages x–ix.

123. Quoted in Dover, *Greek Homosexuality,* page 85.

124. Cantarella, pages 42, 44.

125. Bullough, *Sexual Variance,* pages 109–110; Dover, *Greek Homosexuality,* page 84; Cantarella, page 41; DeBecker, pages 42–45.

126. Eva C. Keuls, *The Reign of the Phallus* (Berkeley: University of California Press, 1985), page 114.

127. Dover, *Greek Homosexuality,* pages 54–55.

128. Vanggaard, page 26.

129. Dover, *Greek Homosexuality,* page 55.

130. Plato, *Charmides,* quoted in ibid.

131. Aeschines, quoted in ibid., 54.

132. *Ibid.,* pages 82–83.

133. Cantarella, page 18.

134. *Ibid.,* pages 28–32; Dover, *Greek Homosexuality,* pages 81–84.

135. Quoted in Cantarella, page 63.

136. Dynes, pages x–xi.

137. Plato, *Symposium,* 217 c–d; 219 b–c–d.

138. Kinsey, Pomeroy, and Martin, page 168; O. Fenichel, *The Psychoanalytic Theory of Neurosis* (New York: W.W. Norton and Co., 1945), pages 334; C.A. Tripp, *The Homosexual Matrix* (New York: McGraw-Hill, 1975), page 81; Vanggaard, page 53–54.

139. Keuls, pages 277–284; Stephen O. Murray, *Homosexualities* (Chicago: University of Chicago Press, 2000), page 101.

140. Murray, *Homosexualities,* page 101.

141. *Ibid.,* page 100.

142. Dover, *Greek Homosexuality,* page 87.

143. Quoted in Greenberg, page 150.

144. Plato, *Symposium,* page 182c-d.

145. Quoted in Vanggaard, page 26.

146. Cantarella, pages 28–32.

147. Quoted in Cantarella, page 32.

148. Plato, *Symposium,* 182b.

149. Quoted in Vanggaard, page 27.

150. Dynes summarizes the prevailing view, page xi; Cantarella notes the same, pages 40–41.

151. In this regard, Robin Scroggs points to nine plates of red-figured vase paintings included and discussed in Dover, "Greek Homosexuality"; Robin Scroggs, *The New Testament and Homosexuality* (Philadelphia: Fortress Press, 1984), page 133.

152. Scroggs.

153. Boswell, *Same-Sex Unions*, pages 60.

154. *Ibid.*, 60, quoting Aristotle, *Politics*, 2.96–97.

155. Cantarella, pages 41–42.

156. *Ibid.*, page 42.

157. Licht, page 462.

158. *Ibid.*, page 434n.

159. Plato, *Symposium*, 189d–192c.

160. Cantarella, pages 54–55.

161. Quoted in Boswell, *Same-Sex Unions*, page 60.

162. Plato, *Symposium*, 193b.

163. Boswell, *Same-Sex Unions*, page 60.

164. Cantarella, page 69.

165. Plato, *Symposium*, 208e–209d.

166. Greenberg, page 141n.

167. Plato, *Symposium*, 192a.

168. Gordon Rattray Taylor, "Historical and Mythological Aspects of Homosexuality," in Judd Marmor, editor, *Sexual Inversion: The Multiple Roots of Homosexuality* (New York: Basic Books, 1965), pages 155–160.

169. Quoted in Arno Karlen, "Homosexuality in History," in Judd Marmor, editor, *Homosexual Behavior: A Modern Reappraisal* (New York: Basic Books, 1980), page 80.

170. *Ibid.*

171. Vanggaard, page 65.

172. Cantarella, pages 28–36.

173. *Ibid.*, page 42.

174. Karlen, page 80.

175. Dover, *Greek Homosexuality*, page 137.

176. *Ibid.*

177. *Ibid.*, page 140.

178. *Ibid.*, page 141.

179. Cantarella, page 46.

180. *Ibid.*, pages 20–21.

181. Dover, *Greek Homosexuality*, pages 142–143; Cantarella, page 64.

182. Cantarella, page 46.

183. Boswell, *Same-Sex Unions*, pages 13–14 n.22.

184. John J. Winkler, "Laying Down the Law: The Oversight of Men's Sexual Behavior in Classical Athens," in David M. Halperin, John J. Winkler, and Froma I. Zeitlin, editors, *Before Sexuality: The Construction of Erotic Experience in the Ancient Greek World* (Princeton, N.J.: Princeton University Press, 1980), page 173.

185. Cantarella, pages 61–63.

186. Boswell, *Christianity*, page 49.

187. Winkler, page 173.

188. John Maxwell O'Brien, *Alexander the Great: The Invisible Enemy* (London and New York: Routledge, 1992), page 58.

189. *Ibid.*, pages 34–35.

190. DeBecker, page 46.

191. O'Brien, page 58.

192. *Ibid.*, pages 57–59.

193. *Ibid.*, pages 57–58.

194. *Ibid.*, page 212.

195. *Ibid.*, page 112, 190.

196. Greenberg, page 123; DeBecker, page 46.

197. O'Brien, pages 117–118.

198. Quoted in Licht, page 421.

199. Boswell, *Same-Sex Unions*, page 43.

200. Quoted in Cantarella, pages 75–76.

201. e.g., George Devereaux, "Greek Pseudo-homosexuality and the 'Greek Miracle,'" *Symbolae Osloenses*, vol. 42 (1967), pages 69–92.

202. C.A. Tripp, *The Homosexual Matrix* (New York: McGraw-Hill, 1975), page 68.

Chapter 8

1. Theopompus, quoted in David F. Greenberg, *The Construction of Homosexuality* (Chicago: University of Chicago Press, 1988), page 152.

2. Stephen O. Murray, *Homosexualities* (Chicago: University of Chicago Press, 2000), page 112.

3. John Boswell, *Christianity, Social Tolerance, and Homosexuality* (Chicago: University of Chicago Press, 1980), pages 71–72; Paul D. Hardman, *Homoaffectionalism: Male Bonding from Gilgamesh to the Present* (San Francisco: GLB Publishers, 1993), pages 59–60.

4. Vern L. Bullough, *Sexual Variance in Society and History* (New York: John Wiley & Sons, 1976), page 127.

5. V. R. Curtis, *Indo-European Origins* (New York: Peter Lang, 1988), page 68.

6. *Ibid.*, pages 69.

7. Greenberg, page 153.

8. *Ibid.*

9. *Ibid.*

10. Bullough, *Sexual Variance*, pages 129–130.

11. Marija Gimbutas, *The Goddesses and Gods of Old Europe* (Berkeley: University of California Press, 1992), pages 227–230, 236.

12. Thorkil Vanggaard, *Phallos: A Symbol and Its History in the Male World* (New York: International Universities Press, 1973), page 61.

13. Greenberg, page 154.

14. Boswell, *Christianity*, page 74n.

15. Greenberg, page 154n167.

16. Eva Cantarella, *Bisexuality in the Ancient World* (New Haven: Yale University Press, 1992), pages 99–100; Murray, *Homosexualities*, page 115.

17. Bernadette J. Brooten, *Love between Women: Early Christian Responses to Female Homoeroticism* (Chicago: University of Chicago Press, 1996), page 43.

18. Cantarella, page 99.

19. Henry W. Prescott, "Inorganic Roles in Roman Comedy," *Classical Philology*, vol. 15 (1931), pages 245–281, quoted in Murray, page 116.

20. Boswell, *Christianity*, page 65.

21. Murray, *Homosexualities*, page 117.

22. Cantarella, pages 101–102.

23. *Ibid.*, page 101.

24. Quoted in Cantarella, page 98.

25. *Ibid.*

26. Livy, *History: Book VIII:27*, quoted online in Paul Halsall, *People with a History: An Online Guide to Lesbian, Bisexual and Trans* History*, http://www.fordham.edu/halsall/pwh/.

27. Cantarella, page 105.

28. *Ibid.*, pages 97–101.

29. Paul Veyne, "Homosexuality in Ancient Rome," in P. Aries and A. Bejin, editors, *Western Sexuality* (Oxford: Oxford University Press, 1985), pages 28–29, quoted in Cantarella, page 99.

30. Cantarella, pages 104–105.

31. Boswell, *Christianity*, page 72; Greenberg, page 154.

32. Cantarella, page 97.

33. Boswell, *Christianity*, page 78.

34. Cantarella, pages 110–111; Boswell, *Christianity*, page 65.

35. Boswell, *Christianity*, pages 63–71; Cantarella, pages 97–106.

36. Boswell, *Christianity*, page 69.

37. Cantarella, pages 106–114.

38. *Ibid.*, pages 115–116.

39. *Ibid.*, page 121.

40. *Ibid.*, pages 123, 248n.

41. The section on Catullus and the other Roman lyric poets, except where noted, follows Cantarella, pages 123–136.

42. Murray, page 118n.

43. Boswell, *Christianity*, page 81.

44. *Ibid.*, page 81n.

45. John R. Clarke, *Looking at Lovemaking: Constructions of Sexuality in Roman Art, 100 B.C.–A.D. 250* (Berkeley: University of California Press, 1998), page 78, quoted in Murray, *Homosexualities*, page 115n.

46. Cantarella, page 133.

47. Greenberg, page 154.

48. Cantarella, page 140.

49. Virgil, *Aeneid*, translated by Robert Fitzgerald (New York: Vintage Classics, 1990), Book X:450–452; on the homosexual relationship between the two, see Cantarella, page 252n60.

50. *Aeneid*, IX:245–248.

51. Murray, page 119.

52. *Aeneid*, IX:249–250.

53. Murray, page 119; Cantarella, page 141.

54. Virgil, *Second Eclogue*, quoted in Hardman, page 68.

55. Murray, *Homosexualities*, page 119.

56. *Ibid.*, pages 121–122.

57. J. P. Sullivan, "Martial's Sexual

Attitudes," *Philologus,* vol. 123 (1979), page 293.

58. Quoted in Greenberg, page 155.

59. Sullivan, page 301.

60. Quoted in Cantarella, page 148.

61. Quotations of Martial from Cantarella, pages 149–152.

62. Boswell, *Christianity,* page 75; Cantarella, pages 156–158.

63. Cantarella, page 163.

64. Amy Richlin, *The Garden of Priapus: Sexuality and Aggression in Roman Humor* (New York: Oxford University Press, 1992), page 88.

65. Cicero, *Philippics,* 2.44–47, quoted in ibid., page 14.

66. Quoted in Greenberg, page 155.

67. Suetonius, *Augustus,* LXVIII.

68. *Ibid.*

69. Cantarella, page 159.

70. Suetonius, *Augustus,* LXVIII; see also Cantarella, pages 158–159.

71. Boswell, *Christianity,* page 80; Cantarella, page 160; Murray, page 117n.

72. Boswell, *Christianity,* page 61.

73. Suetonius, *Tiberius,* XLIII.

74. Murray, page 117n.

75. Boswell, *Christianity,* page 80n.

76. Dio Cassius, quoted in Murray, *Homosexualities,* page 125.

77. Suetonius, *Nero,* XXVIII.

78. Suetonius, *Nero,* XXIX.

79. Suetonius, *Nero,* XXVIII.

80. Suetonius, *Nero,* XXIX.

81. Boswell, *Christianity,* page 81 and note.

82. Cantarella, page 160.

83. Quoted in Hardmann, pages 178–179

84. Bernard W. Henderson, *The Life and Principate of the Emperor Hadrian, A.D. 76–138* (London: Methuen, 1923), pages 131–132, quoted in Boswell, *Christianity,* page 85n.

85. Boswell, *Christianity,* pages 84–85; Hardman, pages 178–179.

86. Cantarella, page 152.

87. *Ibid.*, page 153.

88. Richlin, page 202, Cantarella, pages 154–155.

89. Boswell, *Christianity,* page 79, Murray, *Homosexualities,* page 114.

90. Quoted in Hardman, page 60.

91. Quoted in Bullough, page 128.

92. Murray, *Homosexualities,* page 115.

93. Quoted in Wayne R. Dynes, "Ancient Rome," in Wayne R. Dynes, editor, *Encyclopedia of Homosexuality* (Chicago and London: St. James Press, 1990), 2:1120.

94. Hardman, page 60.

95. Richlin, on page 192, lists the parallels.

96. John Boswell, *Same-Sex Unions in Premodern Europe* (New York: Villard Books, 1994), pages 67, 104, 170.

97. *Ibid.*, page 66n.

98. *Ibid.*, page 67.

99. *Ibid.*, pages 72–73.

100. Boswell, *Christianity,* page 86.

101. Quoted in Cantarella, page 165.

102. *Ibid.*, page 168.

103. *Ibid.*, pages 167–168.

104. Boswell, *Christianity,* page 83.

105. *Ibid.*, page 84.

106. *Ibid.*, page 82.

107. Boswell, *Same-Sex Unions,* pages 81–82.

108. *Ibid.*, page 82.

109. *Ibid.*, pages 97–107.

110. Cantarella, pages 125, 141, 171.

Chapter 9

1. Uta Ranke-Heinemann, *Eunuchs for the Kingdom of Heaven* (New York: Penguin Books, 1990), page 12. Eva Cantarella, *Bisexuality in the Ancient World* (New Haven: Yale University Press, 1992), page 190.

2. John Boswell, *Christianity, Social Tolerance, and Homosexuality* (Chicago: University of Chicago Press, 1980), page 131n.

3. *Ibid.*, page 130n.

4. *Ibid.*, page 130, quoting Sextus Empiricus and Athenaeus.

5. *Ibid.*, citing Epictetus, *Encheiridion,* 33.8.

6. Paul Veyne, "The Roman Empire," in Philippe Aries and Georges Duby, general editors; Paul Veyne, editor, *A History of Private Lives, Volume. I, From Pagan Rome to Byzantium*Paul (Cambridge, Mass.: Belknap Press of Harvard University Press, 1987), page 46.

7. Cantarella, page 189.

8. Vern L. Bullough, *Sexual Variance in Society and History* (New York: John Wiley & Sons, 1976), pages 150–151; Paul D. Hardman, *Homoaffectionalism: Male Bonding from Gilgamesh to the Present* (San Francisco: GLB Publishers, 1993), page 76. .

9. Plotinus, Enneades 3.5.1, quoted in Boswell, *Christianity,* page 129.

10. David F. Greenberg, *The Construction of Homosexuality* (Chicago: University of Chicago Press, 1988), page 224; Bullough, *Sexual Variance,* pages 182–192.

11. I Corinthians 11:14, 13; Epictetus, *Manii,* 1.16.10.

12. Boswell, *Christianity,* page 146.

13. *Ibid.*, page 147.

14. Veyne, page 47.

15. Ranke-Heinemann, pages 75–98.

16. Vern L. Bullough and Bonnie Bullough, *Sexual Attitudes: Myths and Realities* (Amherst, N.Y.: Prometheus Books, 1995), pages 20–21; Greenberg, pages 223–224.

17. W.E.H. Lecky, *History of the Rise and Influence of the Spirit of Rationalism in Europe* (New York: D. Appleton and Company, 1879), Chapter 4, "On Persecution."

18. Robin Scroggs, *The New Testament and Homosexuality* (Philadelphia: Fortress Press, 1983), pages 85–98.

19. Derrick Sherwin Bailey, *Homosexuality and the Western Christian Tradition* (London: Longmans, Green and Co., 1955), page 26; Scroggs, pages 85–98.

20. Bailey, pages 26–27; Scroggs, pages 91–94. The Book of Jubilees of the Palestinian Pseudepigrapha, a reflection of strict Hellenistic Jewish orthodoxy, called the sin of Sodom fornication, uncleanness and "changing the order of nature." The Testament of Naphtali (109–106 BC) also said the people of Sodom "changed the order of nature." See Rictor Norton, *A History of Homophobia, I: The Ancient Hebrews,* 15 April 2002, online at http://www.infopt.demon.co.uk/homophol.htm.

21. Philo Judaeus, *On Abraham,* 26:134–136, translated by F. H. Colson (London: William Heinemann, 1959–1962), vol. 6 of the Loeb Classical Library, quoted in Bullough, *Homosexuality,* page 85.

22. Boswell, *Christianity,* page 131.

23. Bremmer, "Enigmatic," pages 288–289.

24. John 19:26, 20:2, 21:7, 21:20.

25. Boswell, *Same-Sex Unions,* page 139.

26. Boswell, *Christianity,* pages 222–224.

27. *Ibid.*, page 226.

28. Ron Cameron, "The Secret Gospel of Mark," in Willis Barnstone, editor, *The Other Bible: Jewish Pseudepigrapha, Chrstian Apocrypha, Gnostic Scriptures* (San Francisco: Harper & Row Publishers, 1984), pages 339–340.

29. *Ibid.*, page 342.

30. 1 Maccabees 14–15, 49.

31. Galatians 5:16.

32. John Shelby Spong, *Rescuing the Bible from Fundamentalism: A Bishop Rethinks the Meaning of Scripture* (San Francisco: Harper San Francisco, 1991), page 115; 1 Corinthians 7:5.

33. 1 Corinthians 7:1, 9.

34. Spong, pages 117–120.

35. Romans 7:15–25, quoted in ibid., pages 112–113.

36. John Shelby Spong, *Living in Sin? A Bishop Rethinks Human Sexuality* (San Francisco: Harper & Row Publishers, 1988), page 151.

37. Spong, *Rescuing the Bible,* page 117.

38. Galatians 4:10; Colossians 2:18, 20, 23; 1 Timothy 6:3–4; Titus 3:8–9.

39. Kinsey, Pomeroy, and Martin, page 514.

40. Boswell, *Christianity,* page 131.

41. *Ibid.,* pages 131–132.

42. Louis Crompton, *Homosexuality and Civilization* (Cambridge, Mass.: Belknap Press of Harvard University Press, 2003), page 141.

43. Boswell, *Christianity,* page 133.

44. *Ibid.,* pages 132–133.

45. Salvian, *De gubernatione Dei (The Government of God),* translated by Eva M. Sanford (New York: Columbia University Press, 1930), pages 189–223.

46. *Coptic Spell: Spell for a Man to Obtain a Male Lover,* translated by David Frankfurter, from Halsall, *People with a History.*

47. Boswell, *Christianity,* page 135.

48. Veyne, "Roman Empire," page 49.

49. Translation after that in Bailey, page 70.

50. Boswell, *Christianity,* page 119.

51. W. G. Holmes, *The Age of Justinian and Theodora* (London, 1912), 1:121, quoted in Bailey, page 71.

52. Bailey, page 71

53. Cantarella, page 176.

54. *Ibid.,* pages 176–178.

55. *Ibid.,* page 161.

56. William A. Percy, "Roman Emperors," in Dynes, *Encyclopedia,* page 1119.

57. Greenberg, page 229.

58. Cantarella, page 161.

59. Greenberg, page 229.

60. Cantarella, page 177.

61. Bailey, pages 72–73.

62. *Ibid.,* page 73.

63. Cantarella, page 182.

64. Bailey, pages 73–74.

65. *Ibid.,* page 75.

66. *Ibid.,* pages 76–77.

67. See Boswell, *Christianity,* page 173n12.

68. Procopius, *Anecdota,* 11.34–36, quoted in ibid., page 173.

69. Edward Gibbon, *The History of the Decline and Fall of the Roman Empire,* edited by J.B. Bury (New York: Heritage Press, 1946), vol. 2, chap. 44, pages 1450–1451.

70. *Ibid.,* page 1476; see also Boswell, *Christianity,* page 173n14.

71. Boswell, *Christianity,* page 173n15.

72. Procopius, 16:18–22, quoted in ibid., page 173.

73. Boswell, *Christianity* , page 174.

74. Robert Wood, "Sex Life in Ancient Civilizations," in Albert Ellis and Albert Abarbanel, editors, *The Encyclopedia of Sexual Behavior* (New York: Hawthorn Books, 1964), 1:124.

Chapter 10

1. Hinsch, *Passions of the Cut Sleeve: The Male Homosexual Tradition in China* (Berkeley: University of California Press, 1990), pages 1–2.

2. David F. Greenberg, *The Construction of Homosexuality* (Chicago: University of Chicago Press, 1988), page 162.

3. Hinsch, page 2.

4. *Ibid.,* pages 57–59.

5. *Ibid.,* page 147.

6 . *Ibid.,* page 18.

7. R.H. Van Gulik, *Sexual Life in Ancient China* (Leiden: E.J. Brill, 1974), page 50.

8. Hinsch, pages 20–21.

9. *Ibid.,* page 21.

10. *Ibid.,* page 22.

11. *Ibid.,* page 23.

12. *Ibid.,* page 25.

13. *Ibid.,* pages 25–27.

14. *Ibid.,* pages 27–29.

15. *Ibid.,* page 30.

16. *Ibid.,* pages 30–31.

17. *Ibid.,* page 31.

18. *Ibid.*

19. *Ibid.,* pages 16–18.

20. *Ibid.,* pages 17–18.

21. R.H. Van Gulik, *Sexual Life in Ancient China* (Leiden: E.J. Brill, 1974), page 28.

22. Hinsch, page 36.

23. Van Gulik, page 62.

24. Hinsch, page 41; Van Gulik, page 62.

25. Hinsch, page 48–49.

26. *Ibid.,* pages 47–49, 62.

27. *Ibid.*

28. Van Gulik, page 48.

29. Hinsch, page 174.

30. *Ibid.,* page 52.

31. *Ibid.,* pages 45–47.

32. Van Gulik, page 63; Hinsch, pages 52–53.

33. Hinsch, page 56.

34. *Ibid.,* pages 83–85.

35. *Ibid.,* page 56.

36. *Ibid.,* page 60.

37. *Ibid.,* pages 58–59.

38. *Ibid.,* pages 58–61.

39. *Ibid.,* page 90.

40. *Ibid.,* page 62.

41. *Ibid.,* pages 65–66.

42. *Ibid.,* page 64.

43. Van Gulik, page 92–93; Hinsch, pages 68–69.

44. Hinsch, pages 70–71

45. *Ibid.,* pages 75–76.

46. *Ibid.,* page 71.

47. *Ibid.,* pages 71–72.

48. *Ibid.,* page 80.

49. *Ibid.*

50. *Ibid.,* page 87.

51 . *Ibid.,* page 88.

52. *Ibid.,* page 84, 88.

53. *Ibid.,* page 112.

54. *Ibid.,* page 103.

55. *Ibid.,* pages 109–110.

56. *Ibid.,* page 116.

57. *Ibid.,* pages 92–93.

58. Van Gulik, page 163.

59. Hinsch, page 92.

60. *Ibid.,* pages 93–96.

61. *Ibid.,* pages 94–97; Van Gulik, page 163.

62. *Ibid.,* pages 120–121.

63. *Ibid.*

64. *Ibid.,* pages 122–123.

65. *Ibid.,* page 123.

66. *Ibid.,* page 135.

67. *Ibid.,* page 134.

68. Stephen O. Murray, *Homosexualities* (Chicago: University of Chicago Press, 2000), page 184.

69. Hinsch, page 131.

70. *Ibid.,* page 130.

71. *Ibid.,* pages 127–128.

72. Murray, *Homosexualities,* page 181.

73. Hinsch, page 133.

74. Vern L. Bullough, *Sexual Variance in History* (Chicago: University of Chicago Press, 1976), page 299.

75. Hinsch, page 176, Bullough, *Sexual Variance,* page 299.

76. Hinsch, page 175.

77. *Ibid.,* page 143.

78. *Ibid.,* page 141.

79. *Ibid.,* pages 146–147.

80. *Ibid.,* page 146.

81. *Ibid.,* pages 147–148.

82. *Ibid.,* pages 149–150.

83. *Ibid.,* pages 150–151.

84. *Ibid.,* page 152.

85. *Ibid.*

86. Bullough, *Sexual Variance,* page 305.

87. Murray, page 187.

88. Hinsch, page 155.

89. *Ibid.,* page 156.

90. Lu Hsun, *A Brief History of Chinese Fiction* (Beijing: Foreign Language Press, 1976), quoted in Murray, *Homosexualities,* pages 185–196.

91. Hinsch, page 159.

92. *Ibid.*

93. C.A. Tripp, *The Homosexual Matrix* (New York: McGraw-Hill, 1975), page 68.

94. Greenberg, page 161n210.

95. Murray, *Homosexualities,* pages 65–70.

Chapter 11

1. Tsuneo Watanabe and Jin'ichi Iwata, *The Love of the Samurai: A Thousand Years of Japanese Homosexuality,* translated by D.R. Roberts (London: GMP Publishers, 1989), page 11.

2. *Ibid.*

3. *Ibid.,* pages 23–24.

4. *Ibid.*, page 33; see also Murray, *Homosexualities,* page 72n75.

5. Murray, *Homosexualities* page 72.

6. Watanabe, page 32.

7. *Ibid.*, page 35.

8. Murray, *Homosexualities,* page 70.

9. *Ibid.*, pages 70–71.

10. Watanabe, page 46.

11. Murray, *Homosexualities,* page 74.

12. Watanabe, pages 36–38.

13. *Ibid.*, page 38.

14. Murray, *Homosexualities,* page 75.

15. Murasaki Shikibu, *The Tale of Genji,* translated by Edward C. Seidensticker (New York, Alfred A. Knopf, 1976), page 48.

16. Ariwara no Narihira, *The Tales of Ise: Lyrical Episodes from Tenth-Century Japan,* translated by Helen Craig McCullough (Stanford, Calif.: 1968: Stanford University Press), pages 101–102.

17. Gary P. Leupp, *Male Colors: The Construction of Homosexuality in Tokugawa Japan* (Berkeley: University of California Press, 1995), page 25–26.

18. *Ibid.*, page 39.

19. Watanabe, pages 39–41.

20. Leupp, pages 45–46.

21. *Ibid.*, pages 39–40.

22. Watanabe, pages 42–44.

23. Murray, *Homosexualities,* pages 74–75.

24. Edward Carpenter, *Intermediate Types among Primitive Folk, A Study in Social Evolution* (London: George Allen & Co., 1914), page 141.

25. *Ibid.*

26. Leupp, page 51.

27. Murray, *Homosexualities,* pages 84–86.

28. Ian Buruma, *Behind the Mask* (New York: Meridian, 1984), page 128, quoted in Murray, *Homosexualities,* page 84.

29. Watanabe, page 48.

30. Murray, *Homosexualities,* page 87n93.

31. Ihara Saikaku, *The Great Mirror of Male Love* (Stanford, Calif.: Stanford University Press, 1990), page 307, quoted in Murray, *Homosexualities,* page 91.

32. Watanabe, page 48.

33. *Ibid.*, page 113.

34. Murray, *Homosexualities,* page 91.

35. Watanabe page 23, pages 47–48, 52; Murray, *Homosexualities,* page 91.

36. Watanabe, page 47.

37. Murray, *Homosexualities,* page 80.

38. Leupp, pages 127–128; but see also Murray, *Homosexualities,* page 94.

39. Paul Gordon Schalow, "Male Love in Early Modern Japan: A Literary Depiction of the 'Youth,'" in Martin Duberman, Martha Vicinus, and George Chauncey, Jr., editors, *Hidden from History: Reclaiming the Gay and Lesbian Past* (New York: Meridian, 1990), page 122.

40. Murray, *Homosexualities,* pages 78–79.

41. *Ibid.*, page 94.

42. Leupp, page 128.

43. Watanabe, page 116.

44. Murray, *Homosexualities,* page 78.

45. *Ibid.*, pages 82–83.

46. *Ibid.*, page 83.

47. *Ibid.*, page 80.

48. Schalow, pages 124–126.

49. Raymond de Becker, *The Other Face of Love,* translated by Margaret Crosland and Alan Daventry (New York: Grove Press, 1969), page 79.

50. *Ibid.*, page 80.

51. Leupp, page 54.

52. *Ibid.*, pages 52–56.

53. Walter L. Williams, *The Spirit and the Flesh: Sexual Diversity in American Indian Culture* (Boston: Beacon Press, 1992), page 265; Murray, *Homosexualities,* p. 85.

54. Watanabe, page 49.

55. *Ibid.*

56. *Ibid.*, page 50.

57. *Ibid.*

58. Ijiri Chusuke, 1482 "The Essence of Jakudo," quoted in Watanabe, page 109.

59. De Becker, page 82.

60. Watanabe, pages 117–118.

61. *Ibid.*, page 119.

62. *Ibid.*, pages 57–63.

63. *Ibid.*, pages 75–76.

64. *Ibid.*, pages 76–77.

65. *Ibid.*, pages 79–80.

66. *Ibid.*, pages 81–82.

67. *Ibid.*, page 91.

68. *Ibid.*, page 82.

69. *Ibid.*, page 84.

70. Leupp, page 77.

71. *Ibid.*, page 148.

72. *Ibid.*, page 98.

73. Watanabe, pages 111–113.

74. *Ibid.*, page 88.

75. Murray, *Homosexualities,* pages 84–85.

76. Leupp, page 136.

77. Murray, *Homosexualities,* page 85.

78. Leupp, page 137.

79. Murray, *Homosexualities,* page 85.

80. *Ibid.*, pages 93–94.

81. Leupp, page 179.

82. Murray, *Homosexualities,* page 94n108.

83. Leupp, pages 143–144.

84. Yamamoto Tsunetomo, *Hagakure, The Book of the Samurai,* translated by William Scott Wilson (New York and Tokyo: Kodansha International, 2002), page. 58.

85. Leupp, page 124.

86. *Ibid.*, page 128.

87. Murray, *Homosexualities,* page 89.

88. Leupp, page 146.

89. Hiraga Gennai, *Kiku no en,* quoted in Leupp, page 145.

90. Leupp, page 78.

91. Carpenter, pages 141–148.

92. Press quotations are from Watanabe, page 122.

93. Friedrich S. Krausss, *Das Geschlechtsleben in Glauben, Sitte, Brauch under Gewohnheitsrecht der Japaner* (Leipzig, 1910), quoted in Watanabe, page 122.

94. Ferdinand Karsch-Haack, *Das Geschlechtsleben der Japaner* (Leipzig, 1911), quoted in Carpenter, pages 159–160.

95. Tahuro Inagaki, "The Aesthetics of Adolescent-Love," quoted in Watanabe, page 124.

Chapter 12

1. *Al Hadis,* Vol. 4, p. 172, No. 34, Translation and Commentary by Al Haj Maulana Fazlul Karim (New York: Islamic Book Service, 1960).

2. As'ad AbuKhalil, "A Note on the Study of Homosexuality in the Arab/Islamic Civilization," *Arab Studies Journal,* vol. 1, no. 2 (1993), pages 32–48, quoted in Stephen O. Murray and Will Roscoe, editors, *Islamic Homosexualities: Culture History, and Literature* (New York: New York University Press, 1997), pages 14–15.

3. VII:79–81; XXVII:55; XXVI:26.

4. Charles Pellat, "Liwat," in Arno Schmitt and Jehoda Sofer, editors, *Sexuality and Eroticism among Males in Moslem Societies* (New York: Harrington Park Press, 1992), pages 151–153.

5. Helene Kafi, "Tehran: Dangerous Love," in ibid., pages 68–69.

6. Boswell, *Christianity,* pages 279–280.

7. Greenberg, page 176.

8. *Ibid.*, page 178n316.

9. Murray and Roscoe, page 46n23.

10. Stephen O. Murray, "Some Nineteenth-Century Reports of Islamic Homosexualities," in ibid., pages 204–206.

11. Louis Crompton, *Byron and Greek Love* (Berkeley: University of California Press), page 142

12. Greenberg, page 179.

13. Richard Francis Burton, Terminal Essay, *The Arabian Nights* (Lon-

don, 1885), reprinted online in Halsall, *People with a History.*.

14. C.A. Tripp, *The Homosexual Matrix* (New York: McGraw-Hill, 1975), page 38.

15. Vern L. Bullough, *Sexual Variance in Society and History* (Chicago: University of Chicago Press, 1976), page 205.

16. *Ibid.*, page 224.

17. Louis Crompton, *Homosexuality and Civilization* (Cambridge, Mass.: Belknap Press of Harvard University, 2003), pages 161–163.

18. Boswell, *Christianity,* page 197.

19. Crompton, page 187.

20. Boswell, *Christianity,* page 196.

21. Crompton, page 187.

22. *Ibid.*, page 168.

23. Maarten Schild, "Abu Nuwas," in Wayne R. Dynes, editor, *Encyclopedia of Homosexuality* (New York: Garland Publishing Company, 1990), 1:7–8.

24. Ahmad al-Tifashi, "Stories Concerning Young Hustlers," *The Delight of Hearts, or What You Will Not Find In Any Book*, translated by Edward A. Lacey (San Francisco: Gay Sunshine Press, 1988), page 127.

25. Bullough, page 227.

26. Schild.

27. al-Tifashi, pages 128–129.

28. Paul D. Hardman, *Homoaffectualism: Male Bonding from Gilgamesh to the Present* (San Francisco: GLB Publishers, 1993), page 157.

29. Murray and Roscoe, page 107.

30. Maaten Schild, "Sa'di," in Wayne R. Dynes, editor, *Encyclopedia of Homosexuality* (New York: Garland Publishing Company, 1990), 2:1142–1143.

31. Sheikh Muslih-uddin Sa'di Shirazi, *The Gulistan (Rose Garden)*, public domain translation, reprinted online in Halsall, *People with a History.*

32. Boswell, *Christianity,* page 195.

33. Hardman, page 157.

34. Murray and Roscoe, page 23.

35. "The Meadow of the Gazelles," from *The World History of Gay Love*, The Androphile Project, online at http://www.androphile.org/preview/Library/Poetry/aNawaji_islam_%20gayhistory/al-Nawaji_islam_%20gayhistory.htm.

36. Raymond de Becker, *The Other Side of Love*, translated by Margaret Crosland and Alan Daventry (New York, Grove Press, 1969), page 63.

37. *Ibid.*, page 64.

38. *Ibid.*

39. Arno Schmitt, "Different Approaches to Male-Male Sexuality/Eroticism from Morocco to Usbekistan," in Schmitt and Sofer, page 5.

40. Bullough, *Homosexuality,* page 224.

41. Sheikh Muslih-uddin Sa'di Shirazi, *Bustan,* chap. 3.

42. Burton.

43. Murray and Roscoe, page 28.

44. Greenberg, page 31.

45. Bullough, *Homosexuality,* pages 245–261; de Becker, pages 73–74.

46. Hardman, page 143.

47. Stephen O. Murray, "The Mamluks of Medieval Egypt," in *Homosexualities* (Chicago: University of Chicago Press, 2000), page 47.

48. *Ibid.*, pages 44–46.

49. Hardman, page 146.

50. Stephen O. Murray, "Male Homosexuality, Inheritance Rules, and the Status of Women in Medieval Egypt: The Case of the Mamlukes," in Murray and Roscoe, pages 161–165.

51. *Ibid.*, page 170n13.

52. *Ibid.*, pages 162–163.

53. Hardman, page 159.

54. Barnette Miller, *The Palace School of Muhammad the Conqueror* (Cambridge, Mass.: Harvard University Press, 1941), page 78, quoted in Murray (2000), page 52–53.

55. Murray and Roscoe, page 174.

56. *Ibid.*, pages 174–176.

57. Murray, *Homosexualities,* page 55.

58. Albert H. Lybyer, *The Government of the Ottoman Empire in the Time of Sulieman the Magnificent* (Cambridge, Mass: Harvard University Press, 1913), pages 121–122, quoted in Murray, "Homosexuality among Slaves Elites in Ottoman Turkey," in Murray and Roscoe, page 177.

59. Murray, "Homosexuality," page 178.

60. *Ibid.*, page 184n12.

61. Patrick Kinross, *The Ottoman Centuries: The Rise and Fall of the Turkish Empire* (New York: Morrow, 1979).

62. Murray, *Homosexualities,* pages 63–64.

63. Havelock Ellis, *Studies in the Psychology of Sex, Volume I, Part Four: Sexual Inversion* (New York: Random House, 1942), page 10.

64. Murray, *Homosexualities,* page 60.

65. *Ibid.*, page 61.

66. John Boswell, *Same-Sex Unions in Pre-Modern Europe* (New York: Villard Books, 1994), pages 265–267; see page 270n39 in reference to the rite in Montenegro.

67. Greenberg, page 85.

68. Murray and Roscoe, pages 15–16.

69. Rex Wockner, "Homosexuality in the Arab and Moslem World," in Stephen Likosky, editor, *Coming Out* (New York: Pantheon, 1992), page 10.

Chapter 13

1. C.S. Lewis, *The Allegory of Love: A Study in Medieval Tradition* (London: Oxford University Press, 1938), pages 8–9.

2. *Ibid.*, page 10.

3. *The Song of Roland*, CLXXXIV, CLXXXV, translated by John O'Hagan, The Harvard Classics (New York: P.F. Collier & Son, 1910), pages 97–210.

4. Lewis, page 9.

5. *Ibid.*, page 10.

6. Johan Huizinga, *The Waning of the Middle Ages* (Garden City, N.Y.: Doubleday Anchor Books, 1954), page 67.

7. Christon I. Archer, editor, *World History of Warfare* (Lincoln: University of Nebraska Press, 2002), pages 146–147

8. Huizinga, pages 67–69.

9. Archer, pages 146–147.

10. F.J.C. Hearnshaw, "Chivalry and Its Place in History," in Edgar Prestage, editor, *Chivalry: A Series of Studies to Illustrate Its Historical Significance and Civilizing Influence* (London: Kegan Paul, Trench, Trubner, 1928), pages 4–34.

11. *Ibid.*, page 19.

12. Georges Duby, *The Chivalrous Society* (Berkeley: University of California Press, 1977), page 115n19.

13. *Ibid.*, page 115.

14. David F. Greenberg, *The Construction of Homosexuality* (Chicago: University of Chicago Press, 1988), page 259.

15. Boswell, *Christianity,* pages 232–233.

16. *Ibid.*, pages 132–136, 206.

17. Salvian, *De gubernatione Dei (The Government of God)*, translated by Eva M. Sanford (New York: Columbia University Press, 1930), pages 189–223.

18. Homosexual customs among early Germanic tribes are discussed in Chapter 5. On the customs of the Taifali and Heruli, see Jan Bremmer, "An Enigmatic Indo-European Rite: Paederasty," *Arethusa*, vol. 13, no. 2 (1980), pages 288–289; Bernard Sergent, *Homosexualité et initiation chez les peuples indo-européens* (Paris: Éditions Payot, 1996), pages 477–504. On Quintilian, see Louis Crompton, *Homosexuality and Civilization* (Cambridge, Mass.: Belknap Press of Harvard University Press, 2003), page 152.. On the incident concerning the Vandals' capture of Rome, see Greenberg, page 249. On the Scandinavian blood brothers, see Thorkil Vanggaard, *Phallos: A Symbol and Its History in the Male World* (New York: International Universities Press, 1972), page 121.

19. Vern Bullough, *Sexual Variance in Society and History* (Chicago: University of Chicago Press, 1976), pages 348–349.

20. *Ibid.*

21. Michael Goodich, *The Unmentionable Vice: Homosexuality in the Later Medieval Period* (Santa Barbara, Calif.: ABC-Clio, 1979), pages 71–63; Boswell, *Christianity*, pages 176–177; Greenberg, page 250.

22. Arno Karlen, *Sexuality and Homosexuality: A New View* (New York: W.W. Norton & Company, 1971), page 79.

23. Bullough, *Sexual Variance*, page 351.

24. Greenberg, page 253.

25. Vanggaard, figures 15, 20, 21.

26. Greenberg, page 253n64.

27. *Ibid.*, page 248n32.

28. *Ibid.*, page 254.

29. Edward Westermarck, *The Origin and Development of the Moral Ideas*, Second Edition (London: Macmillan and Co.), 2:481–482.

30. Derrick Sherwin Bailey, *Homosexuality and the Western Christian Tradition* (London: Longmans, Green and Co., 1955), page 110.

31. G. Rattray Taylor, *Sex in History: The Story of Society's Changing Attitudes to Sex Throughout the Ages* (New York: Harper & Row, 1954) page 20.

32. Bullough, *Sexual Variance*, page 351.

33. *Ibid.*, page 353.

34. Greenberg, page 254.

35. Crompton, pages 159–160; Greenberg, pages 253–255.

36. For example, Crompton, page 160.

37. Greenberg, page 254.

38. Allen J. Frantzen, *Before the Closet: Same-Sex Love from Beowulf to Angels in America* (Chicago: University of Chicago Press, 1998), page 130; Greenberg, page 264; Bullough, page 357; Crompton, pages 155–156.

39. Taylor, page 51.

40. Pierre J. Payer, *Book of Gomorrah* (Waterloo, Ontario: Wilfrid Laurier University Press, 1982), page 7.

41. Frantzen, pages 173–174.

42. Bullough, *Sexual Variance*, page 357.

43. Frantzen, Chapter 4, Appendix 2, Tables 1, 2; Bullough, *Sexual Variance*, page 360; Bailey, pages 103–108.

44. *Ibid.*, pages 163–165.

45. Greenberg, page 262; Bailey, page 108.

46. James A. Brundage, *Law, Sex, and Christian Society in Medieval Europe* (Chicago: University of Chicago Press, 1987), page 166.

47. Bailey, page 105.

48. Greenberg, page 263.

49. Frantzen, page 168; Greenberg, page 264.

50. Goodich, page 16, quoting the 11th-century Benedictine monk Otloh of St. Emmeram.

51. Greenberg, pages 255–256.

52. Boswell, *Christianity*, page 235.

53. Greenberg, page 260n95.

54. Frantzen, pages 97–104.

55. Michel Rouche, "The Early Middle Ages in the West," in Paul Veyne, editor, *A History of Private Life: Vol. I, from Pagan Rome to Byzantium* (Cambridge, Mass.: Belknap Press of Harvard University Press, 1987), page 425.

56. *Beowulf*, translated by Francis B. Gummere, The Harvard Classics (New York: P.F. Collier & Son, 1910), pages 5–95.

57. Maurice Keen, *Chivalry* (New Haven and London: Yale University Press, 1984), pages 27–30.

58. Georges Duby, "Private Power, Public Power," in Georges Duby, editor, *A History of Private Life: II. Revelations of the Medieval World*, translated by Arthur Goldhammer (Cambridge: Mass.: Belknap Press of Harvard University Press, 1988), pages 20–21.

59. *Ibid.*

60. Georges Duby, *William Marshal: The Flower of Chivalry*, translated by Richard Howard (New York: Pantheon Books, 1985), page 65.

61. Duby, "Private Power," pages 79–80.

62. Rouche, page 486.

63. Duby, *Chivalrous Society*, pages 112–114.

64. Keen, page 19.

65. *Ibid.*, page 20.

66. Duby, *Chivalrous Society*, pages 113–115.

67. *Ibid.*, page 114.

68. *Ibid.*, pages 114–115.

69. *Ibid.*, page 115.

70. *Ibid.*, page 115n22.

71. *Ibid.*, page 116.

72. *Ibid.*, page 115, n19.

73. Boswell, *Christianity*, page 230.

74. Goodich, pages 20–21; also, Guibert de Nogent, *De Vita Sua*, Chatper XV.

75. Frantzen, pages 236–237.

76. Boswell, *Christianity*, pages 228, 235.

77. Bullough, *Sexual Variance*, pages 399–400.

78. Duby (1985), page 38.

79. Lewis, page 9.

80. W.S. Merwin, "The Song of Roland — Introduction," *Medieval Epics* (New York: Modern Library, 1963), pages 90–91,

81. Greenberg, page 257.

82. Duby, *Marshal*, page 25.

83. *Ibid.*, page 32–33, 36.

84. *Ibid.*, page 28.

85. *Ibid.*, page 40.

86. *Ibid.*, page 41.

87. *Ibid.*, pages 77–79.

88. *Ibid.*, pages 79–80.

89. *Ibid.*, pages 49–50.

90. *Ibid.*, pages 50–52.

91. *Ibid.*, page 53.

92. *Ibid.*, page 38.

93. *Ibid.*, page 48.

94. *Ibid.*, page 47.

95. *Ibid.*, pages 34–35.

96. *Ibid.*, pages 141–143.

97. *Ibid.*, page 146.

98. Roger of Hoveden, *The Annals*, translated by Henry T. Riley (London: H.G. Bohn, 1853), 2:63–64, reprinted online in Halsall, *People with a History*.

99. Hoveden, Vol. 2.

100. Bullough, page 399.

101. Hoveden, 2:356–357.

102. Philip Henderson, *Richard Coeur de Lion* (London: Robert Hale, 1958), page 243.

103. Boswell, *Christianity*, page 232.

104. Patricia Terry and Samuel N. Rosenberg, *Lancelot and the Lord of the Distant Isles or, The Book of Galehaut Retold* (Boston: David R. Godine, Publisher, 2006) page 3.

105. *Lancelot-Grail*, Part II, translated by W. Carroll, in Byrne R.S. Fone, editor, *The Columbia Anthology of Gay Literature: Readings from Western Antiquity to the Present Day* (New York: Columbia University Press, 1998), page 112.

106. *Ibid.*, page 111.

107. *Ibid.*, pages 112ff.

108. Simon Gaunt, *Love and Death in Medieval French and Occitan Courtly Literature: Martyrs to Love* (London: Oxford University Press, 2006), page 199.

109. *Lancelot-Grail.*

110. Terry and Rosenberg, pages 80–81.

111. *Ibid.*, pages 81–83; Duby, "Private Power," pages 79–80.

112. Gretchen Mieszkowski, "The Lancelot's Galehot, Malory's Lavin, and the Queering of Late Medieval Literature," *Arthuriana*, vol. 5, no. 1 (Spring 1995), pages 21–51.

113. Boswell (1980), pages 193–194.

114. *Amis and Amile*, translated by William Morris, in *Bibliotheca Elzeviriana*, quoted in Edward Carpenter, *Anthology of Friendship: Iolaus* (London: George Allen & Unwin, 1922), page 106.

115. *Ibid.*, pages 107–108.

116. Boswell, *Same-Sex Unions*, page 154.

117. *Ibid.*, pages 159–160.

118. Duby, *Chivalrous Society*, page 121.

119. Boswell, *Same-Sex Unions*, page 258.

120. *Ibid.*, pages 259–260.
121. Saint Basil, quoted in Andrew McCall, *Medieval Underworld* (New York: Barnes and Noble Books, 1979), page 202.
122. Bailey, page 91.
123. Georges Duby, "The Aristocratic Households of Feudal France," in Georges Duby, editor, *Life: II. Revelations of the Medieval World*, translated by Arthur Goldhammer (Cambridge: Mass.: Belknap Press of Harvard University Press, 1988), page 56.
124. Goodich, page 18.
125. Boswell, *Christianity*, page 190.
126. *Ibid.*, pages 189–191.
127. *Ibid.*, pages 191–192.
128. *Ibid.*, page 213.
129. Richard W. Southern, *Medieval Humanism and Other Studies* (New York: Harper & Row, 1970), page 13; quoted in Boswell, *Christianity*, page 216.
130. Carpenter, pages 104–105.
131. Romans 7:15–25.
132. Richard W. Southern, *St. Anselm: A Portrait in a Landscape* (London: Cambridge University Press, 1992), page 157.
133. Brian P. McGuire, "Monastic Friendship and Toleration in Twelfth Century Cistercian Life," in W. J. Shiels, editor, *Monks, Hermits and the Ascetic Tradition*, Studies in Church History 22 (Malden, Mass.: Blackwell Publishing, 1985).
134. Goodich, pages 31–32; Boswell, *Christianity*, page 213; Greenberg, pages 280–281.
135. Boswell, *Christianity*, pages 214–215.
136. *Ibid.*, pages 220–221.
137. Carpenter, page 103.
138. Boswell, *Christianity*, page 221.
139. *Ibid.*, pages 221–222.
140. *Ibid.*, pages 223–224.
141. *Ibid.*, page 224.
142. Kenneth Clark, *Civilization: A Personal View* (New York: Harper & Row, 1970), page 36.
143. Boswell, *Christianity*, page 250.
144. *Ibid.*, pages 370–371.
145. *Ibid.*, pages 236–237.
146. *Ibid.*, pages 238–239.
147. *Ibid.*, pages 249, 372–373.
148. *Ibid.*, page 244.
149. Greenberg, page 267.
150. Goodich, page 10.
151. Boswell, *Christianity*, pages 254–255, 261–262.
152. *Ibid.*, pages 381–389. Despite the obvious parallels to the similar poetic debates of Plutarch, Lucian and a comparable one in the *Greek Anthologie*, and the familiarity of the literate clergy with the Greek classics, Boswell insists that the anonymous poet of the work did not model his poem after the classical antecedents (pages 256–258).
153. Greenberg, page 286.
154. Goodich, page 10.
155. Brundage, pages 212–213.

Chapter 14

1. Saint Anselm of Canterbury, quoted in James A. Brundage, *Law, Sex, and Christian Society in Medieval Europe* (Chicago: University of Chicago Press, 1987), page 186.
2. Otto Fenichel, *The Psychoanalytic Theory of Neurosis* (New York: W.W. Norton & Company, 1996), page 20.
3. David F. Greenberg, *The Construction of Homosexuality* (Chicago: University of Chicago Press, 1988), page 292.
4. Sigmund Freud, "Psychoanalytic Notes on an Autobiographical Account of a Case of Paranoia (Dementia Paranoids)," *The Standard Edition of the Complete Psychological Works of Sigmund Freud* Volume 12 (London: Hogarth, 1953) Volume 12, pages 1–82; Seymour Fisher and Roger P. Greenberg, *Freud Scientifically Reappraised: Testing the Theories and Therapy* (New York: John Wiley and Sons, 1996), page 71.
5. Brundage, *Law, Sex*, page 186.
6. *Ibid.*, pages 182–183.
7. Brundage, *Law, Sex*, page 185, paraphrasing Guibert and quoting Burchard.
8. *Ibid.*, page 177.
9. Alain of Lille, *The Complaint of Nature*, Yale Studies in English, vol. 36 (1908), translation of *De planctu natura* by Douglas M. Moffat (reprint; Hamden, Conn.: Archon Books/Shoe String Press, 1972), online at Internet Medieval Sourcebook, http://www.fordham.edu/halsall/sbook.html.
10. Byrne Fone, *Homophobia: A History* (New York: Metropolitan Books, 2000), page 139.
11. Derrick Sherwin Bailey, *Homosexuality and the Western Christian Tradition* (London: Longmans, Green and Co., 1955), pages 119–120.
12. Goodich, page 6.
13. James A. Brundage, "Sex and Cannon Law," in Vern L. Bullough and James A. Brundage, editors, *Handbook of Medieval Sexuality* (New York: Garland Publishing, 1996), page 39.
14. Uta Ranke-Heinemann, *Eunuchs for the Kingdom of Heaven: Women, Sexuality and the Catholic Church*, translated by Peter Heinegg (New York: Penguin Books, 1990), page 204.
15. Brundage, "Sex and Canon Law," pages 39–41.
16. G. Rattray Taylor, *Sex in History* (New York: Harper Torchbooks, 1970), page 52.
17. Greenberg, pages 223–224.
18. Taylor, page 55; Brundage, "Sex and Canon Law," pages 39–41.
19. Taylor, page 51.
20. Ranke-Heinemann, page 204.
21. Ibid; Brundage, *Law, Sex*, page 241.
22. Taylor, page 56. See also W.E.H. Lecky, *History of the Rise and Influence of the Spirit of Rationalism in Europe* (New York: D. Appleton and Company, 1879), chap. 4, "On Persecution."
23. Alfred Gallinek, M.D., "Psychogenic Disorders and the Civilization of the Middle Age," *American Journal of Psychiatry*, vol. 99, no. 1 (1942), page 48.
24. *Ibid.*, page 47.
25. *Ibid.*, page 49.
26. Taylor, pages 32–33.
27. Gallinek, page 41.
28. *Ibid.*, pages 42–43.
29. Michael Goodich, *The Unmentionable Vice: Homosexuality in the Later Medieval Period* (Santa Barbara, Calif.: ABC-Clio, 1979), page 18.
30. *Ibid.*, page 19.
31. *Ibid.*
32. Kinsey, Pomeroy, and Martin, page 514.
33. Goodich, page 17.
34. *Ibid.*, page 19.
35. Pierre J. Payer, *Book of Gomorrah* (Waterloo, Ontario: Wilfrid Laurier University Press, 1982), page 27.
36. *Ibid.*, page 29.
37. *Ibid.*, page 44.
38. *Ibid.*, page 63.
39. *Ibid.*, page 68.
40. Goodich, page 30.
41. Greenberg, page 270.
42. Brundage, *Law, Sex*, pages 212–214; Boswell, *Christianity*, page 212.
43. Boswell, *Christianity*, page 211.
44. Ranke-Heinemann, page 204.
45. *Ibid.*, page 205.
46. Goodich, page 33; Boswell, *Christianity*, pages 227–228..
47. Brundage, *Law, Sex*, pages 212–213.
48. Walter Ullman, "Leo IX, Saint and Pope," *The New Encyclopedia Britannica*, 15th Edition, 10:804–805.
49. Alan Clifford, *The Middle Ages* (St. Paul, Minn.: Greenhaven Press, 1980), pages 5–9; Charles L. Mee, *White Robe, Black Robe* (New York: G.P. Putnam Sons, 1972), .pages 64–65, 151–152.
50. Greenberg, page 281.
51. Brundage, *Law, Sex*, page 214.
52. *Ibid.*, page 215.
53. Greenberg, page 281; Brundage, *Law, Sex*, page 215.
54. Brundage, *Law, Sex*, page 219.

55. Greenberg, page 283.
56. Brundage, *Law, Sex*, page 221.
57. *Ibid.*, pages 216–217.
58. *Ibid.*, page 221.
59. Harry J. Byrne, "One Man's Vocation: My 59 Years as a Celibate," *Commonweal*, July 16, 2004.
60. Quoted in Allen J. Frantzen, *Before the Closet: Same-Sex Love from Beowulf to Angels in America* (Chicago: University of Chicago Press, 1998), pages 238–239.
61. Brundage, *Love, Sex*, page 222.
62. Greenberg, pages 282–283.
63. Boswell, *Christianity*, page 278.
64. Ranke-Heinemann, page 110.
65. Derrick Sherwin Bailey, *Homosexuality and the Western Christian Tradition* (London: Longmans, Green and Co., 1955), page 124.
66. Frantzen, pages 237–238.
67. Bailey, page 125.
68. Frantzen page 238.
69. Michael Doe, *Seeking the Truth in Love: The Church and Homosexuality* (London: Darton, Longman and Todd, 2000), p. 18.
70. Bailey, page 124; Boswell, *Christianity*, pages 215–216.
71. Greenberg, page 287.
72. Frantzen, page 237.
73. Kinsey, Pomeroy, and Martin, pages 455–458; Jonathan Ned Katz, *Gay American History: Lesbians and Gay Men in the U.S.A.* (New York: Meridian, 1992), pages 508–512.
74. Goodich, page 44.
75. *Ibid.*, page 43.
76. Boswell, *Christianity*, page 277.
77. Goodich, pages 42–43.
78. Greenberg, pages 288–289.
79. *Ibid.*
80. *Ibid.*, pages 289–90.
81. Goodich, pages 62–63.
82. *Ibid.*, pages 62–63.
83. *Ibid.*, page 64.
84. Boswell, *Christianity*, page 279–280.
85. *Ibid.*, page 281.
86. *Ibid.*, pages 282–283.
87. Andrew McCall, *The Medieval Underworld* (New York, Barnes & Noble Books, 1979), page 219.
88. Boswell, *Christianity*, pages 270–278; Brundage, *Law, Sex*, page 337.
89. "Fourth Lateran Council (1215)," *The Catholic Encyclopedia*, vol. 9 (New York: Robert Appleton Company, 1910).
90. Goodich, page 51.
91. *Ibid.*, pages 52–54.
92. *Ibid.*, pages 44, 51–52, 56–59.
93. *Ibid.*, page 52.
94. Greenberg, pages 286–288; Goodich, pages 45–46.
95. Brundage, *Law, Sex*, page 422.
96. "Inquisition," *The Catholic Encyclopedia*, vol. 8 (New York: Robert Appleton Company, 1910).
97. Goodich, page 89.
98. Gallinek, page 51.
99. John J. McNeill, *Freedom, Glorious Freedom: The Spiritual Journey to the Fullness of Life for Gays, Lesbians, and Everybody Else* (Boston: Beacon Press, 1995), pages 216–217.
100. *Ibid.*, page 218.
101. Bob Altemeyer, *The Authoritarian Specter* (Cambridge, Mass.: Harvard University Press, 1996).
102. Caesarius of Heisterbach, *Caesarius Heiserbacencis monachi ordinis Cisterciensis, Dialogus miraculorum*, edited by J. Strange (Cologne: J.M. Heberle, 1851), 2:296–298.
103. Judith M. Bennett and C. Warren Hollister, *Medieval Europe: A Short History* (New York: McGraw-Hill, 2006), pages 329–330.
104. Emmanuel LeRoy Ladurie, *Montaillou: The Promised Land of Error*, translated by Barbara Bray (New York: Vintage Books, 1979), page 145; McCall, pages 136–137.
105. Robert Ian Moore, *The Formation of a Persecuting Society: Power and Deviance in Western Europe* (Boston: Blackwell Publishing, 1987), pages 124–125.
106. Fone, page 143–144; Boswell, *Christianity*, pages 288–290.
107. Greenberg, pages 296–298.
108. Goodich, page 82.
109. *Ibid.*, pages 83–84.
110. McCall, page 229.
111. Brian Levack, *The Witch-Hunt in Early Modern Europe* (New York: Addison-Wesley / Longman, 1995).
112. McCall, pages 228–229.
113. *Ibid.*, page 85.
114. Fone, page 174; Greenberg, page 314.
115. Boswell, *Christianity*, page 380.
116. Ladurie, page xiii..
117. Goodich, pages 89–92; Fone, pages 155–159.
118. Ladurie, page 144–145.
119. Fone, page 156; Ladurie, page 146.
120. Ladurie, page 146–147; Goodich, page 92.
121. Ladurie, page 147.
122. William A. Percy, "Homosexuality," in Vern L. Bullough and James A. Brundage, editors, *Handbook of Medieval Sexuality* (New York: Garland Publishing, 1996), pages 175–176.
123. Taylor, page 19.

Chapter 15

1. Louis Crompton, *Homosexuality and Civilization* (Cambridge, Mass.: Belknap Press of Harvard University Press, 2003), pages 248–249.
2. *Ibid.*, pages 249–250.
3. *Ibid.*, page 249.
4. Byrne Fone, *Homophobia: A History* (New York: Metropolitan Books, 2000), page 195.
5. David F. Greenberg, *The Construction of Homosexuality* (Chicago: University of Chicago Press, 1988), page 305.
6. Crompton, page 254.
7. *Ibid.*
8. Fone, page 198.
9. Crompton, page 254.
10. Fone, page 198.
11. Crompton, page 258.
12. Fone, page 199.
13. Michael Rocke, *Forbidden Friendships: Homosexuality and Male Culture in Renaissance Florence* (New York: Oxford University Press), page 3.
14. Crompton, page 254.
15. *Ibid.*, page 252.
16. *Ibid.*, page 252.
17. *Ibid.*, page 253.
18. Rocke, page 22.
19. *Ibid.*, page 4.
20. *Ibid.*, page 5.
21. Fone, page 196.
22. Rocke, page 122.
23. J.L. Flandrin, "Repression and Change in the Sexual Life of Young People in Medieval and Early Modern Times," *Journal of Family History*, vol. 2 (1977), page 196.
24. Crompton, page 262.
25. *Ibid.*, page 278.
26. *Ibid.*, page 287.
27. Fone, page 201.
28. Crompton, page 293.
29. Kenneth Clark, *Civilization: A Personal View* (New York: Harper & Row, 1970), page 108.
30. Fone, page 210–211; Crompton, page 326.
31. Fone, page 211–212.
32. Crompton, page 326.
33. Fone, page 217.
34. *Ibid.*, page 216.
35. Arend H. Huussen, Jr., "Prosecution of Sodomy in Eighteenth Century Frisia," in Kent Gerard and Gert Hekma, editors, *Male Homosexuality in Renaissance and Enlightenment Europe* (New York: Harrington Park Press, 1989), page 255.
36. Dirk Jaap Noordam, "Sodomy in the Dutch Republic, 1600–1725," in Gerard and Hekma, pages 214–218.
37. Greenberg, page 317; Fone, pages 238–242..
38. Recent research by Richard Florida and others has shown that social tolerance, and in particular tolerance of homosexuality, strongly correlates with creativity and economic growth. See Richard Florida, *Flight of the Creative Class* (New York: Harper

Collins, 2005), pages 59–60; Richard Florida, *Cities and the Creative Class* (New York: Routledge, 2005), pages 7, 129–132; Richard Florida, *Rise of the Creative Class* (New York: Basic Books, 2002), page xx.

39. Crompton, pages 369–371.

40. Alan Bray, *Homosexuality in Renaissance England* (Boston: Gay Men's Press, Alyson Publications, 1982), pages 63–64; Crompton, page 369.

41. Crompton, page 369.

42. Karlen, pages 118–120; Crompton, page 378–379.

43. Rictor Norton, "Queen James and His Courtiers," *Gay History and Literature, Essays by Rictor Norton,* online at http://www.infopt.demon. co.uk/jamesi.htm.

44. A.L. Rowse, *Homosexuals in History* (New York: Carroll & Graf, 1977), pages 55–56.

45. Norton, "Queen James."

46. Rowse, pages 55–56.

47. Arno Karlen, *Sexuality and Homosexuality: A New View* (New York: W.W. Norton & Company, 1971), page 117.

48. Crompton, page 386.

49. *Ibid.*

50. Rowse, page 44; Karlen, page 115.

51. Karlen, page 115..

52. Bray, page 34.

53. Norton, "Queen James."

54. Greenberg, page 324.

55. *Ibid.*, pages 323–324.

56. *Ibid.*, page 326.

57. *Ibid.*

58. *Ibid.*, page 327, n159.

59. Bray, page 76.

60. *Ibid.*, pages 81–82.

61. Greenberg, page 317.

62. Crompton, page 330.

63. Greenberg, page 316.

64. Crompton, page 337–338.

65. Rowse, pages 71–72; Crompton, page 338.

66. Rowse, page 72; Crompton, page 338.

67. Bullough, page 483; Crompton, page 339–340.

68. Crompton, page 341.

69. Karlen, page 134.

70. Crompton, page 341.

71. *Ibid.*, page 340–341.

72. *Ibid.*, pages 341, 344.

73. *Ibid.*, page 341.

74. Greenberg, page 318n105.

75. *Ibid.*, page 319.

76. Michel Rey, "Police and Sodomy in 18th Century Paris: From Sin to Disorder," in Gerard and Hekma, pages 129–135.

77. Karlen, pages 146–147.

78. *Ibid.*, page 145.

79. Stephen Donaldson, "Seafaring," in Wayne R. Dynes, editor, *Encyclopedia of Homosexuality*, 2:1173.

80. B.R. Burg, *Sodomy and the Pirate Tradition: English Sea Rovers in the Seventeenth-Century Caribbean* (New York: New York University Press, 1983), pages 144–145.

81. Walter Williams, *The Spirit and the Flesh: Sexual Diversity in American Indian Culture* (Boston: Beacon Press, 1992), page 154.

82. Burg, pages 57–58.

83. *Ibid.*, pages 46–51.

84. *Ibid.*, pages 49–50.

85. *Ibid.*, page 63.

86. Williams, page 154.

87. Burg, pages 111–112.

88. *Ibid.*, pages 113–117.

89. *Ibid.*, page 121.

90. *Ibid.*, pages 122–124.

91. *Ibid.*, page 129.

92. *Ibid.*, pages 130–131.

93. *Ibid.*, pages 133–134.

94. Michael Warner, "New English Sodom," *American Literature*, vol. 64, no. 1 (March 1992), pages 19–47

95. Jonathan Ned Katz, *Gay American History: Lesbians and Gay Men in the U.S.A.* (New York: Meridian, 1992), pages 19–20.

96. William Bradford, "Of Plimoth Plantation," *Bradford's History* (Boston: Wright & Potter Printing Co., State Printers, 1900), page 459.

97. Katz, pages 20, 23.

98. Greenberg, page 344.

99. *Ibid.*, page 16.

100. Katz, pages 16–22; Greenberg, page 345.

101. Katz, pages 22–23.

102. *Ibid.*, page 24.

103. *Ibid.*, page 25–26.

104. Emily Stone Whiteley, *Washington and His Aides-de-Camp* (New York: Macmillan Company, 1936); Marcus Cunliffe, *George Washington, Man and Monument* (New York: Mentor Books, 1958).

105. Charley Shively, "George Washington's Gay Mess: Was the Father of Our Country a Queen?" in Leyland, pages 41–45.

106. *Ibid.*, pages 27–28.

107. Washington Irving, *Life of George Washington* (New York: Geo. P. Putnam, 1860), 1:207–208.

108. Shively, pages 28–30.

109. Cunliffe, quoted in Shiveley, page 55.

110. Shively, page 55–57.

111. *Ibid.*, pages 44, 58.

112. *Ibid.*, page 48.

113. *Ibid.*, page 44.

114. Katz, page 453.

115. Shiveley, page 51–53.

116. Katz, page 454.

117. Shively, page 53.

118. Martin Duberman, *Hidden from History: Reclaiming the Gay and Lesbian Past* (New York: Meridian, 1990), pages 153–159.

119. Kinsey, Pomeroy, and Martin, pages 455–459, 631.

120. Williams, pages 159–160, quoting from Winston Leyland, editor, *Flesh: True Homosexual Experiences* (San Francisco: Gay Sunshine Press, 1982), page 14.

121. Williams, pages 161–162.

122. Fone, page 334.

123. Fritz Klein, *The Bisexual Option* (New York: Harrington Park Press, 1993), pages 13–20.

124. Burg, pages 57–58, 111–112, 121.

125. Chris Packard, *Queer Cowboys, and Other Erotic Male Friendships in Nineteenth-Century American Literature* (New York: Palgrave Macmillan, 2005), pages 19–28.

126. Owen Wister, *The Virginian, A Horseman of the Plains* (New York: Macmillan Company, 1903), chap. 1.

127. Packard, pages 46–47.

128. Clifford P. Westermeier, "The Cowboy and Sex," in *The Cowboy: Six-Shooters, Songs and Sex*, edited by Charles W. Harris and Buck Rainey (Norman: University of Oklahoma Press, 1976), pages 85–105.

129. Packard, page 51.

130. *Ibid.*

131. Wister, chap. 6.

132. *Ibid.*, chap. 31.

133. Packard, page 48.

134. *Ibid.*, page 49.

135. Williams, page 159.

136. Charles Badger Clark, "Others," from *Sun and Saddle Leather* (Boston: The Gorham Press, 1922), page 194.

137. *Ibid.*, "The Lost Partner," page 83.

138. Rictor Norton, "The Term 'Homosexual,'" *A Critique of Social Constructionism and Postmodern Queer Theory*, 1 June 2002, online at http://www.infopt.demon.co.uk/social14.htm.

139. Sigmund Freud, "Three Essays on Sexuality," *The Standard Edition of the Complete Psychological Works of Sigmund Freud* (London: Hogarth Press, 1953), 7:145–146.

Chapter 16

1. One study found that up to 91 percent of lesbians have had a heterosexual experience: see Linda Garnets and Douglas C. Kimmel, *Psychological Perspectives on Lesbian, Gay, and Bisexual Experiences* (New York: Columbia University Press, 2003), page 233; studies cited by Massachusetts General Hospital found that up to eighty-seven percent of lesbians and sixty-eight percent of gay men reported heterosexual experiences: see http://www.massgeneral.org/children/

adolescenthealth/articles/aa_gay_and_ transsexual_adolescents.aspx.

2. Stephen J. Ducat, *The Wimp Factor: Gender Gaps, Holy Wars, and the Politics of Anxious Masculinity* (Boston: Beacon Press, 2004), pages 24–83.

3. *Ibid.*, pages 199–203.

4. *Ibid.*

5. Seymour Fisher and Roger P. Greenberg, *The Scientific Credibility of Freud's Theories and Therapy.* (New York: Columbia University Press, 1985, pages 255–269.

6. Remarks of State Representative Sally Kern, Oklahoma House of Representatives, transcribed from videotape by Ace on Tech, www.ace-on-tech.com, March 10, 2008.

7. Bob Altemeyer, *The Authoritarian Specter,* op.cit.

8. Kinsey, Pomeroy, and Martin, page 168.

9. Diane Elze, "It Has Nothing to Do with Me," in Warren J. Blumenfeld, editor, *Homophobia: How We All Pay the Price* (Boston: Beacon Press, 1992), pages 99–101.

10. Elze, pages 98–99.

11. Ibid, page 98.

12. *U.S. Teenage Pregnancy Statistics: National and State Trends and Trends by Race and Ethnicity,* Guttmacher Institute, New York; updated September 2006, page 2.

13. Philip A. Rutter and Emil Soucar, "Youth Suicide Risk and Sexual Orientation," *Adolescence,* Summer 2002.

14. Paul Gibson, *Gay Male and Lesbian Youth Suicide, Report of the Sec-* retary's Task Force on Youth Suicide, DHHS Publication No. ADM89–1623; Vol. 3 (Washington, D.C.: U.S. Government Printing Office, 1989), pages 110–142; a representative conservative critique of the DHHS study is Peter LaBarbera, "The Gay Suicide Myth," at Leadership U, a web site maintained by the Christian Leadership Ministries of the Campus Crusade for Christ International, http://www.leaderu.com/jhs/labarbera.html.

15. Anthony R. D'Augelli and Scott L. Hershberger, "Lesbian, Gay and Bisexual Youth in Community Settings: Personal Challenges and Mental Health Problems," *American Journal of Community Psychology,* vol. 21 (1993), pages 421–447.

16. M. Rotheram-Borus, H. Reid, M. Rosario, R. Van Rossen, and R. Gills, "Prevalence, Course, and Predictors of Multiple Problem Behaviors among Gay and Bisexual Male Adolescents," *Developmental Psychology,* vol. 31 (1995), pages 75–85.

17. Roy Young, "Alcoholism and Addiction in Homosexuals: Etiology, Prevalence and Treatment" (1995), online at http://www.royy.com/pap.html.

18. National Gay and Lesbian Task Force, "Anti-Gay/Lesbian Victimization," New York, 1984.

19. Gary David Comstock, *Violence against Lesbians and Gay Men* (New York: Columbia University Press, 1991), pages 105–106; New York Gay and Lesbian Anti-Violence Report, 1996.

20. Comstock, pages 107–111.

21. Gregory M. Herek and Kevin T. Berrill, *Hate Crimes: Confronting Violence against Lesbians and Gay Men* (Newbury Park, Calif. Sage Publications, 1992), page 160.

22. William R. Greer, "Violence against Homosexuals Rising, Groups Seeking Wider Protection Say," *New York Times,* November 23, 1986.

23. *State of Wisconsin v. Jeffrey L. Dahmer,* Testimony of George B. Palermo, M.D., Thursday, February 6, 1992.

24. National Coalition of Anti-Violence Programs (240 West 35th Street, New York, NY,10001), *Annual Reports, 1998–2006.*

25. Jean S. Gochros, "Homophobia, Homosexuality, and Heterosexual Marriage," in Blumenfeld, page 132.

26. Davenport, quoted in Stephen O. Murray, *Oceanic Homosexualities* (New York: Garland Publishing, 1992), page 357.

27. Martin S. Weinberg and Colin J. Williams, *Male Homosexuals: Their Problems and Adaptations* (New York: Oxford University Press, 1974), pages 270–271.

28. Genesis 2:18, as translated directly from the Hebrew by Phyllis Trible, professor of Old Testament Studies, Union Theological Seminary, New York; quoted in John J. McNeill, *Freedom, Glorious Freedom: The Spiritual Journey to the Fullness of Life for Gays, Lesbians and Everybody Else* (Boston: Beacon Press, 1995).

29. Edward O. Wilson, *On Human Nature* (Cambridge, Massachusetts: Harvard University Press, 1978), pages 140–141.

Bibliography

AbuKhalil, As'ad. "A Note on the Study of Homosexuality in the Arab/Islamic Civilization." *Arab Studies Journal,* vol. 1, no. 2 (1993), pages 32–48. Quoted in Stephen O. Murray and Will Roscoe, editors, *Islamic Homosexualities: Culture, History, and Literature.* New York: New York University Press, 1997.

Adams, Henry E., Ph.D., Lester W. Wright, Jr., Ph.D., and Bethany A. Lohr. "Is Homophobia Associated with Homosexual Arousal?" *Journal of Abnormal Psychology,* vol. 105, no. 3 (1996).

Alain of Lille. *The Complaint of Nature.* Yale Studies in English, vol. 36 (1908). Translation of *De planctu natura* by Douglas M. Moffat. Reprint. Hamden, Conn.: Archon Books/Shoe String Press, 1972. Online at Internet Medieval Sourcebook, http://www.fordham.edu/halsall/sbook.html.

Al Hadis, vol. 4, no. 34, page 172. Translation and Commentary by Al Haj Maulana Fazlul Karim. New York: Islamic Book Service, 1960.

Altemeyer, Bob. *The Authoritarian Specter.* Cambridge, Mass.: Harvard University Press, 1996.

Al-Tifashi, Ahmad. "Stories Concerning Young Hustlers." *The Delight of Hearts, or What You Will Not Find in Any Book.* Translated by Edward A. Lacey. San Francisco: Gay Sunshine Press, 1988.

Alwood, Edward. *Straight News: Gays, Lesbians, and the News Media.* New York: Columbia University Press, 1996.

Amis and Amile. Translated by William Morris, in *Bibliotheca Elzeviriana.* Quoted in Edward Carpenter, *Anthology of Friendship: Iolaus.* London: George Allen & Unwin, 1922.

Archer, Christon I., editor. *World History of Warfare.* Lincoln: University of Nebraska Press, 2002.

Aries, Philippe, and Georges Duby, General Editors. *A History of Private Life.* Cambridge, Mass.: Belknap Press of Harvard University Press, 1988.

Ariwara no Narihira. *The Tales of Ise: Lyrical Episodes from Tenth-Century Japan.* Translated by Helen Craig McCullough. Stanford, Calif.: Stanford University Press, 1968.

Bagemihl, Bruce. *Biological Exuberance: Animal Homosexuality and Natural Diversity.* New York: St. Martin's Press, 1999.

Bailey, Derrick Sherwin. *Homosexuality and the Western Christian Tradition.* London: Longmans, Green and Co., 1955.

Bamberger, Bernard, "Leviticus," in *The Torah: A Modern Commentary,* ed. by W.G. Plaut, New York: Union of American Hebrew Congregations, 1981.

Barker, T.N. "Some Features of Ai'i Society." Ph.D Dissertation, Laval University, 1975. Quoted in Eric Schwimmer, "Male Couples in New Guinea." In Gilbert H. Herdt, *Ritualized Homosexuality in Melanesia.* Los Angeles: University of California Press, 1984.

Bennett, Judith M., and C. Warren Hollister. *Medieval Europe: A Short History.* New York: McGraw-Hill, 2006.

Beowulf. Translated by Francis B. Gummere. The Harvard Classics. New York: P.F. Collier & Son, 1910.

Bethe, Eric. "Die Dorische Knabenliebe: Ihre Ethik und Ihre Idee." *Rheinisches Museum für Philologie,* vol. 62 (1907).

Blount, Ben G., "Issues in Bonobo (Pan paniscus) Sexual Behavior." *American Anthropologist,* vol. 92 (1990).

Blumenfeld, Warren J., editor. *Homophobia: How We All Pay the Price.* Boston: Beacon Press, 1992.

Boswell, John. *Christianity, Social Tolerance and Homosexuality: Gay People in Western Europe from the Beginning of the Christian Era to the Fourteenth Century.* Chicago: University of Chicago Press, 1980.

_____. *Same-Sex Unions in Premodern Europe.* New York: Villard Books, 1994.

Bowers v. Hardwick, 478 U.S. 186.

Bratcher, Dennis. "Speaking the Language of Canaan: The Old Testament and the Israelite Perception of the Physical World." Paper presented at the Consultation on the Relationship between the Wesleyan Tradition and the Natural Sciences, Kansas City, Missouri, October 19, 1991.

Bray, Alan. *Homosexuality in Renaissance England.* Boston: Gay Men's Press, 1982.

Brelich, A. *Paides e Parthenoi.* Rome: Edizioni dell' Ateneo, 1969.

Bremmer, Jan N., "Adolescents, Symposion, and Pederasty." In Oswyn Murray, editor, *Sympotica: A Symposium on the Symposion.* Oxford: Clarendon Press, 1990.

Bremmer, Jan. "An Enigmatic Indo-European Rite: Paederasty." *Arethusa*, vol. 13, no. 2 (Fall 1980).

Brooten, Bernadette J. *Love between Women: Early Christian Responses to Female Homoeroticism.* Chicago: University of Chicago Press, 1996.

Brundage, James A. "Sex and Cannon Law." In Vern L. Bullough and James A. Brundage, editors, *Handbook of Medieval Sexuality.* New York: Garland Publishing, 1996.

Brundage, James W. *Law, Sex, and Christian Society in Medieval Europe.* Chicago: University of Chicago Press, 1987.

Bullough, Vern L. *Homosexuality: A History.* New York: New American Library, 1979.

_____. *Sexual Variance in Society and History.* Chicago: University of Chicao Press, 1976.

_____, and James A. Brundage. *Handbook of Medieval Sexuality.* New York: Garland Publishing, 1996.

_____, and Bonnie Bullough. *Sexual Attitudes: Myths and Realities.* Amherst, N.Y.: Prometheus Books, 1995.

Burg, B.R. *Sodomy and the Pirate Tradition: English Sea Rovers in the Seventeenth-Century Caribbean.* New York: New York University Press, 1984.

Burton, Richard Francis. Terminal Essay. *The Arabian Nights.* London, 1885. Online at People with a History. http://www.fordham.edu/halsall/pwh/burton-te.html.

Buruma, Ian. *Behind the Mask.* New York: Meridian, 1985.

Byrne, Harry J. "One Man's Vocation: My 59 Years as a Celibate." *Commonweal,* July 16, 2004.

Caesarius of Heisterbach. *Caesarius Heiserbacencis monachi ordinis Cisterciensis. Dialogus miraculorum.* Edited by J. Strange. Cologne: J.M. Heberle, 1851.

Cameron, Ron. "The Secret Gospel of Mark." In Willis Barnstone, editor, *The Other Bible: Jewish Pseudepigrapha, Chrstian Apocrypha, Gnostic Scriptures.* San Francisco: Harper & Row Publishers, 1984.

Campbell, Joseph. *Historical Atlas of World Mythology. Vol. 1: The Way of the Animal Powers, Part 2, Mythologies of the Great Hunt.* New York: Harper & Row, 1988.

_____. *The Masks of God: Primitive Mythology.* New York: Penguin Books, 1959.

Cantarella, Eva. *Bisexuality in the Ancient World.* Translated by Cormac O'Cuilleanain. New Haven: Yale University Press, 1992.

Carpenter, Edward. *Anthology of Friendship: Iolaus.* London: George Allen & Unwin, 1920.

_____. *Intermediate Types among Primitive Folk, A Study in Social Evolution.* London: George Allen & Co., 1914.

Cartledge, Paul. "The Politics of Spartan Pederasty." *Cambridge Philological Society, Proceedings,* vol. 27 (1981).

Catlin, George. *Manners, Customs and Condition of the North American Indian.* New York: Dover Publications, 1973.

Churchill, Wainwright. *Homosexual Behavior among Males: A Cross-Cultural and Cross-Species Investigation.* New York: Hawthorn Books, 1967.

Chusuke, Ijiri. "The Essence of Jakudo." 1482.

Clark, Kenneth. *Civilization: A Personal View.* New York: Harper & Row, 1970.

Clarke, John R., *Looking at Lovemaking: Constructions of Sexuality in Roman Art, 100 B.C.–A.D. 250.* Berkeley: University of California Press, 1998.

Clarke, W. M., "Achilles and Patroclus in Love." *Hermes,* vol. 106 (1978).

Clifford, Alan. *The Middle Ages.* St. Paul, Minn.: Greenhaven Press, 1980.

Crompton, Louis. *Byron and Greek Love.* Berkeley: University of California Press, 1985.

_____. *Homosexuality and Civilization.* Cambridge, Mass.: Belknap Press of Harvard University Press, 2003.

Curtis, V.R. *Indo-European Origins.* New York: Peter Lang, 1989.

Deacon, A. Bernard. *Malekula.* London: Routledge Paul, 1934.

de Becker, Raymond. *The Other Face of Love.* Translated by Margaret Crosland and Alan Daventry. New York: Grove Press, 1969.

Denniston, R.H. "Ambisexuality in Animals." In Judd Marmor, editor, *Homosexual Behavior, A Modern Reappraisal.* New York: Basic Books, 1980.

Devereaux, George. "Greek Pseudo-homosexuality and the 'Greek Miracle.'" *Symbolae Osloenses,* vol. 42 (1967).

Devereaux, George. "Institutionalized Homosexuality of the Mohave Indians." *Human Biology,* vol. 9 (1937).

de Waal, Frans B.M., "Bonobo Sex and Society." *Scientific American,* vol. 272 (March 1995, p. 82.

_____. *Peacemaking among Primates.* Cambridge, Mass.: Harvard University Press, 1989.

Di Vito, Robert, "Questions on the Construction of (Homo)sexuality: Same-Sex Relations in the Hebrew Bible," in Beattie Jung, Joseph Andrew Coray, editors, *Sexual Diversity and Catholicism: Toward the Development of Moral Theology,* Collegeville, Minnesota: the Liturgical Press, 2001.

Doe, Michael. *Seeking the Truth in Love: The Church and Homosexuality.* London: Darton, Longman and Todd, 2000.

Dover, K.J. *Greek Homosexuality.* New York: Vintage Books, 1980.

_____. "Greek Homosexuality and Initiation." In K.J. Dover, editor, *The Greeks and Their Legacy: Collected Papers. Vol. 2: Prose, Literature, History, Society, Transmission, Influence.* Oxford and New York: Basil Blackwell, 1988.

Drews, Robert. *The Coming of the Greeks: Indo-European Conquests in the Aegean and the Near East.* Princeton, N.J.: Princeton University Press, 1988.

Duberman, Martin, Martha Vicinus, and George Chauncey, Jr. *Hidden from History: Reclaiming the Gay and Lesbian Past.* New York: Meridian, 1989.

Duby, Georges. "The Aristocratic Households of Feudal France. In Georges Duby, editor, *A History of Private Life: II. Revelations of the Medieval World.* Translated by Arthur Goldhammer. Cambridge, Mass.: Belknap Press of Harvard University Press, 1988.

_____. *The Chivalrous Society.* Berkeley: University of California Press. 1977.

_____. "Private Power, Public Power." In Georges Duby, editor, *A History of Private Life: II. Revelations of the Medieval World.* Translated by Arthur Goldhammer. Cambridge, Mass.: Belknap Press of Harvard University Press, 1988.

_____. *William Marshal: The Flower of Chivalry.* Translated by Richard Howard. New York: Pantheon Books, 1985.

Ducat, Stephen J. *The Wimp Factor: Gender Gaps, Holy Wars, and the Politics of Anxious Masculinity.* Boston: Beacon Press, 2004.

Dynes, Wayne R. *Encyclopedia of Homosexuality.* Edited by Wayne R. Dynes. New York: Garland Publishing Company, 1990.

_____. "Homosexuality in Sub-Saharan Africa: An Unnecessary Question." *Gay Books Bulletin,* vol. 9 (1983).

_____, and Stephen Donaldson. *Ethnographic Studies of Homosexuality.* New York: Garland Publishing, 1992.

_____, and _____. *Homosexuality in the Ancient World.* New York and London: Garland Publishing, 1992.

Edwardes, Allen. *The Jewel in the Lotus, A Historical Survey of the Sexual Culture of the East.* New York: The Julian Press, 1959.

Eglinton, J.Z. *Greek Love.* New York: Oliver Layton Press, 1964.

Eisler, Riane. *The Chalice and the Blade: Our History, Our Future.* San Francisco: HarperCollins, 1988.

_____. *Sacred Pleasure: Sex, Myth, and the Politics of the Body.* San Francisco: HarperSanFrancisco, 1995.

Ellis, Albert, and Albert Abarbanel. *The Encyclopedia of Sexual Behavior.* New York: Hawthorn Books, Publishers, 1964.

Ellis, Havelock. *Studies in the Psychology of Sex. Vol. 1, Part Four: Sexual Inversion.* New York: Random House, 1942.

Epstein, Louis M., *Sex Laws and Customs in Judaism.* New York: Bloch, 1948.

Evans-Pritchard, E.E., "Sexual Inversion among the Azande." *American Anthropologist,* vol. 72 (1970).

Fenichel, Otto. *The Psychoanalytic Theory of Neurosis.* New York, W.W. Norton & Company, 1996.

Fisher, Seymour, and Roger P. Greenberg. *Freud Scientifically Reappraised: Testing the Theories and Therapy.* New York: John Wiley and Sons, 1996.

Fone, Byrne. *Homophobia: A History.* New York: Metropolitan Books, 2000.

Ford, Clellan S., and Frank A. Beach. *Patterns of Sexual Behavior.* Westport, Conn.: Greenwood Press, 1951.

Frantzen, Allen J. *Before the Closet: Same-Sex Love from Beowulf to Angels in America.* Chicago: University of Chicago Press, 1998.

Freud, Sigmund. "Bruchstuck einer Hysterie-Analyse." *Sammlung Kleiner Schrift en zur Neurosenlehre.* Leipzig and Vienna, 1909.

_____. "Three Essays on Sexuality." *The Standard Edition of the Complete Psychological Works of Sigmund Freud.* London: Hogarth Press, 1953.

Friedman, R.E. *Who Wrote the Bible?* San Francisco: Harper Collins, 1997.

Furnish, Victor Paul. "The Bible and Homosexuality: Reading the Texts in Context." In Jeffrey S. Siker, editor, *Homosexuality in the Church: Both Sides of the Debate.* Louisville, Ky.: Westminster John Knox Press, 1994.

Gallinek, Alfred, M.D. "Psychogenic Disorders and the Civilization of the Middle Age." *American Journal of Psychiatry,* vol. 99, no. 1 (1942).

Gambold, Leslie L., "Homosexuality and Lesbianism: Cross-Cultural Perspectives." In Vern Bullough, editor, *Human Sexuality, An Encyclopedia.* New York: Garland Publishing Company, 1994.

Gaunt, Simon. *Love and Death in Medieval French and Occitan Courtly Literature: Martyrs to Love.* London: Oxford University Press, 2006.

Gerard, Kent, and Gert Hekma, editors. *Male Homosexuality in Renaissance and Enlightenment Europe.* New York: Harrington Park Press, 1989.

Gibbon, Edward. *The History of the Decline and Fall of the Roman Empire.* J.B. Bury, editor. New York: The Heritage Press, 1946.

Gimbutas, Marija. "The Beginning of the Bronze Age in Europe and the Indo-Europeans: 3500–2500 B.C." *Journal of Indo-European Studies,* vol. 1, no. 2 (1973).

_____. *The Goddesses and Gods of Old Europe: Myths and Cult Images.* Berkeley: University of California Press, 1982.

Goodich, Michael. *The Unmentionable Vice: Homosexuality in the Later Medieval Period.* Santa Barbara, Calif.: ABC-Clio, 1979.

Greenberg, David F. *The Construction of Homosexuality.* Chicago: University of Chicago Press, 1988.

Guerra, Francisco. *The Pre-Columbian Mind.* New York: Seminar Press, 1971.

Halperin, David M. *One Hundred Years of Homosexuality: And Other Essays on Greek Homosexuality.* New York: Routledge, 1990.

Hardmann, Paul D. *Homoaffectionalism: Male Bonding from Gilgamesh to the Present.* San Francisco: GLB Publishers, 1993.

Hawkes, Jacquetta. *The Atlas of Early Man.* New York: St. Martin's Press, 1976.

_____, and Sir Leonard Woolley. *Prehistory and the Beginnings of Civilization.* New York: Harper & Row, Publishers, 1963.

Hearnshaw, F.J.C. "Chivalry and Its Place in History." In Edgar Prestage, editor, *Chivalry: A Series of Studies to Illustrate Its Historical Significance and Civilizing Influence*. London, Kegan Paul, Trench, Trubner, 1928.

Heidel, Alexander. *The Gilgamesh Epic and Old Testament Parallels*. Chicago: University of Chicago Press, 1971.

Held, George F. "Parallels between the Gilgamesh Epic and Plato's Symposium." *Journal of Near Eastern Studies*, vol. 42 (1983).

Helminiak, Daniel A. *What the Bible Really Says about Homosexuality*. San Francisco: Alamo Square Press, 1994.

Henderson, Bernard W. *The Life and Principate of the Emperor Hadrian, A.D. 76–138*. London, 1923.

Henderson, Philip. *Richard Coeur de Lion*. London: Robert Hale Limited, 1958.

Herdt, Gilbert H. *Guardians of the Flutes*. Chicago: University of Chicago Press, 1981.

_____. *Ritualized Homosexuality in Melanesia*. Los Angeles: University of California Press, 1984.

_____. *Same Sex, Different Cultures*. New York: Westview Press, 1997.

Herm, Gerhard. *The Celts*. New York: St. Martin's Press, 1975.

Hill, Jim, and Rand Cheadle. *The Bible Tells Me So: Uses and Abuses of Holy Scripture*. New York: Anchor Books/Doubleday, 1996.

Hinsch, Bret. *Passions of the Cut Sleeve: The Male Homosexual Tradition in China*. Berkeley: University of California Press, 1990.

Holmes, W. G. *The Age of Justinian and Theodora*. London, 1912.

Homer. *The Iliad*. Translated by Richmond Lattimore. Chicago: University of Chicago Press, 1961.

_____. *The Odyssey*. Translated by Richmond Lattimore. New York: Harper Colophon Books, 1967.

Horner, Tom. *Jonathan Loved David: Homosexuality in Biblical Times*. Philadelphia: Westminster Press, 1978.

_____. *Sex in the Bible*. Rutland, Vt.: Charles E. Tuttle, 1974.

Hoveden, Roger of. *The Annals*. Trans. Henry T. Riley. London: H.G. Bohn, 1853, 2:63–64. Online at People with a History. http://www.fordham.edu/halsall/pwh/hoveden1.html.

Huizinga, Johan. *The Waning of the Middle Ages*. Garden City, N.Y.: Doubleday Anchor Books, 1954.

Jacobsen, Thorkild. "How Did Gilgamesh Oppress Uruk?" *Acta Orientalia*, vol. 8 (1929).

Jung, Beattie and Joseph Andrew Coray, editors, *Sexual Diversity and Catholicism: Toward the Development of Moral Theology*, Collegeville, Minnesota: the Liturgical Press, 2001.

Kafi, Helene. "Tehran: Dangerous Love." In Arno Schmitt and Jehoda Sofer, editors, *Sexuality and Eroticism among Males in Moslem Societies*. New York: Harrington Park Press, 1992.

Karlen, Arno. "Homosexuality in History." In Judd Marmor, editor, *Homosexual Behavior: A Modern Reappraisal*. New York: Basic Books, 1980.

_____. *Sexuality and Homosexuality: A New View*. New York: W.W. Norton & Company, 1971.

Katz, Jonathan Ned. *Gay American History: Lesbians and Gay Men in the U.S.A.* New York: Meridian, 1992.

Keen, Maurice. *Chivalry*. New Haven and London: Yale University Press, 1984.

Keuls, Eva C. *The Reign of the Phallus*. Berkeley: University of California Press, 1985.

Kilmer, Anne Draffkorn. "A Note on an Overlooked Word-Play in the Akkadian Gilgamesh." In G. Van Driel, T.J.H. Krispijn, M. Stol, and K.R. Veenhof, editors, *Zikir Sumim: Assyriological Studies Presented to F.R. Kraus on the Occasion of His Seventieth Birthday*. Leiden: E.J. Brill, 1982.

Kinross, Patrick. *The Ottoman Centuries: The Rise and Fall of the Turkish Empire*. New York: Morrow, 1979.

Kinsey, Alfred C., Wardell B. Pomeroy, and Clyde E. Martin. *Sexual Behavior in the Human Male*. Philadelphia: W.B. Saunders Company, 1948.

_____, Wardell B. Pomeroy, Clyde E. Martin, and Paul H. Gebhard. *Sexual Behavior in the Human Female*. Philadelphia: W.B. Saunders Company, 1953.

Kirsch, John A.W., and James Eric Rodman. "The Natural History of Homosexuality." *Yale Scientific Magazine*, Winter 1977.

_____, and James D. Weinrich. "Homosexuality, Nature and Biology: Is Homosexuality Natural: Does It Matter?" In John C. Gonsiorek and James D. Weinrich, editors, *Homosexuality: Research Implications for Public Policy*. London: Sage Publications, 1991.

Klein, Fritz. *The Bisexual Option*. Binghamton, NY: Haworth Press, 1993.

La Barre, Weston. *Muelos: A Stone Age Superstition about Sexuality*. New York: Columbia University Press, 1984.

Ladurie, Emmanuel LeRoy. *Montaillou: The Promised Land of Error*. Translated by Barbara Bray. New York: Vintage Books, 1979.

Lancelot-Grail, Part 2. Carleton W. Carroll, translator. In Byrne R.S Fone, editor, *The Columbia Anthology of Gay Literature: Readings from Western Antiquity to the Present Day*. New York: Columbia University Press, 1998.

Lecky, W.E.H. *History of the Rise and Influence of the Spirit of Rationalism in Europe*. Chapter 4, On Persecution. New York: D. Appleton and Company, 1879.

Leupp, Gary P. *Male Colors: The Construction of Homosexuality in Tokugawa Japan*. Berkeley: University of California Press, 1995.

Levack, Brian. *The Witch-Hunt in Early Modern Europe*. New York: Addison-Wesley/Longman, 1995.

Levi-Strauss, Claude. *A World on the Wane*. London, 1961.

Lewis, C.S. *The Allegory of Love: A Study in Medieval Tradition*. London: Oxford University Press, 1938.

Licht, Hans (pseudonym of Paul Brand). *Sexual Life in Ancient Greece*. London: Abbey Library, 1932.

Lu Hsun. *A Brief History of Chinese Fiction*. Beijing: Foreign Language Press, 1976.

Lybyer, Albert H. *The Government of the Ottoman Empire in the Time of Sulieman the Magnificent*. Cambridge, Mass.: Harvard University Press, 1913.

Mann, Janet. "Establishing Trust: Sociosexual Behaviour and the Development of Male-Male Bonds among Indian Ocean Bottlenose Dolphin Calves." In P. Vasey and V. Sommer, editors, *Homosexual Behaviour in Animals: An Evolutionary Perspective*. London: Cambridge University Press, 2006.

Manniche, Lise. "Some Aspects of Ancient Egytian Sexual Life." *Acta Orientalia*, vol. 38 (1977).

Marmor, Judd, editor. *Sexual Inversion: The Multiple Roots of Homosexuality*. New York: Basic Books, 1965.

Marrou, H.I. *A History of Education in Antiquity*. Translated by George Lamb. London: Sheed and Ward, 1956.

McBride, A.F., and D.O. Hebb. "Behavior of the Captive Bottlenose Dolphin, Tursiops Truncatus." *Journal of Comparative Physicological Psychology*, vol. 41 (1948).

McCall, Andrew. *The Medieval Underworld*. New York: Barnes & Noble Books, 1979.

McGuire, Brian P. "Monastic Friendship and Toleration in Twelfth Century Cistercian Life." In W. J. Shiels, editor, *Monks, Hermits and the Ascetic Tradition*. Studies in Church History 22. Malden, Mass.: Blackwell Publishing, 1985.

McNeill, John J. *The Church and the Homosexual*. Boston: Beacon Press, 1988.

_____. *Freedom, Glorious Freedom: The Spiritual Journey to the Fullness of Life for Gays, Lesbians, and Everybody Else*. Boston: Beacon Press, 1995.

Mee, Charles L. *White Robe, Black Robe*. New York: G.P. Putnam Sons, 1972.

Mellaart, James. *Catal Huyuk*. New York: McGraw-Hill, 1967.

Merwin, W.S., "The Song of Roland — Introduction." In Roger Sherman Loomis and Laura Hibbard Loomis, editors, *Medieval Epics*. New York: Modern Library, 1963.

Mieszkowski, Gretchen. "The Lancelot's Galehot, Malory's Lavin, and the Queering of Late Medieval Literature." *Arthuriana*, vol. 5, no. 1 (Spring 1995).

Miller, Barnette. *The Palace School of Muhammad the Conqueror*. Cambridge, Mass.: Harvard University Press, 1941.

Moll, Albert. *The Sexual Life of a Child*. Translated by Eden Paul. New York: Macmillan Company, 1919.

Mondimore, Francis Mark. *A Natural History of Homsexuality*. Baltimore: Johns Hopkins University Press, 1996.

Moore, Robert Ian. *The Formation of a Persecuting Society: Power and Deviance in Western Europe*. Boston: Blackwell Publishing, 1987.

Mueller, C.O. *History and Antiquities of the Doric Race*. London: John Murray, 1839.

Murray, Stephen O. *Homosexualities*. Chicago: University of Chicago Press, 2000.

_____. *Oceanic Homosexualities*. New York: Garland Publishing, 1992.

_____, and Will Roscoe, editors. *Islamic Homosexualities: Culture History, and Literature*. New York: New York University Press, 1997.

Nissinen, Martti. *Homoeroticism in the Biblical World: A Historical Perspective*. Translated by Kirsi Stjerna. Minneapolis, Minn.: Fortress Press, 1998.

Norton, Rictor. "The Historical Roots of Homophobia." In Winston Leyland, editor, *Gay Roots: An Anthology of Gay History, Sex, Politics and Culture*. San Francisco: Gay Sunshine Press, 1993.

_____. *A History of Homophobia*. Vol. 1, *The Ancient Hebrews*. April 15, 2002. Online at http://www.infopt.demon.co.uk/homophol.htm.

_____. *The Myth of the Modern Homosexual*. London: Cassell, 1997.

O'Brien, John Maxwell. *Alexander the Great: The Invisible Enemy*. New York: Routledge, 1994.

Olyan, Saul M. "And with a Male You Shall Not Lie the Lying Down of a Woman: On the Meaning and Significance of Leviticus 18:22 and 20:13," *Journal of the History of Sexuality*, Volume 5 (1994), No. 2.

Packard, Chris. *Queer Cowboys: And Other Erotic Male Friendships in Nineteenth-Century American Literature*. New York: Palgrave Macmillan, 2006.

Patai, Raphael. *The Hebrew Goddess*. New York: Avon, 1978.

Payer, Pierre J. *Book of Gomorrah*. Waterloo, Ontario: Wilfrid Laurier University Press, 1982.

Pellat, Charles. "Liwat." In Arno Schmitt and Jehoda Sofer, editors, *Sexuality and Eroticism among Males in Moslem Societies*. New York: Harrington Park Press, 1992.

Pellizer, Elio. *Outlines of a Morphology of Sympotic Entertainment*. In Oswyn Murray, editor, *Sympotica: A Symposium on the Symposion*. Oxford: Clarendon Press, 1990.

Percy, William A. "Homosexuality." In Vern L. Bullough and James A. Brundage, editors, *Handbook of Medieval Sexuality*. New York: Garland Publishing, 1996.

_____. *Pederasty and Pedagogy in Archaic Greece*. Chicago: University of Illinois Press, 1996.

Petronius Arbiter. *The Satyricon*. Translated by J.P. Sullivan. New York: Penguin Books, 1986.

Plaut, W.G., *The Torah: A Modern Commentary*, New York: Union of American Hebrew Congregations, 1981.

Polome, Edgar C. *The Indo-Europeans in the Fourth and Third Millennia*. Ann Arbor: Karoma Publishers, 1982.

Prescott, Henry W. "Inorganic Roles in Roman Comedy." *Classical Philology*, vol. 15 (1931).

Quinn, D. Michael. *Same-Sex Dynamics among Nineteenth-Century Americans*. Chicago, University of Illinois Press, 1996.

Ranke-Heinemann, Uta. *Eunuchs for the Kingdom of Heaven: Women, Sexuality and the Catholic Church*. Translated by Peter Heinegg. New York: Penguin Books, 1990.

Read, Kenneth E. "The Nama Cult Recalled." In Gilbert H. Herdt, editor, *Ritualized Homosexuality in Melanesia*. Los Angeles: University of California Press, 1984.

Richardson, Frank M.. *Mars without Venus: A Study of Some Homosexual Generals*. Edinburgh: William Blackwood, 1981.

_____. *Napoleon: Bisexual Emperor*. New York: Horizon Press, 1973.

Richlin, Amy. *The Garden of Priapus: Sexuality and Aggression in Roman Humor*. New York: Oxford University Press, 1992.

Ricks, Ingrid. "Straight über alles." *Advocate*, May 2, 1995

Rocke, Michael. *Forbidden Friendships: Homosexuality and Male Culture in Renaissance Florence*. New York: Oxford University Press, 1996.

Roscoe, Will. "Precursors of Islamic Homosexualities." In Stephen O. Murray, editor, *Islamic Homosexualities*. New York: Garland Publishing, 1997.

_____. "Precursors of Islamic Male Homosexualities." In Stephen O. Murray and Will Roscoe, editors, *Islamic Homosexualities: Culture, History, and Literature*. New York: New York University Press, 1997.

Ross, Anne. "Celtic and Northern Art." In Philip Rawson, editor, *Primitive Erotic Art*. New York: G.P. Putnam's Sons, 1973.

Rouche, Michel. "The Early Middle Ages in the West." In Paul Veyne, editor, *A History of Private Life. Vol. 1: From Pagan Rome to Byzantium*. Cambridge, Mass.: Belknap Press of Harvard University Press, 1987.

Rowse, A.L. *Homosexuals in History: A Study in Ambivalence in Society, Literature and the Arts*. New York: Carroll & Graf Publishers, 1983.

Saikaku, Ihara. *The Great Mirror of Male Love*. Stanford, CA: Stanford University Press, 1990.

Salvian. *De gubernatione Dei (The Government of God)*. Translated by Eva M. Sanford. New York: Columbia University Press, 1930.

Sandars, N.K. *The Epic of Gilgamesh*. London: Penguin Books, 1972.

Schalow, Paul Gordon. "Male Love in Early Modern Japan: A Literary Depiction of the 'Youth.'" In Martin Duberman, Martha Vicinus, and George Chauncey, Jr., editors, *Hidden from History: Reclaiming the Gay and Lesbian Past*. New York: Meridian, 1990.

Schild, Maarten. "Abu Nuwas." In Wayne R. Dynes, editor, *Encyclopedia of Homosexuality*. New York: Garland Publishing Company, 1990.

_____. "Sa'di." In Wayne R. Dynes, editor, *Encyclopedia of Homosexuality*. New York: Garland Publishing Company, 1990.

Schmitt, Arno. "Different Approaches to Male-Male Sexuality/Eroticism from Morocco to Usbekistan." In Arno Schmitt and Jehoda Sofer, editors, *Sexuality and Eroticism among Males in Moslem Societies*. New York: Harrington Park Press, 1992.

_____, and Jehoda Sofer, editors. *Sexuality and Eroticism among Males in Moslem Societies*. New York: Harrington Park Press, 1992.

Schneebaum, Tobias. *Where the Spirits Dwell: An Odessey in the Jungle of New Guinea*. New York: Grove Press, 1989.

Schwimmer, Eric. "Male Couples in New Guinea." In Gilbert H. Herdt, *Ritualized Homosexuality in Melanesia*. Los Angeles: University of California Press, 1984.

Scroggs, Robin. *The New Testament and Homosexuality*. Philadelphia: Fortress Press, 1984.

Sergent, Bernard. *Homosexualité et initiation chez les peuples indo-européens*. Paris: Éditions Payot, 1996.

_____. *Homosexuality in Greek Myth*. Translated by Arthur Goldhammer. Boston: Beacon Press, 1986.

Shapiro, H.A. "Courtship Scenes in Attic Vase-Painting." *American Journal of Archaeology*, vol. 85 (1981).

Shikibu, Murasaki. *The Tale of Genji*. Translated by Edward C. Seidensticker. New York, Alfred A. Knopf, 1976.

Shirazi, Sheikh Muslih-uddin Sa'di. *The Gulistan (Rose Garden)*. Public domain translation. Online at People with a History. http://www.fordham.edu/halsall/pwh/index.html.

Siker, Jeffrey S., editor. *Homosexuality in the Church: Both Sides of the Debate*. Louisville, Ky.: Westminster John Knox Press, 1994.

Sommer, Volker, and Paul L. Vasey, editors. *Homosexual Behaviour in Animals: An Evolutionary Perspective*. London: Cambridge University Press, 2006.

Sorum, Arve. "Growth and Decay: Bedamini Notions of Sexuality." In Gilbert H. Herdt, *Ritualized Homosexuality in Melanesia*. Los Angeles: University of California Press, 1984.

Southern, Richard W. *Medieval Humanism and Other Studies*. New York: Harper & Row, 1970.

_____. *St. Anselm: A Portrait in a Landscape*. London: Cambridge University Press, 1992.

Spong, John Shelby. *Living in Sin? A Bishop Rethinks Human Sexuality*. San Francisco: Harper & Row Publishers, 1988.

_____. *Rescuing the Bible from Fundamentalism: A Bishop Rethinks the Meaning of Scripture*. San Francisco: HarperSanFrancisco, 1991.

_____. *Resurrection: Myth or Reality? A Bishop's Search for the Origins of Christianity*. San Francisco: HarperSanFrancisco, 1994.

Sullivan, J. P. "Martial's Sexual Attitudes." *Philologus,* vol. 123 (1979).

Symonds, John Addington. *Studies in Sexual Inversion: Embodying a Study in Greek Ethics and a Study in Modern Ethics.* Privately Printed, 1928.

Talayessva, Don C. *Sun Chief: Autobiography of a Hopi Indian.* Edited by Leo W. Summons. Yale College, Institute of Human Relations, 1942.

Taylor, G. Rattray. "Historical and Mythological Aspects of Homosexuality." In Judd Marmor, editor, *Sexual Inversion: The Multiple Roots of Homosexuality.* New York: Basic Books, 1965.

_____. *Sex in History: The Story of Society's Changing Attitudes to Sex throughout the Ages.* New York: Harper & Row, 1954.

Terry, Patricia, and Samuel N. Rosenberg. *Lancelot and the Lord of the Distant Isles or, The Book of Galehaut Retold.* Boston: David R. Godine, Publisher, 2006.

Tripp, C.A., *The Homosexual Matrix.* New York: McGraw-Hill, 1975.

Turley, Hans. *Rum, Sodomy and the Lash: Piracy, Sexuality, and Masculine Identity.* New York: New York University Press, 1999.

Ullman, Walter. "Leo IX, Saint and Pope." *The New Encyclop«dia Britannica.* 15th Edition. 1985.

Vanggaard, Thorkil. *Phallos: A Symbol and Its History in the Male World.* New York: International Universities Press, 1972.

Van Gulik, R.H. *Sexual Life in Ancient China.* Leiden: E.J. Brill, 1974.

Veyne, Paul. "Homosexuality in Ancient Rome." In P. Aries and A. Bejin, editors, *Western Sexuality.* Oxford: Oxford University Press, 1985.

_____. "The Roman Empire." In Philippe Aries and Georges Duby, general editors. Paul Veyne, editor, *A History of Private Lives., Vol. 1: From Pagan Rome to Byzantium.* Cambridge, Mass.: The Belknap Press of Harvard University Press, 1987.

Virgil. *Aeneid.* Translated by Robert Fitzgerald. New York: Vintage Classics, 1990.

Voget, Fred. "American Indians." In Albert Ellis and Albert Abarbanel, editors, *The Encyclopedia of Sexual Behavior,* vol. 1. New York, Hawthorne Books, 1961.

Watanabe, Tsuneo, and Jin'ichi Iwata. *The Love of the Samurai: A Thousand Years of Japanese Homosexuality.* Translated by D.R. Roberts. London: GMP Publishers, 1989.

Weinberg, Martin S., and Colin J. Williams, *Male Homosexuals: Their Problems and Adaptations.* New York, Oxford University Press, 1974.

Weinrich, James D. *Sexual Landscapes.* New York: Charles Scribner's Sons, 1987.

Westermarck, Edward. *Ritual and Belief in Morocco.* London: Macmillan, 1926.

Williams, Walter L. *The Spirit and the Flesh: Sexual Diversity in American Indian Culture.* Boston: Beacon Press, 1992.

Wilson, Edward O. *On Human Nature.* Cambridge, Mass.: Harvard University Press, 1978.

Winkler, John J. "Laying Down the Law: The Oversight of Men's Sexual Behavior in Classical Athens." In David M. Halperin, John J. Winkler, and Froma I. Zeitlin, editors, *Before Sexuality: The Construction of Erotic Experience in the Ancient Greek World.* Princeton, N.J.: Princeton University Press, 1980.

Witcombe, Christopher L.C.E. "Eve and the Identity of Women. Part 6, The Old Testament, Women and Evil." Paper presented at the seminar Images of Women in Ancient Art. Sweetbriar College. Online at http://witcombe.sbc.edu/eve-women/6womenevil.html.

Wockner, Rex. "Homosexuality in the Arab and Moslem World." In Stephen Likosky, editor, *Coming Out.* New York: Pantheon, 1992.

Wood, Charles T. *The Quest for Eternity: Manners and Morals in the Age of Chivalry.* Hanover, N.H.: University Press of New England, 1983.

Wood, Robert. "Sex Life in Ancient Civilizations." In Albert Ellis and Albert Abarbanel, editors, *The Encyclopedia of Sexual Behavior.* New York: Hawthorn Books, 1964.

Yamamoto Tsunetomo. *Hagakure: The Book of the Samurai.* Translated by William Scott Wilson. New York and Tokyo: Kodansha International, 1992.

Yamauchi, Edwin M. "Cultic Prostitution: A Case in Cultural Diffusion." In Harry A. Hoffner, Jr., editor, *Orient and Occident.* Neukirchen-Vluyn: Verlag Butzon and Bercker Kevelaer, 1973.

Zihlman, Adrienne L., John E. Cronin, Douglas L. Cramer, and Vincent M. Sarich. "Pygmy Chimpanzees as a Possible Prototype for the Common Ancestor of Humans, Chimpanzees and Gorillas." *Nature,* vol. 275 (October 26, 1978).

Zuckerman, Solly, Lord. *The Social Life of Monkeys and Apes.* London: Routledge & Kegan Paul, 1981.

Index